# THE GIFTS OF FREEDOM SERIES

## PRISON EDITION

# THE GIFTS OF FREEDOM SERIES

## PRISON EDITION

## GREG RICE

DESTINY IMAGE® PUBLISHERS, INC.
P.O. Box 310, Shippensburg, PA 17257-0310

*"Speaking to the Purposes of God for this Generation and for the Generations to Come."*

Formerly published by Destiny Image as:
*Embracing Life, Spirit, Faith, and Adversity—Book 1*
©2008 ISBN: 978-0-7684-2707-3.
*Understanding Provision, Communication, and Death—Book 2*
©2008 ISBN: 978-0-7684-2723-3.
*Unwrapping Increase, Destiny, Relationships, God, and the Gifts of the Spirit—Book 3*
©2009 ISBN: 978-0-7684-2746-2.

This book and all other Destiny Image, Revival Press, Mercy Place, Fresh Bread, Destiny Image Fiction, and Treasure House books are available at Christian bookstores and distributors worldwide.

For a U.S. bookstore nearest you, call **1-800-722-6774**.

For more information on foreign distributors, call **717-532-3040**.

Reach us on the Internet: **www.destinyimage.com**.

ISBN 13 TP: 978-0-7684-3870-3

ISBN 13 HC: 978-0-7684-3871-0

ISBN 13 LP: 978-0-7684-3872-7

ISBN 13 Ebook: 978-0-7684-8967-5

For Worldwide Distribution, Printed in the U.S.A.

3 4 5 6 7 8 / 17 16 15

# DEDICATED TO

## MY SON, ROBERT RICE

and to the men and women who are spiritual paupers,
men and women behind bars, men and women in rehab,
and

*You*, the reader.

I pray that you will gain greater freedom,
a deeper understanding of God, and a closer relationship
with Him as you read this book.

# TO PRISONERS

✝ *But the Scripture declares that the whole world is a prisoner of sin, so that what was promised, being given through faith in Jesus Christ, might be given to those who believe. Before this faith came, we were held prisoners by the law, locked up until faith should be revealed* (Galatians 3:22-23).

This book is the complete *Gifts of Freedom* compilation, which includes all three books from the series. My prayer is that the twelve God-given gifts found inside will bring you into a closer, more intimate relationship with your Creator. I'd encourage you to accept, unwrap, and use these gifts to restore spiritual, physical, and financial freedom in your life. I realize you may be saying, "You don't know my situation—that kind of freedom is impossible for me!" And you're right, I don't know your story, but I trust that God does. In fact, the Bible says that humankind was originally created for the sole purpose of intimacy with their Creator—our freedom is found in this relationship. Remember, it is not God but us who doubt the power and potential of freedom in our lives. This is why His intimacy is so critical.

Reexamine the Bible verses above and you will see that as a prisoner in physical incarceration, you have something in common with everyone in or out of prison...in fact, we're all born prisoners surrounded by the steel bars of sin that restrain us, both spiritually and physically. Though you are physically incarcerated now, you can still gain the vital spiritual freedoms that others outside of jail don't possess. Indeed, as you read this series about the twelve gifts God is offering, you will learn how receiving, unwrapping, and using these gifts will free you in many areas of your life. In a simple and easy-to-understand way, you will discover what the Bible says about your physical and spiritual life, as well as how they are interrelated to your earthly life and the hereafter.

Look at how much the Bible has to say about prisoners and imprisonment. Read and mark these scriptures for future reference: Psalm 68:6, Psalm 79:11, Psalm 102:19-20, Psalm 142:7, Psalm 146:7, Isaiah 42:6-7; Isaiah 51:14, Isaiah 61:1 (quoted in Luke 4:18-19), Zechariah 9:11-12, Matthew 25:31-46, Galatians 3:22-23, Hebrews 10:34, Hebrews 11:36, Hebrews 13:3, 1 Peter 3:18-19, and Revelation 2:10. As you read and study what this book says about your physical and spiritual life, all these verses will become more meaningful to you; mark them in your Bible so you can go back and read them after you have completed this book.

As an incarcerated prisoner, you may feel inadequate to have a relationship with God and/or feel that you can never be used by Him to affect this world; however, the Bible recounts many people who became imprisoned and then went on to do great things for God. You can read some of their stories using the Bible references as follows:

| | |
|---|---|
| Genesis 37 & 39–41 | Joseph's Imprisonment |
| Judges 16 | Samson's Imprisonment |
| Jeremiah 37 | Jeremiah's Imprisonment |
| Mark 6:17-29 (Luke 3:19-20) | John the Baptist's Imprisonment |
| Acts 4 | Peter & John's Imprisonment |
| Acts 5 | Peter & Other Apostles' Imprisonment |
| Acts 12 | Peter's Imprisonment |
| Acts 16 | Paul & Silas' Imprisonment |
| Acts 22–28 | Paul's Imprisonment |

What's clear after reading these stories is that God uses ordinary people to do great and mighty things even while they're still in prison. Sometimes it is their prison experience that either prepares them or puts them in a position to go on and do great things. It is through receiving, unwrapping, and using the gifts He offers, combined with His power, that you *can* and *will* do great things.

You can use the time you're imprisoned to prepare your heart to develop your relationship with God. It is not what you have done in the past or even what you're doing now that is important to God; it is the process of preparing yourself for the unique destiny God desires you to embrace and live out. Just look at what God says to Jesus after He was baptized (this was before Jesus started His ministry):

✝ *You are My Son, whom I love; with You I am well pleased* (Luke 3:22).

What caused the Father, at this point, to say that He was so pleased with Jesus? At the age of thirty, Jesus hadn't started His ministry yet. He hadn't saved one soul, healed one person, nor performed one miracle. Jesus had been preparing Himself to fulfill God's plan for His life: increasing His knowledge and wisdom, learning from Scripture, and growing *closer* to His Father through prayer. This is where you are as well—preparing yourself so you can fulfill God's will for your life—growing closer to Him so that you can be used by Him.

Once you have begun preparing yourself, you can make an impact right where you are through witnessing, through prayer, and by using the many gifts God offers you. You can always impact others around you no matter where circumstances bring you. Indeed, while still in prison, the apostle Paul was used by God to write four letters to the Christians of his time, which have now become books of the New Testament, known as Ephesians, Philippians, Colossians, and Philemon.

Through reading this book, you will learn that right now, from a prison cell, you can be supernaturally used to impact the world, both spiritually and physically, both indirectly and directly to those around you. Do you believe that God has a specific plan, a true purpose, and clear path for you? Consider the possibility that God's plan begins now by unwrapping His life-changing Gifts of Freedom.

✠ *I will walk about in freedom, for I have sought out your precepts* (Psalm 119:45).

# Contents

# Embracing Life, Spirit, Faith, and Adversity

## Book 1

# Contents

# Understanding Provision, Communication, and Death

## Book 2

# Contents

## UNWRAPPING INCREASE, DESTINY, RELATIONSHIPS, GOD, AND THE GIFTS OF THE SPIRIT

### BOOK 3

# EMBRACING LIFE, SPIRIT, FAITH, AND ADVERSITY

## BOOK 1

# PREFACE

I started writing *The Gifts of Freedom* for my son and other men and women in prisons around the world. While these men and women are lacking physical freedom within cement walls, confined to caged cells, I wrote this book to help set them free in the most important place—the heart. Walking with Jesus Christ and finding intimacy with God and His Spirit is true freedom that cement and steel cannot restrain. Indeed, many who have found this spiritual freedom have also found a miraculous physical freedom.

Yet, as God was guiding me and shaping my writing, I realized that it isn't just the prison system that keeps people jailed in involuntary restraint. The largest "jails" in the world are full of many law-abiding citizens. I'm talking about people who are serving a sentence of loneliness, guilt, sorrow, hopelessness, fear, despair, sickness, disease, anger, confusion, addiction, depression, lack of resources, or a lack of purpose and meaning, just to name a few. *And sadly, even churches are full of people who have not acted on receiving the Gifts of Freedom God offers.*

Consider your own life for a moment. Are you living out your own life sentence? Are you restrained in some areas from living life in the full freedoms God desires for you? Maybe steel bars aren't keeping you from living fully free; but isn't the impact just as devastating? Couldn't prison be defined as "a life devoid of its intended freedoms, a life restrained, a life withheld from the abundance God desires for us"? If you are serving this kind of sentence, then ask yourself: Is this really life?

No. Absolutely not!

Here's the good news. Jesus Christ died to offer you His wonderful Gifts of Freedom, which were designed to set you spiritually free by allowing you to have a more intimate relationship with Him. Will you choose to receive, unwrap, and use all of them to their fullest? In this series of books, we'll explore the life-changing power of God's gifts—gifts for living an abundant, spiritually free life that may even produce physical freedoms.

If you are looking to read something that's full of gimmicks, shortcuts, and tricks to help you make little changes for a better life—then you're holding the wrong book. Jesus shed His blood to radically change and transform our lives. In fact, He offered to take our sentences from us. Jesus doesn't just offer a temporary fix, but a new life. What I've illuminated in these books are God's Gifts of Freedom for those who want to revolutionize their lives. Is that you?

The chapters in this series of three books present twelve gifts that build up to the best gift of all—God Himself. However, this information is only the beginning. The true impact of these books will happen where they end and *you begin*.

Will you choose to receive, unwrap, and use His gift today?

# INTRODUCTION

✠ *[Jesus] left Judea and went back once more to Galilee.*

*Now He had to go through Samaria. So He came to a town in Samaria called Sychar, near the plot of ground Jacob had given to his son Joseph. Jacob's well was there, and Jesus, tired as He was from the journey, sat down by the well. It was about the sixth hour.*

*When a Samaritan woman came to draw water, Jesus said to her, "Will you give me a drink?" (His disciples had gone into the town to buy food.)*

*The Samaritan woman said to Him, "You are a Jew and I am a Samaritan woman. How can you ask me for a drink?" (For Jews do not associate with Samaritans.)*

*Jesus answered her, "If you knew the gift of God and who it is that asks you for a drink, you would have asked Him and He would have given you living water"* (John 4:3-10).

The Bible has been printed more than any other book in history; however, most people don't really understand it. It is my goal to help you explore some of what the Bible teaches and to offer you a better understanding of its message. For instance, what is "the gift" this verse is referring to? And what do we need to know about who Jesus is to receive this living water? Or what kind of freedoms do we obtain when we have received this living water?

What you learn will change your life. The key to this change is being willing to take the time to examine the Bible and listen to what God says to you through its pages—His Word. Consider how much time you spend on what is only temporary. The message of the Bible—and its potential impact on your life—is *eternal*. It's worth the time to know its message.

If you were given the gift of a computer and an e-mail account, but didn't take the time to learn how to use them, then you couldn't use these potentially life-changing tools. Many people who are *set in their ways* don't take the time to learn, and some just don't want to exert the effort. To benefit from these gifts, however, you must take the time to learn about them.

Take a moment to read again the Bible passage at the beginning of this chapter. Samaritans were half-breeds, outcasts whom Jesus' contemporaries would have gone out of their way to avoid. The Samaritan lady was even an outcast among her own people. That is why she was at the well in the heat of the day when no one else would be coming. But Jesus didn't avoid this woman; instead, He engaged her in a conversation that would change her entire perspective. In fact, Jesus went out of His way to speak to her. He left Judea to go to Galilee, which would not be the typical route for a Jew and would leave Jesus exposed to His enemy. Jesus went out of His way to offer the Samaritan lady living water! Jesus offers you the same gift He offered the woman at the well: the Gifts of Freedom. And He has come out of His way to speak to you. It is no coincidence you are holding this book.

God offers us invisible gifts that are receivable and quite usable if we will take the time to understand them. Some are physical gifts and some are spiritual—but all of them give us new freedoms. Consider the natural law of gravity, which is a great gift that we can count on every day to keep the earth in its orbit and our feet on the ground. Over time and with study, scientists have unwrapped the ability to harness gravity's power by building dams and hydroelectric plants that use gravity to create electricity to light cities. Because of their deeper understanding of gravity, we have more freedom to use the night as well as power-speeding trains that, in turn, provide more freedom of time and places to go. We need to be consciously aware of how this invisible law of gravity operates and how it has a profound effect on our everyday lives. Though we *can't see it*, we *can* see and rely on its effects. We organize and adjust our lives counting on and considering its effects. This is why we don't step off a high ledge—we know how gravity would respond to that choice!

There are likewise unseen *spiritual* laws that are just as certain and even more significant and powerful than gravity. These spiritual laws that affect us daily are spoken of in the Bible. There is power in these laws that can bring us great freedom, but in order to receive that benefit from them—to receive the Gifts of Freedom—we understand these laws and our Creator's ultimate purpose for each of us.

Humankind was created to interact in love and friendship with the Creator. You specifically were created out of God's desire to have companionship with His creation, an intimacy in our very interactions with one another that was designed to produce pure love—the God-kind of love that has no restrictions or end.

The problem is that people don't take the time to get to know God. Do you think you could have true companionship with someone who doesn't know you? Who assumes they know you based on rumors or what other people may say about you? In a marriage, could you find real love with your spouse if he or she tried to force you to be someone you're not? Of course not. That would make for a relational disaster. But this is how some people think about God. They don't really know Him. Not being familiar with what the Bible says about God, about who He is and what His nature is, they make Him into the kind of God they *want* Him to be. Therefore, they wind up not becoming a true *companion* of His.

How much do you know about the God of the Bible? Do you think God would say you have been His good companion? Do you think you *know* how to be a good companion to God? I am going to answer these questions and many more by exploring the Bible and helping you discover what the Bible says about who God is, what His nature is, and what He desires. More importantly, I am even going to show you how to get specific answers about your life *directly* from God, answers *only He* can give you.

At the end of each chapter, you'll discover a Meditation Point. When you reach one of these, it's time to think about and soak in what you've read thus far. Then go to the Study Guide at the end of the book where you will find questions that will help you remember the main concepts and give you the opportunity to personalize the concepts and apply them to your own life. To get the fullest benefit from these teachings, take time to honestly answer the questions and carefully consider the action steps. You might want to go back through the chapter and circle key points, things you want to know more about, and things you want to remember.

Imagine that you're sitting in your favorite place in the world, enjoying the comfort of familiar surroundings along with the excitement of learning new ideas. This is your study time. God will be there with you, so be sure to always ask Him to reveal to you what you should be learning from your reading. Learning spiritual lessons is dynamic, like learning to ride a bike. You can't successfully accomplish the goal by just reading the instruction manual. You must at some point get on the bike and try out what you have read to actually master the material. Learning to grow spiritually is no different, and so you will want to read and then act on what you have read as you go.

God created it all, so He is the One who can explain it all. Take your time and allow God to speak to you, elaborate on, and make applicable what you have read. You'll soon learn that He has many ways in which He will speak. You will hear Him best if you follow the instructions in His Book—the Bible—written especially to you.

You'll also discover Action & Visualization instructions throughout where I offer a suggested action that could result in a long-term behavioral change. To make these sorts of changes, it's helpful to practice *visualization*. Think of these sections as park benches where you can rest a bit and visualize what you've learned and what that means for your daily life. Take the time to consider how you might do things *differently* based on what you have learned.

Let me say a few words about this concept of visualization. God designed your mind with two parts: Your conscious mind is like a computer programmer and your subconscious mind and central nervous system are like the computer itself. If your conscious mind had to deal with all the incoming information and demands for action from every part of the body simultaneously, you would be overwhelmed.

Let's use the simple act of driving a car as an example. There are many things you deal with simultaneously while driving. Here are just a few:

- Watch for traffic lights, stop signs, and other directional signs in a continually moving landscape.

- Be aware of other cars that are sometimes traveling at speeds near seventy mph.

- Make the correct turns on streets to get to your destination.

- Juggle distractions such as pedestrians, conversations, weather, or radio chatter.

Though your conscious mind can overlap many of these tasks, it is limited to acting on only one at a time. When you were first learning to drive, you were conscious of everything going on around you. As you drive the first few times, you train your subconscious mind—you teach it how to react subconsciously so you can eventually juggle multiple tasks with less demand. After a few years of driving, you do most of the actions without consciously thinking about them.

Visualization can help program your subconscious mind too. When you observe something (whether it is something actually happening or just the idea of what was pictured in your mind), you begin to program your subconscious mind with how to perform the action. The way our subconscious mind learns is a wonderfully complex system God gave us to help us navigate through life. However, sometimes we use this system to program bad habits.

Once a habit is ingrained in our subconscious, it's difficult to change. It is trained to respond to cues. When one of these cues appears, our subconscious mind reacts in a specific way before our conscious mind has had a chance to think about or debate the merit of the action. Let's say you're brushing your teeth but your conscious mind is thinking about what you're going to do today. When you're done squeezing the toothpaste onto your brush, do you automatically put the cap back on? Or are you one of those people who forgets to replace the cap? Visualization can help. It's as simple as always visualizing ahead of time what you are going to do differently when certain cues appear (like when you finish squeezing the toothpaste tube). If you continually forget to put the cap back on, you would want to take time to picture yourself performing the corrected action and even acting it out in your mind. Over time, as you repeat this visualization, you will teach your subconscious to break the old habit.

Well, we're just about ready to unwrap the Gifts of Freedom. But before we do, we'll take one chapter to explore how and why you were created. The subsequent chapters will present the Gifts of Freedom and show you how to unwrap and use them to impact your relationship with God and your relationship with others. In total, we will unwrap twelve of God's gifts in this book series, ending with an eternal gift—an intimate, loving relationship with God Himself.

There is no need to speed through this book. Take the time you need and allow God to interact with you as you consider the biblical truths He presents to you.

✠ *Every good and perfect gift is from above, coming down from the Father of the heavenly lights, who does not change like shifting shadows* (James 1:17).

Let's get started.

# Chapter 1

# IN THE BEGINNING...

## WHAT'S MY PURPOSE AND WHAT WENT WRONG?

Before you begin to read, pray that the Holy Spirit
will give you understanding and application.

✝ *In the beginning God created the heavens and the earth* (Genesis 1:1).

We celebrate beginnings, don't we? We have birthdays, anniversaries, national holidays, and grand openings to commemorate these events. Do you remember the birth of your children or maybe a niece or a nephew? How about the first date with your spouse, boyfriend, or girlfriend? Maybe you remember your first kiss? Or how about the day you drove your first car home? These events are memorable because they are part of your personal history. These "beginnings" helped shape who you are.

There are even greater "beginnings" that shape us, however, including the beginning of the world and, yes, the beginning of humankind. All our beginnings find their source in God, the Creator of all things, the giver of all good and perfect gifts. The Father is the giver of life—consciousness, self-awareness, and even the free will to live life in the way we decide. So what are we to do now? Why are we here? How should we live? What is our purpose? These questions will be answered in this book.

But I'm not grabbing my answers out of thin air—they are collected from the Author of "In the beginning...." God recorded *the beginning* in His words to us, the Bible. Like all good stories, let's start at the beginning—the creation of humankind.

## Our Beginning

✛ *Let* **Us** *make man in our* **image**, *in our* **likeness**... (Genesis 1:26).

You don't read too far into the first book of the Bible before meeting this foundational verse that answers some of our deepest questions. We were created in the image and likeness of God. If that's true, then why are we so messed up? And if we are made in God's image, why are we so inclined to act so ungodly? To answer these questions, it is important to first learn about God's nature.

Before heading down that path, I'd like to clarify something that may be new to you. Do you find it odd that the verse refers to "Us"? Isn't this God's creation story? Yes, it is. The "Us" in this verse is indeed God. But while God is one, He is also known as the Holy Trinity (God the Father, God the Son [Jesus], and God the Holy Spirit)—three in one. God's use of "Us" here says that all three were present in the beginning.

What does that mean for you personally? It means you were originally designed to be created in God's image, according to His likeness. Let's take a closer look at the words *image* and *likeness*. These words are used in tandem to clarify an overall meaning. *Image* is translated from the Hebrew word *tselem*, which means "a reproductive or duplicative form of a person or object like a statue." This suggests we were created to resemble God in form or appearance. Obviously, this doesn't refer to our physical composition, so it would have to relate to spirit and character. Balancing this is the word *likeness*. This word comes from the Hebrew word *demut*, which does not convey such preciseness as image. To be like someone means "you possess many, but not all of characteristics and qualities."[1]

What, then, does it mean to be created in God's image and likeness? We must first ask some questions about God. What is His composition? What is His character? What is His nature? It is only once we answer these that we can determine in what ways we are like Him or were *intended* to be like Him.

You've probably seen paintings or illustrations depicting God as an old man with a long, white flowing beard. This is a common approach artists take in their attempts to give God a "face." I imagine the image of an old white-bearded man is often chosen because it conjures up a picture of wisdom and, if you have ever read The Lord of the Rings (think of Gandalf), of mystical power. But I'm sure you already know that God is not a human being with a body, head, two arms, and two legs. He is something indefinable and, for lack of a better word, invisible. How can we learn about someone we can't see? The Bible says one way we can better understand God is to examine some of His work:

✟ *God has made it plain to* [humankind]. *For since the creation of the world God's invisible qualities—His eternal power and divine nature—have been **clearly seen, being understood** from what has been **made**, so that men are without excuse* (Romans 1:19-20).

Hmm. These verses say we will be without excuse if we don't examine God's work, so let's examine it carefully.

## GOD IS LIGHT

Look at the first thing God creates, as recorded in Genesis:

✟ *And God said, "Let there be light," and there was light* (Genesis 1:3).

What is light? It is energy. Light rays move at 186,282.397 miles per *second* (over 670 *million* miles per hour). That's a speed we really can't comprehend. Albert Einstein's special theory of relativity (E = mc) states that the speed of light is the same for all observers, even if they are in motion at different speeds relative to one another.[2] Read that again if you need to. Got it? That is significant because the speed of light is not just the velocity of "light" but also a fundamental feature of the way space and time are tied together. God created light—and He is the same to everybody, no matter what race they are, what language they speak, what status they have, or what they have done; He is the fundamental core tying *everything* together.

I once heard a lecture by a Christian physicist who offered this interesting proposition, which is based on Einstein's theory and carefully selected Bible verses: God's essence is light, and if you were to travel the speed of light then you would enter the dimension of Heaven. The physicist was persuasive, but whether his theory has any merit, we can learn a lot about God's attributes and nature by looking at God's first creation—light. God is certainly like light. We'll discover that this theme is significant to God's story and to our understanding of what it means to follow Him.

When we "see" something, anything, our eyes are actually detecting light rays either coming from an object (such as the sun) or reflecting off an object (like the moon). This means that without light we *cannot* see anything at all. Similarly, without God we *cannot* see or experience the spiritual things of this life. The Bible says:

✟ *For with You [God] is the fountain of life; in Your light we see light* (Psalm 36:9).

✟ *The commands of the Lord are radiant, giving light to the eyes* (Psalm 19:8).

✟ *Blessed are those who have learned to acclaim You, who walk in the light of Your presence, O Lord* (Psalm 89:15).

⊕ *What came into existence was Life, and the Life was Light to live by* (John 1:4 MSG).

The sign signifying Jesus entering our world was a bright light in the sky. Jesus Himself says:

⊕ *I am the Light of the world. Whoever follows Me will never walk in darkness, but will have the light of life* (John 8:12).

The Bible describes those who have become Christians in this way:

⊕ *For you were once darkness, but now you are light in the Lord. Live as children of light* (Ephesians 5:8).

God uses light to identify Himself so we can better understand His nature. There are over seventy times in the Bible where God uses this analogy. Because you know the properties of light, you will better understand Him. His light is necessary for spiritual sight, or what is referred to when speaking spiritually as *insight*. This is why I am suggesting that at the beginning of each chapter (or whenever you pick up this book or a Bible) you pray for better understanding before you start reading—so your insight will be *improved*.

## WHO BROUGHT EVIL INTO THE WORLD?

Let's consider another aspect of God's nature by looking at good and evil. Simply put, *good* is what God wills and *evil* is that which is outside of the will of God. Evil therefore *cannot* come from God. For instance, light cannot create darkness; its mere presence negates or *illuminates* darkness. Darkness only exists where light is *not* present. His will (good) negates that which is not His will (evil). The Bible says it succinctly:

✠ *...the Lord is good...* (Psalm 34:8).

✠ *...God is light; in Him there is no darkness at all* (1 John 1:5).

People often ask this question: "If God is so good, then why is there so much evil and pain in the world?" It is a great question, and the answer begins with understanding this truth about God's nature—there is no darkness (or evil) in Him. He could not create any evil (light cannot create darkness).

✠ *For everything God created is good...* (1 Timothy 4:4).

So where does evil come from? Well, we live in a broken world with broken people who are not acting according to God's will—in His image and likeness. We substantially removed God from ourselves and our world, as we will come to understand from this review of our biblical history (the fall of humankind)—and that very absence is why and where evil exists. In other words, the absence of light (God's image and likeness) shining through us into the world allows the darkness to exist. We were created to bring His light (image and likeness) into the world—to *light* the world that humankind collectively decided *not* to do. So it's important to understand that the responsibility for this broken world is collectively ours.

God gave us a wonderful gift—the freedom of choice. However, it is a two-edged sword, and with one edge we have sliced open the curtain that brought evil into this world. But there is good news—the other edge of the sword still works. God invites us to choose the side that leads to Him.

There is a scientific theory on the structure of the universe that says if you aimed yourself in any direction and rocketed that way past all the stars and other galaxies, you would eventually come back to yourself, the original starting point. Since we can't actually do this, it will always remain, like so much of science, just a theory (though a popular theory). Our spiritual lives are similar—the responsibility for the choices we make comes back to us. The law of cause and effect says every choice has consequences. We suffer or enjoy the consequences of all the choices we make individually and corporately.

## GOD IS SPIRIT

The Bible says that God is a spirit being:

✠ *God is spirit...* (John 4:24).

But we're not spirit beings, are we? We have a physical presence. Does that mean we aren't created in the image and likeness of God after all? No. But it does suggest that Adam, the first man, was created different from us, and something changed since creation so we are not the same as Adam. You will see how we are born into one stage, and through our lives here on earth we are afforded the opportunity (by our choice) to move toward what God intended us to be—someone made in His image and likeness. If this is a process, a "moving toward" something, then when are we finished being made, and what will we be upon completion?

Here again God has given clues in His creation that help us understand how such a miraculous change—a metamorphosis—can occur. Consider the butterfly. It begins life as a fertilized egg, then becomes a baby caterpillar, then grows into an adult caterpillar, then forms itself in a cocoon, then goes through a reconfiguring process, and *only* after emerging from that cocoon does it achieve its ultimate purpose—a butterfly full of beauty and fluttering flight. The butterfly has periods of gradual development and times of dramatic change. If you look at the creature in any one of its pre-butterfly stages, you might not believe it could possibly reach the destiny for which God created it.

The same is true for us. God gave His creation, you and me, the gifts of growth and metamorphosis. We, like the butterfly, face transition points that may be gradual or quite dramatic. There is even a kind of death, not unlike the cocoon stage, that immediately precedes a person's emergence as a complete and beautiful new creature. Growth isn't always easy. It may seem impossible to fully appreciate or even believe what God's ultimate purpose is for us during any given step of the process. I doubt you could convince a caterpillar that one day it would fly. And yet God had a plan and purpose for it. God has a plan and purpose for you too.

It's interesting to note that butterflies truly struggle to get out of their cocoons, but that struggle actually helps the butterfly prepare for flight in the new world. The same is true for us as we work through each stage in our development to become people who reflect God's image and likeness. Each trial, challenge, and difficulty we experience can better prepare us for the next stage of our development.

When we look at Adam, we see a man who was created in the image and likeness of God. We also see how his choice (and Eve's) caused humankind to take a *big* step backward in that regard. (A full examination of Adam and Eve's poor choices are found later in this chapter.) And unfortunately, after the fall, they could only pass down to us (their children) what they possessed—a form less than God originally intended.

You might think it would be game over for us at this point; how could we ever find our way back to God's original design? But God already had a plan based on our own failure and free will, one that offers every man and woman the potential to become whole, to become the person He intended and desires us to be. We, the sons and daughters of Adam and Eve, *all* begin life as *less* than God intended. We are in a continual growth process, striving to change into the image and likeness of God. The exact nature of our spiritual growth and stages of our metamorphosis will be understood as we discover what the Bible says about us.

Let's get back to God's composition to find our target as we aim toward growth.

✟ *God is **spirit** and His worshipers must worship in **spirit** and in truth* (John 4:24).

God is a spirit being. But there's more. In this verse, we also learn that we must have a spirit with which to worship Him, or, in essence, to *communicate* with Him. From this, we can deduce that God intended at least some part of us to be *spirit*, and this spiritual component plays a significant role in how God wants to communicate with us.

✟ *Don't you know that you yourselves are God's temple and that God's **Spirit** lives in you?* (1 Corinthians 3:16).

✟ *...he who unites himself with the Lord is one with Him **in spirit*** (1 Corinthians 6:17).

It seems that God intended us to *be* spirit beings *with* a mind *in* a body. We were also made in such a way that God's Spirit and our spirit can be *connected*, or *united*. For Adam, the first man, his spirit was connected to God's Spirit from day one, giving him 20/20 (perfect) insight. However, after Adam's sin, the connection changed because Adam and Eve could not give to their children something they did not possess. Adam and Eve could only create in their own image and likeness so we no longer have a perfect connection between our spirit and God's. But there is good news: God has made a path to redeem that broken connection. He offers a gift that can lead us back to a functioning relationship between our spirit and His. What other attributes or characteristics of God might we receive from this functioning connection with God's Spirit?

## GOD IS LOVE

The apostle John wrote with simplicity and eloquence:

✠ ...*God is **love*** (1 John 4:8).

Of course, *love* can mean different things to different people. And so the Bible offers this definition of love:

✠ *Love never gives up. Love cares more for others than for self. Love doesn't want what it doesn't have. Love doesn't strut, doesn't have a swelled head, doesn't force itself on others, isn't always "me first," doesn't fly off the handle, doesn't keep score of the sins of others, doesn't revel when others grovel, takes pleasure in the flowering of truth, puts up with anything, trusts God always, always looks for the best, never looks back, but keeps going to the end* (1 Corinthians 13:4-7 MSG).

You only have to read the morning newspaper to see how God's creation, humankind, is missing the mark regarding love. Violence, war, terrorism, and countless other evils are clearly the result of people who are *not* living out the biblical definition of love. Each one of us has fallen short of living out this biblical definition at one time or another. But God desires us to reach for and regain His character of love. Thankfully, God also desires to help us get there.

How did we get so far off track from what we were intended to be? Well, in alignment with His desire for us to be in His image and His desire to have an authentic loving relationship with us, God gave us a free will—our own free will with which we could make our *own* decisions. This is the mechanism that allows us to show love. God could have created a companion without a free will. Perhaps a sock puppet.

God: "What are you going to do today, puppet?"

God's "sock puppet" voice: "Whatever You make me do, God."

Can a sock puppet really love its owner? No. But if it had the ability to choose, then yes, it could love with its own free will. However, it could also choose *not* to love. This is an interesting dynamic that is crucial to understanding free will and understanding who is bringing evil into the world. It is this same type of love that God has for us, that He intended for us to have not just for Him but also all others on earth, so that everyone's experience on earth would be wonderful.

Adam and Eve had a choice: to follow God or not. They decided to disobey. This is why John wrote:

✠ *For everything in this world—the cravings of sinful man, the lust of his eyes and the boasting of what he has and does—comes not from the Father but from the world* (1 John 2:16).

With this same free will that Adam and Eve received from God, we too can decide to reject God or to follow God—to pursue the path to becoming more like God's original creation. We can decide if we want to be companions with God. We can also decide how *much* of a companion we want to be. Using my earlier analogy, we can choose to move from being an egg to a caterpillar or a caterpillar to a butterfly. We can even decide if we want to grow at all. We are responsible for our own spiritual growth. As the process unfolds in these pages, you'll discover that while God gives us the means, *we* have to *choose* to go through the *process*.

You may be thinking there is no way to get from here to there, from the person you are today to someone who reflects the image and likeness of God. However, the Bible gives us a clear way to pursue this goal, showing us how to receive, unwrap, and use the Gifts of Freedom.

To start walking down that path, we need to recover an active spirit that God can connect with. This is what happens when we accept the first gift. From there, we begin a slow-growth process to develop God's character of *love*. After we die, we'll be judged by Him based on our decision to follow that path, and how we followed it:

✠ *Just as man is destined to die once, and after that to face judgment...* (Hebrews 9:27).

That may sound a bit daunting, but there is good news for those who have chosen the path to follow God. He loves us so much that He provided a way for His followers to be freed from this judgment, to receive new glorious bodies like the butterflies, allowing them to fly in freedom.

✠ *But our citizenship* [those who accept the first gift] *is in Heaven. And we eagerly await a Savior from there, the Lord Jesus Christ, who, by the power that enables Him to bring everything under His control, will **transform** our lowly bodies so that they will be **like His glorious body*** (Philippians 3:20-21).

This major decision will impact the rest of your life, and determine what happens at the *end* of that life. Choosing to follow God will dramatically change you. Not only will that choice give you the gift of eternal life, but your life in the here-and-now will be completely different. You will be unrecognizable from who you once were by *choosing* growth. But if you refuse to follow God, you will miss having a connection to God that allows you to reach your potential of being able to fully exude His kind of love.

## WHAT WENT WRONG

When Adam and Eve made the decision not to follow God's instructions, their relationship with Him was drastically altered. Let's start at the beginning and see what happened.

Just as God the Father, Jesus, and the Holy Spirit have always been in relationship with each other, so God desired Adam to have a similar relationship of oneness with a companion (marriage).

✟ *The Lord God said, "It is not good for the man to be alone. I will make a helper suitable for him"* (Genesis 2:18).

✟ *So the Lord God caused the man to fall into a deep sleep; and while he was sleeping, He took one of the man's ribs and closed up the place with flesh. Then the Lord God made a woman from the rib He had taken out of man and brought her to the man* (Genesis 2:21-22).

We see in this passage that Eve was also created in God's image and meant to exude His character.

✟ *The man and his wife were both naked, and they felt no shame* (Genesis 2:25).

Adam and Eve were originally created with a physical presence and a mind that could freely choose what to do and how to act; however, Adam and Eve also had a spiritual aspect that connected them with God. God's love flowed in and through them so they would reflect and shine God's light into His creation. We were originally created in the image and likeness of God in essence of spirit (*composition*), freedom of choice (*ability*), and character of *love*.

It is significant that Adam and Eve were naked and yet had no shame. This tells us that God's Spirit was shining through them. With God's shining Spirit *covering* them, they had no reason to feel any shame, even without clothes. Adam and Eve's bodies were like glass light bulbs. The light itself is God's light coming into us through His Spirit, and ours then radiating out of us to exude His image and likeness. When a light bulb is lit, we don't really notice the bulb itself. However, we *do* notice (and desire) the light.

God's character and glory shining through us is to be the essence of our real beauty. I don't want to minimize the importance of our own spirit—God created each of us as unique individuals. But when our spirit and God's Spirit combined in the original design, the light was so strong that it overshadowed the physical body, which is the glass bulb. Our purpose is not merely to exist or to physically look good (about which many people today have so much anxiety); our purpose is to shine His light, represent God in His creation, and to shine His glory into it.

✟ *...he* [man] *is the image and glory of God...* (1 Corinthians 11:7).

✟ *...subdue* [the earth]. *Rule over the fish of the sea and the birds of the air and over every living creature that moves on the ground* (Genesis 1:28).

Adam and Eve had nothing to be ashamed of because God's character exuded from them. To shine with God's love and in His love is to truly feel no shame. Clearly, they were given the authority on earth to execute that responsibility. Understanding that we are given authority over the creation *along with* free will is critical to understand why there is now so much evil in the world despite God's character of love.

We were *not* created to be robots or clones. Moreover, God created each of us as a unique light bulb, a person with a unique mind and personality. When we're connected with Him, as Adam and Eve were in the garden, His light shines through our unique personalities, creating diverse patterns, like light shining through crystals.

Let's get back to the garden. Adam and Eve were living in a paradise garden home, they had full communion with God, and reflected His glory into creation. God had given them clear instructions about how to enjoy and interact with His creation:

✙ *Now the Lord God had planted a garden in the east, in Eden; and there he put the man he had formed. ...And the Lord God commanded the man, "You are free to eat from any tree in the garden; but you must not eat from the tree of the knowledge of good and evil, for when you eat of it you will surely die"* (Genesis 2:8,16-17).

I like to think of the garden of Eden as one of those amusement parks enjoyed by children (and childlike parents). Remember the Ferris wheel? What a great ride. As it slowly revolves, taking you high into the air, it gives both a sense of exhilaration and a wonderful view of the surrounding area. But imagine if you put your hand into the Ferris wheel's machinery—you'd be seriously injured, perhaps even killed. God created a wonderful place for humanity to enjoy, filled with amazing things to see and experience, but He also gave Adam a safety rule to follow so he could enjoy the garden without risk of harm—don't eat of the fruit of the Tree of Knowledge. Sounds simple enough, right? And for a while it probably was. God must have loved it when Adam communicated his enjoyment of the garden with Him and shone His light into the world.

Then satan entered the picture. He was an angel who once led worship over God's throne, but satan developed pride in his beauty and his abilities—desiring to steal God's glory for himself. For this, he was cast from Heaven:

✙ *All your pomp has been brought down to the grave* [meaning death as in separation from God], *along with the noise of your harps. ... How you have fallen from Heaven, O morning star, son of the dawn! You have been cast down to the earth, you who once laid low the nations! You said in your heart, "I will ascend to Heaven; I will raise my throne above the stars of God. ...I will make myself like the Most High"* (Isaiah 14:11-14).

Satan's mistake was in putting *his* will above God's will and considering himself more important than God. As a result, he fell from Heaven; he was separated from God. We will discuss satan's role in a later chapter, but it is important to know that misery loves company. Satan was jealous and fearful of man reflecting God's image into the world. He wanted Adam and Eve to join him in putting their wills and desires above God's. So he approached Eve:

☩ *...[satan] said to the woman, "Did God really say, 'You must not eat from any tree in the garden'?"*

*The woman said to the serpent, "We may eat fruit from the trees in the garden, but God did say, 'You must not eat fruit from the tree that is in the middle of the garden, and you must not touch it or you will die.'"*

*"You will not surely die" the serpent said to the woman. "For God knows that when you eat of it your eyes will be opened, and you will be like God, knowing good and evil"* (Genesis 3:1-5).

Remember that free will that God gave Adam and Eve (and us)? Satan decided to tempt Eve to use her free will to become as God, just like he had tried to do himself. Instead of listening to the Spirit of God in her, Eve was influenced by her senses; her desires caused her mind to make the wrong choice:

☩ *When the Woman saw that the tree looked like good eating and realized what she would get out of it—she'd know everything!—she took and ate the fruit and then gave some to her husband, and he ate* (Genesis 3:6 MSG).

Adam and Eve weren't satisfied just getting their knowledge from God and reflecting His image and likeness into the world. In a similar way, many people today try to get their knowledge through astrology, palm reading, numerology, and even science. When Adam and Eve decided to get their knowledge from another source rather than from God, this broke communication and relationship with God. Simply put, they took their focus off God, who was the source of their life. They set their *own* rules to *be* their own god; they freely chose to disobey *God's will* and subsequently suffered the consequences of a life without taking direction from their Creator.

## Spiritual Death

Since God is the source of spiritual life, Adam and Eve's spirits became functionally dead and their glory was gone. This immediate separation from God's Spirit as a result of sin eventually resulted in physical death. Spiritual, and ultimately physical, death then spread into the world, tainting humanity by multiplying Adam and Eve's sin from that day forward:

✠ *Therefore, just as sin entered the world through one man, and death through sin, and in this way death came to all men, because all sinned* (Romans 5:12).

✠ *Jesus replied, "I tell you the truth, everyone who sins is a slave to sin"* (John 8:34).

The Bible says our slavery to sin will exist until we receive the knowledge of the truth and then *act* on it to escape:

✠ *...leading them to a knowledge of the truth, and that they will come to their senses and escape from the trap of the devil, who has taken them captive to do his will* (2 Timothy 2:25-26).

Continuing with Adam and Eve's story, they knew right away things had changed:

☦ *Then the eyes of both of them were opened, and they realized they were naked; so they sewed fig leaves together and made coverings for themselves* (Genesis 3:7).

There are three things I'd like to point out from this passage of Scripture. The first to note is that the "eyes of both of them were *opened*," meaning they had lost their insight (spiritual sight) and now had to unnaturally rely *only* on their physical eyes for all their sight. Their vision became distorted and solely physical.

Second, have you ever wondered why scientists say we only use such a small fraction of our brain capacity and power? Perhaps it's because we were designed to have substantially more information coming in through our spirits, which needed to be processed and integrated into our daily activities.

Third, with their *spirits* disconnected, the *glory* was gone. Using my light bulb analogy, the light went out. Until you are "born again," until you accept Christ as your personal Savior, the light *source* is unavailable. But after you are born again, the light source is always within reach, but only dimly as we develop this new connection (our intimate relationship with God), and then of course only to the degree we turn it up (become more like Him). As we become closer to His image and likeness by becoming closer to Him, our light brightens. The light does not reach its full potential until we're in Heaven with new bodies, when we will truly be in an intimate relationship and then shine fully in the image and likeness of God.

I do not suggest that God's love is not currently being manifested even by those who have not re-hooked up to the source. God's invisible qualities, including His divine nature, are evident in the world for all to see. However, since the fall we have been infected with sin and self-absorption, which

44

distorts God's kind of love. Unfortunately, many times when people experience each other they may only experience the sin and self-absorption that has grown rampant since the fall.

There may be faint moments when they experience God's love shining, but this low intensity light is merely a reflection or a residue. If people are not hooked up to the source, then the light that God designed for us to reflect will not be of full quality or intensity. The good news is that God can plug us in again and the light can flow to bring healing to those areas in our lives affected by sin.

It is a requirement that you start this healing process before you die so you can assure your entrance into Heaven. This reconnection is necessary because, for Heaven to be the kind of experience that God promises, you and others there must exude His *full* light. There can be no sin or disharmony in Heaven or there can be no true heavenly experience. This is an important point: for us to spend eternity in the kind of Heaven God desires, we all inherently have to be the kind of beings He desires us to be. God leaves that choice up to each of us. Upon agreeing to become a heavenly being, we can enter and become part of that wonderful experience.

Remember God gave us the wonderful gift of choice. Sadly, humanity has chosen not to live with God at the center of their lives and hearts, which has led to us experiencing the world without God's love and light dominating it. Fortunately, we now see what a world without God's love and light at the center of it would look like so the choice He still offers us is easier to make.

After Adam and Eve fell, sin entered the world and their primary communication method was no longer a spiritual one, but physical. Their physical eyes were open and the world as they knew it was not quite so wonderful anymore. They saw the raw weakness of themselves. They must have felt insecure once they'd lost their focus—their connection with God. From that moment forward, they would judge themselves and each other because, for the first time, they were *fully conscious* of the difference between *good* and *evil*.

God's *glory* had been the primary source of their beauty and strength; without it they became ashamed of what they saw—that new evil side, which was the opposite of God's will. Realizing their own frailty, they covered their bodies with fig leaves in an effort to cover their sin and insecurity. This may have given them some comfort; however, we will see that it was not an adequate covering for God. Fig leaves, clothes, and even an appearance of doing the right things aren't enough to hide sin from God.

✠ *Then the man and his wife heard the sound of the Lord God as He was walking in the garden in the cool of the day, and they hid from the Lord God among the trees of the garden* (Genesis 3:8).

Adam and Eve audibly knew the sound of God and God walked with them in the garden on a regular basis. His relationship with Adam and Eve was one of close community. So when they realized their sin, they tried to hide from God. I can imagine them thinking, "Maybe if He doesn't see us, He won't notice our sin." But this would have been only half of the story, because they also feared God because they knew what they had done was wrong. Without that internal connection, the spirit-to-*Spirit* connection, God must have seemed frighteningly different.

## GOD REACHES OUT TO US

This next verse seems almost comical at first, but the significance behind the words is profound:

✠ *But the Lord God called to the man, "Where are you?"* (Genesis 3:9).

Even though Adam and Eve had chosen to go to a different place, God knew where they were at. But this verse tells us several more things about God's relationship with Adam and Eve. First, it was natural for God to speak to them in the garden, which means they enjoyed regular direct audible communications with God. This says something about God's character— He is relational and He desires communication—and that communication should feel as natural as our human-to-human relationships. It also shows us that God desires us to be honest with Him. And finally, it tells us that, though God always knows where we are both physically and otherwise, He wants us—*not* for His sake but for each of our own—to answer the question, "Where are you?" Adam answered God in this way:

✠ *He answered, "I heard you in the garden, and I was afraid because I was naked; so I hid"* (Genesis 3:10).

Adam didn't know he was naked—it wasn't unusual—until he'd sinned. But recognizing that sin (and the fact that the light had gone out and that the glory was gone), Adam desperately wanted to hide from God, knowing God would see his raw self without God's good light covering him.

Many people today do much the same thing; when they recognize they are outside of God's will, they want to hide from Him. Maybe you relate to Adam's answer here. Many people never come to know God because they are afraid of Him. They don't feel they are worthy to have a relationship with their Creator; they believe their sin is too great. As we explore the Bible, you'll find nothing is further from the truth! No matter what you have done or where you are at, God is calling you to receive His unconditional love. There are no sins too large or numerous that God can't forgive.

God's next question to Adam was revealing as well:

✠ *And He said, "Who told you that you were naked?"* (Genesis 3:11).

With this question, God was asking who Adam and Eve were listening to and why was it not His voice that was listened to? God's last question seeks honesty from Adam:

47

✠ *"Have you eaten from the tree that I commanded you not to eat from?"*

*The man said, "The woman you put here with me—she gave me some fruit from the tree, and I ate it."*

*Then the Lord God said to the woman, "What is this you have done?"*

*The woman said, "The serpent deceived me, and I ate"* (Genesis 3:12-13).

When God asked Adam what had happened, Adam did not take responsibility for his actions. Rather, he blamed the woman, and then also blamed God because God gave him the woman. Eve blamed the snake. Both Adam and Eve claimed to be victims. You may be familiar with this type of behavior or reaction. Obviously, Adam and Eve's newly-discovered victim mentality is *not* a character trait found in the image and likeness of God.

While we know Adam and Eve went on after "the fall" to physically populate the world, they did so with the full weight of sin on their shoulders; the result of that sin was eventual physical death to coincide with their newly acquired spiritual death.

✠ *And the Lord God said, "The man has now become like one of Us* [as a result of eating from the Tree of Knowledge of Good and Evil], *knowing good and evil. He must not be allowed to reach out his hand and take also from the tree of life and eat, and live forever." So the Lord God banished him from the garden of Eden to work the ground from which he had been taken"* (Genesis 3:22-23).

The banishment from the garden of Eden (where Adam and Eve were now unable to eat from the Tree of Life, which is now available to us in Jesus Christ) proclaims their physical death sentence. However, this physical death was not the most important issue to God—it was the loss of relationship and spiritual connection with the ones He created in His own image.

God intended for us to be made up of three working parts, as the apostle Paul outlined to the Christians at Thessalonica:

✠ *May your whole **spirit**, **soul**, and **body** be kept blameless at the [second] coming of our Lord, Jesus Christ* (1 Thessalonians 5:23).

The soul, or what I refer to as the "mind," consists of the intellect, emotions, and will. When you become a Christian, your mind, along with your body and your newly-functioning spirit, are bound together as one. It is your will (computer programmer) that decides your course by balancing the input from your intellect, emotions, and bodily desires against that of your spirit's input from God.

God's priority is our spiritual side, not the physical fulfillment and obsession with our bodies' needs, which often become *our* primary focus. Fun, pleasure, and comfort are all temporal, but the spirit is eternal. It's no wonder our minds make physical pleasure and comfort a main priority, because our minds are overwhelmed with information coming through our body's senses. This can distort our view of reality (both spiritual and physical, as well as their relationship to each other) and our sin, then further distorts our perception of reality.

## DISTORTED REALITY

Allow me, for just a moment, to illustrate this skewed perspective that comes from focusing on the importance of our physical being. Have you noticed that we rate sin by its impact on our physical bodies? A little white lie is not as bad as theft, and theft is not as bad as assault, and assault is not as bad as murder. Even in our attempts to understand sin, we end up focusing on how our bodies are affected. However, God is more concerned about how your spirit and your relationship with Him is affected. *All* sin causes you to be out of God's will and therefore equally affects your relationship with Him. This is why James writes:

✝ *For whoever keeps the whole law and yet stumbles at just one point is guilty of breaking all of it* (James 2:10).

When we view the world only through our physical senses and the demands of our bodies, it is like viewing the world through a prism. The picture is distorted. Sin distorts it even further. Some people turn the sin prism into a kaleidoscope, which may be colorful and compelling to look through, but it also makes it impossible to gain even a reasonable perspective of spiritual realities. I want to clarify that nobody has a perfect perspective, because no one, except Jesus Christ, lived in or currently lives in complete obedience to the Father. However, our goal should be to find every possible way to improve our perspective and act on that perception.

You see, it is with our physical senses that we detect, and then with our minds that we understand, physical truth (which is temporal); however, it is through our spirit's insight that we see and understand spiritual truth (which is eternal). What's important to understand is that Truth (with a capital T) will eventually and always trump truth (with a small t). After we get linked back up to God's light, we have the power with our free will to start developing this insight no matter what prisms or kaleidoscopes we currently look through. This will allow us to see the reality that matters the most.

## GOD OF JUSTICE AND MERCY

The Bible repeatedly identifies God as a just God. Because of this, sins must be punished or there is no justice at all. Imagine if judges routinely did not enforce the law! Chaos would be the result. A world without true justice is cruel to its occupants. Also, there can be no love without justice. If you saw someone you love doing something hurtful to themselves, wouldn't your attempt to correct the person be an act of love? Love demands that we correct others when they do wrong. God is indeed a God of love, which makes Him also a God of justice.

✠ *...the Lord disciplines those He loves, as a father the son He delights in* (Proverbs 3:12).

✠ *...Yes, Lord God Almighty,* **true** *and* **just** *are your judgments* (Revelation 16:7).

God desires and created us to live in a Heaven-like environment. Because of the fall, we, like Adam and Eve, live in a world full of evil and pain. When we do finally get to Heaven, we will have established a complete record of evidence on our own failure to live life without Him as He had warned us of in the beginning.

✠ *...I have set before you life and death, blessing and curses. Now* **choose life**, *so that you and your children may live and that you may love the Lord your God,* **listen** *to his voice and* **hold fast to Him**... (Deuteronomy 30:19-20).

Despite our failures, our Father in Heaven loves and wants an eternal relationship with us—for us to *hold fast* to Him. Out of love for us, God did *not* want sin, along with the negative effects of sin (rudeness, violence, wars, terrorism, etc.) to last for an *eternity*; therefore, sin must result in *death* so it can be extinguished once and for all. At the same time, He created a way for sin to be punished without condemning *us* all to *eternal* death. He did this by sending His Son, an *innocent man*, who agreed to take our punishment so that both justice and love would be fulfilled. His innocent blood shed on the cross covers our sin in the sight of God so that when God sees us, He sees Christ's righteousness. Though this story is described in the New Testament, the need for our sins to be covered by the shedding of innocent blood was foreshadowed back in Genesis:

✠ *The Lord God made garments of skin for Adam and his wife and clothed them* (Genesis 3:21).

God took Adam and Eve's fig leaves and replaced them with animal skins. He shed the blood of an innocent goat to cover Adam and Eve's sins. This became a familiar practice for the Jews in the Old Testament—offering animal sacrifices to cover sins. However, they had to continually offer sacrifices because their sacrifices were not perfect or permanent. Jesus Christ became the perfect, final, and complete sacrifice.

✟ *In Him* [Jesus Christ] *we have redemption through His blood, the forgiveness of sins, in accordance with the riches of God's grace...* (Ephesians 1:7).

✟ *To Him* [Jesus Christ] *who loves us and has freed us from our sins by His blood...* (Revelation 1:6).

✟ *...For He* [Jesus Christ] *has clothed me with garments of salvation and arrayed me in a robe of righteousness* [right standing with God]... (Isaiah 61:10).

It is *only* by Jesus' sacrifice that we could re-enter an eternal intimate relationship with God. When we die, this eternal relationship brings us into and indeed is that experience we call *Heaven*. Jesus described eternal life this way:

✟ *Now this is **eternal life**: that they* [you and me] *may **know You** the only true God, and Jesus Christ whom You have sent* (John 17:3).

Hell can simply be defined as an eternity without accepting Christ's reconciliation of an eternal relationship with God.

✠ *Remember that at that time you were separated from Christ, excluded from citizenship in Israel [Heaven] and foreigners to the covenants of the promise, without hope and without God in the world. But now in Christ Jesus you once were far away and have been brought near through the blood of Christ.*

*For He Himself is our peace, who has made the two one and has destroyed the barrier, the dividing wall of hostility, by abolishing in His flesh the law with its commandments and regulations. His purpose was to create in Himself one new man out of two thus making peace, and in this one body to reconcile both of them to God through the cross, by which He put to death their hostility.... For through Him we both have **access** to the Father by one Spirit. Consequently, you are no longer foreigners and aliens, but **fellow citizens with God's people and members of God's household** (Ephesians 2:12-19).*

It is also through Jesus Christ that we eventually get back our glory:

✠ *When Christ, who is your life, appears, then you will also appear with Him in glory (Colossians 3:4).*

By reconnecting with God's Spirit, God can transform us into His image and likeness as He originally intended, and we will receive freedom from the restrictions that kept us from obtaining this glory, a glory we can, to some degree, obtain here and now in this life:

✠ *Now the Lord is the Spirit and where the Spirit of the Lord is, there is freedom. And we, who with unveiled faces all reflect the Lord's glory, are being transformed into His likeness with **ever-increasing** glory, which comes from the Lord, who is the Spirit (2 Corinthians 3:17-18).*

Jesus Christ is the key to reconnecting with God's Spirit and freeing us from the effects of sin in our lives. The process begins with a decision to receive, unwrap, and use the Gifts of Freedom God offers to us. Let's unwrap the first gift.

## MEDITATION POINT

Jesus brings life to you.

Go to the Introduction in the Study Guide section on page 281.

## ENDNOTES

1.  *The Broadman Bible Commentary, Vol. 1* (Nashville, TN: Broadman Press, 1973), 24–25.

2.  "Theory of Relativity," *Encyclopedia Britannica*. 2008. Encyclopedia Britannica Online. Retrieved February 18, 2008, from http://www .britannica.com/eb/article-9109465.

# Chapter 2

# GIFT #1—LIFE THROUGH GRACE (PART 1)

## HOW DO YOU GET IT?

*Before you begin to read, pray that the Holy Spirit
will give you understanding and application.*

☦ *For the wages of sin is death, but the **gift** of God is **eternal life** in
Christ Jesus our Lord* (Romans 6:23).

☦ *For it is by grace you have been **saved**, through **faith**—and this not
from yourselves, it is the **gift** of God—not by works, so that no one can
boast* (Ephesians 2:8-9).

D o you remember what it felt like as a child to wake up on Christmas
day and race from your bedroom to discover presents under the
tree? Anticipation and excitement swirled inside at a dizzying pace
as you reached for each gift with your name on it. Were you a careful un-
wrapper? Or did you tear into the paper with wild excitement? The Bible
says that the first *gift* God offers us is eternal life, which is accepted through
faith alone. Eternal life would be a pretty big Christmas gift to open by
anyone's standard!

Remember your childlike wonder on Christmas Day—the waiting, the expectancy, the genuine expression of surprise and delight? Jesus loves that childlike wonder and excitement, that genuine expression of surprise and delight. In fact, when asked who was the greatest in Heaven, Jesus answered:

☩ *I tell you the truth, unless you **change** and **become** like little children, you will never enter the Kingdom of Heaven. Therefore, whoever humbles himself like this child is the greatest in the Kingdom of Heaven* (Matthew 18:3-4).

God desires us to keep this childlike nature as we get to know Him and unwrap His gifts, because children have an open, accepting, noncritical, and trusting attitude. Having this type of outlook should be easy as God's gifts are so wonderful and are available year-round. The question is, will you receive, unwrap, and use them?

## THE GIFT OF SALVATION

The first gift is the most important of all the gifts. It has an "open this first" sticker on it because it's a prerequisite for all the other gifts. I'm referring to the gift of salvation through God's gift of grace. It is God's gift of grace that allows us to receive the gift of life. It is like it is two gifts that are intertwined together into one wonderful gift.

God's gift of grace is the vehicle for you to receive His gift of life. God clearly offers this two-in-one gift to all of us, but the nature of gift-giving is that you can't receive a gift that you refuse to accept. And it's impossible to receive a gift by force. God does not force us to become His companions. Remember, God gives us free choice in this process of reconciliation and relationship. Jesus talks about this first step of salvation with Nicodemus, a religious ruler in His day. Let's read the exchange they had:

✟ [Nicodemus] *came to Jesus at night and said, "Rabbi, we know you are a teacher who has come from God. For no one could perform the miraculous signs you are doing if God were not with him."*

*In reply Jesus declared, "I tell you the truth, no one can see the Kingdom of God unless he is born again."*

*"How can a man be born when he is old?" Nicodemus asked. "Surely he cannot enter a second time into his mother's womb to be born!"*

*Jesus answered, "I tell you the truth, no one can enter the Kingdom of God unless he is born of water and the Spirit. Flesh gives birth to flesh, but the **Spirit** [God's] **gives birth to spirit** [human's]. You should not be surprised at my saying, 'You must be **born again**'"* (John 3:2-7).

Nicodemus was confused and surprised because it was not the answer he expected. Born again? Of course, Jesus was not speaking physically; rather was speaking about the rebirth of our spirit. Jesus essentially tells Nicodemus that his spirit can't connect with God's Spirit without rebirth. He says, in essence, that while our mother gives us physical life at birth (flesh births flesh), *only* God can give us this spiritual life (Spirit births spirit). If Nicodemus wishes to experience the Kingdom of God, then he needs a fully operational spirit—a spirit that connects with God in the way He intended.

Jesus went on to say:

✟ *...that everyone who believes* [in Jesus] *may have eternal life. For God so loved the world that He gave His one and only Son, that whoever believes in Him shall not perish but have eternal life* (John 3:15-16).

When Jesus speaks of eternal life, He is speaking about both our physical and spiritual lives. Those who believe in Jesus will receive reborn spirits now, as well as glorious new bodies in Heaven, where they will be in an intimate relationship with God for all eternity. John goes on to describe how to experience this rebirth:

✠ *Now this is eternal life: that they may know You, the only true God, and Jesus Christ, whom You have sent* (John 17:3).

And Paul writes:

✠ ...[Jesus Christ] *who, by the power that enables Him to bring everything under His control, will transform our lowly bodies so they will be like His glorious body* (Philippians 3:21).

What happens to those who don't choose to believe in Jesus? They have an eternal destiny too, though one that is separate from God. The Bible refers to this as hell:

✠ *The wicked shall be turned into hell, and all the nations that forget God* (Psalm 9:17 NKJV).

It's important to note what is meant by the word *wicked* here. In the simplest of terms, a wicked person is someone who does evil, someone who does the opposite of God's will. But none of us are perfect. We all fail. If we factor in what Jesus says to Nicodemus, then we can see that it's not only individual actions against God's will that causes someone to experience hell—eternity without God's presence—but it is ultimately the decision to deny God. The decision to reject Jesus is refusing the gift of reconciliation, the heart of salvation.

## WE NEED THIS GIFT

Why do we need to accept this gift of salvation? It is because we have all fallen short of who God intended us to be. The only way to reconnect with God is to acknowledge this truth and choose to receive His free gift through grace. The Bible says:

☩ *...for all have sinned and fall short of the glory of God* (Romans 3:23).

The word for sin in Hebrew is *hamartia* (ham-ar-tee-ah), which means "missing the mark" or "taking the wrong course." The New Testament uses the word in a number of ways: in a generic sense for a concrete wrong-doing; as a principle and quality of action; and as a sinful deed.[1] The word for *sin* was also used as an archers' term for an arrow that misses its target.

Can we hit that target on our own? See if you qualify according to this entry requirement:

☩ [Jesus said], *"Be perfect, therefore, as your heavenly Father is perfect"* (Matthew 5:48).

Working our way to Heaven by being good or following rules is simply *not* an option. This is why grace is so important in our ability to receive the gift of life as a *gift*; we alone are not able to earn it even if we desired. The Old Testament chronicles a long history where men and women did their very best to earn their own salvation. Even then, God required animal sacrifices to atone, or pay, for sin, creating an endless cycle, thus forever missing the mark. But when God sent His Son, the story changed. The author of Hebrews writes:

☩ *For this reason He* [Jesus] *had to be made like his brothers* [you and me] *in every way, in order that He might become a merciful and faithful high priest in service to God, and that He might make* **atonement** *for the sins of the people* (Hebrews 2:17).

The English word *atone* is formed by joining two words together, *at* and *one*. It means to become *at one* with God or reconciled with Him. This is the state where God wishes to see our spirit and His Spirit in oneness. In this verse, Jesus is clearly the way for us to achieve this oneness of spirit. No other way is possible.

While we see it was by the sin of one (Adam) that death was passed to all, it is by the death of One (Jesus) that life is passed to all who accept it. Now, those born once physically die twice (physically and spiritually), but those born twice die only once (physically).

Maybe you're a really good person. You do good things. You don't have any obvious sins in your life. Who knows, perhaps you even go to church every week. However, in God's eyes you have fallen short even if you've only sinned once in your entire existence. Even *one* sin makes you incapable of being holy, pure, and blameless:

✠ *For whoever keeps the whole law and yet stumbles at just **one** point is guilty of breaking **all** of it* (James 2:10).

Let's look at it this way: If you had a reservoir of clean water and you poured even the smallest amount of poison in it, the whole reservoir would be poisoned. No one could drink from it. Since God is perfectly pure, He can't drink from it either. Remember that there is *no* darkness found in Him. Many mistakenly believe that they need to change their lives, stop sinning, and become perfect to receive the gift of salvation. However, the reservoir will always be poisoned and toxic, no matter how little or how much you have sinned, whether you are a hardened criminal or a church-goer—Jesus Christ, the gift through which salvation is received, is the only renewing source to purify our reservoir. And it is by God's grace alone that we are offered this gift.

Remember Jesus asking the Samaritan woman at the well for a drink? He was thirsty for fellowship with her, but her well was not living water. Jesus needs to purify our wells into living water so they can quench that thirst for fellowship. Paul writes:

✠ *As for you, you were dead in your transgressions and sins, in which you used to live when you followed the ways of this world and of the ruler of the kingdom of the air, the spirit who is now at work in those who are disobedient. All of us also lived among them at one time, gratifying the cravings of our sinful nature and following its desires and thoughts. Like the rest, we were by nature objects of wrath. But because of His great love for us, God, who is rich in mercy, made us* **alive with Christ** *even when we were dead in transgressions—it is by* **grace** *you have been saved. And God* **raised us up with Christ** *and seated us with Him in heavenly realms in Christ Jesus in order that in the coming age He might show the incomparable riches of His grace, expressed in His kindness to us in Christ Jesus. For it is by* **grace** *you have been saved, through faith—and this not from yourselves, it is the* **gift** *of God—not by works, so that no man can boast* (Ephesians 2:1-9).

The gift of salvation that Jesus embodies is a *gift*, pure and simple. We can't earn or attain this salvation. We only receive this gift by the *grace* of God.

The concept of grace is unique to the Christian faith. Other religions teach the idea of Karma, which is the philosophy that the quality of people's current and future lives is determined only by *their* behavior in this life. Jesus offers us *grace*, which can be defined as unmerited or undeserved favor. The word for grace, *charis*, comes from the same root as *chara*, which means "joy" or *chairo*, which means "to rejoice."[2] What a perfect origin for such a word!

Grace brings people real joy because it offers freedom from past mistakes, to walk in the truth that God accepts and loves you unconditionally, no matter what you've done in the past, *no matter what you have done in the past.* Jesus Christ's sacrifice cleans the reservoir so you can reconnect with God. If it were up to you to do good works, to earn your salvation, you would become *enslaved* to your efforts. How many good deeds would you need to perform? How would you ever know if you'd done enough?

There are twenty-two letters in the Hebrew alphabet, and the fifth letter is *hei,* which stands for grace. Therefore, the number five stands for grace as well. Every letter in the Hebrew alphabet has a symbol associated with it, except for *hei.* The letter itself looks like a window. The word used for *God* is made up of the letters *hei vav hei yud.* The letter *yud* is a symbol for an open hand, while *vav* means hook or nail. If you read the letters of God's name from right to left, which is how a Hebrew would read them, then the letters making up God's name means "open hand of grace is nailed in grace."

The gospel of John opens with a description of Jesus, which says in part:

*From the fullness of His grace we have all received one blessing after another. For the law was given through Moses; grace and truth came through Jesus Christ* (John 1:16-17).

It is through God's open hand of grace that the gift of life was offered to us and perfected when the open hand of Jesus received the nail of punishment for our sins. It is from this that we are freed when we accept this gift, the ultimate gift of grace.

When the Roman governor ordered Jesus to be crucified at the demands of the religious leaders of the day, he also ordered a sign to be nailed to the cross over Jesus' head, which read, "Jesus (Yeshua) of Nazareth (*Hanazarei*), the King (*Vemelekh*) of the Jews (*Hayhudim*)." The sign was prophetic on two levels. The religious leaders vehemently protested to Pilate (see John 19:19-21) because the sign prophesied Jesus as the King of the Jews. Also, and more profoundly, when you read the first letters of each word, it spells out God's name. The meaning of those letters again is "open hand of grace is nailed in grace."

Jesus' death on the cross paid for our sins under the law. This satisfied the requirement for justice so we no longer have to be perfect to have an eternal relationship with God. Jesus is the embodiment of our achieving eternal life through grace. This is the New Testament message Paul and the other disciples preached as well. God enabled them to perform signs and wonders to confirm His message of grace to the world.

✜ *So Paul and Barnabas spent considerable time there, speaking boldly for the Lord, who confirmed the message of his grace by enabling them to do miraculous signs and wonders* (Acts 14:3).

Specifically, what was their message of grace?

✜ *Therefore, my brothers, I want you to know that through Jesus the forgiveness of sins is proclaimed to you. Through him everyone who believes is justified from everything you could not be justified from by the law of Moses* (Acts 13:38-39).

God's plan is simple: accept His gift and by His grace you are set free! There is only one way to receive eternal life and freedom: we *believe* Jesus was sacrificed to make atonement for our sins. Paul writes, reaffirming this truth:

✜ *God presented* [Jesus] *as a sacrifice of atonement, through faith in His blood. He did this to demonstrate His justice, because in forbearance He had left the sins committed beforehand unpunished* [by those in the Old Testament who had faith in the prophesied Messiah to come]... (Romans 3:25).

Also in the New Testament book of Romans, there is an explanation about how to ask for and receive this gift:

✜ *If you* **confess** *with your mouth, "Jesus is Lord," and* **believe** *in your heart that God raised him from the dead, you will be* **saved**. *For it is with your heart that you believe and are justified, and it is with your mouth that you confess and are saved* (Romans 10:9-10).

We use the word *believe* rather carelessly in the world today. We talk about believing in a cause or Peter Pan, or as a hesitant response to someone's question we say, "I believe so." *Believe* in Romans 10:9-10 is the word *pisteuo* (pist-yoo-oh), the verb form of *pistis*, which means "faith" or "to be fully convinced of" or "to rely on."[3] We are not simply talking about having a belief that Jesus existed. Many people believe He existed, perhaps seeing Him as a prophet or great spiritual leader; however, they *don't* believe in Him for their salvation. Even demons believe Jesus was the Son of God:

✠ *"What do you want with us, Son of God?"* [the demons] *shouted. "Have you come here to torture us before the appointed time?"* (Matthew 8:29).

Perhaps you know people who pray to Jesus in times of trouble, but don't believe in Him for salvation. This is called temporal faith. People with temporal faith believe in Jesus only for temporal things, such as a winning team, a new car, house, job, fame, health, or money, which are all things that are not eternal. This kind of belief in Jesus does *not* give them eternal salvation.

It is important to truly believe and trust in the right source for your eternal salvation. There is a story of a high-wire tightrope artist who asked a man in the crowd if he believed he could cross over the high wire stretched across a deep canyon. The man looked at the situation and nonchalantly said yes. So the high-wire artist asked him to get into a wheelbarrow and he would take him across. What the man *believed* took on a whole new meaning when the stakes were raised and his life *depended* on what he *believed*.

We are all going to die at some point in time. When this happens, we all hope to cross over that canyon of death into a new and better life of some kind. Who are you trusting to get you across that high wire? It's an *important* question; perhaps the *most* important question you will ever have to answer in this life. Both failing to properly answer and procrastinating lead to the same disastrous result—trusting in *yourself*. Are you *really* qualified to be your own master of eternal life and death?

The Bible clearly says the eternal gift of salvation only comes through *believing in Jesus as your Savior*. Nothing more and nothing less.

✠ [Jesus said], *"I tell you the truth, whoever hears My words and believes Him who sent Me has eternal life and will not be condemned; he has* **crossed** *over from death to* **life***"* (John 5:24).

## ACTION & VISUALIZATION

*Accept God's gift of salvation; picture yourself drinking living water.*

## AN EASY GIFT TO RECEIVE

I am belaboring this point because it is important for you to completely understand: there is no way to earn or work your way into salvation; it is an unmerited free *gift*—a gift of grace. Read what happened to a criminal who hung next to Jesus at His crucifixion:

✠ *One of the criminals who hung there hurled insults at Him: "Aren't You the Christ? Save Yourself and us!"*

*But the other criminal rebuked him. "Don't you fear God," he said, "since you are under the same sentence? We are punished justly, for we are getting what our deeds deserve. But this Man has done nothing wrong."*

*Then he said, "Jesus, remember me when You come into Your Kingdom."*

*Jesus answered him, "I tell you the truth, today you will be with Me in paradise"* (Luke 23:39-43).

The sinner on the cross only had to believe in who Jesus was—the Savior—in order to receive the gift of salvation. Jesus said his confession of faith would save him: "Today you will be with Me in paradise." The criminal didn't have the time or the ability to come down from his cross and be a good person, or perform a repentant act. He only had to believe in his heart and confess with his mouth that Jesus was the Savior.

Jesus wants you to come to Him in the same way—just as you are. His entire ministry revolved around reaching out to the most hardened sinners, the broken, downtrodden people of the day. Interestingly, Jesus was criticized by the religious leaders of the time for hanging out with sinful, immoral people. In fact, Jesus wanted the people around Him (and us as well) to understand that He came to forgive the sins of *all* sinners. He told this insightful story, as recorded in the gospel of Luke:

*Now one of the Pharisees invited Jesus to have dinner with Him, so He went to the Pharisee's house and reclined at the table. When a woman who had lived a sinful life in that town learned that Jesus was eating at the Pharisee's house, she brought an alabaster jar of perfume, and as she stood behind Him at His feet weeping, she began to wet His feet with her tears. Then she wiped them with her hair, kissed them and poured perfume on them.*

*When the Pharisee who had invited Him saw this, he said to himself, "If this Man were a prophet, He would know who is touching Him and what kind of woman she is—that she is a sinner."*

*Jesus answered him, "Simon, I have something to tell you."*

*"Tell me, Teacher," he said.*

*He answered, "Two men owed money to a certain moneylender. One owed him five hundred denarii, and the other fifty. Neither of them had the money to pay him back, so he canceled the debts of both. Now which of them will love him more?"*

*Simon replied, "I suppose the one who had the bigger debt canceled."*

*"You have judged correctly," Jesus said.*

*Then He turned toward the woman and said to Simon, "Do you
see this woman? I came into your house. You did not give Me any
water for My feet, but she wet My feet with her tears and wiped them
with her hair. You did not give Me a kiss, but this woman, from the
time I entered, has not stopped kissing My feet. You did not put oil on
My head, but she has poured perfume on My feet. Therefore, I tell you,
her many sins have been forgiven—for she loved much. But he who
has been forgiven little loves little."*

*…Jesus said to the woman, "Your faith has saved you; go in peace"*
(Luke 7:36-47,50).

Jesus told the woman that her faith saved her. The word for *save* in the
original text is *sozo* (sode-zoe), which means "to rescue from danger or destruction" or "to deliver." Perhaps you've heard someone ask the question,
"Are you saved?" They are asking if *the person has accepted God's gift of salvation*.[4] It's a fair and important question, but it would be wrong to assume
a yes answer and to end the discussion there.

To be saved is just the starting point for a renewed relationship with
God; His saving power touches every area of life. He doesn't just want you
to reconnect with Him; He wants you to get to *know* Him, to *learn* to *live life
as He intended*. He wants you to *engage* Him in your life and to receive all
the gifts He offers that lead to an intimate relationship with Him. The role
of free choice continues even after we accept God's *first* gift.

How does this relationship grow? The apostle Paul alluded to this in his
letter to the church at Philippi:

✠ *Therefore, my dear friends, as you have always obeyed—not only in
my presence, but now much more in my absence—**continue to work
out your salvation** with fear and trembling* (Philippians 2:12).

After you accept your gift of salvation, you start a journey, learning how
to walk in relationship with God. This is a relationship that will cause you to

change some of your thinking and ways of acting if you are going to receive the full benefit of this gift and other gifts while you are still on earth. Read what Jesus prayed right before His death:

✠ *My prayer is not for them alone. I pray also for those who will believe in Me through their message, that all of them may be one, Father, just as You are in Me and I am in You. May they also be in Us so that the world may believe that You have sent Me. I have given them the glory that You gave Me, that they may be one as We are One: I in them and You in Me. May they be brought to complete unity* [with God and His will for your life] *to let the world know that You sent Me and have loved **them** even as You have loved **Me*** (John 17:20-23).

Jesus wants to start giving back the glory God intended for you—a flicker at first, and a full blaze in the life to come.

Perhaps you haven't yet accepted Christ as your Savior. You may be wondering, "How do I know that what these verses are saying is true?" That's where faith enters the picture. Read this passage written by the apostle John:

✠ *Anyone who believes in the Son of God **has this testimony in his heart**. Anyone who does not believe God has made Him out to be a liar, because he has not believed the testimony God has given about His Son. And this is the testimony: God has given us eternal life, and this life is in His Son. He who has the Son has life; he who does not have the Son of God does not have life* (1 John 5:10-12).

When your spirit comes alive, you will *know* all this to be true in your heart. Once you begin a relationship with Jesus, your spirit and God's in you will be as real to you as this book you're holding. Until then, the verses may seem empty, words on a page.

Some well-intentioned Christians only throw Bible verses at people to get them to accept Jesus. God's Word certainly is a powerful source. But for some, hearing God's Word alone does little to bring them to Him if they're not open to it. He wants *willing* companions. Even God's Word cannot save you; you are saved only by your faith in Christ alone.

When I walked into a church in 1988, I had plenty of unresolved issues in my life and just as many questions on my mind. No one stood next to me and quoted Bible verses to bring me to Christ. I was seeking God, so God reached out in a real, experiential way. After I accepted Jesus as my Savior, I immediately knew there was something different in me. There was something new in me, a change from the *inside out*, which allowed me to make sense of life. God's method is to work from the inside out, giving us a completely new perspective.

I wanted to tell the world about my new perspective. But how? It was as if I had received sight for the first time in a world filled with blindness. How could I possibly explain that experience to someone who was blind, someone who had always known blindness? What would I tell them about the color blue? About the infinite variations of a smile? About the uniqueness of every sunset?

This also works in reverse. Consider the book you're holding. You are aware of its reality, and there is nothing anybody can say that will convince you it isn't real. You know you are holding this book because you're holding it! Nobody is going to come up with a reasonable argument that will cause you to believe otherwise. This is how being born again works too. You know God is in you because God is in you! Until you experience it for yourself, you can't know what it's like. Someone could describe it to you until they're blue in the face, but without the actual experience it's simply impossible to *fully* understand.

## ACTION & VISUALIZATION
*Reach out to God and trust Him to show you the way.*

## GOD SPEAKS THROUGH HIS CREATION

God knows it can be difficult to accept the truth of His story. While it ultimately takes faith to believe, God has generously given us clues in nature that point to Him:

✠ *God has made it plain to* [humankind]. *For since the creation of the world God's invisible qualities—His eternal power and divine nature—have been clearly seen, being understood from what has been made, so that men are without excuse* [to know He exists and created everything] (Romans 1:19-20).

You only have to look at the complexity of this world to know it was planned and created by an Intelligent Designer. If you were walking along the beach and saw a complex arrangement of sand that spelled out "Jane loves Bill," you would most likely assume it was written by an *intelligent being* and *not* the random rearrangement of sand caused by waves.

Using the same perspective, let's look at the complexity of life itself, which is substantially more complex than just words written in the sand. Protein chains made up in links called amino acids are the most basic ingredients of life. These amino acids line up in exactly the right order and *all* be left handed (which is against the tendency of nature to naturally occur). A small protein with only a hundred amino acids would only have one chance of occurring in 10,000,000,000,000,000,000,000,000,000,000,000,000,000,000,000,000,000, 000,000,000,000,000,000,000,000,000,000,000,000,000,000,000,000,000, 000,000,000,000,000,000,000,000,000 (10 to the 129th power). Proteins with four hundred amino acids would have considerably worse odds than this.[5] Moreover, you need *many different* kinds of proteins to create life and these odds have to be replicated *many, many times* over before resulting in the *simplest* of living organisms. That statistical number would fill this page! If you're betting on luck or some kind of natural process to create life, then stay away from Las Vegas!

If you took these statistical numbers to a mathematician, they would tell you anything that has over 10 to the 50th power of happening is statistically impossible. Yet evolutionists rely on one statistically impossible event after another to supposedly give us a "scientific" view about the origination of life. Sadly, many people today are betting their eternal life on these impossible odds. It is obvious an Intelligent Designer arranges all details in such a way as to allow living things to function in extremely complex and interdependent ways.

Professor Chandra Wickramasinghe and Sir Fred Hoyle—whose ten-year study calculated the statistical odds of our life coming about by chance to 1 in 10 to the 40,000th power—summed it up rather imaginatively with this statistical calculation: the likelihood of a "lucky" circumstance creating life was about the equivalent to the probability of a tornado sweeping through a junkyard and assembling a fully functional Boeing 747 actually in flight out the other side.[6] In fact, it's interesting to note there are approximately 4.5 million nonflying parts (that could not fly alone without being organized in just a certain way with the other parts) in the plane; however, in just *one* human cell there are over *one billion* nonliving parts that *must* be organized in just a certain way for that one cell to function. You would never trust your life on a plane where you didn't know its parts had been organized by an intelligent designer. So why would you put your trust in a theory that has *never* been proven and, according to mathematicians, is statistically impossible to happen?

Moreover, the creation of life itself through evolution would defy the laws of nature as we know them. The Second Law of Thermodynamics (a law fully accepted by all) states in simple terms that the natural tendency is for information to get scrambled—order tends to move into disorder (things are wearing out or breaking down), not organizing into higher more complicated forms. This is one of the most provable laws of physics. Our universe, left to its own natural process, tends toward maximum entropy (a measure of disorder).[7] An example would be if you parked a '57 Chevy on the beach. Eventually it would become a pile of rusted-out junk. But if you took a pile of rusted-out junk onto the beach, you would never end up with a drivable '57 Chevy. Loss of *organization* is the natural progression of nature; organization requires an *organizer*.

God created the earth with precision, and the Bible says that God is focused on every detail of *you*:

✠ *And even the very hairs of your head are all numbered* [by God] (Matthew 10:30).

Let's go even deeper and consider just a *few* of the many amazing details about how you were designed and how the world was created for your benefit. Consider: In the typical human baby, God *organizes* approximately 3,000,000,000,000,000,000,000,000,000 atoms in such a way as to create a living creature that will not remain the same, but will grow or *organize* itself over time in generally the same form, but with some exceptions. To accomplish this growth or *organization*, He has imbedded in each of us a DNA map that guides growth from baby to adult, each according to our own unique plan.

Does this seem like an accident of nature? Evolutionists have *not* come up with any credible theory to explain how or where these plans of construction embedded in our DNA come from. DNA instructs all parts of the body to capture the materials it needs and then *mysteriously* orders the construction of them to make life and grow all living things. I say "mysteriously" because there is one unexplained fact after another in the formation and sustaining of life. Truth is that we can't even fully explain today how He did it, but we do know that God used the DNA mapping plan for the *organization* and construction of plants, animals, fish, birds, and insects—every living thing. In each cell of any seed or living being, one can find the entire growth or *organizing* plan for that specific living thing, a plan that governs how it *organizes* the many new atoms required in its growth.

During a baby's growth to an adult, it will assimilate in an *organized* fashion according to its DNA plan an additional 67,000,000,000,000,000,

000,000,000,000 atoms. Just having the material isn't enough to grow. It's the information and mechanism for arranging that material that is important. Imagine you forgot someone's phone number that had these same twenty-nine digits. How long would it take you to randomly find the right order of numbers? The answer is not in your lifetime or even the earth's age according to evolutionists.

On a different level, however, the immune system, with incredible sophistication and complexity, was designed and *organized* by God to fight germs, viruses, and other microorganisms. The human brain is a natural computer composed of a hundred billion neurons, each of which connects to about ten thousand others, *all* of which function in parallel. Your brain is processing an uncountable amount of information every second. The eye *alone* collects enough data for the brain in just a tenth of a second to keep a Cray supercomputer processing for a hundred years.[8]

The body is designed and *organized* to assimilate the daily required fuel, vitamins, minerals, and nutrients needed to sustain itself. Each one of the processes is unbelievably complex and involved. For example, the body must maintain its internal temperature within a tenth of a degree range or vitamin B won't be assimilated.

All these things, and many more necessities for sustenance, are supplied by an extremely complicated, delicate, and interdependent supply chain within the world in which we live. Many small differences (changes to temperature, the earth's orbit, etc.) would immobilize the structure that supplies our needs and would cause humans to become extinct. Amazingly, the average human heart will beat, in an average lifetime, 2.7 billion times consecutively without interruption or time off.

Given the unbelievable complexity and organization to create and sustain life, it certainly seems unlikely that a statistically *impossible* series of random events created and sustains your life, don't you think? Perhaps, more importantly, how would a soul come about by a random process? Or our self-awareness? Our intellect? Emotions? Desires? Our ability to love? Could *all* of this come from a series of *accidents*?

## THE RELATIONSHIP BETWEEN BODY, MIND, AND SPIRIT

God put an incredible amount of thought and purpose into the inner working of our physical bodies. He put equal thought and purpose into the creation of our minds (our intellect and emotions), with which we make our decisions using our free will, and spirits, which can act like navigation systems when they're connected with the Creator. Just as your body is charged with gathering physical information to help you navigate through life, so your spirit is charged with gathering spiritual information.

Your mind is constantly *balancing* between the *body* and *spirit* on this journey through life. Imagine an airplane cockpit with only half of its vital instruments working. What if the missing equipment included the communications system (there goes your dialogue with the control tower) and the navigational system (there goes your ability to choose a destination and the directions to get there)? This lack of critical equipment is like our condition before we are born again, before we're reconnected with God.

There is a complex interdependent relationship between the physical life (body and mind) and the spiritual life. This becomes especially evident when we begin to consider difficult issues such as sin, immorality, and what happens when we die. Too often we focus on the physical aspects of this life without regard for the spiritual truths that affect our life every day. Our constant focus on pursuing and gratifying our bodies' needs can distract us from discovering spiritual realities. However, *if we're open to God*, He can even use this pursuit of the physical to point us to spiritual truth. One great example of this is found in the story of Bartimaeus:

*Then they came to Jericho. As Jesus and His disciples, together with a large crowd, were leaving the city, a blind man, Bartimaeus (that is, the Son of Timaeus), was sitting by the roadside begging. When he heard that it was Jesus of Nazareth, he began to shout, "Jesus, Son of David, have mercy on me!"*

*Many rebuked him and told him to be quiet, but he shouted all the more, "Son of David, have mercy on me!"*

*Jesus stopped and said, "Call him."*

*So they called to the blind man, "Cheer up! On your feet! He's calling you." Throwing his cloak aside, he jumped to his feet and came to Jesus.*

*"What do you want Me to do for you?" Jesus asked him* (Mark 10:46-51).

At this point in the story, you may be wondering, "Why on earth would Jesus ask him such a question?" It would seem obvious that a blind man would want to see, right? Jesus is aware of another reality, however, a spiritual reality. Bartimaeus had a bigger problem than his *physical* blindness—he was *spiritually* blind! While his physical blindness would only last during his living years, spiritual blindness *affected eternity*. Jesus knew the blind man's *biggest* need was for eternal salvation, to recognize Jesus as the Messiah and choose to follow Him. Bartimaeus did this when he acknowledged Jesus as the "Son of David."

The Jews were expecting a Messiah, a Savior who would bring salvation to their nation. The Old Testament taught that the Messiah would come from the lineage of King David. Jesus was indeed from King David's lineage. He was also the prophesied Messiah, though many Jews did not choose to believe it. However, Bartimaeus, because of his statement, showed belief in Jesus as the Messiah; because of that, he was given the gift of salvation in addition to his sight.

## YOUR STORY SO FAR

"Where are you?" God asked Adam and Eve this question and He asks you now: "Where are you at spiritually?" Have you already chosen to accept God's first gift, the gift of salvation? Or are you still on your spiritual quest? If you're still searching, perhaps it's because you're still unsure how Jesus fits into your story. Perhaps you believe He was just a prophet or a teacher or some sort of philosopher. Read what the Bible says about who Jesus is:

✠ *He is the image of the invisible God, the Firstborn over all creation. For by Him **all** things were created: things in Heaven and on earth, visible and invisible, whether thrones or powers or rulers or authorities; all things were created by Him and for Him. He is before all things, and in Him all things hold together. And He is the **head** of the body, the Church; He is the beginning and the Firstborn from among the dead, so that in **everything** He might have the **supremacy**. For God was pleased to have all **His fullness dwell in Him**, and through Him to **reconcile** to Himself all things, whether things on earth or things in Heaven, by making peace through His blood, shed on the cross.*

*Once you were alienated from God and were enemies in your minds because of your evil behavior. But now He has **reconciled** you by **Christ's physical body through death** to present you holy in His sight* [Christ's blood covers your sins], *without blemish and free from accusation…* (Colossians 1:15-22).

Jesus is *the* key to our reconciliation with God because we can accept His blood to cover us. So then, when God sees us He sees the holiness of Christ in us, not our sins. Those sins are now covered with Christ's blood. Accepting the gift of salvation is as simple as doing what Bartimaeus did or what the criminal next to Jesus on the cross did. They *recognized* and *trusted* Him as their *Savior*.

What about you? Where are you? You may not be blind like Bartimaeus or hanging on a cross like the thief, but do you feel as helpless as they did? Jesus, have mercy on me. Jesus, remember me. Have you trusted in Jesus as the *only one* who can save you? This is the first gift that *must be accepted and used* for any of the others to have any *value*. This is what brings us back on course. Jesus Christ is *the* way to life. Perhaps *now* is the time for you to make that decision.

If you're ready for this gift and wish to begin a relationship with God, all you have to do is believe in your heart and respond in prayer, much like the following:

*Jesus, I confess that I'm a sinner and I come to You through faith. I invite You into my heart and into my life right now. I confess with my mouth that You are Lord of my life. I believe You died for my sins and that God raised You from the dead so that I might have everlasting life with You. Thank You for taking my place on the cross and for paying the full price for my sins. Fill me with Your Holy Spirit and make my life pleasing and fruitful in Your sight. I am praying in the name of Jesus. Amen.*

If you just took that first step, congratulations! It is your birthday, the first day of your new life connected to God. The Bible tells us in Luke 15:22-24 that whenever someone accepts the gift of salvation, a celebration breaks out in Heaven. God throws a party just for you. We find the beautiful picture of this celebration in the story of the prodigal son, which Jesus relays to us in the gospel of Luke.

It is the story of a man and his two sons. One son leaves home abruptly, taking all his inheritance with him and abandoning his family to live life on his own, the way he wants to. Eventually, he ends up broke, empty, and alone. Out of sheer desperation he returns home, expecting very little from his father because of all the wrongs he has done. Jesus continues the rest of the story:

[The prodigal son says], *"I will set out and go back to my father and say to him: Father, I have sinned against Heaven and against you. I am no longer worthy to be called your son; make me like one of your hired men."* So he got up and went to his father.

    *But while he was still a long way off, his father saw him and was **filled with compassion for him**; he ran to his son, threw his arms around him and kissed him* (Luke 15:18-20).

Did you notice what it says about the father? He saw his son while he was *a long way off*. The father was looking for him, *expecting* him, ready to accept him whenever he chose to return. What a beautiful picture. Your heavenly Father has been compassionately expecting you too. Jesus continues the story:

✠ *The son said to him, "Father, I have **sinned** against Heaven and against you. I am no longer worthy to be called your son."*

*But the father said to his servants, "Quick! Bring the best robe and put it on him. Put a ring on his finger and sandals on his feet. Bring the fattened calf and kill it. Let's have a **feast** and **celebrate**. For this son of mine was dead and is **alive again**; he was lost and is found." So they began to celebrate (Luke 15:21-24).*

While this is a marvelous story of reconciliation, it also shows God accepts, even welcomes, those of us who accept the gift of salvation, despite our sin against Him. Those of us who were spiritually dead are made alive, we're "born again." Jesus continues:

✠ *Meanwhile, the older son was in the field. When he came near the house, he heard music and dancing. So he called one of the servants and asked him what was going on. "Your brother has come," he replied, "and your father has killed the fattened calf because he has him back safe and sound."*

*The older brother became angry and refused to go in. So his father went out and pleaded with him. But he answered his father, "Look! All these years I've been slaving for you and never disobeyed your orders. Yet you never gave me even a young goat so I could celebrate with my friends. But when this son of yours who has squandered your property with prostitutes comes home, you kill the fattened calf for him!" (Luke 15:25-30).*

Some people may have a hard time accepting the fact that God has *accepted you.* They might look at the way you've lived—the actions that preceded your acceptance of this first gift—and question your salvation or your right to it. Here's a truth that's important to understand: your salvation is between *you* and *God*. It doesn't matter what other people believe; if you've been saved, then you've been saved. Don't be discouraged or offended by what others may say, even others who profess to be Christians. Some people may even be jealous of your new life. But read what the father says to the son who had not run away:

⊕ *"My son," the father said, "you are always with me, and everything I have is yours. But we had to celebrate and be glad, because this brother of yours was **dead** and is **alive again**; he was lost and is found"* (Luke 15:31-32).

## SATAN'S PLAN

Yes, God is celebrating, but, as you might guess, there is another who gets angry when someone accepts the gift of salvation. Reconnecting to the source of light allows people to bring God's light into the world at an ever-increasing level. Satan's goal is to stop or limit your light from shining in the world because light limits him in the world. The parable of the sower, which Jesus told, reveals this reality:

⊕ *As he was scattering the seed, some fell along the path, and the birds came and ate it up. Some fell on rocky places, where it did not have much soil. It sprang up quickly, because the soil was shallow. But when the sun came up, the plants were scorched, and they withered because they had no root. Other seed fell among thorns, which grew up and choked the plants, so that they did not bear grain. Still other seed fell on good soil. It came up, grew and produced a crop, multiplying thirty, sixty, or even a hundred times* (Mark 4:4-8).

When asked to explain the parable, Jesus said:

✠ *The farmer sows the word [of God]. Some people are like seed along the path, where the word is sown. As soon as they hear it, satan comes and takes away the word that was sown in them. Others, like seed sown on rocky places, hear the word and at once receive it with joy. But since they have no root, they last only a short time. When trouble or persecution comes because of the word, they quickly fall away. Still others, like seed sown among thorns, hear the word; but the worries of this life, the deceitfulness of wealth and the desires for other things come in and choke the word, making it unfruitful. Others, like seed sown on good soil, hear the word, accept it, and produce a crop—thirty, sixty or even a hundred times what was sown* (Mark 4:14-20).

This parable explains how people respond when presented with the gift of salvation. And it's clear from Jesus' explanation that satan would love to "take away the Word that was sown" in you. He despises those who follow God and he will do anything to keep you from reflecting the image and likeness of God into the world.

One of satan's greatest tactics is to sow uncertainty in your heart. Perhaps you begin to wonder, "Am I really accepted by God?" Surely you've failed too many times. Right? *Wrong.* That's satan talking. Don't listen to him:

✠ [Jesus said], "*He [the devil] was a murderer from the beginning, not holding to the truth, for there is no truth in him. When he lies, he speaks his native language, for he is a liar and the father of lies*" (John 8:44).

The truth is:

✠ *If we confess our sins, He is faithful and just and will forgive us our sins and purify us from **all** unrighteousness* (1 John 1:9).

Uncertainty and doubt aren't the only methods satan uses to keep that seed from growing all-important roots in your heart. He also sends tribulation and persecution to make you stumble. Choosing to follow God by accepting this gift doesn't magically make life perfect. We still live in an imperfect world and life will be full of trials and challenges. You will still face temptation. Salvation does not make you immune to greed, sexual immorality, pride, addiction, the desire to satisfy the flesh. However, God gives you the power through the Holy Spirit to resist temptations and to weather the storms of life.

You will come to realize that physical cravings don't satisfy. Just like the prodigal son, the thief on the cross, the blind man, and you and I—we know the Way, the Truth, and Life; all these worldly desires pale in comparison.

If you've accepted God's gift of salvation, then you are a seed in the "good ground" Jesus referred to in the parable, and you have become imperishable and eternal. The only question that remains is how much *you* will *choose* to grow in this life:

✝ *For you have been born again, not of perishable seed, but of imperishable...* (1 Peter 1:23).

How much you grow depends on how much you cultivate the seed planted in you by God and follow the instructions you are given:

✝ [Jesus said], *"But the seed on good soil stands for those with a noble and good heart, who hear the word, retain it, and by* **persevering** *produce a crop"* (Luke 8:15).

As we go through the Bible together, you will grow spiritually and your light will shine more brightly through *perseverance*. One of the properties of light is being a conveyer of the energy that enhances life in the world. Likewise, enhancing life in the world is our ultimate purpose.

## MEDITATION POINT

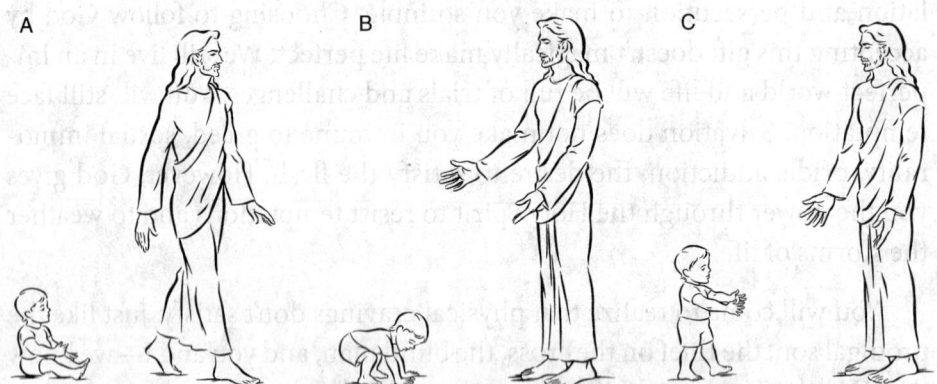

Trials, errors, and determination will allow you to walk like Him. As spiritual babies you must first make the attempt before you can ever learn to do it.

Go to Chapter 2 in the Study Guide section on page 293.

Go to Chapter 2 in the Study Guide section on page 293.

## ENDNOTES

1.  Jack Hayford, ed., *Spirit-Filled Life Bible for Students* (Nashville, TN: Thomas Nelson, 1995), 1339.

2.  Ibid., 1510.

3.  Ibid., 1453.

4.  Ibid., 1297–1298.

5.  Duane T. Gish, *The Amazing Story of Creation: From Science and the Bible* (Green Forest, AR: Master Books, 1996).

6.  Ibid., 34–35.

7.  Paul S. Taylor, *The Illustrated Origins Answer Book, Fifth Edition* (Gilbert, AZ: Eden Communications, 1995), 7–8.

8.  Michael Denton, *Evolution: A Theory in Crisis* (Chevy Chase, MD: Adler & Adler Publishers, Inc., 1986), 310.

# Chapter 3

# Gift #1—Life through Grace (Part 2)

## How Do You Get the Most from It?

> Before you begin to read, pray that the Holy Spirit
> will give you understanding and application.

✠ *You've all been to the stadium and seen the athletes race. Everyone runs; one wins. Run to win. All good athletes train hard. They do it for a gold medal that tarnishes and fades. You're after one that's gold eternally.*

*I don't know about you, but I'm running hard for the finish line. I'm giving it everything I've got. No sloppy living for me! I'm staying alert and in top condition. I'm not going to get caught napping, telling everyone else all about it and then missing out myself* (1 Corinthians 9:24-27 MSG).

### "Okay, I've Opened This Gift of Life. Now What?"

As a child, when you got that brand-new bike for Christmas, did you quickly put it in a storage closet? Or how about now if you received a new fifty-inch plasma television or state-of-the-art laptop computer—would you leave them in the boxes? Would you toss a velvet jewelry box in a drawer, unopened? Of course not! These new gifts cry out to be opened, examined, and used.

Even if it happened to be snowing outside on Christmas day, you probably rode your new bike around the living room. After tearing open the boxes, I remember calling friends in excitement about my new gifts—it was a joyful and exciting occasion. I could hardly wait to unwrap and use the new gifts.

What about this wonderful *gift of life*? Well, *unlike* toys and clothing we eventually grow out of or get tired of, the gift of life will make our lives exciting, every day here on earth and especially after we die. The gift of life that God offers enriches our daily lives, giving us purpose and meaning by allowing us to fulfill our destiny. The gift of life assures us that we will spend eternity in the presence of a God who loves us unconditionally, who has only our best interests at the top of His priority list. Unwrapping and using this gift will bring you joy and confidence. God gives you this gift, so if you choose to use it daily, then you can have an abundantly joyful life now and an eternal life of blessings with Him.

✝ [Jesus said], *"I have come that they may have **life** and that they may have it more **abundantly"** (John 10:10 NKJV).

✝ [Jesus said to His disciples before He was crucified], *"In My Father's house are many rooms; if it were not so, I would have told you. I am going there to prepare a place for you, I will come back and take you to be with Me that you will also may be where I am"* (John 14:2-3).

When we're born again, we're in many ways like newborn babies. We need to grow up, to mature into adulthood. In our case, that means deepening our relationship with God, which enables us to grow into His image and likeness. This is a *daily* choice—something we are encouraged, even commanded, to pursue. Paul writes:

✦ *For we are God's workmanship, created in Christ Jesus to do good works, which God prepared in advance for us to do* (Ephesians 2:10).

This kind of growth doesn't just happen magically; it requires *your active involvement*. It will also require you to deepen your relationship with God. You can only overcome your human weaknesses and become more in His image and likeness when you invest the time to get to know Him better and to allow His power into your life.

What are you pursuing? What is most important to you? We can't pursue everything all the time and be successful and fulfilled. We must make choices with our time and efforts to be successful in our pursuits.

The desire for happiness is always near the top of the list in any survey exploring what people want out of life. We put great effort into what we think will make us happy, spending most our time earning money to buy things to bring us closer to this elusive feeling of happiness. This is one of life's core desires. But here's the problem: we were not created to be fulfilled from the *outside in*. God originally designed us to achieve our fulfillment from the *inside out*. God has "hardwired" His creation for something far greater than happiness; He designed us for *joy* and *blessings*, which have eternal qualities.

As you grow in faith, which is the substance of your life, finding fulfillment will shift from the pursuit of outer activities to an inner fulfillment. This comes through a new life in God, a relationship that is initially internally developed. Beyond happiness, a dynamic and growing relationship with Christ will allow you to cultivate joy from within and receive blessings from your Creator as He intended for you.

Consider the word *happy* for a moment. It has the same root as the word *happenstance* or *happening*. With this meaning in mind, we could assume that to be happy we must *make fun things happen* continually, forever chasing that goal. However, this obsession with "making fun things happen" turns us into mice running on wheels trying to keep the good times rolling.

Eventually, bad things will *always* happen and therefore the pursuit of happiness is ultimately destined to *fail*. Regardless of how many times we try and fail, we are relentless. We're running, we're working, we're always busy, but we can't seem to get any closer to our goal of real sustained happiness because "being happy" is a momentary or temporal state. It doesn't last. The real question is, how do we find joy?

As Christ grows within, you'll discover that *joy* and *blessings* surpass happiness because they come from within. Read what the Bible says about this:

✝ *...strength and joy* [are] *in* [God's] *dwelling place* (1 Chronicles 16:27).

✝ *Do not grieve, for the joy of the Lord is your strength* (Nehemiah 8:10).

✝ *You have filled my heart with greater joy than when their grain and new wine abound* (Psalm 4:7).

✝ *You* [God] *have made known to me the path of life; You will fill me with joy in Your presence...* (Psalm 16:11).

✝ [Jesus said], *"I have told you this* [the instructions in the Bible] *so that My joy may be in you and that your joy may be complete"* (John 15:11).

✝ *Blessed is he who comes in the name of the Lord...* (Psalm 118:26).

✠ *But the man who looks intently into the perfect law* [the Bible] *that gives freedom, and continues to do this, not forgetting what he has heard, but doing it—he will be blessed in what he does* (James 1:25).

✠ [God said], *"If you follow My decrees and are careful to obey My commands, I will send you rain* **in its season***, and the ground will yield its crops and the trees of the field their fruit. Your threshing will continue until the grape harvest and the grape harvest will continue until planting, and you will eat all the food you want and live safely in your land. I will grant peace in the land, and you will lie down and no one will make you afraid. I will remove the savage beasts and the sword* [enemies in life] *will not pass through your country"* (Leviticus 26:3-6).

There are physical blessings and there are spiritual blessings. It is also important to note in the last verse in the Leviticus passage that blessings come "in season," which is a season that God determines. Physically we may have bad times but our God-given joy and blessings will get us through the bad circumstances as well as the good because they come from within and are not reliant on outside circumstances. Happiness is temporary, bound by circumstances and feelings. Blessings and joy are infinite, without change, when we access them from within. The root word for *blessing*, which is *makar*, means "the same" or "permanent." This is the nature of God—eternal.

As I've previously mentioned, you will not be immune to bad circumstances after you become a Christian; however, when they happen you can have an *inner* peace, strength, and joy. This probably sounds unbelievable to you now. But just like the experience of coming to know Christ, once you've experienced it you'll know exactly what I'm talking about. Joy is deep within and does not depend on external circumstance—it comes when you are living *in* His image and likeness, *in* close relationship with Him. When you do this, you will see for yourself what I mean. The root word for happy in the Hebrew language says it aptly: "to get in touch with what is real." We lose an important concept of the word *happy* when we translate the word into English.

## RUNNING THE RACE

This chapter began with a verse where the apostle Paul compares our life here on earth to running a race. Preparing for a race is a lot like the way we're to approach our spiritual development. It is something we need to *pursue*, something we have to work at with *purpose*. If you set out to run a marathon, you would have to change your habits so your body and mind are in peak condition. Your lifestyle would have to change for you to be successful. The same principle holds true for spiritual development. We need to pursue with purpose, aligning our body and mind to the new spirit, so we can live out an abundant life in Christ on this earth.

Paul reminds us that our current physical life is only temporal, a millisecond, when compared to the eternal life we received with the gift of salvation. Our pursuits should be for things of eternal consequence, not temporal happiness.

When you make an immediate purchase on a credit card, and get immediate gratification and happiness, the result is debt. And heavy debt makes us slaves. Another way to look at it is by considering those long-lasting light bulbs. You can buy a regular bulb for a relatively low price that will last for several months, or you can pay a bit more for one that will last for years. Don't you think you'd be better off initially spending the extra money for a quality bulb that will give you better results in the long run? In our spiritual pursuit, the extra effort is worth the *longer-lasting results.* Therefore, our *main* focus and efforts should be on the things with long-lasting earthly or eternal significance, not the temporal comforts of this world.

Let's take a closer look at some important elements of this growth process toward finding your earthly significance.

## FIND A CHURCH

An essential element for Christian maturity is finding a community or fellowship of believers; a group of like-minded, supportive Christians who are hungry to grow, learn, and enjoy rich relationships. *Fellowship* is the sharing of similar interests, ideas, or experiences. When we do this as Christians, we enjoy encouragement in our faith that takes us toward a more intimate relationship with God. Finding a church is *not* finding a building; it is finding people like you who are seeking to grow their relationship with God. Think of church as a fellowship of people with whom you want to share part of your life.

The early Christians sold all their possessions and pooled their resources in a sort of "communal living" arrangement. During this time, the church experienced rapid growth. The church's style and structure has changed over the years and will continue to change, but one thing is clear: finding a community of fellow believers isn't just a good idea, it's a *biblical* idea.

✟ *And let us consider how we may spur one another on toward love and good deeds. Let us not give up meeting together...* (Hebrews 10:24-25).

When I say "like-minded," I don't mean that you need to find a group of people who think, look, or live just like you. Some of our greatest spiritual growth comes from the interchange with other believers who have different life experiences and unique perspectives on living a life in the image and likeness of God. By like-minded, I mean believers who are also seeking a deeper relationship with God. You might want to avoid people who believe they have already arrived at ultimate spirituality in their relationship with God, for they will lack a certain amount of humility and hunger for a deeper relationship, both of which are important for you to see and copy.

A good church is a lot like a barbecue pit filled with hot coals. When you remove a coal from the pile, it quickly cools. Find a good church to regularly attend and it will help keep the embers of your faith burning hot and vibrant.

Choosing a church can seem like a daunting task. But it's important to take your time and find one that is a good fit for you, one where you can worship, learn, and grow in your faith. Do you have friends who go to church? Start your search there. Invite yourself to join them for one of their services. You might find a church that feels "right" on your first visit, or it could take weeks of searching. That's okay. Take the time you need. Church-shopping is fine when you're a new believer (or new to a community), but after you've found a good one it's best to grow roots there. Frequent church-hopping or transplanting after you've started to settle in isn't conducive to spiritual growth. A church fellowship where others know you well can help you get the most out of your experience.

One of the first things you'll notice about churches is the diversity of worship styles. By "worship style" I'm referring to the part of the service where we sing to and about what God has done and is doing in our lives. You may feel most comfortable in a church that has a contemporary service, complete with a rock band, dynamic drama performances, and creative multimedia content. Or perhaps you'll be drawn to a more traditional service with hymns instead of modern choruses. Worship is an important part of developing a strong relationship with God, so your comfort level with worship is *important*.

You'll find churches of all sizes too. A small church might feel more like a "family" to you, while a larger church will likely provide more specialized teaching and ministry opportunities. No matter where you go, you're not going to find a community of perfect people. Churches are filled with sinners who are working on their spiritual lives just like you, a community working together toward spiritual growth. This includes the leadership of the church. While leaders have been given spiritual authority, they are still imperfect people working on their spiritual growth. God can only use imperfect people to build His church, growing together in Him toward that goal of perfection. So be wise and *understanding* when it comes to the church family.

It's important to feel a sense of belonging wherever you end up. Look for people who are authentic about the ups and downs of their walk, and ones with whom you can be authentic about yours. Remember that Jesus accepted us the way we are with our sins, funkiness and all. His church, also known as the body of Christ, should show the same *grace* to all that He shows to all…no matter what they have done or are doing. It is important to find such a church so you can both receive that kind of grace while you are developing your Christian walk as well as learn how to show it to others.

That said, it is also critical to your growth to be challenged and have your faith stretched. Being comfortable with the teaching and the worship will make it easy to want to go to church, but being challenged by the teaching and inspired by the worship will make it worth the trip. Stepping out of your comfort zone forces more reliance on God, which is both what He desires for you and how you will better find Him. You'll know when you've found the right one—stick with it even when the *inevitable* challenges arise.

## ACTION & VISUALIZATION

*Find a church or fellowship of Christians and attend regularly.*

## BAPTISM

After you've found a church that feels like a match, it's time to consider baptism. Just before He began His ministry, Jesus Himself was baptized by John the Baptist. Though Jesus didn't need to repent of sin, Him being baptized shows us the importance of baptism. And at the end of His ministry, Jesus commissioned His disciples to continue baptizing others:

✚ *Therefore go and make disciples of all the nations, baptizing them*
*in the name of the Father and of the Son and of the Holy Spirit…*
(Matthew 28:19).

What is baptism? Essentially, it is a public confession of a private decision. It is a way to identify with Jesus' death (going under the water) and resurrection (coming out of the water with a new resurrected life). It is a beautiful event that can be a powerful experience for you and for those who are observing the public confession of your faith. Baptism points us to one of the most significant aspects of our new lives in Christ—Jesus' resurrection, which is sometimes overshadowed by His death for our sins. Read what Paul says in Romans:

✚ *Or don't you know that all of us who were baptized into Christ Jesus were baptized into His death? We were therefore buried with Him through baptism into death in order that, just as Christ was* **raised** *from the dead through the glory of the Father,* **we** *too may live a* **new life.**

*If we have been united with Him like this in His death, we will certainly also be* **united with Him in His resurrection.** *For we know that our old self was crucified with Him so that the body of sin might be done away with, that we should* **no longer be slaves** *to sin...* (Romans 6:3-6).

Jesus' death and resurrection gave us freedom from slavery to sin and are the mechanism that will one day give us complete freedom in Him. It is your choice to set this mechanism in motion by accepting Jesus' sacrifice on the cross; however, you must also decide *daily* to *avoid* sin so that you can take advantage of *freedom from sin.*

Some theologians believe baptism is no more than a symbol of the inward change that happened the moment you accepted Christ as your Savior. But I believe Paul is suggesting that baptism actually plays a role in *creating* inward spiritual change. If nothing else, the courage it takes to publicly express your identification with Christ's death and resurrection certainly creates more of an *expectation* of change and freedom. Because we must daily choose to exercise that freedom, this *expectation* of change helps *make* those changes.

You will discover when we get to the gift of faith chapters that any action done in faith can have an impact in the spiritual world, and that in turn has an impact on the physical world. The act of water baptism can in some ways help free you from slavery to sin or at least allow you to better exercise your freedom from it, as well as deepen your relationship with Him. Look at how Paul reinforces this concept:

✠  *...because anyone who has died has been freed from sin.*

> *Now if we died with Christ, we **believe** that we will also **live** with Him. For we know that since Christ was raised from the dead, He cannot die again; death no longer has mastery over Him. The death He died, He died to sin once for all; but the life He lives, He lives to God.*
>
> *In the same way, count [baptize] yourselves dead to sin but alive to God in Christ Jesus (Romans 6:7-11).*

During Christ's ministry and within the first-century church, the decision to accept Jesus as Savior and water baptism went hand in hand. When a person was saved, he or she was immediately baptized. In today's churches, it seems that more emphasis is placed on the verbal spiritual commitment rather than the physical act of baptism. Our public expression of our faith commitment is meant to occur in conjunction with the verbal spiritual commitment, representing the death of the old life and the resurrection into a new life in Christ. It is a symbol of what we are verbally confessing.

If you grew up in certain Christian denominations, you may have been baptized as a baby or a young child. Obviously, at the time you were not making a voluntary public identification with Jesus' death and resurrection. God wants you to knowingly memorialize your relationship with Him.

✠  *Peter replied, "Repent and be baptized, every one of you, in the name of Jesus Christ" (Acts 2:38).*

Throughout the New Testament, people were instructed to receive Christ and to be baptized, as we see in this account when the apostle Paul was saved:

✠ [Ananias said], *"And now what are you waiting for? Get up, be baptized and wash your sins away, calling on His name"* (Acts 22:16).

I encourage you to be baptized so its purpose can be fulfilled in your life. God is as excited about this decision as you are. Think about it!

## Action & Visualization

*Arrange with a pastor to be baptized.*

## Change Old Habits

When you accept the gift of salvation, you are immediately *changed*:

✠ *Therefore, if anyone is in Christ, he is a **new creation**; the old has gone, the new has come!* (2 Corinthians 5:17).

The word *new* in this passage is *kainos* (kahee-noss), which means unused, fresh, or novel. It's used here in regards to form and quality, rather than in reference to time (a thought conveyed by a similar-sounding word, *neos*). One of the Bible's wonderful, transforming truths is that Jesus offers everyone a chance to start over in life. No matter what you have done in the past or who you may have been, when you accept Jesus Christ your past is forgiven. You become a brand-new person with a totally *new identity* in Him![1]

✠ *As far as the east is from the west, so far has* [God] *removed our transgressions from us* (Psalm 103:12).

This change happens immediately; it's a heart change that occurs the moment you accept Jesus. But old *habits* die hard. Even though you are a new creation in spirit, you continue to live in the old world and in your old body under the direction of a mind with old programming. To get the full effect of *all* the *freedoms* this first gift of life can bring, you will need to work at *reprogramming* your mind and your body.

This is one of the main reasons to find a good church or fellowship with other believers. Here you can surround yourself with friends who are also striving to become a "new creation" and learning how to do that daily. It may be equally important to move away from some old friends—friends and habits that tie you to the old life. Here's what the Bible advises:

✠ **Blessed** *is the man who does* **not** *walk in the counsel of the wicked or stand in the way of sinners or sit in the seat of mockers* (Psalm 1:1).

✠ *He who walks with the wise grows wise, but a companion of fools suffers harm* (Proverbs 13:11).

✠ *Do not be misled: "Bad company corrupts good character"* (1 Corinthians 15:33).

When you accepted Jesus Christ as your Savior, you received your new insight—spiritual sight—which is dim at first. There is another story in the Bible of a blind man who was healed that presents interesting spiritual parallels for our own story:

✠ *They came to Bethsaida, and some people brought a blind man and begged Jesus to touch him. He took the blind man by the hand and **led him outside the village**. When He had **spit** on the man's eyes and put His hands on him, Jesus asked, "**Do you see anything?**"*

*He looked up and said, "I see people; they look like trees walking around."*

*Once more Jesus put His hands on the man's eyes. Then his eyes were opened, his sight was restored, and he saw everything clearly.*

*Jesus sent him home, saying, "**Don't go into the village**"* (Mark 8:22-26).

Jesus first led the blind man outside the village. Your spiritual sight is a personal matter between you and God. Without God, the world can't understand what you are now seeing. The next thing that happened would have been considered offensive by the world—Jesus spit on the man's eyes. The gospel is likewise offensive to some and therefore they don't come to Jesus to get insight.

Jesus then asks the blind man a question, "Do you see anything?" to which the man replied that he saw something, but not clearly. This is where we are now. We see spiritually, yet not clearly. We now know we have an eternity within us, yet we don't see everything.

✠ *[God] has made everything beautiful in its time. He has also set eternity in the hearts of men; yet they cannot fathom what God has done from the beginning to end* (Ecclesiastes 3:11).

Jesus continues to work with us, but we must choose to learn from Him that which we do not know and to grow in Him. It's a lifelong growth process. Jesus sends us home with the instruction not to go back into the world *for our sight.*

Take a moment to think about each of your current relationships. Do they encourage behaviors or actions that are contradictory to your new relationship with God? How wise would it be to continue those relationships? Remember how your computer (subconscious and central nervous system) works. When you see familiar faces and places, your computer will automatically run old programs. Don't be discouraged that this is happening; the apostle Paul struggled with this very thing too:

✛ *For I have the desire to do what is good, but I cannot carry it out. For what I do is not the good I want to do; no, the evil I do not want to do—this I keep on doing* (Romans 7:18-19).

Just like Paul, you will not always be able to stop old programs from running, programs that lead you into sin. But you can make it easier on yourself by saying no to some of those old faces, places, and habits. Visualize yourself doing this. In time, with a regular commitment to positive influences, you'll develop new computer programs that avoid old patterns. In time, old programming will become obsolete so you won't be prompted by the old cues. At this time your new programming will allow you to shine God's light in those very same old dark places.

## ACTION & VISUALIZATION

*Where necessary, avoid old friends and old places*
*that lead a new creation back to old habits.*

## READ THE BIBLE

To continue your journey toward spiritual growth, you need to know your history. The most important history you can know is "His story"—God's story, written in the Bible. God is part of your past, present, and future, so the Bible is also *your* story. It is life's ultimate direction manual for those who are serious about seeking wisdom.

✝ *I write these things to you who believe in the name of the Son of God*
*so that you may know that you have eternal life* (1 John 5:13).

✝ *Always be prepared to give an answer to everyone...for the hope that*
*you have...* (1 Peter 3:15).

The B-I-B-L-E is our "Believers Instruction Book for Living on Earth."
I recommend reading the Bible every day. You don't have to read dozens of
chapters to get something valuable out of it. Sometimes a single verse can
have a powerful impact on you; all Scripture has meaning on some level if
you consider it carefully. As you study the Bible, read expectantly and look
for ways you can apply the truths to your life. Here's another amazing thing
about God's Book: you can read the same passage dozens of times and still
find something new each time. God's Word is rich and alive!

✝ *God means what He says. What He says goes. His powerful Word*
*is sharp as a surgeon's scalpel, cutting through everything, whether*
*doubt or defense, laying us open to listen and obey. Nothing and*
*no one is impervious to God's Word. We can't get away from it—no*
*matter what* (Hebrews 4:12-13 MSG).

Are you new to the Bible? Does the size of the Book, the tiny print,
and the seemingly overwhelming amount of content intimidate you? Well,
know that you're not alone. To make it easier, here's how it all breaks down.
Basically, the Bible is divided into *two* parts, the Old and New Testaments.
The Old Testament tells the story of the creation of the world and the history
of God's interaction with the world until about 400 B.C. (before Christ). The
books in the Old Testament, while important for their historical content
and the unique stories they tell, also play a role in the foretelling of Jesus
Christ's place in God's larger story. There are many specific prophecies in
the Old Testament that accurately predicted the details of Jesus' life, along

with many symbolic references in stories, events, and peoples' lives that predicted Jesus' ministry and purpose. Some of these predictions occurred more than a *thousand years before* Jesus' birth. *It's truly amazing!*

The New Testament tells the story of Jesus who was the Messiah foretold by the Old Testament, and the story of the early Christian church. Until recently, time was divided into two parts based on the life of Jesus (B.C., before Christ, or A.D., *anno domini*, which means "the year of our Lord"). Peoples' lives have revolved around Jesus for over two thousand years, whether they believe in Him or not. (Only recently it has become "politically correct" in the secular world to denote time periods with B.C.E., Before Common Era, and C.E., Common Era.)

The Old Testament may initially seem like stories of ancient people in another time that hold little relevance to your spirituality; however, as you develop your spiritual insight you will see that these people's stories can guide you in your spiritual walk. Paul, in writing about his Israelite forefathers from the time of Moses, said the following:

*They were all baptized into Moses in the cloud and in the sea. They all ate the same spiritual food and drank the same spiritual drink; for they drank from the spiritual rock that accompanied them, and that rock was Christ. Nevertheless, God was not pleased with most of them; their bodies were scattered over the desert.* **Now these things occurred as examples to keep us from setting our hearts on evil things as they did** (1 Corinthians 10:2-6).

The Bible (from the Greek word *biblios*, meaning "book"), is made up of sixty-six smaller books written by forty authors over 1,600 years. Although it was written over such a long period of time by different authors, all the books from Genesis, which is the first book, to Revelation, which is the last book, have a *consistent* and relevant message. This in and of itself is a *miracle*, showing the *divine hand of God* on its *writing*.

When you see a quote from the Bible, it is usually followed by a reference that identifies where you can find the quote. Just a side note: chapter and verse numbers were not part of the original writings; they were added to later translations for easier reference. I have included references throughout this book so you can go straight to the source and study the subject and context yourself. Context is an important consideration when studying the Bible. As with any written work, simply pulling a sentence or two out of the whole can sometimes lead to an incorrect interpretation. Get to know the entire story and each verse will make more sense.

You will want to choose a Bible that fits your reading style and level. There are many versions of the English Bible available today, some dating back hundreds of years. Since we don't use the same words as we did in 1700, for example, it's usually a good idea to begin with a Bible that has been translated into modern English. I have used the New International Version for most of my verses throughout this book, unless otherwise noted. *The Message Bible* is one that has been translated to everyday language, which I recommend and have occasionally used. There are also study Bibles that, in addition to the Bible text, footnote some context based on customs of the time and other verses, as well as the meaning of names of people and places—all of which may add a better understanding of the Bible. The best way to choose a Bible is to go to a local *Christian* bookstore and have a conversation with the Bible specialist there. This person is familiar with the different versions of Bibles and can help you choose the one that best fits you.

The Old Testament was written in Hebrew. Jewish custom says that there are seventy levels on which the Torah (first five books of the Bible) can be read and understood as we gain more knowledge. Hebrew is the language in which God spoke the world and all of life into existence. It is the language with which God wanted to communicate with man about the world, about Himself, and about man's relationship with Himself.

Within the Hebrew language there is the DNA that makes up everything that physically exists and all actions in the world. Hebrew is made up of twenty-two letters comprised of seven shapes—some letters are made by combining other letters together. Each letter has a name, a sign (except the one letter that means grace), a shape or combination of shapes, a numerical value, a pronunciation, and a meaning based on the context where it is first used as the first letter in a word in the Bible. These attributes will be clues to the further understanding of the word they are within.

Hebrew is the only language where the letters within a word tell you something about the makeup of what the word identifies. It is the only conceptual language that resembles the chemical language of science where we all know immediately that $H_2O$ is the name for water; however, we also know by simply looking at the scientific name that water is made up of two hydrogen atoms and one oxygen atom.

An interesting example is the word *truth*, which is made up of the first, middle, and last letters of the alphabet. This indicates that truth must take everything into consideration. The first letter means God and the last means empty or the physical world empty of God while the middle letter in the word means move. We can say truth is moving God's principles into the world. The value of the three letters added together is 441 and the sum of those is nine. When you multiply nine by any number, the sum of that number when added together will again equal nine, which suggests truth in any form or variation is still truth.

In *Or Tohah*, Rabbi Dov Ber, the Maggid of Mezritch, explained the first words of Torah: *Bereshit Bara Elohim Et*—"In the beginning God created *et*" (Genesis 1:1)—that the *et* is an untranslatable word used to indicate that "a definite direct object is next," much like the word *the* (thus there needs to be an *et* before *the* heavens and *the* earth). But Dov Ber points out that *et* so spelled with the two letters—*aleph* and *tav*—is an abbreviation for the Hebrew alphabet. *Aleph* is the first letter of the Hebrew alphabet and *tav* the last; so he reasoned, in the beginning, God created the Hebrew alphabet. Since God did this *before* creating *the* heaven and *the* earth, the letters are considered to be the primordial "building blocks" of all creations.

Words in Hebrew are generally made up of root words typically containing three letters, and each root word can have one to two hundred uses within a larger word. The three letters each have their own meaning and can create up to twelve thousand root words, each being used an average in two hundred words can make in total 2.4 million word. We modern English speakers use about six hundred thousand English words. Since letters in words we use don't have any meaning, we don't have any clue as to the meaning of a word we see by only looking at it if we don't already know the word. This is not the case with Hebrew. In fact, the Hebrew language already had words for things that had not yet been invented. As an example, the root word of *computer* means "that which does the thinking for you." The root word of *camera* means "copies of image." If you had shown these words to someone three thousand years ago, they would not know what you meant, but when you show them the object they would automatically have a word for it.

The Hebrew word for *letter* is *ot*, which can also mean sign or wonder. There is even meaning within the construction of a letter or word works on every level. Even the high level attributes of the language means something like when you divide twenty-two into seven you get the infinite number π (known as Pi), which is the ratio of a circle's circumference to its diameter, commonly approximated as 3.14. It is amazing how God has tied everything together on multiple levels.

You'll find that letters or sounds of words will be found as the root words of other languages since Hebrew is God's language to create the world. It was only after the Tower of Babel where God mixed up their language. The letters and sounds were mixed up so humankind could not go against God's will. There is one word that sounds the same and/or has similar lettering in most all languages, and that is *abracadabra*, which magicians say when they are going to make something appear from nothing. The exact meaning in ancient Hebrew is "I will create as I speak."

Conventional wisdom say that all languages were created over time, beginning with grunts and sounds and developing into a more sophisticated language. However, there is not a record of Hebrew being used before 3,500 years ago, and it was from the beginning the most sophisticated highly technical language ever used, even to this day. It could not possibly have evolved over time. And within its grammatical structure are all the words that will ever be needed. In this book, I will dip into the Hebrew spelling of a few key words to show you this amazing way of understanding the Bible. There are many interesting books and web sites with information on the Hebrew language which will give you a better understanding of God and help build up your faith.

The Bible is filled with God's words to us—it is not just any old collection of writings. The ideas and the wisdom found in the Bible are to be taken not like good advice but as the words of our Creator! The Bible has this to say about that:

✟ *All Scripture is **God-breathed** and is useful for teaching, rebuking, correcting and training in righteousness* (2 Timothy 3:16).

✟ *Above all, you must understand that no prophecy of Scripture came about by the prophet's own interpretation. For prophecy never had its origin in the will of man, but men spoke from God as **they were carried along by the Holy Spirit*** (2 Peter 1:20-21).

We read the Bible because God asks us to. He wants us to get to know Him better. Knowledge of someone would be required to improve any relationship. The better we know and understand Him as He is revealed in the Bible, the better friend we can be to Him. Jesus points out how important it is to learn and understand what God is doing so we can know how to be a true friend to Him:

✟ *You are my friends if you do what I command. I no longer call you servants, because a servant does not know his master's business. Instead, I have called you friends, for everything that I learned from My Father I have made known to you* [through the Bible] (John 15:14-15).

In the gospel of John, Jesus is referred to as the Word (Bible) because both the Old and New Testaments are all about Him. We also read the Bible because it gives us great knowledge on how to live this earthly life. The key is being diligent and open-minded when reading the Bible. Jesus said:

✝ *...seek and you will find* (Matthew 7:7).

If you are reading God's living Word with expectancy, diligence, and faith, then you will find something new every time you open your Bible. (We'll learn later how the Holy Spirit also helps us to get the most out of our Bible reading.) This new information will help reprogram your mind, establishing new habits. Choose a reading time and place you can return to regularly; however, I caution you not to develop your reading of the Bible into a mindless habit. Seek to keep it *fresh*. Supplement your Bible reading with other Christian reading material on subjects that interest you.

While the Bible has a beginning, middle, and an end, it's not necessary to begin reading Genesis. I recommend starting at the gospel of John in the New Testament, then read through to the end of Revelation. Beginning with John gives you the details of the life of Jesus, His ministry, death, and resurrection. Remember, this isn't a book you read once and put on the shelf—you'll come back to the Bible repeatedly for the rest of your life. It is always *new* and *alive* for those who diligently seek the Truth.

✝ *Do not let this Book of the Law depart from your mouth; meditate on it day and night, so that you may be careful to do everything written in it* (Joshua 1:8).

## Action & Visualization

*Start reading your Bible daily.*

# TAKE COMMUNION

Jesus Himself asked us to participate in something called the Lord's Supper:

*And He took bread, gave thanks and broke it, and gave it to them, saying, "This is My body given for you; do this in remembrance of Me." In the same way, after the supper He took the cup [of wine], saying, "This cup is the new covenant in My blood, which is poured out for you" (Luke 22:19-20).*

Jesus indicated here through this analogy that He is the sole and complete sustainer of our lives. Eating with others is a way of developing intimacy with them. So Jesus, by indicating He is the meal that is to be eaten, points us to the *highest* form of *intimacy*…living life with *Him* as our sustainer.

Many churches refer to this act of eating bread and drinking wine in remembrance of Him as communion. It is a powerful place to meet God because it is a vivid reminder of Jesus' sacrifice on the cross. While churches vary in how they present communion, you will find that most (if not all) place a high value on this experience. It's a time to reflect not only on Jesus' death but also on our own lives. We are asked to confess our sins before we come to the communion table. When we approach the table to drink Jesus' blood (usually represented by grape juice or wine) and eat of His flesh (represented by the bread), our thought ought to be on giving up our lives to live them through Him and developing this greater intimacy.

## ACTION & VISUALIZATION

*Regularly participate in communion,
remembering the sacrifice Jesus made for you.*

## REMEMBER THE SABBATH

God set aside one day of the week for us to honor Him, to focus on the spiritual side of life, and rest from our physical activities. In the book of Exodus is where this is first clearly commanded:

✟ *Remember the Sabbath day by keeping it holy. Six days you shall labor and do all your work, but the seventh day is a Sabbath to the Lord your God. On it you shall not do any work, neither you, nor your son or daughter, nor your manservant or maidservant, nor your animals, nor the alien within your gates. For in six days the Lord made the heavens and the earth, the sea, and all that is in them, but He rested on the seventh day. Therefore the Lord blessed the Sabbath day and made it holy* (Exodus 20:8-11).

✟ *And God blessed the seventh day and made it holy, because on it He rested from all the work of creating that He had done* (Genesis 2:3).

If you keep this day for rest and spiritual rejuvenation, then you'll soon discover how it helps both your spirit and your attitude. Taking time to reflect on the spiritual things can also bless the other days of your week too. The more you diligently follow this instruction, the more you will see His life-giving results in your life.

Consider these two principles regarding the day of rest. First, if you happen to have a job that requires you to work on Sunday, then choose another day of the week as your "Sabbath." The goal of Sabbath is rest and focus on God for a day, not adherence to a pointless religious exercise. Second, taking one day a week to rest and focus on spiritual things doesn't mean we are free to forget God on the other days of the week. The Christian life is a 24-7 proposition. Keeping the Sabbath gives us energy and wisdom and a rejuvenated spirit, making it easier to honor God with our words and actions the other six days of the week. It also gives us an opportunity to do some reprogramming through meditation and visualization.

With the coming of Jesus in the New Testament, we have been give grace and no longer fall under the law. The reason we now celebrate the Sabbath on Sunday and not Saturday, as was the custom of the Jews in the Old Testament, is because Jesus rose from the dead on Sunday. So we celebrate Jesus' resurrection and ours with Him because He has brought us alive in Him.

Spiritually speaking, the number six represents the flesh of man, which means we exert our flesh in labor for six days throughout the week. The number seven represents Heaven, which stands for perfection. Jesus is the perfect sacrifice to cover all our sins. He did all the work of being perfect for us so we can rest in Him after we have done what we can do. Jesus in also alive in us to help us complete our destiny, so again when we have done what we can do, we can find rest in Him at our most difficult moments. In Jesus and only in Jesus will we obtain perfect rest. As New Testament Christians, we don't have just a day in which to rest as the Old Testament Jews did, but we have a person in which we can rest—and that person is Jesus in which we find our rest. When we have worked and done everything we can, we should then turn it over to Jesus and rest. Jesus will do the rest.

For Christians, Sabbath should be set aside for us to celebrate what Jesus has done, is doing, and will do in our lives, so we can find that refreshing rest for a day. In so doing, this allows God the space to both work for and on us during that day.

## ACTION & VISUALIZATION
*Rest and honor God on the Sabbath.*

## REDEDICATE YOUR LIFE

If you already accepted the gift of salvation at some point in your life but drifted away from your relationship with Jesus, it's never too late to return. You might feel unworthy, like the first time you came to Him, but all that is asked of you is to repent of your sins. God promises that He is faithful to forgive. John writes:

> *If we confess our sins, He is faithful and just and will forgive us our sins and purify us from all unrighteousness* (1 John 1:9).

Because we're imperfect people—we still make bad choices and we still sin—we may find ourselves needing to return to Christ more than once over the course of our lives. We're in good company. Consider one of Jesus' disciples, Simon Peter, who was the first to identify Jesus as the Savior. When Jesus asked His disciples who people thought He was, they suggested multiple Old Testament prophets. But then:

> *Simon Peter answered, "You are the Christ, the Son of the living God."*
> *Jesus replied, "Blessed are you, Simon son of Jonah, for this was not revealed to you by man, but by My Father in Heaven. And I tell you that you are Peter, and on this rock I will build My church, and the gates of Hades will not overcome it"* (Matthew 16:16-18).

This same person, not too long after the above interaction, as a solid follower of Christ, turned around and denied Jesus three times just prior to His death:

> *Now Peter was sitting out in the courtyard, and a servant girl came to him. "You also were with Jesus of Galilee," she said.*
> *But he denied it before them all. "I don't know what you're talking about," he said.*
> *Then he went out to the gateway, where another girl saw him and said to the people there, "This fellow was with Jesus of Nazareth."*
> *He denied it again, with an oath: "I don't know the man!"* (Matthew 26:69-72).

Sometimes the term *backsliding* is used to describe a time when people turn from their previously held views or direction. Simon Peter was the first to correctly identify Jesus as the Son of God—he served, lived with, and followed Jesus for three years—yet he denied Him three times in a moment of weakness.

Here is the good news about Simon Peter's story (and ours as well): After Jesus rose from the dead, He came to Simon Peter and encouraged him, reaffirming His love, and sent him out to preach the gospel with confidence. This renewed faith was underscored when Simon Peter spoke to a crowd (as recorded in the book of Acts) and more than five thousand people became believers as a result:

✦ *But many who heard* [Peter's] *message believed, and the number of men grew to about five thousand* (Acts 4:4).

If you have turned away from God for a season, Jesus knows your past; however, He is more interested in your future, in helping you fulfill your destiny. When you ask to be forgiven, Jesus forgets all the stuff you did and welcomes you into His arms so that together you can look at where He wants you to walk next. He knows what you can be and what you can do if you align your will with His, because He is the one who can give you the power and ability.

If you need to come back to Jesus and repent, then say a prayer like this:

*Father God, I need to rededicate my life to You. I believe in my heart that Your Son, Jesus Christ, died to redeem me from my sins. I know I am a sinner and I ask You to forgive me. Help me to obey and follow You all the days of my life so that my life will be pleasing to You. I ask this in Jesus' name, amen.*

## DEVELOP AN ONGOING RELATIONSHIP

Whether you have prayed to receive the gift of salvation for the first time, or have prayed a prayer of rededication, you now have a brand-new relationship with Jesus. He wants to grow and expand this relationship always into a more intimate one. Jesus said:

✠ *Here I am! I stand at the door and knock. If anyone **hears My voice** and opens the door, I will come in and eat with him, and he with Me* (Revelation 3:20).

For many Christians, Revelation 3:20 is used to present the salvation message; however, Jesus is clearly speaking to people who are *already* Christians. He is saying that He wants to *build an intimate relationship with all believers,* even those who have *already* accepted Him. It's not simply receiving Christ that creates the intimate relationship God desires. Receiving Jesus into your heart is the starting point from which to develop that relationship. It's like moving into the same house with someone else. That alone doesn't create an intimate relationship, as one can see from the divorce rate. To develop intimacy, one must also *daily* hear His voice and open the door to his or her heart to respond to it.

Jesus is making the analogy that dining with someone is a great way to develop greater intimacy with them, which is what lovers and families do over a shared meal. Even business people use a shared meal to establish trust and build relationships. At the Last Supper, Jesus called His disciples (and us) to greater intimacy, in a representative way, by eating His flesh and drinking His blood. The gospel of Luke (chapter 24) includes another story that illustrates the power of dining together.

Just after Jesus' resurrection, He comes across a couple of disciples walking along the road. They walk and talk with Him, but they don't recognize Him as the Savior *until* they share a meal with Him. We too at times don't recognize *He is with* us until we share a meal with Him, or to put it another way...*develop that more intimate relationship* with Him.

What is important to God is *not* your position, power, or abilities—for all those things come from Him. Nor is it your past—that's *behind* you. What is *most* important to God is developing a relationship with Him that *grows* with time. *Anyone* can grow closer by simply opening that door *whenever* he or she hears His voice.

You can hear His voice and get to know Him better through prayer and reading the Bible (remember, Jesus is the Word). Both intimacy-building activities should be done daily. In fact, you should be speaking to Him and listening for His voice throughout the day. The relationship God desires with you will open many opportunities during the day for the two of you to grow closer together.

God offers this more intimate relationship for your benefit. Whether you're actively seeking this, God still has never-failing love for you. Your standing with God is not measured by what you do for Him; your relationship is solely based on the decision you made to accept what Jesus did for you.

## ACTION & VISUALIZATION

*Regularly seek more time to be with Jesus so you can get to know Him better.*

## CONFORM YOUR IMAGE AND LIKENESS

As you seek a more intimate relationship with Jesus Christ, you'll learn that He desires us to make certain changes to our lives. I have been asked by some Christians, "If I don't have to quit sinning to be accepted by God, then why would I want to stop sinning at all?" It's actually a fair question. One answer is that obedience to God is a form of *gratitude* for God giving you eternal life and salvation in the first place. Paul writes:

*Therefore, I urge you, brothers, **in view of God's mercy**, to offer your **bodies** as living sacrifices, holy and pleasing to God—this is your spiritual act of worship. Do not conform any longer to the pattern of this world, but be transformed by the renewing of your **mind**. Then you will be able to test and approve what God's will is—His good, pleasing and perfect will* (Romans 12:1-2).

These verses tell us that after we are saved, as an act of gratitude for eternal life, we conform our old bodies and minds to a new spirit. This is the process of working out our own salvation, which we read about previously. You will not be able to make some of the more difficult changes by your own effort alone; in fact, you will have to develop a deep and intimate relationship with God that allows you to rest in Him. And through this resting in Him, you can rely on God to assist you in making some of the more difficult changes. God is only asking you to decide to accept what He offered you and what He wants you to be. This is why Jesus offers us this invitation:

*Are you tired? Worn out? Burned out on religion? Come to Me. Get away with Me and you'll recover your life. I'll show you how to take a real rest. Walk with Me and work with Me—watch how I do it. Learn the unforced rhythms of grace. I won't lay anything heavy or ill-fitting on you. Keep company with Me and you'll learn to live freely and lightly* (Matthew 11:28-30 MSG).

A second reason for not sinning is because, as a new creation, sinning goes against our new nature—it doesn't satisfy us anymore. As fallen people, we did completely fallen things and thought nothing of it. As born-again believers, however, we are completely different. Sure, we can live in, and do often live in, sin, but for a Christian close to God, it's like a married man with another woman—he knows it's wrong and will feel the weight of guilt until he makes it right.

The third reason is that this change of becoming more Christlike allows you to experience more intimacy and vice versa. In the process of conforming yourself to God's image through obedience, you will receive, unwrap, and use all the Gifts of Freedom God offers. And ultimately, dwelling in His *image and likeness* is only accomplished when you are in an *intimate relationship* with Him where your identity is truly found in Him. These go hand in hand. When I reference "image and likeness," I am also talking about this "most intimate relationship."

✠ *...and have put on the **new self**, which is being renewed in **knowledge** in the **image of its Creator** (Colossians 3:10).*

I want to be clear here. I am not saying you have to be sinless in order to have intimacy with God. You are already seen as pure in God's eyes because you are covered with the blood of Christ (see Isaiah 61:10). You remember what Jesus told the Samaritan lady at the well?

✠ *Jesus answered her, "If you knew the gift of [grace] and who it is that asks you for a drink, you would have asked him and he would have given you living water" (John 4:10).*

Now that you have been born again, you have pure water living in you—living water—which is water of which God can partake. No longer does sin separate you from God. What hurts your intimacy with God is when you sin, you lose time and focus on Him, who is your life.

The fourth reason to avoid sin is that by living in His image and likeness in an intimate relationship with Him, you will certainly live an abundant life, experiencing all the things God intended for you. Unfortunately, many Christians who receive the gift of salvation do not go on to receive, unwrap, or use all the additional gifts God offers. Some Christians don't pursue what it means to be Christlike, what it means to conform our image and likeness to Christ's; some Christians try to achieve His image and likeness, but only through their own efforts. Both result in lives less than what God desires.

Christians who diligently seek an intimate relationship with God and seek Christlikeness discover the amazing, supernatural ways God can meet them and help them grow. Your desire to avoid sin will allow you to grow a closer, more intimate relationship with God, especially when you allow Him to remove that sin from your life. Dwelling in this place is to know a joyful life, more than you have ever experienced.

Pursuing Christlikeness is just what it sounds like—*choosing* daily to be like Jesus. Jesus is the living expression of all that God wants to communicate to us. Jesus was fully man (He walked this earth in a body like yours and mine); He was also fully God (He had the Spirit of God in Him). By God's intent, Jesus is the perfect model for us to observe, emulate, and conform. This is why Paul writes:

✝ *And just as we have borne the likeness of the earthly man* [Adam], *so shall we bear the likeness of the Man from Heaven* [Jesus] (1 Corinthians 15:49).

Jesus Himself said we should do as He does. After He demonstrated how to be a servant by washing His disciple's feet, Jesus said:

✝ *Now that I, your Lord and Teacher, have washed your feet, you also should wash one another's feet* (John 13:14).

Jesus wants you to use Him as a model as you seek to become more in the image and likeness of your Creator. God does not care what you look like on the outside or even about the good deeds you do to make yourself look good, deeds that are not coming from your heart. Jesus had this insightful exchange with the religious leaders of the time.

✙ *Then some Pharisees and teachers of the law came to Jesus from Jerusalem and asked, "Why do your disciples break the tradition of the elders? They don't wash their hands before they eat!"* [A tradition set up that did not come from the Word of God or from the heart.]

*Jesus replied, "And why do you break the command of God for the sake of your tradition?…*

*"You hypocrites! Isaiah was right when he prophesied about you:*
*'These people honor Me with their lips,*
*but their hearts are far from Me.*
*They worship Me in vain;*
*their teachings are but rules taught by men.'"*

*Jesus called the crowd to Him and said, "Listen and understand. What goes into a man's mouth does not make him 'unclean,' but* **what comes out of his mouth, that is what makes him 'unclean'"** (Matthew 15:1-3,7-11).

God's desire is that we surrender ourselves over to Him so that He can begin remaking us into His image and likeness, starting with what He sees—the *inside.*

✙ *As water reflects a face, so a man's heart reflects the man* (Proverbs 27:19).

This will not be done by our own efforts alone. This transformation will only be accomplished by Jesus when our focus is on His power and glory.

✙ *And we, who with unveiled faces all reflect the Lord's glory, are being transformed into His likeness with ever-increasing glory, which comes from the Lord, who is the Spirit* (2 Corinthians 3:18).

The road to becoming like Jesus is a lifelong one. Just look at what God says to Jesus after He was baptized (this was before Jesus started His ministry):

✝ *You are my Son, whom I love; with you I am well pleased* (Luke 3:22).

What caused the Father to say He was so pleased with Jesus? At the age of thirty, Jesus hadn't yet started His ministry. He hadn't saved one soul, healed one person, nor performed one miracle. An earlier verse in Luke tells us:

✝ *And Jesus grew in wisdom and stature, and in favor with God and men* (Luke 2:52).

Jesus had been *preparing* Himself to fulfill God's plan for His life; *increasing* in knowledge and wisdom, *learning* from Scripture, and *growing closer to His Father through prayer.* This is where you are too—*preparing yourself* so you will fulfill God's will for your life—growing *closer* so you can be used by Him.

As unique individuals, each of us has a *different* purpose in life that, once fulfilled, leads us to our personalized abundant life; however, to fulfill our noble purposes we must prepare ourselves first by being born again then by seeking to conform ourselves to His image and likeness.

✝ *In a large house there are articles not only of gold and silver, but also of wood and clay; some are for noble purposes and some for ignoble. If a man cleanses himself from the latter, he will be an instrument for noble purposes, made holy, useful to the Master and prepared to do any good work. Flee the evil desires of youth, and pursue righteousness, faith, love and peace, along with those who call on the Lord out of a pure heart* [other like-minded believers] (2 Timothy 2:20-22).

The fifth reason that conforming to the likeness of Christ will build up and strengthen your spiritual life is that it will be necessary to fully achieve your unique purpose and the abundant life that comes with it. This will allow you to be balanced in your Christian walk, which is important as you are a human *being* not a human *doing*. God is most interested in who you are, not what you do. If you take time to prepare your heart and strengthen your relationship with Him, then God will be close to you. That's not to say that He will not want you to act a certain way, to preach or teach or share the gospel message with others—but *who* you *are* is most important. This will ultimately determine *what* you *do* as God guides you *personally*.

There is an order to this process. It's like when you get on a plane and the flight attendant tells parents, "In the event of an emergency, secure your oxygen mask before your children's." This is because the chance for survival is much greater if the parent cares for himself or herself first. We need to *prepare ourselves first* so we can help others.

Jesus demonstrated a life of servanthood for us to follow, as exemplified in washing His disciples' feet. This is an important aspect of spiritual growth. Helping others brings us closer to God and therefore spiritual growth occurs. But remember that Jesus wants you to rest in Him and find your strength in Him. Even Jesus withdrew from the crowds and people in need at times, and spent time alone in prayer, renewing Himself with God. Jesus said we should not be so busy, even doing good, that we don't focus on God, who is our source of life, love, and destiny.

✝ *As Jesus and His disciples were on their way, He came to a village where a woman named Martha opened her home to Him. She had a sister called Mary, who sat at the Lord's feet listening to what He said.*
*But Martha was distracted by all the preparations that had to be made. She came to Him and asked, "Lord, don't you care that my sister has left me to do the work by myself? Tell her to help me!"*
*"Martha, Martha," the Lord answered, "you are worried and upset about many things, but only one thing is needed. Mary has chosen what is better, and it will not be taken away from her"* (Luke 10:38-42).

Remember, God is more interested in growing you from the inside out, which only happens in solitude through listening, study, and prayer. He should always be the primary object of your focus in all matters. If you do this, then He will work out everything else in your life for your good. Don't ever let "doing a bunch of Christian activities" distract you from your priority, which is developing your spiritual relationship with God. This can be a difficult and delicate balancing act at times, as you will also want and need to grow as a servant too.

Jesus' life was a perfect example for us to follow. The degree to which we can follow in His footsteps is the degree we can live a powerful, *supernatural, Spirit-filled life* and have a significant *impact* on the world as we become *like* Him and become His *evidence* in the world. This is the sixth reason to conform to the image of Christ.

☩ *For you were once darkness, but now you are light in the Lord. Live as children of light* (Ephesians 5:8).

☩ *You* [Christians] *are the light of the world. A city on a hill cannot be hidden. Neither do people light a lamp and put it under a bowl. Instead they put it on its stand, and it gives light to everyone in the house. In the same way, let your light shine before men, that they may see your good deeds* [actions in the will of God] *and praise* [or come to know] *your Father in Heaven* [because they are seeing Him in you] (Matthew 5:14-16).

We begin our relationship with God by identifying ourselves with Jesus' death and resurrection. Our relationship with Him grows by receiving, unwrapping, and using the additional Gifts of Freedom. We then must diligently conform ourselves to His image and likeness in all aspects of our lives. In doing so, our lives will reveal and reflect Him to others. While the apostle Paul says we will never fully achieve perfection in this life, it should still be our aim:

✠ *Aim for perfection, listen to my appeal, be of one mind, live in peace. And the God of love and peace will be with you* (2 Corinthians 13:11).

If we want to follow God, then we are called to model our lives after His beloved Son.

✠ *For those God foreknew* [you] *He also predestined to be conformed to the likeness of His Son, that He* [Jesus] *might be the Firstborn among many brothers* (Romans 8:29).

## ACTION & VISUALIZATION

*Conform yourself to the image and likeness of Jesus Christ.*

## MEDITATION POINT

Follow in His steps.

Go to Chapter 3 in the Study Guide section on page 301.

## ENDNOTE

1.  Jack Hayford, ed. *Spirit Filled Life Bible for Students* (Nashville, TN: Thomas Nelson Publishers, 1995), 1502.

# Chapter 4

# GIFT #2—THE HOLY SPIRIT (PART 1)

## WHAT DOES THE HOLY SPIRIT MEAN IN YOUR LIFE?

Before you begin to read, pray that the Holy Spirit
will give you understanding and application.

✠ *Peter replied, "Repent and be baptized, every one of you, in the name
of Jesus Christ for the forgiveness of your sins. And you will receive the
**gift** of the **Holy Spirit**"* (Acts 2:38).

### THE HOLY SPIRIT AND YOU

When you fell in love with your husband or wife, you probably couldn't wait to introduce him or her to your friends and family. This person was so wonderful you just had to share him or her with others—you couldn't keep this gift to yourself. When Jesus was departing the world and introduced us to the Holy Spirit, it was much the same. Jesus was saying, "Yes, you know and have seen Me, but though I am leaving, just wait until you meet this wonderful Counselor, Guide, and Helper—the Holy Spirit." He said:

✝ *I will not leave you as orphans... (John 14:18).*

Jesus' promise was fulfilled by the next Gift of Freedom: the gift of the Holy Spirit.

✝ *And I will ask the Father, and He will give you another Counselor to be with you **forever**... (John 14:16).*

When Jesus promised the coming of the Holy Spirit to believers, what He was promising was a new connection with God, a gift for those who would believe in Him through faith:

✝ *[Jesus said], "When the **Counselor** comes, whom I will send to you from the Father, the Spirit of truth who goes out from the Father, He will testify about Me" (John 15:26).*

✝ *[Jesus said to His disciples], "Now I am going to Him who sent Me. ...It is for your good that I am going away. Unless I go away, the **Counselor** will not come to you; but if I go, I will send Him to you" (John 16:5,7).*

✝ *By this He meant the **Spirit**, whom those who believed in Him were later to receive. Up to that time the **Spirit** had not been given, since Jesus had not yet been glorified (John 7:39).*

You may be feeling a bit overwhelmed right about now. Perhaps you're wondering how you can absorb these new thoughts, feelings, and information being presented. Perhaps you're asking, "What else do I need to know? How will I apply these new concepts to my daily life? How do I go about making necessary life changes (especially difficult ones)?" Rest assured, these questions are familiar to most new believers—I asked them myself after I accepted the first gift of salvation. The all-encompassing simple answer to these questions is the *Holy Spirit,* which is a gift you *automatically* receive when you *accept* the gift of life.

## WHO IS THE HOLY SPIRIT?

Before we see how the Holy Spirit is going to help you, let's understand who the Holy Spirit is and where the Holy Spirit came from. The Holy Spirit was present at the creation of the world:

✢ *Now the earth was formless and empty, darkness was over the surface of the deep, and the Spirit of God was hovering over the waters* (Genesis 1:2).

✢ *Then God said, "Let Us [the Father, the Son, and the Holy Spirit] make man in our image, in our likeness..."* (Genesis 1:26).

The Holy Spirit is an important part of the Holy Trinity. Jesus said:

✢ *The Spirit gives life...* (John 6:63).

Elsewhere in Scripture, this theme of life is repeated:

✢ *The Spirit of God has made me; the breath [Spirit] of the Almighty gives me life* (Job 33:4).

The Holy Spirit also was involved in the creation of Jesus' human life:

125

✠ *This is how the birth of Jesus Christ came about: His mother Mary was pledged to be married to Joseph, but before they came together, she was found to be with child through the Holy Spirit* (Matthew 1:18).

And the Holy Spirit brings Jesus to life after His death on the cross:

✠ *For Christ died for sins once for all, the righteous for the unrighteous, to bring you to God. He was put to death in the body but made alive by the Spirit...*" (1 Peter 3:18).

✠ *And if the Spirit of Him who raised Jesus from the dead is living in you, He who raised Christ from the dead will also give life to your mortal bodies through His Spirit, who lives in you* (Romans 8:11).

And finally, when *you* become a new Christian—a born-again believer—God gives you a new heart and a regenerated spirit as well as the Holy Spirit to guide you:

✠ *I [God] will give you a new heart and put a new spirit in you; I will remove from you your heart of stone and give you a heart of flesh. And I will put my Spirit in you and move you to follow My decrees and be careful to keep My laws* (Ezekiel 36:26-27).

## FOR EVERY CHRISTIAN

Jesus promises *every* Christian the indwelling power of the Holy Spirit, to lead and reveal God's truth within you. Remember what I said earlier about the Holy Trinity? God is made up of three persons: God the Father, Jesus the Son, and the Holy Spirit. The word used in the original text to refer to the Holy Spirit is *parakletos* (par-ak-lay-toss). *Parakletos* comes from the word *para*, which means "beside," and *kaleo*, which means "to call." Together they suggest someone called to one's side. The word signifies a comforter, a helper, an advocate, and a *counselor*. In nonbiblical literature, the word *parakletos* often referred to an attorney, someone who would appear in court on another's behalf.[1]

The Holy Spirit helps us in several key ways. He leads believers to a greater understanding of gospel truths, gives us strength to endure the hostility of the world, and helps us communicate with God. Isaiah prophesied:

*"For My thoughts are not your thoughts, neither are your ways My ways," declares the Lord. "As the heavens are higher than the earth, so are My ways higher than your ways and My thoughts than your thoughts"* (Isaiah 55:8-9).

We can't understand the ways and nature of God because we have been shaped by earthly circumstances. Our minds have been, in a sense, grounded, and that grounding leads us to death or a disconnection with God. Still, we desperately need a way to communicate with Him. Our earthly bodies and minds block us from intimacy with a holy, sinless God. The Holy Spirit helps us connect to God's ways, which are unreachable on our own.

Read what else Jesus said of the Holy Spirit:

*And I will ask the Father, and He will give you another Counselor to be with you forever—the Spirit of truth. The world cannot accept Him, because it neither sees Him nor knows Him. But you know Him, for He lives **with** you and will be **in** you* (John 14:16-17).

When you are born again, the Holy Spirit becomes your companion for life, literally dwelling within you. The moment you accept the gift of salvation, you receive a gift the world doesn't have: a Comforter and Counselor you can call on to help you face life's many challenges. The Holy Spirit, or what John refers to as the anointing, can show you truth when the world offers lies and uncertainty. John wrote:

✝ *As for you, the anointing* [Holy Spirit] *you received from Him remains in you, and you do not need anyone to teach you, but as His anointing teaches you about all things and as that anointing is real, not counterfeit—just as it has taught you, remain in Him* (1 John 2:27).

How does the Holy Spirit bring you to truth? How can you listen and follow the Spirit in your life? You should be receptive to the Holy Spirit speaking to you through your spirit. He will speak to you through other people, and He will speak to you through events and circumstances. Become sensitive to the Holy Spirit's communications with you and reprogram yourself to receive them by consciously opening your mind and spirit to Him—become childlike.

Remember how you programmed yourself to drive? Your eyes and mind learned to pick out important information as you drove: the red or green traffic lights, the red octagonal sign, and countless other traffic instructions, not to mention other vehicles, street signs, roadwork, etc. Now you process this information automatically, without conscious thought, right? It has almost become second nature. We've reprogrammed our minds and bodies to detect, think, react, and process data as drivers. Similarly, will you program your mind and body to detect, think, react, and process the Holy Spirit's active voice and signs as a Christian seeking a deeper relationship with God?

✝ *When He* [the Holy Spirit] *comes, He will convict the world of guilt in regard to sin and righteousness and judgment* (John 16:8).

If we do not program ourselves to recognize these signs or choose *not* to follow them once detected, then we're like a reckless driver behind the wheel. Our lives become chaotic with potentially devastating results, giving new meaning to the term "hell on wheels." The Holy Spirit not only gives us divine insight to help us avoid unnecessary trouble, but He is also our Guide, drawing us back toward the image and likeness of God.

Without the Holy Spirit, we, in our own ability, are *powerless to change*. Changing into His image and likeness can only happen by the guidance and through the *power* of the Holy Spirit; we need to accept His *leading* and *power*. And, of course, the complete fulfillment of this change will occur solely by Him in the next life. But we can still discover what this means for us in our earthly lives; the degree to which we follow the Holy Spirit's lead determines how far we get toward our goal of being transformed to God's image and likeness while on earth.

✠ *Now the Lord is the Spirit, and* **where the Spirit of the Lord is**, *there is* **freedom**. *And we, who with unveiled faces all reflect the Lord's glory, are being transformed into His likeness with ever-increasing glory, which comes from the Lord, who is the Spirit* (2 Corinthians 3:17-18).

We are profoundly changed when we unite ourselves with the Spirit of God, who gives us the *freedom* to change in ways we can't fully imagine right now. This is assuming, of course, we *choose* to change. Read what the apostle Paul wrote to the church in Corinth:

✠ *But he who unites himself with the Lord is one with Him in spirit. ... Do you not know that your body is a temple of the Holy Spirit, who is in you, whom you have* **received** *from God?* (1 Corinthians 6:17,19).

This does not mean, of course, that we become Jesus or that we become God. But because of the Holy Spirit dwelling within us, we have access to all three aspects of the Holy Trinity. We have Jesus within us; God is within us, which allows us the right to be called children of God and joint-heirs with Christ for what our heavenly Father owns. Paul writes:

✠ *Because you are sons, God sent the Spirit of His Son **into our hearts**, the Spirit who calls out, "Abba, Father." So you are no longer a slave, but a son; and since you are a son, God has made you also an heir (Galatians 4:6-7).*

✠ *Now if we are children, then we are heirs—heirs of God and **co-heirs with Christ**, if indeed we share in His suffering in order that we may also share in His glory (Romans 8:17).*

What does it mean to be an heir of God? Under the Mosaic law—the law of the Old Testament—a father's property was divided among the sons of his legitimate wives. Succession to property was a matter of *right, not favor*. The Bible says Jesus Christ, God's only begotten Son, is the "heir of all things" and that Christ-followers are "joint heirs with Christ." Yes, as a believer, there will come a day when you will share in all things not just spiritually but also physically.

## ACTION & VISUALIZATION

*Consider your new standing with God and how that will affect your life.*

## MORE THAN BEFORE

This brings us to a most important point. Now that you're a Christian, you are *more* than you were *before*. You are a child of God, an heir to the King of kings and Lord of lords.

We have already read that the Holy Spirit is the same Spirit who raised Jesus from the dead and gave Him life. *This same Spirit within you now becomes part of your new identity.* God wants us to listen to the Spirit.

Before you were a Christian, you primarily listened to the desires of your mind and the needs and wants of your body. But as a Christian, your real power doesn't come from your mind or your body; rather, it comes from the Holy Spirit. As we restrain our minds and bodies and offer ourselves up to the *leading* and *shaping* of the Holy Spirit, we are *bringing* the Kingdom of Heaven within us. This is the place where Jesus Christ can take His place as King of our lives. Read what the apostle Paul wrote in Romans:

✠ *And if the Spirit of Him who raised Jesus from the dead is living in you, He who raised Christ from the dead will also give life to your mortal bodies through His Spirit, who lives in you* (Romans 8:11).

Are you wrestling with an issue in your life that seems dead and hopeless? If so, remember that the same Spirit who raised Christ from the dead can provide resurrection power in all parts of your life. Whether you need a physical, mental, social, or financial resurrection, reliance on God is your only hope. His workspace is faith; this is where He can shape a fulfilling life for you. It also provides a forum where He can hear and respond to your desires. Your mind will put *limits* on what you can do, but God's will for your life is *limitless*. Connect yourself to God's Spirit in a meaningful relationship and watch your new identity start falling into place.

✠ *Flesh gives birth to flesh, but the Spirit gives birth to spirit* (John 3:6).

The Holy Spirit is a life-giving power.

✠ *The Spirit Himself testifies with our spirit that we are God's children* (Romans 8:16).

While we have a new spirit, we're much like children. We have a lot to learn. We need a teacher, someone to instruct us in this new life as God's children. We need someone to help us change all our old programming. Who better than God to teach us? Remember Romans 12:1-2 says God wants us to realign our minds and bodies with His will so His will and purpose can be completed in our lives, and through us in the world. He has given us the Holy Spirit to help teach, lead, and empower us to do that.

## ACTION & VISUALIZATION

*Consider how the Holy Spirit can change your identity.*
*You need to visualize and embrace the change before*
*you can fully manifest your new identity.*

## THE POWER OF THE SPIRIT

Being in sync with God will put His power in sync with our efforts, much like a plane or kite uses the wind to achieve its goal of flight. The Holy Spirit can lift us to do God's will so we can soar in life. This power allows us to accomplish what we could not accomplish otherwise: blessings, long life, benefits for our descendants, a closer relationship with God, and much more.

✝ *All these blessings will come upon you and accompany you if you obey the Lord your God. ...You will be **blessed when you come in** and **blessed when you go out** (Deuteronomy 28:2,6).*

✝ *See that what you have heard from the beginning remains in you. If it does, you also will remain in the Son and in the Father (1 John 2:24).*

✝ *And if you walk in My ways and obey My statutes and commands as David your father did, I will give you a long life* (1 Kings 3:14).

✝ *Oh, that their hearts would be inclined to fear Me and keep all My commands always, so that it might go well with them and their children forever!* (Deuteronomy 5:29).

✝ *Now if you obey Me fully and keep My covenant, then out of all nations you will be My treasured possession...* (Exodus 19:5).

✝ *But seek first His Kingdom and His righteousness and all these things* [your needs] *will be given to you as well* (Matthew 6:33).

✝ *...because those who are led by the Spirit of God are sons of God* (Romans 8:14).

This is exciting stuff. But what does it take to get into alignment with God's will? How do we get into sync? We *begin* by understanding how the Holy Spirit works!

✝ *But the Counselor, the Holy Spirit, whom the Father will send in My name, will teach you all things and will remind you of everything I have said to you* (John 14:26).

✝ *You gave Your good Spirit to instruct them...* (Nehemiah 9:20).

> *This is what we speak, not in words taught us by human wisdom but in words taught by the Spirit, expressing spiritual truths in spiritual words* (1 Corinthians 2:13).

> *...I will put My law in their minds and write it on their hearts. I will be their God, and they will be My people* (Jeremiah 31:33).

When you read the Bible, you should always pray and invite the Holy Spirit to reveal spiritual and practical life application. The Holy Spirit illuminates the truth that we are often too blind to see. For example, Paul wrote:

> *The man without the Spirit does not accept the things that come from the Spirit of God, for they are **foolishness** to him, and he **cannot understand** them, because they are **spiritually** discerned* (1 Corinthians 2:14).

The Holy Spirit sheds spiritual light and understanding, giving us revelation that could only be seen with the Holy Spirit's help. What the Holy Spirit has revealed to you is supernatural and not understandable by the human mind. This is why it may seem crazy to your nonbelieving friends or family members.

> *For the message of the cross is **foolishness to those who are perishing**, but to **us** who are being saved it is the **power of God*** (1 Corinthians 1:18).

After I became a Christian, my unsaved friends accused me of being brainwashed when I spoke to them about my newfound belief. I told them, "I'm glad you noticed...because my brain needed washing." Of course, it was the Holy Spirit who did this cleansing.

The Holy Spirit teaches us and reveals God's laws or His ways of guiding us morally and spiritually. This allows us to use the *power* of these laws for our benefit and, of course, avoid being harmed. As an example, adhering to the law of sowing and reaping will allow you to use its power to better reap the things you want in life and better avoid the things you don't.

The Holy Spirit also imprints these laws on our mind and heart to help us adjust to our new spirit:

✠ *The Holy Spirit also testifies to us about this. First He says: "This is the covenant I will make with them after that time, says the Lord. I will put My laws in their hearts, and I will write them on their minds"* (Hebrews 10:15-16).

To accomplish God's overall mission, the Bible says that the Holy Spirit's presence is everywhere. David lamented:

✠ *Where can I go from Your Spirit? Where can I flee from Your presence? If I go up to the heavens, You are there; if I make my bed in the depths, You are there. If I rise on the wings of the dawn, if I settle on the far side of the sea, even there Your hand will guide me, Your right hand will hold me fast* (Psalm 139:7-10).

The Holy Spirit leads us into the completely fulfilling life God offers to all His children. There may be times when we make some wrong turns from God's plan, but just like the new guidance systems on cars, the Holy Spirit is ever-present, ready to get us back on track when *we're* ready to follow His leading again. This is important: You will make some wrong turns in this new life, but even then you won't be left alone without guidance. Even when you feel down or sad or like you've failed, the Holy Spirit is working to restore you just like your body does in such a marvelous way when you cut yourself.

✟ *But when He, the Spirit of truth, comes, He will guide you into all truth... (John 16:13).*

✟ *The Spirit gives life; the flesh counts for nothing. The words I have spoken to you are spirit and they are life (John 6:63).*

Paul, when explaining God to the Romans, says God had created and arranged everything in such a way that we might seek Him.

✟ *God did this so that men would seek Him and perhaps reach out for Him, though He is not far from each of us (Acts 17:27).*

## ACTION & VISUALIZATION

*Look and listen for the leading of the Holy Spirit in your life.*

## PROMPTED BY THE HOLY SPIRIT

When I became a Christian, I didn't know any other Christians, so there wasn't anyone who told me to read the Bible. Instead, I was prompted by the Holy Spirit to do so. The Holy Spirit also testified to me that the Bible is indeed the inspired Word of God—that all truth in the Bible was given by God. However, as I began reading, I discovered many difficult concepts that my natural mind could not fully understand. Sometimes, I didn't have someone to help me comprehend, so I would simply pray for the Spirit to help. Sure enough, something would happen to illuminate the Bible passage—whether it came through the sermon that week or a life experience. God regularly used and still uses circumstances to teach me, bringing understanding when there seemingly was none.

When you prepare to read the Bible, ask the Holy Spirit to shed light on truth. Guidance from the Holy Spirit, however, is *not* limited to reading the Bible. Ask Him to illuminate truth in every circumstance and in all of life's situations. You will find truth as you read, and keep your eyes open long after you've closed your Bible—look for God's truth in everyday life.

There were times when I didn't clearly hear God's voice in my reading or even soon thereafter. But even on those occasions I received a confirmation in my spirit that I was not ready to understand. The process of spiritual growth is like that of physical or mental development. We're just not meant to understand everything from "day one." For instance, it would be pointless to discuss the relative educational merits of attending UCLA or Harvard with a two-year-old. But when that toddler matures and is a student in high school, then yes, that student could understand conversation regarding higher education. Likewise, we grow in understanding as we grow closer to God. Remember what Jesus said to His disciples:

✠ *I have much more to say to you, more than you can **now** bear* (John 16:12).

God packages and times His information when we are ready for it and truly capable of understanding and using it. However, we must be open and look for it. Jesus spoke in parables much of the time—those whose hearts were open and eager for the truth understood.

✠ [Jesus said], *"That's why I tell stories: to create readiness, to nudge the people toward receptive insight. In their present state they can stare till doomsday and not see it, listen till they're blue in the face and not get it. I don't want Isaiah's forecast repeated all over again: Your ears are open but you don't hear a thing. Your eyes are awake but you don't see a thing. The people are blockheads! They stick their fingers in their ears so they won't have to listen; they screw their eyes shut so they won't have to look, so they won't have to deal with me face-to-face and let Me heal them"* (Matthew 13:13-15 MSG).

An open heart assists our growing relationship with God, which enables us to *understand* the spiritual matters we see and hear. That maturity as Christians and the process of developing spiritual muscle and growth is expressed this way in Hebrews:

✠ *We have much to say about this, but it is hard to explain because you are slow to learn. In fact, though by this time you ought to be teachers, you need someone to teach you the elementary truths of God's word all over again. You need milk, not solid food! Anyone who lives on milk, being still an infant, is not acquainted with the teaching about righteousness. But solid food is for the mature, who by constant use have trained themselves to distinguish good from evil* (Hebrews 5:11-14).

The book you're holding is filled with a variety of foods—some milk and lots of meat. It's okay if you don't understand everything right away. Perhaps the next time you pick up this book you'll find a truth you didn't see the first time. Of course, you should be reading and rereading the Bible as often as you can. Each time you read the Bible, the Holy Spirit will give you new understanding. Consistent study of God's teaching will help you better distinguish between good and evil.

## ACTION & VISUALIZATION

*Read the Bible daily and study other Christian resources often.*
*Keep your eyes and heart open when you read and the*
*Holy Spirit will reveal fresh truth to you.*

## ALL IN GOD'S TIME AND WAY

Sometimes God chooses to withhold information in order to protect us. He did this with the Israelites when they were escaping from Egypt:

✠ *It so happened that after Pharaoh released the people, God didn't lead them by the road through the land of the Philistines, which was the shortest route, for God thought, "If the people encounter war, they'll change their minds and go back to Egypt." So God led the people on the wilderness road, looping around to the Red Sea. The Israelites left Egypt in military formation...* (Exodus 13:17-18 MSG).

God always does things the *right* way, which is in His loving way. And that's not always the quickest way or the way we might think is most logical. The Israelites, having just been freed from a long period of captivity, didn't have enough faith to face the enemy they would have to fight to possess the Promised Land. At that point, God knew they were spiritually underdeveloped—weak in faith they would be fearful and run back to Egypt, even if that meant back into slavery. Of course, they would ultimately have to battle the Philistines to obtain possession of the Promised Land, but God nurtured and matured their faith over time to prepare them to fearlessly attack the enemy in battle.

New and even maturing Christians are a lot like the recently freed Israelites, still in need of nurturing. As with music, comedy, sports, and many other areas in life, timing is *important* and God's plan is all about timing. God has *perfect* timing. The more you grow in faith, the more you'll learn to trust in *His perfect timing.*

## ACTION & VISUALIZATION

*Pray that the Holy Spirit will reveal things you don't understand in your life.*

## BE OPEN TO ANSWERS YOU DON'T EXPECT

If you pray for revelation, then you will receive answers when God determines you are ready for them. When you ask for answers, ask with confidence and expectancy that the Holy Spirit will reveal truth, but also with the understanding that God sometimes answers in surprising, unexpected ways. Do not be overly influenced by what you *want* or *think* should happen.

Perhaps you've heard this little story that illustrates this point: Once there was a Christian man whose neighborhood was flooding. He prayed and asked God to save him and God assured him he would be saved. As the waters rose, a fire truck came by and the firemen offered the man a ride out of the neighborhood. The man was convinced God would save him, so he said, "No thanks." As the waters continued to rise, the man had to climb up onto his roof. A boat came by and offered him a ride. Still trusting God, he again replied, "No thanks." The flood kept rising and the man found himself balancing on his chimney, the water now moving up around his neck. A helicopter dropped a rope ladder and offered a flight to safety. With his faith still strong, the man said, "No thanks, God is going to save me." Well, the waters didn't stop and the man finally drowned. When he got to Heaven he immediately went to God to complain, "I thought You said You were going to save me! What happened?" To that God replied, "I sent a fire truck, a boat, and a helicopter—what else did you expect Me to do?"

God will not always speak to you in a way and through a circumstance you expect. The prophet Elijah discovered this when he was scared and on the run. After having just seen God do great miracles on his behalf, God found Elijah hiding in a cave from his enemies.

*The Lord said, "Go out and stand on the mountain in the presence of the Lord, for the Lord is about to pass by."*

*Then a great and powerful wind tore the mountain apart and shattered the rocks before the Lord, but the Lord was not in the wind. After the wind there was an earthquake, but the Lord was not in the earthquake. After the earthquake came a fire, but the Lord was not in the fire. After the fire came a gentle whisper. When Elijah heard it, he pulled his cloak over his face and went out and stood at the mouth of the cave.*

*Then a voice said to him, "What are you doing here, Elijah?"* (1 Kings 19:11-13).

God spoke to Elijah in a gentle whisper. When you're in a place you shouldn't be, God will ask you the same question, "What are you doing here?" It is essentially the same question God asked Adam after he had sinned: "Where are you?" If you always listen for God's soft, still voice, then you too will hear it when you're going in the wrong direction.

We need to be open and sensitive to God's voice so we can recognize God's direction and answers when they come. Unfortunately, sometimes we have to be hit over the head before we're ready to hear God. I can assure you, it is a lot easier when you get in tune with God's still, soft voice and learn to recognize Him and the signs He leaves you during life's circumstances. With time, study, prayer, and the guidance of the Holy Spirit, you can get better and better at hearing His voice and finding Him amid troubling circumstances. Like so much of our faith, this too is a growth process.

Here's a story that has helped me understand this idea of hearing God's voice in our daily circumstances:

✢ *Now Moses was tending the flock of Jethro his father-in-law, the priest of Midian, and he led the flock to the far side of the desert and came to Horeb, the mountain of God. There the angel of the Lord appeared to him in flames of fire from within a bush. Moses saw that though the bush was on fire it did not burn up. So Moses thought, "I will go over and see this strange sight—why the bush does not burn up."*

*When the Lord saw that he had **gone over to look**, God called to him from within the bush, "Moses! Moses!"* (Exodus 3:1-4).

This story begins with Moses going about his daily work of shepherding. But in the middle of a typical day, he sees something unusual. Having an *inquisitive* and *open* spirit, he takes a *closer* look. It's only *after* God sees that he is taking a closer look that He speaks to Moses. That last sentence could almost be rewritten like this: "When the Lord saw that Moses had gone to take a closer look *in the circumstance,* that's when He chose to speak to Moses!" You will have to take a closer look at the circumstances in your life so you don't *just see,* but also *perceive,* God's voice speaking to you through those circumstances.

Somewhere in the middle of your day, the Holy Spirit might be trying to get your attention. When we're open to taking a closer look, God can, and often does, speak to us through circumstances. If we don't take a closer look, sometimes the Holy Spirit will diligently repeat the clues until we hear Him. If you've been getting the same message over and over, it is possible God is trying to get your attention. Look for Him there. Otherwise you may suffer the same fate as the Israelites on the way to their Promised Land.

After crossing the Red Sea, which God parted for the children of Israel in a miraculous way, they were only eleven days away in distance from being able to enter Promised Land. However, because they did not listen to God, they wound up walking around and around and around the same mountains for forty years. Because of that needless wandering from not listening to God's direction, they were never able to enter their Promised Land and simply died in the desert.

Jesus scolded His disciples when they repeatedly missed the signs too:

✝ *Aware of their discussion, Jesus asked them: "Why are you talking about having no bread? Do you still not see or understand? Are your hearts hardened? Do you have eyes but fail to see, and ears but fail to hear? And don't you remember?"* (Mark 8:17-18).

The word for *hardened* in this passage, *poroo* (po-rah-oh), means "to petrify" or "to form a callous." It was sometimes used metaphorically to refer to spiritual deafness and blindness. Jesus was making the point that those who hear the gospel and repeatedly resist its truth soon become insensitive and numb to the power of real understanding. Sinful lifestyles, false sophistication, intellectual pride, and self-reliance can also harden a heart toward the kind of truth the Holy Spirit brings.[2] Sins we repeat can make us calloused, as we repeatedly ignore the Holy Spirit's urging to do otherwise. In essence, we program ourselves to tune out the signs and therefore they will become of no benefit to us.

Our environment and experiences also condition us to automatically act and react in a certain, often godless, way. Influences such as our race, parents, upbringing, education, physical abilities, size, mental abilities, and economic standing impact the way we think. But with salvation and the Holy Spirit's guidance and power, we can have real impact in the world beyond our life's experiences and influences.

The changes I have seen in my own life and in the lives of other believers are dramatic, even unbelievable, considering human abilities. Miraculous freedoms from bondages, physical and/or emotional healings, supernatural favor, and God's power and presence in you can completely reshape your story if you are open to it. *All things are possible with God* by seeking, unwrapping, and using His life-changing *gifts*. God has much He would like to tell you and many gifts He would like to give you. It is the Holy Spirit who delivers or reveals God's gifts at His appointed time. Will you have your eyes and arms open when those times come?

✠ *However, as it is written: "No eye has seen, no ear has heard, no mind has conceived what God has prepared for those who love Him"—but God has revealed it to us by His Spirit.*

*The Spirit searches all things, even the deep things of God. For who among men knows the thoughts of a man except the man's spirit within him? In the same way no one knows the thoughts of God except the Spirit of God. We have not received the spirit of the world but the Spirit who is from God,* **that we may understand what** *[gifts]* **God has freely given us.** *This is what we speak, not in words taught us by human wisdom but in words taught by the Spirit, expressing spiritual truths in spiritual words* (1 Corinthians 2:9-13).

The Holy Spirit will teach us and confirm to our spirits all the spiritual laws of nature, along with an understanding of the gifts God offers should we choose to receive, unwrap, and use them. The offer and receiving is done through God's *Spirit* to your spirit. So be attentive and listen.

## Action & Visualization

*Be open and ready for truth and answers
beyond your current expectations.*

## Seeking Direction

Beyond an openness to God, it's beneficial to *actively seek* direction from the Holy Spirit in both the small and big decisions you face. Consider this passage from the Old Testament book of Judges:

✙ *In those days Israel had no king; everyone did as he saw fit* (Judges 21:25).

Does this sound familiar? Apart from a relationship with God, people set their own standards of right and wrong. They are not basing these standards on God's absolute truth, but instead on relative standards—standards that teach that most anything is okay depending on the circumstances. This approach didn't work for the Israelites; instead, chaos and disaster ruled because it led them down the wrong path, a direction God did not want them to go. The same is still true today. However, as a follower of King Jesus, we can overcome this chaos in our life, and with the Holy Spirit's help we can keep Jesus on the throne at the center of our lives.

The Holy Spirit also helps you choose the right paths to take, even when the road forks. He leads us down the path to *abundant life*. I want to clarify that an abundant life does not necessarily mean riches, perfect health, no disappointments, and so on. An *abundant life* is when you achieve the things you were uniquely *destined by God* to achieve—being in the center of His will, which allows you to experience the fullest life possible for you to achieve—the one for which you were made.

There is no greater joy in life than to know and live out the experiences and achievements for which you were uniquely designed and destined. Reaching that destiny usually involves pain and struggle. The heroes, prophets, apostles, and disciples in the Bible would testify to this fact. Remember that the runner in a great race goes through great pain and struggle to prepare himself. That struggle makes victory that much sweeter and more fulfilling.

As you pursue God's wonderful plan for your life, remember that there would be no fulfillment without the struggle. Keep in mind that the greater the struggle, the greater the reward. Part of our reward is eternal and will come later. But here and now our reward is joy, true satisfaction, and real love. Those things that the world is trying to buy, acquire, or take pills to find, we have in Jesus through the Holy Spirit and our relationship with God.

Our path may not always be obvious. In fact, it is a narrow road, so partner with the Holy Spirit and journey toward your destiny. Consider these words from Jesus:

*Enter through the narrow gate. For wide is the gate and broad is the road that leads to destruction, and many enter through it. But small is the gate and narrow the road that leads to life and only a few find it* (Matthew 7:13-14).

## Action & Visualization

*When deciding, pray that the Holy Spirit will guide you down the narrow road.*

## MEDITATION POINT

The Holy Spirit is your guide to a more intimate relationship with God—not the crowd.

Go to Chapter 4 in the Study Guide section on page 309.

## ENDNOTES

1. Jack Hayford, ed., *Spirit Filled Life Bible for Students* (Nashville, TN: Thomas Nelson Publishers, 1995), 1370.

2. Ibid., 1260.

# Chapter 5

# GIFT #2—THE HOLY SPIRIT (PART 2)

## HOW DO YOU MAKE THE HOLY SPIRIT RELEVANT IN YOUR LIFE?

Before you begin reading, pray that the Holy Spirit
will give you understanding and application.

✠ [Jesus said], *"When the Counselor comes, whom I will send to you
from the Father, the Spirit of truth who goes out from the Father, He
will testify about Me"* (John 15:26).

✠ [Jesus said], *"Therefore go and make disciples of all nations, baptizing
them in the name of the Father and of the Son and of the Holy Spirit,
and teaching them to obey everything I have commanded you. And
surely I am with you always, to the very end of the age"* (Matthew
28:19-20).

I f you have ever done any public speaking, then you probably had to
overcome a certain amount of fear: "What if I blank out and forget what
I was going to say? What if I freeze? What if I get people's names wrong?
Is there spinach in my teeth?" It's nerve-racking to say the least. On a grand
scale, we as believers are destined to fail, freeze, and blank out at times

without the power of the Holy Spirit involved in our witnessing. Truth is, we need the help. We want to live with purpose and passion, we want our lives to stand for truth, we want to love and be loved, but how do we do all that? How do we find that power?

To feel some level of anxiety when you hear about your responsibility in the Great Commission (see Matthew 28:19-20) is normal, and in line with what Jesus expects. It is your calling as a believer to make disciples and bring others to Christ. This may seem overwhelming at times (especially if you're still reeling from all the stuff you're learning as a new Christian), but once again, you're not alone. The Holy Spirit testifies and gives witness to who Jesus is; He helps you relay this to your friends, your family, and to the whole world.

✟ [Jesus said], *"But you will receive power when the Holy Spirit comes on you; and you will be My witnesses in Jerusalem, and in all Judea and Samaria, and to the ends of the earth"* (Acts 1:8).

This is an important aspect in becoming a mature Christian. You have become part of the Christian body, so it is important for you to be unified with a body of believers who are passionate about bringing God's plan for salvation to the world. You will find true fulfillment in reflecting God's image and likeness with others, shining His light into the world together so others can see Him. This evidence of Him in us is our strongest testimony. *Actions speak louder than words.* That means *you* have a *big* part to play in this plan.

Dedicated Christians are called disciples. Yes, when you dedicate yourself to Christ, you become one of His disciples—not unlike those who spent time with Him while He taught, preached, and healed during His earthly ministry. Disciples not only work at improving their own spirituality but also reach out to others, encouraging, supporting, teaching, and training them in the things of God. In other words, disciples are charged with duplicating themselves by helping create others who can be equipped to duplicate themselves too. No matter what profession you are in or what God's plan for your life is, if you are a Christian you will still be a disciple and hopefully a dedicated one.

Jesus lived and died, never leaving a 300-mile radius. He left only twelve disciples to bring His message to the whole world, and now today there are approximately two billion Christians worldwide.[1] At some point you will want to see that you are impacting twelve others who are going out and doing the same so that you can be an active part of the expansion of God's presence on earth. God asks us to be His hands, arms, legs, and mouth—to serve and witness to unbelievers as well as grow and help others grow in Christ. Like Christ's disciples, you are *not only* to affect *your* generation but also those to come.

God doesn't expect you to be a brilliant speaker. The first step to making a disciple is to simply be a witness to what Christ has done in your life. A witness is someone who tells what he or she has *experienced*. If you accepted Christ as your Savior, then you already have an *experience* to talk about. What is *your story*? How did Jesus find you? How did He draw you to Himself? How is He changing you? What is He doing for you?

When you share what God has done or is doing in your life, you will not only make a positive impact on others, but you will also reinforce your own faith. That anxiety you feel? It's a spiritual prompting to tell others what you have experienced. That urging is a God-planted desire to share what you know is a wonderful (and eternal) gift.

## LET THE HOLY SPIRIT WORK

There are two points to remember about being a witness for Jesus. First, don't condemn others or start arguments; instead, simply give your testimony, tell what you have *experienced*, and let the Holy Spirit give them understanding as *only* He can. People may argue with your theories or theology, but they can't argue with *your story*. A person's salvation is usually a process that ends in a decision. The Bible says this process is like growing a plant—someone plants a seed, someone waters the plant, but only God makes it grow. Paul wrote:

✝ *I planted the seed, Apollos watered it, but **God made it grow**. So neither he who plants nor he who waters is anything, but only God, who makes things grow. The man who plants and the man who waters have one purpose, and each will be rewarded according to his own labor* (1 Corinthians 3:6-8).

You will not know ahead of time whether you are a "sower" or a "waterer" in the process. Pray for guidance from the Holy Spirit as you testify about your faith, then trust that He, in His timing, will do what only He can do. The Holy Spirit will give you the words to say. Jesus promised His disciples and, therefore, us:

✝ *Whenever you are arrested and brought to trial, do not worry beforehand about what to say. Just say whatever is given you at the time, for it is not you speaking, but the Holy Spirit* (Mark 13:11).

You may be tempted to look for immediate results from the seeds you've planted or watered, but God's timing is not the same as ours. The truth is that we can become impatient, especially when we're reaching out to a loved one.

My wife was saved before me, but her words weren't taking root in my heart. In fact, she and two of our children moved to Hawaii to live with my mom. However, she continued to water her words with prayer, which led me to mysteriously stop at a church one Sunday morning. Ultimately, she was rewarded with an interesting phone call. My wife intended to tell me that she was going to be water baptized the next Sunday at Calvary Chapel in Honolulu, but before she could tell me her exciting news, I interrupted her with news of my own: I had arranged to be water baptized that same Sunday at Calvary Temple in Denver! Interesting coincidence? The Holy Spirit gives us the understanding to follow His perfect path at His perfect time.

Remember, it can take time for a seed to grow. Just look at nature—all plants blossom, bear fruit, and harvest according to their unique timetables. In the natural world, you can't circumvent that process; however, you can cultivate the spiritual seed you've planted in someone by praying for them and relating to them in *God's love*. Love is the key. Judgment, on the other hand, will *kill* anything you or others have planted. Here's a reminder of the kind of love we are to project to others:

*Love is patient, love is kind. It does not envy, it does not boast, it is not proud. It is not rude, it is not self-seeking, it is not easily angered, it keeps no record of wrongs. Love does not delight in evil but rejoices with the truth. It always protects, always trusts, always hopes, always perseveres. Love never fails…* (1 Corinthians 13:4-8).

Do you remember the story of the Samaritan woman in the Introduction? This is how the story continues:

*Jesus said to her, "You are right when you say you have no husband. The fact is, you have had five husbands, and the man you now have is not your husband. What you have just said is quite true"* (John 4:18).

Jesus, who was the seventh man in her life, told her something that went straight to her heart. Because of this, she immediately believed in Him as the Savior. Seven is the number of heavenly perfection that always satisfies—that which is produced in a fallen world will never completely satisfy. Jesus' words came right to the heart of the woman's issue, which immediately made her a believer when she heard those words.

✞ *Many of the Samaritans from that town believed in Him because of the woman's testimony: "He told me **everything** I ever did"* (John 4:39).

Jesus didn't literally tell the Samaritan woman everything she ever did in her life; but what she felt was Jesus touching her at the core of who she was. She knew from what He said that He knew her. He identified the empty part of her life that she had repeatedly tried to fill with men. The Samaritan woman was excited because Jesus revealed that her emptiness could now be filled with living water—Jesus Himself.

✞ *The Spirit and the bride say, "Come!" And let him who hears say, "Come!" Whoever is thirsty, let him come; and whoever wishes, let him take the free gift of the water of life* (Revelation 22:17).

We all have multiple issues in our lives that, if touched, could make a dramatic impact on us and bring us to a revelation that Jesus is God and the source of life. Sometimes all we need to hear is one word. This was true for me. The word I needed to hear was *simplify*. Life had become complex because I had no absolute truth, no compass to guide me. Everything was a shade of gray. God simplified things by providing one truth to navigate my life. When I walked into church that Sunday morning, I was seeking an answer. I was primed to listen to God, and because of that I heard Him. The Bible says that the seed (the Word of God) needs to fall on good soil if it is to grow. That "good soil" is a heart that's open to hear God.

Sometimes the task we have as a disciple is *not* to plant, but to *till* the soil, to encourage people to ask questions. How do you till the soil? It's done through praying, loving, and caring as well as being there to lend a helping hand. Remember this saying: People don't care about what you know unless they know you care. God says:

✝ *"Break up your unplowed* [hard] *ground* [heart] *and do not sow among thorns* [conflicting ideas]*"* (Jeremiah 4:3).

Indeed, people often ignore answers to questions they did *not* ask. In fact, all of us have built-in defense mechanisms to justify what we do and what we believe. Offering answers to someone who hasn't even asked a question will only trigger his or her defense mechanisms and likely create an argument—at this point you're trying to plant in hard soil.

Instead, these people first need your love to till the soil. After hard soil is tilled, then seeds will grow much better, especially if planted in the right season. Allow the Holy Spirit to guide you in His time and in His way. After all, only He can lead us to a blind spot in a person's defense system or give us divine insight to simply offer our friendship, our service, or resources that will till the ground and position us for the right timing, making others receptive to future seeds.

It is critical to trust and listen to the Holy Spirit when we testify to others. It may be tempting to speak to a specific issue we know a friend or family member has. We might think this is the issue where God can reach them best, but it may *not* be as obvious as we think. Be cautious and make sure your anxiety doesn't turn to desperation, which will often override wisdom.

A desperate attitude can be counterproductive. As a salesman, I know through experience that if you need a sale badly, projecting this attitude can negatively impact the ability to "close the deal." Just do your part—share what you believe the Holy Spirit wants you to share—then let the Holy Spirit *complete* the work you started. As we see with the Samaritan woman, Jesus' words can penetrate a person's heart like no others.

As the Holy Spirit gives you spiritual witness to Christ, make sure your physical witness does the same. In other words, is your lifestyle reflecting Christ? If people can see changes in your life, your actions will testify in ways words cannot. Mahatma Gandhi noted, "I like your Christ, I do not like your Christians. Your Christians are so unlike your Christ."[2] If you want to make a real impact on the people you care about, then start growing into His image and likeness. It will be hard to deny His presence and power when others *see* and *feel* it flowing *out* of you.

## ACTION & VISUALIZATION

*Be a witness of Jesus Christ whenever possible.*
*Pray for the Holy Spirit to give you the words to say and the*
*actions to do, as well as to give them the ears to hear and the sight to see.*

## BOLDNESS

Perhaps you're feeling a bit uncertain about sharing your testimony. Are you concerned you will fumble with your words? Or maybe you're fearful or shy around those who don't know about your salvation. Do you have family members who are hostile toward believers? If so, you are feeling what many of the early Christians felt. Like them, step out in *faith* to witness under the prompting of the Holy Spirit, and the Holy Spirit will give you *boldness*.

✝ *After they prayed, the place where they were meeting was shaken. And they were all **filled** with the Holy Spirit and spoke the word of God **boldly** (Acts 4:31).*

The word for boldness used here, *parrhesia* (par-rhay-see-ah), means "outspokenness" or "freedom of speech, with frankness, candor, cheerfulness, and courage." It's the opposite of cowardice, timidity, or fear. In this context, it denotes a divine enablement giving ordinary people spiritual authority and power. It also refers to a clear and understandable presentation of the gospel. *Parrhesia* is not a human quality but the result of following the leading of the Holy Spirit. It is not emotional hype, hysteria, or fanaticism.

It is a *confidence* produced by the Holy Spirit that moves through a person, allowing that person to act as a conduit for divine power and ability.[3]

You will feel this when you step out and follow the leading of the Holy Spirit, sharing your story. And He *will* lead you:

✠ *While Peter was still thinking about the vision, the Spirit said to him, "Simon, three men are looking for you. So get up and go downstairs. Do not hesitate to go with them, for I have sent them"* (Acts 10:19-20).

## POWER

The Holy Spirit enhances our abilities. The "heroes" of the Bible were regular people just like you and me; however, the Holy Spirit came upon them and allowed them to do great things. Read what the Bible says about some of these men:

✠ *Then the Spirit of the Lord came upon Gideon…* (Judges 6:34).

✠ *The Spirit of the Lord came upon* [Samson] *in power so that he tore the lion apart with his bare hands as he might have torn a young goat. But he told neither his father nor his mother what he had done* (Judges 14:6).

✠ *As* [Samson] *approached Lehi, the Philistines came toward him shouting. The Spirit of the Lord came upon him in power. The ropes on his arms became like charred flax, and the bindings dropped from his hands* (Judges 15:14).

✝ *Then the Lord said, "Rise and anoint [David]; he is the one." So Samuel took the horn of oil and anointed him in the presence of his brothers, and from that day on the Spirit of the Lord came upon David in power...* (1 Samuel 16:12-13).

✝ *The power of the Lord came upon Elijah and, tucking his cloak into his belt, he ran ahead of Ahab* [who was on a chariot] *all the way to Jezreel* (1 Kings 18:46).

I am not suggesting you will suddenly slay lions, defeat thousands, and heal people like these men did. But I *am* saying that as you grow spiritually and start learning to work with the Holy Spirit, you can and will experience spiritual power in your life *beyond* your natural power, intellect, and abilities. The possibilities are truly limitless, even if they are unimaginable to you right now.

## HOPE AND MORE

I'm sure you're starting to get the picture that the Holy Spirit plays a huge role in our lives as Christians. But there's still more! The Holy Spirit also gives us hope. Paul writes:

✝ *Oh! May the God of great hope fill you up with joy, fill you up with peace, so that your believing lives, filled with the life-giving energy of the Holy Spirit, will brim over with hope!* (Romans 15:13 MSG).

It is hope that allows us to experience joy and peace even as we go through trials, challenges, or battles. The Holy Spirit knows the future, so He can tell you things yet to come that you can use to build up your hope.

✝ [Jesus said], *"But when He, the Spirit of truth, comes, He will guide you into all truth. He will not speak on His own; He will speak only what He hears, and **He will tell you what is yet to come**"* (John 16:13).

The Holy Spirit is the conduit for prophecy:

✝ *For prophecy never had its origin in the will of man, but men spoke from God as they were carried along by the Holy Spirit* (2 Peter 1:21).

The Holy Spirit prays God's will for us:

✝ *In the same way, the Spirit helps us in our weakness. We do not know what we ought to pray for, but the Spirit Himself intercedes for us with groans that words cannot express. And He who searches our hearts knows the mind of the Spirit, because the Spirit intercedes for the saints in accordance with God's will* (Romans 8:26-27).

And it is the Holy Spirit who gives us favor with others:

✝ *The king had granted [Ezra] everything he asked, for the Hand of the Lord [Holy Spirit] his God was on him* (Ezra 7:6).

A restored connection to God through the Holy Spirit brings you access to God's guidance, power, and knowledge. It's important to note that the Holy Spirit prays God's will for us; although we still have a free choice, we can pursue or ignore this new life-enhancing relationship. Choosing to listen to the Holy Spirit will give us access to all the things He can provide us, including power, love, hope, confidence, joy, and peace.

## Subjecting Your Will

God's guidance, power, and knowledge are not the only benefits of a connection with Him. Some other benefits are known as fruits of the Spirit. The fruits of the Spirit can flow into you and out from you into other people's lives in large measure. What are these fruits? They are the attributes and the nature of God that were intended for us in His original design. The Bible describes these fruits of the Spirit as follows:

✠ *But the fruit of the Spirit is love, joy, peace, patience, kindness, goodness, faithfulness, gentleness and self-control...* (Galatians 5:22-23).

We consume these attributes from the Holy Spirit so we can give them away to *all* those around us. When we live out these attributes in our lives now and help others see Jesus, we become fruit-bearers. Imagine if everyone in the world was bearing fruit. That's the world God intended for us to live in and benefit from—a world where everyone we meet demonstrates love. Read what Jesus said about bearing fruit:

✠ *This is to My Father's glory, that you bear much fruit, **showing yourselves to be My disciples*** (John 15:8).

We have read that at our spiritual birth we are given a new heart. With this new heart and God's Spirit now within us, God expects this newly empowered us will have opportunities in everyday life to choose to bear fruit. Jesus told His disciples a parable:

✠ *A man had a fig tree, planted in his vineyard, and he went to look for fruit on it, but did not find any. So he said to the man who took care of the vineyard, "For three years now I've been coming to look for fruit on this fig tree and haven't found any. Cut it down! Why should it use up the soil?"*

"Sir," the man replied, "leave it alone for one more year, and I'll dig around it and fertilize it. If it bears fruit next year, fine! If not, then cut it down" (Luke 13:6-9).

From this we can see that God expects us to bear fruit, but He gives us time to do it. He also offers us His help to accomplish our fruit-bearing mission. Jesus describes it this way:

✠ I am the true Vine, and my Father is the gardener. He cuts off every branch in Me that bears no fruit, while every branch that does bear fruit He prunes so that it will be even more fruitful. You are already clean because of the word I have spoken to you. Remain in Me, and I will remain in you. No branch can bear fruit by itself; it must remain in the vine. Neither can you bear fruit unless you remain in Me.

I am the Vine; you are the branches. If a man remains in Me and I in him, he will bear much fruit; apart from Me you can do nothing" (John 15:1-5).

The pruning can be painful, yet it is an important process that allows the Holy Spirit to flow freely in all aspects of our lives. Our focus on bearing fruit will become important. I can tell you from experience that pruning can be painful, but like the pruning of plants, it's always beneficial. When you bear much fruit, you will benefit because you will receive much fruit— what you sow, you will also reap in due time. Did you notice from this passage that you can't produce the fruit alone? (He is the Vine and we are the fruit that grows off it.) This concept of God being the source of the good things that we produce is found throughout the Bible.

✠ If anyone does not **remain in Me**, he is like a branch that is thrown away and withers; such branches are picked up, thrown into the fire and burned (John 15:6).

This is a good reason to be actively working together with God to bear fruit. You are merely a conduit through which God's attributes will flow. To do this, you must seek God's will above your own—you must subject your will to His. How do you do this? Start with prayer. Ask God to *show* you His will. Then *listen* to the Holy Spirit who will help you recognize God's will and complete the work by giving you *strength* and the ability to follow through on His prompting.

Being in sync with God's will allows you to fire up His power, much like the distributor in a car. If the spark plugs don't fire in sync with the release of fuel into the piston chamber, then the car won't start. When you consider God's will and count on the Holy Spirit to help with your decision making, you'll discover something that will guide you—*wisdom*.

✠ *...And the breath of the Almighty* [the Holy Spirit] *gives* [man] *understanding. Great men are not always wise...* (Job 32:8-9 NKJV).

✠ *To the man who pleases Him, God gives wisdom, knowledge and happiness...* (Ecclesiastes 2:26).

Wisdom is much better than knowledge. Knowledge is simply possessing information, but wisdom leads to the correct use of that information. Wisdom for Christians means taking knowledge and applying God's guidelines and truths to it.

✠ *My* [wisdom's] *fruit is better than fine gold...* (Proverbs 8:19).

✠ *Wisdom makes one wise man more powerful than ten rulers in a city* (Ecclesiastes 7:19).

✠ *A prudent [wise] man sees danger and takes refuge, but the simple keep going and suffer for it (Proverbs 22:3).*

✠ *Blessed is the man who finds wisdom, the man who gains understanding, for she [wisdom] is more profitable than silver and yields better returns than gold. She is more precious than rubies; nothing you desire can compare with her. Long life is in her right hand; in her left hand are riches and honor. Her ways are pleasant ways, and all her paths are peace. She is a tree of life to those who embrace her; those who lay hold of her will be blessed (Proverbs 3:13-18).*

When faced with a choice, I recommend you always ask yourself the defining question: "What is the *wise* thing to do?"

## BAPTISM IN THE SPIRIT

We choose to be baptized into Jesus' death and resurrection. Baptism in the Holy Spirit is done in much the same way—it is a choice that each of us must make. This second baptism, much like the first, is a stepping-stone on our journey toward the image and likeness of Christ:

✠ *Therefore let us leave the elementary teachings about Christ and go on to maturity, not laying again the foundation of repentance from acts that lead to death, and of faith in God, instruction about baptisms...* (Hebrews 6:1-2).

You will note the "s" on the word baptism, which suggests more than one. Actually, there are two baptisms in our Christian walk. We see this recorded in several instances in the Bible where people who had already been water baptized are encouraged to be baptized in the Holy Spirit.

161

✠ *When the apostles in Jerusalem heard that Samaria had accepted the word of God, they sent Peter and John to them. When they arrived, they prayed for them that they might receive the Holy Spirit, because the Holy Spirit had not yet come upon any of them; they had simply been baptized into the name of the Lord Jesus* [which means they did have the Holy Spirit in them already]. *Then Peter and John placed their hands on them, and they received the Holy Spirit* (Acts 8:14-17).

I like to think of our developing relationship with God as a three-step process: accepting Christ, water baptism, and then Holy Spirit baptism. The first step is to simply accept Christ as your personal Savior and Lord. This is what reconnects God's Spirit within you and provides you with the promise of eternal life. The second step is to identify with and commit yourself to Jesus by being baptized in water. This is important to symbolize and memorialize your relationship with Jesus. Think of it as a wedding ceremony that publicly announces the commitment between husband and wife. And step three is being baptized in the Holy Spirit.

Holy Spirit baptism happens when you memorialize your relationship with the Holy Spirit. While the details or process may vary from one church to the next, typically an elder of the body of Christ will lay hands on you and ask the Holy Spirit to be present and active in guiding you through life. Or in a time of spiritual closeness, you may simply ask the Holy Spirit to come into your life and guide you. Baptism in the Holy Spirit is your action of faith, a way to express your intent and desire to follow the Holy Spirit's prompting not just initially but *daily*.

Some believers put too much emphasis on the ceremonial aspect of the baptism in the Holy Spirit versus its intended daily application of following the Holy Spirit. Following the Holy Spirit's daily leading allows the Him to work through you beyond your natural talents, intellect, and abilities. Indeed, many believers who have not specifically opted to go through the ceremonial baptism of the Holy Spirit still lead supernatural lives by faithfully following the Holy Spirit's daily leading.

## THE ROOTS OF THE STORY

This three-step progression of faith was foretold in the Old Testament book of Exodus. In fact, this Old Testament story, which outlines this three-step progress of faith, is prominent in understanding the Gifts of Freedom. Let's explore this story together.

First a little background. In the Old Testament book of Genesis, we learn that God promised Abraham that he would have many descendants. He also promised that these descendants (which are referred to as Israelites) would inherit a rich and fertile land—the Promised Land.

✛ *The Lord had said to Abram [Abraham], "Leave your country, your people and your father's household and go to the land I will show you. I will make you into a great nation and I will bless you; I will make your name great, and you will be a blessing"* (Genesis 12:1-2).

Skip ahead a few years, and the Israelites have been taken into captivity in Egypt and forced to live as slaves under the harsh rule of Pharaoh; however, they still had a promise from God.

✛ *And I have promised to bring you up out of your misery into the land [the Promised Land], …a land flowing with milk and honey* (Exodus 3:17).

God then raises up Moses (an Israelite) from within Pharaoh's household and charges him with setting the Israelites free to bring them back to the Promised Land. One of the ways God does this is by granting Moses the power to perform dramatic miracles intended to convince Pharaoh to let the people go free. (Perhaps you recall the ten plagues on Egypt? See Exodus 7–11.) These miracles get Pharaoh's attention, but it's only the last one—a plague intended to kill all the firstborn in Egypt—that convinces Pharaoh to let the Israelites leave his kingdom. It's important to note how

God protected the Israelites' sons from this plague. God instructed them to sacrifice an unblemished (innocent) lamb and apply the blood from that lamb to the doorpost and lintel of their homes.

*When the Lord goes through the land to strike down the Egyptians, He will see the blood* [of the innocent lamb] *on the top and sides of the doorframe and will pass over that doorway, and He will not permit the destroyer* [death] *to enter your houses and strike you down. Obey these instructions as a lasting ordinance for you and your descendants. When you enter the land that the Lord will give you as He promised, observe this* [Passover] *ceremony* (Exodus 12:23-25).

You are probably familiar with the next part of the story. When Pharaoh's firstborn son dies, he finally relents and lets the Israelites go. Moses leads the Israelites out of Egypt, but they didn't get far before Pharaoh had a change of heart and started chasing after them. Backed up against the Red Sea, God gave Moses the power to part the sea and let the Israelites cross, narrowly escaping the Egyptian armies. Then the sea destroyed the pursuing army that was seeking to take them back into captivity. Exodus tells us what happened next:

*Moses stretched out his hand over the sea, and at daybreak the sea went back to its place. The Egyptians were fleeing toward it, and the Lord swept them into the sea. The water flowed back and covered the chariots and horsemen—the entire army of Pharaoh that had followed the Israelites into the sea. Not one of them survived* (Exodus 14:27-28).

After such a miraculous feat, one would think the Israelites would have been ready to trust God with anything. Yet despite the great miracles they saw God do on their behalf, they still complained and did not listen to His direction. As a result, they traveled around and around the same mountains to make what should have been an eleven-day journey into what turned out to be an eventual forty-year journey.

Even as Moses led them to the Jordan River, near the Promised Land, they still failed to have the faith to enter. Moses sent twelve spies to scout out the land. Ten of the spies returned with reports of unbeatable foes—they even called them "giants"—and the Israelites were *frightened* by those reports. Because they weren't ready to trust God when facing new enemies, they had to continue to wander in the wilderness. They all died and only their children could enter the Promised Land.

There's more to this story, but let's step back for a moment to see how the overall story up to this point applies to the Gifts of Freedom. Before we accept the gift of salvation, you and I—and all people—are like the enslaved Israelites. We escape the angel of death not by the blood of an innocent lamb on our doorposts, but by the blood of Jesus on the post of the cross.

✞ *...For Christ, our Passover Lamb, has been sacrificed* (1 Corinthians 5:7).

We're captives, not to Pharaoh but to sin. Just as God sent Moses to save the people from their slavery, so He sent Jesus to save us and set us free from the bondage of sin. Like the Israelites, we are free. But to live in that freedom, we need to follow Jesus just as the Israelites had to follow Moses out of their slavery in Egypt. It's interesting that the first miracle Moses performed for Pharaoh was turning the waters of Egypt into blood. Likewise, the first recorded miracle Jesus performed was turning water into wine (which is a symbol of blood) at a wedding ceremony (see John 2:1-11).

The Red Sea crossing represents our water baptism. Though we are set free by Jesus Christ, we are called to identify with Him through baptism. As the Israelites went into the "water" and then came up out of it on the other side freed from their captives who were buried in the water, so we do the same when we are baptized. Noted in an earlier chapter, this baptism is a way of identifying with Jesus' death (shedding of His blood) and resurrection. It is no coincidence then that the sea is called the Red Sea.

Now what about the Promised Land? For the Israelites, this was a geographical land they would call their own—a home and place where they could become the nation God intended. For you and me, the Promised Land is the place where we can become the people God intended us to be, a home where we can conform to the *image and likeness of God*. Remember, we are spirit beings, and there are areas we must conquer in this life to more fully inhabit our Promised Land—*our minds and bodies.*

The Israelites didn't cross the Jordan River the first time they encountered it because there were giants in the land they did not think they could conquer. God had promised them the land! Shouldn't it have been a forgone conclusion that God would supernaturally give them victory against any occupants in the land, even "giants"? One would think so, but they didn't have enough faith. The writer of Hebrews tells us:

✠ *So we see that they were not able to enter, because of their unbelief* (Hebrews 3:19).

The Israelites were afraid to go into the land because they didn't think they could defeat the inhabitants, even with God's promise to help. God had set them free from Egypt; however, the restraints of Egypt were still in their minds. This overrode what God was showing and telling them, so they wandered around aimlessly for the rest of their lives seeking the Promised Land, which that generation would never have the faith to enter. This is the same with us. Upon our salvation, God sets us free from sin and the enemy; however, because of our old thinking patterns, our minds keep us out of the Promised Land until we are free in each area of our thinking.

Many believers don't have the faith it takes to seek entry into their Promised Land (image and likeness of God) because they don't believe they can be successful at subduing the enemy in their mind and body. Perhaps you're a little fearful about what it will take to conform to the image and likeness of Christ. But fear not, for you have a promise from God to help you.

The first step for the Israelites to achieve the occupation of the Promised Land was to cross the Jordan River. For you and me, this river crossing represents the baptism of the Holy Spirit, or our commitment to following the leading of the Holy Spirit in our daily lives. It's an act of faith to trust God to lead us to victory so we can safely inhabit our Promised Land.

Looking at this Old Testament account spiritually, we see God's promise to bring us back into His image and likeness (into the Promised Land). However, the degree to which you have faith in the Holy Spirit—to ascertain God's will for your life and then rely on Him to help you regain possession of your Promised Land—is the degree to which you can start taking possession of that land.

Ten spies didn't have that faith, but two of them did. Two of the spies knew that it was possible because God had promised it to them.

✠ *Then Caleb* [one of the two faith-filled spies] *silenced the people before Moses and said, "We should go up and take possession of the land, **for we can certainly do it**"* (Numbers 13:30).

Caleb spoke from his faith in God. But it wasn't enough to convince the Israelites, and so they continued to wander through the wilderness. This is where many Christians are today—wandering through life, just getting by, and not entering their God-promised Promised Land.

It's important to note that despite their undeveloped faith, the Israelites weren't wandering alone—God was still in their midst. He even provided them with food when they needed it, raining down manna from the heavens. God gave them a cloud to follow them during the day, which protected them from the hot desert sun, and at night He provided a pillar of fire that gave them heat to get through the cold desert nights. This was God's way of training the Israelites' faith by showing them that He was their daily Provider. And so it is for some of us today.

We accept Christ and get baptized in Christ, and then we find ourselves wandering around and around the same mountains in the wilderness, doing the same old habits with the same old disbeliefs we had before we were saved and freed by Christ. However, we're called to seek guidance, strength, and joy from the Holy Spirit, not letting worldly ups and downs or its physical constraints affect our drive and faith in God to help us through the Holy Spirit to become all He wants us to be. And still, all this time we wander around God is giving us our daily provision.

## Entering the Promised Land

When the Israelites finally crossed the Jordan to enter the Promised Land, they did so by letting go of their fears and trusting God's leading. Life didn't suddenly become perfect and pain-free—they would face many battles to possess the land—but they trusted God's power to help them overcome obstacles. This is same for us too. When we are baptized in the Spirit, we need to let go of the fears produced by our natural mind and instead trust the Holy Spirit's leading and power.

The story of the Israelites' first major battle in the Promised Land is a great illustration of this trust. Jericho was a well-fortified city, a stronghold surrounded by high walls. God told the Israelites to march around the city once for six days in a row, and then to march around the city seven more times on the seventh day, blowing their horns and shouting. Does this seem like a sound military strategy to you? No, at least not to our natural minds. But they did this anyway *in faith* and *obedience* to God, and the walls crumbled to the ground (see Joshua 6:1-20).

In a spiritual sense, we face strongholds in our lives. What are strongholds? Spiritually speaking, strongholds are the thoughts and habits that are contrary to God's will—godless thinking we have built up over time with our natural minds and physical desires. They keep us from fully occupying our Promised Land and from conforming to the *image and likeness of God*. When we trust the Holy Spirit's guidance and power, we can defeat these strongholds in our lives and bring them down.

The most critical step in any endeavor is to find God's will. Ask yourself this question: Am I in sync with God's will for my life? The Holy Spirit is always available to help you get in sync with God's will. He reveals where you need to be and what you need to do in order to bring down the strongholds that are holding you back. Don't be surprised when the Holy Spirit leads you to do the unexpected. It's His style!

The Israelites could not bring down Jericho with their own efforts, weapons, or intellects, but once they accepted the fact that God knew what He was doing (and obeyed Him), they received victory. In this case, it was as simple as the Israelites confessing their faith in God in obedience to what He asked of them. God can do unbelievable things in our lives, both physically and spiritually, if we obediently work with Him and His representative in us, the Holy Spirit.

It is not simply crossing the Jordan (receiving the baptism of the Holy Spirit) that allows us to fully possess the Promised Land. To occupy it, we must take the territory that is inhabited by enemy strongholds—thoughts and habits that are not aligned with God's will. God will supply the knowledge and power to take them down *if* we continually seek His will and trust the Holy Spirit to lead us.

Here's one more thought on this subject that helps to tie the Old Testament and New Testament stories together as they relate to the baptism of the Holy Spirit. Just prior to starting His ministry, Jesus was baptized in water. It is at this water baptism when He was simultaneously baptized in the Spirit, as was the case much of the time in the early New Testament church.

✠ *Then Jesus came from Galilee to the Jordan to be baptized by John [the Baptist]. ...As soon as Jesus was baptized, He went up out of the water. At that moment Heaven was opened, and He saw the Spirit of God descending like a dove and lighting on Him* (Matthew 3:13,16).

This is the same Jordan River we just read about that represented the baptism of the Spirit for the Israelites 1,400 years earlier. Amazing, don't you think? God's story is an intricate weaving designed to send us a clear message. Would you like to seek this intimate relationship with the Holy Spirit and give Him your allegiance?

## Action & Visualization

*Arrange with a pastor or church elder for prayer to receive the baptism of the Holy Spirit, or simply pray for it yourself.*

## Effects of the Baptism of the Spirit

What does it look like to be baptized in the Spirit? We get a glimpse of this in the book of Acts, where the Holy Spirit comes upon the disciples for the very first time:

*When the day of Pentecost came, they were all together in one place. Suddenly a sound like the blowing of a violent wind came from Heaven and filled the whole house where they were sitting. They saw what seemed to be tongues of fire that separated and came to rest on each of them. All of them were filled with the Holy Spirit and began to speak in other tongues as the Spirit enabled them (Acts 2:1-4).*

When you are baptized in the *Holy Spirit*, you probably won't experience this dramatic of a Pentecost experience due to the spiritual season we are in. However, it is not unusual to have a manifestation of the *gift* of tongues and/or other specific gifts residing in you. I will speak more about these other gifts of the Spirit in Book 3, but I'd like to talk a bit about the gift of tongues now, which is a heavenly language many receive at their baptism in the Spirit.

✢ *While Peter was still speaking these words, the Holy Spirit came on all who heard the message. The circumcised believers who had come with Peter were astonished that the gift of the Holy Spirit had been poured out even on the Gentiles. For they heard them speaking in tongues and praising God.*

*Then Peter said, "Can anyone keep these people from being baptized with water? They have received the Holy Spirit just as we have"* (Acts 10:44-47).

When you accept the gift of salvation, the Holy Spirit enters you and begins speaking with you in a language your natural mind can understand. But the gift of tongues is something different—it is a language God understands and your spirit understands; however, your natural mind does not understand what is being spoken. The Holy Spirit gives these utterances— we don't choose the words, but we choose to let these utterances flow out of our mouths.

✢ *This is what they speak [tongues], not in words taught to us by human wisdom but in words taught by the Spirit, expressing spiritual truths in spiritual words* (1 Corinthians 2:13).

The gift of tongues is something that will flow out when the Holy Spirit comes upon us. While I may have received the language from God when I was baptized in the Holy Spirit, I did not actually let it start flowing until a short time later. Initially, it came from my spirit when I fell into deeper worship and concentration on God. This heavenly language was prophesied about in the Old Testament:

✢ *For then I will restore to the peoples a pure language, that they may all call on the name of the Lord, to serve Him with one accord* (Zephaniah 3:9 NKJV).

And the apostle Paul said:

✠ *For anyone who speaks in a tongue does not speak to men but to God. Indeed, no one understands him; he utters mysteries with his spirit* (1 Corinthians 14:2).

## Action & Visualization

*Pray that you may receive your heavenly language and learn to flow with the Spirit's outpouring of that language.*

The Holy Spirit can lead you to use this language in prayer when you don't know what else to pray for. Keeping your natural mind out of the way, this allows the Holy Spirit to pray in agreement with God's will, because the Holy Spirit knows what to pray for:

✠ *In the same way, the Spirit helps us in our weakness. We do not know what we ought to pray for, but the Spirit Himself intercedes for us with groans that words cannot express* (Romans 8:26).

✠ *For if I pray in a tongue, my spirit prays, but my mind is unfruitful. So what shall I do? I will pray with my spirit, but I will also pray with my mind; I will sing with my spirit, but I will also sing with my mind* (1 Corinthians 14:14-15).

✠ *But you, dear friends, build yourselves up in your most holy faith and pray in the Holy Spirit* (Jude 1:20).

It is good when the Holy Spirit leads us to pray and sing to God in tongues. Indeed, this is a way for us to allow God's will to be prayed into our lives without the interference of our wills.

As this chapter ends, I'd like to turn your attention to something Jesus teaches and that helps us understand more about the Holy Spirit. This lesson is recorded in two of the Gospels, but there is a subtle difference between them that speaks volumes. In the gospel of Luke, Jesus says:

✠ *So I say to you: Ask and it will be given to you; seek and you will find; knock and the door will be opened to you. For everyone who asks receives; he who seeks finds; and to him who knocks, the door will be opened.*

*Which of you fathers, if your son asks for a fish, will give him a snake instead? Or if he asks for an egg, will give him a scorpion? If you then, though you are evil, know how to give good gifts to your children, how much more will your Father in Heaven give the* **Holy Spirit** *to those who ask Him!* (Luke 11:9-13).

The lesson is repeated in the gospel of Matthew almost verbatim, except in the last sentence the Holy Spirit's name is replaced with the name of what He means to us. Matthew writes:

✠ *How much more will your Father in Heaven give* **good gifts** *to those who ask Him!* (Matthew 7:11).

It is clear that the Holy Spirit is our source for all good gifts. In fact, the Holy Spirit is a really *big* gift, for He assists us in receiving and using the rest of the Gifts of Freedom. Partnership with the Holy Spirit is essential to bring freedom into all areas of our lives. He leads us to receiving all God's gifts so we can gain the *freedom* to fully occupy the land God desires especially for us.

# MEDITATION POINT

The Holy Spirit will deliver to you the Gifts of Freedom. If you wear them, they will prepare you for an intimate relationship with God Himself.

Go to Chapter 5 in the Study Guide section on page 317.

# ENDNOTES

1. About.com. "Denominations." Retrieved April 5, 2008, from http://christianity.about.com/od/denominations/p/christiantoday.htm.

2. Brainyquote.com. "Quotes." Retrieved April 5, 2008, from http://www.brainyquote.com/quotes/quotes/m/mohandasga107529.html.

3. Jack Hayford, ed., *Spirit Filled Life Bible for Students* (Nashville, TN: Thomas Nelson Publishers, 1995), 1392.

# Chapter 6

# GIFT #3—FAITH (PART 1)

## WHY IS FAITH NEEDED TO UNWRAP GOD'S GIFTS?

Before you begin to read, pray that the Holy Spirit
will give you understanding and application.

✟ *...think soberly, as God has dealt to each one a measure of faith*
(Romans 12:3 NKJV).

C an you truly capture the immensity of the Grand Canyon based on a postcard? Can the grandeur of Niagara Falls truly be described with words alone? How about your favorite beach—do your vacation pictures do it justice? If you've been to these or other amazing places, you may have snapshots you can show your friends, but two-dimensional images always pale in comparison to the firsthand experience. "You have to check this out for yourself!" you might say as you show them the pictures.

Honestly, this book, as well as all Christian books and even the Bible, can only go so far in presenting what faith is all about. Words, pictures, and instructions are only snapshots. If you want the real thing, you'll have to receive, unwrap, and use faith for yourself. Indeed, unless you do, the Bible and God's words will be little more than just that—mere words—to you.

✠ *For we also have had the gospel preached to us, ...**but** the message they heard was of **no** value to them, because those who heard did not **combine** it with **faith** (Hebrews 4:2).*

While the Spirit gives you *access* to all the other Gifts of Freedom, your faith is the catalyst that brings them *alive*. It was faith that brought to life or allowed you to unwrap the first two gifts—eternal life and the Holy Spirit. The Holy Spirit allows you to understand the message; however, you still need to use your faith for the messages to become real to you and have an impact on your life. The Holy Spirit delivers you the gifts, and your faith is what you use to unwrap and use them.

So what is faith? The writer of Hebrews defines it for us when he writes:

✠ *Now **faith** is being sure of what we hope for and certain of what we do not see (Hebrews 11:1).*

That's an interesting phrase, "certain of what we do *not* see." This could be a definition of trust too. It's *not* easy to be certain of what you don't see, especially when what you *see* sometimes is the opposite of what you were hoping for. In fact, we couldn't be certain of anything we don't see—whether spiritually or worldly—without God's gift of faith.

What about these "things we do not see"? When used in the spiritual context, this phrase applies to two different aspects of our lives. The first is the Kingdom of God, a place where God Himself lives: this includes the spirit realm where invisible truths shape and influence our relationship with Him. Obviously, we cannot see Him or His truths with our natural eyes, so we must have faith in them.

The second aspect is our physical realm—the place where we live and breathe on this earth. There are things we have faith in God for in the physical realm that haven't been manifested. Maybe you'd like to have many kids, or you have been going through financial difficulty, yet believe by faith that God will provide. Remember being sure of what we hope for doesn't necessarily mean getting the exact results or the ideal timeframe we were expecting. God works in such complex ways beyond our understanding that many times it seems mysterious. In these instances, we must have faith in Him and His intentions—that in the end He will work out everything for our ultimate good.

⊕ *And we know that in **all things** God works for the **good** of those who love Him, who have been called according to His purpose* (Romans 8:28).

Keep in mind that even outside your relationship with God, you currently act in faith every day. You get up and go to work because you have faith that a paycheck you can't currently see will show up at the end of the week or month. You plant seeds in anticipation that they will grow. Whether you realize it or not, you're using your faith mechanism every time you do anything based on the expectations of producing a specific result. Your actions of faith based on God's Word and your love for Him please Him. The more you act without seeing the result you expect, the more you are *exercising* your faith. It takes stronger, better-developed faith to continue to act longer or more in faith before seeing a result. The more we exercise this idea of *acting in faith*, the *stronger* our faith gets in that area.

How important is faith in our relationship with God? Again, the writer of Hebrews says:

⊕ *And without faith it is **impossible** to please God because anyone who comes to Him must believe that He exists and that He rewards those who earnestly seek Him* (Hebrews 11:6).

Faith is paramount to God. It breathes life into our relationship and all the other gifts, helping us conform to His image and likeness. When we act in faith, we please God because our actions of faith reflect our trust and surrender to Him. *Faith is the key to His heart.* It takes faith to unwrap all the other gifts because they are spiritual in nature, not readily identifiable by our senses or minds. Therefore, faith is required to act on them and to even make them real to us. The manifestation of the gift inside that we unwrap with our faith becomes our *reward* for our *action* of faith in unwrapping it.

On the surface, the verse in Romans (*"think soberly, as God has dealt to each one a measure of faith"*) and the verse in Hebrews (*"and without faith it is impossible to please God"*) seem to create an interesting conflict. Romans 12:3 clearly states that God determines the amount of faith each of us is to receive, while Hebrews 11:6 seems to say it takes faith to please Him. If God determines the amount of faith we each have, then doesn't that mean He alone programs within us how much we can please Him? Sounds like a catch-22, right? Thankfully, it's not. It is not simply faith that pleases God. Rather, it is when we have faith in God's Word on which we will base our actions that pleases God—*faith is action.* It doesn't matter how much faith we are given; it only matters if we *act* on it.

✝ *...faith by itself, if it is not accompanied by action, is dead* (James 2:17).

God gives us the inanimate ability to have faith; however, it is up to us to *animate* that faith by *acting* on it. God gives us faith as a noun and we give it back to Him as a verb so He is pleased. While you can't "work" for more faith through your deeds (remember, it is a gift), you can and are expected to *express* what you were given. It is acting in faith on *His* words that makes faith pleasing to God and at the same time allows you to grow, increase, and strengthen your faith.

Remember that it was through faith and *only* faith that you were saved so that you could have right standing with God:

✠ *For it is by grace you have been saved, through* **faith***...* (Ephesians 2:8).

✠ *...to the man who does not work* [trust in his own good works] *but trusts God who justifies the wicked, his* **faith** *is credited as righteousness* (Romans 4:5).

Think about it. Faith has been given to us by God; however, we were not automatically saved by that faith. No, we had to *use* it. As it says in Romans 10:9, we had to exhibit an *action* of faith by *confessing* with our mouths and *believing* in our hearts that Jesus is our Lord and Savior. This is what many Christians call "saving faith." The word *saving* suggests the action that was taken because of a decision that we made to be saved. But our exhibition of saving faith was only the *initial* step that began our journey, which calls us to exhibit *daily* what I call a *living faith*.

✠ *...but the righteous will live by his faith* (Habakkuk 2:4).

As you do this, you'll begin to see an interesting phenomenon: *when you accept and use a gift God offers, you are in turn giving a gift back to God—the gift of fulfilling His will for your life.*

## Using Your Faith

Imagine staring at a snapshot of the Grand Canyon taken by a friend and wanting to see and experience it for yourself. Simply hoping or wanting to see the Grand Canyon doesn't make it happen. Doing so requires action. We must pack the car, fill it with gas, check the tires and the engine, get directions to the Grand Canyon, and then drive there. Doing all this careful preparation in *faith* and *hope* that we will experience what we saw in the snapshot doesn't ensure an easy, event-free trip. We still might run into bad weather or heavy traffic. And yet, our faith moves us forward toward our goals, despite the obstacles. What if you are in an accident along the way and end up in the hospital? You can give up hope of experiencing the Grand Canyon, or you can, based on your faith of being able to get there, *resume* your journey when you're released.

It's important to remember that we live in a fallen world brought about by our rejection of God and His intentions for the world. Therefore, we are going to face obstacles along this journey. This is one of the reasons God said to Adam after the fall:

✠ *Cursed is the ground because of you; through painful toil you will eat of it all the days of your life* (Genesis 3:17).

Humankind's disruption of God's plan for the world is why it's going to be a struggle sometimes to have our hope manifest before we give up. But just as it takes persistence to make that journey to the Grand Canyon, so it is our *persistent actions of faith* that allow us to fully experience what we hope for in God as well as the gifts God *offers* us. To *fully* experience the gifts He offers, we must continue with our actions of faith to unwrap them until we get the results He promises. Indeed, the Hebrew word for *faith* indicates *persistence*.

## Growing Your Faith

Because our lives are not suddenly perfect and trouble free when we accept the gift of life, we now have plenty of opportunities to live by faith. All living things grow and develop, even spiritual things. The way we grow our faith is similar to the way we grow our muscles—through exercise. If everything you ever wanted in life was brought to you on a silver platter, and you didn't have to move physically to reach for anything, eventually the muscles in your legs and arms would grow weaker until your sedentary lifestyle made it more difficult to walk. The same is true of our faith.

What causes us to exercise faith?

- When there is something we hope for but we can't see it yet.

- When we continue to believe God will fulfill His promises.

- When we rely on God to provide for us, answer our prayers, and show up in challenging circumstances.

- When we wait for and act in anticipation of God's physical manifestation of that for which we hope.

- When, in any circumstance, we base our actions on God's nature and good intentions for us—even when we don't understand the reason for what's happening.

Exercising faith in all these situations will be the key to achieving new freedoms by the unwrapping and use of additional gifts.

✟ *For we walk by faith, not by sight* (2 Corinthians 5:7 NKJV).

Again, we live in a fallen world full of fallen people doing things *not* in the will of God, so we'll encounter *many* circumstances we don't expect to see—circumstances we don't understand—and many of them will be painful or difficult physically, relationally, or circumstantially. Some of what we'll encounter is the result of humanity's fall, which allowed evil into the world, because we ignore spiritual laws, because of our sin, or sometimes it is even evidence of God's discipline in our lives; and just sometimes it simply an attack by satan or evil forces now prevalent in the world.

Regardless of the cause, the trials and sufferings we encounter in life, despite the pain, are actually the material God uses to build our faith when we're working with Him.

## God Builds Our Faith on Multiple Levels

Painful circumstances and situations can help build up our faith if we choose to use our faith to get through those tough times. If we don't use it, then we won't develop the strong faith God desires us to have. This whole process of exercising our faith *can* be a painful process. The saying "no pain, no gain" is appropriate as it relates to faith-building. God may not have brought you out of all your trials, but He will use them to build you up. So rather than pray God will take you out of the trial, pray that God will come into the trial with you so He can change you in a way that will allow you to complete your destiny.

As we all know, challenging circumstances are inevitable; however, God wants you to use your faith to get through them. You may be thinking, "That's easy for you to say—you're not going through what I am." Well, it's not always easy for me to say either. But I believe for both of us that the greater the trials, the greater the potential for using the gift of faith (and, therefore, the greater the pleasure you will bring to God). Consider this verse again:

✟ *And we know that in all things* [human events and circumstances] *God works for the good of those who love Him, who have been called according to His purpose* (Romans 8:28).

This is an important truth to remember, a promise to be trusted. No matter how painful, tragic, heartbreaking, or challenging a situation is, God can redeem it into something good. Note that this verse doesn't say, "God makes all things happen to you." It says, despite the circumstances, whether the result of a fallen world, someone else's actions, or even your own, God uses everything to benefit those *"who love Him and have been called according to His purpose."*

Allow me to share a personal example of a bad situation God ultimately used for my good. The first job I had after high school graduation was developing apartments with my brother in San Antonio. In 1974 and 1975, an overabundance of apartment units suddenly and dramatically drove rents down. This downturn in revenues, combined with skyrocketing utility rates, sent many apartment complexes into foreclosure. It wasn't a pleasant experience for those of us who chose to build apartments during that time. This was obviously a challenging time for me, where I felt alone and vulnerable.

But because of that experience, I learned some important lessons about real estate, especially how easy it was to inadvertently box myself into a bad situation. Since that time, I've watched other developers (who didn't have the benefit of a painful learning experience like mine) lose large sums of their own money and that of others who trusted them. God can use our difficult experiences to teach and grow us in many ways, not only relating to our physical situation (as in this example) but in a spiritual sense as well.

These challenges in life will give you needed experience and knowledge to help you in business, personal relationships, and ministry, as well as allowing you to relate and empathize with others experiencing similar circumstances. You will learn later that developing empathy and relatability is an important part of drawing other people to Christ.

## ACTION & VISUALIZATION

*When you encounter difficult circumstances, act in faith,*
*hope, and trust that God has a plan for your good.*
*This will foster a closer relationship with Him.*

## ACTING ON FAITH

Let's dig a little deeper by looking at the New King James Version of Hebrews 11:1:

✝ *Now **faith** is the substance of things hoped for, the evidence of things not seen* (Hebrews 11:1 NKJV).

The "things we hope for" are what have not manifested themselves in this world. However, if you could peek into the Kingdom of God, you would find that faith is a "substance" used to make what you hope for in this world. Therefore, this substance is evidence that what you hope for exists somewhere. But how does it come into existence in our world? Jesus gives us a hint when He says:

✝ *I will give you the keys of the Kingdom of Heaven; whatever you bind on earth will be bound in Heaven, and whatever you loose on earth will be loosed in Heaven* (Matthew 16:19).

What we do here on earth (either good or bad) can have an effect in the Kingdom of God (Heaven) and vice versa. Do you remember reading that faith must be combined with our actions to actually work? James writes:

✝ *...faith by itself, if it is not accompanied by* **action,** *is* **dead** (James 2:17).

We must *act* on faith as if what we hope for is going to manifest, otherwise our faith is dead and what we hoped for will not happen (unless it is in God's predetermined will). For faith to be alive, we must accompany it with actions that are congruent with what we are having faith for.

*Faith is an action!* Your action should be lined up with what you believe, because your actions influence what's being "bound and loosed" in the spiritual realm, in the Kingdom of God, where what we encounter in this life is being "manufactured." God sees your actions, and your actions speak louder than words. Acting in faith on God's promises is the relationship God desires with you—and, therefore, doing this *pleases God!*

So how can you please God in your day-to-day life? You can please Him by walking in faith and trusting God's Word, principles, promises, and nature. This also places us on solid ground so we're able to withstand the inevitable storms that come our way.

✠ [Jesus said], *"Therefore **everyone who hears these words of Mine and puts them into practice** is like a wise man who built his house on the **rock**. The rain came down, the streams rose, and the winds blew and beat against that house; yet it did not fall, because it had its foundation on the rock"* (Matthew 7:24-25).

The faith you show in God by doing what He says gives you the ability to withstand the inevitable storms, even helping you discover *joy* during those storms. Jesus goes on to explain what happens to someone who does not act in faith, basing their life on His promises:

✠ [Jesus said], *"But **everyone who hears these words of Mine and does not put them into practice** is like a foolish man who built his house on the sand. The rain came down, the streams rose, and the winds blew and beat against that house, and it fell with a great crash"* (Matthew 7:26-27).

Jesus is saying that it is up to *us* to prepare for the storm by *acting* on His Word. Moreover, when we *do* act in faith on what we know from God, we'll receive a blessing:

✠ [Jesus said], *"Now that you know these things, you will be **blessed if you do them**"* (John 13:17).

Just a reminder: when you act on God's Word, that doesn't mean He'll eliminate the storms in life. Jesus says you will still have storms, but He also says that if you are obedient to His Word—if you *act* in faith—the storms won't blow away your house, or blow away any part of your life. Hearing and acting on God's Word will also bring you closer to God and allow Jesus to better *manifest* Himself in your life circumstances.

✝ [Jesus said], *"He who has My commandments and **keeps** them, it is he who loves Me. And he who loves Me will be loved by My Father, and I will love him and **manifest** Myself to him"* (John 14:21 NKJV).

## ACTION & VISUALIZATION
*Act in faith on God's Word.*

## WHAT IS UNSEEN

There is a concept woven throughout the Bible that states we will be blessed by God when our belief is *not* dependent on what we see. For example, Jesus says:

✝ *...blessed are those who have not seen and yet have believed* (John 20:29).

This is why I will remind you again of this important verse:

✝ *We live by **faith**, not by sight* (2 Corinthians 5:7).

Living by faith means we shouldn't be overly influenced by what we see, because, among other things, what we see or experience is only *temporal*. God wants us to reestablish our spiritual insight and strengthen it so we can see Him. The Bible says Adam's physical eyes were opened at the fall when his spiritual eyes died. God wants to build our spiritual eyes back up because, as this is done, we can walk more effectively by faith.

What is physical in this world will come and go, but God and His spiritual truths are eternal. It may be that time now when you are experiencing

186

a difficult circumstance, but God's truth will eventually trump it. You and God are in this together for the long haul, so that's where your vision should be focused—on the *future*. The present is only a moment, but your future is for an eternity. Therefore, Paul could say with confidence:

✠ *So we fix our eyes not on what is seen, but on what is unseen. For what is seen is temporary, but what is unseen is eternal* (2 Corinthians 4:18).

You must *not* let the facts you see today overly influence you, confuse you, or rule you. Facts are real in the physical, temporal realm, but God's truths are spiritual and eternal. If we believe only in facts as if they are permanent, then they likely will be; however, if we believe God's truths and walk in *faith* based on His truth, then truth will *trump* facts in time.

Living by faith will keep you on God's path, which will please Him and bring you a reward at the same time. Again, another important verse you will want to hang on to in your spirit as you go through life is this:

✠ *But without faith it is impossible to please Him, for he who comes to God must believe that He is, and that He is a **rewarder** of those who **diligently** seek Him* (Hebrews 11:6 NKJV).

We see in this verse that it is not just important that we believe in God, but also that God is a *rewarder* of those who *diligently* seek Him. Every Easter, I hid eggs for our children all over *our* yard, not our neighbor's yard and not in the street where I told our children never to go. The eggs were only where they were *supposed* to look. Sure enough, when Easter morning came, my kids would enthusiastically dash out into our yard in search of the eggs.

When they first ran into the yard, they didn't see any eggs; however, even though they did not *see* the eggs, my kids were excited because they had *faith* and *confidence* in their earthly father. They knew that on Easter I was a *rewarder*. My kids knew they just had to keep looking in the area they were supposed to, and despite what they *initially* didn't see, they would *eventually* be rewarded. Eventually, they would find the eggs I hid.

Shouldn't we have this same childlike *faith* and *confidence* in God our Father? The lesson is simple: If we stay on the path our heavenly Father planned for us, then we can have confidence that He has left our rewards along *that* path for us to find—if not today, then tomorrow or the next day. Certainly, there will be days when we come up empty; however, we should continue to search *His path* enthusiastically, knowing that God is a *rewarder* when we are on the path we are *supposed to be on*. All other paths lead to wandering, frustration, and danger.

What is God's path? Well, it's all the instruction God gives you through His Word, through pastors, and directly to you. When asked a question about what was the most important commandment to follow, Jesus answered in this way:

*Jesus said, "The first in importance is, 'Listen, Israel: The Lord your God is one; so love the Lord God with all your passion and prayer and intelligence and energy.' And here is the second: 'Love others as well as you love yourself.' There is no other commandment that ranks with these"* (Mark 12:29-31 MSG).

Let me remind you again that developing your relationship with God is a *process*. Diligently seeking Him means seeking His will and intentions daily. When we know His will and intentions, and act on them, we receive great rewards, even though the rewards may not always be what we expect. His will and intentions are *always* good for us. God said through Jeremiah:

*For I know the thoughts that I think toward you, says the Lord, thoughts of peace and not of evil, to give you a future and a hope* (Jeremiah 29:11 NKJV).

And Jesus said:

✠ *The thief does not come except to steal, and to kill, and to destroy. I have come that they may have life, and that they may have it more **abundantly*** (John 10:10 NKJV).

If we are seeking Him and staying on His path, then we can expect that God will use our experiences to perfect us in the way He desires, helping us fulfill our destiny and living the abundant life He desires for us.

## ACTION & VISUALIZATION

*Seek to stay on God's path always, and expect God
to reward you along the way, according to His will.*

## TRIALS AND TESTING OF FAITH

Not only are we called to walk in faith when faced with challenging circumstances, but we're also called to something else that may seem impossible at first. The Bible tells us repeatedly that we are to rejoice in our trials and tests.

✠ *Consider it pure **joy**, my brothers, whenever you face trials of many kinds, because you know that the testing of your faith develops perseverance. Perseverance must finish its work so that you may be **mature** and **complete, not lacking anything*** (James 1:2-4).

✠ *…we also **rejoice** in our **sufferings**, because we know that suffering produces perseverance; perseverance, character; and character, **hope*** (Romans 5:3-4).

Yes, you read that right. God desires that we rejoice *in* our sufferings, because, among other things, they provide us with spiritual and physical development. Before going any further, please realize that we are *not* being instructed to rejoice *about* our troubles. The writer of Ecclesiastes tells us:

✝ [There is] *a time to weep and a time to laugh, a time to mourn and a time to dance...* (Ecclesiastes 3:4).

Suffering is painful; however, God has put *gifts* within our troubles that *those living in faith* can unwrap and use to *grow* their *faith, character, experiences,* and *knowledge*—but most of all, grow *closer to Him.* Our joy, peace, and trust in Him helps us build up our hope to greater levels.

✝ *May the God of hope fill you with all joy and peace as you trust in Him, so that you may overflow with hope by the power of the Holy Spirit* (Romans 15:13).

You can probably imagine difficult circumstances where it might seem impossible to experience joy. That's okay to think at this point. However, you can begin to discover joy in challenging circumstances by starting small. For example, at the airline ticket counter when the attendant says, "I'm sorry, we've lost your reservation and the flight is full." Can you imagine what it would be like to maintain joy in that circumstance? You'll be surprised what happens when you do.

If you are relaxed, joyful, and going with the flow, then you will often discover that God has a *better* plan for your day. Sometimes you will flat-out experience a miracle. And if nothing else, you will grow closer to God because you acted in faith and trusted God to work everything out for your good, even though you may not be fully aware of why or how He did it. As we continue to explore what it means to stay joyful, remember that it's okay to start with small circumstances and work up from there. These verses sound like they are asking you to eat a lot; however, you've probably heard that the best way to eat an elephant is one bite at a time.

People tend to let their challenging circumstances get them down or influence their *outlook*. When I ask people who are going through tough times how they're doing, they invariably say, "Under the circumstances, I'm doing okay." I then say to them, "Wouldn't you be better off to get out from under those circumstances? You may have to continue to live with them, but your view or *outlook* would be much better if you were on top of them rather than under them."

My point is that we don't let an adverse situation enslave our attitudes. Our attitude and thought-life will affect our hope, and our hope is essential for our faith. In turn, our faith will be important in shaping the things that we will eventually run into, which are being created in that other realm. Most importantly, remember that you serve a God of redemption who has a history of restoring, healing, and promoting people in lowly places, in peril, or in distress.

The Bible is overflowing with this message. If He has overcome the world, why should we live subject to temporal circumstances? Circumstances come and go. As believers, we are eternal, we have Him in us growing as an incorruptible seed:

✠ *Who is it that overcomes the world?* **Only** *he who believes that Jesus is the Son of God* (1 John 5:5).

✠ *I've told you all this so that trusting Me, you will be unshakable and assured, deeply at peace. In this godless world you will continue to experience difficulties. But take heart! I've conquered the world* (John 16:33 MSG).

*Regardless* of the reason something bad happens, God embeds in it an opportunity for us to get back to our Promised Land (redemption), both physically and spiritually. We may need some preparation before we enter it, or we may need to do something before entering it. Remember, we have a promise from a loving God "that all things are working together for our good."

In the Chinese language, the word *disaster* is made up of two symbols. One conveys danger and the other is the symbol for *opportunity*. This is a good way to view our challenging circumstances, for there is always a gift, an opportunity, we can unwrap. When we find our barn full of horse crap, we can view it as a problem or we can see it as fertilizer for our garden.

I'm not suggesting this is easy, or even possible sometimes, until after the challenging circumstance is over. In some cases, it may take years to see restoration and the gift God has designed from it. However, trust God's perfect timing today and diligently choose to unwrap the opportunity in disaster. Admittedly, this is a difficult subject for our earthly minds to understand, but we'll benefit more from the gifts He offers *when* we do, and in the meantime have a better attitude while waiting in expectation of it. To help us better grasp this concept, we'll go deeper into this subject and explore many examples of this as we go through this series of books. Have faith for now!

## ACTION & VISUALIZATION

*Practice maintaining joy when experiencing small troubles*
*so you will be prepared when facing bigger challenges.*

## TRUSTING GOD WITH WHAT YOU DON'T UNDERSTAND

How do we develop the ability to have joy in challenging circumstances, which we would otherwise see as major setbacks or even devastating situations? Answering this question will take time and trust as we grow in our relationship with God. There are many things that cannot be described in this book. But that's part of God's plan—you'll understand and accept these truths better when God is the teacher, *not me*.

Remember that the core truth of this life of faith is your relationship with *God*. Though pastors and books and other sources can help you discover new truths, it's ultimately *your direct relationship with God* that allows you to grow into the person God wants you to be. The core definition of faith for us as God's children is having a childlike focus on God as our all-encompassing Provider. *Aman* is the Hebrew root that is translated in the Old Testament "faith." The word is found the first time in the book of Numbers, when God had given Moses the Israelites to look after, and it is translated into two words: nursing father.

✛ *And Moses said unto the Lord, Wherefore hast thou afflicted thy servant? and wherefore have I not found favour in thy sight, that thou layest the burden of all this people upon me? Have I conceived all this people? Have I begotten them that thou shouldest say unto me, Carry them in thy, as a **nursing father** beareth the sucking child, unto the land which thou swarest unto their fathers?* (Numbers 11:11-12 KJV).

A nursing child is the best understanding of the word *faith* as it relates to God. It confidently and openly relies on everything from the parent. Remember Jesus said in Matthew 18:3, "Unless you change and become like little children, you will never enter the Kingdom of Heaven"? This is the nature of faith God is seeking—an open, humble, and completely dependent faith. When things happen you don't understand, then talk to God. He longs for you to be honest with Him. Then *listen*. Be open for God's answer and know that it will come in His time and according to His plan. Be open and prepared, for the answer could be a surprise to you! From your vantage point, you only see a small part of God's overall plan, which is too complex for the human mind to comprehend.

✝ *"For My thoughts are not your thoughts, neither are your ways My ways," declares the Lord. "As the heavens are higher than the earth, so are My ways higher than your ways and My thoughts than your thoughts"* (Isaiah 55:8-9).

All of science and human knowledge accumulated over thousands of years by billions of people still has not given us a full understanding of how God created our complex physical bodies to function. So it's not likely that we, apart from Him, are going to know how He has our life planned.

To help you through your lack of understanding, God will sometimes give you glimpses of the future *beyond* your current trial and tribulation. Having faith in these previews can make it much easier to know joy while you're still in the midst of your challenging circumstances. Also, you already know your ultimate destiny—Heaven—where you will become the image and likeness of God, spending an *eternity with Him.*

✝ *...we are looking forward to a new Heaven and a new earth, the home of righteousness* (2 Peter 3:13).

This thought in 2 Peter can help us keep the temporal challenges in proper perspective. If you knew and fully understood your future, I believe you'd be smiling right now. It is my belief that we have a hard time hanging on to joy and a victor's mentality in difficult times *not* because of the things that are happening but because we don't fully understand *why* these things are happening. If we understood why, then we might better exhibit an unusual faith to *lift* us above our circumstances. In the meantime, the best way to hang on to a good attitude of joy is to believe in God's goodness and that He is working all things for our good. Look at what the apostle Paul wrote to the Colossian church:

✝ *...we have not stopped praying for you and asking God to **fill you with knowledge of His will through all spiritual wisdom and***

**understanding.** *And we pray this in order that you may live a life worthy of the Lord and may please Him in every way: bearing fruit in every good work, growing in the knowledge of God, being strengthened with all power according to His glorious might so that you may have great endurance and patience, and joyfully giving thanks to the Father, who has qualified you to share in the inheritance of the saints in the Kingdom of Light* (Colossians 1:9-12).

When we don't understand, when faith is difficult, this is part of God's refining fire, showing our humanity and our need for a Savior. Peter, who followed and lived with Christ, mistakenly believed that at one point God had abandoned Him and that he could better survive some particularly difficult circumstances on his own. At the time, circumstances seemed like they were going out of control with Jesus' arrest and impending crucifixion, but God had the situation *perfectly* under control. Through the trials he experienced, Peter's faith grew and his more-developed faith eventually allowed him to do some unusual and dramatic things for God.

There will be times when you don't fully understand what is happening, and in those scariest and most confusing moments your only *comfort* may be the knowledge of your eternal life that God has placed in you. Have faith in His love for you.

*He has made everything beautiful in its time. He has also set eternity in the hearts of men; yet they cannot fathom what God has done from the beginning to end* (Ecclesiastes 3:11).

In Hebrew, God's name spelled backward is the word *wonder*. There will be some things that you never know; however, you should still pray often that you might grow in the knowledge and understanding of God's will, especially as it relates to dealing with challenging circumstances. This is also a good thing to pray for your loved ones.

## Action & Visualization

*Even when you don't fully understand the reason,*
*act in faith when facing challenging circumstances*
*and pray for God to come into them.*

## God Lays a Foundation for Your Faith

Our faith can also be built up by studying God's omnipotence and omniscience. Let's start at the beginning:

✠ *...And there was evening, and there was morning—the first day* (Genesis 1:5).

✠ *...And there was evening, and there was morning—the second day* (Genesis 1:8).

✠ *...And there was evening, and there was morning—the third day* (Genesis 1:13).

✠ *...And there was evening, and there was morning—the fourth day* (Genesis 1:19).

✠ *...And there was evening, and there was morning—the fifth day* (Genesis 1:23).

✠ *God saw all that **He had made**, and it was very good. And there was evening, and there was morning—the sixth day. Thus the heavens and earth were **completed** in their vast array (Genesis 1:31–2:1).*

The very first chapter of the first book of the Bible demonstrates quite clearly that God created *everything* within the heavens and the earth. This foundational chapter can act as a strong foundation for your daily living faith if you truly believe it. Though there are many theories about the actual timeframe, Genesis' account is six days—I don't see how God could have made it clearer that it was six *literal* twenty-four-hour days. To leave no doubt it was six twenty-four hour periods, God separated each day in the Bible with an evening and a morning. Indeed, *every* time in the Bible the word *day* (*yom*) follows a numerical number, it means a twenty-four-hour period.

Imagine if you had complete *confidence* in this account of the creation of the whole universe as we know it. How would that change everyday trials for you? Those seemingly insurmountable troubles? Wouldn't you have to say, "Certainly, a God who can create the world and everything in it in six days can handle any problem I might face"? By remembering the power God had to create *all* things in *just* six days, you can be confident that God can and will deliver on His promises to you.

Some Christians believe that the creation story should not be taken literally, or that a person can believe that God somehow used evolution to make His creation within the context of what the Bible says. However, the Bible in both the Old and New Testaments says God spoke the world into existence:

✠ *By the word of the Lord were the heavens made, their starry host by the breath of His mouth. ...For He **spoke and it came to be** (Psalm 33:6-9).*

✠ *By faith we understand that the universe was formed at God's **command**, so that what is seen was **not** made out of what **was visible** (Hebrews 11:3).*

On the other hand, the evolution theory purports that all was made over long periods of time, random chance, and natural processes. Does this sound like a description of the same thing? Let's look deeper. God says He began earth's creation with water, while evolution says a fiery ball from an explosion came first. How about the order of creation? God says He created the earth first and then the stars on the fourth day, while evolution says the order was the reverse. God says He created the birds first and then the reptiles on the sixth day, while evolution says the order was reverse.

There is no way the evolution theory will fly with the biblical account. In fact, flight itself, from an evolutionary standpoint, is impossible because from a purely scientific perspective flight requires too many complex things to occur *all* at the *same time*: among them a unique light bone structure (using honeycomb design *not* found in other animals), a unique joint structure, unique muscles, perfectly aerodynamically designed wings, an interlocking but flexible feather design, and a completely unique lung design allowing for maximum lung capacity to support the extra oxygen requirement to the blood for energy. All birds and only birds have a put-through system of air going continuously through the lung system instead of the in and out dead-end system found in all other animals.[1]

Again, *all* these mutations would be required to happen at the same time according to the law of natural selection. If only *one* did not occur in that mutation, there could be no flight and the mutations would vanish because it did not serve a useful purpose—that's the law of natural selection.[2] If you took the time to study all the additional details that would need to happen for birds to fly, you would probably agree that the complex combination would be impossible to be achieved by random chance, even *once*. Remember though, it would have had to occur three times: once for birds, once for mammals, and once for insects.

There is no way you can believe that God used evolution to create the world if you believe the Bible to be the inspired Word of God. There are only two ways the world and everything in it came about—creation by the Creator as recorded in Genesis, or evolution by man's theory. One is right and one is *wrong*.

The most important question raised when trying to combine evolution with the Genesis account is this: What came first, sin or death? Again, we see an irreconcilable difference in the two outlooks. In the evolution model, death came first because you had to have billions of years of death to create humanity; only once created could a human then sin. However, Paul in Romans says:

✠ *Therefore, just as sin entered the world through one man, and death through sin, and in this way death came to all men, because all sinned* (Romans 5:12).

The order is clear here—first man, then sin, and then death. In the evolution model, God would have had to give the creation death rather than man (who brought it about by disobeying God's will). Then how could we make sense of God's description of His new creation?

✠ *God saw all that He had made, and* **it was very good**. *And there was evening, and there was morning—the sixth day. Thus the heavens and earth were* **completed** *in their vast array* (Genesis 1:31–2:1).

If His creation was achieved through billions of years of death and decay, then how could God have said it was *very good*? He couldn't—and He didn't.

Though believing theories other than the literal six-day creation story doesn't take away anyone's salvation; it is clearly God's intent that we believe He *did* create the world in six days. In so doing, our faith is strengthened, and thus might allow us to exhibit stronger actions of faith that please God. Our stronger actions of faith will also allow us to make a bigger impact on other people!

Whether you believe God created everything in six days, or in an evolutionary process lasting hundreds of billions of years, you will have to rely on faith. No human witnessed creation. However, we Christians do have a witness—God. His account is written in the Bible. When you match scientific evidence against God's account and the evolutionists' theory, there is actually a better scientific fit with the biblical account. It's vastly more logical and compatible with scientific facts.

As part of your supplemental reading, I encourage you to examine the *scientific case* for creation science. I believe you will see, based on the *evidence*, that the "six-day creation model" is substantially *more credible* than the evolution model. Seeing this for yourself will build your confidence in the literal interpretation of creation. Taking this on just faith, however, will not build your faith as much as doing your *own study* and coming to your *own conclusions* based on science. When you see for yourself the unbelievable complexity and beauty in God's design of everything He made, it will *encourage* your faith because:

✝ *The heavens* [His creation] *declare the glory of God; the skies proclaim the work of His hands* (Psalm 19:1).

Your built-up faith will give you more freedom and power in your walk with God, as well as a closer relationship. It is also important that we have a clear and concise answer for our faith and beliefs.

✝ *...Always be prepared to give an answer to everyone...for the hope you have* (1 Peter 3:15).

Therefore, it is important you do your own study of this all-important question of how our existence came about. Don't take someone else's word or listen to so-called experts. It is important your answer does not make God's Word a lie, for how then can the world believe God's other promises? Peter said:

✠ *First of all, you must understand that in the last days scoffers will come, scoffing and following their own evil desires. They will say, "Where is this 'coming' he promised? Ever since our fathers died, everything goes on as it has since the beginning of creation." But they **deliberately forget** that long ago by God's **word** the heavens existed and the earth was formed out of **water** and by **water**. By these waters also the world of that time was deluged and destroyed [Noah's flood]. By the **same word** the present heavens and earth are reserved for fire, being kept for the day of judgment, and destruction of ungodly men* (2 Peter 3:3-7).

By now you probably see how important it is for you to spend some time studying this subject. A great book to begin with is *The Amazing Story of Creation: From Science and the Bible* by Duane T. Gish (Master Books). Another good book is *The New Answer Book* by Ken Ham (Master Books). Other creation science material can be found at www.icr.org, www.creationev idence.org, and www.answersingenesis.com. Two of these groups operate museums where you can see scientific evidence that supports the six-day creation model.

It is important that you view Genesis and the other books of the Bible as accurate accounts of God's history. They are designed to give you knowledge and encouragement—and to build your faith in God. God showed His power through regular people like you and me for edification, knowledge, and encouragement in an effort to build up our faith. Throughout the book of Exodus, God told the Israelites to tell their children about the great and powerful things He had done. We have much to learn from these accounts in the Bible's rich history of people who lived by faith.

If Adam and Eve's story was just a fairy tale, then who made the choice to violate God's will and bring evil into the world? The foundation for the entire gospel message is found in the story of Adam and Eve's creation and fall. Jesus spoke of them in Mark 10:6. Indeed, Jesus quoted Genesis more than any other book in the Bible. Here is what Jesus said about Moses, who was the author of Genesis:

✠ *If you believed Moses, you would believe Me, for he wrote about Me.*
*But since you do not believe what he wrote, how are you going to*
*believe what I say* (John 5:46-47).

Out of Genesis comes the principles for marriage, sin, death, the
Sabbath (day of rest), and even the reason Jesus had to die on the cross.
Satan knows that if you can undermine the foundation of a building, then
you can collapse the entire building. A believer's foundation is the Bible,
and the Bible's foundation is the book of Genesis.

✠ *When the foundations are being destroyed, what can the righteous*
*do?* (Psalm 11:3).

It is critical to trust what God says to us in His Word so our faith can be
built on the most solid foundation.

## ACTION & VISUALIZATION
*Knowing and believing in God's Word will give you*
*power to trust Him in every situation.*

## WALKING TOWARD GOD

Walking is a two-step process. First, you move your right leg and then
your left as you make movement forward. Walking toward God is essentially the same in that our first step is an action of faith, allowing us to begin
to enter a relationship with Him. The first step of faith is important, but
if we are going to achieve intimacy and closeness within the relationship,
then we have to go many steps further.

The next step is to start removing whatever blocks and hinders you
from achieving intimacy. This is a step of faith because you have to rely on

God to remove that which you were not able—diligently putting your faith into action *every day*—to *habitually* take step after step of faith from the first step to the last. Paul wrote:

✠ *For in the gospel a righteousness* **from** *God is revealed, a righteousness that is* **by** *faith from the first to last, just as it is written: "The righteous will live by faith"* (Romans 1:17).

Faith should always be the lead step as you journey through life. It was by Abraham's faith, *not* his virtuous living, that he became righteous in God's eyes. Likewise, our faith in Jesus was our first step—for this is the only avenue that brings us into right standing with God, not our good works or virtuous living. When our relationship with God is reestablished through faith alone, does God completely shift His emphasis to grow the relationship on virtue alone? Of course not, because we will never be perfect and therefore we will always rely on Jesus to cover us so that we will have His perfection in God's eyes. In spite of this, we find many Christians and churches making living a purely righteous life their primary focus—primarily focused on exhorting Christians to stop sinning. In essence, their message becomes, "Stop making God mad!" But not making Him mad isn't necessarily pleasing Him. Remember:

✠ *For we walk by faith not by sight* (2 Corinthians 5:7 NKJV).

✠ *And without faith it is impossible to please God...* (Hebrews 11:6).

✠ *Does God give you His Spirit and work miracles among you because you observe the law, or* **because you believe what you heard** [God's Word]? *Consider Abraham: "He believed God, and it was credited to him as righteousness."*

*Understand, then, that those who believe are children of Abraham. The Scripture foresaw that God would justify the Gentiles by faith, and announced the gospel in advance to Abraham: "All nations will be blessed through you." So those who have faith are blessed along with Abraham, the man of faith.*

*All who rely on observing the law are under a curse, for it is written: "Cursed is everyone who does not continue to do everything written in the Book of the Law." Clearly no one is justified before God by the law, because, "The righteous will **live by faith**"* (Galatians 3:5-11).

Our greatest mandate is to use faith in everything we do and continue to diligently walk in faith, going beyond our first step of faith, which will sometimes lead us beyond our comfort zone. God is calling us to this greater goal—to continue stepping out in faith, above and beyond our first step of faith, which was salvation. To say it another way, we simply need to put the things we are working on into God's hands and trust Him with the reins of our live. I am not saying the effort to quit sinning is not essential in cultivating an intimate walk with God. After all, we must do this to conform ourselves to the image and likeness of God. Also, sin is a poison that kills many areas of our lives—it counteracts faith. Unresolved sin also limits us, keeping us imprisoned in areas of our lives, which results in death, sickness, disease, depression, poverty, and literal imprisonment.

Here's the point: Walking requires both legs. Continuously taking steps of faith toward God multiplies faith, building it even stronger, which in turn pleases God. Indeed, unless you strengthen your faith, you will crumble under the pressure of the sins—that which holds you captive.

Remember the Israelites whom God brought out of their slavery from Egypt in a marvelous way through the parting of the Red Sea? God fed them daily with manna from Heaven and provided water from rocks. Yet despite all of this, they were still afraid and at times wanted to go back to Egypt—back to captivity. To them, bondage was familiar surroundings, safer than trusting God's promises in the face of an unseen and unknown future.

This is the same with our walk today. We were not freed from the Egyptians but from sin; however, we wind up voluntarily going back into bondage. Sin is not the only thing we have a hard time letting go of. There is also our general lack and loss of freedoms. While conditions in our life may be bad and we may be suffering from lack, we are used to living with it—it's *familiar*. So when God speaks to us to have faith for something great—to strike a rock for water, to blow a horn and shout to bring down walls, to step out of the boat and walk on the water, to love somebody who is seemingly unlovable—it can be hard to trust God and take steps toward a future we can't physically see. However, it is through those steps that our faith is built up, manifesting the freedoms we've been offered.

You also need a strong faith because some sin is buried *deep*; without a strong faith, it can be impossible to dislodge. God's presence must become vivid in your life, so you involve Him in your every move. As you strive to construct a solid foundation for your relationship with God, remember:

✠ *Unless the Lord builds the house, its builders labor in vain...* (Psalm 127:1).

You alone will *never* be able to get sin out of your life and conform yourself to the image and likeness of God. There are strongholds in your body and mind that are like impenetrable fortresses with high walls. The Israelites needed God's plan for victory to take possession of these areas in their Promised Land, and so do we. Just like the Israelites, it is our actions in faith connecting with God's power that will make us victorious. As our faith grows, God becomes clearer and clearer in our everyday lives. As His presence becomes more *evident*, then the following verse will have more meaning and *impact*:

✝ *Nothing in all creation is hidden from God's sight. Everything is uncovered and laid bare before the eyes of Him to whom we must give account* (Hebrews 4:13).

If you continually rest in God and let Him do the work, then you will see results in your life—and those results will build faith. If His presence was more *real* to you in your everyday life when temptations came, wouldn't it be *easier* to resist them, knowing confidentially He is looking over your shoulder at the time? And for those temptations too difficult for you to overcome on your own, wouldn't it be easier to confidently give those over to God to take out of your life? Your built-up faith will help you remove sin from your life. Indeed, your built-up faith will help you remove many unwanted things from your life. In your walk toward an intimate relationship with God, make sure each alternating step is a step of faith. Those alternating steps in faith will keep you looking good in God's eyes as you can become closer to who He desires you to be.

When you fall in your walk of faith, just take a rest and ask God to help you get up and try again. In so doing, God will be pleased with you. Remember, spiritually speaking, on this side of heaven, God will always see you as His baby who is learning to walk. You know how you feel when your baby falls when he or she is trying to walk—so you can see it is okay to fall while you are learning this new walk of faith.

## ACTION & VISUALIZATION
*Lead each step in life with a step of faith.*

## EXERCISE YOUR FAITH

God wants us to take what measure of faith He has given to us and *use* it, therein growing its strength. This gift of faith is just like the talents and other abilities God gives to us. He desires to build and multiply them through our actions. Jesus expressed this concept in a story He told His disciples:

✝ *Again, it will be like a man going on a journey, who called his servants and entrusted his property to them. To one he gave five talents of money, to another two talents, and to another one talent, each according to his ability. Then he went on his journey. The man who had received the five talents went at once and put his money to work and gained five more. So also, the one with the two talents gained two more. But the man who had received the one talent went off, dug a hole in the ground and hid his master's money.*

*After a long time the master of those servants returned and settled accounts with them. The man who had received the five talents brought the other five. "Master," he said, "you entrusted me with five talents. See, I have gained five more."*

*His master replied, "Well done, good and faithful servant! You have been faithful with a few things; I will put you in charge of many things. Come and share your master's happiness!"*

*The man with the two talents also came. "Master," he said, "you entrusted me with two talents; see, I have gained two more."*

*His master replied, "Well done, good and faithful servant! You have been faithful with a few things; I will put you in charge of many things. Come and share your master's happiness!"*

*Then the man who had received the one talent came. "Master," he said, "I knew that you are a hard man, harvesting where you have not sown and gathering where you have not scattered seed. So I was afraid and went out and hid your talent in the ground. See, here is what belongs to you."*

*His master replied, "You wicked, lazy servant! So you knew that I harvest where I have not sown and gather where I have not scattered seed? Well then, you should have put my money on deposit with the bankers, so that when I returned I would have received it back with interest.*

207

*"Take the talent from him and give it to the one who has the ten talents. For everyone who has will be given more and he will have an abundance. Whoever does not have, even what he has will be taken from him. And throw that worthless servant outside, into the darkness, where there will be weeping and gnashing of teeth"* (Matthew 25:14-30).

This is sort of like the "use it or lose it" concept regarding exercise. When you stop using muscles, they will become smaller. Think about how this applies to your faith. Wouldn't you rather hear God tell you, "Well done, good and faithful servant; you have used your faith, so I will give you more," rather than, "Take from him what he has and cast him into the darkness"? It was *fear* that caused the unprofitable servant to bury his talent and choose not to make an investment. Fear is also what keeps us from exercising faith. The good news is that faith, like muscles, can start being built up at any time by your *actions*. How are you investing or exercising your specific God-given faith and talents?

## ACTION & VISUALIZATION

*Look for opportunities to use and exercise your faith.*

## HAVE FAITH IN WHO GOD IS

When, despite our circumstances, we come to God in faith of who He is, our faith pleases God—giving us the opportunity to fully experience Him and His power. We see this in many instances in the Bible. Here are just a few. Note the role that faith plays in each.

✠ *Some men brought to Him a paralytic, lying on a mat. When Jesus saw their **faith**, He said to the paralytic, "Take heart, son; your sins are forgiven."…*

*"But so that you may know that the Son of Man has authority on earth to forgive sins..." Then He said to the paralytic, "Get up, take your mat and go home." And the man got up and went home* (Matthew 9:2,6-7).

✠ *A Canaanite woman from that vicinity came to [Jesus], crying out, "Lord, Son of David, have mercy on me! My daughter is suffering terribly from demon-possession."*

*Then Jesus answered, "Woman, you have great **faith**! Your request is granted." And her daughter was healed from that very hour* (Matthew 15:22,28).

✠ *Jesus said to the woman, "Your **faith** has saved you; go in peace"* (Luke 7:50).

✠ *Then [Jesus] said to him, "Rise and go; your **faith** has made you well"* (Luke 17:19).

✠ *Jesus said to [the blind man], "Receive your sight; your **faith** has healed you"* (Luke 18:42).

✠ *There a centurion's servant, whom his master valued highly, was sick and about to die. The centurion heard of Jesus and sent some elders of the Jews to Him, asking Him to come and heal his servant. When they came to Jesus, they pleaded earnestly with Him, "This man deserves to have you do this, because he loves our nation and has built our synagogue." So Jesus went with them.*

*He was not far from the house when the centurion sent friends to say to Him: "Lord, don't trouble Yourself, for I do not deserve to have*

*You come under my roof. That is why I did not even consider myself worthy to come to You. But say the word, and my servant will be healed. For I myself am a man under authority, with soldiers under me. I tell this one, 'Go,' and he goes; and that one, 'Come,' and he comes. I say to my servant, 'Do this,' and he does it."*

*When Jesus heard this, He was amazed at him, and turning to the crowd following Him, He said, "I tell you, I have not found such great **faith** even in Israel." Then the men who had been sent returned to the house and found the servant well* (Luke 7:2-10).

Imagine what it would be like to have Jesus marvel at how you have built up your *faith*! As you can tell, there are many examples in the Bible when someone's faith *moves* God to act. There are also many examples in the Bible when a *lack* of faith discourages God. In the beginning of Mark 6, Jesus is in Nazareth where He grew up as a young boy. They knew Jesus as the carpenter's son, and did not know Jesus for who He truly was—the Savior and Son of God. Read what happens:

*Jesus left there and went to his hometown, accompanied by His disciples. When the Sabbath came, He began to teach in the synagogue, and many who heard Him were amazed.*

*"Where did this man get these things?" they asked. "What's this wisdom that has been given Him, that He even does miracles! Isn't this the carpenter? Isn't this Mary's son and the brother of James, Joseph, Judas and Simon? Aren't His sisters here with us?" And they took offense at Him.*

*Jesus said to them, "Only in his hometown, among his relatives and in his own house is a prophet without honor." **He could not do any miracles there, except lay His hands on a few sick people and heal them**. And He was amazed at their **lack of faith*** (Mark 6:1-6).

Later in the same chapter, Jesus crosses the Sea of Galilee to Gennesaret, where it says the people recognized Him for who He was—the Messiah:

*When they had crossed over, they landed at Gennesaret and anchored there. As soon as they got out of the boat, people **recognized Jesus**. [Acting in faith] they ran throughout that whole region, and carried the sick on mats to wherever they heard He was. And wherever He went—into villages, towns or countryside—they placed the sick in the marketplaces. **They begged Him to let them touch even the edge of His cloak, and all who touched Him were healed*** (Mark 6:53-56).*

Because they had faith in who Jesus was, exhibited by them wanting to touch the edge of His cloak (tallit), many were healed. To fully understand this, it's important to know the customs of the day. A tallit was a rectangle scarf-like garment that hung down from around the neck; however, it was wider so that when praying a man could put it over his head to create a tent-like effect, a holy place to meet with God. At the hem of the cloak, on the four corners, there was a tassel (*tzitzit*) made of eight strands with five knots, which represented all of God's commandments and the names of God (the five knots represent His grace). In addition, one thread in the tassel was blue, which represented the Messiah. The full manifestation and embodiment of God was represented by these tassels. When praying, they were to hold on to these tassels as a reminder of God and His Word to them.

*The Lord said to Moses, "Speak to the Israelites and say to them: 'Throughout the generations to come you are to make tassels on the corners of your garments, with a blue cord on each tassel. You will have these tassels to look at and so you will remember all the commands of the Lord, that you may obey them and not prostitute yourselves by going after the lusts of your own hearts and eyes'"* (Numbers 15:37-39).

When one held the corners of their tallit, it created wings and they knew from prophecy that in the wings of the Messiah there was healing.

✛ *But for you who revere my name, the sun of righteousness will rise with healing in its wings...* (Malachi 4:2).

Their faith in Jesus, for who He is, produced the result of many being healed when He crossed over to Gennesaret. We see this same faith again in the story of the woman with an issue of blood:

✛ *A large crowd followed and pressed around Him. And a woman was there who had been subject to bleeding for twelve years. She had suffered a great deal under the care of many doctors and had spent all she had, yet instead of getting better she grew worse. When she heard about Jesus, she came up behind Him in the crowd and touched His cloak [tallit], because she thought, "**If I just touch His clothes** [tallit], **I will be healed.**" Immediately her bleeding stopped and she felt in her body that she was **freed** from her suffering.*

*At once Jesus realized that power had gone out from Him. He turned around in the crowd and asked, "Who touched My clothes?"*

*"You see the people crowding **against You**," His disciples answered, "and yet You can ask, 'Who touched Me?'"* (Mark 5:24-31).

Having an issue with blood for *twelve years* would have made her an outcast by the people around her. Note that she was saying to herself, "If I just touch His clothes, I will be healed." You need to always continue to speak the promises of God to your spirit, because faith comes by hearing God's words (see Romans 10:17). The other thing to note is that although there were many people touching and crowding around Jesus, only one received healing power from Him. She was not one whom Jesus had a pre-determination to heal, but because of her faith, and her acting to reach out to Him, her faith drew healing power from Him. In many churches today, people are crowded around Jesus touching Him; however, they are not receiving His full power because they are not reaching out in persistent faith to Him as their Healer, Provider, Comforter, and Strengthener.

Many people perceive God incorrectly, so they don't experience all that He has to offer. It is important to know and to have faith in His attributes, for that is how you unwrap these attributes, which are gifts in your life. The parable of the talents illustrates how the servants' perceptions of God caused them to act in a way that blessed two of them with the fullness of God, while the one with the wrong perception of God got nothing but trouble. What was this servant's perception of God that caused him to come up empty-handed?

✠ *Then the man who had received the one talent came. "Master," he said, "I knew that you are a **hard** man, harvesting where you have not sown and gathering where you have not scattered seed. So I was **afraid** and went out and hid your talent in the ground..."* (Matthew 25:24-25).

It's important for us to have faith in God's character and attributes. Our faith in God begins with the belief that God *is* love and therefore can only exude *love*. Our faith in His unfailing love pleases God:

✠ [God's] *pleasure is not in the strength of the horse, nor His delight in the legs of man; the Lord delights in those who fear Him, who put their hope in His **unfailing love*** (Psalm 147:10-11).

Although God is a just God, He is not a *hard* God—we should not be *afraid* of God's intentions for us. He is a God of love and mercy, and we are to trust in His unfailing love and *power*.

✠ *Wealth and honor come from You; You are the ruler of all things. In Your hands are strength and power to exalt and give strength to all* (1 Chronicles 29:12).

✝ *And we know that all things God works for the good of those who love Him who have been called according to His purposes* (Romans 8:28).

You also can trust that God is *everywhere* and *knows everything.*

✝ *Acknowledge and take to heart this day that the Lord is God in Heaven above and on earth below...* (Deuteronomy 4:39).

✝ *Nothing in all creation is hidden from God's sight...* (Hebrews 4:13).

✝ *Does [God] not see my ways and count my **every** step?* (Job 31:4).

✝ *[God's] eyes are on the ways of men; He sees their **every** step* (Job 34:21).

✝ *Great is our Lord and mighty in power; His understanding has **no** limit* (Psalm 147:5).

And you can have faith in the truth that there are *no limits to what God can do.*

✝ *I know that You can do **all things**; no plan of Yours can be thwarted* (Job 42:2).

✠ *Our God is in Heaven; He does **whatever** pleases Him* (Psalm 115:3).

✠ *The Lord does **whatever** pleases Him, in the heavens and on the earth...* (Psalm 135:6).

✠ *For **nothing** is impossible with God* (Luke 1:37).

Having faith in each of these attributes of God will help *manifest* that attribute into your own life. Of course, the opposite is also true: acting in a lack of faith in these attributes will cause you to miss out on the full benefits they can bring you. Finally, the more you know and trust in Jesus, the more He will bring His supernatural power into your life. Just like all the other gifts, you must unwrap faith and use it to ignite and dramatically affect your life. Most of all, as you grow in faith, God will be pleased.

✠ *"If you can?" said Jesus. "Everything is possible for him who believes"* (Mark 9:23).

✠ *...My righteous one will live by faith. And if he shrinks back, I will not be pleased with him* (Hebrews 10:38).

To develop the kind of faith that will allow you to not shrink back in times of suffering and attack, you must fully develop your *intimate* relationship with God.

✠ *...because I **know** whom I have believed, and am convinced that He is able to guard what I have entrusted to Him for that day* (2 Timothy 1:12).

## MEDITATION POINT

Walk through life in faith, trusting your heavenly Father's loving intentions for you.

Go to Chapter 6 in the Study Guide section on page 325.

## ENDNOTES

1.  Michael Denton, *Evolution: A Theory in Crisis* (Chevy Chase, MD: Adler & Adler Publishers Inc., 1985), 210–212.

2.  Ibid.

# Chapter 7

# GIFT #3—FAITH (PART 2)

## HOW CAN YOU STRENGTHEN YOUR FAITH?

Before you begin to read, pray that the Holy Spirit
will give you understanding and application.

✝ [Jesus said], *"I tell you the truth, if you have* **faith** *as small as a mustard
seed, you can say to this mountain, 'Move from here to there' and it
will move. Nothing will be impossible for you"* (Matthew 17:20).

Do you believe Jesus' words in Matthew 17:20? Can our faith truly
be limitless? If so, how does that change our lives? If you have ever
watched a spider crawling, perhaps you've noticed that some spi-
ders can move surprisingly fast, their swift legs coordinated in a sweeping
motion, moving gracefully along the ground. What if the spider's eight legs
moved in different directions, some forward, some backward, and others
sideways? The spider would go nowhere. Likewise, James tells us:

✝ *Faith by itself, if it is not accompanied by* **action,** *is dead* (James 2:17).

Just as the spider must coordinate all eight legs to move toward a goal,
so we must line up *all* our actions to have a *functioning* faith, a unified faith
in forward motion. Remember that you are made up of a spirit, a mind,

and a body. These three aspects of our make-up need to move in harmony with one another, in one cohesive direction toward what Jesus calls "mountain-moving" (limitless) faith. The necessary direction is, of course, to move in sync with the will of God. Let's take a closer look at what the apostle Paul wrote to the Roman church about the acceptance of that initial gift of life:

✝ *That if you confess with your mouth, "Jesus is Lord," and believe in your heart that God raised Him from the dead, you will be saved. For it is with your heart that you believe and are justified, and it is with your mouth that you confess and are saved* (Romans 10:9-10).

Paul says that to have "saving faith," we must align our *verbal* confession to what we believe in our *heart* to receive eternal life. *Living faith* works in much the same way. To move mountains, we must unify faith and action, our *words* and our *heart*. We might be able to confess anything, but we can't hide our heart's true feelings from God.

✝ *...but God knows your hearts* (Luke 16:15).

✝ *...but the Lord looks at the heart* (1 Samuel 16:7).

✝ *...for the Lord searches every heart...* (1 Chronicles 28:9).

✝ *The crucible for silver and the furnace for gold, but the Lord tests the heart* (Proverbs 17:3).

What's in your heart? Is it in alignment with what you're saying? Is it aligned with your desires? Your actions? God's will? What needs to change—your heart, your words, or your actions? How about all three? To get mountain-moving faith, we need to learn to trust God completely, taking hold of hope over doubt.

✝ *But when he asks, he must **believe** and **not doubt**, because he who doubts is like a wave of the sea, blown and tossed by the wind* (James 1:6).

✝ *Let us hold unswervingly to the hope we **profess,** for He who promised is faithful* (Hebrews 10:23).

✝ *Trust in the Lord with all your heart...* (Proverbs 3:5).

Pockets of *doubt* will leave you directionless and open to paths that are *not* aligned with God's will. To shed doubts, repeatedly confess your hope as if you believe it will happen. Your thought life is powerful; it can connect you to fear or build within you a fearless faith. You must align your mind, desires, heart, words, and actions with your hope in God. This is why the Bible says:

✝ *For as he thinks in his heart, so is he...* (Proverbs 23:7 NKJV).

✝ *...the Lord searches every **heart** and understands every motive behind the thoughts...* (1 Chronicles 28:9).

Our words are *powerful* and have a *big* impact on our lives. Consider this:

✝ *If anyone considers himself religious and yet does not keep a tight rein on his tongue, he deceives himself and his religion is worthless* (James 1:26).

✝ *Reckless words pierce like a sword, but the tongue of the wise brings healing* (Proverbs 12:18).

✝ *He who guards his mouth and his tongue keeps himself from calamity* (Proverbs 21:23).

✝ *The mouth of the righteous man utters wisdom, and his tongue speaks what is just* (Psalm 37:30).

✝ *Or take ships as an example. Although they are so large and are driven by strong winds, they are steered by a very small rudder wherever the pilot wants to go. Likewise the tongue is a small part of the body, but it makes great boasts. Consider what a great forest is set on fire by a small spark* (James 3:4-5).

The words you say to others as well as to yourself have great power over your physical *and* spiritual life. Words can change the direction of your life, either for the better or for the worse. Consider how God used words to create all things in this world, including us.

✝ *And God **said**, "Let there be light;" and there was light...* (Genesis 1:3).

God went on to *speak* each thing He created into existence. There is *creative* power in the spoken word that comes from God's mouth. This is also confirmed in the New Testament:

✟ *By faith we understand that the universe was formed at God's* **command***, so that what is seen was* **not** *made out of what was visible* (Hebrews 11:3).

Just as God spoke light into existence, and all creation into existence, from things not seen, we, on a smaller scale, are "creating" in our own lives daily. Despite what you believed up until now, the circumstances you encounter in your earthly life are *not* made from what is visible in this world. Remember, they begin in the unseen world, where faith is a substance, and then materialize a change in our own world.

✟ [God said], *"So is My word that goes out from My mouth: It will not return to Me empty, but will accomplish what I desire and achieve the purpose for which I sent it"* (Isaiah 55:11).

Outside of God's specific will, what is going to happen is that what we *believe* and *say* is going to happen, or the result of what we say will be set in motion by the invisible laws of our universe. Words spoken in *faith*, and therein believed by the heart, can influence the spirit realm. Faith is a substance in the spiritual realm that affects the physical. Indeed, I like to say that godly desires mixed with faith are memories of the future.

How can living out this idea truly affect your prayer life? Do you pray, then believe, then live out your life with the faith that what you have been praying for is going to come to pass? Do you speak words of faith over your children? Your marriage? Your finances? Your next meeting? Just saying positive affirmations from God's Word can build on your overall faith. Listen to some of these statements that were made by godly men:

✝ *I can do everything through [God] who gives me strength* (Philippians 4:13).

✝ *...Do not grieve, for the joy of the Lord is your strength* (Nehemiah 8:10).

✝ *...If God is for us who can be against us?* (Romans 8:31).

There is real power you can lay hold of with this sort of faith. Don't get me wrong. I am not saying you can just tell the rain to stop and it will stop. Your words must not be contradictory to God's will. However, Jesus made it clear that our faith can accomplish limitless things. Believe in your heart and speak it forth with your mouth, for you are equipped with life-changing, supernatural power.

Are you conscious of the words that you are speaking over your life? Indeed, carelessness can lead to unintentionally speaking negativity into your life, and into the lives of others. As much as possible, speak positive words and positive affirmations into your life and into those around you.

✝ *Do not let any unwholesome talk come out of your mouths, but only what is helpful for building others up according to their needs, that it may benefit those who listen* (Ephesians 4:29).

## ACTION & VISUALIZATION

*Align your words and your heart, and speak positive things into your life and the lives of others.*

## THE POWER OF THE WORD OF GOD

You will remember from Chapter 2 that Jesus Christ came as the Word. John wrote of Him:

✝ *In the beginning was the Word, and the Word was with God, and the Word was God....*

*The Word became flesh and made His dwelling among us. We have seen His glory, the glory of the One and Only, who came from the Father, full of grace and truth* (John 1:1,14).

This power of the spoken word is how Jesus Christ sustains all things, including our spirit and our life. The writer of Hebrews tells us:

✝ *The Son is the radiance of God's glory and the exact representation of His being, sustaining all things by His powerful word...* (Hebrews 1:3).

And Moses reminds us:

✝ *...man does not live on bread alone but on every word that comes from the mouth of the Lord* (Deuteronomy 8:3).

In the previous chapter, we learned that the catalyst to get the most benefit from the Word is to combine it with our faith:

✝ *...the message they heard was of no value to them, because those who heard did not combine it with faith* (Hebrews 4:2).

As God's creation, who is made in His image and likeness, we have access to our Creator's power and authority. Though our words spoken in faith can never trump God's Word, the Bible suggests ways in which that power can be enacted. Let's look back to Genesis for God's original plan of who has dominion over the earth:

✠ *God blessed them* [Adam and Eve] *and said to them, "Be fruitful and increase in number; fill the earth and subdue it.* **Rule over** *the fish of the sea and the birds of the air and* **over every** *living creature that moves on the ground"* (Genesis 1:28).

✠ *You have made them a little lower than the angels and crowned them with glory and honor. You made them rulers over the works of your hands; you put everything under their feet* (Psalm 8:5-6).

We temporarily lost this authority to satan when Adam and Eve sinned. But Jesus came on our behalf and took back that authority, then passed it along to us.

✠ *Then Jesus came to them and said, "All authority in Heaven and on earth has been given to Me"* (Matthew 28:18).

✠ [Jesus said], *"I will give you the keys to the Kingdom of Heaven; whatever you bind on earth will be bound in Heaven, and whatever you loose on earth will be loosed in Heaven"* (Matthew 16:19).

Jesus gave a special authority to His disciples.

✠ *Jesus said, "Peace be with you! As the Father has sent Me, I am sending you," And with that He breathed on them and said, "Receive the Holy*

*Spirit. If you forgive anyone his sins, they are forgiven; if you do not forgive them, they are not forgiven"* (John 20:21-23).

You have already learned that we regained authority over our lives and our world when we were set free from sin. Therefore, our tongues can have a life-and-death effect on us and others, both physically and spiritually. Proverbs tells us:

✝ *The tongue has the power of life and death...* (Proverbs 18:21).

✝ *The tongue that brings healing is a tree of life, but a deceitful tongue crushes the spirit* (Proverbs 15:4).

✝ *He who guards his lips guards his life, but he who speaks rashly will come to ruin* (Proverbs 13:3).

And Peter and Paul tell us much the same thing in the New Testament:

✝ *Whoever would love life and see good days must keep his tongue from evil and his lips from deceitful speech* (1 Peter 3:10).

✝ *Avoid godless chatter, because those who indulge in it will become more and more ungodly* (2 Timothy 2:16).

Look at some of the faithless statements we often make: "Nothing good ever happens to me," or "I can't get a break," or "I can't get anywhere because of my lack of education," or even "My childhood experiences create too many problems for me." Does this sound like someone who has been given power and authority by God, the Creator of the universe? Of course not, so be diligent about *eliminating* this type of negativity from both your *thoughts* and your *speech*. You should even work toward eliminating clichés like "This is killing me," or "This always happens to me."

It takes time and effort to systematically break old speech habits and develop new ones. Don't feel bad when you make a mistake. Whenever you catch yourself slipping into an old habit, stop and visualize yourself in the same circumstance but saying the *right* thing. Keep working at it. The Bible itself, the very Word of God, can be our greatest ally when we face difficult situations:

✠ *For the Word of God is **living** and **active**. **Sharper than any double-edged sword**...* (Hebrews 4:12).

To get an idea just how life-saving this weapon truly is, look at Jesus' response when He was confronted directly by satan, as recorded in Matthew 4:1-11. In this passage, we learn that Jesus quoted God's Word to satan in response to each of his temptations. There is power in God's Word. It would be wise for us to follow Jesus' example here and counter satan's advances and all of life's trials with the Word of God spoken in faith.

You can build on your faith simply by listening to God's Word, coming either from your own mouth, in your personal study, in community with others, during a church service, or even in Sunday school. You can even take advantage of an audio Bible too, and fill your drive by listening to God's Word so your faith can be built up. The lyrics of effective worship should be your positive confessions, which in turn will thereby reinforce your faith. Hearing God's Word will build faith that will bring His power in your life.

✠ *In Lystra there sat a man crippled in his feet, who was lame from birth and had never walked. He **listened** to Paul as he was speaking. Paul* *looked directly at him, saw that he had **faith** to be healed and called out, "Stand up on your feet!" At that, the man jumped up and began to walk (Acts 14:8-10).*

Spend time listening to God's Word, just as this crippled man did, and not to other voices; for it is only then that you'll be able to effectively deal with and overcome the challenges you face. Remember the adage in computer programming: "Garbage in, garbage out; good in, good out." Speaking God's Word out loud has an additional benefit because

✟ *...faith comes from hearing the message, and the message is heard through the Word of Christ (Romans 10:17).*

## ACTION & VISUALIZATION

*Listen to and speak God's Word in your life, trusting in the Word's power to help you face difficult times.*

## YOUR VISION OR FORESIGHT

Foresight is seeing ahead of time where to go in life. If you want to run in life, not walk, crawl, or stand still, then you need to have a clear vision of your desired future.

✟ *Where there is no vision, the people perish... (Proverbs 29:18 KJV).*

✟ *Then the Lord answered me and said: "Write the vision and make it plain on tablets, that he may run who reads it" (Habakkuk 2:2 NKJV).*

If you are walking through the woods but not sure where you're going, then you need to move slowly and hesitantly to find your destination. However, if you have a clear vision of where you want to go, then by hearing instructions or looking at a map ahead of time, you can move quickly toward your goal. This is why I have inserted Action & Visualization reminders throughout this book. It is my hope that when you encounter these, you put the book down, close your eyes, and visualize a specific change in your life as if you are actually acting it out.

Every so often it's good to visualize the things that have occurred because of your salvation and the changes you desire for the future. This allows you to plan for your life. Also, consider these in your visualization: 1) how you *see* yourself as different; 2) how you will *act* differently than you did before when you find yourself in certain situations; and 3) how you imagine God fulfilling His promises to you, leading you to the fulfillment of His unique and special plan for your life.

Having a clear picture of your desired actions in situations ahead of time can allow you to automatically and subconsciously restrain your internal programming to respond in kind to bad acts against you. Visualizing a desired outcome will help break mindless habits. Remember the Israelite spies who saw themselves as grasshoppers compared to the giants? They did not visualize themselves properly and they became how they visualized themselves: *insignificant*. What you see, you will be!

Visualizing God's promises growing in your life will help line up your actions with your words, because you're then speaking what you are already seeing. Lining up your words, actions, thoughts, and heart is the key to having limitless faith. I'm not saying this is easy to do or that it will come quickly. You wouldn't expect a newborn baby to be able to run—the child needs to grow and then, through trial and error, discover the ability to first walk before he or she runs.

What are you wishing or hoping for? Do you want to break an addiction? Restore a broken relationship? Find a new job? Then visualize it. Dwell on it and confess it before God as you pray. Hope and confession are inexplicably tied together and can help encourage and build the other in crafting that unwavering faith required to move mountains. When you are successful at visualizing your future, even when times get rough, you will see the promise of hope, power, and authority *no matter* the circumstances.

✢ *So we fix our eyes not on what is seen, but on what is unseen. For what is seen is **temporary**, but what is unseen is **eternal*** (2 Corinthians 4:18).

## ACTION & VISUALIZATION

*Have a clear vision of what you hope for, as well as who you are in Christ.*

## ALIGN YOURSELF WITH GOD

God wants your actions and words to be congruent with your faith in Him. This puts you in sync with Him and allows the two of you to share a joyful and powerful life together—*your life*. What happens when you're not in sync with God? Suppose your spouse left town for a week. You would not actually *see* him or her for that week; however, to keep your relationship strong, wouldn't your spouse expect your actions to continue as if he or she were still at home? Even though you may be apart, you both would expect the love you have for each other to continue. And you would expect actions that backed this up, right? But what if they didn't? What if either one of you decided "out of sight, out of mind" and chose to act as if you were single? Sound like a recipe for trouble? Absolutely!

Your relationship with God works in much the same way. Though you may speak to Him occasionally and perhaps listen even less, He still exists between those times. God still expects us to remember His love for us and our love for Him—this keeps the relationship *vibrant* and *real*. This also keeps us on the right path for our lives, where our rewards are located.

A real relationship with God demands that we line up our actions *each* day, not just when it seems convenient. Perhaps you know this scenario: It's Sunday morning and you're open and engaged to experience God in a real way. You feel great—inspired, joyful, encouraged. It's almost as if you're "high" on God when you're worshiping Him at church. Your problems and circumstances seem to grow dimmer in His presence. But then Monday comes. And Tuesday. And so on. The energy and excitement of shared worship or challenging teaching gives way to the stress of work and the demands of a busy life. Did God leave? Not at all. He's just as real and available on Wednesday morning in the middle of a workday as He is on Sunday morning when the music is lifting your spirit.

It takes a conscious awareness to develop an ongoing connection with God's presence, beyond a "church high." This is part of the maturation process of your faith—learning to feel and trust God's nearness when life seems to push Him far away. But He isn't far away! In fact, God is right by your side always. Having faith in this fact will bring a better awareness of Him in your daily life. Look at what the apostle Paul says about mature faith:

*No, in all things we are more than conquerors through Him who loved us. For I am **convinced** that neither death nor life, neither angels nor demons, neither height nor depth, nor anything else in all creation, will be able to separate us from the love of God that is in Christ Jesus our Lord (Romans 8:37-39).*

## ACTION & VISUALIZATION

*Learn to trust in God's nearness and stay connected with Him throughout each day.*

## YOU HAVE ENOUGH FAITH

You might wonder at times if God gave you enough faith. Jesus' disciples certainly did, and on one occasion they asked Jesus for more.

✛ *The apostles said to the Lord, "Increase our faith!"*
*He replied, "If you have faith as small as a mustard seed, you can say to the mulberry tree, 'Be uprooted and planted in the sea,' and it will obey you"* (Luke 17:5-6).

Mustard seeds are tiny, so Jesus responded by saying they didn't need any more because it takes only a *small* amount of faith to do a *big job*.

## LEVERAGE YOUR FAITH

Some may have faith in something that you do not have faith in, or they may even have faith in the opposite. We have collectively been given dominion over the earth. You will recall reading in the previous chapter that Jesus Himself could not do many healings in the area where He grew up because the local people did not believe in Him as a Healer. They saw Him as the son of a local carpenter, so He could perform only a few miracles. Yet when He went across the sea where they saw Him as the Christ, He healed many people there. This group of people's collective faith in His power and their desire to see Jesus manifest that power is what acted as a catalyst to release it.

You too will find times when the disbelief that is around you stifles your faith. And yet at other times, miracles will come easy when people who see Christ in you also believe in His limitless power. This is why it is important to leverage your faith with others of strong faith. And likewise, you should avoid situations where other people's faith will work against yours.

*Regularly*, when Jesus and His disciples were healing, they would remove disbelief from the area. Here is one example:

✛ *Peter went with them, and when he arrived he was taken upstairs to the room* [where Tabitha, a disciple, lay dead]. *All the widows stood around him, crying and showing him the robes and other clothing that Dorcas had made while she was still with them.*

*Peter sent them all out of the room; then he got down on his knees and prayed. Turning toward the dead woman, he said, "Tabitha, get up." She opened her eyes, and seeing Peter she sat up* (Acts 9:39-40).

When there are people around you whose faith contradicts yours, in these times it is not always wise to let them know what you are believing, for their faith will only 1revolt against yours. Likewise, you can use other people's faith to help you accomplish God's permissive will.

✝ *A few days later Jesus again entered Capernaum, the people heard that He had come home. They gathered in such large numbers that there was no room left, not even outside the door, and He preached the Word to them. Some men came, bringing to Him a paralyzed man carried by four of them. Since they could not get him to Jesus because of the crowd, they made a hole in the roof above Jesus by digging through it and then lowered the mat the man was lying on. When Jesus **saw their faith**, He said to the paralyzed man, "Son, your sins are forgiven"* (Mark 2:1-5).

This is why it is good to surround yourself with people of strong faith who are believing in what you are believing for so you can leverage each other's faith. There is a synergy in faith, which is why it's so *important for the church to become unified.*

## ACTION & VISUALIZATION
*Seek out others of strong faith who will support your faith.*

## FACING CIRCUMSTANCES WITH FAITH

Faith is dynamic—it's something we need to have 24-7. It's easy to have faith when things are going well, but what about the times where our faith is challenged? The prayers that go unanswered? The relationships that continue to go unhealed? What do we do when we hope and see nothing change? Do we desire and hope in vain?

Understanding what causes challenges to your faith will help you ready a faithful response when adversity comes. The following are some common hurdles, or challenges, to our faith:

- Sin in the world and in us.

- The enemy.

- Reaping what we sow.

- Loving discipline.

- God's purpose and perspective.

## SIN IN THE WORLD AND IN US

As we have already discussed, we live in a fallen world. Sin entered the world because of free will and it reaches all the way to you and me. The Bible also states that even the earth itself is in travail or pain. Perhaps this is the reason our world suffers from deadly hurricanes, tsunamis, and other such things. We daily face the effects of that sin, whether because of the world's state of imperfection or the freewill choices of other sinners. Did someone curse at you today? Cut you off in traffic? Ignore you? In these ways and many others our faith is challenged by sin.

We also cause self-inflicted wounds when we sin. Maybe you reacted wrong to being cursed out, or maybe *you* were the person cursing someone out or cutting them off in traffic. These may seem like little things (and in the scheme of things, perhaps they are), but they are still examples of an imperfect heart and the power of free will to choose right or wrong in any given circumstance. When we sin, we undermine our faith. In fact, we toss it out the window, choosing not God's will but our own. The more our faith is built up, the less allure sin has—Jesus can then reign supreme in our lives. The effects of sin are delayed, allowing us time to seek redemption. So when you sin, be quick to seek forgiveness and redemption.

## YOU HAVE AN ENEMY

The Bible says you have an enemy in this world.

✝ *Be self-controlled and alert. Your enemy, the devil, prowls around like a roaring lion looking for someone to devour. Resist him, standing firm in the* **faith,** *because you know that your brothers throughout the world are undergoing the same kind of sufferings* (1 Peter 5:8-9).

Clearly you have an enemy in this world who will bring challenges your way; however, your actions of faith give you the power to overcome him. I believe that says it all.

## REAPING WHAT WE SOW

Simply put, what you dish out to others will be served back to you at some point. If you smile a lot and are a positive, giving person, then generally people will respond in a similar way. While many believe this on some level, it's surprising to see how often they act in ways that suggest otherwise. We can get so caught up in our own "stuff" that we forget everything we do affects those around us. Therefore, it cycles back around to affect us as well, both in a direct obvious way and in spiritual ways that are often hard to see. As we learn to walk in faith, we plan positive and God-honoring attitudes and actions, knowing that what goes around comes around.

## LOVING DISCIPLINE

✠ *...the Lord disciplines those He **loves**, as a father the son he delights in* (Proverbs 3:12).

There are several aspects to this concept of being disciplined that we need to understand so we can fully appreciate and recognize when we are being disciplined, but primarily we need to understand the word *love*. Again, Paul gives us a good definition of it in 1 Corinthians 13:

✠ *Love is patient, love is kind. ...It is not rude, it is not self-seeking, it is not easily angered, it keeps no record of wrongs. ...It always protects, always trusts, always hopes, always perseveres. Love never fails...* (1 Corinthians 13:4-8).

Since God *is* love, He only disciplines in love—patiently, kindly, not based on the past, not self-seeking, and protectively. Though it is true that our earthly parents sometimes discipline in this way, they may have also disciplined out of frustration, in anger, out of self-interest, or they are (or were) just plain in the *wrong*. Some people believe God disciplines us by swatting us every time we get out of line. That's an interesting image, but it is a *wrong* one! One way God disciplines is with the invisible laws He set up to benefit, serve, and protect us. However, we must work within these invisible laws for them to have their intended effect.

Is physical pain a good thing? It hurts! But pain is created by the central nervous system God designed in you and does have a beneficial purpose. If you put your hand on a hot stove, without the shock of pain, would you move it? The pain caused by the hot burner may not feel good, but it is essential for your body's preservation. Pain alerts you that something is *wrong*.

God designed many systems (immune, nervous, digestive, thought, sight, hearing, and emotions), and layers upon layers of physical laws and spiritual laws that work together for the good of His children. I imagine in the garden, when the whole world was in perfect harmony, Adam and Eve never received feedback that was sharp or "painful"—perhaps a gentle coaxing. In this fallen world, however, there are many things that can bring sharp pain, devastating harm, and even death.

When we do something or expose ourselves to something that could permanently damage us physically, psychologically, or spiritually, we will often encounter uncomfortable or even painful events. These are warnings to adjust behavior before we're badly damaged. Some people try to cover these uncomfortable feelings with painkillers like drugs, drinking alcohol to excess, or other behaviors intended to deflect or distract. Even the pursuit of happiness can be an attempt to avoid an uncomfortable or empty feeling. These are vain attempts to plug our ears so we can't hear God speaking to us.

God presents to us these spiritual laws through the Bible, through His Spirit, and through everyday circumstances. Trial and error is a painful way to learn, and it is often needless since God allows "open book" tests, using the Bible. That's one more reason why it is important to read the Bible and soak up all of God's truth—we can avoid some of those damaging and painful experiences. Out of this learning and trusting, we change our hearts, minds, and actions—our very lives. Remember:

✟ *Keep your heart with **all** diligence, for out of it spring the issues of life* (Proverbs 4:23 NKJV).

Let's see what the author of Hebrews said about discipline.

✟ *And you have forgotten that word of encouragement that addresses you as sons: "My son, do not make light of the Lord's discipline, and* *do not lose heart when He rebukes you, because the Lord disciplines those He loves, and He punishes everyone He **accepts as a son.***"

*Endure hardship as discipline; God is treating you as sons. For what son is not disciplined by his father? If you are not disciplined (and everyone undergoes discipline), then you are illegitimate children and not true sons. Moreover, we have all had human fathers who disciplined us and we respected them for it. How much more should we submit to the Father of our spirits and live! Our fathers disciplined us for a little while as they thought best; but God disciplines us for **our good**, that we may **share in His holiness**. No discipline seems pleasant at the time, but painful. **Later on,** however, it produces a harvest of righteousness and peace for those **who have been trained by it*** (Hebrews 12:5-11).

God's discipline is for your benefit as it brings circumstances intended to adjust your behavior in ways that will allow you to live a more abundant life. God's discipline is *not* just to punish you for punishment's sake. God doesn't love us because we are perfect or even close to being perfect, just like your love for your children is not based on what they do, but on who they are—your children. God's love is so much stronger than yours to your children, because God's love is never in the slightest way affected by frustration, impatience, or pride. It is only through His perfect will and perfect timing that we can receive His gifts, finding long-term growth and restoration. Indeed, God has circumvented our negative actions against Him to hardwire a system that points us back to restoration and eternal life, away from destruction and death. So when things take a turn from the outcome you had hoped, be open to what God may be saying. In fact, seek the answer from Him alone, and eventually you will find it if you're patient, diligent, and remain open to hear His answer.

✝ *...seek and you will find...* (Matthew 7:7).

Remember, Jesus said of some people of His time:

✝ *...though seeing, they do not see; though hearing they do not hear or understand* (Matthew 13:13).

You will not want this said of you, so it is important to carefully *look* and *listen* for God in *all* your circumstances so you can benefit from what He is saying to you.

Some of the trials and tribulations in life are like bumps in the road. Imagine driving with a coffee cup in your lap. When you hit a bump, what's *already in the cup splashes out*. It's these bumps in the road of life that allow us to see what's in us as well. When you're on "easy street," it's natural to have faith, praise God, be generous, and love others. But what comes out when you hit a bump in life? Does a confident, praising, and loving spirit overflow? Or does a fearful, retreating, complaining, and self-focused spirit splash out?

It's common to put on a "Why me, God?" attitude when we hit those bumps. Don't feel condemned when this happens, because none of us has been perfected yet. These bumps are actually part of the process of being perfected. They help *you* see what's *in you* or what you're *made of* so you can continue to *adjust*. It is interesting to note that the word in Hebrew that is translated into *punishment* is a three-letter word that's first letter means eye and next two mean falling back. The word indicates a circumstance that allows you to see that you have fallen back.

I want to reiterate that I am not saying God is designing *all* the trials, tribulations, and suffering to train you. Some things we bring on ourselves, some are a correction from God, and some are outright attacks by satan. But I *am* saying that no matter what created the bump, there is in *each* one a good gift we can use to improve ourselves if we *choose* to see it and use it. In each circumstance, there is an opportunity for us to take the high road on which we will not be likely to encounter that *same* bump.

It may be difficult to fully appreciate this now, but there are things in you (habits, thoughts, and desires) that need to change before you can be conformed to the image and likeness of God. Some of these problems are deeply embedded in us, and change will not come easily (or without pain). Adversity can be a purifying process intended to filter bad habits, thoughts, and desires in order to refine a new kind of purity in you.

✟ *Therefore this is what the Lord Almighty says: "See, I will refine and test them, for what else can I do because of the sin of My people?"* (Jeremiah 9:7).

✟ *But He knows the way that I take; when He has tested me, I will come forth as gold* (Job 23:10).

The only way to get impurities out of gold and silver is to heat them up to a very high temperature so that the impurities float to the surface and are thus burned away. Physically we are designed in the same way. When we are infected with bacteria that is not good for us, our bodies naturally rise to a higher temperature (a fever) to help us kill that bacterial infection so we can be healthy and purified again. The same idea of a refining process seems to be true as it relates to our character and spirit. Sometimes it takes a high heat to burn away those sins embedded deep in our hearts. Proverbs tells us:

✟ *The crucible for silver and the furnace for gold, but the Lord tests the heart* (Proverbs 17:3).

When the heat comes, and it will come, you will want to remember:

✟ *Blessed is the man whom God corrects; so do not despise the discipline of the Almighty* (Job 5:17).

✠ *Blessed is the man who perseveres under trial, because when he has stood the test, he will receive the crown of life that God has promised to those who love Him* (James 1:12).

✠ *Whoever loves discipline loves knowledge, but he who hates correction is stupid* (Proverbs 12:1).

✠ *He who scorns instruction will pay for it, but he who respects a command is rewarded* (Proverbs 13:13).

✠ *He who ignores discipline despises himself, but whoever heeds correction gains understanding* (Proverbs 15:32).

## Action & Visualization
*Expect and accept discipline willingly and thankfully.*

## God's Purpose and Perspective

Sometimes things happen in your life that may simply be part of God's greater plan. Although you may not understand these now, they have a purpose. Sometimes that purpose looks like a delay, another detour away from hope. However, though seemingly late to us, God's timing is always perfect.

✠ *For the revelation awaits an appointed time...though it lingers, wait for it; it will certainly come and will not delay* [past God's appointed time] (Habakkuk 2:3).

Consider this story from the book of Acts:

✠ *One day Peter and John were going up to the temple at the time of prayer—at three in the afternoon. Now a man crippled from birth was being carried to the temple gate called Beautiful, where he was put **every day** to beg from those going into the temple courts. When he saw Peter and John about to enter, he asked them for money. Peter looked straight at him, as did John. Then Peter said, "Look at us!" So the man gave them his attention, expecting to get something from them.*

*Then Peter said, "Silver or gold I do not have, but what I have I give you. In the name of Jesus Christ of Nazareth, walk." Taking him by the right hand, he helped him up, and instantly the man's feet and ankles became strong. He jumped to his feet and began to walk. Then he went with them into the temple courts, walking and jumping, and praising God. When all the people saw him walking and praising God, they recognized him as the same man who used to sit begging at the temple gate called Beautiful, and they were filled with wonder and amazement at what had happened to him* (Act 3:1-10).

The lame man sat at the entrance of the gate called Beautiful every day. People knew him—even Jesus Himself would have passed this man as we know He went through this gate. But for some reason, Jesus did not heal him when He passed by. Instead, in God's time and for God's purpose, Peter and John were called upon to heal the lame man in the name of Jesus, and in front of a large crowd. The account goes on to say that Peter started preaching to the crowd of people who were suddenly intrigued because of the miracle. Here was the ultimate result of the delay in the blind man's healing:

✠ *But many who heard the message believed, and the number of men grew to about five thousand* (Acts 4:4).

From a worldly perspective, it may seem odd that Jesus didn't heal this man much earlier. Perhaps it's even a bit perplexing that God would allow him to be lame in the first place. However, look at this story from a larger spiritual perspective and see how the lame man could be part of God's plan and purpose of bringing him and others to Christ.

Let's look at another story—this one of a man who had been blind from birth—whom Jesus and His disciples encounter. Jesus' disciples ask Him who sinned—who caused the man's blindness—the blind man or his parents? Read Jesus' answer from the gospel of John:

✝ *"Neither this man nor his parents sinned," said Jesus, "but this happened so that* **the work of God might be displayed in his life"** (John 9:3).

When the blind man received salvation and sight from God's "display in his life," his neighbors and those who observed the healing spread the word of the miracle until it even caught the attention of the Pharisees, who were leading the people astray from God. As a result of this circumstance, Jesus was able to teach an important spiritual lesson to the blind man and countless others that had eternal consequences of life and death for them.

How would you feel if you knew your blindness or other infirmity was for the sole purpose of giving God the opportunity to reveal Himself to you and to others? Or perhaps so you could have a closer and more intimate relationship with Him? These are difficult questions to wrestle with, for they force us to admit that some spiritual things are simply beyond our natural mind's understanding. We can't fully comprehend how secondary in importance this life we live on earth is compared to the eternal life that follows. The physical things in life are minor when compared to the spiritual truths God seeks to teach us.

Yes, God could heal everyone in the blink of an eye. He could stop all alcoholics from craving liquor and mend every broken marriage. Yet

He doesn't always correct the problems we have brought upon ourselves. Instead, He uses every adversity, sickness, addiction, accident, and challenging relationship to draw us and others closer to Him. Is it more important for us to have complete comfort in this temporal life without developing a relationship with God, or is developing an internal relationship with our Creator the most important? God didn't create, nor does He want battery-powered robot believers, which is what we would be if He changed us whenever we didn't do His will. He wants you, out of your own free will, to grow close to Him and be like Him—that is why He created you. This is important because, ultimately, it is where you find your true source of sustenance, joy, life, and fulfillment.

☩ *Woe to him who quarrels with his Maker, to him who is but a potsherd among the potsherds on the ground. Does the clay say to the potter, "What are you making?" Does your work say, "He has no hands?"* (Isaiah 45:9).

God is playing out a great plan for the world that involves billions of souls. There is interplay between God and satan, good and evil, as it relates to our wills, both individually and corporately, that we cannot fully appreciate. Consider Job, who the Bible indicates was a righteous man. Job became involved in a high-stakes contest where it was ultimately proven to satan that Job did not love God *merely because* God gave him many earthly possessions and good health. Job was faithful, even when he was stripped of his family, money, career, and left alone, homeless, covered in boils and body sores. The question that comes to each of us is, could we do the same?

And yet we learn in the book of Job that Job's faith was *strengthened* because of and through this initially *devastating* process. Job also developed a deeper understanding of God and a more intimate relationship with Him. Are you willing to give up some comfort and possessions for a deeper understanding and closer relationship with God?

243

In the Old Testament story of Job, it says God spoke to him in the midst of his troubles. It is often amid your troubles when God is most likely to speak to you. There is a saying that God whispers in your pleasure, speaks in your comfort, but shouts in your pain. Sometimes hardship gives God the opportunity to teach you significant lessons. In the face of adversity, in the height of the storm, look at Job's understanding and faith in his ultimate destiny with God:

✛ *I know that my Redeemer lives, and that in the end He will stand upon earth. And after my skin has been destroyed yet in my flesh I will see God; I myself will see Him with my own eyes—I, and not another. How my heart yearns within me!* (Job 19:25-27).

In the midst of Job's troubles, God was speaking, helping him know that in "the end" he would receive in the resurrection a new body by which he would physically see God. God is always speaking to us, but in the midst of our biggest troubles we simply are more open to hearing His voice.

✛ *For God does speak—now one way, now another—though men may not perceive it* (Job 33:14).

Through these troubles, Job and God brought their relationship to a *higher level*. After Job had fully unwrapped the trials and tribulations, for all his suffering, he was physically rewarded *double* the possessions he started with. Job accepted God's will for his life, stayed on God's path, and found his reward. You too will have trials that, if handled properly, will allow you to see God and receive your reward.

✛ *I know how great this makes you feel, even though you have to put up with every kind of aggravation in the meantime. Pure gold put in the fire comes out of it proved pure; genuine faith put through this suffering comes out proved genuine. When Jesus wraps this all up, it's your faith, not your gold, that God will have on display as evidence of*

*His victory. You never saw Him, yet you love Him. You still don't see Him, yet you trust Him—with laughter and singing. Because you kept on believing, you'll get what you're looking forward to: total salvation* (1 Peter 1:6-9 MSG).

God has a purpose for everything and plans to work everything out for the good of those He loves. We just don't always understand how or why, nor do we understand God's perfect timing. Remember that God moves according to a timetable we can't comprehend. While we may sometimes think He is slow to respond, it may be that we're simply not ready to hear an answer from Him, or the particular answer God is giving. Our calling at these times is to just stay on His path even if we don't understand where it is going.

## ACTION & VISUALIZATION

*See God's hand in both good and bad circumstances;*
*align your heart and actions with God's purposes.*

If you have felt confined by life with habits, thoughts, and actions you can't seem to break out of, then take heart! Do you remember the caterpillar and the struggle from cocoon to flight? Let this physical struggle lead you to receive, unwrap, and use the Gifts of Freedom He offers. They will give you the freedom and spiritual wings that allow you to fly.

*…We were under great pressure, far beyond our ability to endure, so that we despaired even of life. Indeed, in our hearts we felt the sentence of death. But this happened that we might not rely on ourselves but on God, who raises the dead. He has delivered us from such a deadly peril, and He will deliver us.* **On Him we have set our hope** [with actions of faith] **that He will continue to deliver us…** (2 Corinthians 1:8-10).

We must understand that the fallen world we have created will wear us down and defeat us without God's intervention. It is our hope in Him and our unwrapping of *all* the gifts He offers that brings His strength into our lives, giving us freedom and victory.

☩ *He gives strength to the weary and increases the power of the weak. Even youths grow tired and weary, and young men stumble and fall; but those who* **hope in the Lord** *will renew their strength. They will soar on wings like eagles; they will run and not grow weary, they will walk and not faint* (Isaiah 40:29-31).

In summary, acting in faith—even strong faith—won't eliminate problems in your life, *nor* will it trump God's will. However, acting in faith *will* allow you to overcome adversities and discover joy along the way. Most importantly, using your gift of faith by putting it into action opens His heart so you can enjoy intimacy between you and your Maker.

## MEDITATION POINT

Put your faith in opening His gifts and He will give you a spiritual way out— sometimes a physical way out too.

Go to Chapter 7 in the Study Guide section on page 333.

- Without adversity and trials, you could not refine your character.

- Without adversity, great testimonies could not be created to lead others to Jesus.

- Without adversity, how would we know our daily need for God?

Indeed, the biggest gift found within adversity is that it drives us *closer* to God. And that closeness allows us to take our eyes off the present, the earthly here and now, and to envision something much greater—our eternal future with Him.

David recognized that he was only passing "through" a valley; it wasn't his permanent home. He knew and believed in a promise from the Creator of the universe that he would eventually rest in a better place. Our foresight and our faith doesn't rest in the physical—in selling millions of chicken wings or tickets to an amusement park. Our foresight and faith rests in Christ's statement, "I go to prepare a place for you," a place beyond our imagination. And this is the kind of vision, the only kind of faith, that can see one through life's *darkest, deepest valleys*, much like David experienced.

Painful lows and struggles here on earth should also remind us that this world is not our permanent home. Jesus wants to comfort us in this truth:

✠ *Do not let your hearts be troubled. Trust in God; trust also in Me. In My Father's house are many rooms; if it were not so, I would have told you. I am going there to prepare a place for you. And if I go and prepare a place for you, I will come back and take you to be with Me that you also may be where I am* (John 14:1-3).

Don't forget that God's original intent was for us to live in the garden of Eden here on earth, not in the valley of the shadow of death. Our choices and the natural consequences of sin have led us through the valleys. Through His resurrection power, our destination will be like the garden, a place where we live in God's presence and enjoy the splendor He intended for us, a place without the adversities we now face. In this place, the city of God,

☩ *there will be no more night.* [We] *will not need the light of a lamp or the light of the sun, for the Lord God will give* [us] *light…* (Revelation 22:5).

Imagine it: You'll be remade in God's image and likeness, experiencing the fullness of His love with no distortion of sin, in harmony with all that is around you. And God's presence will be enough to provide you with light! But because of sin that we brought on ourselves, we have work to do before we get to this glorious city; however, the very adversities we run into while getting there have gifts inside to better equip and prepare us. The question remains: will you choose to unwrap all the gifts God gives you, even those found within adversity? Your proper handling of adversity can be a powerful witness of God's love and a vehicle to bring life to a dying world.

## KEEP A GOOD PERSPECTIVE

If your exercise coach told you he was giving you a free exercise machine to use at home, you'd probably feel good about that. However, to use this gift to its full benefit, you'd have to work out, sweat, and train, perhaps experiencing some pain along the way. Likewise, we should be joyful when trials and adversities come our way because they give us a chance to exercise our faith. In essence, adversity is your exercise machine, and you can't build up your faith and/or refine yourself without it. There is no way to build up your muscles without resistance; likewise, it takes resistance to build up your faith. You also need to stretch your muscles *regularly* to retain full range and use of them, and faith is the same. We must have the proper knowledge and perspective to get the most out of the opportunities life offers.

Sometimes when we fail at reaching one of our goals, or experience challenges or adversities, we feel as if we are out of God's will and nothing good is happening. However, consider this story about a man's faith. God asked the man to push a large rock. In faith, the man obediently started pushing the rock with all his strength, yet it would not move. The man had such a high level of faith that he went out every day diligently pushing on the rock for an hour. After a month of seeing no movement, he decided to also start studying the Bible to see if he could find people in similar situations and learn how they dealt with it. After another month of pushing on the rock and reading the Bible every day, yet seeing no movement, the man started talking to God about it daily. He continued to see no movement.

He questioned God: "Is it me? Are there changes in my life I need to make to complete Your will? Why am I failing to move the rock?" After a month of dialogue with God, God said to the man, "I asked you to push the rock, *not move it*. By obediently pushing it, you moved yourself into a better position." In his faithful efforts of pushing on the rock, the man improved his physical strength, his mental knowledge of the Bible, and intimacy with God. While the man thought he was losing, he was really winning!

God has also given you a rock to push. You live on it—it is called *earth*. By pushing on this rock to move it in His way, though you may not always be successful at your goal, you will *certainly* be successful in building yourself up into a better person by faithfully pushing on the world in which you live.

Along with the gift of faith, God gives us a promise to help us *embrace* the adversities of life. Romans 8:28 gives us this perspective: *"all things are working together for our good."* Therefore, it is up to us to use faith and act on this promise. God wants us to be joyful, which is an enduring state that abides with us, unlike happiness. Remember this discussion in Chapter 3?

You start growing your strength, confidence, and joy from the *inside*, not the outside. It is done by knowing where and how our blessings come. In Hebrew, the noun word for blessed, *barak*, is spelled with three Hebrew letters; the first two relate to the word *son* and the third is the letter that's symbol stands for a clasped or cupped hand, symbolizing the Son standing over us with His hand on our forehead pronouncing a blessing over us. Interestingly, the verb blessing, *baraka*, is spelled in Hebrew by adding the letter *hay* or grace at the end to make it an action word—the action of grace. The good news is that our receiving blessings does not solely rely on us doing things that make us deserving of it. When seemingly bad things happen, you should *not* be driven to a place of fear and defeat; instead, have confidence in God's love, grace, and resurrection power. Out of this response, we are positioned to see the gifts imbedded within adversity. From this vantage point, adversities become testimonies of God's power, blessings, and growth.

This is an important point to grasp. We as Christians are designed to work from the inside out, not the outside in. Our joy and peace should *not* come from the physical world or any accomplishments we achieve in this world, because when we were saved, the real world, the world that matters, was created in us that day. It begins with our heart. We are to project God's love and light from it outward.

✝ *Once, having been asked by the Pharisees when the kingdom of God would come, Jesus replied, "The Kingdom of God does not come with your careful observation, nor will people say, 'Here it is,' or 'There it is,' because **the Kingdom of God is within you**"* (Luke 17:20-21).

You will learn and experience God through prayer, worship, praise, spiritual achievements, and even adversity. Your experiences with God can give you an inner peace that allows you to receive the joy God desires for you. Jesus said:

✝ *Do not fear, little flock, for it is your Father's good pleasure to give you the Kingdom* (Luke 12:32 NKJV).

If you have faith in God and trust that God can use your adversity for good—physical, mental, or spiritual—then you will know that your trials and sufferings are only temporary. Trusting God now—before, during, and after your troubles—provides you with supernatural joy. Even in the hardest of times, blue skies will open within you when you unwrap all His gifts.

Let's recap. Why is having a strong faith important? Faith in action shows our belief in God, both in His promises and in His nature. Faith in action helps us get through difficult times, holding on to God's promises and nature. And most importantly, faith pleases God and brings us closer to Him. So how is your faith built up and exercised? It is done through adversity.

## DON'T GIVE UP

Beyond joy, we need to believe that trials and adversities will result in something to help us achieve our purpose. When you graduated from school, your goal may have been to run a company. However, without first having the trials and challenges of actual business experience, you are likely to fail. We need personal experience to develop the skill and talent we need to reach our goals. This applies to our spiritual development as well. God is building into us the tools, friendships, and character we need to become what He wants us to be. A reminder: "All things God works for the good of those who love Him."

Don't let adversity rattle your faith—don't give up before you get *through* the valley to where God desires you to be. Some people lose faith in the face of adversity and turn an opportunity for victory into defeat. They pitch their tent in the valley or even start building their house there. When trouble is surrounding you, I believe in following this old adage: "If you find yourself going through hell, don't stop—keep going!" You need to understand things in this temporal world are subject to change. Tomorrow is another day. This is why the psalmist could write:

✠ *...weeping may remain for a night, but rejoicing comes in the morning* (Psalm 30:5).

The Old Testament is filled with stories about people who kept moving through the valleys, and they saw their faith and relationships continually increase as they moved through to the other side. One of the most familiar stories is David and Goliath. David's story begins when he was merely a shepherd boy. The destiny God was shaping for David to become the king of Israel brought him through a truly monumental valley—a confrontation with a warrior named Goliath:

✠ *A champion named Goliath, who was from Gath, came out of the Philistine camp. He was over **nine feet** tall. He had a bronze helmet on his head and wore a coat of scale **armor** of bronze weighing five thousand shekels [about 125 pounds]; on his legs he wore bronze greaves, and a bronze javelin was slung on his back. His spear shaft was like a weaver's rod, and its **iron point** weighed six hundred shekels [about 15 pounds]. His shield bearer went ahead of him.*

*Goliath stood and shouted to the ranks of Israel, "Why do you come out and line up for battle? Am I not a Philistine, and are you not the servants of Saul? Choose a man and have him come down to me. If he is able to fight and kill me, we will become your subjects; but if I overcome him and kill him, you will become our subjects and serve us." Then the Philistine said, "This day I defy the ranks of Israel! Give me a man and let us fight each other." On hearing the Philistine's words, Saul and all the Israelites were **dismayed** and **terrified** (1 Samuel 17:4-11).*

David would probably have been too terrified to fight this nine-foot giant had it not been for the way God prepared him through *other challenges* they overcame together. See how David used them to build up his faith and confidence in God.

✠ *Saul replied* [to David's request to be the one to fight Goliath], *"You are not able to go out against this Philistine and fight him; you are only a boy, and he has been a fighting man from his youth."*

> *But David said to Saul, "Your servant has been keeping his father's sheep. When a **lion** or a **bear** came and carried off a sheep from the flock, I went after it, struck it and rescued the sheep from its mouth. When it turned on me, I seized it by its hair, struck it and killed it. Your servant has killed both the **lion** and the **bear,** this uncircumcised Philistine will be **like one of them,** because he has defied the armies of the living God"* (1 Samuel 17:33-36).

David overcame a lion and a bear, as God was building his faith to handle the giant. These attacks by the lion and bear certainly would have seemed like problems at the time, but in reality they were building up his faith, his trust in God. What seemed bad at the time was preparing David so he would not give up when a much bigger challenge or adversity came into his life. Because David did not give up or run from these previous battles, he was prepared to fulfill the will of God—to defeat the *giant* in his life, the one seeking to enslave the nation of Israel.

Each of David's prior adversities led to victory and created trust and depth in his relationship with God, because he knew he didn't kill the lion and bear—*God did*. Each adversity also created a *compelling* testimony to help others build up their faith in God because they knew God would do the same again. Do you believe your actions of faith in the face of adversity will do the same? The only difference between David and the other Israelites is that David acted on the faith he was given while the others didn't. And just like David, you too can daily choose to act in faith, thus building up your relationship with God to have the faith to stand up to your own giants and allow Him to conquer them for you.

## CREATING TESTIMONIES

There is no question that you will face adversity. There may be attacks on you, your family, and your possessions. Perhaps you are experiencing some of these right now. Are you facing your own "lions" and "bears"—perhaps preparing you for an even greater challenge that lies ahead?

If you are in sync with God's will, then it is by faith that you can attack and with God's help defeat these lions, bears, and, eventually, giants. In the physical realm, you may not see a way to defeat them; however, as you receive God's supernatural Gifts of Freedom, then, like David, you will find a supernatural *victory*. Instead of running away or giving up, you can find joy and strength in overcoming these circumstances. David knew God would be his Savior if he trusted and rested in God as he had done in the past. The verse says David *ran quickly* at Goliath when they fought. *Over time* David built up a fearless faith that allowed him to say:

✝ *I will not fear the tens of thousands drawn up against me on every side* (Psalm 3:6).

It may be a long journey for you to get to this level of faith, but this is what God desires. This may even seem impossible today, but keep in mind that God doesn't give us circumstances that are too difficult to handle. Paul wrote:

✝ *No temptation had seized you except what is common to man. And God is faithful; He will not let you be tempted beyond what you can bear. But when you are tempted, He will also provide a way out so that you can stand up under it* (1 Corinthians 10:13).

God puts a gift in adversity so that we can have a way out *if we choose*. This way out doesn't come in our own strength, but in His. This is where we find rest and confidence.

✝ *Haven't I commanded you? Strength! Courage! Don't be timid; don't get discouraged. God, your God, is with you every step you take* (Joshua 1:9 MSG).

✝ *For God did not give us a spirit of timidity, but a spirit of power, of love and of self-discipline* (2 Timothy 1:7).

✠ *...in all things we are more than conquerors through Him who loves us* (Romans 8:37).

We will have setbacks and adversities because of choices we have made, sins we've committed, and because the world in which we live is populated with fallen people doing evil deeds—things not in the will of God. We will be knocked down but not defeated. Be confident in this.

✠ ***Do not gloat over me, my enemy! Though I have fallen, I will rise.*** *Though I sit in darkness, the Lord will be my light. Because I have sinned against Him, I will bear the Lord's wrath, until He pleads my case and establishes my right. He will bring me out into the light; I will see His righteousness. Then my enemy will see it and will be covered with shame, she who said to me, "Where is the Lord your God?" My eyes will see her downfall; even now she will be trampled underfoot like mire in the streets* (Micah 7:8-10).

✠ *We are hard pressed on every side, but not crushed; perplexed, but not in despair; persecuted, but not abandoned; struck down, but not destroyed* (2 Corinthians 4:8-9).

So how do we turn our defeat into victory? Well, it is important to be open to God's leading because many of the biggest victories will *not* occur how and when our natural minds might expect. Remember the Israelites at Jericho? They were led by God to do something unusual, to walk around the walls and shout for seven days to receive their victory. Your spiritual solution to the physical battles you face may be hidden from your natural mind. When problems, battles, and adversities arise, look for and be open to the supernatural. Don't automatically assume and rely on conventional thinking. Remember that God's primary objective is for you to express your faith while at the same time creating a testimony for others to see. His ways are higher than ours—don't rule out God's often unorthodox approach to overcoming adversity.

Before David, a shepherd boy, fought Goliath, Saul offered David his own armor and weapons. While this would have been the traditional method of preparing for battle, David refused Saul's armor because of the way God had trained him. David instead armed himself in a very surprising and unnatural way:

Then [David] *took his staff in his hand, chose five smooth stones from the stream, put them in the pouch of his shepherd's bag, and with his slings in hand, approached the Philistine....*

*[Goliath] looked David over and saw that he was only a boy, ruddy and handsome, and he despised him. He said to David, "Am I a dog that you come at me with sticks?" And the Philistine cursed David by his gods. "Come here," he said, "and I'll give your flesh to the birds of the air and the beasts of the field!"*

*David said to the Philistine, "You come against me with sword and spear and javelin, but I come against you in the name of the Lord Almighty* [in His will], *the God of the armies of Israel, whom you have defied. This day the Lord will hand you over to me, and I'll strike you down and cut off your head. Today I will give the carcasses of the Philistine army to the birds of the air and the beasts of the earth, and the whole world will know that there is a God in Israel. All those gathered here will know that it is not by sword or spear that the Lord saves; for the battle is the Lord's, and He will give all of you into our hands."*

*As the Philistine moved closer to attack him, David ran quickly toward the battle line to meet him. Reaching into his bag and taking out a stone, he slung it and it struck the Philistine on the forehead. The stone sank into his forehead, and he fell facedown on the ground* (1 Samuel 17:40-49).

The number five represents God's grace (the fifth Hebrew letter), and stones (the Rock) represent Jesus. We could say David relied on God's grace and Jesus' power as his weapons to take down Goliath. *Hay*, which is the fifth letter of the Hebrew alphabet, also represents God's breath. So we could also say that David's proclamation of God spoken in faith activated God's power. In your life, it will never be the weapons of the world that give you your greatest victories. It will be your reliance on the Rock, on His Word, His grace, His power and speaking His will in your life that will give you all the supernatural victories in your life.

When Goliath was down, David used Goliath's own sword to kill him and cut off his head. At times, God will allow you to use the weapons of your enemies to defeat them. On seeing their hero killed, the other Philistines ran and were therefore easily defeated by the Israelites. They ran because they put their faith in a man, albeit a man who was over nine feet tall. Today we still have the tendency to idolize people of great strength, beauty, talent, and speech. When they fall, their followers will also be scattered like Goliath's. In your walk of faith, it's important to stay focused on Jesus and not a pastor or minister, regardless of their seemingly great spiritual strength.

David was focused on God and only on God. This strong faith David exhibited in God's will for him created a *testimony* to the world that God did indeed exist and was with David and the Israelites. God wants to build testimonies that reflect God's strength in you, giving you victory over your "giants." Your testimony, just as David's was, will be a light in a dying world for others to see the God you serve.

Some of what I have written here is in contradiction to a popular notion among many Christians that after we're saved, life should be smooth sailing. After all, as some Christians say, "God gives us the victory!" This statement is certainly true; however, what many Christians miss is that without a battle, how can there be a victory? Battles exist because there is an enemy of God, a force opposed to obedience to the will of God. God will use that very attack of the enemy to defeat him. Your faith in the battles gives you victory. And each victory you obtain will help you in the next battle.

We see in David's story later in 1 Samuel 21 that he was fleeing for his life weaponless as the king's men were chasing David so they could kill him. Arriving in Nob, David asked the priest if they had a sword for him to defend himself, and the priest replied that they only had the sword of Goliath, whom he had killed. Success in one battle will prepare you and give you the weapon for the next battle. God will give you success in the battles; however, what He requires is for you to use your faith to *enter* them. Therefore, start developing a warrior's spirit, much like David. Warriors carry shields to help defend themselves in battle. The Bible says *faith* is our *shield*—it's the one David used in his battle against the giant.

✝ *...take up the shield of faith, with which you can extinguish all the flaming arrows of the evil one* (Ephesians 6:16).

Did you catch that? The enemy isn't just shooting arrows at you—these are *flaming* arrows. It is up to you, with God's help, to raise your shield of faith and defend yourself when adversity comes.

✝ *...If you do not stand firm in your faith, you will not stand at all* (Isaiah 7:9).

## ACTION & VISUALIZATION

*Stand strong in your faith when the inevitable attacks come and thereby create a testimony with God.*

## YOU ARE HIS GLORY ON EARTH

You live in a fallen world with an enemy who wants to bring you down. Jesus left you here as His occupation force for at least one specific purpose:

to *show* the world God's love. Jesus Himself prayed this prayer to His Father before He died and was resurrected:

⊕ *My prayer is not that You take [believers] out of the world but that You protect them from the evil one. They are not of the world, even as I am not of it. Sanctify them by the truth; Your word is truth....*

*My prayer is...that all of them may be one, Father, just as You are in Me and I am in You. May they also be in Us so that the world may believe that You sent Me. **I have given them the glory that You gave Me**, that they may be one as We are One: I in them and You in Me. May they be brought to **complete unity to let the world know that You sent Me** and have loved them even as You have loved Me* (John 17:15-23).

When the world and your enemy take shots at you, will you follow David's example? Will you choose the road of faith in the face of fear? Will you choose to show the world God's love, resurrection power, and glory? Truly, this is your mission as a Christian. What's the point if our lives do not reflect the glory of God? Moses pointed this out to God Himself when he said to Him:

⊕ ***If your Presence does not go with us***, *do not send us up from here. How will anyone know that You are pleased with me and with Your people unless You go with us? What else will distinguish me and Your people from all the other people on the face of the earth?* (Exodus 33:15-16).

In our case, as born-again believers, we all have God's presence *in us*; however, the world cannot see it unless *we act* in faith to show it to them. This is another reason why your action of faith pleases God—it shines His light into a dying world. It brings others closer to Him. We will have struggles, but it is those struggles that allow us to show God's presence in us and distinguishes us from all other people. When these challenges come, we can choose to either quit and allow our lives to be defined by our mistakes and losses, or we can keep moving forward in faith until we have found God's purpose and victory.

## BE AN EXAMPLE

The more you exercise your faith, the closer you will grow to God. You may have heard people refer to this relationship as "walking with God." Walking is an action, an exercise, a forward movement. That's why we don't ask, "How's your nap with God?" Faith in action is a catalyst for intimacy with Him. Enoch is an example of someone who walked closely with God. The book of Genesis tells us:

> *Enoch walked with God; then he was no more, because God took him away* (Genesis 5:24).

The phrase "walking with someone" denotes a constant and familiar interaction. This is the kind of relationship God desires us to have with Him, a *oneness* where the *end* of Him and the *beginning* of us is hard to discern. The Hebrew word for *took* in this verse is *laqach* (law-kakh), which means to get, lay hold of, snatch away, or marry, as in take a wife. The image we get from this verse is that Enoch walked so closely and in alignment with God that God enveloped him—they became *one* as in the marriage of a husband and wife. *Intimacy* with our Creator also leads us to joy in adversity that others will notice, because it is completely contradictory to the world's standards—it's supernatural! The apostle Paul wrote about it in this way:

> *We are hard pressed on every side, but not crushed; perplexed, but not in despair; persecuted, but not abandoned; struck down, but not destroyed. We always carry around in our body the death of Jesus, so*

*that the life of Jesus may also be revealed in our body. For we who are alive are always being given over to death for Jesus' sake, so that His life may be revealed in our mortal body. So then, death is at work in us, but life is at work in you.*

*It is written: "I believed; therefore I have spoken." With that same spirit of faith we also believe and therefore speak, because we know that the One who raised the Lord Jesus from the dead will also raise us with Jesus and present us with you in His presence. All this is for your benefit, so that the grace that is reaching more and more people may cause thanksgiving to overflow to the glory of God.*

*Therefore we do not lose heart. Though outwardly we are wasting away, yet inwardly [spiritually] we are being renewed day by day. For our light and momentary troubles are achieving for us an eternal glory that far outweighs them all. So we fix our eyes not on what is seen, but on what is unseen. For what is seen is temporary, but what is unseen is eternal* (2 Corinthian 4:8-18).

All circumstances can help us build better spiritual muscles. Believers who have successfully built up faith through trials are a *powerful testimony* to young believers and nonbelievers alike. Their spiritual muscles are beautiful in the sight of God. In fact, God can do great works *in* you and *through* you when *you choose* to become the person He wants you to be.

✝ [Jesus said], *"...let your light shine before men..."* (Matthew 5:16).

We are warned that for some, the stakes will be high:

✝ [Jesus said], *"Do not be afraid of what you are about to suffer. I tell you, the devil will put some of you in prison to test you, and you will suffer persecution for ten days. Be faithful, even to the point of death, and I will give you the crown of life"* (Revelation 2:10).

## ACTION & VISUALIZATION

*Shine your light for others to see by exercising faith in adversity.*

## DON'T LOOK AT YOUR CIRCUMSTANCES

When you have a word from God, keep your faith in it, regardless of your circumstances.

☦ *During the fourth watch of the night Jesus went out to [the disciples in a boat], walking on the lake. When the disciples saw Him walking on the lake, they were terrified. "It's a ghost," they said, and cried out in fear.*

*But Jesus immediately said to them: "Take courage! It is I. Don't be afraid."*

*"Lord, if it's You," Peter replied, "tell me to come to You on the water."*

*"Come," He said.*

*Then Peter got down out of the boat, walked on the water and came toward Jesus* (Matthew 14:25-29).

Peter, whose name incidentally means rock, gets his word and in stepping out of the boat in faith he achieves a miracle.

☦ *But when [Peter] saw the wind [his current circumstances] he was afraid and beginning to sink and cried out, "Lord, save me!"*

*Immediately Jesus reached out His hand and caught him. "You have little faith," He said. "Why did you doubt?"* (Matthew 14:30-31).

Peter initially had faith in the word he received, but when he saw his circumstances he became fearful—fear is the opposite of faith—and he lost his miracle. Instead of putting his faith in the supernatural word of God and the supernatural dimension in which it exists, Peter shifted his faith to the circumstances he was experiencing at the time. Though Peter did not hold on to his word from Jesus to keep from sinking, Jesus still held on to Peter so he wouldn't be overcome by the world's circumstances. Jesus' last words are important ones to ask ourselves when we get caught up in our circumstances: "Why did I doubt?"

## ACTION & VISUALIZATION

*Look beyond your circumstances to keep God's Word in sight.*

## AN ASTOUNDING FAITH

Though it's impossible to assign a measurable value to faith or to rank biblical heroes according to their level of faith, I would be remiss if I didn't examine the life of the man who is often referred to as the "father of our faith"—Abraham. Abraham received a promise from God:

> *Then the Lord said, "I will surely return to you about this time next year, and Sarah your wife will have a son."*
>
> *Now Sarah was listening at the entrance to the tent, which was behind him. Abraham and Sarah were already old and well advanced in years, and Sarah was past the age of childbearing. So Sarah laughed to herself as she thought, "After I am worn out and my master is old, will I now have this pleasure?"*
>
> *Then the Lord said to Abraham, "Why did Sarah laugh and say, 'Will I really have a child, now that I am old?' Is anything too hard for the Lord? I will return to you at the appointed time next year and Sarah will have a son" (Genesis 18:10-14).*

Despite the fact Sarah had never been able to have a child and now was too old to have one, God gave Abraham a promise that he would have a son with her. And Abraham's faith did not fail:

✠ *Against all hope, Abraham in hope believed and so became the father of many nations, just as it had been said to him, "So shall your offspring be." Without weakening in his faith, he faced the fact that his body was as good as dead—since he was about a hundred years old—and that Sarah's womb was also dead. Yet he did not waver through unbelief regarding the promise of God, but was strengthened in his faith and gave glory to God, being fully persuaded that God had power to do what He had promised. This is why* **"it was credited to him as righteousness"** *(Romans 4:18-22).*

Abraham's faith was accounted to him as righteousness. The word *accounted* is the Greek word *logidzomai* (log-id-zom-ahee), which refers numerically to "adding up" or metaphorically to the concept of drawing a conclusion. The idea here is that when God added up the sum total of Abraham's life, he was considered righteous *not* because he was perfect but because of his faithful belief in God's promise. Abraham didn't *earn* righteousness; he simply received the gift of righteousness because of his great *actions* of faith in God.[1]

Abraham, who was originally called Abram, followed God from the beginning of his life. Genesis tells us of God's initial promise to him:

✠ *The Lord had said to Abram, "Leave your country, your people and your father's household and go to the land I will show you. I will make you into a great nation and I will bless you; I will make your name great, and you will be a blessing. I will bless those who bless you, and whoever curses you I will curse; and all people on earth will be blessed through you." So Abram left, as the Lord had told him... (Genesis 12:1-4).*

When God called Abraham to leave his country, his people, and his family, he simply obeyed and left. This was a big step of faith. Can you imagine? Abraham had never seen God face to face, yet he trusted Him. Look at how Abraham kept his final destination in view as he exercised his faith:

✠ *By faith Abraham, when called to go to a place he would later receive as his inheritance, obeyed and went, even though he did not know where he was going. By faith he made his home in the promise land like a stranger in a foreign country; he lived in tents, as did Isaac and Jacob, who were heirs with him of the same promise.* **For he was looking forward to the city with foundations, whose architect and builder is God** *(Hebrews 11:8-10).*

God may not ask you to leave your country, your people, or your family, but God is asking you to follow Him *wherever* He leads. And just as Abraham followed God through a wilderness to his Promised Land, so you too can take hold of the same kind of faith. Our journey is headed toward our Promised Land, though the route may first take us through valleys, into some battles with giants, and cause us to leave some things behind.

God fulfilled His promise to Abraham and made him the physical father of the Jewish nation, as well as the spiritual father to all who would believe. However, this did not come easily. As the story continues, we discover the *amazing* depths of Abraham's faith in God.

✠ *Some time later God tested Abraham. He said to him "Abraham!"*
*"Here I am," he replied.*
*Then God said, "Take your son, your only son, Isaac, whom you love, and go to the region of Moriah. Sacrifice him there as a burnt offering on one of the mountains I will tell you about" (Genesis 22:1-2).*

Did you feel the weight of that request as you read it? God asked Abraham to give up his only son, something God Himself would do for all of us thousands of years later. How did Abraham feel about God's request? He loved Isaac and believed the promised "great nation" would be fulfilled through him. Did Abraham wonder if God was asking him to give up his destiny?

Abraham faced a choice between God's will and his own. Likewise, we will face that choice often on a smaller scale, and maybe someday at this same magnitude. God may ask us to destroy our view of the future so He can build a better one, the one we were designed and destined for. He loves us and we are His creation; therefore, He knows the perfect future for us. God's plan for our future is often beyond our comprehension. Sometimes we need to "bite the bullet" and trust God. We need to combine "action" with our faith to bring it alive.

⊕ *You foolish man, do you want evidence that faith without deeds is useless? Was not our ancestor Abraham considered righteous for what he did when he offered his son Isaac on the altar? You see that his faith and his actions were working together, and his faith was made complete by what he did. And the scripture was fulfilled that says, "Abraham believed God, and it was credited to him as righteousness," and he was called God's friend. You see that a person is justified by what he does and not by faith alone....*

*As the body without the spirit is dead, so faith without deeds is dead* (James 2:20-24,26).

Let's continue with Abraham's story.

⊕ *When they reached the place God had told him about, Abraham built an altar there and arranged the wood on it. He bound his son Isaac and laid him on the altar, on top of the wood. Then he reached out his hand and took the knife to slay his son. But the angel of the Lord called out to him from Heaven, "Abraham! Abraham!"*

*"Here I am," he replied.*

*"Do not lay a hand on the boy," he said. "Do not do anything to him. Now I know that you fear God, because you have not withheld from Me your son, your only son."*

*Abraham looked up and there in a thicket he saw a ram caught by its horns. He went over and took the ram and sacrificed it as a burnt offering instead of his son. So Abraham called that place The Lord Will Provide. And to this day it is said, "On the mountain of the Lord it will be provided"* (Genesis 22:9-14).

This is a powerful passage and a prophetic snapshot of the ultimate sacrifice God made when He gave His only Son Jesus to redeem the world. Abraham was willing to sacrifice his only son, yet God provided an alternate sacrifice—a lamb, symbolic of Jesus Christ—so Abraham's lineage could live on eternally. Note Abraham's words to us: "God will provide." Know that even in the toughest and most challenging of circumstances, God will provide a way so when you have done all you can, it is up to you to then rest and let God do the rest. God expects you to trust the story of Abraham and others in the Bible to build your confidence, because the star in all these stories is God. He is the one who helped these broken people like us through their most difficult moments. God knows how broken we all are, and He wants us to know He can do what we can't do for ourselves.

✝ *These things happen to them* [faith heroes in the Bible] *as examples and were written down as warnings for us, on whom the fulfillment of the ages has come. So, if you think you are standing firm, be careful that you don't fall! No temptation has seized you except what is common to man. And God is faithful; He will not let you be tempted beyond what you can bear. But when you are tempted, He will also provide a way out so that you can stand up under it* (1 Corinthians 10:11-13).

## Turning Defeat into Victory

It was the morning of Jesus' crucifixion and Pilate spoke to the people:

*"But you have a custom that I should release someone to you at the Passover. Do you therefore want me to release to you the King of the Jews [Jesus]?"*

*Then they all cried again, saying, "Not this Man, but Barabbas!" Now Barabbas was a robber* (John 18:39-40 NKJV).

Not only was Barabbas a robber, but Luke 23:25 says he was also described as a lawless man and murderer. You could say Barabbas represented satan (who is described in John 10:10 as a thief, in Matthew 16:23 as a lawless man, and in John 8:44 as a murderer). That morning the choice Pilate was giving humankind was between the only begotten Son of God, whom they had seen bring healing and love into the world, or the crowd could choose satan who brought theft, murder, and lawlessness. As in the garden, Adam and Eve made the wrong choice. They chose what satan offered them over what God offered. Humanity sent God's only Son—the only sinless Man, guilty of nothing—to His death on the cross.

It would have seemed to Jesus' followers that His death would be the ultimate defeat of His movement and ministry, but the story doesn't end here. There was a bigger spiritual reality taking place that the world did not see. It's not the end of your story either, because there is always a greater spiritual reality taking place. Jesus took the punishment for your sin that day, bringing you back into right standing with God. Then, three days later, He defeated sin and death to rise from the dead. This is why your story isn't over. Jesus' sacrifice and resurrection gives you eternal life, as well as the opportunity to eventually be transformed into the image and likeness of God.

What looked like the greatest defeat ever became God's greatest victory—salvation for you and me. God uses the actions of His adversaries to defeat them, and He will use the actions of your adversaries to allow you to defeat them too, just as David used Goliath's own sword to cut off His head.

You may have been surprised to see adversity among the gifts as one of the twelve Gifts of Freedom God offers. Just consider this, Jesus had twelve disciples to help Him change an entire world forever. One of those twelve betrayed Jesus, causing Him the biggest adversity in His life, Jesus' physical death. However, wrapped in that very adversity was Jesus' greatest *victory*, the defeat of sin and death in the world—*our redemption*. You have been offered twelve gifts to bring God to your world, and one of them is wrapped in adversity.

Because of Jesus' resurrection power within *you*, your seemingly greatest adversities can become your biggest victories. Look at Abraham and Jesus—when you're willing to give up your future, God can give you the destiny He designed especially for you. Even death is a victory for those who follow Christ, a step closer to our Promised Land in Heaven and eternal life with God!

Sometimes we practice an uncertain or tentative faith. We believe God's Spirit can breathe resurrection power into one or two specific areas of our lives, yet we feel other areas are hopelessly dead, or we can handle things better than God. However, Jesus wants us to harness His resurrection power in our lives *completely*. The same Spirit who raised Him from the dead is in us. With this power, we can bring to life all that seems dead. It only takes a little faith to go to Heaven; however, with a lot of faith, you can be a vehicle to bring Heaven to earth.

## ACTION & VISUALIZATION

*In your worst times, look for your victory.*

## RESURRECTION POWER

There is a story in the Bible about a friend of Jesus' named Lazarus, who had two sisters, Mary and Martha. Lazarus became sick and ultimately died. But when he first became sick, the two sisters sent a messenger to Jesus.

✠ *So the sisters sent word to Jesus, "Lord, the one you love is sick."*

*When He heard this, Jesus said, "This sickness will not end in death. No, it is for God's glory so that God's Son may be glorified through it" (John 11:3-4).*

Again we see God's plan to use someone's sickness for a greater glory. You may ask, "Who brings sickness and death—God?" I say no. Satan and man bring sickness and death. Just read these three passages:

✠ *...[satan] was a murderer from the beginning, not holding to the truth, for there is no truth in him... (John 8:44).*

✠ *For the wages of sin is death... (Romans 6:23).*

✠ *The thief comes only to steal, kill and destroy: I have come that they may have **life** and have it to the **full** (John 10:10).*

Our sin brought on sickness and death, and indeed God sacrificed His only Son to reverse this curse we have brought on ourselves. Though God may implant redemption in them, He is not the root cause of sickness and death in our lives.

Read what happens next in the story of Lazarus:

✠ *Jesus loved Martha and her sister and Lazarus. Yet when He heard that Lazarus was sick, He stayed where He was two more days (John 11:5-6).*

Yes, He loved them, but even though He knew Lazarus was near death, Jesus still waited *two days* before going to see him. Surely the messenger would have had time to report what Jesus said to Mary and Martha— Lazarus would not die! But why the two-day wait? You would think if Jesus loved him and knew Lazarus was sick, He would have left immediately. Jesus' disciples were probably confused by this delay as well:

✠ *After He had said this, He went on to tell them, "Our friend Lazarus has fallen asleep; but I am going there to wake him up."*

*His disciples replied, "Lord, if he sleeps, he will get better." Jesus had been speaking of his death, but His disciples thought He meant natural sleep.*

*So then He told them plainly, "Lazarus is dead, and for your sake I am **glad** I was not there, so that you may believe. But let us go to him"* (John 11:11-15).

Jesus knew this unfolding story was bigger and more important than Lazarus' sickness or even death. Why was He *glad* that He wasn't there when Lazarus was dying? I think it's so He could *bring His disciples' faith alive*, along with *Lazarus' faith*. Jesus would demonstrate for them the res- urrection power that would change their lives and yours too. The story continues:

✠ *Then Thomas (called Didymus) said to the rest of the disciples, "Let us also go, that we may die with him"* (John 11:16).

Many Christians have Thomas' defeated attitude in life. Thomas is the same disciple who, after the other disciples had seen Jesus after His resur- rection, said he doubted them (see John 20:24-25). Thomas became known as "doubting Thomas," which has now become a well-known phrase for unbelief. A week after Thomas expresses his unbelief, the Bible records the following:

✟ *A week later His disciples were in the house again, and Thomas was with them. Though the door was locked, Jesus came and stood among them and said, "Peace be with you." Then He said to Thomas [and all Christians], "Put your finger here, see My hands. Reach out your hand and put it into My side. **Stop doubting and believe**" [in My resurrection power].*

*Thomas said to Him, "My Lord and my God!"*

*Then Jesus told him, "Because you have seen Me, you have believed; blessed are those who have not seen yet have believed"* (John 20:26-29).

Jesus wants us to believe in His resurrection power without seeing, because it is our steadfast faith in that power and knowing it is within us that will allow us to continue in the face of seemingly impossible circumstances. It is through that faith and continuing to press on that will allow us to experience His resurrection power in each difficult circumstance in our lives and therefore come into the blessings God desires for us.

Let's go back to our unfolding story of Lazarus.

✟ *On His arrival, Jesus found that Lazarus had already been in the tomb for four days. Bethany was less than two miles from Jerusalem, and many Jews had come to Martha and Mary to comfort them in the loss of their brother* (John 11:17-19).

There is great encouragement in these verses: They remind us that we are not alone in our journey. There are many other believers who are ready to comfort and walk alongside us in difficult times. However, remember the messengers would have already reported that Jesus had said the sickness would not *end* in death. Everyone missed the fact that when Jesus' resurrection power is involved, death and defeat are *not the end*. Make sure you are not burying something God wishes to be alive, like His Word to you.

✠ *When Martha heard that Jesus was coming, she went out to meet Him, but Mary stayed at home.*

*"Lord," Martha said to Jesus, "if You had been here, my brother would not have died. But I know that even now God will give You whatever You ask."*

*Jesus said to her, "Your brother will rise again."*

*Martha answered, "I know he will rise again in the resurrection at the last day."*

*Jesus said to her, "I am the resurrection and the life. He who believes in Me, though he may die, he shall live. And whoever lives and believes in Me shall never die. Do you believe this?"*

*"Yes, Lord," she told Him, "I believe that You are the Christ, the Son of God, who was to come into the world"* (John 11:20-27).

Here's what I find most interesting about this passage: Martha doesn't answer Jesus' question. She says what is certainly an important belief—*You are the Christ*—yet seemingly ignores the resurrection power that we can all access through Jesus in this life now, for ourselves, our families, our friends, our country, and those whom God puts in our path. Isn't this the way many people approach faith? They believe that Jesus is the Christ, the Savior, but they don't understand or embrace the resurrection power that He brings into their daily lives.

The apostle Paul spoke about getting ahold of this power:

✠ *I want to know Christ **and** the power of the resurrection **and** the fellowship of sharing in His sufferings, becoming like Him in death, and so somehow, to attain to the resurrection from the dead* (Philippians 3:10-11).

The story goes on to say that Martha told her sister Mary that Jesus had arrived. Mary went to Jesus:

275

*When Mary reached the place where Jesus was and saw Him, she fell at His feet and said, "Lord, if You had been here, my brother would not have died."*

*When Jesus saw her weeping, and the Jews who had come along with her also weeping, He was deeply moved in spirit and troubled (John 11:32-33).*

Jesus was moved by their mourning, certainly, but I believe He was most troubled by their lack of faith that caused the mourning. He had faith He would raise Lazarus from the dead. Jesus was not mourning the loss of Lazarus but was mourning their lack of faith. Didn't they know He was the Son of God? Couldn't the Creator of life bring Lazarus back to life? Jesus became even more troubled when He saw that they had buried Lazarus, essentially rolling a stone in front of the word that He had given to them through the messengers:

*Jesus, once more deeply moved, came to the tomb. It was a cave with a stone laid across the entrance. "Take away the stone," He said.*

*"But, Lord," said Martha, the sister of the dead man, "by this time there is a bad odor, for he has been there four days" (John 11:38-39).*

Some of the promises God made to you have been locked away so long that they are dead and now they stink; however, this does not mean they can't be brought to life by the resurrection power of Jesus. Remember the message Jesus sent?

*Then Jesus said, "Did I not tell you that if you believed, you would see the glory of God?" (John 11:40).*

In the face of adversity, if you believe in His power and that His power is within you, then you too can see the glory of God manifest in your life.

✟ *So they took away the stone. Then Jesus looked up and said, "Father, I thank You that You have heard Me. I knew that You always hear Me, but I said this for the benefit of the people standing here, that they may believe that You sent Me."*

*When He had said this, Jesus called in a loud voice, "Lazarus, come out!" The dead man came out, his hands and feet wrapped with strips of linen, and a cloth around his face.*

*Jesus said to them, "Take off the grave clothes and let him go"* (John 11:41-44).

When you act on faith, you can be in a place to receive God's promises in your life. You must give over *all* areas of your life to God so that you can receive His life-giving resurrection power in those areas. The areas you keep to change by your own power can only be rehabilitated at best. Which do you desire to attain, *rehabilitation* or *resurrection*?

✟ *...The Lord is faithful to all His promises and loving toward all He has made* (Psalm 145:13).

## ACTION & VISUALIZATION

*Jesus said, "I am the resurrection and the life. He who believes in Me will live even though He dies; and whoever lives and believes in Me will never die." Do you believe this?*

## PUT YOUR FAITH IN GOD

Do you believe Jesus is working in the midst of your adversity and that no adversity is too great for Him to overcome? Do you believe the valley you may be walking through right now is not your home? Do you believe

God can resurrect that seemingly lifeless circumstance in your life? It is only to the degree that you have faith in God's love for you that you can clearly see the gift He implants in adversities. Reacting to these adversities with a strong action of faith allows you to receive the gifts of God within and sometimes even turn those circumstances around, as told in the story in Acts:

*On the first day of the week we came together to break bread. Paul spoke to the people and, because he intended to leave the next day, kept on talking until midnight. There were many lamps in the upstairs room where we were meeting. Seated in a window was a young man named Eutychus, who was sinking into a deep sleep as Paul talked on and on. When he was sound asleep, he fell to the ground from the third story and was picked up dead. Paul went down, threw himself on the young man and put his arms around him. "Don't be alarmed," he said. "He's alive!" Then he went upstairs again and broke bread and ate. After talking until daylight, he left. The people took the young man home alive and were greatly comforted (Acts 20:7-12).*

Notice that when tragedy struck, Paul didn't ask for other people to help him pray for Eutychus, nor did he stand over Eutychus to pray. Paul both literally and figuratively laid it all out and was clearly, 100 percent committed to calling on God and putting his in faith in God. Likewise, when God leads you to an action of faith, you too should lay it all out in much the same way Paul did. If you are open, God can use what seems like a bad circumstance to move you toward your destiny or to create a powerful witness, as He did with Job. God can make what looks to be dead come alive, as well as what seems like a bad circumstance change into a good one. It is interesting to note that the meaning of Eutychus' name is "good fortune." So it would be good for you to think and visualize what you will do the next time *good fortune* goes out the window in your life?

Words such as *faith* and *belief* may be easy to read off the page and nice to think about, but they may be harder to practice and live out. Remember that we are called to a *living faith*, and amid adversity our living faith can truly come to life where there was once death, thus radiating God's presence for the world to see.

## MEDITATION POINT

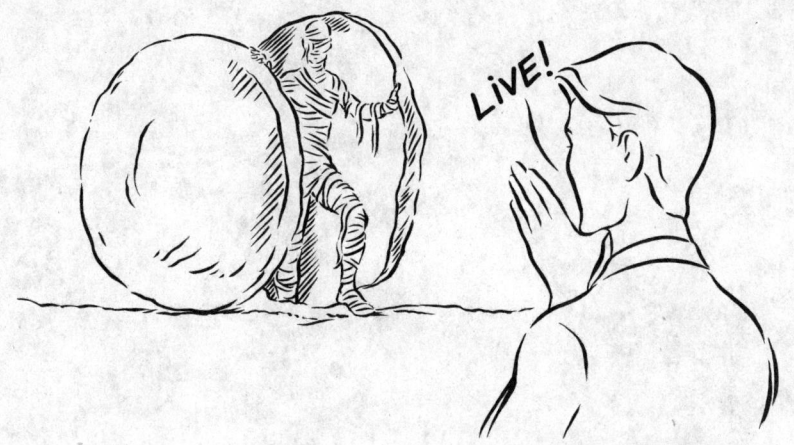

Your faith in action will manifest God's promises to come alive in your life.

Go to Chapter 8 in the Study Guide section on page 339.

## ENDNOTE

1.   Jack Hayford, ed., *Spirit Filled Life Bible for Students* (Nashville, TN: Thomas Nelson Publishers, 1995), 1443.

# Study Guide

# INTRODUCTION

P lease don't think of this study guide as a homework assignment. It *isn't* about giving the "right answer"—it's about giving an honest answer. It *isn't* about "getting it done"—it's about letting the questions stir your heart. It *isn't* about "filling in the blanks," but instead letting the Holy Spirit speak to your soul. Think of this as a spiritual experience or potential encounter between you and God rather than an exercise to check off your to-do list.

We are conditioned to believe that our answers to questions in a textbook will be graded; however, that mind-set stifles the purpose of this study guide. This is an opportunity to write honestly about your faith, to grow and go deeper in God's Word, to pray earnestly about His will for your life, and most of all to cultivate an intimate relationship between you and your Creator.

If possible, devote time for quiet reflection as you read the material, think about your life, and write accordingly. Answer the questions as you truly feel, even if it seems wrong or troubling. Remember that "the truth will set you free" and that growth can only happen when the soil is soft. You get what you give. You could burn through this entire study guide in half an hour if you'd like, but it would offer little to no lasting benefit.

I pray that you will put in the time and effort to maximize this material and actualize the full impact of His Gifts of Freedom into your life. Use the study guide to find the spiritual growth and maturity God desires you to have in your life.

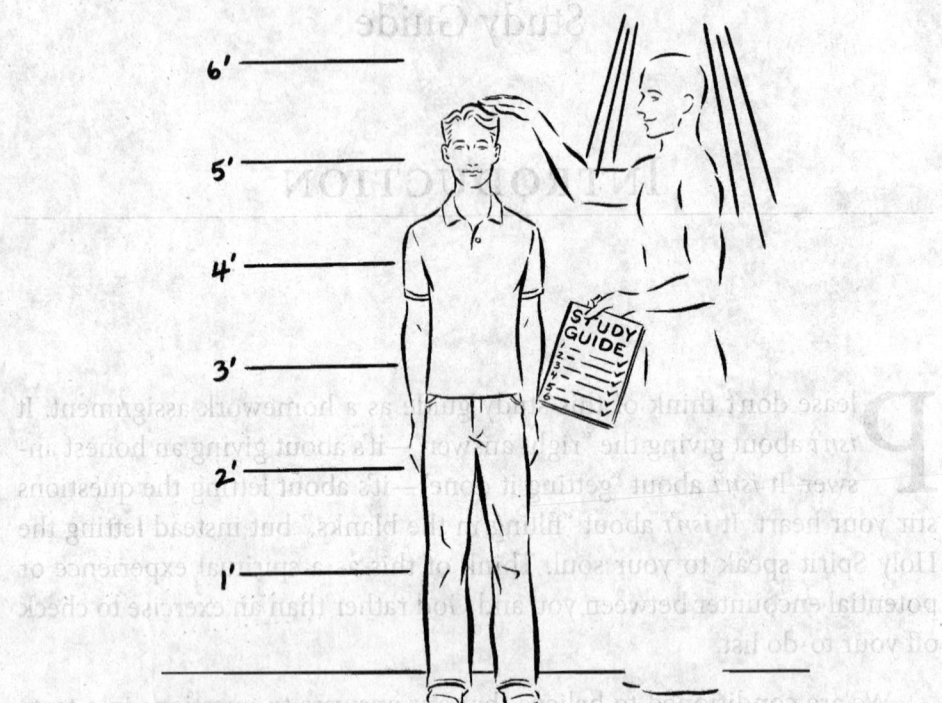

# The Gifts of Freedom Study Guide

# BOOK 1

## GIFTS OF LIFE, HOLY SPIRIT, FAITH, AND ADVERSITY

### HOW TO USE THE STUDY GUIDE

You can use this study guide in a variety of ways, including individually, as part of a small group Bible study, or in a Sunday school setting. If you are working through this book on your own, then use this study guide to record your personal growth journey. Take the time after each chapter to answer the questions. Some are designed to help you remember the main concepts in the chapter, while others are designed to help you personalize the content and apply it to your own life. At the end, seriously pray in closing that God will fill you with His gifts, and that you will recognize and accept them. You can also visit our website at www.giftsoffreedom.com and see how others have applied this information to their lives.

If you're reading this book in a small group, then use the study questions to prompt lively discussion. Discuss the action steps with at least one other group member to build accountability in your plans for action, then close your time together with prayer. For more information on how to lead a group or Sunday school class and get additional resources, visit our website at www.giftsoffreedom.com.

If you are not currently in a group study of the book, you might want to consider starting one after you finish, so you can spread to others the new freedoms you have discovered. As you help others, you will deepen your understanding and relationship with God, gaining even more freedoms.

Go to www.giftsoffreedom.com for additional resource materials and instructions.

# Chapter 1

# In the Beginning...

## What's My Purpose and What Went Wrong?

### Study Questions

1. What was God's original plan when He created man?

   To have a relationship with Him. We were
   made in His likeness (with his spirit) by
   which He used to fellowship with Him
   in a more organic way.

2. What changed, and how does that change (the fall) affect your life on a daily basis?

   _____

   _____

   _____

   _____

   _____

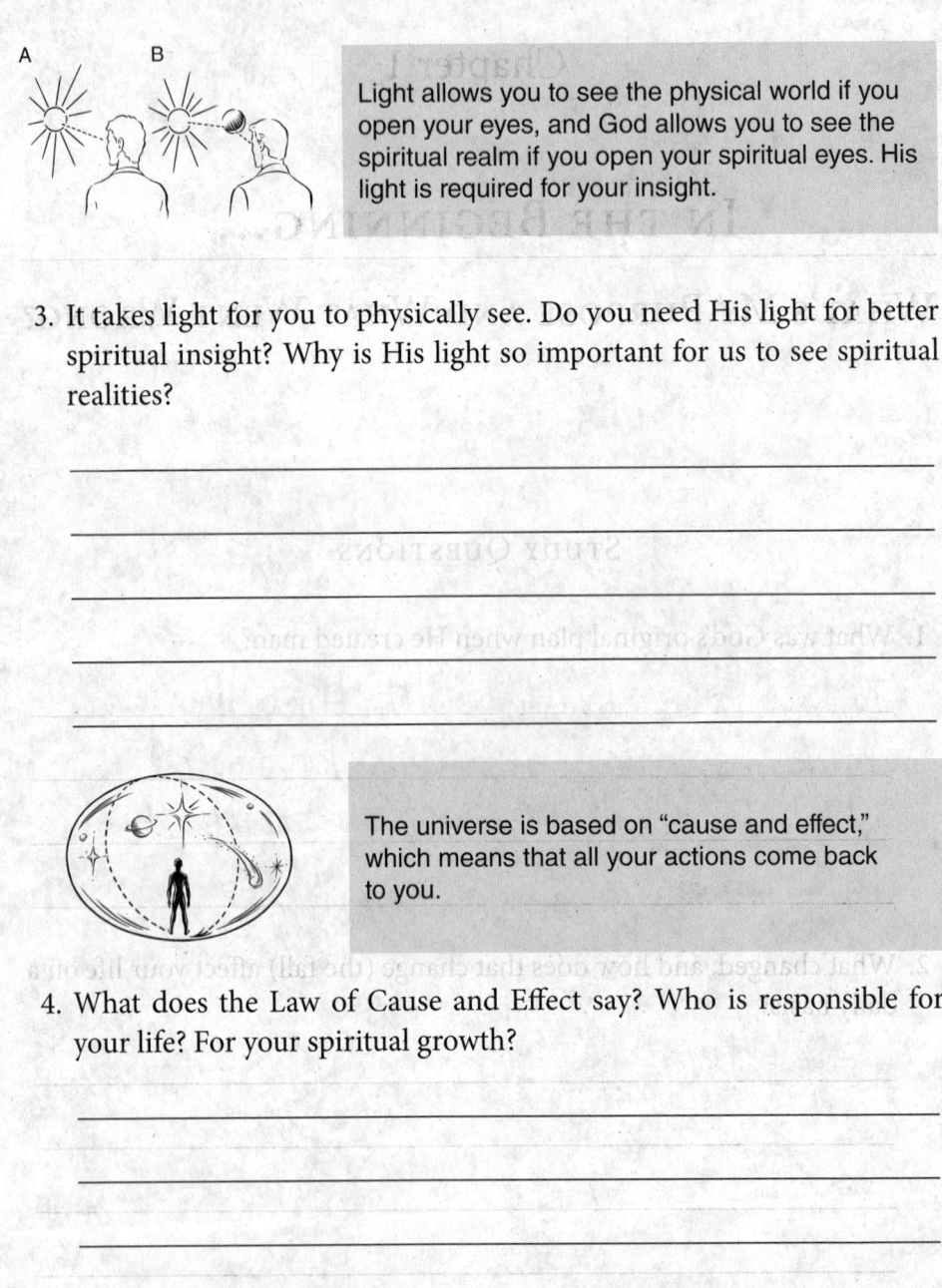

Light allows you to see the physical world if you open your eyes, and God allows you to see the spiritual realm if you open your spiritual eyes. His light is required for your insight.

3. It takes light for you to physically see. Do you need His light for better spiritual insight? Why is His light so important for us to see spiritual realities?

_____

_____

_____

_____

The universe is based on "cause and effect," which means that all your actions come back to you.

4. What does the Law of Cause and Effect say? Who is responsible for your life? For your spiritual growth?

_____

_____

_____

_____

_____

God's beautiful illustration of the kind of meta-morphosis, we too can choose to experience—a spiritual then physical metamorphosis.

5. How is the butterfly's metamorphosis like the way Christians grow into the people God created them to be?

_____

_____

_____

_____

A        B

You must plug in to shine His light.

6. Why did God make us in His image and likeness? Where do you see His image and likeness manifesting itself in your own life? Are there any areas where it is not?

_____

_____

_____

_____

_____

_____

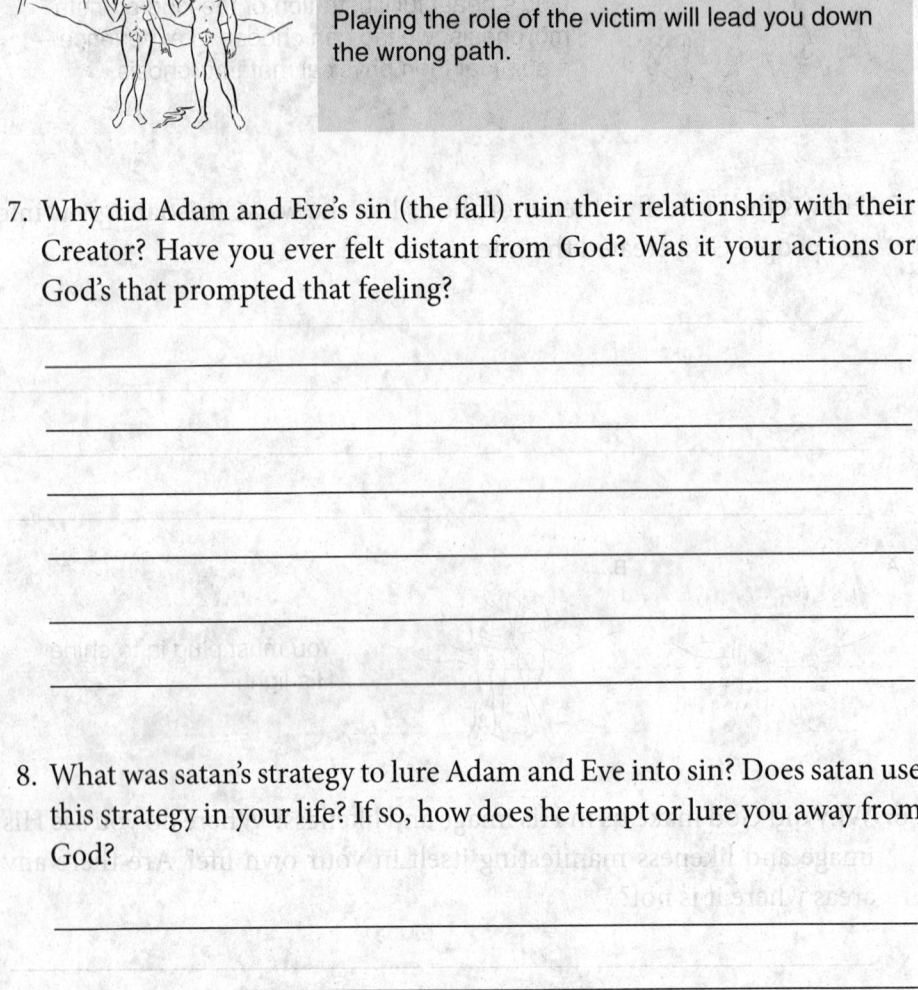

Playing the role of the victim will lead you down the wrong path.

7. Why did Adam and Eve's sin (the fall) ruin their relationship with their Creator? Have you ever felt distant from God? Was it your actions or God's that prompted that feeling?

_____

_____

_____

_____

_____

_____

8. What was satan's strategy to lure Adam and Eve into sin? Does satan use this strategy in your life? If so, how does he tempt or lure you away from God?

_____

_____

_____

_____

_____

_____

9. Can a person really hide from God? What are some of the ways you try to hide from Him?

_____

_____

_____

_____

_____

_____

10. Respond to the following quote: "God's priority is our spiritual side, not the physical fulfillment and obsession with our bodies' needs." How might this play out in your own life?

_____

_____

_____

_____

_____

_____

_____

11. What is the difference between God creating us with a free will versus God creating us like "sock puppets"? Why wouldn't God just program us to automatically love Him?

_____

_____

_____

_____

_____

His blood covers your sin so that when God looks at you He only sees Jesus' righteousness.

12. To have a perfect world, wouldn't we all need to act according to His image and likeness? Do you see the need for the consequences of sin to be death so the cancer of evil won't last forever? Is a just God required for us to live in a just world? In what ways and why? How did God satisfy justice and love at the same time?

_____

_____

_____

_____

## ACTION STEPS

Summarize the content of Chapter 1. Based on what you've learned, do you know God better? Do you understand His path, essence, intent, and His plan for you? What are things you can do in the pursuit of His destiny for you?

_____

_____

_____

_____

_____

## CLOSING PRAYER

(Pray this prayer or pray your own to close this study time.)

Lord, thank You for the Gifts of Freedom. Open my heart and mind as I begin to learn more about these gifts and how they can help me reconnect with Your Spirit.

# Chapter 2

# Gift #1—Life through Grace (Part 1)

## How Do You Get It?

## Study Questions

1. What memories do you have of unwrapping gifts when you were a child? Why does God desire a childlike nature from His children?

_____

_____

_____

_____

2. The first Gift of Freedom is eternal life—salvation. How much work do you need to do before you can receive this gift? Why should you open it first?

_____

_____

_____

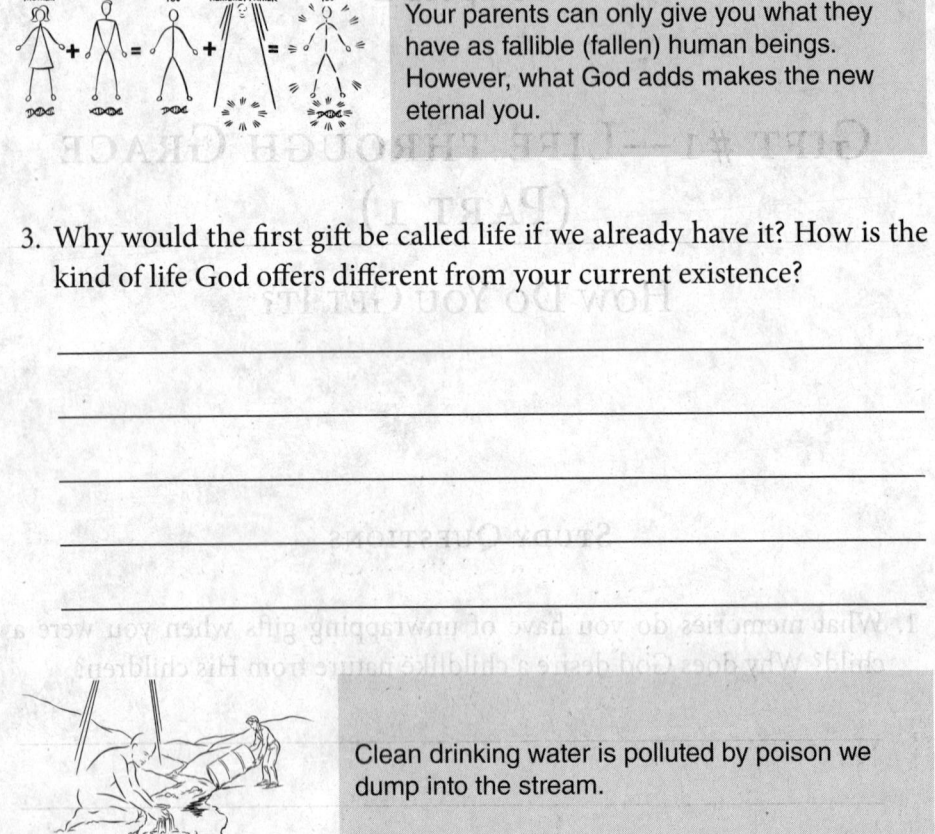

Your parents can only give you what they have as fallible (fallen) human beings. However, what God adds makes the new eternal you.

3. Why would the first gift be called life if we already have it? How is the kind of life God offers different from your current existence?

_____

_____

_____

_____

_____

Clean drinking water is polluted by poison we dump into the stream.

4. What does the image in this diagram say about sin? Can God drink of an intimate relationship with us in our present condition? What is the only way to purify our reservoir?

_____

_____

_____

_____

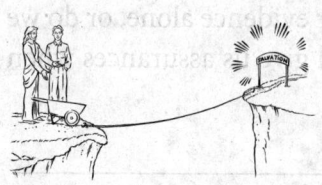

You must not only believe that Jesus existed and is great but also that He is the only One who will get you across to your salvation.

5. What is grace? Why is grace important in salvation? Can we save ourselves? Why not?

_____

_____

_____

_____

_____

A                          B                          C

Pull yourself closer to the source (God) and your light will shine brighter.

6. What role does our salvation play in beginning our relationship with God? How about in exuding His image in likeness? How do we continue to work out our salvation?

_____

_____

_____

7. Is it possible to accept the gift of life on fact or evidence alone, or do we need faith to do so? Once accepted, will God give us assurances when we ask?

_____

_____

_____

An accidental or purposeful creation?

8. When looking at God's creation, why is it hard to believe that there is no Creator? What evidence do you find in creation that God exists and loves you?

_____

_____

_____

_____

9. What is one way that you have personally seen God speaking and revealing Himself in His creation?

_____

_____

_____

Flying blind is dangerous for you and others aboard your plane.

10. How does your physical mind and body distract you from the spiritual? What part does your spirit play in helping you navigate through life? How do you find the eternal?

_____

_____

_____

_____

_____

_____

11. Is it difficult for you to believe that God accepts you the way you are? Why or why not?

_____

_____

_____

_____

_____

_____

_____

Satan does not want you to shine God's light into the world.

12. Do you think satan is attacking God's seeds growing in you? Is there anything you can do about it? What is your counter-attack plan?

_____

_____

_____

_____

## ACTION STEPS

Have you received and opened the first gift? If not, what is stopping you from accepting and unwrapping the gift of salvation? If you have, then what does this change mean in your daily life? What changes do you see coming as you seek to grow spiritually? Plan for how you will begin to grow and write your initial thoughts here.

_____

_____

_____

_____

_____

_____

## CLOSING PRAYER

(Pray this prayer or pray your own to close this study time.)

Lord, thank You for the gift of life. Help me to accept it by faith and learn to avoid the temptations satan puts in my way as I seek to grow closer to You.

# Chapter 3

# GIFT #1—LIFE THROUGH GRACE (PART 2)

## HOW DO YOU GET THE MOST FROM IT?

STUDY QUESTIONS

1. In what ways can you relate to the "now what" question at the beginning of this chapter? Is it clear to you how you will get the answer to that question? What are some of the ways God will use to provide the answers?

_____

_____

_____

_____

_____

_____

_____

_____

You will never get a firm hold on worldly happiness, so stop running in vain and look inside to find joy.

2. What are three things you are pursuing in your life? Ultimately, what do you plan to gain from these pursuits? How have you made the pursuit of happiness a priority? What do you think should be your highest priority? What can you do to start pursuing this priority?

_____

_____

_____

_____

_____

3. Using the analogy of preparing for a race, what are you doing today to prepare for eternal life? What behaviors are you starting? What are you stopping in order to make room for those things you are starting?

_____

_____

_____

_____

_____

Don't isolate yourself; stay where it is hot!

4. How does finding and attending a church help you "stay hot" in your faith? Is it possible to "stay hot" and be alone, isolated from other believers? Why or why not? What are some important aspects to finding a good church?

_____

_____

_____

5. What does baptism symbolize? What are some other actions we can take that symbolize and memorialize our life-changing decisions?

_____

_____

6. Why do you think the Bible uses the phrase "new creation" when describing a follower of Jesus Christ? What has God changed or made new in you? What aspect of your life has not changed immediately and is left up to you?

_____

_____

_____

7. What are some of the ways we can take advantage of our new life?

_____

_____

_____

_____

_____

_____

Prepare yourself to start running beneficial mental programs. Your actions will follow.

8. Consider the fact that the Bible is an ancient Book. So why is it still relevant today? What makes the Bible so special? How does God use it to affect the way we live today?

_____

_____

_____

_____

_____

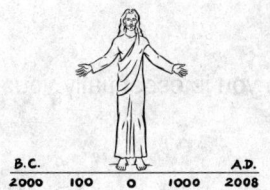

Even time itself revolves around Jesus.

9. What kind of relationship does Jesus want you to have with Him? What are some of your personal obstacles that can get in the way?

_____

_____

_____

_____

_____

_____

He wants to focus with you on where you are going.

10. How does your past factor into this relationship?

_____

_____

_____

_____

His image and likeness in you is essentially your relationship with Him.

11. List some things that come to mind when you think of Jesus. Is this accurate with the biblical account of His life and ministry? Write six reasons why you believe it is important to walk in the image and likeness of Jesus.

_____

_____

_____

_____

_____

12. Respond to this statement: "God is most interested in who you are, not what you do." What does God think of "who you are"? Can you find scriptural support for your answer?

_____

_____

_____

_____

_____

## ACTION STEPS

Think about what it means to embrace the "new life" you've been given. What are some practical actions you can take to become more like Jesus? Are there some habits you need to change? How might you begin reprogramming yourself to change those habits? List those action steps here.

_____

_____

_____

_____

## CLOSING PRAYER

(Pray this prayer or pray your own to close this study time.)

Lord, You have made me a new creation. Help me to take steps toward living out that new creation in daily life. Give me wisdom as I seek to become more like You every day.

# Chapter 4

# GIFT #2—THE HOLY SPIRIT (PART 1)

## WHAT DOES THE HOLY SPIRIT MEAN IN YOUR LIFE?

### STUDY QUESTIONS

1. Why does Jesus offer us the Holy Spirit? How is this a "new connection with God"? What is the Holy Spirit's role in your life?

_____

_____

_____

_____

_____

_____

_____

_____

A

B

The Holy Spirit lets you see God's perspective above your grounded state.

2. Which word used to describe the Holy Spirit has the most meaning to you right now (some examples would be Comforter, Helper, Advocate, and Guide)? Why did you choose this word?

_____

_____

_____

Follow the Holy Spirit's signs, for they lead to becoming formed in His image and likeness. Any other way will eventually lead to death.

3. What are some areas of your life that could use divine help, guidance, or counsel? Do you know some ways the Holy Spirit will speak to you? List them.

_____

_____

_____

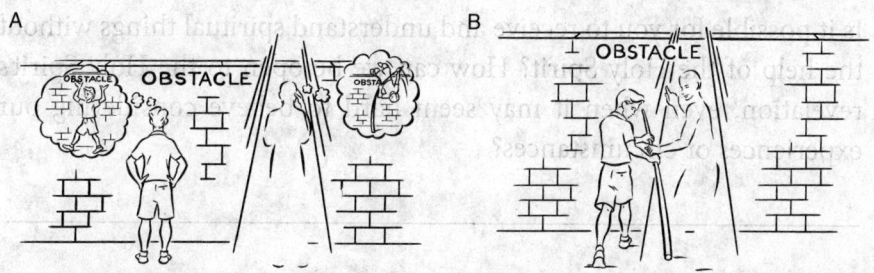

> Only God can show you the way through your obstacles in life—only He can turn dead ends into beginnings and bring death to life.

4. Given the fact that God knows everything and is all-powerful, can you see areas in your life where He could provide supernatural resurrection power?

   _____

   _____

   _____

5. Read again the Scripture passages in the Power of the Spirit section of this chapter. Which verses speak to you most powerfully about your life? Why? Have you fully considered how other passages may apply to your life?

   _____

   _____

   _____

   _____

   _____

6. Is it possible for you to receive and understand spiritual things without the help of the Holy Spirit? How can we be open to the Holy Spirit's revelation, even when it may seem hard to believe considering our experiences or circumstances?

_____

_____

_____

_____

_____

_____

_____

7. Have you ever felt prompted by the Holy Spirit? Describe that experience. If not, in what areas of your life do you hope to experience His prompting?

_____

_____

_____

_____

_____

_____

_____

A    B    C

God will expose you to what you will need to know when you're capable of using it. You will need to pay attention always and be open to learning or you will not have the information when you need it. God places information for you everywhere, *if* you're looking and open to it.

8. How can it be difficult or even troubling to wait on "God's timing"? Why is God's timing perfect, and how does faith play a role in waiting?

_____

_____

_____

_____

9. Consider the story of the man in the flood. What kind of crisis do you face today? What are three ways God could provide a way out or might already be answering that request? Could something you need to do be the answer? Are you looking and open to perceive Him in your circumstances?

_____

_____

_____

_____

God places information for you everywhere, if you're looking and open to it.

10. Does God bring us divine insight and information in places beyond church? Is it difficult to separate God's information from worldly information? Why or why not?

_____

_____

_____

When you seek answers as to your direction, God will provide them if you look for them.

11. What are some of the sins in your life where you may have become calloused to the Holy Spirit's leading? How can and will you change toward becoming open again to Him speaking to you in these areas?

_____

_____

_____

_____

12. At the end of the chapter, the verse in Matthew says that "narrow is the road that leads to life and few find it." Why do you think only "a few" find the road to life? Are you striving to be one of the few?

_____

_____

_____

## ACTION STEPS

Think about what you've learned about the Holy Spirit's role in your life. What are some things you know now that can help you grow closer to God? List some practical steps you can take to better understand the Holy Spirit's role, and to pursue the wisdom, comfort, and guidance He offers.

_____

_____

_____

_____

## CLOSING PRAYER

(Pray this prayer or pray your own to close this study time.)

Father, thank You for the gift of the Holy Spirit. Lead me in my understanding of the Spirit's role in my life, and help me to see and hear His promptings.

# Chapter 5

# Gift #2—The Holy Spirit (Part 2)

## How Do You Make the Holy Spirit Relevant in Your Life?

### Study Questions

1. In the Great Commission, Jesus says, "Go and make disciples." Does this mean we are single-handedly responsible to convince and force people to become disciples? What is a disciple? How are true disciples made? In what ways can you be part of that process?

_____

_____

_____

_____

_____

_____

_____

_____

People can argue about your doctrine and religion, but they can't argue with your experience because you're the sole expert. They didn't experience it.

2. If you've accepted Christ, you already have a story. In as few words as possible, tell that story here.

_____

_____

_____

_____

_____

3. List some of the people in your life who have not heard your story/ testimony. How do you think they would respond? Have you worked out a plan with the Holy Spirit to share your story with each of them?

_____

_____

_____

_____

_____

_____

Do the part you are assigned and let God orchestrate the rest.

4. If we plant "spiritual seed" and see little or no growth, what does that mean? What can we do to till the ground? How can timing be a factor? Once a seed starts taking root, how can we water it?

_____

_____

_____

5. Is boldness really God-given? If so, when does God give you supernatural boldness? What would that look like for you?

_____

_____

_____

6. Does the Holy Spirit offer His power only to overseas missionaries, pastors, and heroes in the Bible? Why will the Holy Spirit offer this same power to you?

_____

_____

_____

_____

Imagine for a minute the world God desired you to live in where everyone treated you with real love. Do your part now to start bringing that world into existence—it's called Heaven on earth.

7. What is Jesus talking about when He instructs us to "bear much fruit"? How do we do this, and why is it important?

_____

_____

_____

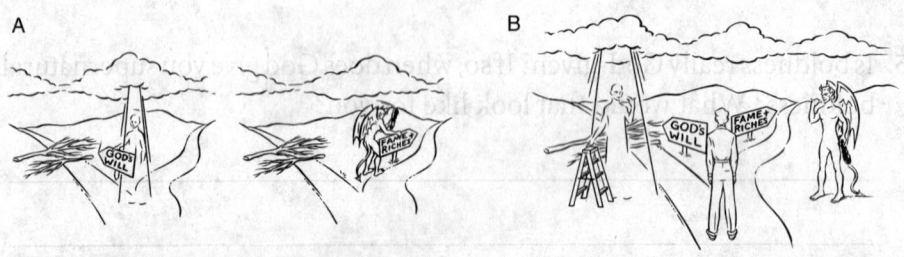

Stay on the path called "His will," where the obstacles have already been worked out.

8. What does it mean to "subject your will" to God? When you do so, does that mean you want to encounter obstacles in life? Why will the Holy Spirit offer His power and assistance when you're operating in "God's will"?

_____

_____

_____

_____

9. Which is more valuable, wisdom or knowledge? What are the qualities and characteristics that separate the two? Have you witnessed wisdom instead of knowledge emerging in your own life? How will it help you in decisions to ask yourself this question, "What would be the wise thing to do?"

_____

_____

_____

_____

_____

_____

Follow the Holy Spirit into battles to possess your Promised Land.

10. What is the third step in the progression of faith? How does this memorialize your relationship? You are already a Christian and have the Holy Spirit dwelling within you, so why should you need to be baptized in the Spirit?

_____

_____

_____

_____

_____

Let God speak directly from His Spirit to yours without interference.

11. What are the benefits of praying in the Spirit, if any?

_____

_____

_____

_____

12. In what ways does the Holy Spirit help prepare you to receive the other gifts of the Spirit?

_____

_____

_____

_____

## ACTION STEPS

If you haven't yet received the baptism of the Spirit, meet with other Christians to learn what you must do to embrace this baptism. Also, if you haven't been water baptized, consider the steps necessary for doing this at your church.

Review your answer to the second question. Think of ways you can share your story in everyday circumstances. Though it's best to tell your story naturally (not in a scripted manner), it might help to say it out loud a few times so you can think about the parts that matter most, and organize it in a way that is simple to understand. Consider "role-playing" a conversation where you have an opportunity to share your testimony with another believer.

_____

_____

_____

_____

_____

## CLOSING PRAYER

(Pray this prayer or pray your own to close this study time.)

Father, thank You for the many ways the Holy Spirit partners with me as I seek to gain the freedom You desire for me. Help me to receive and embrace the Holy Spirit as I continue to grow my intimate relationship with You.

# Chapter 6

# GIFT #3—FAITH (PART 1)

## WHY IS FAITH NEEDED TO UNTIE GOD'S GIFTS?

### STUDY QUESTIONS

It takes faith to please God, so when we are living our lives by faith we are pleasing God all the time.

1. Is faith something you can acquire or receive through personal prayer, teaching, and study? If not, where does it come from and how do you make it work for you?

   _____

2. The Bible says that "without faith it is impossible to please God." Can't you simply please God by "being good" and going to church? How do you personally live by faith? What does that look like in your life?

   _____

   _____

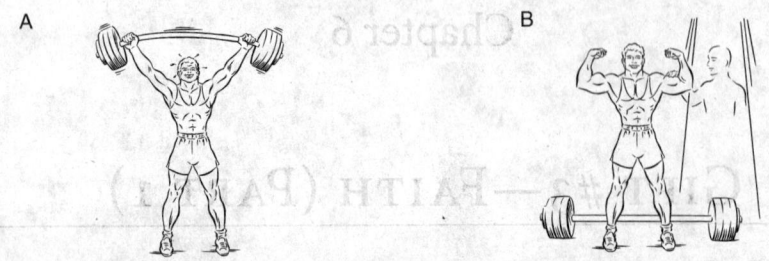

"No pain, no gain"; however, when you do gain you please God.

3. If exercising your faith is similar to physical exercise, what causes you to "break a sweat" spiritually speaking? What benefits do you receive from this exercise and how do you receive them?

_____

_____

_____

Praying in what you hope for is an action of faith.

4. How does the analogy of the Grand Canyon apply to faith? What does it mean in your life to "pack the car" or "fill it with gas"? Briefly describe a few ways you have acted or will act in faith.

_____

_____

_____

5. Most people take great care and pride in their homes; most would never invest money in a property with a bad, unstable foundation. Yet what are some ways that you have invested in property built on sand?

_____

_____

_____

Have faith in going down God's path, for that is where your heavenly Father has hidden your rewards.

6. Do you have faith to stay on the path God lays out for you until you reach your reward? What about when the path is tiring or painful, or the rewards don't initially seem apparent? How about when you have to wait a long time? Can you think of some examples where you've struggled to walk down God's path of faith?

_____

_____

_____

_____

_____

_____

7. Is it possible for you to find joy during a trial? Is it possible to "count it pure joy" in the midst of pain? Based on your response to trials, do you think that would change the way others thought of you in those trials? Who is the best source to get answers from when trials come your way?

_____

_____

_____

Look for the opportunity in your trouble—a good attitude alone will always be a witness of Him in you to others.

8. Can having faith in God's good intentions allow you to have joy during troubles? How can faith encourage you to find the good in those trials, or build you up? Can faith encourage you to better please God?

_____

_____

_____

_____

9. How can looking to God's history within the Bible help build your faith?

_____

_____

_____

EVOLUTION

CREATION

Are all your beliefs consistent with God's story you're telling?

10. Are you prepared to give an account for the hope you have within you that is consistent with the Bible?

_____

_____

_____

_____

_____

11. The Bible says that "faith without action is dead." You read many stories in the Bible where people's actions of faith moved God. What does an action of faith look like in your own life? Think also beyond church-related activities.

_____

_____

_____

_____

_____

What seems bad to you at times often brings good things.

12. Has this fallen world tested your faith through a major trial? Has this change brought you closer to God or have you let it drive you further away? In what ways? How could you have used these circumstances to make your relationship closer and more intimate? Can you visualize this in future circumstances?

_____

_____

_____

## ACTION STEPS

What are some ways you currently act on faith? What are practical steps you can take to be more intentional in your actions of faith? Are there some things you're currently struggling with that you need to trust God for? List those here and take a moment to pray for faith and God's will in these areas of your life.

_____

_____

_____

_____

## CLOSING PRAYER

(Pray this prayer or pray your own to close this study time.)

Father, thank You for the gift of faith. Help me to grow in faith and learn to trust You with the things I don't understand.

What seems bad to you at times often brings good things.

# Chapter 7

# GIFT #3—FAITH (PART 2)

## HOW CAN YOU STRENGTHEN YOUR FAITH?

### STUDY QUESTIONS

1. In Matthew 17:20, Jesus says that with faith "nothing is impossible for you." If you believed this without reservation, what would change?

_____

_____

_____

2. What does it take to get mountain-moving faith? Is mountain-moving faith different from what you are doing now? Why or why not? What are the key components to a mountain-moving faith?

_____

_____

_____

_____

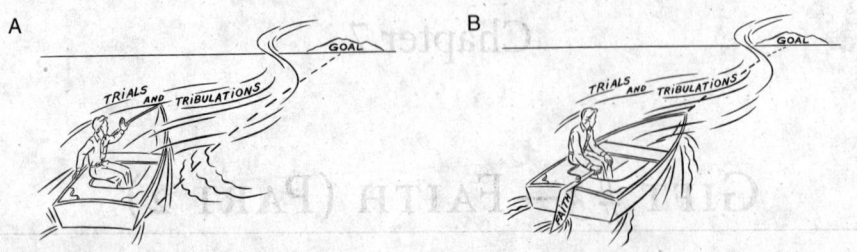

Your unwavering faith will act as a rudder to keep you on course.

3. How can pockets of doubt affect your mind, desires, heart, words, and actions? How can that affect your faith?

_____

_____

_____

_____

_____

4. What does it mean to "align your words and heart"? How do you do that? Write an example of this from your own life.

_____

_____

_____

_____

_____

_____

_____

Faithless words can stop you from reaching your goals.

5. Our faithless speech has an impact on our hearts and minds. Are there some nonverbal ways you live faithlessly? What can you do to change those areas?

_____

_____

_____

A       B

To reach your goals, you need a clear vision of who you are in Christ. This will then be reflected in your actions and the results you achieve.

6. How can you use the visualization process to get to the place God wants you to be? How will you work this into your daily life?

_____

_____

_____

_____

7. Respond to this statement: A real relationship with God demands that you line up your actions each day, not just when it seems convenient.

_____

_____

_____

He is there all the time wanting to be engaged in your life.

8. What are ways you can develop a daily, ongoing connection with God's presence? If this is something you would like, what are some steps you can take?

_____

_____

_____

9. Do you see examples in your life of the "five challenges" to your faith discussed in the chapter? List examples to each of the challenges.

_____

_____

_____

When you hit bumps in life, does God's love come out of you?

10. Do you hear what God is saying to you through your daily circumstances? Are you making a genuine attempt to listen? List some areas where you think God may be speaking to you (i.e., job, friendship, family, or events).

_____

_____

_____

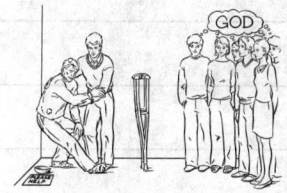

There is resurrection power in your testimony.

11. What was your reaction to the story of the lame man at the gate called Beautiful? Maybe you're not paralyzed, but in what way could your life be related to his?

_____

_____

_____

12. Does God ultimately offer us grace and mercy with the thoughts, actions, and habits we're having trouble eliminating? Why? What is ultimately most important to Him?

_____

_____

_____

## ACTION STEPS

List some of the current struggles you're facing. Could they be pointing you back to God? Think of the caterpillar and its struggle from cocoon to flight. How does your faith in God's good intentions help you deal with those struggles? Are there actions you can do today to help build a stronger faith for facing difficult times? Make a note of those here.

_____

_____

_____

_____

## CLOSING PRAYER

(Pray this prayer or pray your own to close this study time.)

Lord, thank You for placing a gift in all the struggles I'm facing, and for letting me know how I can unwrap them. Help me to align my heart and actions so they are in line with Your will for my life.

# Chapter 8

# GIFT #4—ADVERSITY

## HOW CAN FAITH TURN ADVERSITY INTO VICTORY?

1. Does God bring adversity, or do you mostly bring it on yourself? When you do something stupid that causes adversity, does God put some form of gift in it to offer you redemption?

_____

_____

_____

2. If you are facing adversity, has God turned His back on you? If God is good and loving, then why does He allow adversity in your life?

_____

_____

_____

Everybody knows experience helps you reach your goals, which, in turn, will help you reach your purpose.

3. What are some of the gifts God puts within adversities that can help strengthen and redeem your life and relationship with Him?

_____

_____

4. List the adversities you are facing right now. Will you look for a gift in them?

_____

_____

5. Are you letting life experiences govern your attitude and vision? In what ways are you letting life circumstances affect you from the outside in? What does a life that works from the inside out look like?

_____

_____

6. Look at the story of David and Goliath. David's character exhibited an extraordinary faith. What are some Goliath-like problems or struggles that seem insurmountable? How could they be strengthening you or creating a testimony?

_____

_____

7. How did David develop his faith over time? How did overcoming the problems build up his faith? What made him different from the others in Saul's army? What makes you different from the rest of the world?

_____

_____

_____

> Act in faith when you're hit. Act in faith when you get knocked down. Act in faith when God provides the path to victory, even if it seems unusual.

8. In your trials, battles, and adversities, are you open to using untraditional weapons or solutions that God may offer you? Like David, are you open to creating a new testimony with Him?

_____

_____

_____

_____

_____

Abraham was willing and Jesus was willing in faith to sacrifice their futures for God's will in their lives—are you?

9. What causes you to doubt? What is the remedy for that doubt?

_____

_____

_____

_____

_____

10. Consider your own relationship with those you love. How has your faith in them cultivated your relationship? How does this relate to developing intimacy with God?

_____

_____

_____

_____

_____

_____

Your greatest defeat could be your greatest victory!

11. In the case of relationships between a loving Creator and His created, wouldn't it make sense for the created to yield to the Creator for its own good and the good of the relationship? How can you align yourself with God's will today? What areas in your life are you currently holding off limits?

_____

_____

_____

_____

12. God's resurrection power turns adversity into victory. How do you turn adversity into victory? What are some areas of your life that need victory?

_____

_____

_____

_____

## ACTION STEPS

Spend some time reading about David's faith. Consider what impresses you most about his actions. What can you learn from his faith? How can you work toward building up a similar faith? If there are some obstacles or adversities in your life today, think of ways to use them for your benefit. List your thoughts here.

_____

_____

_____

_____

_____

## CLOSING PRAYER

(Pray this prayer or pray your own to close this study time.)

Father, thank You so much for the gift of faith and the role it plays in helping me open the gift of adversity. Allow me to clearly see the gifts in all my adversities. Grant me a portion of faith that will allow me to do all those things You desire for me to do, and let me see how to use that faith to accomplish them.

# Understanding Provision, Communication, and Death

## Book 2

# PREFACE

During the Christmas season, gold, frankincense, and myrrh may not be on your shopping list, but they represent priceless gifts God offers you—just as He gave His Son two thousand years ago. Fully understanding what these gifts represent (provision, communication, and death) will allow you to release God's fullness into your life.

In a society that appears to be abundant and wealthy, why is it that so many people lack purpose, peace, and true intimacy with their Creator? Without this essential connection to truth, isn't real, heartfelt wealth impossible? Well, the book you're now holding seeks to untangle the freedom-giving gifts, which, if accepted, will connect you to your Creator in a new, life-changing way—a true bond even most believers fail to make.

This holiday season, growing in His likeness and regaining purpose and meaning does not need to be merely a Christmas "wish." Jesus did not die to make you and me "wish" for freedom; instead, He freely offers abundance, healing, and wholeness to each of us—this is the life He destined for us to receive. Will you accept His gifts that will lead you to this new life?

# INTRODUCTION

## BOOK 1: IN THE BEGINNING

In Book 1, we looked at how we were created by God to be in relationship with Him—a relationship of mutual love. Originally, this was easy because Adam and Eve were created in His image and likeness, and they enjoyed a spirit-to-Spirit connection with Him. This allowed them to keep His essence of love alive within them. They radiated with God's love in a pure and intimate relationship with their Creator. God gave them freedom of choice, with free will that allowed them to love and choose perfect love or to reject His will for their lives and thus sin. They rebelled and chose to reject God (see Genesis 3).

Today many people still reject Him, much like Adam and Eve, because they believe they are wiser, they can work their lives out on their own, and have a better plan than their Creator. However, God's desire is for His creation to *thrive* by walking with His Spirit's guidance and according to instruction from His Word.

When Adam and Eve disobeyed God, they brought sin into the world—that is, they brought into this world things that were outside God's perfect plan. They opened Pandora's Box. With sin came death and humankind's bondage in and to this world. Then humanity had to toil, work, and sweat in order to survive, having lost a functioning spirit-to-Spirit connection with God. As humans, we brought this curse upon ourselves, and our daily experience of it brings us back to the truth—we need God. The trouble is that we can't find God on our own. Our only hope of getting back on course is in salvation through Jesus Christ. His death on the cross, through the gift of grace, gives us the opportunity for new life and complete forgiveness of our sins—if we will accept it.

When we receive this first gift of life through the gift of grace, we accept the second with it—the gift of the Holy Spirit. Indeed, this spirit-to-Spirit connection is the vehicle for achieving real intimacy with Him. His image and likeness can once again exude from our lives with a real-time connection. It is through the Holy Spirit that we receive the other gifts, too, except for the gift of faith.

The gift of faith is given to everyone at birth, but it must be received, unwrapped, and used in our relationship with God if it is to bring forth life. Faith is a verb, an action word; that's the only way to use it! An action of faith in God pleases Him; it's the key to His heart (see Hebrews 11:6). This means that we live out and act upon His promises as if our lives depended on it. Our actions please God because the gift of faith is the foundation on which we live, allowing us to unwrap and unleash all the other gifts available to us while we're here on earth.

The first gift we can unwrap with our faith is the gift of adversity. In all adversity, no matter what the cause, God has embedded some form of potential redemption that we can unwrap.

## BOOK 2: WHERE DO WE GO FROM HERE?

The gift of new life in Jesus is just that—a new and unfamiliar way of living. Jesus called it becoming "born again." If that is truly what you are, just like a newborn, you now need to learn how to crawl, walk, run, live, and eat. How do children learn these essential components to life? They learn them by being willing to accept guidance, teaching, and help until they are mature and can stand on their own.

If Book 1 is about building a spiritual foundation, then Book 2 involves assessing and using the materials to build a solid spiritual home. What will you need to construct a strong, vibrant relationship with Him? How do we assemble our lives around God's specific plan and the destiny He has given to you and me? How is God's power made alive in us? At Jesus' birth, the wise men brought Him gifts of gold, frankincense, and myrrh. These gifts were symbolic and practically used by Jesus and His family. They were vital gifts. Today, these gifts are still just as essential to His family—you and me!

Gold represents God's commitment to provide for our needs; frankincense is our primary means of contact with Him through praise, worship, and prayer; and myrrh represents the building blocks for a Spirit-filled life—dying to self so we can correctly see the Creator's plan for our lives and how to overcome the struggles we face getting there. God has made these gifts available to you today. Will you open and receive them?

If you are hungry for growth, spiritual nourishment, and guidance in life's most important relationship, then this is the place to begin. Our calling is to intimacy, strength, and diligence to run with God—not to limp and crawl through life as so many have chosen to do.

This is the second book in The Gifts of Freedom series. These three books were written to help and guide you along your spiritual journey. They were written to connect you with the missing pieces that have kept many churchgoers spiritual infants. As you read these three books in unison, and dig deeper with the study guide, you can and will find your true calling—becoming a warrior for God.

Remember, there is no need to speed through this book. Take the time you need and allow God to interact with you as you consider the biblical truths He presents to you. Also consider how each of the Action and Visualizations I offer throughout each chapter can work for a long-term change in your life. These are meant to be a time to pause and apply to your life what you read. Perhaps sometimes it's a good point to lay the book down and live out what you just read.

Let's unwrap these next three gifts.

*Therefore, holy brothers, who share in the heavenly calling, fix your thoughts on Jesus, the apostle and high priest whom we confess. He was faithful to the one who appointed Him [God], just as Moses was faithful in all God's house. Jesus has been found worthy of greater honor than Moses, just as the builder of a house has greater honor than the house itself. For every house is built by someone, but* **God is the builder of everything.** *Moses was faithful as a servant in all God's house, testifying to what would be said in the future. But Christ is faithful as a son over God's house.* **And we are His house, if we hold on to our courage and hope of which we boast** (Hebrews 3:1-6).

# Chapter 1

# GIFT #5—GOLD (PART 1)

## HOW DOES YOUR RELATIONSHIP WITH GOD RELATE TO GETTING YOUR NEEDS MET?

Before you begin to read, pray that the Holy Spirit
will give you understanding and application.

✞ *After Jesus* [who in John 6:35 said He is the Bread of Life] *was born in Bethlehem* [which means the "house of bread"] *in Judea, during the time of King Herod, Magi* [wise men] *from the east came to Jerusalem and asked, "Where is the One who has been born King of the Jews? We saw His star in the east and have come to worship Him."...*

*On coming to the house, they saw the Child with His mother Mary, and they bowed down and worshiped Him. Then they opened their treasures and presented Him with **gifts of gold** and of **incense** and of **myrrh*** (Matthew 2:1-2,11).

We've all felt the anxiety that goes together with gift giving. We fear the recipient will not like the gift, will return it, or simply find it unusable. As the recipient is tearing open the package, questions buzz through our minds: "Did I get the right size sweater?" "Does he already have a cordless drill?" "Does she even wear pierced earrings?" We can't hide the truth that we want to give those we love the perfect gift—something that says, "I know you and I know what you like." This is why we often ask, "How do you like it?" Well, God wants His gifts to be perfect as well. He knows where you are and what you need. The Bible tells us His gifts are good, though sometimes they may seem unusable until we bring our faith into play.

You've probably heard the Christmas story about the wise men who brought gifts to baby Jesus. But have you ever wondered why these men gave gifts of gold, frankincense, and myrrh to a newborn? When you think of baby gifts, you probably think of rattles, colorful toys, and baby clothes—age-appropriate items that have a practical purpose. Gold, frankincense, and myrrh seem like foolish gifts, right? I hope they saved the receipt. Yet we know the men who brought these gifts weren't fools; they were *wise* men. The Bible tells us God was leading them in their journey; they were also following God's leading in their gift selections.

Clearly the gifts were to send a larger message to people, both then and now, that a King had been born. Upon a closer look, these three gifts also hold a deeper meaning, with a life-changing application. Each of the three gifts relays an important message, an essential truth that is critical to our journey with God—just as the bright star did for the wise men.

## GOLD

Immediately after Jesus' birth, the Lord appeared to Joseph in a dream, saying:

✝ *Arise, take the young Child and His mother, flee to Egypt, and stay there until I bring you word; for Herod will seek the young Child to destroy Him* (Matthew 2:13 NKJV).

Satan was out to destroy Jesus at His birth, just as he is out to destroy all people who follow God now. The gift of gold Jesus was given turned out to be an immediately usable gift, as it filled Jesus' and His family's financial needs. It gave them the means to flee to Egypt and stay there so King Herod would not be able to kill Jesus. As you go through life as a Christian, you will learn time and time again that God will fulfill your needs (sometimes just as they arise).

Let's look at the primary message God is offering us with this gift. In Jesus' day, gold was used as a means of monetary exchange—a type of currency. Today we use money as our currency, as our medium of exchange to fulfill needs. God used this gift to illustrate that He would fulfill Jesus' physical needs and likewise that He would fulfill *our* physical needs. Now it's important to note that these needs are often fulfilled as they arise. This keeps our relationship with God dynamic and intimate. Throughout Jesus' life and ministry, God met His needs. We catch glimpses in the Bible that Jesus' ministry was well provided for by those who surrounded Jesus.

The gospel writer Luke relays an event where Jesus was preaching and ministering to a large crowd (about five thousand men, plus women and children). As the day went on, the disciples were worried about the crowd getting fed since they were miles from a food supply. Even McDonald's wouldn't have been able to fill such a huge order on the spot! Jesus said to His disciples:

*"You give them something to eat."*
*They answered, "We have only five loaves of bread and two fish—* **unless we go and buy food for all this crowd"** (Luke 9:13-14).

The disciples' response here is significant: it wouldn't have been cheap to buy food for five thousand men (plus women and children, who were not counted among that five thousand; in the culture of the time, women and children did not have the same importance as men). However, the implication is that Jesus' disciples had the money to do this if it was necessary. Remember, Jesus said that buying food would *not* be necessary. Luke 9:16-17 tells us that Jesus and the disciples could use just five loaves of bread and two fish *with the blessing of God,* supernaturally multiplying it to fulfill the needs of more than five thousand people.

This story reminds us that it is *not* money itself that is important, but money's ability to be exchanged for the things that satisfy our physical needs. If you were banished to a country where money was not used as a medium of exchange, then money would lose its importance or value. Money simply represents the *fulfillment* of your physical needs. In the feeding of the five thousand, God shows us He can supernaturally fulfill needs. Think about it: God wants you to understand that neither gold nor money can satisfy your needs—*only* He can do that. Another great example of God's model of provision was during a road trip Jesus took with His disciples.

✠ *After this, Jesus traveled about from one town and village to another, proclaiming the good news of the Kingdom of God. The Twelve were with Him, and also some women. ...These women were helping to support them out of their own means* (Luke 8:1-3).

Matthew includes a story in his gospel about Peter's and Jesus' discussion of paying a temple tax. The discussion concludes with Jesus saying to Peter:

✠ *But so that we may not offend them, go to the lake and throw out your line. Take the first fish you catch; open its mouth and you will find a four-drachma coin. Take it and give it to them for My tax and yours* (Matthew 17:27).

God doesn't need money to meet needs. Remember, He used words to create the world and everything within it. The wise men's gift of gold represents God's commitment (His word) that He will fulfill Jesus' needs. In addition, those needs will be fulfilled in whatever way *God chooses.*

Through the wise men, God gave the gift of gold as a symbolic message. And this two-thousand-year-old message is still relevant for us today: God is going to meet our physical needs, just as He did for His Son. Joseph and Mary knew that a baby showered with gold was going to be well cared for. The Bible is filled with stories in which God fulfilled Jesus' needs. Do you believe He can and will meet your needs in much the same way?

This relationship between God and Jesus is important to understand because the Bible says we, as Spirit-born children of God, have the same basic position with God that Jesus had.

✠ *But as many as received Him, to them He gave the right to become children of God, to those who believe in His name: who were born, not of blood, nor of the will of the flesh, nor of the will of man, but of God* (John 1:12-13 NKJV).

And as we have already read:

✠ *You can tell for sure that you are now fully adopted as His own children because God sent the Spirit of His Son into our lives crying out, "Papa! Father!" Doesn't that privilege of intimate conversation with God make it plain that you are not a slave, but a child? And if you are a child, you're also an **heir**, with complete access to the inheritance* (Galatians 4:6-7 MSG).

As heirs of God, we inherit what He has. And God certainly owns and produces everything we need. One of the most important things we inherit is provision for our lives.

✠ *[Jesus said], "So do not worry, saying, 'What shall we eat?' or 'What shall we drink?' or 'What shall we wear?' For the pagans [people without God] run after all these things, and your heavenly Father knows that you need them"* (Matthew 6:31-32).

✟ *Though* [the wicked person] *heaps up silver like dust and clothes like piles of clay, what he lays up the righteous will wear, and the innocent will divide his silver* (Job 27:16-17).

✟ *To the man who pleases Him, God gives wisdom, knowledge and happiness, but to the sinner He gives the task of gathering and storing up wealth to hand it over to the one who pleases God. This too is meaningless, a chasing after the wind* (Ecclesiastes 2:26).

✟ *The Lord does not let the righteous go hungry...* (Proverbs 10:3).

## THE PEACE OF GOD

God promises provision to all the righteous ones. When you accepted the gift of salvation, you were given that right standing through your *personal* relationship with Jesus; you were made righteous. It's not just that God gives you the representative gift of gold, the gift of fulfilling your needs; God also wants you to have faith that you have received this gift, that His promises are real, and that you are His child. For it is in *this* confidence that you can begin to experience the *peace of God*, which is another gift God gives to us.

✟ *You will keep in **perfect peace** him whose mind is steadfast, because he **trusts** in You* [God] (Isaiah 26:3).

✳ *May the God of hope fill you with all **joy** and **peace** as you **trust** in Him, so that you may overflow with **hope** by the **power of the Holy Spirit*** (Romans 15:13).

Our complete trust in God for our provision not only gives us peace and joy, but it also allows the Holy Spirit to fill us with great hope. Jesus, the One who makes this peace possible, personally offers it to us with the encouragement to use it.

[Jesus said], *"Peace I leave with you; My peace I give you. I do not give to you as the world gives. Do not let your hearts be troubled and do not be afraid"* (John 14:27).

[Jesus said], *"I have told you these things, so that in Me you may have **peace**. In this world you will have trouble. But take heart! I have overcome the world"* (John 16:33).

You can't experience this gift of peace unless you have *faith* to unwrap the gift of provision. In other words, you must have expectancy for God to *deliver* on His *gift of gold*. To live out this kind of faith is to know, without a shadow of a doubt, that God is the ultimate Provider of our lives. This was Paul's point to Timothy when he wrote:

*Tell those rich in this world's wealth to quit being so full of themselves and so obsessed with money, which is here today and gone tomorrow. Tell them to go after God, who piles on all the riches we could ever manage—to do good, to be rich in helping others, to be extravagantly generous. If they do that, they'll build a treasury that will last, gaining life that is truly life* (1 Timothy 6:17-19 MSG).

Peace is the key to God's power, provision, and health in your life. You need to feel it deep in your heart and speak it from your mouth. This is how we received salvation (see Romans 10:9), and it is how we receive the kind of peace that leads to God's power in our lives.

In 2 Kings 4, there is a story of a well-to-do Shunammite woman who noticed that the prophet Elisha regularly came by her and her husband's place. So she provided a room in which he could stay and food whenever he came through town. Elisha wanted to do something kind for her, but she had everything she needed. Elisha's servant told Elisha she had no child and that her husband was old. Elisha called her and told her she would have a child by this time next year, and she did. The story goes on:

> *And the child grew. Now it happened one day that he went out to his father, to the reapers. And he said to his father, "My head, my head!"*
>
> *So he said to a servant, "Carry him to his mother." When he had taken him and brought him to his mother, he sat on her knees till noon, and then died. And she went up and laid him on the bed of the man of God, shut the door upon him, and went out.*
>
> *Then she called to her husband, and said, "Please send me one of the young men and one of the donkeys, that I may run to the man of God and come back."*
>
> *So he said, "Why are you going to him today? It is neither the New Moon nor the Sabbath."*
>
> *And she said, "It is well" (2 Kings 4:18-23 NKJV).*

In the Old Testament, before Jesus was crucified for our sins, people did not have an internal connection to God. Rather, they sought out priests and prophets if they wanted to speak to or hear from God. When trouble hit, the first thing the Shunammite woman sought after was God. When her husband asked what was happening, she replied amid her deepest trouble that all was well. In Hebrew, she said one word—*shalom*—which translates to "all is well" or "peace." The story then goes on:

> *And so she departed, and went to the man of God at Mount Carmel.*
>
> *So it was, when the man of God saw her afar off, that he said to his servant Gehazi, "Look, the Shunammite woman! Please run now*

*to meet her, and say to her, 'Is it well with you? Is it well with your husband? Is it well with the child?'"*
*And she answered, "It is well" (2 Kings 4:25-26).*

When the average mother would be in historical fear about this situation, the Shunammite spoke out the peace that all would be well. How was she not terrifyingly afraid? It's because she spoke what she believed and believed what she spoke.

In Hebrew, the word for *fear* is *pehed,* which is spelled with three letters—*pey,* which sign is a mouth; *chat* represents fence or shut in; and *dilet's* symbol is a door or an opening. What we see in the word *fear* is a closed mouth or a paralyzed state. However, the Shunammite woman spoke her confidence in God. In Hebrew, the word *fearless* or *lopaxad* has the same three letters, with two additional ones: *vav* or nail is in the center of the word *fear,* and *tav* or the symbol of the cross or complete work is at the end. There is a wonderful illustration of these words in the gospel of John. After Jesus was killed, the disciples were shut up inside for fear of what would happen next:

*Then, the same day at evening, being the first day of the week, when the doors were shut where the disciples were assembled, for fear of the Jews, Jesus came and stood in the midst, and said to them, "Peace be with you." When He had said this, He showed them His hands and His side. Then the disciples were glad when they saw the Lord (John 20:19-20 NKJV).*

We see an example of the word *fear* here when the disciples were huddled behind the shut door; however, the picture changes to fearlessness when Jesus is added to the midst of them and they see the proof of the work of the cross by looking at the nail and spear holes in His body. In a similar way, the Shunammite woman's peace was rewarded when Elisha laid on her son and brought him back to life. Peace is a God-centered dependence, a position of surrender to the Lord. It is only in this place where you can experience His supernatural peace in the face of any storm.

How could you possibly enjoy an amusement park roller-coaster ride if you didn't have faith in its tracks and structure? In fact, you'd probably be too afraid to ride if you felt that the roller coaster could spontaneously spin out of control and derail. You can enjoy the ride because you trust the tracks will keep you from careening off the ride to certain death. This is the same kind of trust and faith we need to have in God. He is our "track" in life. Yes, life has a lot of ups and downs, as well as sharp corners, but those who earnestly seek Him, listen, and obey can know they will not fly off His track and therefore have peace in life. Even during the scarier parts of this ride, your spirit connection with God can intimately connect to God's Spirit so that you will know His peace—that peace will allow for life to be both *exciting* and *joyful* at the same time.

It is much easier for us to fulfill our purpose when we know the *peace of God*. This peace brings *patience* as God works out and unfolds His plan for our lives. It keeps us from acting out of desperation and doing something that goes against God's will. Confidence that God will come through (though in *His* time, not ours) helps us resist the temptation to lie, steal, or prostitute ourselves to get what we need. We have *power* and *freedom* when we truly enter this *peace*—power *over* satan and freedom *from* temptation. This is why James tells us:

✠ *Resist the devil, and he will flee from you* (James 4:7).

Right after I became a Christian, I went through a difficult financial time. I lost my nonessential possessions one by one. I had all the reasons in the world to worry about how our family would survive. And I did worry—I worried as all my hopes seemed to derail. However, thankfully, I also experienced many moments—when in prayer, in worship, or while reading the Bible—when my spirit enjoyed faith. This gave me confidence in God's ability to meet my needs despite the seemingly impossible circumstances. It was in these moments when I reached out to God by faith. He sustained me and gave me hope that He would provide a way out so that the peace of God came over me. This certainly was supernatural *peace*, considering the circumstances. It was the type of peace that Paul talks about:

> *Do not be anxious about anything, but in everything, by prayer and petition, with thanksgiving, present your requests to God. And the* **peace of God***, which transcends all understanding, will* **guard your hearts** *and* **your minds** *in Christ Jesus* (Philippians 4:6-7).

There is a reason God tells us to be anxious for nothing. It is because anxiety takes us out of our rightful zone, which is the zone in which the supernatural happens! We know something is wrong in our hearts when we don't have peace. If everything in our lives were lined up with God's Word, we would have peace; the more we line up our lives with His Word, the more peace we will have.

> *Great peace have they who love Your law, and nothing can make them stumble* (Psalm 119:165).

Peace makes it easier to do God's will, and doing God's will gets you more peace. When you have *peace* in your heart, you will be protected from thoughts that are contrary to God's will. It will be easier for you to walk in God's will and not stumble. Faith and trust lead to peace—and peace leads to doing God's will.

There were many times when I was going through this financial valley that I was *not* able to find that peace of God on my own. God still wanted me to have the *peace*, though, so He often led me down surprising paths where I could find it. During the most difficult circumstance in my life as a young Christian, my wife gave me a plaque with this familiar poem:

*One night I dreamed I was walking along the beach with the Lord.*
*Many scenes from my life flashed across the sky.*
*In each scene I noticed footprints in the sand.*
*Sometimes there were two sets of footprints,*
*other times there was only one.*
*This bothered me because I noticed that during the low periods of my life,*
*when I was suffering from anguish,*
*sorrow or defeat,*
*I could see only one set of footprints,*
*so I said to the Lord,*
*"You promised me Lord,*
*that if I followed You,*
*You would walk with me always.*
*But I have noticed that during the most trying periods of my life*
*there has only been one set of footprints in the sand.*
*Why, when I needed You most, have You not been there for me?"*
*The Lord replied,*
*"The years when you have seen only one set of footprints,*
*My child, is when I carried you."*[1]

Remember that in the toughest times of life, you are not going at it alone, but God is carrying you through. And while you may cling to Him at critical times in your life to make it through, it will be Him never letting go that will actually allow you to make it.

In retrospect, the things that happened to me in this period were a necessary part of allowing me to reach my destiny. My career took a big and necessary shift in direction. Some things had to be taken away so that God could get me to focus on what ultimately developed into a new direction. I didn't realize at the time that old habits, thoughts, and mind-sets had to die in order to make way for God's work. It felt like I was losing at the time. Obviously, these experiences were building my faith; however, the building process often involves demolition of that which is not useful. In retrospect,

I am glad I walked this path of loss and hardship; without the struggle, I could not have seen where God had "carried me"—places I would not otherwise have gone.

Today I can see how critical these lessons were to my career and life, even leading and preparing me to write this book. My circumstances shaped my story, and the seeming setbacks became advances that brought my faith to life. Your heavenly Father is with you and watching you *all* the time; His Spirit is within you to guide your every step. When you learn to trust His leading, then *He will take you where you need to go to fulfill the plan He has for your life.*

When you face times in life when circumstances overwhelm you, you're only seeing *half* of the picture. God is always working in the spiritual realm to manifest His will in the physical—the world in which we live. If we could see what was going on "behind the scenes," we'd have a different perspective on these circumstances. There is an example of this in the Old Testament where God provides for His prophet Elisha:

⊕ *When the servant of the man of God got up and went out early the next morning, an army with horses and chariots had surrounded the city. "Oh, my lord, what shall we do?" the servant asked.*

*"Don't be afraid," the prophet answered. "Those who are with us are more than those who are with them."*

*And Elisha prayed, "O Lord, open his eyes so he may see." Then the Lord opened the servant's eyes, and he looked and saw the hills full of horses and chariots of fire all around Elisha* [called by God to help him from the invisible spirit realm] (2 Kings 6:15-17).

As God provided victory for Elisha, so He will also provide for your needs. There is always more to the picture than we can physically *see*. That is why God instructs us to walk by faith and *not* by sight.

## ACTION & VISUALIZATION

*Ask God to reveal the spiritual aspect of your circumstances. Though you may not always see it, continue to trust God for your provision.*

## GOD USES CIRCUMSTANCES

As God gave Elisha's servant a more complete vision of reality, so God sometimes uses circumstances in our daily lives to give us a more complete vision of the reality in which we are living. As I was leaving the house one morning, I thought my wife's car was blocking mine. Out of the kitchen window, it appeared that way, but when we walked outside we saw that it wasn't. I could clearly pass by unobstructed. It hit us both simultaneously: this was a picture of our financial situation! It appeared that we could *not* get the money required to meet our current financial needs. Yet in *truth*, it was just a matter of *perspective*. When I get in a tight spot now, I picture this analogy God gave me. This provides a shortcut to the place of God's peace. With His help, I have reprogrammed myself to more easily find that place of peace when adversity comes.

We have power when we achieve this peace because we are close to God. When we find this place of *peace,* it communicates to God in a meaningful way our dependence on Him. Remember that God is your Father, and though things may look troubling at times, He wants you to rely on Him as your Provider. Proverbs reminds us:

✠ *Trust in the Lord with all your **heart** and lean **not** on your own understanding* (Proverbs 3:5).

## LEARN TO TRUST GOD

When my son was young, he had an old brass bed that was quite high off the ground. While I was lying on the floor below, he liked to stand on the edge, lean out, and fall forward. He had complete faith I would catch him. This is the kind of faith God is seeking from us. Can you see how this kind of faith will give you freedom to live without the shackles of fear? You will be able to go farther out on the tree limbs in your life—out to the place where the best fruit grows. You will also be able to lean out and take more chances when you trust in Him and know His will. God is there below you always. This kind of faith and confidence is what Jesus spoke of when He said:

> *Let the little children come to Me, and do not hinder them, for the Kingdom of God belongs to such as these. I tell you the truth, anyone who will not receive the Kingdom of God like a little child will never enter it* (Mark 10:14-15).

What did Jesus mean when He said we could only enter the Kingdom of God by becoming like little children? He was saying we should not let our knowledge of the world and the prejudices we have built up over time hinder us from believing that God can do anything. You cannot *fully* enter the Kingdom of God, which is within you, without childlike faith—in the case of this verse, that He will provide for you. Just like a child is completely dependent on his or her parents for every need, so we too should express a childlike faith in Him as our Provider. We rely on Jesus completely, and He provides, sustains, and protects. It is like a continuing conversation each day as both do their part—indeed, it is the most intimate relationship of trust because it revolves around our most basic needs being met.

Not only do we gain the peace of God through faith that God has given us this gift of gold, but it is also possible for us to unwrap more of His gifts. We can know the full depth and richness of this gift through expectancy.

> *Therefore do not cast away your **confidence**, which has great **reward*** (Hebrews 10:35 NKJV).

It is important not to merely believe *in* God, but also believe that He is our *Provider* and *Rewarder* if we seek an intimate relationship with Him.

Do you remember worrying as a child about where your next meal might come from? More than likely, you assumed your parents would provide for you. You had a childlike trust in them that this would happen. And this trust strengthened your relationship. In fact, faith and expectancy strengthens any interactive relationship. It communicates to the provider in a meaningful way that you have placed your trust in his or her care and concern for you. Your actions of confidence and expectancy speak louder than words:

[Jesus said], *"What do you think? There was a man who had two sons. He went to the first and said, 'Son, go and work today in the vineyard.'*
*'I will not,' he answered, but later he changed his mind and went.*
*Then the father went to the other son and said the same thing. He answered, 'I will, sir,' but he did not go.*
*Which of the two did what his father wanted?"*
*"The first,"* they answered (Matthew 21:28-31).

It's important to express faith not only in words but also in *actions*. One such action is to have a faith and *peace* in God as your Provider when *circumstances* dictate *otherwise*.

A lack of faith and expectancy communicates a much different message. A child who hordes sandwiches because he or she worries about being fed is saying to his or her parents, "I don't trust you to feed me tomorrow." Likewise, if we horde our possessions out of fear that God will not provide for our needs, then we communicate a *faithless* message to God as well.

When God wants us to grow spiritually, He often puts us through a training process to remove disbelief, a lack of trust in Him as the Provider. You've already read about the dramatic fashion in which God delivered the

Israelites out of Egypt. The Israelites saw God's provision again and again, and yet, after each time, they still questioned God's ability.

✟ *Yes, they spoke against God: They said, "Can God prepare a table in the wilderness? Behold, He struck the rock, so that waters gushed out, and the streams overflowed. Can He give bread also? Can He provide meat for His people?"* (Psalm 78:19-20 NKJV).

The result of this constant questioning represented a lack of faith in God. It limited God from fulfilling the desires He had for their lives. This is why the same psalm goes on to say:

✟ *...[they] limited the Holy One of Israel* (Psalm 78:41 NKJV).

Despite the exceptional way God revealed Himself to the Israelites, they showed a lack of faith in Him as their Provider. Therefore, they wandered around in circles because they could not enter the Promised Land where they would have peace. Indeed, a lack of peace or fear is the opposite of faith; by definition, you must have faith to enter and you will receive peace when you enter the Promised Land.

✟ *So we see that they were not able to enter, because of their unbelief* (Hebrews 3:19).

Instead, God put the children of Israel on a daily training routine to build up their faith enough to enter the Promised Land. Food came from Heaven every night, but the sun would melt it during the day. God didn't allow them to store up the food for the following day. This taught the Israelites to see how God provided for their *daily* needs. Eventually their faith and confidence in God grew. But until it did, they were not able to enter their Promised Land. Even though it was a short distance, their journey to the Promised Land took forty years to complete.

The Israelites had to learn in stages, trusting God completely and then moving forward. This process was repeated time and again to stretch the Israelites' faith. We are the same. We may feel like we're wandering around in life, experiencing the same things repeatedly. If that is us, then we need to *look for the lesson*. We cannot successfully enter our Promised Land unless we truly have faith in God as our *sole* Provider.

We could also say that is why Adam and Eve were not able to stay in their Promised Land, the garden of Eden. They lacked faith that God would provide *everything* they needed. They felt they needed more knowledge than God provided and went against God's will by seeking knowledge through another source…the Tree of the Knowledge of Good and Evil that led us to evil. God wants us to have only good thoughts so that we are only led to good things, not evil ones that lead to death and destruction. It's only through the knowledge that God provides that we find life, yet today people continue to seek knowledge from other sources, as did Adam and Eve.

Jesus used this same training technique with His twelve disciples when He sent them out the first time on their own.

☩ *Then Jesus went around teaching from village to village. Calling the Twelve to Him, He sent them out two by two and gave them authority over evil spirits.*

*These were His instructions: "Take nothing for the journey except a staff—no bread, no bag, no money in your belts. Wear sandals but not an extra tunic"* (Mark 6:6-9).

These instructions forced the disciples to trust that God would provide food, shelter, and clothing each day as they traveled to new places. How easy would it be for you to do this? Do you need a certain amount of money in your bank statement, a certain amount in your IRA, and so on? Is that how you feel confident that your needs are going to be met each day? If it is, then you're going to have a *more* stressful life than if your *trust* and *faith* are in *God*. In fact, sometimes when we have nothing at all, we are drawn closer to God. The disciples were completely dependent on their relationship with Jesus to provide food and shelter each day, and therefore they were forced to exercise and build up their faith. Through this strong *daily* faith came a more *intimate* relationship with their Creator—and with that came supernatural demonstrations of God's power, because with God's intimate presence comes the manifestation of His provision and power.

✝ [The disciples] *drove out many demons and anointed many sick people with oil and healed them* (Mark 6:13).

Wouldn't you like to obtain this kind of relationship with God? It is built on a foundation of *childlike* faith—a foundation of complete confidence in Him as your Provider. By offering to meet all our needs, God is offering Himself as the best companion one could ever hope for. God wants us to *wholeheartedly* accept this gift so we will gain the freedom to fulfill our purposes.

## ACTION & VISUALIZATION

*Show a wholehearted faith and confidence in God as your Provider. Then, when trouble and adversity come, diligently seek out the peace of God.*

As a father, I can relate to what our Father God must feel with us. My children's faith and confidence in me as their provider inspires me. I will never forget the time I overheard my youngest daughter and my son talking about how I was investing *money* in a trust fund I had set up for each of them. They were probably about ten and thirteen at the time. My daughter added an edge of expectancy to her faith and confidence when she said with excitement, "I don't know what Dad is doing with [the money in the trust fund], but I know it will be good!" I can't begin to tell you how inspirational my child's simple exhibition of faith and expectancy was for me. Not only was it moving, but it also moved me to do things differently than I might otherwise have done. She raised the stakes for me.

## Action & Visualization

*Add an edge of excited expectancy to your faith and confidence.*

## An Attitude of Gratitude

The next step with our Provider is to add gratitude to our faith and expectancy. My youngest daughter has developed this virtue as it relates to our relationship. Many of you fathers know how powerfully persuasive thankfulness can be.

People who know my youngest daughter might say that she is spoiled. I really don't say this as a negative thing. She has high expectations for me, and I am inspired to meet those expectations. In turn, I can always count on her gratefulness. Because of what I have learned through our relationship, I now seek to be God's spoiled child. The path to this result is *faith*, *expectancy*, and *gratitude*. You should be careful in your relationship with God, though, *not* to take on the negative connotation sometimes implied in the word "spoiled"—that of *entitlement*. In other words, we should feel expectant and grateful, but *not* that God *owes* us.

I want to further make it clear that I don't believe the *gift* of *gold* means every Christian is going to be rich by the world's standards. We are all designed to experience differences because we are different people who have different purposes. Look at what the apostle Paul mockingly said in a letter to the Corinthian Christians who had developed a belief that when they became Christians, they automatically became "entitled." In essence, they believed that when they were saved they would instantly be spiritually and physically enriched and reigning with God:

✠ *Already you have all you want! Already you have become rich! You have become kings—and that without us! How I wish that you really had become kings so that we might be kings with you* (1 Corinthians 4:8).

372

Keep in mind that Paul went through his own grueling and challenging experiences in which he worked out his salvation. His "riches" did not come from a pile of gold given to him when he chose to follow God. Consider what Paul went through *because* of his faith:

✠ *From the Jews five times I received forty stripes minus one* [lashes with a whip]. *Three times I was beaten with rods; once I was stoned; three times I was shipwrecked; a night and a day I have been in the deep; in journeys often, in perils of waters, in perils of robbers, in perils of my own countrymen, in perils of the Gentiles, in perils in the city, in perils in the wilderness, in perils in the sea, in perils among false brethren; in weariness and toil, in sleeplessness often, in hunger and thirst, in fastings often, in cold and nakedness...* (2 Corinthians 11:24-27 NKJV).

God allowed Paul to grow through trials and develop into a spiritual warrior. That was *his destiny.* His riches were to be found in his *close relationship* with God and in the words God gave him to write. (Twenty-three percent of the New Testament was written by Paul.) God gave Paul a warrior's spirit, and he found joy and satisfaction in the battles. Through these trials and tribulations, he maintained an expectant and thankful attitude. This is the same Paul who suffered through numerous and unimaginable trials and who also wrote these words to the church at Corinth:

✠ *But thanks be to God! He gives us the victory through our Lord Jesus Christ* (1 Corinthians 15:57).

✠ *But thanks be to God, who always leads us in triumphal procession in Christ and through us spreads everywhere the fragrance of the knowledge of Him* (2 Corinthians 2:14).

In the last verse, Paul is indicating that it is through our tribulations that God reveals Himself to the world. Since we are all on a spiritual battlefield, it's good to learn from the apostle Paul's warrior attitude. However, God has a unique destiny for each of us. Not all are called to intense physical suffering as Paul was, just as not all are called to be ministers of finance for the gospel with large sums of money.

In nature, though there are an incomprehensible number of snowflakes, there are *no* two that are *the same*; likewise, *no two people are the same*. It's important to understand each person is unique and has his or her *unique purpose* according to the unique gifts God has given to him or her. It takes many people with many different gifts for humankind to meet *all* its goals and its purpose. We each have a purpose in the overall big picture of God's great plan.

We were not created as God's robots or clones to receive and experience the same circumstances. For example, if you study the lives of Bible heroes, it will become clear that God does not intend all of us to be rich, or to become kings, or to do missions work, or to become shepherds. However, we can be certain that God has a *specific* calling for each of us, an individual *destiny*—whatever that looks like in your life.

I don't want to imply that we don't have roles to play. The fact is, how could we live out our callings if we never answered the call? We still need to sow diligently. But as we do this in faith, God can then parlay our efforts into meeting our needs and sometimes exceeding them. God may give some farmers the capacity to work harder than others, but those who work harder do *not* necessarily get the best harvest. At the end of the day, *God* brings the sun and rain and gives the increase. This truth ought to point us *back to thanksgiving*.

Nehemiah, an Old Testament hero whom God called to rebuild the walls around Jerusalem, organized a thanksgiving choir to thank God as they worked despite their enemy's attempts to stop them:

✠ *I had the leaders of Judah go up on top of the wall. I also assigned two large choirs to give thanks* (Nehemiah 12:31).

The Bible is clear that what sets spiritual forces in motion to assist us is our thanks and gratefulness toward God.

✠ *Give thanks to the Lord…* (1 Chronicles 16:8).

✠ *May the peoples praise You, O God; may all the peoples praise You.* **Then** [the world] *will yield its harvest, and God, our God, will bless us* (Psalm 67:5-6).

We should thank God for these incredible gifts of freedom, regardless of our circumstances at any given time.

✠ *Thanks be to God for His indescribable gift* (2 Corinthians 9:15).

✠ *Enter His gates* [presence] *with thanksgiving and His courts with praise; give thanks to Him and praise His name* (Psalm 100:4).

Thankfulness communicates to God that we recognize Him as the source of the gift. We're acknowledging the giver, and He responds. However, the opposite is also true. An ungrateful attitude is a selfish position that reveals a lack of faith—"I'm the one running the show."

✠ *For although they knew God, they neither glorified Him as God nor gave thanks to Him, but their thinking* **became** *futile and their foolish hearts were darkened. Although they claimed to be wise, they* **became** *fools* (Romans 1:21-22).

It is important to give God thanks in all things; otherwise, your thinking will *become* futile and foolish. Those who don't thank God in the good times foolishly think they have a bigger part to play than they really do. And those who don't thank God in the challenging times are foolish for not trusting in God's good intentions for us and therefore will not find and use the gift God put in those circumstances. Simply be thankful in all circumstances that God has a plan and a purpose for your life that will unfold according to *His will.*

✝ *Though the fig tree does not bud and there are no grapes on the vines, though the olive crop fails and the fields produce no food, though there are no sheep in the pen and no cattle in the stalls, yet I will rejoice in the Lord, I will be joyful in God my Savior* (Habakkuk 3:17-18).

✝ *Give thanks in **all** circumstances, for this is God's will for you in Christ Jesus* (1 Thessalonians 5:18).

We show reliance on God by having a *sacrificially* thankful attitude toward Him. God does not need us for anything. He is simply seeking a loving relationship with us. He is lovingly providing *all* our basic needs. We should acknowledge this, rely on Him, and be thankful always. Look at what God Himself says in Psalms:

✝ *I have no need of a bull from your stall or of goats from your pens, for every animal of the forest is Mine, and the cattle on a thousand hills. I know every bird in the mountains, and the creatures of the field are Mine. If I were hungry I would not tell you, for the world is Mine, and all that is in it. Do I eat the flesh of bulls or drink the blood of goats? **Sacrifice thankful offerings to God, fulfill your vows to the Most High, and call upon Me in the day of trouble; I will deliver you, and you will honor Me*** (Psalm 50:9-15).

## ACTION & VISUALIZATION

*Have a grateful and thankful attitude in all circumstances.*

A thankful attitude knows that God is in control, that His will for your life is good and perfect, regardless of the circumstances you and/or the world is creating. Of course, we don't thank Him for pain or suffering because God wants an *honest*, close relationship with us. If one of your children gets hurt or receives a cut, you would expect them to show it to you and agonize over it with you. God expects this as well, and indeed wants us to do this when our circumstances seem to turn for the worse.

Remember in your times of suffering that He can and will use every circumstance for your good. It is because of this that we can be thankful to Him when we are crying out. When we are crying because of a painful circumstance, this time of "shared hurt" can be a special, close time to bond with God, because it is in those moments we realize we need God more than ever.

## SEEK GOD DILIGENTLY

Acting on faith and being thankful allows us to unwrap the gifts we receive. But you may still be asking, "How do I find these gifts that are sometimes hidden or not apparent?" or "What other attribute encourages God to give and reveal more?" or "What else does God want from me that will prepare me to receive provision from Him?" The psalmist says:

✠ *The Lord looks down from Heaven on the sons of men to see if there are any who understand, any who **seek** God* (Psalm 14:2).

God loves those who *seek* Him. The Bible says He will provide for and never forsake those who seek Him:

✠ *The lions may grow weak and hungry, but those who* **seek** *the Lord* **lack no good thing** *(Psalm 34:10).*

✠ *Those who know Your name will trust in You, for You, Lord, have never forsaken those who* **seek** *You (Psalm 9:10).*

A constant, consistent, and continual seeking helps you sustain your success:

✠ *He sought God during the days of Zechariah, who instructed him in the fear of God. As long as he* **sought** *the Lord, God gave him success (2 Chronicles 26:5).*

Let's go back to the story of the wise men for a moment. It's important to note that they were *seeking* the Son of God—the Messiah. Indeed, this diligent seeking is what led them to travel such a long distance. It's what led them to *find* the Son of God—their Savior and Provider. This same desiring spirit is how you and I will *find* our Provider and the gifts of freedom He offers. And it is in this *unquenchable* seeking that we will possess the territory of our Promised Land (conforming to His image and likeness as well as finding peace that surpasses understanding) here in this life. Conforming to His image and likeness and finding peace is integral to intimacy with God. Seeking is an important part of gift giving and receiving in our developing relationship with God. *Diligent* and *heartfelt* seeking is how we get to know Him better:

✠ [Jesus said], *"Ask and it will be given to you; seek and you will find; knock and the door will be opened to you"* (Matthew 7:7).

✟ *But if from there you **seek** the Lord your God, you will find Him if you **look** for Him with **all your heart** and with **all your soul** (Deuteronomy 4:29).*

✟ *You will seek Me and find Me **when** you seek Me with **all your heart** (Jeremiah 29:13).*

✟ *I love those who love Me, and those who seek Me **diligently** will find Me (Proverbs 8:17 NKJV).*

Those who do not wholeheartedly seek God will be left to their own devices and will not receive the same provision as those who do.

✟ *But for those who are self-seeking and who reject the truth and follow evil, there will be wrath and anger (Romans 2:8).*

✟ *He did evil because he had **not** set his heart on **seeking** the Lord (2 Chronicles 12:14).*

You read in Book 1 that people who are *not* seeking or asking questions will *not* understand the message of the cross or their need for Jesus. Likewise, Christians who are *not* diligently seeking a *deeper* relationship with God will lack spiritual knowledge and understanding—they will be unable to receive, unwrap, and use the Gifts of Freedom to the fullest. Diligent seeking *precedes* a spiritual harvest, an outpouring of gifts and healing. We see from the Bible that when we stop seeking, we open the door for evil. The Bible tells us to be hungry for this kind of spiritual life.

✝ *My son, if you accept My words and store up My commands within you, turning your ear to wisdom and **applying** your heart to understanding, and if you **call out** for insight and **cry aloud** for understanding, and if you **look** for it as for silver and **search** for it as for hidden treasure, **then** you will understand the fear of the Lord and find the knowledge of God. For the Lord **gives** wisdom, and from His mouth **come** knowledge and understanding* (Proverbs 2:1-6).

Seeking is a key to knowing and understanding spiritual principles. When we seek to know God, we are open to hearing what He says, which is a vital part of communication. We bring ourselves into a position to have the most intimate relationship possible. Let the story of Zacchaeus be your example in seeking Jesus with all your heart:

✝ *Jesus entered Jericho and was passing through. A man was there by the name of Zacchaeus; he was a chief tax collector and was wealthy* (Luke 19:1-2).

Note that Zacchaeus was not described as a religious leader or particularly special in any way. Indeed, he was a *wealthy* man and a tax collector (which was considered by his peers as a negative position to hold). Luke tells us:

✝ *He wanted to see who Jesus was, but being a short man he could not, because of the crowd. So he ran [not walked] ahead and climbed a sycamore-fig tree to see [Jesus], since Jesus was coming that way* (Luke 19:3-4).

We too have the same problem as Zacchaeus: God's ways are so much higher than our minds can understand or see. The crowds of influence in this world will always hinder a proper view of Jesus. Zacchaeus did something others did *not* do—he climbed a tree to get a better view. He "went out on a limb" to seek Jesus.

✠ *When Jesus reached the spot, He looked up and said to him, "Zacchaeus, come down immediately.* **I must stay at your house today**" (Luke 19:5).

Zacchaeus was seeking, and therefore Jesus picked him out of the crowd. Did you notice that Jesus said He *must* stay at Zacchaeus' house? Would you like Jesus to come to your house today? Well, *you* are your house, and He is at the door.

## THE KEY TO LIFE IS TRUSTING GOD

Our reliance and trust in our relationship with God is above everything and everyone else—our boss, our friends, our teachers, our pastors, and even our families. Our trust in God as our Provider should be at the center of our lives. There are 1,188 verses in the Bible. It's interesting to note that Psalm 118:8 reads, "It is better to take refuge in the Lord than to trust man." It is no coincidence that Psalm 118:8 is the 594th verse in the Bible and there are 594 verses after it. The message you should "rely on God, not man" is at the center of God's Word.

# MEDITATION POINT

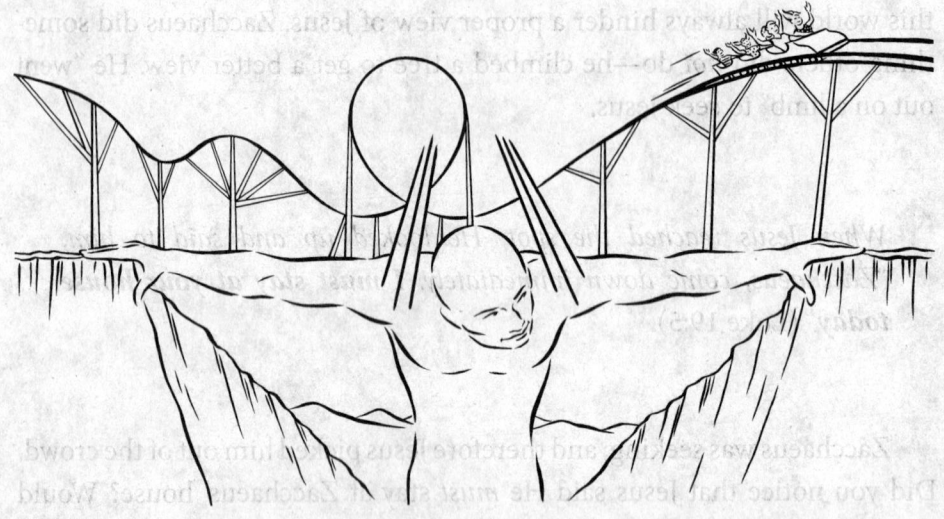

Trusting in God "to provide" sets us free, making the ride of life much more enjoyable.

Go to Chapter 1 in the Study Guide section on page 591.

# ENDNOTE

1. Adapted from a well-known poem called "Footprints" by Margaret Fishback Powers.

# Chapter 2

## Gift #5—Gold (Part 2)

### How Does Faith in God's Gift of Provision Bring This Gift into Full Bloom?

*Before you begin to read, pray that the Holy Spirit will give you understanding and application.*

[Jesus said], *"Therefore I tell you, do not worry about your life, what you will eat or drink; or about your body, what you will wear. Is not life more important than food, and the body more important than clothes? Look at the birds of the air; they do not sow or reap or store away in barns, and yet your heavenly Father feeds them. Are you not much more valuable than they? Who of you by worrying can add a single hour to his life?*

*"And why do you worry about clothes? See how the lilies of the field grow. They do not labor or spin. Yet I tell you that not even Solomon in all his splendor was dressed like one of these. If that is how God clothes the grass of the field, which is here today and tomorrow is thrown into the fire, will He not much more clothe you, O you of little faith? So do not worry, saying, 'What shall we eat?' or 'What shall we drink?' or 'What shall we wear?' For the pagans run after all these things, and your heavenly Father knows that you need them. **But seek***

*first His Kingdom and His righteousness, and all these things will be given to you as well. Therefore do not worry about tomorrow, for tomorrow will worry about itself. Each day has enough trouble of its own"* (Matthew 6:25-34).

I magine what it would sound like if one of your coworkers decided to give this speech at your next office meeting: "Don't worry about tomorrow, for tomorrow will worry about itself." Or what if a movie star got up at the Academy Awards this year and said, "Don't worry about your life, what you will eat or drink; or about your body, what you will wear." Do you think these people would get more than a few strange glances? Some people would call them crazy, naive, or just plain foolish. Well, the Kingdom of God is foreign to the kingdom of this world. Seeking Jesus first is a revolutionary idea, thus shifting our focus from our own work ethic and bank account as our primary means of provision.

Jesus said the birds of the air don't worry about how they'll get their needs met. Why should you? In a world that is often anything but predictable and comfortable, Jesus is offering a greater truth—God's abiding provision as a gift; however, if you unwrap this gift with your faith, then you find an even bigger gift—the peace of God. He is releasing you from worry, that oppressive stress you so often find yourself living under. Does worrying about the future ever make you feel better? Does dwelling on these things add any time or joy to your life? No, it doesn't, which is why Jesus offers us this gift of freedom if we choose to accept it and unwrap it with our faith.

It is common knowledge in the medical field that worry weakens our internal systems. A sense of peace, however, not only helps the body work like a well-oiled machine but it can also speed up the healing process for those who are sick.

✢ *A heart at peace gives* **life** *to the body, but envy rots the bones* (Proverbs 14:30).

Worrying about getting things we want, desire, or envy puts stress on the immune system and makes us susceptible to disease. It also puts stress on many internal organs and thereby causes them to age much faster. There's some truth in the expression, "I'm so worried about my future that it's killing me!" In Hebrew, the root word for heal is relax, so if we want to keep good health God is telling us to trust, relax, and not to worry.

One of the items Jesus tells us not to worry about is clothing. Again, He uses an example in nature where He compares us to the lilies in the field, for which God takes sole responsibility. He clothes them with amazing beauty. Remember the creation story from Genesis? God clothed *us* in amazing beauty too. We had no need to concern ourselves with traditional clothing (or designer clothing, for that matter) while in the garden of Eden. Though we gave up the perfect clothing God had given us in the garden (our light or glory), we will be completely clothed in it once again when we reach our Promised Land. Though we won't know the fullness of that "clothing" (new, perfect bodies) until Heaven, we can get glimmers of it by seeking the Kingdom of God while here on earth. Until then we are clothed in Jesus' righteousness; we don't have to worry if God still likes us when we do wrong or go astray. He is still looking at the righteousness of His Son.

Even though Adam and Eve gave up the perfect clothing when they sinned, God still provided for them—and He does for you as well.

✞ *The Lord God made garments of skin for Adam and his wife and clothed them* (Genesis 3:21).

God also provided food for them in the perfect garden, which the Bible says took care of itself. The garden grew more than just what was required for subsistence. It had a great variety of fruits, vegetables, and nuts to make life more interesting for Adam and Eve. They had what God wanted to give them, you, and me—abundance, so that we can live life fully. When Adam and Eve chose to disobey Him, God said it would suddenly be a struggle to get food. Adam and Eve were out of sync with God, disconnected from Him. This shows up in the way God pronounces a curse on the man:

✠ *Cursed is the ground **because of you**; through painful toil you will eat of it all the days of your life. It will produce thorns and thistles for you, and you will eat the plants of the field. By the sweat of your brow you will eat your food until you return to the ground, since from it you were taken; for dust you are and to dust you will return* (Genesis 3:17-19).

While on the one hand, God says not to worry about what we are to eat and drink for tomorrow will take care of itself, He also says that because of our sin, it will be more difficult for us to meet our daily needs. By definition, a *curse* is that which "calls or brings evil down," and evil is the *opposite* of God's will. God cannot do or make evil because it is the opposite of His will. Given this definition, it is clearly humans who brought down the curse or evil. In response to humanity's chosen actions to defy the system God created, God had to change the way things operated because God is love. Isn't love God's nature, His essence? How is this struggle to get our needs met an act of love?

Well, this difficulty we brought on ourselves by the curse was also embedded with God-written purpose. God made sure it would direct us back to Himself, and it gave us reason to become more reliant on Him, to build our faith in Him as our Provider. In other words, we are more likely to come back into a relationship with Him and grow that relationship in ways that help us physically and spiritually. His loving intentions really are manifested through this curse we created and brought on ourselves.

Since Adam and Eve's sin, no matter how advanced the world has become technologically (better tractors, combines, harvesters, irrigation systems) and scientifically (new strains of drought-tolerant plants or high-producing seeds), there *always* has been and *always* will be a shortage of food, shelter, and water to meet the world's needs. We're on a constant treadmill to gain food, shelter, and clothing because of sin, and it will remain that way until the fullness of God's Kingdom comes—until Heaven manifests itself on the earth.

While God works through our self-imposed curse to bring people to Himself and to grow believers' faith in Him as Provider, we are also called by Him to put that faith into action. By faith, we can make a difference in the world around us—not only in bringing others to God, but also in helping to face the worldwide challenge of providing food and shelter for those less fortunate. This allows God's love to flourish and be seen by others. Consider the way the disciples responded to a season of famine:

✠ *During this time some prophets came down from Jerusalem to Antioch. One of them, named Agabus, stood up and through the Spirit predicted that a severe famine would spread over the entire Roman world. (This happened during the reign of Claudius.) The disciples, each according to his ability, decided to provide help for the brothers living in Judea. This they did, sending their gift to the elders by Barnabas and Saul (Acts 11:27-30).*

We're called to reflect God's love in the world.

## ACTION & VISUALIZATION

*Be thankful for God's provision and seek ways
to show others His provision for them.*

## LESSONS LEARNED

While I was writing this chapter, I received a call from a friend in the hotel business. He'd just received news that a lucrative deal he expected to complete had hit the wall. Knowing I was writing this book, he hoped I might have some spiritual advice for him. He asked, "What are you supposed to think when God brings a deal like this into your life and then, after working on it for some time, it fizzles out?" He went on to say, "It would be easy for me to keep up my faith if I were around when God did miracles by feeding people with daily bread." He was surprised when I told him that the people in Moses' time were much like us—their faith was weak, even after witnessing God's miraculous provision. They only focused on where it looked like God might not provide for them, *not* on all the countless days and ways He had *already* provided for them.

I even surprised myself when I asked him, "Hasn't God done a miracle by providing food every day of your life?" I continued, boldly stating, "When you were a child, you were not able to provide any food for yourself. Yet God gave you the miracle of parents as an extension of Himself to provide for you in that vulnerable period. Like clockwork every day, you were provided for just like the Israelites. Beyond that, God gave your mother the ability to feed you from her own body. And despite the ups and downs in life that may have come since, you have still managed to eat every day." I then asked, "Is that not a miracle?"

As a side note, just days after this conversation, I got a call from a common client who needed to work a deal rather quickly. I lined up something as fast as possible—something that could net me a significant commission. I *knew* this must be God because of the surrounding circumstances! After working extremely hard, this deal blew up in a surprising way. I questioned God, "Wasn't that You in the deal?"

Well, I am certain God was in the deal, but He was *not* doing what I predicted or for what I had hoped. He wasn't helping me get a significant commission but was teaching me a significant lesson: compassion and understanding. The next time I share my lesson on faith with a friend in a difficult circumstance, I will be doing so with much more compassion and understanding. Even though I was telling my friend the truth, it doesn't seem like the truth unless the other party feels you've been through something similar—*that you know what he or she is going through.*

That is why *hard truths* are better given in *compassion* and *understanding*. If the truth is going to be spread and become accepted by the world, then we, as Christians, must experience what the world experiences so we can credibly empathize with the world. Jesus (part of God the Trinity) came as a *Man* to do just that; therefore, shouldn't we? This is one reason why we don't automatically become rich and reign with God in a problem-free state when we are saved. Jesus Himself (the Redeemer), prayed to God the Father that God would *not* take us out of the world but would protect us while we remain in this world. This would allow us to do as He did in the world—gain compassion and understanding, only through which we can effectively show others the way as Jesus was able to do for us. Jesus prayed:

✝ *My prayer is* **not** *that You* [God] *take them out of the world but that You protect them from the evil one. They are not of the world, even as I am not of it. Sanctify them by the truth; Your word is truth. As You sent Me into the world, I have sent them into the world* [to bring Your light and love to those who do not know You] (John 17:15-18).

When we personalize our words with *experiences*, we gain *authenticity*. As we mix the authority of His Word with compassion, we find a powerful balance that is the most persuasive—truly following in the footsteps of Jesus.

## ACTION & VISUALIZATION

*Be confident in God as your Provider, and when things seem to go wrong, be open to the lesson you can unwrap from within.*

## MORE THAN PHYSICAL COMFORT

God will always meet your basic needs, but not always in the *way* you expect or *when* you expect Him to. Remember, our Father is all-knowing, seeing the greater purpose while at the same time exercising your faith. An intimate relationship with Him is His ultimate priority, not your comfort. This doesn't mean God isn't concerned about your physical comfort—He is; it's just that He knows your *character* and *spiritual development* are *more* important. He is walking and leading you toward the Promised Land, where you will ultimately find perfection. In turn, as you get closer to your Promised Land, you will be in a position where you can help others get to theirs. Lastly, God knows your intended destiny; He knows that certain desires you have at times will only slow you down on your journey toward it.

Keep in mind that we don't always see the whole picture. What might seem like a tough road today may lead to an easier one tomorrow. Of course, the opposite is also true. What may seem like an easier road today could lead to a more difficult one tomorrow. For example, not going to grade school, high school, and college might seem to make the first twenty years of your life easy, but the rest of your life will likely be much more difficult. Life on earth is a lot like school. The more you *use* your experiences and learn from them in positive ways, the easier it will be for you later. Since you are going to be in this class of life, whether you like it or not, it's important to pay attention so you get something out of it for your time, trouble, and attendance.

## ENTERING HIS REST

Just as you can receive the *peace of God* through confidence in Him, so you can also enter into His *rest* through faith in Him as your Provider. Remember that God rested on the seventh day after creating the universe in six days, because what He created was finished. God desires that *we* rest as well. On that seventh day, God wants us to have faith in Him that He will honor the work we've done during the previous six days. Because our work in not compete after our six days of work, He wants us to rest in Him on the seventh day, trusting that *He* will give the *increase* to our six days of labor:

*Therefore, since the promise of entering His rest still stands, let us be careful that none of you be found to have fallen short of it. For we also have had the gospel preached to us, just as they did; but the message they heard was of no value to them, because those who heard did not combine it with faith. Now we who have believed enter that rest, just as God has said,*

> *"So I declared on oath in My anger,*
> *'They shall never enter My rest.'"*

*And yet His work has been finished since the creation of the world. For somewhere He has spoken about the seventh day in these words: "And on the seventh day God rested from all His work"* (Hebrews 4:1-4).

*...for anyone who enters God's rest also rests from his own work, just as **God did from His*** (Hebrews 4:10).

God looked at His work after six days, said it was good, and then He rested. On the seventh day, when God rested, everything was not yet final, but He knew it would all fall into place. God made the seventh day available for us to enjoy that same kind of rest, if we have the *faith*:

*By the seventh day God had finished the work He had been doing; so on the seventh day He rested from all His work. And God blessed the seventh day and made it holy, because on it He rested from all the work of creating that He had done* (Genesis 2:2-3).

I can attest from personal experience that this is an important aspect of our faith. This is an area where I've failed, which has resulted in problems for my family and me.

Unless we have faith and focus on God as the center of our lives, it is impossible to enter a restful state because we are too anxious for what we are hoping our work will accomplish, to rest and allow God to provide the increase. Resting in God is an act of faith—one that may seem impossible during trials and tribulation, yet one that we will be blessed for doing. As you have learned, faith is an action. In the case of *rest,* it is an action of waiting and of quiet expectation. When you rest in God, you are saying to Him, "I've done my part (planted the seed and watered); now I am relying on You to do Your part (give the increase)." Your rest creates room for God to work—a sort of "vacuum" He can fill. There is power in rest—God's power. God said through Isaiah:

✠ *If you keep your feet from breaking the Sabbath and from doing as you please on My holy day, if you call the Sabbath a delight and the Lord's holy day honorable, and if you honor it by not going your own way and not doing as you please or speaking idle words,* **then** *you will find your joy in the Lord, and* **I will cause you to ride on the heights of the land**... (Isaiah 58:13-14).

It's when we are in His will, in His presence—walking with Him as Enoch did and becoming one with Him—that we enter His perfect rest.

✠ *The Lord replied, "My presence will go with you, and I will give you rest"* (Exodus 33:14).

## ACTION & VISUALIZATION

*Rest from work on your Sabbath and experience the rest only
He can give you by continually walking in His presence.*

## SEEK GOD FIRST

Jesus said to seek first the Kingdom of God and His righteousness. Once this is established, then all the things we need will be added to us.

Those things we need—like money, for example—should *not* be our priority. Rather, God said that He should be our first and main priority. Job said:

✚ *I have not departed from the commands of His lips; I have treasured the words of His mouth more than my daily bread (Job 23:12).*

I like to say it this way: "Don't look for the bread; hunger for the Word, because one word from God, acted on in faith, can change your world. After all, He used words to create the world." Your world can be changed by God's Word too. God has a plan and purpose that is complementary and compatible with the way He made you. If you are *pursuing* His will, then you are going to receive what He intended. This certainly ought to lead us to thankfulness for God's provision.

Paul writes about another way we ought to respond to God's provision.

✚ *But godliness with contentment is great gain. For we brought nothing into the world, and we can take nothing out of it. But if we have food and clothing, we will be content with that. People who want to get rich fall into temptation and a trap and into many foolish and harmful desires that plunge men into ruin and destruction. For the **love** of money is a root of all kinds of evil. Some people, eager for money, have wandered from the faith and pierced themselves with many griefs.*
*But you, man of God, flee from all this, and pursue righteousness, godliness, faith, love, endurance and gentleness. Fight the good fight of the faith. Take hold of the eternal life [Gift #1] to which you were called when you made your good confession in the presence of many witnesses (1 Timothy 6:6-12).*

Contentment with God's provision communicates to God that we trust the plan He is unfolding in our lives. Our trust and hope allow us to be satisfied, content, and willing to receive His provision that will unfold in the fullness of His timing. Conversely, when we are not satisfied with God's provision, this also communicates something to God. The Bible shows us that God is not pleased with those who complain about their circumstances. Complaining is actually criticizing God's plan. They have forgotten that God has embedded hope and redemption in all events—even the ones for which He is *not* responsible. The apostle Paul said it this way:

✠ *Do everything without complaining or arguing* (Philippians 2:14).

## ACTION & VISUALIZATION
*Be joyful with circumstances, and don't complain.*

In the middle of Paul's discourse on being satisfied and grateful for God's plan, we come to a highly-misquoted verse: *"For the love of money is the root of all kinds of evil."* How many times have you heard, "Money is the root of all evil"? This is *not* what the verse says, however. The verse reads, *"The **love of money** is the root of all kinds of evil."* Some Christians misunderstand the verse to propagate the idea that you can't serve God unless you are poor. This is *not* the truth, *nor* is this concept found anywhere in the Bible.

While many people are poor and serve God, there are also those in poverty who love and worship money. The truth is that you don't have to be rich to *love* money to a *fault*. On the other hand, I know some wealthy people who are generous with their riches, freely giving to the Kingdom. Indeed, it takes money to accomplish many good works. Some of God's people are called to use their money to grow God's Kingdom as God's ministers of finance. Paul had this to say to them.

✠ *Command those who are rich in this present world not to be arrogant nor to put their hope in wealth, which is so uncertain, but to put*

394

*their hope in God, who richly provides us with everything for our enjoyment. Command them **to do good, to be rich in good deeds, and to be generous and willing to share**. In this way they will lay up treasure for themselves as a firm foundation for the coming age…* (1 Timothy 6:17-19).

Paul is speaking to rich people in this verse, and there is a clear pre-supposition embedded at the end that rich people on earth can enjoy Heaven. Rich people are part of God's plan; the *more* money they have, the *more* good works they can do when they invest in God's Kingdom. Here is the overall point in Paul's discourse on "the love of money": don't let your love or concern for wealth come even remotely close to your love for the Provider.

The question is, rich or poor, where are you investing? You may invest in the stock market, real estate, or a business venture, hoping that you see a profitable return. However, an investment in the Kingdom of God is an eternal investment with eternal returns. Listen to what Jesus says about what you are doing when you invest in His Kingdom:

✠ *Provide purses for yourselves that will not wear out, a treasure in Heaven that will not be exhausted, where no thief comes near and no moth destroys. For where your treasure is, there your heart will be also* (Luke 12:33-34).

Jesus also struggled with keeping money in perspective. We have seen that Jesus' ministry had ample money. In fact, His ministry had enough resources to have its own treasurer.

✠ *Judas Iscariot, one of [Jesus'] disciples, even then getting ready to betray Him, said, "Why wasn't this oil sold and the money given to the poor? It would have easily brought three hundred silver pieces." He said this not because he cared two cents about the poor but because he was a thief. He was in charge of their common funds, but also embezzled them* (John 12:4-6 MSG).

The ministry must have had enough money that Judas' pilfering could go unnoticed by the others. Despite His treasurer being a thief, there is nothing in the Bible to suggest Jesus' ministry ever lacked provision (food, money, or clothes) to accomplish its mission. In fact, because Jesus put His total trust in His heavenly Father for provision, all things seem to be provided for in one way or another when needed to accomplish His goals.

✝ *Then the soldiers, when they had crucified Jesus, took His garments and made four parts, to each soldier a part, and also the tunic. Now the tunic was without seam, woven from the top in one piece.*

*They said therefore among themselves, "Let us not tear it, but cast lots for it, whose it shall be," that the Scripture might be fulfilled which says:*

*"They divided My garments among them, and for My clothing they cast lots"* (John 19:23-24 NKJV).

There is a prophecy in Psalm 22:12-18 that predicted a little over a thousand years before Jesus' crucifixion how Jesus would die, and even what would happen to His clothes:

✝ *They divide My garments among them and cast lots for My clothing* (Psalm 22:18).

We often skim right over the little details in passages like this, but I want to pause for a moment and look closely at them. Note that Jesus' tunic was made without seams and sewn from top to bottom. In Jesus' day, only royalty and the wealthy could afford clothes like this. One of either two things had to be the case: either Jesus did not walk around in common clothes during His ministry as is sometimes depicted in pictures, or the expensive royal clothing He was wearing at the time of His crucifixion was put on Him by Herod and the Roman soldiers. Luke tells us:

✠ *Then Herod and his soldiers ridiculed and mocked Him. Dressing Him in an elegant robe, they sent Him back to Pilate* (Luke 23:11).

In Jesus' last hours, His mission was clear: wearing a royal robe, He was clothed in a manner befitting His role as the coming King, perhaps provided for by the hands of His worldly enemy. Jesus was indeed the Messiah the Jews were seeking, but His mission wasn't to rule an earthly kingdom—yet! It was to establish a spiritual Kingdom and to provide us access to that Kingdom through His life, death, and resurrection. In following God's will, Jesus went from wearing a kingly robe to nothing, to death, to rising again in a life without death. Jesus sought God's will first above His own, and God provided *all things* needed in the fulfillment of His purpose in miraculous ways. This He can do for you as well.

Yes, Jesus reached out to the poor, and He had an equally strong message for those who were rich, but, no matter His audience, the focus to both was all about seeking God *first*.

## ACTION & VISUALIZATION

*Seek first the Kingdom of God and then all things will follow.*

## CONTENTMENT

God also wants us to be clothed in a way that is befitting of our destiny. Remember the flowers in the field? There are many types and colors of flowers, and each in its own way helps to create a beautiful mosaic in a field. There is nothing wrong in dressing well or in living well, just as there is nothing wrong in dressing modestly or living modestly—depending on your *unique* destiny. It takes all colors to make up that beautiful mosaic—humankind. God has a role for each of us to grow into. We go wrong when we don't accept our *God-intended* role. We can also go wrong when we start placing more importance on what's provided rather than on the Provider. The *love of what is provided* is the root of all kinds of evil. The verse goes on to say:

✠ *Some people, eager for money, have wandered from the faith and pierced themselves with many griefs* (1 Timothy 6:10).

Seeking riches over God's will causes never-ending problems.

✠ *People who want to get rich fall into temptation and a trap and into many foolish and harmful desires that plunge men into ruin and destruction* (1 Timothy 6:9).

Plus, people who seek riches over God's Kingdom will never be satisfied, find rest, or have joy, no matter how much they obtain.

✠ *Whoever loves money never has money enough; whoever loves wealth is never satisfied with his income. This too is meaningless* (Ecclesiastes 5:10).

So be satisfied with what you have always:

✠ *Keep your lives free from the love of money and be content with what you have, because God has said, "Never will I leave you; never will I forsake you"* (Hebrews 13:5).

## ACTION & VISUALIZATION

*Be content with what God gives you, and do not put seeking riches before your relationship with God and others.*

## KEEP YOUR PRIORITIES STRAIGHT

Paul expanded on this idea of putting the provision above the Provider in this passage from Romans:

✢ *Therefore God gave them over in the sinful desires of their hearts to sexual impurity for the degrading of their bodies with one another. They exchanged the truth of God for a lie, and worshiped and served created things **rather** than the Creator...* (Romans 1:24-25).

We need to keep our focus on God and not the things He creates or provides for us, no matter how interesting, satisfying, or good they seem. It is important to be satisfied with what He gives us each day. In that satisfaction, we will *please God* and *find a blessing.*

Do you have an attitude of expectancy for tomorrow? God is a God of increase, growth, and multiplication; however, getting *more* should not be our primary focus. That should be left up to Him. Nor should we be concerned when possessions come and go. Our attitude, love, and joy should *not* be based around possessions that come and go; rather, our joy should come from within. Its roots should be deeply grounded in our relationship with God—a God-centered confidence that His will for our lives is to prosper us, with or without money or earthly possessions. After all, we came into the world penniless, with no possessions at all; we should be ready, willing, and able to give up everything we own at any time.

Sadly, in our world today, people often subscribe to an attitude that is very un-Job-like. Jesus told a story about this type of attitude.

✠ *A certain ruler asked him, "Good teacher, what must I do to inherit eternal life?"*

*"Why do you call me good?" Jesus answered. "No one is good— except God alone. You know the commandments: 'Do not commit adultery, do not murder, do not steal, do not give false testimony, honor your father and mother.'"*

*"All these I have kept since I was a boy," he said.*

*When Jesus heard this, He said to him, "You still lack one thing. Sell everything you have and give to the poor, and you will have treasure in Heaven. Then come, follow Me."*

*When he heard this, he became very sad, because he was a man of great wealth* (Luke 18:18-23).

Jesus didn't care if the man was rich; He wanted to uncover the source of the man's hope. Was his hope in wealth and possessions, or was his faith in his relationship with God, like Abraham's—willing to follow God to another country, even to offer up his own son as a sacrifice? However, the rich ruler didn't want to give up control of his life or his possessions.

The message of this passage is significant when we think about this Gift of gold, the gift of God's promise to fulfill our needs. We need to "let go" of control and trust God with our lives. This is what Jesus' disciples had to do when He sent them out two by two with no money, no food, and no change of clothes. They had to trust God daily for all their provision. At the end of the story of the rich ruler, Jesus offers this conclusion:

✠ *Jesus looked at him and said, "How hard it is for the rich to enter the Kingdom of God! Indeed, it is easier for a camel to go through the eye of a needle than for a rich man to enter the Kingdom of God"* (Luke 18:24-25).

This is a frequently misunderstood passage of Scripture, mainly because we are not familiar with the context and customs of the time. It is, of course, impossible for an actual camel to go through the eye of a needle, yet we know from 1 Timothy 6:17-19 that rich people can see the Kingdom of God. Indeed, Jesus Himself, who was given many treasures at birth and might have been considered rich by His peers, clearly entered the Kingdom of Heaven. Jesus is *not* saying He has an issue with someone being rich. After all, He is the Provider, and we have seen that money is required to accomplish His goals as it was used in His very own ministry. He *is* saying that people with money, position, power, or fame can easily become their own god, or at least believe they don't need God. They worship and put their faith in that which is temporal. Having more can make you feel like you don't need to be reliant on Him or follow His will for your life because you are providing for yourself just fine. It is important to be willing to "let go" of your possessions or position at any time if God asks this of you. If you can do this, then He may allow you to have more without hurting yourself or your relationship with Him.

One popular explanation for Jesus' parable would have made perfect sense to you had you lived during that time. In Jesus' day, cities had great walls around them for protection. Inside the walls, depending on the size of the city, there were one or more large gates. During the day, these large gates were left open. However, the gates were closed at night for protection. Within the large gate was a small door that was used by anyone wishing to enter or exit the city at night. It has been recorded that this door was called the "eye of the needle."

If someone came with a camel at night to the "eye of the needle" and wanted to enter the city, he or she would have quite a challenge before him or her. The only way to get the camel through the door, or through the "eye of the needle," was to take *all* the baggage *off* the camel so the camel could get through the door. What Jesus was saying was that the rich man must be willing to "let go" of his possessions or baggage if he wished to follow in God's path. The second thing the camel does to get through the "eye of the needle" is kneel, which is another interesting aspect to this analogy, don't you think?

Most of us have problems when asked to "let go" of possessions we have obtained from God. Sometimes we value our possessions so much that they become *part of our identity*, which can negatively affect our perception of our *identity* in Christ. Our trappings and baggage can also negatively impact our ability to reach our God-planned destiny. Do you see this in areas of your own life?

Of course, this problem of "letting go" extends beyond possessions—it extends to habits and even relationships. We all have things God says we should "let go" of so we can enter our Promised Land (the image and likeness of God). Do you know what these things are for you? These earthly goods, relationships, and habits hinder you from entering doors God wants you to go through. We can avoid damage to ourselves and our destiny if we develop the ability to quickly, easily, and without regret "let go" of everything God requires.

Does what you have acquired or what you are holding on to seem beneficial? Remember that just because something is not a sin does *not* mean it is necessarily beneficial. Paul wrote to the church of Corinth:

*"Everything is permissible for me"—but not everything is beneficial. "Everything is permissible for me"—but I will not be mastered by anything* (1 Corinthians 6:12).

He is saying that having some money, possessions, relationships, or habits are not a sin; however, being mastered by these things—loving these more than God—*is* a sin. This includes many areas—even football, which was a favorite pastime of mine that was sometimes in competition with God on Sundays.

The *desire* for possessions is another problem we need to face head-on. This desire, as well as a fear that God won't provide the necessities in life, can drive people to work too long and too hard, leading to an unbalanced life. I can attest to this firsthand that workaholics can damage families, relationships, and health. If people aren't willing to "let go" of whatever it is they are holding on to, they will damage their joy, their relationships with loved ones, and even their relationship with God.

As we go through the process of growing into the likeness and image of God, we'll experience plenty of pain, but our ability to handle that pain will grow along with the challenges. God takes us through different levels of spiritual development, and each level has its own set of requirements. Don't hang on to things that will weigh you down. This only slows your growth process as you move toward your destiny.

*And we, who with unveiled faces all reflect the Lord's glory, are being transformed into His likeness with ever-increasing glory, which comes from the Lord, who is the Spirit (2 Corinthians 3:18).*

## ACTION & VISUALIZATION

*Be ready and willing to "let go" of all things always.*

## GOD'S PLAN BEHIND THE SCENES

We may *think* we know God's plan, but our vision is often flawed—we are often near-sighted because of external realities that can blind spiritual insights. When things look off-track, we may be right on God's intended plan for our lives. Our human vision is just that—only human. If we love and seek God, we are always being transformed into the image and likeness of Him, even when we may think otherwise.

*And we know that in all things God works for the good of those who love Him, who have been called according to His purpose. For those God foreknew He also predestined to be conformed to the likeness of*

403

*His Son, that He might be the Firstborn among many brothers. And those He predestined, He also called; those He called, He also justified; those He justified, He also glorified* (Romans 8:28-30).

We are in a process, a painful one at times, yet we are being restored, healed, and supernaturally changed into Christlike people. When you were a baby cutting your teeth, you suffered growing pains; however, aren't you glad you have your teeth now? I will freely admit it's hard to understand at times; however, God gives us this assurance:

✟ *...being confident of this, that He who began a good work in you will carry it on to completion until the day of Christ Jesus* (Philippians 1:6).

We must unlearn the obsession we have with our physical efforts. In its place, let's learn His way for us and rest in His power, thus being carried to our destinies like a current drawing river water toward the ocean.

✟ [Jesus said], *"Come to Me, all you who are weary and burdened, and I will give you rest. Take My yoke upon you* [have a strong faith in Me] *and learn from Me, for I am gentle and humble in heart, and you will find rest for your souls. For My yoke is easy and My burden is light"* (Matthew 11:28-30).

When things seem too much for you to handle, do you rest and let God be God and do *all* the work? Do you have joy as you live out God's plan for your life? Joseph, from the Old Testament, is a vivid example of this surprising joy and confidence during working through life to achieve his destiny.

Joseph and his eleven brothers were the sons of Isaac (who was the son of Abraham). Joseph had a dream from God that one day his family would come and bow down to him. As you would expect, his brothers became jealous when Joseph shared this dream with them, so they put him in a hole to die. However, one of the brothers eventually talked the others out of killing him, and, instead, Joseph was sold as a slave to a man traveling to Egypt.

When this traveling man arrived in Egypt, he sold Joseph to Potiphar, who was officer in the Egyptian army. Joseph did well for Potiphar and God gave him favor, so Potiphar asked him to run his household. Despite the evil done to Joseph by his brothers, he was elevated and promoted. However, things took a turn for the worse when Potiphar's wife wrongfully accused him of trying to make advances on her. The real story was that Joseph had rejected *her* advances, which made her angry and scornful.

Because of these accusations, Joseph was put in jail. He was down and out again. Perhaps this is beginning to sound like your own story—I know it sounds a lot like mine. While in jail, Joseph met Pharaoh's cook and wine taster and was eventually given an opportunity to interpret a dream for the pharaoh himself. God gave Joseph the interpretation of the dream—that there would be seven years of plenty followed by seven years of famine.

Pharaoh recognized Joseph's supernatural ability in interpreting the dreams, and Joseph was put in charge of all Pharaoh's possessions. This would not have happened unless Joseph had been sold as a slave by his brothers, then subsequently wrongfully accused by Potiphar's wife and thrown into jail, where he would meet Pharaoh's cook and wine taster. Joseph managed the crops well in the years of plenty and stored them up. In the drought years that followed, the country still thrived because Joseph had correctly interpreted a prophetic dream about seven years of plenty and seven years of drought.

During the drought, Joseph's father and brothers learned that Pharaoh had food, so they went to Joseph to buy some, not realizing who he was. They came to him and bowed down before him, just as in the dream God had given Joseph years earlier. When his brothers discovered who this great man in Egypt was, they became afraid.

✝ *But Joseph said to them, "Don't be afraid. Am I **in** the place of God? [I am fulfilling God's purpose for my life.] You intended to harm me, but **God intended it for good** to accomplish what is now being done, the saving of many lives* (Genesis 50:19-20).

We see in the verse that God had been using Joseph's circumstances *all along* through this process to position him to greatness so he could save his family, his people, and many other lives. (Ultimately, he and his brothers would become the heads of the twelve tribes of Israel.) This was Joseph's *destiny*.

On the road to his destiny, God built up Joseph's character. There were many points in Joseph's life where he was seemingly defeated, points when he could have given up or complained about God. He was left in a hole to die. He was sold as a slave to a foreigner. He was wrongfully accused and put in jail. Through it all, though, he never cursed God for these pitfalls or gave up his faith that God had a better plan for his life. He believed even in the bad circumstances that God was somehow behind the scenes working for his ultimate good—being his ultimate Provider. *All* these negative events were required to position Joseph into fulfilling his destiny. And what a great destiny it was—saving his family and the entire nation of Israel.

Fulfilling your destiny will also benefit others, for this is the way God chooses to work. If you look around now, maybe you're stuck in a relational or emotional hole. Or maybe you're in a financial prison—or a real one. Take heart! Just like Joseph, if you keep *heart*, your destiny will be fulfilled regardless of the trial that surrounds you. If it's not good where you are now, then it is *not* the end of your story. Also remember that it is harder to go up the stairs than down them, but going up the stairs gets you to the top.

Look at the story of Job for a moment. He was an upright man whom God allowed satan to test. In the course of that testing, Job lost all his possessions and his children through a series of horrible disasters. Job responded to this calamity not by cursing God but with praise. Job said:

406

⊕ *"Naked I came from my mother's womb, and naked I will depart. The Lord gave and the Lord has taken away; may the name of the Lord be praised." In all this, Job did not sin by charging God with wrongdoing* (Job 1:21-22).

Not satisfied with his testing of Job, satan pointed out to God that Job still had his health, which was why Job could still praise God. To try and prove his point, satan took away Job's good health, but Job still *didn't* curse God. In the end, God fulfilled Job's hope and restored his life with a double portion of the possessions he'd lost.

Through all of this, Job's relationship with God was dramatically improved. Job came to know God as his source of life, his Provider and Sustainer, as well as his eventual Redeemer. Because of his great faith in God, which he maintained through many trials and tribulations, Job has been memorialized in the Bible as an inspiration for all Christians to emulate.

You may ask yourself, "Why did God allow satan to test Job?" God ultimately allowed this to bring His light back into the world. When we take a close look at Job's story, we see that God brought Job into a sort of cosmic arena, knowing Job would crank up the "light" (the image and likeness of God) for all to see, even as satan attacked him. God allowed Job to become an example for us to emulate when things go bad. He was allowing Job to be positioned to give a testimony to all on earth and in Heaven. Seeing Job's light in the face of darkness has become an inspiration for us to do the same. This is why it was important for Job to be an upright man, because a weaker man would not likely have responded in the same God-honoring way. Because God chose Job, satan's plan backfired.

⊕ *Then the Lord said to satan, "Have you considered my servant, Job? There is no one on earth like him; he is blameless and upright, a man who fears God and shuns evil"* (Job 1:8).

The circumstances Job faced were not the consequences of sin. Satan was responsible for the attacks; they were not the result of reaping what he had sown. Satan accused Job of loving God only because of the good things he'd received from Him. While in Job's case, satan learned this wasn't true, this story does remind us that satan is a force to be reckoned with. How do you think you will do?

✠ *One day the angels came to present themselves before the Lord, and satan also came with them. The Lord said to satan, "Where have you come from?"*

*Satan answered the Lord, "From roaming through the earth and going back and forth in it" (Job 1:6-7).*

Satan is at war with God; therefore, as a follower of God, you will be attacked because he is still roaming the earth. Your faith in God as your Provider will *surely* be *tested* at times. Remember that there are examples throughout the Bible where God uses satan's own actions to defeat him. It is in these defeats that testimonies of trust are created. It happened with Job because Job didn't curse God. Instead, *he grew closer* to Him. It happened to Joseph in Egypt, and it can happen to you in your life as well if you keep the faith.

Ultimately, God provided for Job and Joseph even when satan was attacking them. This is the gift of gold that God gives to each one of us—God's promise of provision. Even when it seems all *hell* is breaking loose, we serve a Provider who has our best interests in mind. Paul reminds us:

✠ *And my God will meet **all your needs** according to His glorious riches in Christ Jesus (Philippians 4:19).*

When you are in doubt about whether God will provide for you, remember this passage from Romans:

✟ *He who did not spare His own Son, but gave Him up for us all— how will He not also, along with Him, graciously **give us all things**? (Romans 8:32).*

And when life's circumstances seem to be working against you, ask yourself this question that Paul raises:

✟ *If God is for us, who can be against us? (Romans 8:31).*

## ACTION & VISUALIZATION

*Have faith and confidence in God's provision.*
*And, like Job, praise God in all circumstances.*

## MEDITATION POINT

Even when life pushes you to the edge, God will always be your help and salvation in your time of need.

Go to Chapter 2 in the Study Guide section on page 603.

# Chapter 3

# GIFT #6—FRANKINCENSE (PART 1)

## HOW CAN PRAISE AND WORSHIP CHANGE YOUR LIFE?

Before you begin to read, pray that the Holy Spirit
will give you understanding and application.

☩ *Then they opened their treasures and presented* [the baby Jesus] *with
gifts of gold and of incense and of myrrh* (Matthew 2:11).

☩ *When anyone offers a grain offering to the Lord, his offering shall be
of fine flour. And he shall pour oil on it, and put **frankincense** on it.
He shall bring it to Aaron's sons, the priests, one of whom shall take
from it his handful of fine flour and oil with all the **frankincense**. And
the priest shall burn it as a memorial on the altar, an offering made
by fire, a **sweet aroma to the Lord**. ...It is **most holy** of the offerings
to the Lord made by fire* (Leviticus 2:1-3 NKJV).

The sense of smell has a powerful relationship with the mind, specifically the memory. A special perfume or cologne, the smell of your favorite food fresh from the oven, pine trees, the home you grew up in, your mom or your dad, or wood fire or the beach air—all these ignite our memories. Is there a scent that you love? Most likely, it is something you associate with someone, something, or a time or a place you love—something you like to dwell on. This is the essence of worship—dwelling on God, letting your mind rest exclusively on His greatness, love, and good intentions for you. The Bible says that God loves this aroma we offer up to Him. The scent of our dwelling on God brings Him pleasure.

Incense is used several times in the Bible to represent worship, praise, and prayer. In the example above, frankincense was combined with the grain offering, which was an offering symbolizing God's provision of *all* our needs. Clearly, God is telling us something about the importance of worship, praise, and prayer—our primary means of contact with Him, our source for everything. In this chapter, we are going to look at the sweet aroma we offer to God with our lives, specifically through *praise, worship,* and *sacrifice.*

✠ *That they may offer sacrifices of sweet aroma to the God of Heaven* (Ezra 6:10 NKJV).

✠ *...now that I received from Epaphroditus the gifts you sent. They are a fragrant offering, an acceptable sacrifice,* **pleasing** *to God* (Philippians 4:18).

✠ *Through Jesus, therefore, let us continually offer to God a sacrifice of praise—the fruit of lips that confess His name. And do not forget to do good and to share with others, for with such sacrifices* **God is pleased** (Hebrews 13:15-16).

Jesus offering up His life in worship to God is described this way:

✠ ...[Christ] *gave Himself up for us as a* **fragrant** *offering and sacrifice to God* (Ephesians 5:2).

## CALLED TO WORSHIP

We are called and encouraged to pursue praise and worship. Here are a number of verses from the Bible to show this fact:

✠ *Speak to one another with psalms, hymns and spiritual songs. Sing and make music in your heart to the Lord, always giving thanks to God the Father for everything, in the name of our Lord Jesus Christ* (Ephesians 5:19-20).

✠ *Ascribe to the Lord the glory due His name; worship the Lord in the splendor of His holiness* (Psalm 29:2).

✠ *Bow before the beauty of God, then to your knees—everyone worship!* (Psalm 96:9 MSG).

✠ *Exalt the Lord our God and worship at His footstool; He is holy* (Psalm 99:5).

✠ *Let every living, breathing creature praise God!* (Psalm 150:6 MSG).

✠ *Jesus said to him, "Away from me, satan! For it is written: 'Worship the Lord your God, and serve Him only'"* (Matthew 4:10).

✠ [An angel of God] *said in a loud voice, "Fear God and give Him glory, because the hour of His judgment has come. Worship Him who made the heavens, the earth, the sea and the springs of water"* (Revelation 14:7).

✠ *...ascribe to the Lord the glory due His name. Bring an offering and come before Him; worship the Lord in the splendor of His holiness* (1 Chronicles 16:29).

✠ *Let every creature praise His holy name for ever and ever* (Psalm 145:21).

✠ [Jesus said], *"God is Spirit, and His worshipers must worship in spirit and in truth"* (John 4:24).

✠ *Rejoice always* (1 Thessalonians 5:16 NKJV).

We are called to unity with one another in our praise and worship, because unity brings God's presence in which resides God's power, perfect love, and will. Paul wrote about this to the Romans:

✠ *May the God who gives endurance and encouragement give you a spirit of **unity** among yourselves as you follow Christ Jesus, so that* *with **one** heart and mouth you may glorify the God and Father of our Lord Jesus Christ. Accept one another, then, just as Christ accepted you, **in order** to bring praise to God* (Romans 15:5-7).

This spirit of unity by God's people brings an enveloping presence of God as exhibited when Solomon brought the chest of the covenant into the Temple.

✠ *The priests then left the Holy Place. All the priests there were consecrated regardless of their rank or assignment and all the Levites who were musicians were there; ...the choir and orchestra assembled on the east side of the alter and were joined by 120 priests blowing trumpets. The choir and trumpets made **one voice** of praise and thanks to God—orchestra and choir in **perfect harmony** singing and playing praise to God:*

    *Yes! God is good!*

    *His loyal goes on forever!*

    *Then a billowing cloud filled The Temple of God. The priests couldn't even carry out their duties because of the cloud—glory of God!—that filled the Temple of God* (2 Chronicles 5:11-14 MSG).

The priests worshiping in *one voice* and *perfect harmony* of belief is what caused the glory of God to fall with such a profound presence in the Temple of God. They spoke with *oneness* that God is good and His mercies endure forever. This unity of spirit with God's Spirit is what brings His presence to a church service during worship. You are also God's Temple, so your unity with His Spirit is also powerful and can bring His presence in a powerful way.

Jesus also praised, worshiped, and rejoiced.

✠ [Jesus said], *"I praise you, Father, Lord of Heaven and earth...* (Luke 10:21).

Our connection with God was severed at the fall of Adam and Eve. After sin entered the world, our spirit and God's Spirit could no longer commune and communicate in the direct, intimate way for which we were originally designed. Therefore, we had to meet God at man-made altars. From the time of Adam and Eve until the time of Jesus, humans could only meet God in these specially designated places, and even then, only the high priests could enter God's presence. Jesus' life, death, and resurrection gave all of us access to worship Him freely—a place of intimacy with our Creator. Jesus made it possible for men and women (no matter race or class) to become a temple for God's Spirit to dwell within them.

Jesus told the Samaritan woman at the well about this new change that would take place:

✠ *"Sir," the woman said, "I can see that You are a prophet. Our fathers worshiped on this **mountain**, but You Jews claim that the place where we must worship is in Jerusalem [at the temple]."*

*Jesus declared, "Believe Me, woman, a time is coming when you will worship the Father **neither** on this **mountain** nor in Jerusalem [at the temple]. You Samaritans worship what you do not know; we worship what we do know, for salvation is from the Jews. Yet a time is coming and has **now come** when the true worshipers will worship the Father **in spirit and truth**, for they are the kind of worshipers the Father seeks. **God is Spirit, and His worshipers must worship in spirit and in truth**"* [within the new temple...all those who accept Him] (John 4:19-24).

Jesus was explaining that because of Him, people, with their newly birthed spirits, could reestablish their internal connection with God by accepting Jesus as their Savior. This is what changed the nature of worship again to an inward-driven expression. Praise and worship is for the spiritual realm, where God exists. We must go there *regularly* if we really wish to experience God in an intimate way, which will position us to receive the fullness of Him in our daily lives.

It is important to note that God is *not* seeking worship, praise, or exaltation because He *needs* our praise. God doesn't need anything from us. Paul said:

✞ *The God who made the world and everything in it is the Lord of Heaven and earth and does not live in temples built by hands. And He is not served by human hands, as if He needed anything, because He Himself gives all men life and breath and everything else* (Acts 17:24-25).

✞ *Oh, the depth of the riches of the wisdom and knowledge of God! How unsearchable His judgments, and His paths beyond tracing out! "Who has known the mind of the Lord? Or who has been His counselor?" "Who has ever given to God, that God should repay him?" For from Him and through Him and to Him are all things…* (Romans 11:33-36).

God desires us to worship Him because it's essential in the relationship for us to gain our complete well-being and joy in life. However, worship is of no use to us if it is done in a ritualistic, robotic spirit that only goes through the motions. Meaningful worship requires authenticity of the heart; worshiping in *spirit* and in *truth*.

✞ *Glory in His holy name; let the **hearts** of those who seek the Lord rejoice* (1 Chronicles 16:10).

And in so doing we will receive the desires of our hearts:

✞ *Delight yourself in the Lord and **He will give you** the desires of your heart* (Psalm 37:4).

## True Worship Is from the Heart

Please follow this carefully. The act of serious worship gives us a proper perspective on our place in relationship with God. Just like in any human relationship, we must fully understand and accept the other's position and intentions for the relationship to be beneficial. In the case of our relationship with God, that means fully understanding and accepting that He is our *Creator* and we are the *creation*.

In true worship, it is easier for us to see that we need to yield to Him and His desires if we want to live out His perfect plan. This is a dramatic perspective shift in the way we *view our lives*. It is a shift in our core paradigm, a heart change that needs to happen before God can bring into view His destiny and will for us. Worship is the vehicle that brings our Creator's glory, lordship, and supremacy into *clear view*, and therefore our earthly will and desires fade in the light of His Kingdom, leaving our destiny in sight. Worship counterbalances our body's and mind's natural tendency to focus on itself by shifting our focus on to God, our Creator and planner. When we worship, we are drawn into God's presence, and in this place of power we have direct access to *prophecy, victory, freedom, provision, healing,* and *comfort*. These are things we *need* to live an abundant life on earth.

King David, who is credited with writing most of the psalms, stands out as a model worshiper in the Old Testament. He comes from the tribe of Judah, and *Judah* means "worship." First Samuel 16 says that God picked David and anointed him as king *because of his heart*. Throughout his life, David was a consummate worshiper of God. It is recorded that:

✠ *David...danced before the Lord with **all** his might* (2 Samuel 6:14).

The Bible says David was so focused on the Lord when he worshiped that he lost sight of himself—he danced before the Lord, having no pride. David communicated with God from his *innermost* being, from his *heart*.

Indeed, we see this vividly in the psalms David wrote—psalms that illustrate David's heart for worship. Let's look at some of the attributes from the psalmists that we can incorporate into our own lives. How do we develop a true worshiper's heart?

Praise and worship is something we're called to do *always*.

✠ *...I will **ever** praise you* (Psalm 71:6).

However, we must be careful that our praises don't become mindless repetitions. Don't program it into your computer to just start up in repetition when the music starts. Worship is not merely something that precedes the sermon or part of some religious checklist. It is not a program your subconscious mind starts running at the beginning of a service while your conscious mind reviews the day or week or checks out what's happening around you at church. Praise and worship is *alive* when your *mind* and *heart* are in it, because that is when you can experience God's Spirit in a meaningful way. How effective would your communication be with your boss or spouse if your mind was on something else the whole time you were talking to him or her? Moreover, what if that fact was obvious to the other person? Therefore, God, your Creator and the holder of the grand plan for your life, should have your full attention, thus allowing your communication to be *alive* and *new* every day so you can know His secrets.

✠ *Praise the Lord. Sing to the Lord a **new** song, His praise in the assembly of the saints* (Psalm 149:1).

And God will show up in your praise.

✠ *But You are holy, enthroned in the praise of* [God's people] (Psalm 22:3 NKJV).

We don't have to wait until we get to church on Sunday to worship Him, to find that place of joy, safety, and comfort in His presence. Most of us get in the habit of worshiping God on Sunday, so we're surviving from Sunday to Sunday to find God's presence. However, you can set up your own altar to Him anytime by praising and worshiping Him, with music or without, in your car, in your shower, in your bed, or wherever you are and before and after whatever you are doing.

Remember that going through the motions is *not* true worship. We move our minds and God's heart when our praise and worship comes from a heart that is seeking an intimate relationship with Him. God is in those expressions of worship. And where God *is*, there you can find *prophecy, victory, freedom, provision, healing, understanding*, and *comfort*. Isn't that what you long for in life?

In fact, God is upset when people worship ritualistically with their mouths and not with their hearts. Listen to these important words from the Lord:

✠ *The Lord says: "These people come near to Me with their mouth and honor Me with their lips, but their hearts are far from Me. Their worship of Me is made up only of rules taught by men. Therefore once more I will astound these people with wonder upon wonder; the wisdom of the wise will perish, the intelligence of the intelligent will vanish." Woe to those who go to great depths to hide their plans from the Lord, who do their work in darkness and think, "Who sees us? Who will know?" You turn things upside down, as if the potter were thought to be like the clay! Shall what is formed say to Him who formed it, "He did not make me?" Can the pot say of the potter, "He knows nothing"? (Isaiah 29:13-16).*

It is important in times of worship to be *fully* engaged and not consumed by the distractions around you. Your view of the world should reflect the truth: He created you and every physical thing in the world.

✠ *Come, let us bow down in worship, let us kneel before the Lord our* **Maker** *(Psalm 95:6).*

Allow your heart, soul, and mind to be in sync with what your mouth is singing. Indeed, what your mouth is saying *should* be flowing from your heart.

David was an effective worshiper. His worship came from the depth of his heart; he poured himself out completely to God. God responded to David's worship, which is why we have so many rich and wonderful psalms in the Bible. This same presence of God is available to you in your worship, as it was to David in his. You have the ability, with God through your worship, to create your own psalms particular to *your life*. In fact, much of this book you're now holding came to me through worship. I started keeping a pen and paper with me, taking notes of what God would reveal to me in my praise and worship.

David wrote many of his psalms to express worship, praise, and thanks to God. He wrote a song of thanksgiving that illustrates some important elements of worship and praise. David uses the word *thanks* or *yadah* [yah-dah] in his songs. This Hebrew word means "to revere or worship with extended hands, to praise, to give thanks, or to declare the merits of someone." *Yadah* appears over a hundred times in the Old Testament.[1] Let's look at the first part of this song of thanksgiving:

✠ *Give thanks to the Lord, call on His name; make known among the nations what He has done. Sing to Him, sing praise to Him; tell of all His wonderful acts. Glory in His holy name; let the hearts of those who seek the Lord rejoice. Look to the Lord and His strength; seek His face always. Remember the wonders He has done, His miracles, and the judgments He pronounced (1 Chronicles 16:8-12).*

The verse repeats three major instructions: *seek God, remember and make God's works known,* and *thank God.* Not only that, but there are two repeated themes throughout: *who* God is and *what* He does. By declaring who God is, we confirm what He is capable of doing—we are embracing His nature in our spirits. Exulting God's nature reminds us that He is good and He cannot do evil. This allows us to find His will in the confusing circumstances in a world full of evil and equips us to execute it. And by declaring the good deeds God does and giving Him thanks, we build our confidence and show Him our appreciation for what He has done and who He is. Without a clear picture of who God is, our circumstances will overwhelm us and get us turned around.

## FIND GOD IN YOUR PRAISE AND WORSHIP

Psalm 22 tells us that God dwells in the praises of His people. If we wish to experience God's presence in a real and powerful way, then praise and worship is the answer. The first step to entering God's presence is to become a temple of God with a reborn spirit that has been made alive (become "born again," spiritually speaking).

✝ *Death* [spiritual] *cannot praise You...the living man, he shall praise You* (Isaiah 38:18-19 NKJV).

✝ *A man is not a Jew* [true spiritual child of God] *if he is only one outwardly, nor is circumcision merely outward and physical. No, a man is a Jew if he is one inwardly; and circumcision is circumcision of the* **heart**, *by the* **Spirit** [born again spiritually], *not by the written code* [by doing the law]. *Such a man's praise is not from men, but from God* (Romans 2:28-29).

True praise and worship does not come from the flesh and mind but from our spirit tied to God's Spirit. It's through your spirit connected to

God's Spirit that you begin to understand Him. Remember that praise and worship is meant to give us a better understanding of our place in relation to God. And God Himself must be the one, through His Spirit, to reveal Himself to you. When Peter first told Jesus that He was the Lord and Savior, Jesus' response was that flesh and blood did *not* reveal that to Him but the Spirit of God. It will be by this same Spirit that you will more correctly and intimately worship Him because the Spirit will lead you in areas where you don't fully understand.

True praise and worship is entering God's courtyard, where He dwells, and creating a deeper closeness with our Creator.

*Shout for joy to the Lord, all the earth. Worship the Lord with gladness;* **come before Him** *with joyful songs. Know that the Lord is God. It is He who made us, and we are His; we are His people, the sheep of His pasture.* **Enter His gates with thanksgiving and His courts with praise...** (Psalm 100:1-4).

*Great is the Lord, and greatly to be praised* **in the city of our God, in His holy mountain** (Psalm 48:1 NKJV).

We come before God, the Creator of all things, when we praise and worship Him. That is truly astounding!

## PRAISE AND WORSHIP IN THE HEART

It is wonderful, powerful, and beneficial to praise and worship God in your heavenly language (also referred to as tongues). When you do this, you are communicating spirit (yours) to Spirit (God's) without the distractions of your mind or flesh. Paul wrote:

✠ *I will pray with my spirit, but I will also pray with my mind; I will sing with my spirit, but I will also sing with my mind* (1 Corinthians 14:15).

✠ *Do not get drunk on wine, which leads to debauchery. Instead, be **filled** with the **Spirit**. Speak to one another with psalms, hymns and spiritual songs. Sing and make music in your **heart** to the Lord...* (Ephesians 5:18-19).

✠ *For it is we who are the circumcision, we who worship by the Spirit of God, who glory in Christ Jesus, and who put no confidence in the flesh* (Philippians 3:3).

## ACTION & VISUALIZATION

*Allow the Holy Spirit to lead you to praise and worship in the Spirit.*

## UNDERSTANDING WORSHIP AND PRAISE

What exactly is praise and worship? To find out more, let's look at the meaning of the original Hebrew words used in the Bible. There are two words used for *worship* in the Bible. The first one is *shachah* (shah-chah), which means to bow before someone as an act of submission or reverence. The primary meaning is "to *make* oneself bow." This is a vivid illustration of what it means to take our proper place before the King of the Universe, our Maker. When we are in the presence of God, we can do nothing less than fall on our faces and worship Him, because He is worthy to be praised.[2]

The other word used for *worship* in the Bible is *proskuneo* (pros-koo-neh-oh). It comes from the word *pros,* which means "toward," and the word *kuneo,* which means "to kiss." Worship means moving toward God. In the New Testament, the word especially denotes homage rendered to God and the ascended Christ. Worship is a supernatural act. In the act of worship, we unite with our Creator on a deep, indescribable level. It's a wondrous, mysterious, awesome, and beautiful experience.[3]

Likewise, there are two words used for *praise* in the Bible. The first is *shabach* (shab-uach) which means "to adore," "to glory in something," or "to still, quiet or pacify someone." *Shabach* has two meanings in the Old Testament: praising and calming.[4] The other word used for praise is *halal* (hah-lahl), which means "to thank, rejoice, or boast about someone." In our contemporary Christian culture, we often use the expression, "Praise the Lord!" But what does the term "praise" mean? *Halal* usually conveys the idea of speaking or singing about glories or virtues, or honoring of someone or something. *Halal* is the root from which hallelujah is formed. The phrase is a command, hallelujah ("all of you must praise").[5] The word *tehillah* is derived from *halal*; it is a praise, a psalm, or a song. The Hebrew title of the book of Psalms is the plural of *tehillah*, which is *tehellim*, literally meaning "praises."[6]

## PRAISE AND WORSHIP IS GOOD PREPARATION

When you have effective praise and worship, you break strongholds in the spiritual realm, receiving spiritual clarity in God's presence. That is why good worship at church is so critically important. It plows the field and prepares the soil (heart) before planting the seed (Word of God). Prepare your soil, and then spiritual understanding and growth will follow.

✙ [God says], *"Break up your unplowed ground* [hard ground] *and do not sow among thorns* [conflicting thoughts]*"* (Jeremiah 4:3).

425

Don't think praise and worship is only for Sundays, though. You can praise and thank the Lord every day of the week for the things He is doing in your life.

✟ *Through Jesus, therefore, let us **continually** offer to God a sacrifice of praise—the fruit of lips that confess His name* (Hebrews 13:15).

✟ *But thanks be to God! He gives us the victory through our Lord Jesus Christ* (1 Corinthians 15:57).

✟ *After a meal, satisfied, bless God, your God, for the good land He has given you* (Deuteronomy 8:10 MSG).

✟ *Let them sacrifice thank offerings and tell of His works with songs of joy* (Psalm 107:22).

✟ *Giving thanks to the Father, who has qualified you to share in the inheritance of the saints in the Kingdom of Light* (Colossians 1:12).

## PRAISE IN LACK BRINGS PLENTY

Do you only offer praise to God when your circumstances are praise-worthy? Praising God for the good you experience is great, but remember, praising God amid difficult circumstances invites His presence into that situation. You have the opportunity to access divine perspective, making it easier to take advantage of the gifts within that trial or tribulation.

✝ *Give thanks in all circumstances, for this is God's will for you in Christ Jesus* (1 Thessalonians 5:18).

✝ *We also rejoice in our sufferings, because we know that suffering produces perseverance; perseverance, character; and character, hope* (Romans 5:3-4).

✝ *Consider it pure joy, my brothers, whenever you face trials of many kinds, because you know that the testing of your faith develops perseverance. Perseverance must finish its work so that you may be mature and complete, not lacking anything* (James 1:2-4).

When Jesus was in a place of lack, He still always thanked God for the little He had. You can see the results of this thankful spirit recorded in the gospel of Matthew when Jesus had only five loaves of bread and two small fish to feed over five thousand followers:

✝ *Taking the five loaves and the two fish and looking up to Heaven, [Jesus]* **gave thanks** *and broke the loaves. Then He gave them to the disciples, and the disciples gave them to the people. Then* **all** *ate and were* **satisfied***, and the disciples picked up twelve basketfuls of broken pieces that were left over. The number of those who ate were about 5,000 men, besides women and children* (Matthew 14:19-21).

Remember Job blessed God in his time of loss and lack, and by fully embracing God's plan in the low point, Job could live out God's entire plan for His life…a doubling of everything in the end. Job's thankful attitude also memorialized him in all of eternity by his story being recorded in the Bible. Praise God in your lack, believing in God to manifest His good intentions and destiny for you.

## There Is Prophecy in Your Praise and Worship

When we are experiencing true praise and worship, we are participating in an intimate communication with God. We share secrets with Him and He reveals truth about Himself and about our future together. The Bible says He is the Alpha and Omega, the beginning and the ending. God is not restricted by the dimension of time, which we experience only in the present.

Imagine we are a dot moving down a timeline that includes the past, present, and future. We can only experience the point where we currently are at during any given time (the present), while God stands outside the line simultaneously seeing the *whole* line (past, present, and future). God is seeing *now* at this moment all the things that have happened, are happening, and will happen. He often gives us a glimpse of the what He is seeing on the timeline in our moments of true praise and worship.

Read this prophetic vision given to the psalmist, written as many as a thousand years before it happened, of Jesus speaking to His Father in His darkest hour of torment.

✝ *My God, my God, why have You forsaken Me [Jesus]? ...All who see Me mock Me; they hurl insults, shaking their heads: "He [Jesus] trusts in the Lord; let the Lord rescue Him. Let [God] deliver Him, since He delights in Him." Yet you brought Me out of the womb; You made Me trust in You even at My mother's breast. From birth I was cast upon You; from My mother's womb You have been My God. Do not be far from Me, for trouble is near and there is no one to help. Many bulls surround Me; strong bulls of Bashan encircle Me. Roaring lions tearing their prey open their mouths wide against Me. I am poured out like water, and all My bones are out of joint. My heart has turned to wax; it has melted away within Me. My strength is dried up like a potsherd, and My tongue sticks to the roof of My mouth; you lay Me in the dust of death. Dogs have surrounded Me; a band of evil men has*

encircled Me, they have pierced My hands and My feet. I can count all
My bones; people stare and gloat over Me. They divide My garments
among them and cast lots for My clothing* (Psalm 22:1,7-18).

In all, there are about two dozen prophecies in the Psalms regarding
Christ's birth, life, ministry, and death. Over a thousand years before they
occurred, they foretold with great accuracy the details of these events.
These important communications from God came to us through a seeker's
heart in praise and worship. In your heartfelt worship, prophetic insight
will often come to you as well.

## YOUR DESTINY IS IN YOUR PRAISE AND WORSHIP

If you have this same sort of seeker's heart, then you can open personal
prophecy from God. When you are in true praise and worship, God will
share with you about your destiny.

✠ *You have made known to me the path of life; You will fill me with joy
in Your presence, with eternal pleasures at Your right hand* (Psalm
16:11).

✠ *But when He, the Spirit of truth, comes, He will guide you into all
truth...**He will tell you what is yet to come*** (John 16:13).

## YOUR VICTORY IS IN YOUR PRAISE AND WORSHIP

David regularly accessed God's knowledge and power through his
praise and worship. When David was tormented, he would go to the Lord
in praise and worship.

✠ *Be merciful to me, O God, for man would swallow me up; fighting all day he oppresses me. My enemies would hound me all day, for there are many who fight against me, O Most High. Whenever I am afraid, I will trust in You. In God (I will praise His word), in God I have put my trust; I will not fear. What can flesh do to me?* (Psalm 56:1-4 NKJV).

David shifted the responsibility from himself to God to deal with his enemies.

✠ *They gather together, they hide, they mark my steps, when they lie in wait for my life. Shall they escape by iniquity? In anger cast down the peoples, O God! You number my wanderings; put my tears into Your bottle; are they not in Your book?* **When I cry out to You, then my enemies will turn back;** *this I know, because God is for me* (Psalm 56:6-9 NKJV).

As David indicates, his praise will turn back his enemies and keep him from falling.

✠ *In God (I will praise His word), in the Lord (I will praise His word), in God I have put my trust; I will not be afraid. What can man do to me? Vows made to You are binding upon me, O God; I will render praises to You, for You have delivered my soul from death. Have You not kept my feet from falling, that I may walk before God in the light of the living?* (Psalm 56:10-13 NKJV).

Jehoshaphat is another king described in the Bible as seeking the Lord with all his heart. In 2 Chronicles 20, a great multitude came to battle against Jehoshaphat. This caused him to seek the Lord. As Jehoshaphat sought God's help, he thanked God for all the great things He had already done for His people. He then reminded God of His promises about the

Promised Land. Jehoshaphat acknowledged that they didn't know what to do, but that they were watching God for His direction. God answered:

✦ *"Do not be afraid or discouraged because of this vast army. For the battle is not yours, but God's. …You will not have to fight this battle. Take up your positions; stand firm and see the deliverance the Lord will give you, O Judah and Jerusalem. Do not be afraid; do not be discouraged. Go out to face them tomorrow, and the Lord will be with you."*

*…After consulting the people, Jehoshaphat appointed men to sing to the Lord and to praise Him for the splendor of His holiness as they went out at the **head** of the army, saying:*

*"Give thanks to the Lord, for His love endures forever."*

**As they began to sing and praise, the Lord set ambushes against the men of Ammon and Moab and Mount Seir** *who were invading Judah, and they were defeated. The men of Ammon and Moab rose up against the men from Mount Seir to destroy and annihilate them [the three united forces who were coming against Judah began attacking each other]. After they finished slaughtering the men from Seir, they helped to destroy one another.*

*When the men of Judah came to the place that overlooks the desert and looked toward the vast army, they saw only dead bodies lying on the ground; no one had escaped. So Jehoshaphat and his men went to carry off their plunder, and they found among them a great amount of equipment and clothing and also articles of value—more than they could take away. There was so much plunder that it took three days to collect it* (2 Chronicles 20:15,17,21-25).

When you praise God in your lack and you're seemingly on the verge of defeat, that very praise can bring multiplication and victory. There is an abundance of wisdom about praise and worship in these verses. First, even though Jehoshaphat didn't think so at the time, this battle was necessary so they could end up with the spoils. They simply needed to get God involved.

On the surface, what appeared to be a bad situation became an opportunity to offer praise and worship to God, which would then result in them obtaining spoils from the enemy.

Second, they kept a positive attitude; they maintained hope in the midst of the challenges. This is something we as Christians often have difficulty with. Instead of believing that God will *not* let us down, we simply give up. But we *always* lose when we give up.

Jehoshaphat employed an unusual battle strategy in that he sent worshipers out before his army. Some people put their emphasis on first developing a conventional battle strategy. They make the tragic mistake of thinking, "God helps those who help themselves." Though a popular adage, this teaching is not found anywhere in the Bible! These believers vainly struggle against all kinds of problems, desperately using their own strength, wisdom, and resources. They may enjoy a small measure of success, but they will miss the incredible victory and potential God has for them. Why would anyone want to miss out on that?

You will never soar like an eagle by "clawing your way up" in the fleshly struggle. Instead, you will only reap exhaustion and disappointment. On the other hand, through praise and worship and waiting upon God, you can be brought into His presence and *receive victory.*

✠ *From the lips of children and infants you have ordained praise because of your enemies, to silence the foe and the avenger* (Psalm 8:2).

✠ *He is your praise; He is your God, who performed for you those great and awesome wonders you saw with your own eyes* (Deuteronomy 10:21).

✠ *Therefore I will praise you among the nations, O Lord; I will sing praises to Your name. He gives His king great victories; He shows unfailing kindness to His anointed, to David and His descendants forever* [Jesus was a descendant of King David; therefore, spiritually speaking, so are you considered to be a descendant] (Psalm 18:49-50).

✚ *After the death of Joshua, the Israelites asked the Lord, "Who of us is to go up first to fight against the Canaanites?"*

*The Lord answered, "Judah shall go up; I have given the land into their hands"* (Judges 1:1-2).

Judah means worship, so God told them to first send worshipers to re-cover their land. The same is true with you. When you want to recover your Promised Land in your mind and in your body, God is telling you to first worship. The same is true of any possessions the enemy has taken from you.

## YOUR FREEDOM IS IN YOUR PRAISE AND WORSHIP

Praise and worship can break the *spiritual* chains and bondage the enemy wraps around you. This freedom will *eventually* manifest itself in the physical realm. The story of Paul and Silas illustrates the freeing power of praise and worship.

✚ *After they had been severely flogged, they were thrown into prison, and the jailer was commanded to guard them carefully. Upon receiving such orders, he put them in the inner cell and fastened their feet in the stocks.*

*About midnight Paul and Silas were **praying and singing hymns to God**, and the other prisoners were listening to them. Suddenly there was such a violent earthquake that the foundations of the prison were shaken. At once all the prison doors flew open, and everybody's chains came loose. The jailer woke up, and when he saw the prison* *doors open, he drew his sword and was about to kill himself because he thought the prisoners had escaped. But Paul shouted, "Don't harm yourself! We are all here!"*

*The jailer called for lights, rushed in and fell trembling before Paul and Silas. He then brought them out and asked, "Sirs, what must I do to be saved?"*

*They replied, "Believe in the Lord Jesus, and you will be saved— you and your household." Then they spoke the word of the Lord to him and to all the others in his house. At that hour of the night the jailer took them and washed their wounds; then immediately he and all his family were baptized* (Acts 16:23-33).

Their praise and worship freed them from spiritual bondage and brought them into the throne room of God. They found reason to rejoice despite this bad circumstance. In this case, not only were their spirits soaring despite physical incarceration, but they were also ultimately broken free from their physical chains by the Spirit of God. Moreover, their praise and worship amid bad circumstances broke free others around them, both physically and spiritually speaking.

You may be in some kind of physical bondage, in an addiction, in a bad job, jobless, in poverty, homeless, or even in jail. But no matter your circumstances, you can have *spiritual freedom*. Paul and Silas went to go to jail in part so they could spiritually free others. Are you in a similar situation? Consider if there might be some good that could come from the bad location in which you find yourself. If so, be alert and watch for opportunities God may be giving you in those circumstances.

It's important to know that you may not discover physical freedom from your circumstances in the timetable you had hoped for, or possibly not at all. Learn to accept your circumstances and remain joyfully, pursuing whatever God leads you to do. Even though your body is still captive to bondage, remember your spirit is free to visit the throne room of God at any time you desire. Trust God's ultimate plan for you. Remember, He always has perfect timing. It took the Israelites 430 years to get out of bondage:

✠ *And it came to pass at the end of the four hundred and thirty years—on that **very same day**—it came to pass that all the armies of the Lord went out from the land of Egypt (Exodus 12:41 NKJV).*

## YOUR PROVISION IS IN YOUR PRAISE AND WORSHIP

You learned in the last chapters that God is your Provider. You can enhance your provision when you praise and worship God.

✠ *May the peoples praise You, O God; may all the peoples praise You. **Then** the land will yield its harvest, and God, our God, will bless us (Psalm 67:5-6).*

✠ *The lions may grow weak and hungry, but those who seek the Lord lack no good thing (Psalm 34:10).*

## YOUR HEALING IS IN YOUR PRAISE AND WORSHIP

You can also find healing when you praise and worship God. We can see this in the story of the ten lepers. Remember that only one of the lepers came back to thank Jesus for the healing he received:

✠ *One of them, when he saw he was healed, came back, praising God in a loud voice. He threw himself at Jesus' feet and thanked Him—and he was a Samaritan.*

*Jesus asked, "Were not all ten **cleansed**? Where are the other nine? Was no one found to return and give praise to God except this foreigner?" Then He said to him, "Rise and go; your faith has made you **well**"* (Luke 17:15-19).

Not only was this one leper who praised God cleansed, but he was also healed.

✠ *For you who **revere** [praise] My name, the sun of righteousness [Jesus] will rise with healing in its wings [His tallit or cloak]. And you will go out and leap like calves released [freed] from the stall* (Malachi 4:2).

## Your Understanding Is in Your Praise and Worship

When circumstances in your life seem perplexing or you're struggling to discern God's will, then you can gain understanding through praise and worship.

✠ *If I had said, "I will speak thus," I would have betrayed your children. When I tried to understand all this* [the circumstances of his life], *it was oppressive to me **till** I entered the sanctuary of God; then I understood their final destiny* (Psalm 73:15-17).

If you recall, it was in the midst of challenging circumstances, while still praising God, that Job received understanding, finding clarity involving his final destiny. We saw in Book 1 that challenging circumstances can come from several areas: they can come from sin in the world, sin in us, the enemy, harvesting what we sow, God's loving discipline, and as a result of God's greater purpose and plan. God knows the source, and as you get yourself closer to God through your praise and worship, then you can better receive this understanding of your circumstances directly from Him.

Paul, in his letter to the church in Ephesus, associated worship with understanding God's will.

✠ *Don't live carelessly, unthinkingly. Make sure you understand what the Master wants. Don't drink too much wine. That cheapens your life. Drink the Spirit of God, huge draughts of Him. Sing hymns instead of drinking songs! Sing songs from your heart to Christ. Sing praises over everything, any excuse for a song to God the Father in the name of our Master, Jesus Christ* (Ephesians 5:17-20 MSG).

## YOUR COMFORT IS IN YOUR PRAISE AND WORSHIP

There is no comfort like that which God gives. As much as I or anyone else might want to offer you empathy, the truth is that we haven't lived your story. I could never fully understand the pain and sorrow you're experiencing in your life. But God *has* lived your story, and He *does* understand. Jesus suffered pain, endured betrayal, intense sorrow, excruciating pain, and death to overcome and rise again; He will comfort you in your times of praise and worship, and, in time, He will raise and redeem your painful circumstances as well. Cling to God in praise and worship through your trials; He is the only one who can really *comfort* your heart.

✠ *Shout for joy, O heavens; rejoice, O earth; burst into song, O mountains! For the Lord comforts His people and will have compassion on His afflicted ones* (Isaiah 49:13).

✠ *In this you greatly rejoice, though now for a little while you may have had to suffer grief in all kinds of trials. These have come so that your faith—of greater worth than gold, which perishes even though refined by fire—may be proved genuine and may result in praise, glory and honor when Jesus Christ is revealed* (1 Peter 1:6-7).

✣ *I will praise the Lord, who **counsels** me...* (Psalm 16:7).

## Action & Visualization

*Praise and worship God in spirit and truth so you can obtain a more intimate relationship with Him, as well as prophecy, victory, freedom, healing, understanding, and comfort.*

## Sacrifice Is Praise and Worship with Action

Our sacrifices can be a fragrant worship offering to God.

✣ *But the Lord, who brought you up out of Egypt with mighty power and outstretched arm, is the One you must worship. To Him you shall bow down and to Him offer **sacrifices*** (2 Kings 17:36).

✣ *When Solomon finished praying, fire came down from Heaven and consumed the burnt **offering** and the **sacrifices**, and the glory of the Lord filled the temple* (2 Chronicles 7:1).

✣ *Let them sacrifice thank **offerings** and tell of His works with songs of joy* (Psalm 107:22).

Abraham gave up his home and country, and he was prepared to worship God with the sacrifice of his only son. It was these great actions of faith, trust in God's provision and love that made Abraham the father of our faith.

Just days before Jesus' death, a woman gave Jesus a sacrificial worship offering. This is described by Mark:

✠ *Now the Passover and the Feast of Unleavened Bread were only two days away, and the chief priests and the teachers of the law were looking for some sly way to arrest Jesus and kill Him. "But not during the Feast," they said, "or the people may riot."*

*While He was in Bethany, reclining at the table in the home of a man known as Simon the Leper, a woman came with an alabaster jar of very expensive perfume, made of pure nard [this perfume's scent is said to last seven days]. She broke the jar and poured the perfume on His head.*

*Some of those present were saying indignantly to one another, "Why this waste of perfume? It could have been sold for more than a year's wages and the money given to the poor." And they rebuked her harshly.*

*"Leave her alone," said Jesus. "Why are you bothering her? She has done a beautiful thing to Me. The poor you will always have with you, and you can help them any time you want. But you will not always have Me. She did what she could. She poured perfume on My body beforehand to prepare for My burial. I tell you the truth, wherever the gospel is preached throughout the world, what she has done will also be told, in memory of her"* (Mark 14:1-9).

Jesus said this woman did a beautiful act because she sacrificially offered to recognize Jesus' lordship. Her actions are now memorialized in the Bible and would certainly be remembered days later by Jesus as He was nailed to the cross. The sweet fragrance of that sacrificial perfume she poured on Him would have risen to His nostrils, offering a real encouragement in this most difficult of circumstances. At that time, Jesus also knew the future, so the *fragrance* of your *sacrificial offerings* can also be an encouragement to Jesus while He hangs on the cross dying for your sins. You should always have this in mind when you prepare your sacrificial offerings.

✠ *Let us fix our eyes on Jesus, the author and perfector of our faith, who for the **joy** [of your sacrificial offering] set before Him endured the cross...* (Hebrews 12:2).

Indeed, Jesus Himself, of His own free will, became a *sacrificial fragrant offering* of incense to God for you.

✠ *And live a life of love, just as Christ loved us and gave Himself up for us as a **fragrant** offering and **sacrifice** to God* (Ephesians 5:2).

✠ *The high priest carries the blood of animals into the Most Holy Place as a sin offering, but the bodies are burned outside the camp. **And so Jesus also suffered outside the city gate to make the people holy through His own blood.** ...Through Jesus, therefore, let us continually offer to God a sacrifice of praise—the **fruit** of lips that confess His name* (Hebrews 13:11-12,15).

What will you give God as a sacrificial worship offering? You may or may not have material things to give. However, His primary desire is intimacy, a deep relationship with you, and a life *submitted* to Him.

✠ *Therefore, I urge you, brothers, in view of God's mercy, to offer your bodies as living sacrifices, holy and pleasing to God—**this is your spiritual act of worship**. Do not conform any longer to the pattern of this world, but be transformed by the renewing of your mind* (Romans 12:1-2).

God treasures your *obedience* over your sacrifices because obedience is the sacrifice of your *life* to Him.

✠ *But Samuel replied: "Does the Lord delight in burnt offerings and sacrifices as much as in obeying the voice of the Lord? To obey is **better** than sacrifice, and to heed is better than the fat of rams"* (1 Samuel 15:22).

✠ *The sacrifices of God are a broken spirit; a broken and contrite [obedient] heart...* (Psalm 51:17).

God likes your obedience more because giving God your obedience will bring God's love, His image, and His likeness back into the world through your life. There will be times where being obedient will seemingly be beyond your own power, but these are times God wants you to surrender to His power.

## ACTION & VISUALIZATION

*Worship God by presenting your life as a sacrificial love offering to Him.*

## MEDITATION POINT

Worship is an outward expression that allows you to express inner feelings to God, which is a sweet-smelling gift to Him, and positions you to fulfill your purpose.

Go to Chapter 3 in the Study Guide section on page 611.

## Endnotes

1. Jack Hayford, Ed. *Spirit-filled Life Bible for Students* (Nashville, TN: Thomas Nelson, 1995), 521.

2. Ibid., 743.

3. Ibid., 1665.

4. Ibid., 717.

5. Ibid., 529.

6. Ibid., 562.

# Chapter 4

# Gift #6—Frankincense (Part 2)

## What Are the Key Elements of Intimate Communications with God?

Before you begin to read, pray that the Holy Spirit
would give you understanding and application.

✠ *The four living creatures and the twenty-four elders fell down before
the Lamb. Each one had a harp and they were holding golden bowls
full of incense, which are the prayers of the saints* (Revelation 5:8).

✠ *Another angel, who had a golden censer, came and stood at the altar.
He was given much incense to offer, with the prayers of all the saints,
on the golden altar before the throne* (Revelation 8:3).

✠ *May my prayer be set before You like incense...* (Psalm 141:2).

### Reestablishing Our Communication Link

C ommunication is the adhesive that bonds people together. It turns
an acquaintance into a friend, and it makes a date into a marriage.
It's the steady, continual, rich conversations where you are actively
seeking to get to know one another. Think about your best relationships.

What do they all have in common? Most likely, these people are open, willing to listen, available, and share a mutual trust and commitment. You are confident that they have your best interests at heart.

On the flip side, how would you feel if your spouse, girlfriend, boyfriend, or best friend ignored you? How would you feel if this person showed no interest at all in your life and he or she never called you to see how you were doing? What if this person seemed disinterested in your concerns or your needs? What if this person spoke openly with others but wouldn't give you the time of day? What if he or she hid important information from you? Ultimately, we discover that the same adhesive that brings us close together can also tear us apart. This is the raw power of communication—to intimately bond or break relationships. This is also true in our relationship with our Creator.

We see from the opening verses above that incense, one of the three gifts Jesus received at His birth, is also representative of prayer. This is, of course, an important means of communication with God. God created each of us to have a relationship with Him—an *intimate* relationship. The cornerstone of an intimate relationship with anyone, let alone God, is communication. Just like we do in our earthly relationships, God also shares His secrets with His closest friends. Are you a close friend of God when you don't regularly communicate with Him? Are you talking to God about your day, your concerns, and your needs? Or are you talking to everyone else *but* God about these things? God wants to be in communication with us and involved in our lives as we live them out on the earth. What does it say if we don't talk to Him? Do we think He doesn't care? Or perhaps it reveals that we question whether He really *exists*.

## REESTABLISHING OUR COMMUNICATION LINK

Communication with God began in the garden of Eden. Adam and Eve had real and personal communication with God until the fall took place and sin entered the world. After they sinned, everything changed. That communication system became distorted. Of course, God could still hear them just as He can hear us. In fact, He already knows what's in our hearts and minds before we speak to Him. But what has been distorted is our method of communication with God and our perspective of Him. These distortions caused Adam and Eve to hide from God rather than come to Him.

After the fall, God's Spirit no longer lived in humans as His temples—humans became unholy. Therefore, in obedience to God, humanity built a holy physical structure (altar or temple) where they and God could meet to communicate. God's people would request His presence in this building through prayer. When Solomon dedicated the temple to the Lord many years later, he prayed:

> *May Your eyes be open toward this temple day and night, this place of which You said You would put Your name there. May You hear the **prayer** Your servant prays toward this place* (2 Chronicles 6:20).

The Hebrew word for *prayer, tephillah* (the-feel-lah), means "supplication or intercession." Prayer is a means of communication with God. It is not difficult or far off, for even a little child can effectively pray.[1] Prayer can be a brief and casual dialogue with God or a formal conversation offered on your knees with hands folded and your head bowed.

Jesus Christ went to the cross to pay for our sins so we could once again become God's temple wherein His Spirit would dwell. This reestablished a direct and personal relationship with God *through Him*.

> [Jesus said], *"Until now* [Jesus' coming to earth] *you have not asked for anything in **My name**. Ask and you will receive, and your joy will be complete"* (John 16:24).

Because Jesus justified us so that we could have a reestablished standing with God, so Jesus instructed us to ask the Father for anything in His name. He said again:

✟ *I tell you the truth, My Father will give you whatever you ask in* **My name** (John 16:23).

Our reestablished link through Him gives us direct access to the Father.

✟ [Jesus said], *"In that day* [when I am gone from the earth] *you will ask in* **My name***. I am not saying that I will ask the Father on your behalf. No, the Father Himself loves you because you have loved Me and have believed that I came from God* (John 16:26-27).

The early apostles regularly called on the Father in Jesus' name as well:

✟ *Then Peter said, "Silver or gold I do not have, but what I have I give you.* **In the name of Jesus Christ of Nazareth, walk"** (Acts 3:6).

✟ [Paul said], *"***In the name of Jesus Christ** *I command you* [the evil spirit] *to come out of her!" At that moment the* [evil] *spirit left her* (Acts 16:18).

Jesus also says our communication with our heavenly Father should be personal. When teaching His disciples about prayer, He told them:

✟ *When you* **pray***, go into your room, close the door and pray to your Father, who is unseen. Then your Father, who sees what is done in secret, will reward you* (Matthew 6:6).

Prayer creates intimacy between you and God so that He draws close as you draw close to Him. James tells us:

✟ *Draw near to God and He will draw near to you...* (James 4:8 NKJV).

Communication is further enhanced, and therefore intimacy is enhanced as well, when you listen and respond to what God is saying to you. Remember what Jesus instructed us to do in order to build intimacy with Him:

*Here I am! I stand at the door and knock. If anyone **hears** My voice and opens the door [responds to what I'm is saying], I will come in and eat with him, and he with Me [enjoy intimacy together]* (Revelation 5:20).

We must work at developing greater intimacy with God each day because the more we *know* Him the better we will be able to stand in times of trouble. This is why Paul told Timothy:

*I **know** whom I have believed and [therefore] am convinced that He is able to guard what I have entrusted to Him for that day* (2 Timothy 1:12).

To pray means many things to many people, but prayer basically is *simply* talking audibly, silently, or even spirit to Spirit with God. Prayer is a vital communication link with God, and, as we all know, good communication takes the *full* participation of two individuals. It is not a one-sided event; it is a progressive, continual concept. We are not only called to direct our requests toward God, which most of us believers are naturally good at, especially when trouble arises. But here's the part that we often neglect, miss, or ignore: *we are also called to expect Him to give an answer when we pray in His name.* God said through Jeremiah:

*Call to Me and I will answer you and tell you great and unsearchable things you do not know* (Jeremiah 33:3).

Call on God when you need answers or don't understand what you are facing. Through your intimate relationship with Him, you can receive, in due time, answers to the unsearchable truths of life. As you have already read, His answers may come in many ways or take many different forms, which is why you need to be open and expectant so you don't miss the answer.

## Prayer Is for You

Prayer can be a mysterious business, but the Bible spells out some key concepts that will help us understand why we are called to pray. It's important to understand that God already knows our needs even before we ask Him.

✝ *Your Father knows what you need before you ask Him* (Matthew 6:8).

Also, God already knows what we're thinking before we ever put those thoughts to words:

✝ *The Lord knows the thoughts of man...* (Psalm 94:11).

✝ *...God knows your hearts* (Luke 16:15).

✝ *...the Lord searches every heart and understands every motive behind the thoughts* (1 Chronicles 28:9).

If God already knows everything, then why does He want us to pray? It's because He loves us and knows *we* need prayer to have an intimate relationship with Him. Prayer allows us to organize and cleanse our thinking and perspective so we can have a dialogue with God. And catch this: when we begin that communication through prayer, we create an *expectation of a response*. This anticipation for a response (in faith) prepares us for an answer from God.

✠ *In the morning, O Lord, You hear my voice; in the morning I lay my requests before You and* **wait in expectation** (Psalm 5:3).

Prayer also allows us to exercise our faith in God through this *action*. Then we begin building on that faith by *acting* on that for which we have just prayed. Still, we don't merely pray to organize our thinking, begin the dialogue, and to exercise our faith; rather, we pray because God commands us to pray. It is a point of obedience. The New Testament is full of admonitions to prayer—here are just a few of those:

✠ *Devote yourselves to prayer* [speaking with God], *being watchful and thankful* (Colossians 4:2).

✠ *Then Jesus told His disciples a parable to show them that they should always pray* [speak to God] *and not give up* (Luke 18:1).

✠ *Cast all your anxiety on Him because He cares for you* (1 Peter 5:7).

✠ [Jesus said], *"Watch and pray* [speak to God] *so that you will not fall into temptation. The spirit is willing, but the body is weak"* (Matthew 26:41).

## Elements of an Effective Prayer Life

What are some of the elements of effective prayer? Prayer begins by *seeking* God.

✠ But Moses sought the favor of the Lord his God. "O Lord," he said, "why should Your anger burn against Your people, whom You brought out of Egypt with great power and a mighty hand?" (Exodus 32:11).

✠ Look to the Lord and His strength; seek His face always (1 Chronicles 16:11).

✠ If My people, who are called by My name, will humble themselves and pray and **seek** My face and turn from their wicked ways, then will I hear from Heaven and will forgive their sin and will heal their land (2 Chronicles 7:14).

✠ One thing I ask of the Lord, this is what I **seek**: that I may dwell in the house of the Lord all the days of my life, to gaze upon the beauty of the Lord and to **seek** Him in His temple (Psalm 27:4).

✠ He will receive blessing from the Lord and vindication from God his Savior. Such is the generation of those who **seek** Him, who **seek** Your face, O God of Jacob (Psalm 24:5-6).

✠ **Seek** the Lord while He may be found; call on Him while He is near (Isaiah 55:6).

[Jesus said], "**Ask** and it will be given to you; **seek** and you will find; **knock** and the door will be opened to you. For everyone who asks **receives**; he who seeks **finds**; and to him who knocks, the door will be **opened**" (Matthew 7:7-8).

Your *actions* of faith must be another element for successful prayer.

Let us then approach the throne of grace with **confidence**, so that we may receive mercy and find grace to help us in our time of need (Hebrews 4:16).

"**Have faith in God**," Jesus answered. "I tell you the truth, if anyone says to this mountain, 'Go, throw yourself into the sea,' and does not doubt in his heart but believes that what he says will happen, it will be done for him. Therefore I tell you, whatever you ask for in prayer, **believe** that you have received it, and it will be yours" (Mark 11:22-24).

Praying isn't like putting money in a vending machine and punching the item you want. Nor is it like a slot machine where you put in money with absolutely no idea of the potential result and just hope for the best. There are things you can do for your prayers to be effective, or to "improve your odds," of receiving the answer you seek. For prayer to be effective, it first must be *within* God's will. And let's not forget the spiritual laws that God set up for our good even when He structured the universe. All this is to say, when our prayers are contrary to His will or spiritual laws, we will not see the answer for which we're hoping:

This is the confidence we have in approaching God: that if we ask anything according to **His will**, He hears us. And if we know that He hears us [faith]—whatever we ask—we know that we have what we asked of Him (1 John 5:14-15).

✞ [Jesus said], *"If you remain **in Me** and **My words** remain **in you**, ask whatever you wish, and it will be given you"* (John 15:7).

Being *in Him* is the best way to be sure you are praying according to God's will. It is therefore beneficial to pray *in the Spirit*, so our spirit and God's Spirit can directly communicate.

✞ *And pray in the **Spirit** on all occasions with all kinds of prayers and requests. With this in mind, be alert and always keep on praying for all the saints* (Ephesians 6:18).

✞ *In the same way, the Spirit **helps us** in our weakness. We do not know what we ought to pray for, but the Spirit Himself **intercedes** for us with groans that words cannot express* (Romans 8:26).

✞ *For if I pray in a tongue, my spirit prays, but my mind is unfruitful. So what shall I do? I will pray with my spirit, but I will also pray with my mind; I will sing with my spirit, but I will also sing with my mind* (1 Corinthians 14:14-15).

✞ *But you, dear friends, build yourselves up in your most holy faith and pray in the **Holy Spirit*** (Jude 20).

Not only that, but prayer should also be offered wholeheartedly.

✞ *You will seek Me and find Me when you seek Me with **all** your heart* (Jeremiah 29:13).

Our *obedience* can lead to successful prayer too:

✠ *And receive from Him anything we ask, because we* **obey** *His* **commands** *and* **do** *what pleases Him* (1 John 3:22).

Obedience not only has a direct positive influence on our prayers, but it also helps build our confidence and faith in our prayers' results. John writes:

✠ *Dear friends, if our hearts do not condemn us, we have confidence before God and receive from Him anything we ask, because we* **obey** *His commands and* **do** *what pleases Him* (1 John 3:21-22).

We need to always pray with a merciful and nonjudgmental attitude:

✠ *I want men everywhere to lift up holy hands in prayer,* **without** *anger or disputing* (1 Timothy 2:8).

✠ *And when you stand praying, if you hold anything against anyone,* **forgive** *him, so that your Father in Heaven may forgive you your sins* (Mark 11:25).

James tells us that the prayer of the *righteous* will have a powerful impact:

✠ *Therefore confess your sins to each other and pray for each other so that you may be healed. The prayer of a* **righteous** *man is* **powerful** *and* **effective** (James 5:16).

## Pray with Structure

The spirit we bring to prayer is not insignificant to God. In His Sermon on the Mount, Jesus offered us a model of the kind of attitude to bring to our prayer life. Read what He said:

*And when you pray, do not be like the hypocrites, for they love to pray standing in the synagogues and on the street corners to be seen by men. I tell you the truth, they have received their reward in full. But when you pray, go into your room, close the door and pray to your Father, who is unseen. Then your Father, who sees what is done in secret, will reward you. And when you pray, do not keep on babbling like pagans, for they think they will be heard because of their many words. Do not be like them, for your Father knows what you need before you ask Him.*

*"This, then, is how you should pray: 'Our Father in Heaven, hallowed be Your name, Your Kingdom come, Your will be done on earth as it is in Heaven. Give us today our daily bread. Forgive us our debts, as we also have forgiven our debtors. And lead us not into temptation, but deliver us from the evil one.'*

*"For if you forgive men when they sin against you, your heavenly Father will also forgive you. But if you do not forgive men their sins, your Father will not forgive your sins"* (Matthew 6:5-15).

Do you remember in Book 1 that we mentioned a debtor who had his debts forgiven but wouldn't forgive someone who was indebted to him? This parable is calling us to grace, mercy, and forgiveness. It warns us against holding on to offense, as this hinders our prayer life. Holding on to offenses only hardens our hearts. Strive to approach prayer with a pure heart.

The model prayer Jesus gives us in this passage is most commonly known as the Lord's Prayer. Let's look at it more closely. The prayer begins with, "Our Father in Heaven," which acknowledges God's superiority over humankind—His kingship. It continues with "hallowed be Your name," which reminds us to regard God as *holy*. In so doing, we are confirming that His will is perfect and is that which we seek. It goes on to say, "Your Kingdom come, Your will be done on earth as it is in Heaven." This is both a call to have God's perfect will in our lives (even if it does not match our goals), and a call for Jesus' Kingdom to be reestablished on the earth. There is nothing more powerful than praying for God's perfect will to manifest itself in every area of our lives.

Following on with the model prayer, we discover the phrase, "Give us today our daily bread." This is both a reminder of God's provision and a request for God to help fulfill our earthly needs. "Forgive us our debts, as we also have forgiven our debtors" tells us to resolve any unforgiveness issues we have with others so we can stand before God, honest and pure-hearted. Last, the prayer closes with an acknowledgment of our weakness, along with a request for God's intervention: "Lead us not into temptation, but deliver us from the evil one."

The Lord's Prayer is a good template to use for our own prayers. Start here with this prayer, and then personalize it for your own life, focusing on the needs and issues you're encountering on a day-to-day basis.

## ACTION & VISUALIZATION

*Incorporate the elements of the Lord's Prayer into your prayers, along with the spirit in which Jesus suggested your prayers are to be offered.*

## GOD HEARS YOU

When you pray, you can have confidence that God hears you:

*They caused the cry of the poor to come before Him, so that He **heard** the cry of the needy (Job 34:28).*

✝ *Know that the Lord has set apart the godly for Himself; the Lord will* **hear** *when I call to Him* (Psalm 4:3).

✝ *In my distress I called to the Lord; I cried to my God for help. From His temple He* **heard** *my voice; my cry came before Him, into His ears* (Psalm 18:6).

✝ *The righteous cry out, and the Lord* **hears** *them; He delivers them from all their troubles* (Psalm 34:17).

✝ *But as for me, I watch in hope for the Lord, I wait for God my Savior; my God will* **hear** *me* (Micah 7:7).

✝ *And how bold and free we then become in His presence, freely asking according to His will, sure that He's listening. And if we're confident that He's listening, we know that what we've asked for is as good as ours* (1 John 5:14-15 MSG).

✝ *Don't fret or worry. Instead of worrying, pray. Let petitions and praises shape your worries into prayers, letting God know your concerns. Before you know it, a sense of God's wholeness, everything coming together for good, will come and settle you down. It's wonderful what happens when Christ displaces worry at the center of your life* (Philippians 4:6-7 MSG).

Did you catch that? The last verse is saying that if we pray or petition God without anxiety, then He will give us confirmation of His presence through a peace that will guard our hearts. This invisible affirmation gives us confidence to know God is not only listening to our prayers, but that He is also concerned about the outcome. Having confidence and peace about this helps us to not be tempted to do something stupid or self-destructive while waiting for God's answer. Keep an open, willing spirit with a heightened awareness to God and embrace the spirit of peace He gives, for He will answer your prayers.

## ACTION & VISUALIZATION
*Have confidence your prayers are heard by God.*

## ANSWERS DELAYED

If God hears our prayers, then why does it seem like He doesn't always answer them? This is a good question! You have already read that we sometimes need more internal growth before God answers a prayer. And honestly, sometimes we may be asking for something that would harm us if He gave it to us.

✠ *Then Moses said, "Now show me Your glory."*
*And the Lord said, "I will cause all My goodness to pass in front of you, and I will proclaim My name, the Lord, in your presence. I will have mercy on whom I will have mercy, and I will have compassion on whom I will have compassion. But," He said, "you cannot see My face, for no one may see Me and live"* (Exodus 33:18-20).

The best prayer we can ever pray is simply for God's will to be manifest in our lives. God not only knows what's best for us, but He also knows what will ultimately bring us the greatest joy and satisfaction. Praying for God's will is an act of faith and trust in God that He has our best interests at heart and will execute them.

Sometimes what seems like God's silence is an issue of timing. Remember from Book 1 the lame man at the Gate called Beautiful? He'd been waiting to be healed for a long time, and God's perfect timing allowed many people to come to know Jesus Christ because of his healing. Spiritual battles can also cause a delay. It is recorded that Daniel once fasted and prayed for three weeks for God to help him understand a message that came to him through a vision. On the twenty-first day, a man dressed in linen with a belt of the finest gold around his waist came to him.

✟ *Then he continued, "Do not be afraid, Daniel. Since the **first day** that you set your mind to gain understanding and to humble yourself before your God, your words were **heard**, and I have come in response to them. But the prince of the Persian kingdom resisted me twenty-one days. Then Michael [the archangel], one of the chief princes, came to help me, because I was detained there with the king of Persia. Now I have come to explain to you what will happen to your people in the future, for the vision concerns a time yet to come* (Daniel 10:12-14).

## ELEMENTS OF PRAYERS DENIED

Of course prayer will be refused if it is *not* according to God's will.

✟ [Paul said], *"Three times I pleaded with the Lord to take [an affliction] away from me. But He said to me, 'My grace is sufficient for you, for My power is made perfect in weakness...'"* (2 Corinthians 12:8-9).

✟ *But because of you [the Israelites] the Lord was angry with me [Moses] and would not listen to me. "That is enough," the Lord said. "Do not speak to Me anymore about this matter"* (Deuteronomy 3:26).

If we pray with the *wrong motives*, then our prayers may *not* be answered.

✠ *What causes fights and quarrels among you? Don't they come from your desires that battle within you? You want something but don't get it. You kill and covet, but you cannot have what you want. You quarrel and fight. You do not have, because you do not ask God. When you ask, you do not receive, because you ask with* **wrong motives***, that you may spend what you get on your pleasures* (James 4:1-3).

Sometimes our prayers aren't answered because of *sin*.

✠ *If I had been cozy with evil, the Lord would never have listened* (Psalm 66:18 MSG).

✠ *God has no use for the prayers of the people who won't listen to Him* (Proverbs 28:9 MSG).

✠ *Ah, sinful nation, a people loaded with guilt, a brood of evildoers, children given to corruption! They have forsaken the Lord; they have spurned the Holy One of Israel and turned their backs on Him.*
    *…"When you spread out your hands in prayer, I will hide My eyes from you; even if you offer many prayers, I will not listen"* (Isaiah 1:4,15).

✠ *So Saul asked God, "Shall I go down after the Philistines? Will You give them into Israel's hand?" But* [because of Saul's disobedience] *God did not answer him that day* (1 Samuel 14:37).

☩ *God keeps His distance from the wicked; He closely attends to the prayers of God-loyal people* (Proverbs 15:29).

If we seek forgiveness, then God is quick to forgive us of our sin. John reminds us:

☩ *If we confess our sins, [God] is faithful and just and will **forgive** us our sins and purify us from all unrighteousness* (1 John 1:9).

But sometimes, even though we've sought forgiveness and therefore been fully *forgiven*, the law of *sowing and reaping* can cause us to receive the fruits of what we have sowed (which may differ from what we're praying for).

☩ *As long as the earth endures, seedtime and harvest, cold and heat, summer and winter, day and night will never cease* (Genesis 8:22).

Sometimes our prayers may not be answered because of *indifference* to God.

☩ *Then they will call to Me but I will not answer; they will look for Me but will not find Me. Since they hated knowledge and did not choose to fear the Lord, since they would not accept My advice and spurned My rebuke, they will eat the fruit of their ways and be filled with the fruits of their schemes* (Proverbs 1:28-31).

And sometimes prayers may not be answered because we are unmerciful.

☩ *If you stop your ears to the cries of the poor, your cries will go unheard, unanswered* (Proverbs 21:13 MSG).

Our prayers may not be answered because of stubbornness.

✛ *"When I called, they did not listen; so when they called, I would not listen," says the Lord Almighty (Zechariah 7:13).*

And finally, our prayers sometimes may not be answered because of *unstable* faith. James reminds us:

✛ *But when he asks, he must believe and not doubt, because he who doubts is like a wave of the sea, blown and tossed by the wind. That man should not think he will receive anything from the Lord; he is a double-minded man, unstable in all he does (James 1:6-8).*

## ACTION & VISUALIZATION

*Present your prayers to God with a pure heart
and wait in expectation for His answer. If it seems your
prayers aren't being answered, then ask God why.*

## WHEN TO PRAY?

When should we pray? Both James and Paul give us instructions concerning when we should pray. James writes:

✛ *Is any one of you in trouble? He should pray. Is anyone happy? Let him sing songs of praise. Is any one of you sick? He should call the elders of the church to pray over him and anoint him with oil in the name of the Lord. And the prayer offered in faith will make the sick person well; the Lord will raise him up. If he has sinned, he will be forgiven.*

*Therefore confess your sins to each other and pray for each other so that you may be healed. The prayer of a righteous man is powerful and effective* (James 5:13-16).

And Paul writes:

✝ *And pray in the Spirit on* **all occasions** *with all kinds of prayers and requests...* (Ephesians 6:18).

Many people are led to pray only when they have pressing needs. Indeed, the bigger the need, the more likely someone will decide to seek God and pray. But doesn't that seem like a lopsided relationship with God? If we only pray when we have big needs, are we tempting God to make sure we always have needs so that we continue to converse with Him? God desires a more comprehensive and well-rounded conversation with His children. Certain problems we typically face can be avoided, and thus we allow Him to give His children more freedom. Get in the habit of praying around the clock, praying always and on all occasions:

✝ *In the* **morning**, *O Lord, You hear my voice; in the morning I lay my requests before You and wait in expectation* (Psalm 5:3).

✝ **Evening, morning** *and* **noon** *I cry out in distress, and He hears my voice* (Psalm 55:17).

✝ *Be joyful always; pray* **continually**; *give thanks in all circumstances, for this is God's will for you in Christ Jesus* (1 Thessalonians 5:16-18).

✠ *Devote yourselves to prayer, being watchful and thankful* (Colossians 4:2).

Yes, we are to *pray all the time.* Remember that we're building a relationship with our heavenly Father. The more we communicate with Him, the closer we'll grow. Prayer doesn't need to be a formal or a special event. God wants to be in the real-time, everyday circumstances of your life. Your prayers throughout the day can be casual and conversational, inviting God to be involved in all aspects of your life right down to the smallest detail. This is what it means to pray continually. Keep your dialogue going always and on all occasions.

## JESUS IS OUR MODEL FOR WHEN TO PRAY

We can look to Jesus as our model for when we should pray. Jesus had a *prayerful lifestyle*, meaning that he prayed *always* and *on all occasions.* And if Jesus, the very Son of God, prayed on all occasions, how much more should we?

✠ *Very **early in the morning**, while it was still dark, Jesus got up, left the house and went off to a **solitary** place, where He prayed* [for God's direction on where He should go that day]. *Simon and His companions went to look for Him, and when they found Him, they exclaimed: "Everyone is looking for you!"* [Jesus had to get away from the crowd of ideas to find the direction His Father wanted Him to go.]
*Jesus replied, "Let us go somewhere else—to the nearby villages—so I can preach there also. That is why I have come"* (Mark 1:35-38).

✠ [After a physical and spiritual victory from feeding five thousand with five loaves of bread and two fish, Jesus]...*went up on a mountainside to pray* [alone] (Mark 6:46).

✝ *Yet the news about [Jesus] spread all the more, so that crowds of people came to hear Him and to be healed of their sicknesses. But Jesus* **often** *withdrew to* **lonely places** *and prayed* [so He could find God's will and have His own spirit sustained and recharged by God] (Luke 5:15-16).

✝ *One of those days Jesus went out to a mountainside to pray, and* **spent the night** *praying to God* [so He could discern God's will in an important decision]. *When morning came, He called His disciples to Him and chose twelve of them, whom He also designated apostles* (Luke 6:12-13).

✝ *Once when Jesus was praying in private* [to discern God's direction of spiritual teaching for His disciples] *and His disciples were with Him, He asked them, "Who do the crowds say I am?"* (Luke 9:18).

✝ *When all the people were being baptized, Jesus was baptized too. And as He was praying* [during this spiritual event], *Heaven was opened and the Holy Spirit descended on Him in bodily form like a dove* (Luke 3:21-22).

✝ *Jesus, once more deeply moved, came to the tomb* [where Lazarus was buried]. *It was a cave with a stone laid across the entrance. "Take away the stone," He said.*

*"But, Lord," said Martha, the sister of the dead man, "by this time there is a bad odor, for he has been there four days."*

*Then Jesus said, "Did I not tell you that if you believed, you would see the glory of God?"*

*So they took away the stone. Then Jesus looked up and said* [in open prayer to God for the benefit of the onlookers, Jesus spoke an appeal that God would answer to build their faith], *"Father, I thank You that You have heard Me. I knew that You always hear Me, but I said this for the benefit of the people standing here, that they may believe that You sent Me."*

*When He had said this, Jesus called in a loud voice, "Lazarus, come out!" The dead man came out...* (John 11:38-44).

[Jesus] *withdrew about a stone's throw beyond* [the disciples], *knelt down and prayed* [before His greatest spiritual battle to ask about God's will and His own destiny in that battle], *"Father, if You are willing, take this cup from Me; yet not My will, but Yours be done"* (Luke 22:41-42).

## ACTION & VISUALIZATION
*Like Jesus, pray all the time and on all occasions.*

## BE PERSISTENT IN YOUR PRAYER

*Persistence* is an important part of what Jesus taught regarding prayer. I want to encourage you to not give up until you get an answer.

*Then Jesus told His disciples a parable to show them that they should always pray and not give up. He said: "In a certain town there was a judge who neither feared God nor cared about men. And there was a widow in that town who kept coming to him with the plea, 'Grant me justice against my adversary.'*

*"For some time he refused. But finally he said to himself, 'Even though I don't fear God or care about men, yet because this widow*

465

*keeps bothering me, I will see that she gets justice, so that she won't eventually wear me out with her coming!"*

*And the Lord said, "Listen to what the unjust judge says. And will not God bring about justice for His chosen ones, who cry out to Him day and night? Will He keep putting them off? I tell you, He will see that they get justice, and quickly. However, when the Son of Man comes, will He find faith on the earth?"* (Luke 18:1-8).

Remember, the Hebrew word for faith means *persistence*.

## POWER IN UNITY AND NUMBERS

There is power when people *agree together* in prayer, because God promises that He will be in their midst.

✠ *For where two or three come together in My name, there am I with them* (Matthew 18:20).

When we are united in prayer together, we create a special synergistic, multiplied power—removing evil thoughts and powers in the spiritual realm that are contrary to the will of God.

✠ *Five of you shall chase a hundred, and a hundred of you shall put ten thousand to flight; your enemies shall fall by the sword before you* (Leviticus 26:8 NKJV).

The early church demonstrated this kind of spiritual power because there was a spirit of *one* accord. As a result of unity in prayer, the first churches witnessed many signs, wonders, and miracles:

✟ *When the Day of Pentecost had fully come, they were **all** with **one accord** in **one place**. And suddenly there came a sound from Heaven, as of a rushing mighty wind, and it filled the whole house where they were sitting. Then there appeared to them divided tongues, as of fire, and one sat upon each of them. And they were all filled with the Holy Spirit and began to speak with other tongues, as the Spirit gave them utterance* (Acts 2:1-4 NKJV).

✟ *They devoted themselves to the apostles' teaching and to the fellowship, to the breaking of bread and to prayer. Everyone was filled with awe, and many wonders and miraculous signs were done by the apostles. **All** the believers were together and had everything in common* (Acts 2:42-44).

The phrase *with one accord* comes from the Hebrew word *homothumad* (homoth-oo-mad-on), which means "being unanimous" or "having one mind and purpose." In each of its occurrences, *homothumad* shows harmony, which leads to action. There was generally harmony among leadership in the early church. This spiritual unity among God's people released unusual spiritual power.[2] Why do you suppose satan spends most of his efforts trying to divide and destroy unity among believers?

Shortly before His death, Jesus prayed this prayer to the Father on behalf of all believers to come:

✟ *May they be brought into **complete unity** to let the world know that You sent Me...* (John 17:23).

Our *complete* unity will be an important part of the world clearly coming to know Him. All believers will need to emphasize that in which they agree upon and deemphasize that in which they do not.

## ACTION & VISUALIZATION

*Pray in agreement and in one accord with others.*

## HOLDING OTHERS UP IN PRAYER
## AND INTERCESSION

With our earthly authority, God wants us to intercede for others, to pray for His will to blossom in their lives so that they will grow closer to Him and His Spirit. Moses had to do this when the Israelites disobeyed and began to worship a golden calf. He pleaded with God for their forgiveness. Exodus tells us the story:

✛ *So Moses went back to the Lord and said, "Oh, what a great sin these people have committed. They have made themselves gods of gold. But now, please forgive their sin—but if not, then blot me out of the book You have written."*

*The Lord replied to Moses, "Whoever has sinned against Me I will blot out of My book. Now go, lead the people to the place I spoke of, and my angel will go before you. However, when the time comes for Me to punish, I will punish them for their sin."*

*And the Lord struck the people with a plague because of what they did with the calf Aaron had made.*

*...Then the Lord said to Moses, "Leave this place, you and the people you brought up out of Egypt, and go up to the land I promised on oath to Abraham, Isaac and Jacob, saying, 'I will give it to your descendants.' I will send an angel before you and drive out the Canaanites, Amorites, Hittites, Perizzites, Hivites and Jebusites. Go up to the land flowing with milk and honey. But I will not go with you, because you are a stiff-necked people [God's presence could not coexist with disobedience to His will] and I might destroy you on the way"* (Exodus 32:31-35; 33:1-3).

✠ *Moses said to the Lord, "You have been telling me, 'Lead these people,' but You have not let me know whom You will send with me. You have said, 'I know you by name and you have found favor with Me.' If You are pleased with me, teach me Your ways so I may know You and continue to find favor with You. Remember that this nation is Your people."*

*The Lord replied, "My presence will go with you, and I will give you rest."*

*Then Moses said to Him, "If your Presence does not go with us, do not send us up from here. How will anyone know that You are pleased with me and with Your people unless You go with us? What else will distinguish me and Your people from all the other people on the face of the earth?"*

*And the Lord said to Moses, "I will do the very thing you have asked, because I am pleased with you and I know you by name"* (Exodus 33:12-17).

It is up to Christ-followers to use their God-given authority and promises to stand in the gap between God and humanity, just as Moses did. We have promises from God that we are to use to support others spiritually, especially when they are going through spiritual battles. John writes:

✠ *If anyone sees his brother commit a sin that does not lead to death, he should **pray** and God will give him life* (1 John 5:16).

There is a beautiful example of support with Moses joining Joshua's battle. At the same time, Aaron and Hur supported Moses in his support of Joshua. This is how God unifies His followers in power!

✠ *The Amalekites came and attacked the Israelites at Rephidim. Moses said to Joshua, "Choose some of our men and go out to fight the Amalekites. Tomorrow I will stand on the top of the hill with the staff* [type and shadow of Jesus] *of God in my hands."*

*So Joshua fought the Amalekites as Moses had ordered, and Moses, Aaron and Hur went to the top of the hill. As long as Moses held up his hands [with the staff in it], the Israelites were winning, but whenever he lowered his hands, the Amalekites were winning. When Moses' hands grew tired, they took a stone and put it under him and he sat on it. Aaron and Hur held his hands up—one on one side, one on the other—so that his hands remained steady till sunset. So Joshua overcame the Amalekite army with the sword [in the physical realm]* (Exodus 17:8-13).

It is important to lift your spiritual leader, pastor, husband, and father to gain spiritual and physical victories. If you let their hands drop, then you too will suffer consequences when the enemy overruns your territory. In addition to our spiritual authority, we need to pray for our earthly authority—both elected and appointed officials. Paul reminded Timothy of this very fact:

*I urge, then, first of all, that requests, prayers, intercession and thanksgiving be made for **everyone**—for kings and **all** those in authority, that we may live peaceful and quiet lives in all godliness and holiness* (1 Timothy 2:1-2).

It doesn't matter who is physically in authority over you because you can appeal to God for His will to be done in his life. God ultimately reigns, and with your prayers of agreement He can help you accomplish the goals He has for you and your city, county, state, province, or country. The psalmist reminds us of His sovereignty:

*All kings will bow down to Him and all nations will serve Him* (Psalm 72:11).

✚ *The Lord has established His throne in Heaven, and His Kingdom rules over all* (Psalm 103:19).

## INTERCESSORY PRAYER

Intercession is the act of praying for someone else. The Hebrew word for *intercession* is *enunchano* (en-toong-khan-oh), which means to "fall in with" or "to meet with in order to converse." The word conveys the idea of pleading with a person on behalf of another. Jesus is the ideal intercessor because He is constantly praying for His people—interceding for them. Just as Jesus intercedes for His people, so we too as believers are to enter intercessory prayer for one another.[3]

✚ *Who is he that condemns? Christ Jesus, who died—more than that, who was raised to life—is at the right hand of God and is also **interceding** for us* (Romans 8:34).

Jesus was interceding for *our salvation*.

✚ *Therefore He is able to save completely those who come to God through Him, because He always lives to **intercede** for them* (Hebrews 7:25).

Jesus interceded for *weak* believers.

✚ [Jesus said], *"But I have prayed for you, Simon, that your faith may not fail. And when you have turned back, strengthen your brothers"* (Luke 22:32).

✚ [Jesus said], *"I pray for them [believers]. I am not praying for the world, but for those You have given Me, for they are Yours"* (John 17:9).

Jesus interceded for His *enemies*.

✝ *Jesus said, "Father, forgive them, for they do not know what they are doing." And they divided up His clothes by casting lots (Luke 23:34).*

Jesus interceded for us to receive the Holy Spirit:

✝ *And I will ask the Father, and He will give you another Counselor to be with you forever (John 14:16).*

There is a sowing and reaping effect when we intercede. Solomon gave us an example of the power and reward in a selfless, servant attitude. After he became king over the Israelites, God appeared to Solomon to fulfill any request he would ask of Him. Look at Solomon's response.

✝ *At Gibeon the Lord appeared to Solomon during the night in a dream, and God said, "Ask for whatever you want Me to give you."*

*Solomon answered, "You have shown great kindness to Your servant, my father David, because he was faithful to You and righteous and upright in heart. You have continued this great kindness to him and have given him a son to sit on his throne this very day."*

*Now, O Lord my God, You have made Your servant king in place of my father David. But I am only a little child and do not know how to carry out my duties. Your servant is here among the people You have chosen, a great people, too numerous to count or number. So give Your servant a discerning heart to govern Your people and to distinguish between right and wrong. For who is able to govern this great people of Yours?"*

*The Lord was pleased that Solomon had asked for this. So God said to him, "Since you have asked for this and not for long life or wealth for yourself, nor have asked for the death of your enemies but for discernment in administering justice, I will do what you have asked. I will give you a wise and discerning heart, so that there will **never** have been anyone like you, nor will there **ever be**. Moreover, I will give you*

**what you have not asked for**—*both riches and honor—so that in your lifetime you will have no equal among kings"* (1 Kings 3:5-13).

Solomon's request was a selfless one designed to benefit *others,* so he received *not only* what he asked for but also what *he did not ask for.* Test this principle for yourself and intercede for others as Job did when he was experiencing the darkest moment of his life.

✠ *After Job prayed for his friends, the Lord restored his fortunes and gave him twice as much as he had before* (Job 42:10).

How can we grow our relationship with God without understanding what He desires? Effective communication and joining with Him in one spirit will allow us to do just that. God has given us authority here on earth, and He is seeking us to join with Him to bring His will back to earth so that all may know Him. I encourage you to bookmark this page and reference this Action and Visualization often. Continue to revisit this section and intercede for others. Your mind and heart will be refreshed, God's Word will come alive, and the Holy Spirit will move in your life as well as the lives of those you love. You will also receive that for which you did not ask. It all begins with you reaching out to your heavenly Father in spirit and truth with a heartfelt prayer.

## ACTION & VISUALIZATION

*Pray for those to whom you have given this book series and all who read it, that they might understand and apply what they have learned.*

*Pray that those who read this book series will unwrap each gift to the fullest.*

*Pray for those who might stall out in reading this book series, that they would be filled with a hunger for more.*

*Pray for those readers who are not yet believers, that they might receive a full revelation of Jesus Christ.*

*Pray for those who talk about this book series with others,*
*that they may be led by the Holy Spirit.*

*Pray for the book series to attract the attention and interest of those*
*for whom it is intended.*

*Pray for the men and women behind bars, in rehab, in poverty,*
*and those who are spiritual paupers, that this book series*
*will help them to discover God's will.*

*Pray as you are otherwise led by the Holy Spirit.*

## MEDITATION POINT

Communication with God through prayer will give you an expectation for an answer. Expectation gives birth to hope, and hope acted upon will bring about that which is in God's will.

Go to Chapter 4 in the Study Guide section on page 619.

## Endnotes

1.   Jack Hayford, Ed. *Spirit-filled Life Bible for Students* (Nashville, TN: Thomas Nelson, 1995), 546.

2.   Ibid., 1384.

3.   Ibid., 1597.

# Chapter 5

# GIFT #7—MYRRH (PART 1)

## WHY IS DYING THE FIRST STEP TO LIVING IN FREEDOM?

Before you begin to read, pray that the Holy Spirit will give you and all readers of this book understanding and application.

✝ *Then [the wise men] opened their treasures and presented Him with gifts of gold and of incense and of **myrrh** (Matthew 2:11).*

We don't like "the end," do we? The end of our weekend or vacation; the end of childhood; the end of a great movie or concert. In fact, that's the reason for an encore, right? We don't want the show to stop. When our checking and savings accounts run low, we pull out one of our many credit cards because we don't want our spending ability to end. How about life? Death is the biggest "the end" of them all. However, that was Jesus Christ's purpose on earth—to die.

Myrrh was an herb commonly used to embalm a dead body. Jesus' very purpose was being foretold by this unusual baby gift given to Him at birth. However, "the end" of Jesus' life marked the beginning of ours. As believers, because of Jesus' sacrifice unto death and then resurrection into life, we are given the same resurrection power. Through Jesus' earthly "end" we find victory over our "end," and in its place, we are given eternal life and are therefore free from the fear of "the end," as we know we will one day live with Him—living better than anyone could ever dream or imagine. Indeed, the closer we come to God in this life, and the more time we spend in His Kingdom while we're still on earth, the less and less fearful death will seem to us.

To complete the circle, we also read that myrrh was among the last gifts Jesus received in His life:

✠ *Later, Joseph of Arimathea asked Pilate for the body of Jesus. Now Joseph was a disciple of Jesus, but secretly because he feared the Jews. With Pilate's permission, he came and took the body* [of Jesus] *away. He was accompanied by Nicodemus, the man who earlier had visited Jesus at night. Nicodemus* [who asked Jesus the question, "How do I get to Heaven?"] *brought a mixture of* **myrrh** *and aloes, about seventy-five pounds. Taking Jesus' body, the two of them wrapped it, with the spices, in strips of linen. This was in accordance with Jewish burial customs* (John 19:38-40).

The life, death, and subsequent resurrection of Christ changed human history forever. It reversed the way we look at life and death. Jesus defeated death and thus rose again, transforming life's end into a better, joy-filled beginning. Therefore Paul could tell us:

✠ *For the perishable* [you and I] *must clothe itself with the imperishable* [blood of Jesus], *and the mortal* [you and I] *with immortality* [of a reborn spirit connected to God's Spirit]. *When the perishable has been clothed with the imperishable, and the mortal with immortality, then the saying that is written will come true: "Death has been swallowed up in victory."*
*"Where, O death, is your victory?*
*Where, O death, is your sting?"*

> *The sting of death is sin, and the power of sin is the law. But thanks be to God! He gives us the victory through our Lord Jesus Christ* (1 Corinthians 15:53-57).

It is just as important to understand that during Jesus' life, He brought about life into a dying world by also letting His will die to the will of His Father.

☩ [Jesus said], *"For I have come down from Heaven not to do My will but to do the will of Him who sent Me"* (John 6:38).

So how does this strange embalming herb apply to you and me today? What significance does it have in our world? Well, it is vital because it symbolizes two types of death. The first is the death of Jesus' will. Remember, Jesus was both God and man. He endured the same kinds of trials and tests that we do. Jesus, in "dying to His will" or "dying to self," made a way for *God's will* to be done through Him. "Dying to self" also meant Jesus had to die to the flesh—He had to overcome fleshly desires and enslavement to sin. This brought Him absolute freedom and clarity to follow the leading of the Spirit, the Spirit that brings *life*:

☩ *Those who live according to the sinful nature have their minds set on what that nature desires; but those who live in accordance with the Spirit have their minds set on what the Spirit desires. The mind of sinful man is death, but the mind controlled by the Spirit is life and peace* (Romans 8:5-6).

Through dying to self, Jesus could spiritually establish His Kingdom on the earth, and our dying to self brings life to our earthly life as well as further establishing His Kingdom on earth.

The second death symbolically foretold by the gift of myrrh was Jesus' physical death. His death on the cross paid for all of humanity's debt to sin and gave us a way to life in His Kingdom. Paul tells us in Romans:

✝ *For what the law was powerless to do in that it was weakened by the sinful nature, God **did** by sending His own Son in the likeness of sinful man to be a sin offering. And so He condemned sin in sinful man, in order that the righteous requirements of the law might be fully met in us, who do not live according to the sinful nature but according to the Spirit* (Romans 8:3-4).

In doing this, Jesus changed our biggest ending into a new beginning and gave us a way to see and experience glimpses of His Kingdom now. As we will learn in this chapter, Jesus wants us to follow His example so we can indeed enter that Kingdom now:

✝ *Then Jesus said to His disciples, "If anyone would come after Me, he must deny himself and take up his cross and follow Me. For whoever wants to save his life will lose it, but whoever loses his life for Me will find it"* (Matthew 16:24-25).

Of course we can't die for someone else's sin—that was something only Jesus, a perfect man, could do. But we can start experiencing some of God's life and freedom now in this dying world, which will allow us to be examples for others to show them the way. In this passage, Jesus tells us we need to deny ourselves, take up our crosses, and follow Him.

What does that mean? To answer this, let's get some context on why Jesus came to earth—how He lived and what He did—so we can then understand how to walk and live this out in our lives. Who was Jesus anyway?

## THE EXPECTED MESSIAH

Jesus did not come to earth as a typical king. His life even surprised those who followed Him. The Jews were awaiting a Messiah, and they expected Him to come and set up His earthly reign as referenced up to fifteen hundred years before in the Old Testament:

✠ *Therefore the Lord Himself will give you a sign: The virgin will be with child and will give birth to a son, and will call Him Immanuel* (Isaiah 7:14).

✠ *For to us a Child is born, to us a Son is given, and the government will be on His shoulders* (Isaiah 9:6).

✠ *In the time of those kings, the God of Heaven will set up a Kingdom that will never be destroyed, nor will it be left to another people. It will crush all those kingdoms and bring them to an end, but it will itself endure forever* (Daniel 2:44).

✠ *"Shout and be glad, O Daughter of Zion. For I am coming, and I will live among you," declares the Lord. "Many nations will be joined with the Lord in that day and will become My people. I will live among you and you will know that the Lord Almighty has sent Me to you"* (Zechariah 2:10-11).

✠ *In love a throne will be established; in faithfulness a Man will sit on it—one from the house of David* [Jesus' lineage was from the house of David]—*one who in judging seeks justice and speeds the cause of righteousness* (Isaiah 16:5).

✟ *The Lord swore an oath to David, a sure oath that He will not revoke: "One of your own descendants I will place on your throne..."* (Psalm 132:11).

✟ *A Shoot will come up from the stump of Jesse* [David's lineage was from the house of Jesse, thus, Jesus' was too]; *from his roots a Branch will bear fruit. The Spirit of the Lord will rest on Him—the Spirit of wisdom and of understanding, the Spirit of counsel and of power, the Spirit of knowledge and of the fear of the Lord—and He will delight in the fear of the Lord.*

*He will not judge by what He sees with His eyes, or decide by what He hears with His ears; but with righteousness He will judge the needy, with justice He will give decisions for the poor of the earth. He will strike the earth with the rod of His mouth; with the breath of His lips He will slay the wicked. Righteousness will be His belt and faithfulness the sash around His waist* [then when His earthly reign is established].

*The wolf will live with the lamb, the leopard will lie down with the goat, the calf and the lion and the yearling together; and a little child will lead them. The cow will feed with the bear, their young will lie down together, and the lion will eat straw like the ox* [all death will end]. *The infant will play near the hole of the cobra, and the young child put his hand into the viper's nest. They will neither harm nor destroy on all My holy mountain, for the earth will be full of the knowledge of the Lord as the waters cover the sea. In that day the Root of Jesse will stand as a banner for the peoples; the nations will rally to Him, and His place of rest will be glorious.*

*In that day the Lord will reach out His hand a second time to reclaim the remnant that is left of His people from Assyria, from Lower Egypt, from Upper Egypt, from Cush, from Elam, from Babylonia, from Hamath and from the islands of the sea. He will raise a banner for the nations and gather the exiles of Israel; He will assemble the scattered people of Judah from the four quarters of the earth* (Isaiah 11:1-12).

✠ *Then the sovereignty, power and greatness of the kingdoms under the whole Heaven will be handed over to the saints, the people of the Most High. [Jesus'] Kingdom will be an everlasting Kingdom, and all rulers will worship and obey Him* (Daniel 7:27).

## THE UNEXPECTED OUTCOME

At the time of Jesus' birth, Israel was under the oppressive rule of the Roman Empire. The Jews were anxious for this prophesied Savior to come, free them, and then set up His Kingdom. They desired a king and the victorious savior described in the Bible to answer their cry. While they may have understood the need for a spiritual savior, what they expected was a king and savior who would respond to their physical needs—freedom from physical oppression. We too are often misled in asking God simply for physical freedom. We pray for financial freedom and for other physical freedoms, but what about spiritual freedom? What about asking God to release us from spiritual oppression and bondage? This is true freedom, and it *must* clearly be established before the other freedoms can follow.

Jesus didn't come with an army and a plan to overthrow the Roman Empire. There would actually be two "comings." The first is when He came to be our spiritual Savior—to live a perfect life and then die for our sins, triumphing over death and rising once again. This was humankind's only hope to restore our relationship with God. Indeed, in Jesus' first coming, He *contradicted* humanity's sin nature that was a result of the fall as recorded in the book of Genesis. His purpose was to reverse the curse and the cause of sickness and death that humankind brought about through its own actions. The spiritual cause that initiated the curse had to be resolved before the physical consequences of it could be resolved and reversed. Therefore, we needed a perfect sin offering, which Jesus became for us.

The arrival of Jesus, the sacrificial Lamb (the spiritual requirement), was also prophesied in the Old Testament, *but* it was overlooked by Jesus' contemporaries because their physical needs blinded them from this other facet God was trying to show them.

✠ *Abraham answered, "God Himself will provide the Lamb for the burnt offering..."* (Genesis 22:8).

✠ *And I will pour out on the house of David and the inhabitants of Jerusalem a spirit of grace and supplication. They will look on Me, the **One they have pierced**, and they will mourn for Him as one mourns for an only child, and grieve bitterly for Him as one grieves for a firstborn son* (Zechariah 12:10).

As we sometimes do, they believed what they wanted, what fit into their *physical* need rather than what God's Word said. The prophet Isaiah had prophesied Jesus' death on the cross over five hundred years before the event with surprising accuracy. Isaiah declared:

✠ *Who has believed our message and to whom has the arm of the Lord been revealed? He [Jesus] grew up before Him [God] like a **tender** shoot, and like a root out of dry ground. He had no beauty or majesty to attract us to Him, nothing in His appearance that we should desire Him. [Jesus looked just like everyone else—an ordinary man in appearance.] He was despised and rejected by men, a man of sorrows, and familiar with suffering. Like one from whom men hide their faces He was despised, and we esteemed Him not.*

*Surely He took up our infirmities and carried our sorrows, yet we considered Him stricken by God, smitten by Him, and afflicted. But He was pierced* [in His side on the cross with a spear] *for our transgressions, He was crushed for our iniquities; the punishment that brought us peace* [with God] *was upon Him, and by His wounds we are healed. We all, like sheep, have gone astray, each of us has turned to his own way; and the Lord has laid on Him the iniquity of us all.*

*He was oppressed and afflicted, yet He did not open His mouth* [in defense of Himself at His trial]; *He was led like a **lamb** to the slaughter, and as a sheep before her shearers is silent, so He did not open His mouth. By oppression and judgment He was taken away* [tried by the Roman authority]. *And who can speak of His descendants? For He was cut off from the land of the living; for the transgression of My* [God's] *people He was stricken. He was assigned a grave with the wicked* [crucified with two criminals], *and with the rich in His death* [buried in a rich man's tomb], *though He had done no violence, nor was any deceit in His mouth.* [Though it seemed He was being punished and cut off by God for sins He did not do, He was standing in for us.]

*Yet it was the Lord's will to crush Him and cause Him to suffer, and though the Lord makes His life a guilt offering* [requiring a lamb without blemish to be sacrificed—in Jesus' case, a perfect and complete offering requiring no other], *He will see His offspring and prolong His days, and the will of the Lord will prosper in His hand. After the suffering of His soul, He will see the light of life and be satisfied; by His knowledge My righteous servant will justify many, and He will bear their inequities. Therefore I will give Him a portion among the great, and He will divide the spoils with the strong, because He poured out His life unto death, and was numbered with the transgressors* [hung on a cross with criminals]. *For He bore the sin of many, and made intercession for the transgressors* [us] (Isaiah 53:1-12).

The New Testament also confirms Jesus would not be coming as a worldly king, but rather as a sacrificial Lamb—a sacrifice for our sins.

✝ *The next day John saw Jesus coming toward him and said, "Look, the **Lamb of God**, who takes away the sin of the world!"* (John 1:29).

✝ *Get rid of the old yeast that you may be a new batch without yeast— as you really are. For Christ, our **Passover Lamb**, has been sacrificed* (1 Corinthians 5:7).

✝ *...but with the precious blood of Christ, a **lamb** without blemish or defect* (1 Peter 1:19).

Jesus was destined to die these two deaths so He could establish His spiritual Kingdom and bring salvation and life. During His life, Jesus fulfilled the requirement for righteousness by letting the will of His flesh die:

✝ *...I may gain Christ and be found in Him, not having a righteousness of my own that comes from the law* [from us being able to keep to every letter of the law—impossible], *but that which is through faith in Christ—the righteousness that comes from God and is by faith* (Philippians 3:8-9).

✝ *I will raise up for them a prophet like you from among their brothers; I will put my words in* [Jesus'] *mouth, and He will tell them **everything** I command Him* (Deuteronomy 18:18).

Prior to His death, Jesus even told His adversaries that His Kingdom was not yet an earthly Kingdom.

✠ *Jesus said, "My Kingdom is not of this world. If it were, My servants would fight to prevent My arrest by the Jews. But now My Kingdom is from another place" (John 18:36).*

And though Jesus had to die to set up His Kingdom here on earth, He was not abandoned by God, even in death. It was prophesied approximately a thousand years in advance that God would raise Jesus to everlasting life to rule over His everlasting Kingdom. Psalm 16:10-11 foretold this:

✠ *Because You will not abandon Me [Jesus] to the grave, nor will You [Father] let Your Holy One see decay. You have made known to Me the path of life; You will fill Me with joy in Your presence, with eternal pleasures at Your right hand (Psalm 16:10-11).*

Again, at Jesus' first coming, His contemporaries did not see this because their immediate need for a physical savior from the oppression of Roman rule blinded them; however, it is through His spiritual victory over sin and death that we can now follow Him on the same path to a "death" that really is a metamorphosis into real life—spiritual life.

✠ *"Death has been swallowed up in victory." …The sting of death is sin, and the power of sin is the law. But thanks be to God! He gives us the victory through our Lord Christ Jesus (1 Corinthians 15:54-57).*

✠ *Therefore, there is now no condemnation for those who are in Christ Jesus, because through Christ Jesus the law of the Spirit of life set me free from the law of sin and death (Romans 8:1-2).*

## FOLLOWING JESUS

How then do we follow Jesus? The apostle Paul describes denying ourselves, taking up our crosses, and following Him this way:

☦ *So here's what I want you to do, God helping you: Take your everyday, ordinary life—your sleeping, eating, going-to-work, and walking-around life—and place it before God as an offering. Embracing what God does for you is the best thing you can do for Him. Don't become so well-adjusted to your culture that you fit into it without even thinking. Instead, fix your attention on God. You'll be changed from the inside out. Readily recognize what He wants from you, and quickly respond to it. Unlike the culture around you, always dragging you down to its level of immaturity, God brings the best out of you, develops well-formed maturity in you (Romans 12:1-2 MSG).*

☦ *For you were once darkness, but now you are the light in the Lord. Live as children of light (for the fruit of the light consists in all goodness, righteousness and truth) and find out what pleases the Lord [His will]. Have nothing to do with the fruitless deeds of darkness, but rather expose them. For it is shameful even to mention what the disobedient do in secret. But everything exposed by the light becomes visible, for it is light that makes everything visible. This is why it is said: "Wake up, O sleeper, rise from the dead, and Christ will shine on you" (Ephesians 5:8-14).*

☦ *I want to know Christ and the power of His resurrection and the fellowship of sharing in His sufferings, becoming like Him in His death, and so, somehow, to attain to the resurrection from the dead (Philippians 3:10-11).*

Jesus' first coming was a humble one, as a man destined to die. But Jesus is coming a second time, as prophesied in Revelation, to physically establish a new Heaven and new earth for all who follow Him.

✝ *They will make war against the Lamb, but the Lamb will overcome them because He is Lord of lords and King of kings—and with Him will be His called, chosen and faithful followers* (Revelation 17:14).

✝ *Coming out of His mouth is a sharp sword with which to strike down the nations. "He will rule them with an iron scepter"* (Revelation 19:15).

Like His disciples, we are following Him in what sometimes appears to be a losing situation. However, when He physically establishes His Kingdom, we, His faithful followers, are His chosen. Our lives here on earth are much like Jesus' first coming—we are called to live in humility and endure suffering, denying ourselves and taking up our crosses. We are also called to follow in Jesus' footsteps and live in contradiction to this world. But our second coming—our entrance with Him when He establishes His Kingdom—will be a glorious and triumphant occasion. Paul reminds us:

✝ *When Christ, who is your life, appears, then **you** also will appear with Him in **glory*** (Colossians 3:4).

## THE HUMBLE ARRIVAL

While Jesus' second coming will be in glory and majesty (probably the sort of arrival the Jews originally hoped for while suffering under Roman rule), He came first in humility and suffering to die and bring salvation. Hebrews tells us:

✝ *Just as man is destined to die once, and after that to face judgment, so Christ was sacrificed once to take away the sins of many people; and He will appear a second time, not to bear sin, but to bring salvation to those who are waiting for Him* (Hebrews 9:27-28).

Jesus' first coming was to take the load of sin off our backs. This is the spiritual cornerstone for the ultimate physical manifestation of our salvation—transformation into the image and likeness of God.

*So this is what the Sovereign Lord says: "See, I lay a stone in Zion, a tested stone, a precious Cornerstone for a sure foundation; the one who trusts will never be dismayed"* (Isaiah 28:16).

*The stone the builders* [the spiritual leaders of Jesus' day] *rejected has become the capstone* (Psalm 118:22).

Because Jesus was God physically present on earth, when we follow Jesus, we are actually following God. John tells us:

*In the beginning was the Word* [Jesus]*, and the Word was with God, and the Word was God. He was with God in the beginning. Through Him all things were made; without Him nothing was made that has been made* (John 1:1-3).

This verse confirms Jesus was part of the Holy Trinity and was there at creation. Of course, this suggests Jesus was Spirit at the time prior to His manifestation on earth, at which time He took on human form to be one of us. As one of us, He could then sacrifice His perfect life—what we were incapable of doing ourselves.

## RECOGNIZING JESUS

The "wisdom" of the world does not understand or recognize Jesus. There is not a mathematical or a scientific formula that can prove or disprove His existence. Jesus says, however, that His followers will know Him:

✝ *Therefore Jesus said again, "I tell you the truth, I am the gate for the sheep. All who ever came before me were thieves and robbers, but the sheep did not listen to them. I am the gate; whoever enters through Me will be saved. He will come in and go out, and find pasture [joy]. The thief [satan] comes only to steal and kill and destroy; I have come that they may have life and have it to the full. I am the Good Shepherd. The Good Shepherd lays down His life for the sheep. ...I am the Good Shepherd; I know My sheep and My sheep know Me"* (John 10:7-11,14).

Did you catch that? Our spirit will recognize Him. Jesus says that when you accept Him, you will become aware of His presence and voice. And this is true; remember Simon Peter, who was the first to identify Jesus as the Son of God:

✝ *Jesus replied, "Blessed are you, Simon son of Jonah, for this was not revealed to you by man, but by My Father in Heaven"* (Matthew 16:17).

## ENTERING THE KINGDOM

First and foremost, Jesus came to the Jewish race and they rejected Him. But Jesus also came for the non-Jews (the Gentiles).

✝ *[Jesus] came to that which was His own, but His own did not receive Him* (John 1:11).

✝ *I am not ashamed of the gospel, because it is the power of God for the salvation of everyone who believes: first for the Jew, then for the Gentile* (Romans 1:16).

✠ *Yet to all who received Him, to those who believed in His name, He gave the right to become children of God—children born not of natural descent, nor of human decision or a husband's will, but born of God* (John 1:12-13).

Isaiah, of the Old Testament, prophesied that Jesus would bring salvation, not only to the Jews but also to the Gentiles.

✠ *[God] says, "It is too small a thing for You to be My servant to restore the tribes of Jacob* [whose twelve sons make up the twelve tribes of Israel (Israel also became Jacob's name)] *and bring back those of Israel I have kept. I will also make You a light for the Gentiles, that You may bring My salvation to the ends of the earth"* (Isaiah 49:6).

Again, we see that birth into the Kingdom of God is a spiritual one and not a physical one. Jesus was already spirit and took on a fleshly form so He could come to earth and live fully as a man and fully God.

✠ *The Word became flesh and made His dwelling among us. We have seen His glory, the glory of the one and only, who came from the Father, full of grace and truth* (John 1:14).

Living as fully man allowed Jesus to take our place, to be the sacrifice on our behalf. He was one of us. Remember that death itself is the result or penalty of sin. Jesus didn't sin, so why did He have to die? He died and overcame death to pay the price for you and me to have everlasting life—to be able to receive God's Spirit in us and make a way for us to intimately know Him.

✠ *Jesus answered, "I am the way and the truth and the life. No one comes to the Father [God] except through Me"* (John 14:6).

⊕ *Jesus said, "My Kingdom is not of this world..."* (John 18:36).

So where is the Kingdom of God and how do we get there?

⊕ *Once, having been asked by the Pharisees when the Kingdom of God would come, Jesus replied, "The Kingdom of God does not come with your careful observation, nor will people say, 'Here it is,' or 'There it is,' because the Kingdom of God is **within you**"* (Luke 17:20-21).

This parallel universe lies within you! The Kingdom of God is found through the Holy Spirit within us, not by physical observation. We don't have to die physically to get to the Kingdom of God. We have access to it today by first accepting Jesus and then *subjecting our wills* to the Spirit dwelling within us (dying to ourselves).

⊕ *Not everyone who says to Me, "Lord, Lord," will enter the Kingdom of Heaven, but only he who does the will of My Father who is in Heaven* (Matthew 7:21).

⊕ [Jesus said], *"For I tell you that unless your righteousness surpasses that of the Pharisees and the teachers of the law, You will certainly not enter the Kingdom of Heaven"* (Matthew 5:20).

⊕ *"We must go through many hardships to enter the Kingdom of God,"* [Paul and Barnabas] *said* (Acts 14:22).

How do we access His Kingdom *in this life*? We access it by following the way He got there, which is through *obedience* to the will of God. In other words we need to sync ourselves with heaven to be able to experience it here on earth.

✟ *Jesus gave them this answer: "I tell you the truth, the Son can do nothing by Himself; He can do only what He sees His Father doing, because whatever the Father does the Son also does"* (John 5:19).

✟ *By Myself I can do nothing; I judge only as I hear, and My judgment is just, for I seek not to please Myself but Him who sent Me* (John 5:30).

We become Jesus' family members in Heaven by doing the will of God, just as He did.

✟ *For whoever does the will of My Father in Heaven is My* **brother** *and* **sister** *and* **mother** (Matthew 12:50).

And through this obedience we also gain a greater understanding of *Him* and *His teachings*—that is to say, we gain a more intimate relationship with Him.

✟ [Jesus said], *"If anyone chooses to do God's will, he will find out whether My teaching comes from God or whether I speak on My own"* (John 7:17).

✟ [Jesus said], *"He who has My commandments and keeps them, it is he who loves Me. And he who loves Me will be loved by My Father, and I will love him* **and manifest Myself to him**" (John 14:21 NKJV).

Remember what Jesus' instructions were to His disciples (and us), when He said to them all:

✟ *If anyone would come after Me, he must deny himself and **take up his cross daily and follow Me*** (Luke 9:23).

Jesus, in this same discourse, went on to say this:

✟ *I tell you the truth, some who are standing here will not taste death before they see the Kingdom of God* (Luke 9:27).

This verse was immediately fulfilled, because days later after Jesus told them this, Jesus took Peter, John, and James with Him up a mountain where they would witness the Kingdom of God, just as Jesus had prophesied.

✟ *As [Jesus] was praying, the appearance of His face changed, and His clothes became as bright as a **flash of lightning**. Two men, Moses and Elijah, appeared in glorious splendor, talking with Jesus…* (Luke 9:29-31).

Both the gospels of Matthew and Mark record that Jesus was transformed before the disciples' eyes. This description of the temporary advent of the Kingdom of God parallels what is described as the second coming to the disciples.

✟ *Then [Jesus] said to His disciples, "The time is coming when you will long to see one of the days of the Son of Man, but you will not see it. Men will tell you, 'There He is!' or 'Here He is!' Do not go running off after them. For the Son of Man in His day will be like the **lightning, which flashes** and lights up the sky from one end to the other"* (Luke 17:22-24).

Heaven is not some remote place beyond the sky. Jesus, when He was translated, did not rise into the sky and get smaller and smaller until they could not see Him. Heaven, for the lack of a better word, is a parallel universe, and Jesus was *transformed* into it. Moses and Elijah were temporarily transformed from it, and Jesus will be transformed from it as well in His second coming. Indeed, God is all around us as Paul described to the Romans:

*God did this so that men would seek Him and perhaps reach out for Him and find Him, though He is not far from each one of us* [no matter where we are physically located]. *For in Him we live and move and have our being...* (Acts 17:27-28).

When we're doing the will of God, we're moving and acting in the *Kingdom of God*. We are going to that intimate place with God where He is always dwelling—this place all around us no matter where we are—our home in Him. This is our only real home on earth where we can truly feel safe and at peace. Jesus points this out to a potential follower:

*Then a teacher of the law came to Him and said, "Teacher, I will follow You wherever You go."*
*Jesus replied, "Foxes have holes and birds of the air have nests, but the Son of Man has no place to lay His head"* (Matthew 8:19-20).

Nor do you have a place to lay your head in this world. However, when we follow Jesus and live in God's will, we are in a place (in Him) to gain His peace and power, by subjecting all of ourselves to Him. Indeed, Jesus' full commitment to God's will is why you and I have the gift of salvation.

*All that the Father gives Me will come to Me, and whoever comes to Me I will never drive away. For I have come down from Heaven **not***

**to do My will but to do the will of Him who sent Me**. *And this is the will of Him who sent Me, that I shall lose none of all that He has given Me, but raise them up at the last day. For my Father's will is that everyone who looks to the Son and believes in Him shall have* **eternal life**, *and I will raise him up at the last day* (John 6:37-40).

Doing the will of God was what sustained Jesus.

✠ *Meanwhile His disciples urged Him, "Rabbi, eat something."*

*But He said to them, "I have food to eat that you know nothing about."*

*Then His disciples said to each other, "Could someone have brought Him food?"*

*"**My food**," said Jesus, "**is to do the will of Him who sent Me and to finish His work**" (John 4:31-34).*

Jesus didn't get sufficient nourishment from His circumstances, nor will your circumstances satisfy you. As was the case with Jesus, only doing the will of your Father in Heaven will give you true sustenance and satisfaction.

✠ *Jesus answered, "It is written: 'Man does not live on bread alone, but on every word that comes from the mouth of God'" (Matthew 4:4).*

In Jesus' last open prayer to God, He said this:

✠ *I have brought You glory on earth by* **completing** *the work You gave Me to do* (John 17:4).

Yes, doing God's will and thereby bringing Him glory *is* also the charge He gives to you and to me.

497

> *Now all has been heard; here is the conclusion of the matter: Fear God and keep His commandments, for this is the **whole duty of man*** (Ecclesiastes 12:13).

In that final public prayer to His Father as recorded in the book of John, Jesus appealed to God that we be left in the world as He was, so we could show others the way to *His Kingdom* (not of this world) by showing His glory in doing and seeking His will. Jesus prayed:

> *My prayer is not that You take them out of the world but that You protect them from the evil one. They are not of the world, even as I am not of it. Sanctify them by the truth; Your Word is truth. As You sent Me into the world, **I have sent them into the world**. For them I sanctify Myself, that they too may be truly sanctified.*
>
> *...May they also be in Us so that the world may believe that You have sent Me. I have given them the glory that You gave Me, that they may be **one** as **We are one**: I in them and You in Me. May they be brought to complete **unity** to let the world know that You sent Me and have loved them even as You have loved Me* (John 17:15-19,20-23).

Seeking and becoming obedient to God's will should be our goal each day; however, this requires a fight against the temptation that follows, because our fleshly will and desires wage war against the things of God. This is why James writes:

> *When tempted, no one should say, "God is tempting me." For God cannot be tempted by evil, nor does He tempt anyone; but each one is tempted when, by his own evil desire, he is dragged away and enticed. Then, after desire has conceived, it gives birth to sin; and sin, when it is full-grown, gives birth to death* (James 1:13-15).

Our minds have also been shaped by our earthly circumstances—in a sense, grounded—and that grounding leads us to death.

⊕ *There's a way of life that looks harmless enough; look again—it leads straight to hell* (Proverbs 14:12 MSG).

God is above all. We need a way to communicate with Him so we can maintain our lives in His Kingdom. The Holy Spirit is that way. As spirit beings with the Holy Spirit within us, we strive to reject the desires of the flesh and accept the leading, prompting, and indwelling of the Holy Spirit.

⊕ *...we who worship by the Spirit of God, who glory in Christ Jesus, and who put no confidence in the flesh* (Philippians 3:3).

⊕ *So I say, live by the Spirit, and you will not gratify the desires of the sinful nature* (Galatians 5:16).

⊕ [Jesus said], *"The Spirit gives life; the flesh counts for nothing. The words I have spoken to you are spirit and they are life"* (John 6:63).

The Hebrew word for flesh, *sarx* (sarks), is used throughout the New Testament, and it refers to more than our skin. Although in a literal sense *sarx* refers to the substance of the body, in its idiomatic use the word indicates humanity or personhood. In an ethical or spiritual sense, *sarx* is the lower physical nature of a person, in contrast to a person's spiritual side.[1] Jesus crucified His flesh on the cross, and, because of that, we can and should daily crucify ourselves. This is the "taking up our cross" Jesus spoke about. Our focus and full reliance on Jesus will assist us in our efforts to do this.

✚ *For this reason [Jesus] had to be made like His brothers [us] in every way, in order that He might become a merciful and faithful high priest in service to God, and that He might make atonement for the sins of the people. Because He Himself suffered when He was tempted, **He is able to help those who are being tempted*** (Hebrews 2:17-18).

While you will not achieve this a 100 percent of the time, God sees this honest pursuit of seeking purity in your heart. King David wanted to do God's will; however, he had his moments of weakness just like you and I. He fell into adultery and even had the husband of the woman he was having the affair with killed. Yet David is often referred to as a man after God's own heart. He didn't let his failures keep him down. He stayed in a *continual* pursuit of God. David desired God and, as a result of that pursuit, he ultimately fulfilled God's desire for his life.

✚ *After removing Saul, He made David their king. He testified concerning him: "I have found David son of Jesse a man after My own heart; he will do everything I want him to do"* (Acts 13:22).

Remember, imitating Jesus is what is referred to as becoming Christlike (following Him). This is our earthly goal.

✚ *Rather, clothe yourselves with the Lord Jesus Christ, and do not think about how to gratify the desires of the sinful nature* (Romans 13:14).

It is the Holy Spirit who will help you get there.

✚ *Teach me to do Your will, for You are my God; may Your good Spirit lead me on level ground* (Psalm 143:10).

Doing this will allow you to enter God's Kingdom in the here and now. Being in sync with God's will also put you in sync with His power. This begins by placing yourself on the tracks of righteousness. God can't give you His full power until this is first in place. Otherwise, if you're on the wrong tracks, He could be powering you right into a train wreck—and you're the train. His will in your life and His power, combined with your faith, can move mountains. You and God need to be heading in the same direction— His direction. This is the key to mountain-moving faith.

## ACTION & VISUALIZATION

*With the Holy Spirit's leading and power, deny your will,*
*take up your cross, and follow Him as you live out your life.*

## GOD IS BUILDING YOUR TESTIMONY

You can have a dramatic impact on others through your own personal testimony, if it is telling others about God's power and love in your life. Good testimonies have more power than words alone can ever have. Jesus gave us an example of this, giving glory to His Father in Heaven and giving us His testimony to grab hold of for our salvation:

✢ *That if you confess with your mouth, "Jesus is Lord," and believe in your heart that God raised him from the dead, you will be saved* (Romans 10:9).

Prior to Jesus, humankind had the Word of God; however, Jesus became a living manifestation of the Word of God, and we can make the Word come alive when our actions line up with the Word. There are two types of testimony: one you make by your actions and reactions to what the world brings your way, while the other is when people see the power of God working in or through your life. Jesus said:

✠ *You are the light of the world. A city on a hill cannot be hidden. Neither do people light a lamp and put it under a bowl. Instead they put it on its stand, and it gives light to everyone in the house. In the same way, let your light shine before men, that they may see your good deeds and praise your Father in Heaven* (Matthew 5:14-16).

And Paul said:

✠ *You groped your way through that murk once, but no longer. You're out in the open now. The bright light of Christ makes your way plain. So no more stumbling around. Get on with it! The good, the right, the true—these are the actions appropriate for daylight hours. Figure out what will please Christ, and then do it. Don't waste your time on useless work, mere busywork, the barren pursuits of darkness. Expose these things for the sham they are* (Ephesians 5:8-11 MSG).

We are compared to salt and light in the way we are to be perceived by the world. Salt can awaken flavor, create thirst, and heal. We are to be an agent in the world who does these things too. Just like God, we also have the properties of light. Genesis shows us some of those properties.

✠ *And God said, "Let there be lights in the expanse of the sky to **separate** the day from the night, and let them serve as signs to mark seasons and days and years, and let them be lights in the expanse of the sky to give light on the earth." And it was so* (Genesis 1:14-15).

We should make conscious choices to separate ourselves from the kingdom of evil so there is a clear divide for the world to see. As His followers, our lives should point out the coming season of God, a light in this world to cancel out the darkness.

You too will be given opportunities to testify to the light within you for the world to see—to serve as a witness of God's indwelling power. Like Jesus, you too will suffer and even sometimes appear to be defeated by the world. However, what will be important is how you *react* to these events, for if you fully receive and use the gift of myrrh—walk in God's will *instead of your own*, even through trials like Job and Joseph experienced—your testimony will be powerful and speak truth to many lives. John writes:

✠ [Christians] *overcame* [satan] *by the blood of the Lamb and by the* **word** *of their* **testimony**... (Revelation 12:11).

A testimony can be your action of good in response to evil against you.

✠ *Do not repay anyone evil for evil* (Romans 12:17).

In doing this, we are showing the world the selfless, God-kind of love that will be complete in our Heaven experience to come. In other words, we are bringing them a slice of Heaven now to see and experience through us. Even our "Random Acts of Kindness" (ARK) can create an ark for someone's salvation *if we will create them*.

Your testimony may be a miracle or simply living against the grain of the world and your flesh. God can even take your mistakes and weaknesses, then redeem them so the world will see Him as you testify to that turnaround or contradiction.

✠ *Let the weak say, "I am strong"* (Joel 3:10 NKJV).

✠ *But God chose the foolish things of the world to shame the wise; God chose the weak things of the world to shame the strong* (1 Corinthians 1:27).

No matter what you have done or what weaknesses and failings there have been in your life, God can use you in creating testimonies to inspire others. As we are all weak in different areas, so we can relate best to people like us, ones who are not perfect. When relaying your testimony, be open and transparent about your weaknesses and flaws, because then your testimony will be most effective.

Your testimony can be a physical healing.

✟ [Jesus] *said to the paralytic, "I tell you, get up, take up your mat and go home." He got up, took his mat and walked out in full view of them all. This amazed everyone and they praised God, saying, "We have never seen anything like this!"* (Mark 2:10-12).

Your testimony of God's power causes the enemy to stop and stand back.

✟ *When* [the Sanhedrin] *saw the **courage** of Peter and John and realized that they were unschooled, **ordinary men**, they were **astonished** and they took note that these men had been with Jesus. But since they could see the man who had been **healed** standing there with them, **there was nothing they could say**. So they ordered them to withdraw...* (Acts 4:13-15).

Bringing salt or light into the world with your testimony is persuasive, causing others to take notice and then to turn on their own light. Because of this, satan will try to stop you from fully developing your testimony or speaking it out to others. You will need to use your faith to fully develop your testimony as well as find the courage, wisdom, and skill to speak it out. The above story is continued below, demonstrating this principle.

✟ *...and then* [the Sanhedrin] *conferred together. "What are we going to do with these men?" they asked. "Everybody living in Jerusalem knows they have done an **outstanding miracle**, and we cannot deny* *it. But to stop this thing from spreading any further among the people, we must warn these men to speak no longer to anyone in this name"* (Acts 4:15-17).

Here is yet another example:

✟ *Meanwhile a large crowd of Jews found out that Jesus was there and came, not only because of Him but also to see Lazarus, whom He had raised from the dead. So the chief priests made plans to kill Lazarus as well, for on account of him many of the Jews were going over to Jesus and putting their faith in Him* (John 12:9-11).

God's desire is for your fully-developed and spoken testimony to bring other people to Jesus, although you will need to walk in God's will to fully develop and speak out your testimony.

✟ *Always be prepared to give an answer to everyone who asks you to give the reason for the hope that you have. But do this with gentleness and respect* (1 Peter 3:15).

✟ *Come and listen, all you who fear God; let me tell you what He has done for me* (Psalm 66:16).

✟ *You will be His witness to all men of what you have seen and heard* (Acts 22:15).

Like Jesus, you will need to "die to yourself"—like Abraham, leave your old land behind and look forward to your Promised Land. As Paul says, this will fully manifest the testimony God offers you:

✚ *Brothers, I do not consider myself yet to have taken hold of it. But one thing I do: Forgetting what is behind and straining toward what is ahead, I press on toward the goal to win the prize for which God has called me heavenward in Christ Jesus* (Philippians 3:13-14).

We are to look heavenward and point others heavenward to Jesus. The Old Testament stories, one after another, point us to Jesus, who died on a cross on a hill called Calvary. In the story of Sodom and Gomorrah, God found a city full of evil and darkness. In fact, there was no light at all. God agreed with Abraham not to destroy the city if ten good men could be found to light the city, but other than Lot, none were found. Lot and his family escaped the city, which was on a plain, by fleeing up a hill. God told them not to look back, but to press on, focused on what was ahead, looking forward up the hill (symbolic of Calvary) where they were going. However, Lot's wife looked back.

✚ *But Lot's wife looked back, and she became a pillar of salt* (Genesis 19:26).

For you and me, we see the parallels and warnings for our lives and testimonies. God has called us to Himself through Jesus' crucifixion on the hill of Calvary. The world, or more to the point, our desires for what it offers, will inhibit us from developing and/or speaking out our testimony. Because of that, we are to keep our eyes fixed on Him—not on the world He wants us to leave—never looking back as Lot's wife did. By doing so, she became an *absurd* example of what she was supposed to become—the salt for the world. A Christian still focusing on and looking back desiring the *things* of this world (riches, fame, power, etc.), will also become an *absurd* testimony of God, a dead pillar of salt looking the *wrong* way. You, like Lot's wife, can make yourself into dead pillars of salt if you choose to keep riches, fame, power, and other things of the world as your primary focus over God.

Jesus Himself referred to Lot's wife.

✠ *Remember Lot's wife! Whoever tries to keep his life will lose it, and whoever loses his life will preserve it (Luke 17:32-33).*

Our charge then? The author of Hebrews reminds us:

✠ *Let us fix our eyes on Jesus the author and perfecter of our faith, who for the joy set before Him endured the cross, scorning its shame, and sat down at the right hand of the throne of God (Hebrews 12:2).*

We are to look to our true home and toward the things of the Kingdom, "letting go" of the world; not to look back as Lot's wife did, but to make ourselves into a real testimony of God—true salt and light.

## ACTION & VISUALIZATION

*Allow yourself to "let go" and work at becoming a real living testimony of God.*

## LETTING GO

The whole idea of "dying to self" is something crucial to grabbing ahold of God's will for your life. This is how Jesus did it.

✠ *Your attitude should be the same as that of Christ Jesus: Who, being in very nature God, did not consider equality with God something to be grasped, but made Himself nothing, taking the very nature of a servant, being made in human likeness. And being found in appearance as a man, He **humbled** Himself and became **obedient** to death—even death on a cross! **Therefore** God exalted Him to the highest place and gave Him the name that is above every name, that* *at the name of Jesus every knee should bow, in Heaven and on earth and under the earth, and every tongue confess that Jesus Christ is Lord, to the glory of God the Father* (Philippians 2:5-11).

Because Jesus "let go" of His own *reputation* and *desire*, because He *humbled* Himself to the will of God, God exalted Him above everyone and everything. The verse goes on to say that there will be a day when *everyone*, saved and unsaved, will kneel before Jesus Christ. We too can be exalted when we *humble* ourselves, *let go* of our egos, and align our lives with God's will. Of course, the opposite is also true, as we see in the story Jesus tells at a prominent Pharisee's house:

✝ *When [Jesus] noticed how the guests picked the places of honor at the table, He told them this parable: "When someone invites you to a wedding feast, do not take the place of honor, for a person more distinguished than you may have been invited. If so, the host who invited both of you will come and say to you, 'Give this man your seat.' Then, humiliated, you will have to take the least important place. But when you are invited, take the lowest place, so that when your host comes, he will say to you, 'Friend, move up to a better place.' Then you will be honored in the presence of all your fellow guests. For **everyone who exalts himself will be humbled**, and **he who humbles himself will be exalted**"* (Luke 14:7-11).

Jesus was rewarded for His decision to do the will of God despite the impact on His reputation. Be confident that you too will be rewarded when you do the will of God, despite any perceived negative impact on your reputation. We should not seek honor and praise, but rather to honor and praise the Lord:

✝ *Let another praise you, and not your own mouth; someone else, and not your own lips* (Proverbs 27:2).

✢ *...nor is it honorable to seek one's own honor* (Proverbs 25:27).

✢ *The crucible for silver and the furnace for gold, but man is tested by the praise he receives* (Proverbs 27:21).

It is on the other side of obedience where you will find your blessing. However, you must get *through* it if you are to receive it.

✢ *But [Jesus] said, "More than that, blessed are those who hear the word of God and keep it!"* (Luke 11:28 NKJV).

✢ *He replied, "Blessed rather are those who hear the Word of God and obey it"* (Luke 11:28).

Obedience takes persistence and perseverance:

✢ *You need to persevere so that when you have done the will of God, you will receive what He has promised* (Hebrews 10:36).

## ACTION & VISUALIZATION

*In humility, persevere in obedience to God so that you can find the real place of honor He ascribes for you.*

## READY TO DIE

Throughout the Bible, we run across the concept of readiness to surrender to God's will. We've already explored how we're called to "die to self" and give up our wills and physical desires. Moreover, we should even be prepared to give up our physical lives for God if we are called upon to do so. These thoughts are embodied in the verses that follow, perhaps all of which have the *dual* meaning of death to self too.

✠ *Here is a trustworthy saying: If we died with Him, we will also live with Him...* (2 Timothy 2:11).

✠ *Precious in the sight of the Lord is the death of His saints* (Psalm 116:15).

✠ *They overcame [satan] by the blood of the Lamb and by the word of their testimony; they did not love their lives so much as to shrink from death* (Revelation 12:11).

✠ *The man who loves his life will lose it, while the man who hates his life in this world will keep it for eternal life* (John 12:25).

When you are following Jesus, you can't lose. Think about it. In the end, death is the way to your new life. Yes, this is yet another contradiction to the way the world thinks. If we follow our own wills or our fleshly desires instead of the Holy Spirit's leading, we meet a different kind of death—a real *death*—not a metamorphosis.

✠ *There is a way that seems right to a man, but in the end it leads to death* (Proverbs 14:12).

✠ *For when we were controlled by the sinful nature, the sinful passions aroused by the law were at work in our bodies, so that we bore fruit for **death** (Romans 7:5).*

✠ *I declare to you, brothers, that flesh and blood cannot inherit the Kingdom of God, nor does the perishable inherit the imperishable (1 Corinthians 15:50).*

✠ *The mind of sinful man is **death**, but the mind controlled by the Spirit is life and peace (Romans 8:6).*

✠ *Therefore, brothers, we have an obligation—but it is not to the sinful nature, to live according to it. For if you live according to the sinful nature, you will **die**; but if by the Spirit you put to death the misdeeds of the body, you will live, because those who are led by the Spirit of God are the sons of God (Romans 8:12-14).*

✠ *But you have planted wickedness, you have reaped evil, you have eaten the fruit of deception. Because you have depended on your own strength and on your many warriors, the roar of battle will rise against your people, so that all your fortresses will be **devastated**... (Hosea 10:13-14).*

The Bible is clear that we need to be led by the Spirit of God. However, this was not always easy, even for Jesus Himself. Read what happened in the garden of Gethsemane when in the last moments of His life, Jesus wrestled with His decision to embrace death:

✠ *And being in anguish, [Jesus] prayed more earnestly, and His sweat was like drops of blood falling to the ground* (Luke 22:44).

As His follower living in contradiction to the world, you will be met with pressure to give in, compromise, and give up your conviction and calling. Gethsemane means "olive," and you *cannot* extract the oil (Holy Spirit) from the olive without extreme pressure on the olive itself. If we are living in *obedience*, don't we feel this same pressure as well? Don't we feel the pressure to die to our flesh and release the Holy Spirit (oil) who resides within us? Also, in giving our lives up to God, we find our path to Him and true fulfillment in life.

✠ *You were bought at a price. Therefore honor God with your body* (1 Corinthians 6:20).

✠ *[Jesus said], "The Spirit gives life; the flesh counts for nothing. The words I have spoken to you are Spirit and they are life"* (John 6:63).

## ACTION & VISUALIZATION

*Always walk in life, even when it means the death of your will—even when it means death in this life.*

## THE SERVANT'S HEART

One of the attributes that led Jesus to obedience was that He saw Himself as a *servant*—a servant to God and a servant to humans. This is also your charge:

✛ [Jesus said], *"You know that the rulers of the Gentiles lord it over them, and their high officials exercise authority over them. Not so with you. Instead, whoever wants to become great among you must be your servant, and whoever wants to be first must be your slave—just as the Son of Man did not come to be served, but **to serve**, and to give His life as a ransom for many"* (Matthew 20:25-28).

Forsaking one's life is the ultimate act of servanthood. You won't find that sort of service standards in even the best five-star hotel. Yet God charges us to deliver this sort of ultimate service to God and to one another. Paul wrote:

✛ *Your attitude should be the same as that of Christ Jesus: Who, being in very nature God, did not consider equality with God something to be grasped, but made Himself nothing, taking the **very nature of a servant**, being made in human likeness. And being found in appearance as a man, He humbled Himself and became obedient to death—even death on a cross!* (Philippians 2:5-8).

Paul speaks of what it means to be a servant in his letter to the Ephesians. This letter didn't merely apply to slaves but to anyone who was under the authority of another—an officer, a boss, a teacher, a parent, or a husband. Paul wrote:

✛ *Slaves, obey your earthly masters with respect and fear, and with sincerity of heart, just as you would obey Christ. Obey them not only to win their favor when their eye is on you, but like slaves of Christ, doing the will of God from your heart. Serve wholeheartedly, as if you were serving the Lord, not men, because you know that the Lord will reward everyone for whatever good he does, whether he is slave or free* (Ephesians 6:5-8).

It should go without saying that this does not mean we are to commit sin on someone's order. Rather, it means we are to be helpful and respectful to those who are in positions of authority.

In Jesus' time, the Roman occupation force in Israel could rightfully require an Israelite to carry his backpack for one mile. Jesus told His contemporaries this:

✠ *If someone forces you to go one mile, go with him two miles* (Matthew 5:41).

Jesus was telling them to be servants to their enemies, even if it meant going in the wrong direction for an extra mile.

## ACTION & VISUALIZATION

*Be a servant to God and to others.*

## TRUE FULFILLMENT

Our true fulfillment is in living out God's will, living out that for which He designed us. Shouldn't your Creator know how to maximize His creation's purpose? Wouldn't that be the plan of greatest fulfillment and joy? We simply can't achieve that plan and purpose unless we are in His will, and we can't know His will unless we are in relationship with Him. God's entire plan is beyond our comprehension, and that is why we must be led by the Holy Spirit and not by our own minds.

We are to put on the attitude Jesus had while on earth:

✠ *Therefore, since Christ suffered in His body, arm yourselves also with the **same attitude**, because he who has suffered in his body is done with sin* (1 Peter 4:1).

Is this an easy process? Of course, it isn't. While on this earth and in this life, we'll fall short, never achieving it completely. We'll never be perfect as Jesus was. However, in the next life we'll experience the result of this process: our Promised Land—being formed in the image and likeness of God. In the meantime, however, it is our charge to have a seeking heart occupy as much of that Promised Land as we can.

Stay alert to and aware of the attacks by satan and those battles between your mind and body and your spirit. Daily seek God's understanding and guard yourself; these are keys to your victory. When I was finalizing this chapter, Mel Goebel, who operates a prison ministry, Daughters of Destiny (www.daughtersofdestiny.com), sent me this:

When God leads, we experience an exciting adventure around every corner. When God leads, all provision and individuals are put in place. When God leads, humility is being developed in our character. When God leads, our heart is the most important thing to Him. When God leads, angels are there to work on your behalf. When God leads, joy is always with us. When God leads, contentment resides. When God leads, there is peace. When God leads, self is denied.

## ACTION & VISUALIZATION

*Submit your will to God and walk in the Spirit, not your flesh.*

In summary, the gift of myrrh is all about death, but not a death that is sad or empty. It is about Jesus' death that leads to life, a rebirth if you will. It is about the death of our wills and pursuit of God's will, bringing *purpose* and *meaning* to our lives. For some, it is even the act of giving up our physical lives for someone else or for God.

When we receive, unwrap, and use this gift, we grow much closer to God. This process gives us a glimpse of what it will be like some day to finally enter our Promised Land. Physical death may be the end of life on this earth, but for those who have received the gift of salvation, it is only the beginning of true life—the best life possible—an eternal one with Jesus in Heaven.

## MEDITATION POINT

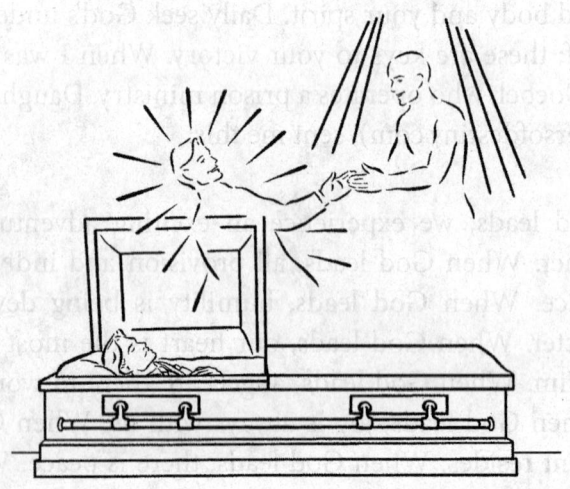

For a believer, physical death is only the beginning of a new heavenly life.

Go to Chapter 5 in the Study Guide section on page 627.

## ENDNOTE

1.  Jack Hayford, Ed. *Spirit-filled Life Bible for Students* (Nashville, TN: Thomas Nelson, 1995), 1237.

# Chapter 6

# Gift #7—Myrrh (Part 2)

## What Are Good Strategies for Successful Living?

Before you begin to read, pray that the Holy Spirit will give you
and all readers of this book understanding and application.

✟ *Let us fix our eyes on Jesus*, *the author and perfecter of our faith,
who for the joy set before Him endured the cross, scorning its shame,
and sat down at the right hand of the throne of God. **Consider Him
who endured such opposition from sinful men, so that you will not
grow weary and lose heart*** (Hebrews 12:2-3).

When you woke up today, you had a strategy. If you were tired, it
may have been as simple as drinking a strong cup of coffee to
wake you up. If you have kids, it probably had something to do
with getting them fed and off to school. If you were running late for work,
you probably quickly deduced the fastest route and a way to eat breakfast
on the go. How does your favorite football team score a touchdown? How
do you go about remodeling a house? Losing weight? Raising kids? Starting
a business?

It all comes down to one word: strategy. A specific, ordered plan to reach your goal. As believers, we need to have a specific plan to accomplish what our Creator has laid out for us here on earth—to move into our Promised Land. We make battle strategies based on the nature of the opposition. Waking up sleepy and getting a latte at Starbucks requires little planning. But engaging in a spiritual battle where your soul, body, spirit, and heart are at stake requires a clear, well-thought-out, informed, and powerful strategy. It is critical for us to receive, unwrap, and use the gift of myrrh to implement God's strategies for success in our lives.

Let's first step back to gain insight and understanding about the larger story that is unfolding around us. With this information, we can then start building a plan.

## Satanic Struggle

God wants us to have a fully connected relationship with Him. This is vital. Because of the distortion sin causes in our lives, we can't know and fully manifest His image and likeness in the world without an intimate relationship with God. Satan fights diligently against this connection. Why? Because God's image and likeness (light) overcome evil (darkness). This means, whether we know it or not or whether we like it or not, we are in the midst of an intense daily battle that we will either win or lose. There is no draw. Paul writes to the Romans:

✠ *Do not be overcome by evil, but overcome evil with good* (Romans 12:21).

Jesus' goodness is so perfect that dwelling in His brightness cancels darkness. We can overcome and outshine evil with good. Indeed, it will be that brightness on Jesus' second coming that will eventually destroy and completely cancel satan's darkness.

✟ *And then the lawless one will be revealed, whom the Lord will consume with the breath of His mouth [words] and destroy with the **brightness** of His coming* (2 Thessalonians 2:8 NKJV).

Until then, however, we are left here to fight evil and darkness with our actions and spiritual weapons, standing firm and holding our ground in this effort.

✟ *Be on your guard; stand firm in the faith; be men [and women] of courage; be strong. Do everything in love [which defeats darkness]* (1 Corinthians 16:13-14).

Our actions create God's light, which overcomes evil in the spirit realm. Therefore, when we bring God's light into the world, we essentially reduce satan's areas of freedom. Satan's goal is to *provoke, intimidate,* or *trick* us into going against God's will in an effort to reduce our light, and especially to keep it from spreading to others which further limits satan's area of freedom to wander. God has set boundaries, a "hedge of protection," that satan is always trying to lure us away from. It's when we leave God's will that we needlessly expose ourselves to evil by succumbing to satan's influence.

## DEVELOP A BATTLE PLAN

Any successful general will tell you that it is important to 1) know your enemy, 2) know his strengths and weaknesses, 3) know your strengths and weaknesses, and 4) know the territory in which the fighting will take place. We will examine each of these in this and the following chapter; however, simply put: our enemy is satan, and his strength is in his cunning and apparent beauty, which enables him to turn our flesh and minds into his allies.

Cartoons depict satan as a little red monster with a spiked tail and a pitchfork. Of course, this cartoonish version is nothing at all like the real

519

satan. We know from Isaiah and Ezekiel that satan at one time was God's worship leader—he was beautiful and made beautiful music—and we know from Genesis that he is crafty. He can and will use all these attributes against us. Sin can look and sound beautiful, even romantic at times. It is pleasurable for a season, but eventually it leads to death. That is why we need to be alert, even if something looks, sounds, or feels good. I urge you to wisely consider the consequences of all your actions. You, of course, will have to eventually deal with the aftermath of them. Remember what the Bible says about satan's first approach to humankind:

✠ *Now the serpent* [satan] *was **more crafty** than any of the wild animals...* (Genesis 3:1).

✠ *When the woman saw that the fruit of the tree was **good** for food and **pleasing to the eye,** and also **desirable** for gaining wisdom, she took some and ate it* (Genesis 3:6).

Satan and sin will be attractive and desirable at times, unless you develop *spiritual* discernment (insight), which you will gain as your relationship with God grows. However, satan's weakness is that he has already been defeated. His only hope of winning is to provoke, lure, coerce, or intimidate your flesh and/or mind to make the wrong choice, quit, or surrender. What Jesus did on the cross has given *you* the freedom to choose victory or defeat.

Your strength is God within you, and your weakness is your mind and your flesh. For this reason, it is vital that you gain control over yourself (the flesh) to be able to overcome each attack by the enemy.

✠ *Therefore do not let sin reign in your mortal body so that you obey its evil desires* (Romans 6:12).

✟ *Like a city whose walls are broken down is a man who lacks self-control* (Proverbs 25:28).

You will allow satan to overrun you if you do not maintain self-control in your life. Along with self-control, you will need to sharpen your spirit so you can more easily cut through this life.

✟ *If the ax is dull and its edges unsharpened, more strength is needed but skill will bring success* (Ecclesiastes 10:10).

Lest we forget, we must remember that the battlefield is in our minds.

## GOOD AND EVIL

The fight we're in is between good and evil. Before we go any further, I want to remind you of God's definitions of these words:

- **Good:** All that is in line with God's character and purpose.
- **Evil:** Anything that is not in line with God's character and purpose.

These definitions are in stark contrast to humanity's definitions:

- **Good:** All that is in line with what pleases me.
- **Evil:** Anything that displeases me or negatively impacts the fulfillment of my desires.

Keep in mind that when I use these terms, I'm referring to God's definitions, *not* humanity's.

God's will, and therefore our path to a successful battle plan, is understood through the Bible and the Holy Spirit. Following God's will is the way to *life*. On the other hand, humanity's ways are based on self-interest, human reason, circumstance, emotion, philosophy, religious tradition, what others think, our habits, and so on. Following humanity's will to its conclusion is a path that eventually leads to *death*. However, because we have God within us, we can understand His will, and it is in *contradiction* to our flesh, our natural impulses. We are to act on this contradiction to gain more territory in our Promised Land. In so doing, our light can show the world the way to go.

## Inevitable Battles

The Bible makes it clear: we're going to face battles here on earth as a result of this contradiction. Satan wants to either dim or extinguish our light. Jesus said:

✢ *But before all this, they will lay hands on you and persecute you. They will deliver you to synagogues and prisons, and you will be brought before kings and governors, and all on account of My name. This will result in your being witnesses to them. But make up your mind not to worry beforehand how you will defend yourselves. For I will give you words and wisdom that none of your adversaries will be able to resist or contradict. You will be betrayed even by parents, brothers, relatives and friends, and they will put some of you to death. All men will hate you because of Me. But not a hair of your head will perish. By standing firm you will gain life (Luke 21:12-19).*

And Paul reminded Timothy:

✢ *Fight the good fight of the faith…* (1 Timothy 6:12).

Though you may not have run into this level of persecution because of your faith, I can tell you that if you are following God and living by faith, then you'll eventually have skirmishes. But don't forget that God gives the victory (or increase) in this world. We need to follow God's instructions so that we're on the winning side of the battle. The writer of Proverbs says:

> *There is no wisdom, no insight, no plan that can succeed against the Lord. The horse is made ready for the day of battle, **but victory rests with the Lord*** (Proverbs 21:30-31).

The first rule of battle is to make sure that you are in sync with God so you don't find yourself fighting *against* Him. This is what the Pharisees—the religious leaders of the day—found themselves doing with the early church. A Pharisee named Gamaliel had this to say when the other Pharisees were trying to figure out what to do about this new Christian movement that was threatening their religious traditions:

> *Therefore, in the present case I advise you: Leave these men alone! Let them go! For if their purpose or activity is of human origin, it will fail. But if it is from God, you will not be able to stop these men; you will only find yourselves fighting against God* (Acts 5:38-39).

We face circumstances like this every day. And each time we do, we need to determine which side of the battle God is on. The side He is on is not always as apparent as one might think. This can apply to situations at work, school, home, church, social events, or anywhere else. There are battles going on around us all the time. We read many Bible verses where we are likened to soldiers in a battle, who are at war with our adversary. We need to follow our Commander's instruction in each of our own battles:

> *Endure hardship with us like a good soldier of Christ Jesus. No one serving as a soldier gets involved in civilian affairs—he wants to please his commanding officer. Similarly, if anyone competes as an athlete, he does not receive the victor's crown unless he competes according*

*to the rules. The hardworking farmer should be the first to receive a share of the crops. Reflect on what I am saying, for the Lord will give you **insight** into all this* (2 Timothy 2:3-7).

Isn't it easy to get caught up in the physical and emotional aspects of this world? It is so easy to keep our sights on this world and thus lose sight of the other world in which we live, the spiritual world God has placed within us. Strengthening your spiritual vision and insight will be a first step in your success. As you already know, the spiritual world intersects and influences the physical world in which we live. One affects the other and vice versa (see Matthew 16:19).

Therefore, when you are dealing with problems in the physical world, you need to identify their source. The root problems are always spiritual in nature, and so you need to deal with them spiritually before you can obtain a physical resolve. This is an act of faith, to overcome our real adversary in a spiritual battlefield and not a physical one. Then your victory, once obtained spiritually, is manifest in the physical world. As a *spiritual* being, your battle plan should be different than those who solely rely on their mind and body. The apostle Paul told early Christians this:

✠ *I beg you that when I come I may not have to be as bold as I expect to be toward some people who think that we live by the standards of this world. For though we live in the world, we do **not** wage war as the world does* (2 Corinthians 10:2-3).

✠ *For our struggle is **not** against flesh and blood [others], but against the rulers, against the authorities, against the powers of this dark world and against the spiritual forces of evil in the heavenly realms* (Ephesians 6:12).

How do we act in contradiction to the world? How do we respond in the face of the many challenges we face daily? We need to understand that though we may have problems with people (bosses, family members, neighbors, friends, or others), what we see as the problem has its root cause in something we *can't* see. The cause of conflict is a stronghold in *them* or in *ourselves*, which is set against the will of God—or likely both to some degree.

God is a God of *order* and *harmony*. You can see it in how God, the Father, Jesus and the Holy Spirit act together in perfect harmony as one. If conflict exists, it is due to forces set against His will. If two people were both acting according to the will of God, then they would *not* collide into one another. It is only because of a spiritual stronghold that problems arise and manifest themselves in the physical realm. We'll always have relationship problems if we simply rely on argument or leveraging a person with physical means rather than attacking the real cause of the problem. If we are to have victory over a problem, we need to attack these spiritual strongholds directly and spiritually. Look at what the Bible says about the best way to take a city:

✢ *A wise man attacks the city of the mighty and pulls down the stronghold in which they trust* (Proverbs 21:22).

When you attack and have victory over a stronghold in which a city trusts, you will immobilize an entire city and minimize the damage to property or people. This is a clear example for us to follow in all our interpersonal relationships. It is a swift, clear victory. It is a way to have victory over a problem with someone without damaging relationship. It is a way to attack the spiritual issues at the core of the problem. You do this through prayer, fasting, seeking wise counsel, and through other spiritual endeavors. At first you may feel unsuccessful at this—yet once again, I'll remind you we are to live by faith and *not by sight*. Faith is one of our most effective spiritual weapons and the one that allows us to have confidence to depend only on the other spiritual weapons in our battles. Remember:

✢ *The weapons we fight with are not the weapons of the world. On the contrary, they have divine power to demolish strongholds* (2 Corinthians 10:4).

Unfortunately, our bodies' senses and minds have trained us to use physical means to solve conflicts. But Paul told the Corinthians that this would cause them to lose the battle even before it started:

✝ *The very fact that you have lawsuits among you means you have been* **completely** *defeated already. Why not rather be wronged? Why not rather be cheated? Instead, you yourselves cheat and wrong, and you do this to your brothers* (1 Corinthians 6:7-8).

## ACTION & VISUALIZATION
*Seek spiritual answers to your problems or challenges.*

## YOU'RE NOW FREE

Not only do you have an enemy in satan, but your own habits and thinking can attack and defeat you too. Indeed, your habits and thinking can keep you enslaved. Before we were saved, we were slaves to sin. We did not have the ability to free ourselves. It was Jesus' sacrifice that gave us freedom from sin:

✝ *For we know that our old self was crucified with [Jesus] so that the body of sin might be done away with, that we should no longer be slaves to sin—because anyone who has died has been* **freed from sin**.
*Now if we died with Christ, we believe that we will also live with Him. For we know that since Christ was raised from the dead, He cannot die again; death no longer has mastery over Him. The death He died, He died to sin once for all; but the life He lives, He lives to God.*
*In the same way, count yourselves* **dead to sin** *but alive to God in Christ Jesus* (Romans 6:6-11).

What about our flesh, our old habits? Yes, the habits and addictions of the "old self" are still there although Jesus has set us free from sin; however, freedom in Christ gives us the *ability* to overcome these habits and addictions. We live in a body with old habits and a thought life that opposes the things of God—even as a follower of Jesus Christ. Indeed, even believers can remain in slavery to old habits and thinking patterns if they don't make a committed decision to change, as well as a thought-out plan of action to execute that change.

A friend of mine had an invisible fence set up around his property for his dog. Through sensors buried in the ground, the dog would receive an uncomfortable shock through a collar around his neck, jolting him to stay within this invisible fence. The dog learned its boundaries. In fact, even when the invisible fence was removed, the dog still stayed confined! The dog had complete freedom yet remained in *self-imposed* slavery. Its own thinking and habits kept it confined because it reacted not to its current reality, but to the memory of its old boundaries.

For believers, Christ removed our invisible fence, the place we were once confined to live. Our bodies and our thinking patterns shock us through seductions and desires into returning to habitual sins, to dwell in thoughts and actions that keep us from running free. Christians may receive, hear, and know the good news of freedom, yet like the dog *they* stop *themselves* from taking advantage of it. Even though their hearts, minds, and spirits have been set free, they still stay confined by old habits.

If you've found yourself in this place, know you are not powerless—you have the ability to take advantage of the freedom He offers. You don't have to give your mind and body over to sinful actions or thoughts as you once were in the habit of doing. Through the power of Christ, we can take control of our thought life, destructive mind-sets, and toxic habits—reprogramming and washing ourselves with truth. Pray and visualize yourself in situations that usually lead to sin—but choose to respond differently. You have been set *free* to have a *choice*—you are *not helpless* or *defeated*. You can choose to take hold of the power you have been given as a child of the living God:

✠ *Therefore do not let sin reign in your mortal body so that you obey its evil desires. Do not offer the parts of your body to sin, as instruments of wickedness, but rather offer yourselves to God, as those who have been brought from death to life; and offer the parts of your body to Him as instruments of righteousness. For sin shall **not** be your master, because you are not under law, but under grace* (Romans 6:12-14).

## ACTION & VISUALIZATION
*Change your thinking and systematically start reprogramming those old habits that led you to sin.*

## INSIGHT

Being a Christian does *not* assure you an easy life or assure you of His power and provision when you are pursuing your own goals. However, God does assure you His power and provision when you lay down your ambitions and pick up the desires He has for you.

There is an Old Testament story of Jacob, who was the father of twelve sons who made up the twelve tribes of Israel. Indeed, Jacob would go through changes that developed him into the person God wanted him to be. These changes led God to change his name to Israel. Jacob's given name means "first," and that is what he did in life—he sought his will "first," over that of others and over God's will. He even obtained, through trickery, his father's blessing, which was meant for his older brother, Esau. Shortly after he received this blessing, we see Jacob on the run from his brother:

✠ *Jacob left Beersheba and set out for Haran. When he reached a certain place, he stopped for the night because the sun had set. Taking one of the stones there, he put it under his head and lay down to sleep. He had a dream in which he saw a stairway resting on the earth, with its top reaching to Heaven, and the angels of God were ascending and descending on it. There above it stood the Lord, and He said: "I am the Lord, the God of your father Abraham and the God of Isaac. I will give you and your descendants the land on which you are lying"* (Genesis 28:10-13).

Maybe your life at times seems like you're on the run from your enemies. Are you lacking comfort and rest—in essence, using stones as pillows? We see two important lesson we can take from these verses. The first is that though life seemed hard and out of control for Jacob, God showed him that He was active on the earth, with angels in Jacob's dreams ascending and descending on the earth to fulfill His will for His chosen people. Second, God reaffirmed His commitment to Jacob and his descendants, that they would find their Promised Land. Likewise, we as believers know our Promised Land is our bodies and minds becoming transformed into His image and likeness.

God goes on to reaffirm to Jacob His active involvement and presence, delivering on His promise:

*I am with you and will watch over you wherever you go, and I will bring you back to this land. I will not leave you **until I have done what I have promised you*** (Genesis 28:15).

Let's see what Jacob does next in this story:

*Early the next morning Jacob took the stone he had placed under his head and set it up as a pillar and poured oil on top of it. He called that place Bethel [which means "House of God"], though the city used to be called Luz* (Genesis 28:18-19).

Jacob used the same stone pillow, which was symbolic of his hardship and trouble, to build an altar of worship to God. The oil he used represents the Holy Spirit, who is our source of praise, comfort, and new life in the midst of hardship, pain, and trouble. Most of the time, hardship is the result of loss and change, *or* it leads us to change—to the death of our old self and old ways. Truly, the process of dying to ourselves is a metamorphosis, letting some things go so that we can make room for growth and the fulfillment of our purpose. You will have to let go of some things and make sacrifices in the physical realm to make room for spiritual growth and maturity. There sometimes must be a sowing of physical seeds if we are to achieve spiritual growth. Read how Jacob did this:

✠ *Then Jacob made a vow, saying, "If God will be with me and will watch over me on this journey I am taking and will give me food to eat and clothes to wear so that I return safely to my father's house, then the Lord will be my God and this stone that I have set up as a pillar will be God's house, and of all that You give me I will give You a tenth* [now referred to as tithes] (Genesis 28:20-22).

In following Jacob's example, we should not be discouraged by our current circumstances. We will be attacked, go on the run at times, and have resistance in life when we are going in God's direction. When these occur, however, we must *not* focus on the physical but the spiritual for our comfort, direction, and strength. God in His mercy and love is struggling with us to bring us into our specific destiny. Indeed, the new name God gave Jacob was Israel, which means "God struggle."

God came to Jacob another night and *struggled* with him all night. It is not always easy for God to get us to realize certain changes we need to make so that our lives can become all they were intended to be. In Jacob's (Israel's) case, he developed a *limp* from this struggle that became a constant reminder of his weakness. And ironically, it was Jacob's limp that led him to a better walk—connected to God's will for his life.

## MAKING A STAND

God has freed us from the power of evil and given us spiritual insight. How do we use these to fulfill His purpose? We are to make a stand so He can reveal Himself for all the world to see. For Shadrach, Meshach, and Abednego, it was nearly being burned to death in a blazing fire. The king of the time, King Nebuchadnezzar, had given an edict that all must worship a false god or be thrown into a blazing furnace of fire, much like society today sets up all sorts of false gods so that we will have pressure to acknowledge them over God. However, Shadrach, Meshach, and Abednego would not worship the false god King Nebuchadnezzar had required, so in his rage the king ordered the furnace to be heated seven times hotter for their execution. The Bible says that the furnace became so hot that the guards who threw the three Jews into the furnace were instantly killed.

✠ *Then King Nebuchadnezzar leaped to his feet in amazement and asked his advisers, "Weren't there three men that we tied up and threw into the fire?"*

*They replied, "Certainly, O King."*

*He said, "Look! I see four men walking around in the fire, unbound and unharmed, and the fourth looks like a son of the gods."*

*Nebuchadnezzar then approached the opening of the blazing furnace and shouted, "Shadrach, Meshach and Abednego, servants of the Most High God, come out! Come here!"* (Daniel 3:24-26).

As Shadrach, Meshach, and Abednego stood in the face of trials and would not bow down or succumb to a false god, Jesus was with them—active even within their trial. As they stood in the fire, Jesus became visible to the king, causing him to recognize and worship the one true God. When you follow your spiritual insight, staying rooted in Christ, and are *not* moved by the pressures of the world, then you will reveal Christ as well as create a witness for the whole world to see.

531

*So Shadrach, Meshach and Abednego came out of the fire, and the satraps, perfects, governors and royal advisers crowded around them. They saw that the fire had not harmed their bodies, nor was a hair of their heads singed; their robes were not scorched, and there was no smell of fire on them (Daniel 3:26-27).*

Remember that as a believer God intended our clothes be our ability to shine the light of the Holy Spirit within us. That is the covering God intended us to have so we would have no shame. We see here in this verse that the world or satan *cannot* affect our covering or ability to shine our light as long as we are walking with Jesus. Regardless of the trial, we can exude a joyous and victorious attitude—there'll be no scorched clothes or smell of fire on us even when we are amid the fire.

## ACTION & VISUALIZATION

*Stand on God's Word, and know God is with you in all things you do in His will. And in so doing, your light will shine to others.*

## FASTING

Before we start using our spiritual weapons, we need to know our battle strategy. There are four things you can do that are helpful in discerning God's will: knowing God's Word, worship, prayer, and fasting. We have already studied the merits of knowing God's Word, worship, and prayer, so let's look at the spiritual implications and benefits of fasting.

The first thing Jesus did after He was baptized and just before He started His three-year ministry was go on a forty-day fast. Luke tells us:

*Jesus, full of the Holy Spirit, returned from the Jordan and was led by the Spirit in the desert, where for forty days He was tempted by the devil. He ate nothing during those days, and at the end of them He was hungry* (Luke 4:1-2).

Note that Jesus' fasting was *led by the Spirit*. I believe a fast needs to be truly Spirit-led to have a significant spiritual impact. We don't always understand God's will, but the Spirit leads us to the right reasons. Being led by the Spirit is key, because so often God's will, *from our perspective*, doesn't match up with what we might expect.

✠ *Now John's disciples and the Pharisees were fasting. Some people came and asked Jesus, "How is it that John's disciples and the disciples of the Pharisees are fasting, but Yours are not?"*

*Jesus answered, "How can the guests of the Bridegroom fast while He is with them? They cannot, so long as they have Him with them. But the time will come when the Bridegroom will be taken from them, and on that day they will fast"* (Mark 2:18-20).

Much like Jesus, Moses, who ushered God's people into a new Promised Land (though the one Moses led them to was an earthly land), also fasted for forty days before he brought God's word down from the mountain:

✠ *Moses was there with the Lord forty days and forty nights without eating bread or drinking water. And he wrote on the tablets the words of the covenant—the Ten Commandments* (Exodus 34:28).

Both the New and Old Testaments include stories of men who fasted anywhere from three days to forty days as a means to get spiritual clarity and growth, along with gaining greater intimacy with God. Fasting will suppress your flesh and earthly desires, both of which want to eat and feed on that which is outside of God's will and nourishment. This is a powerful way to clean out the spiritual impurities of the flesh and mind. When you fast from food, you force your body on a cellular level to eject impurities. In a sense, fasting does the same thing for you spiritually as it does physically—it helps purify. The suppression of your will allows you to have clearer vision and spiritual clarity. This, of course, helps you to see and do God's will and connect with His power.

Some spiritual issues can *only* be resolved by fasting, as we read in the book of Matthew:

✚ *And when they had come to the multitude, a man came to Him, kneeling down to Him and saying, "Lord, have mercy on my son, for he is an epileptic and suffers severely; for he often falls into the fire and often into the water. So I brought him to Your disciples, but they could not cure him."*

*Then Jesus answered and said, "O faithless and perverse generation, how long shall I be with you? How long shall I bear with you? Bring him here to Me." And Jesus rebuked the demon [fallen angel], and it came out of him; and the child was cured from that very hour.*

*Then the disciples came to Jesus privately and said, "Why could we not cast it out?"*

*So Jesus said to them, "Because of your unbelief; for assuredly, I say to you, if you have faith as a mustard seed, you will say to this mountain, 'Move from here to there,' and it will move; and nothing will be impossible for you. However, this kind does not go out except by* **prayer** *and* **fasting***"* (Matthew 17:14-21 NKJV).

David believed fasting was a way to move God as well:

✚ *David pleaded with God for the child. He fasted and went into his house and spent the nights lying on the ground* (2 Samuel 12:16).

Then just a few verses later, we read:

✠ *His servants asked him, "Why are you acting this way? While the child was alive, you fasted and wept, but now that the child is dead, you get up and eat!"*

*He answered, "While the child was still alive, I fasted and wept. I thought, 'Who knows? The Lord may be gracious to me and let the child live.' But now that he is dead, why should I fast? Can I bring him back again? I will go to him* [in Heaven at my death], *but he will not return to me"* (2 Samuel 12:21-23).

God spoke to David in his fasting and allowed him to see clearly so that he would be comforted.

If you are on a complete fast from all food, it is important to drink plenty of water so the impurities being jettisoned from your cells don't accumulate in your liver and kidneys. (It's also a good idea to consult a physician before fasting if you have a history of health problems.) But fasting completely from food isn't the only way to fast. A "Daniel fast" is a fast from one or more items you typically enjoy; it is done to show honor to God as well as to show your faith in Him.

✠ *But Daniel resolved not to defile himself with the royal food and wine, and he asked the chief official for permission not to defile himself this way. Now God had caused the official to show favor and sympathy to Daniel, but the official told Daniel, "I am afraid of my lord the king, who has assigned your food and drink. Why should he see you looking worse than the other young men your age? The king would then have my head because of you."*

*Daniel then said to the guard whom the chief official had appointed over Daniel, Hananiah, Mishael and Azariah, "Please test your servants for ten days: Give us nothing but vegetables to eat and water to drink. Then compare our appearance with that of the young men who eat the royal food, and treat your servants in accordance with what you see." So he agreed to this and tested them for ten days.*

*At the end of the ten days they looked healthier and better nourished than any of the young men who ate the royal food. So the guard took away their choice food and the wine they were to drink and gave them vegetables instead.*

*To these four young men God gave* **knowledge** *and* **understanding** *of all kinds of literature and learning. And Daniel could understand visions and dreams of all kinds.*

*At the end of the time set by the king to bring them in, the chief official presented them to Nebuchadnezzar. The king talked with them, and found none equal to Daniel, Hananiah, Mishael and Azariah; so they entered the king's service. In every matter of wisdom and understanding about which the king questioned them, he found them* **ten times** *better than all the magicians and enchanters in his whole kingdom* (Daniel 1:8-20).

A Daniel fast can be powerful in gaining spiritual vision, wisdom, knowledge, understanding, and favor. The concept of this type of fast can extend beyond food into other areas of life. For example, some people take a vow of poverty, celibacy, or simply quit something they enjoy doing for a set period.

The truth is that fasting is a powerful and personal action between you and God. Therefore, fasting should be done in the quiet of your relationship with God—not publicly. The religious leaders of Jesus' day would fast and pray publicly *not* to grow closer to God but to "show off" their pious spirituality. This is why Jesus said:

✠ *When you fast, do not look somber as the hypocrites do, for they disfigure their faces to show men they are fasting. I tell you the truth, they have received their reward in full* [by doing it to get other people's respect, thus requiring nothing from God]. *But when you fast* [for only God], *put oil on your head and wash your face, so that it will not be obvious to men that you are fasting, but only to your Father, who is unseen; and your Father, who sees what is done in secret, will reward you* (Matthew 6:16-18).

Jesus begins His instruction with the words *"when* you fast" not *"if you* fast." This is because fasting should in some ways be part of every Christian's life, just like eating, breathing, and sleeping. There are many good resources available on fasting. I would encourage you to visit your local Christian bookstore or check online to find one suited to your situation or needs.

The benefits of fasting can be great. But what's most important is listening to God—allowing Him to lead you in the timing, type, and length of the fast. Wait for a confirmation in your spirit before fasting. And when you fast, spend time in worship and prayer. Then be sure to listen for God to speak and give you spiritual clarity.

## ACTION & VISUALIZATION

*Use God's Word, worship, prayer, and fasting to discern God's will and to knock down strongholds in your life and in the lives of others.*

## BRING EVERY THOUGHT CAPTIVE

We must not only stand against strongholds in the spirit realm, but we must also understand those in our minds and in our actions. Paul told the early church that when we wage war, we must use spiritual weapons with the *goal* of bringing every thought *captive* to the will of God:

✠ *For though we live in the world, we do not wage war as the world does [nonbelievers]. The weapons we fight with are not the weapons of the world. On the contrary, they have divine power to* **demolish strongholds**. *We demolish arguments and every pretension that sets itself up against the knowledge of God, and we take captive* *every thought to make it obedient to Christ. And we will be ready to punish every act of disobedience, once **your obedience is complete*** (2 Corinthians 10:3-6).

What do you think these verses are saying? Well, they are suggesting that *obedience* is a prerequisite for victory over strongholds. Obedience means we give up our own wills and suppress the sinful desires of our flesh and do the will of God. This is what Jesus did to take back authority on earth for humankind. He had to come and spiritually fulfill the law so He would then have a foundation on which to establish justice. Jesus said:

✠ *Do not think that I have come to abolish the Law or the Prophets; I have **not** come to abolish them but to **fulfill them*** (Matthew 5:17).

He could not execute justice without first *being* just. And neither can you.

Remember that once we receive Jesus Christ as our Savior, the evil forces warring against the light will only increase. Satan aims to steal your Promised Land here on earth. In the present sense, the battles for obtaining your Promised Land are only just beginning. It is a lifelong process that is fought in your mind. Paul describes this process as working out our own salvation:

✠ *Therefore, my dear friends, as you have always obeyed—not only in my presence, but now much more in my absence—continue to work out your salvation in fear and trembling* (Philippians 2:12).

✠ *Remember those earlier days after you had received the light, when you stood your ground in a great contest in the face of suffering* (Hebrews 10:32).

✠ *So let us put aside the **deeds** of darkness and put on the armor of light* [which will help protect us, because light overcomes darkness] (Romans 13:12).

✠ *Timothy, my son, I give you this instruction in keeping with the prophecies once made about you, so that by following them you may **fight the good fight**...* (1 Timothy 1:18).

The reason it is critical to fight the good fight of faith is because *we ourselves* are the battlefield, and our minds are where the battle is the hottest. To have victory, we must possess the territory where the fight rages. Possession of that territory comes when all thoughts and actions are pulled into obedience God's will. Paul says it this way:

✠ *But I see another law at work in the members of my body, waging war against the law of my mind and making me a prisoner of the law of sin at work within my members* (Romans 7:23).

That territory is sometimes referred to as "God's temple," which is why Paul said in another place:

✠ *Don't you know that you yourselves are God's temple and that God's Spirit lives in you?* (1 Corinthians 3:16).

You and you alone will be held responsible for the cleaning of your temple. Jesus illustrated the need to "clean out His temple" with a rare display of righteous anger, as described by Mark. Remember when reading these verses that we *are* His temples, the place where His Spirit dwells:

✠ *On reaching Jerusalem, Jesus entered the temple area and began driving out those* [in our cases, thoughts] *who were buying and selling there* [putting worldly affairs over relationships with God]. *He overturned the tables of the money changers and the benches of those selling doves, and would not allow anyone to carry merchandise through the temple courts. And as He taught them, He said, "Is it not written: 'My house will be called a house of prayer* [communication with God] *for all nations?' But you have made it 'a den of robbers'"* (Mark 11:15-17).

As evidenced in this story, cleaning up a temple can be uncomfortable at times. Symbolically, we are God's temples, not to be corrupted (by *any* thought that is not in the will of God), but used solely for the work of God's Spirit living within us. If we give over our wills to Jesus, then He can help us drive those demons out and break down those strongholds. The story goes on to suggest, however, that while Jesus is on our side in this battle, we are facing a powerful and determined enemy:

✠ *The chief priest and the teachers of the law heard this* [what Jesus was doing in the temple] *and began looking for a way to kill Him, for they feared Him, because the whole crowd was amazed at His teaching* (Mark 11:18).

Satan and his minions will try to stop you when you start working with Jesus to clean up your temple. You may be attacked, persecuted, ridiculed, and, most of all, tempted, because with a "clean temple" you *brightly* radiate the light of God's love to the world.

This can come by one simple word of kindness, one selfless deed, or one small act of submission (Act of Random Kindness or ARK). God uses each of these ARKs to bring His light and therefore salvation into the world. He can turn the tiniest of seeds we plant into a full revelation of Jesus Christ (God gives the increase to the seeds *you and I* plant). As more and more people are saved by these ARKs and come to this revelation of Jesus and exude God's light with each of our own individual rainbow of colors, satan's darkness becomes eclipsed. This is why satan considers the cleaning of your temple—the very battle for your attention—a life-and-death struggle for both you and him. At each encounter one wins, the other loses.

Jesus warned Simon Peter of satan's designs for him; however, Jesus said He would stand with him in his time of temptation.

✠ *Simon, Simon, satan has asked to sift you as wheat. But I have prayed for you, Simon, that your faith may not fail. And when you have turned back, strengthen your brothers* (Luke 22:31-32).

Let's look at Jesus' life as an example we are to follow. The Bible tells us that He is the author and finisher of our faith:

✠ *And having been perfected, He became the author of eternal salvation to all those who obey Him...* (Hebrews 5:9 NKJV).

If we want to work toward obedience, then we will need the power of God through Jesus Christ to win the battles in our minds. Sin begins in the mind, and it is powered by our desires.

✠ *But each one is tempted when, by **his own** evil* [out of the will of God] *desire, he is dragged away and enticed. Then, after desire has conceived, it gives birth to sin...* (James 1:14-15).

If we seek obedience, then we must examine our thought life first, taking *each* thought captive to the will of God before it has a chance to lead us to action. This is why even thoughts against the will of God are sin. This is seen in the Sermon on the Mount:

✠ *You have heard that it was said, "Do not commit adultery." But I tell you that anyone who looks at a woman lustfully has **already** committed adultery with her in his heart* (Matthew 5:27-28).

We sin *not* just by our actions but also by our thoughts and what's in our hearts. As a result of our unholy obsessions, desires, and lusts of the physical world, our spiritual lives take a back seat. Jesus said it like this:

✠ *If your right eye causes you to sin, gouge it out and throw it away. It is better for you to lose one part of your body than for your whole body to be thrown into hell* (Matthew 5:29).

Obviously, throwing away your eye wouldn't keep you from sinning, because sight isn't a requirement for sinning—it occurs in the mind and in the heart. Jesus was merely making a point in a dramatic way to catch our *attention* that *we need to address* our spirituality as a first and foremost order of business. Even the loss of our eye is less important than our relationship with God. For us to overcome sin, we must reprioritize, with "growing closer to God" taking *first* place. As we do this, our desires and His desires become one and the same, and *temptations lose their hold.*

## ACTION & VISUALIZATION

*Invite Jesus to help you clean your temple and bring every thought captive to God; follow the leading of the Holy Spirit in doing this.*

## DON'T BE TRICKED INTO PHYSICAL BATTLES

We need to be on guard and always remember that the battle we fight is spiritual. God has not called us to fight a spiritual battle with natural weapons. For example, if someone is unkind to you, the natural response might be to respond with similar unkindness—they deserve it! However, the spiritual response calls us to return evil with good. God's will is *always* goodness, as His very essence and nature is love:

✠ *Do not repay anyone evil for evil* (Romans 12:17).

✠ *Avoid every kind of evil* [deserved or not] (1 Thessalonians 5:22).

✠ [Jesus said], *"You have heard that it was said, 'Eye for eye, and tooth for tooth.' But I tell you, Do not resist an evil person. If someone strikes you on the right cheek, turn to him the other also. ...You have heard that it was said, 'Love your neighbor and hate your enemy.' But I tell you: Love your enemies and pray for those who persecute you"* (Matthew 5:38-39,43-44).

Remember God's response to our sins and rejection of Him. He responded with the greatest love and sacrifice of all—the death of His Son.

We have been *tricked* into believing that it's okay to return evil with evil if someone wrongs us. But let's look at what this is suggesting. Essentially, if someone else acts against God's will, then this way of thinking tells us we can act against God's will too. Obviously, two wrongs don't make a right. Jesus tells us that when we suffer a physical attack, we are to make a spiritual counterattack by doing good and praying for our enemies. Jesus admonishes us *not* to correct someone else, because this puts us on the spiritual high ground, so we're in position to get a spiritual victory. Remember, we can't punish disobedience without first being obedient ourselves. This does not mean, however, that we can judge other people just because we have improved our behavior. Jesus wants us always to be focused on getting our temple clean and not judging the cleanliness of others' temples. Jesus said:

> *Why do you look at the speck of sawdust in your brother's eye and pay no attention to the plank in your own eye? How can you say to your brother, "Let me take the speck out of your eye," when all the time there is a plank in your own eye? You hypocrite, first take the plank out of your own eye, and then you will see clearly to remove the speck from your brother's eye* (Matthew 7:3-5).

Jesus is saying that it is important for you to *not* judge others unless you are *completely* sinless, which of course will not happen until His return. One of several reasons you aren't capable of effectively getting the speck out of someone else's eye is that the sin in your own has distorted your vision. When you're in church listening to a sermon, are you sometimes thinking about how it applies to the person next to you? Our zeal to do some cleaning should only reside with our own temple.

There is another account in Jesus' ministry that demonstrates our need to deal with our own sin, *not* that of others:

> *At dawn He appeared again in the temple courts, where all the people gathered around Him, and He sat down to teach them. The teachers of the law and the Pharisees brought in a woman caught in adultery. They made her stand before the group and said to Jesus, "Teacher, this woman was caught in the act of adultery. In the law Moses commanded us to stone such women. Now what do You say?" They were using this question as a trap, in order to have a basis for accusing Him.*
>
> *But Jesus bent down and started to write on the ground with His finger. When they kept on questioning Him, He straightened up and said to them, "If any one of you is without sin, let him be the first to throw a stone at her." Again He stooped down and wrote on the ground.*
>
> *At this, those who heard began to go away one at a time, the older ones first, until only Jesus was left, with the woman still standing*

*there. Jesus straightened up and asked her, "Woman, where are they? Has no one condemned you?"*

*"No one, sir," she said.*

*"Then neither do I condemn you," Jesus declared. "Go now and leave your life of sin"* (John 8:2-11).

Are you sinless? Do you have the right to throw a stone, an insult, or an accusatory word at anybody else? Jesus' temple *was* perfectly clean, which is something we will never have in this lifetime. He had the *right* to judge. But Jesus didn't come to judge; instead, He came to love us and protect us even from ourselves.

The first thing Jesus did was to protect the woman who was accused of adultery from the crowds, and then He attempted to protect her from herself by telling her to sin no more. Jesus also came to live as we live and experience what we experience so that He could then establish spiritual salvation.

✟ *For God did not send His Son into the world to condemn the world, but to save the world through Him* (John 3:17).

✟ [Jesus said], *"As for the person who hears My words but does not keep them, I do not judge him. For I did not come* [this time] *to judge the world, but to save it"* (John 12:47).

We are to follow in Jesus' footsteps and not judge people for what they do, but to love them and protect them, as well as feel and experience what they experience, much like Jesus did. In doing so, we are in a better position to show them grace, the same grace we were extended by Him. Remember that final judgment has been reserved by Him for a later time:

✞ *Do not judge, or you too will be judged. For in the same way you judge others, you will be judged, and with the measure you use, it will be measured to you* (Matthew 7:1-2).

✞ *You, then, why do you judge your brother? Or why do you look down on your brother? For we will all stand before God's judgment seat* (Romans 14:10).

Be aware that even your grumbling against others is a form of judgment:

✞ *Don't grumble against each other, brothers, or you will be judged. The Judge is standing at the door!* (James 5:9).

There will be a day when Jesus will return, and on that day—at Jesus' second coming—He will judge the world:

✞ *For [God] has set a day when He will judge the world with justice by the Man [Jesus] He has appointed. He has given proof of this to all men by raising Him from the dead* (Acts 17:31).

✞ *Moreover, the Father judges no one, but has entrusted all judgment to the Son* (John 5:22).

✞ *[Jesus] will judge the world in righteousness; He will govern the peoples with justice* (Psalm 9:8).

## ACTION & VISUALIZATION

*Do not judge others; rather, only extend to them God's love and grace.
Strive for personal obedience to God and attack others' disobedience
through your good deeds, worship, prayer, and with fasting.*

## LET GOD DO THE WORK

How can we possibly have victory in the physical realm until we have
it in the spiritual realm? God must give us the knowledge and power to be
victorious in battles. It even sometimes means letting God do all the work
while we remain silent and stand back.

✠ *The Lord will fight for you; you need only to be still* (Exodus 14:14).

One of the most powerful ways to reconcile with others is to be *silent*
and let God work. This often means humbling yourself and not arguing,
even when your reputation is at stake. Consider the story that brought the
greatest reconciliation to this world—Jesus' sacrifice. During the events
leading up to His crucifixion, Jesus was falsely charged. Look at how Jesus
answered those charges:

✠ *When [Jesus] was accused by the chief priests and the elders, He gave
no answer. Then Pilate asked him, "Don't You hear the testimony
they are bringing against You?" But Jesus made no reply, not even to
a single charge—to the great amazement of the governor* (Matthew
27:12-14).

Indeed, Jesus didn't answer or argue with false charges. He was not
concerned about His reputation; rather, He was concerned about the

reconciliation of humankind to God. Jesus had to "let go" of His reputation at this trial to gain the spiritual victory—*reconciliation* with the Father. Jesus could have proved Himself right and vindicated His name. But do you think Jesus is thought any less of today because of not defending Himself? Of course not. And while Jesus may have lost the trial, He won the *real* victory—reconciliation for you and me.

✚ *Therefore God also has highly exalted [Jesus] and given Him the name which is above every name* (Philippians 2:9 NKJV).

We need to grab hold of this spiritual contradiction for success in our earthly relationships. Sometimes we need to have a worldly "loss" in order to have a spiritual win. We need to give up what may seem important in the physical realm to gain a great victory spiritually. Sometimes we simply need to be still and lose the argument—we need to die to ourselves—to find spiritual victory and freedom.

✚ *Be still, and know that I am God...* (Psalm 46:10).

## ACTION & VISUALIZATION

*Learn to stand still and allow God to be God.*

Following God's will in your life allows God to bring life to you and life through you to the world around you.

# MEDITATION POINT

Our light gets brighter as we "die to ourselves" and choose to follow God further down His path.

Go to Chapter 6 in the Study Guide section on page 635.

# Chapter 7

# Gift #7—Myrrh (Part 3)

## Who Is Your Enemy, and How and Where Will He Attack?

Before you begin to read, pray that the Holy Spirit will give you and all readers of this book understanding and application.

✟ [Jesus said], "*Watch and pray, lest you enter into temptation. The spirit indeed is willing **but** the flesh is weak*" (Matthew 26:41 NKJV).

There's a story of a man who found a cocoon. One day, a small opening appeared. He sat and watched the butterfly for several hours as it struggled to force its body through that little hole. Then it seemed to stop making progress. It appeared as if it had gotten as far as it could and could go no further. The man decided to help and used a pair of scissors to snip off the remaining part of the cocoon. The butterfly emerged easily. But it had a swollen body and small, shriveled wings. The man continued to watch the butterfly, because he expected that, at any moment, the wings would enlarge and expand to be able to support the body, which would contract to a normal size. Neither happened. In fact, the butterfly spent the rest of its life crawling with a swollen body and shriveled wings—never able to fly.

God is preparing us for something wonderful. However, God does not operate like the man in this story. He sees our struggles, He sees how we're restricted, and He even knows our desire for flight. Yet God knows the natural struggle is how we find life in Him alone. Our flesh is just like the man who didn't understand the necessity of the butterfly's struggle to escape the cocoon. That was God's design—pressing through that tiny opening is how the butterfly forces fluid from its body into the wings in preparation for flight. Likewise, God has a plan to bring us to our potential. Focusing on our knowledge and our will can blind us to God's plan, while dying to self allows us to see God's hand amid struggle. This is the gift of myrrh—surrendering our will to God's, persevering, and recognizing that only through Him and His plan can we develop.

Jesus instructs us that we are to watch and pray. What a great way to start *every* day. An intense battle for your mind is going on all the time, and your weakest point is the desires of your flesh. With that in mind, what if you also began the day with a review of yesterday's battles? How well did you fight the good fight of faith? Are there strategic things you need to do today to correct mistakes or make amends?

It's important to learn from our mistakes and then to make appropriate adjustments. Remember the point at which things went wrong and then visualize what you could have done differently. Some changes won't come easy because the flesh is weak; they require God's involvement. So be persistent, be prayerful, and take one step at a time. Also take note of your victories so you can praise God and acknowledge Him in your journey toward life-altering changes.

How much has your life changed since you were first saved? Imagine the "then" and "now" together to encourage you on the spiritual growth you've made. And when you do suffer setbacks, no matter the size or kind of trials, press on as did David, Peter, and others. If your heart is in it, God will know. He understands that the flesh is weak.

A wise battle commander puts his strengths on the frontlines and sends his weaknesses to the back. As you grow in your relationship with God, His

Spirit within you will quickly become your greatest battle strength. This is why it's important to stay "walking in the Spirit" in constant communication as you encounter trials and tribulations. Let the Spirit lead you into your battles.

## BE ALERT

The battle for your mind continues as you're still living on this earth. Satan is sly; he will provoke, tempt, and seduce you, trying every angle to find your weakness. And then, once he finds that weakness, he will target it again and again and again. It's important to understand the nature of your enemy and his schemes:

✝ *...in order that satan might not outwit us. For we are not unaware of his schemes* (2 Corinthians 2:11).

✝ *...that ancient serpent called the devil, or satan, who leads the whole world astray...* (Revelation 12:9).

Satan is relentless and a master opportunist. If you're a new Christian, you're just beginning the battle to retake your territory. If you have been a Christian for some time, are you still recovering new territory? Whether you're starting your battle for territory or taking more, satan will always be there to trick, discourage, intimidate, or tempt you from pursuing that fight.

Let's look at some battles Jesus faced at the beginning of His ministry:

✝ *Jesus, full of the Holy Spirit, returned from the Jordan and was led by the Spirit in the desert, where for forty days He was tempted by the devil. He ate nothing during those days, and at the end of them He was hungry* (Luke 4:1-2).

We've already noted that Jesus fasted for forty days before He began His ministry. This is a good way to start a battle. Fasting will help you focus on spiritual matters, which is where the real battle rages. And as you can see from this passage of Scripture, satan is ready to pounce on anything new you do for God. Just as he was right there at the beginning of Jesus' ministry, so satan is eager to tempt, trick, or intimidate you away from your mission.

Shortly after I was saved, I took some classes as part of a program called Evangelism Explosion. These classes were designed to teach us how to give someone a quick-and-simple presentation of the gospel message using Bible verses and analogies. Every Tuesday evening after we finished the class, we went to the homes of people who had visited the church the week before. This gave us the chance to practice our presentations and an opportunity to meet these people's needs in other ways as well.

After a while, problems requiring me to work late at the office started to crop up like clockwork *every* Tuesday. Coincidence? I made the decision to ignore or delay my response to the problems and went to the classes anyway. On one Tuesday, I was told I would be needed to work through the night and help put together a proposal for a major client. We desperately needed to land this client, but I elected *not* to take the bait and went to class instead. I trusted God's reasons—that class took first place. The next morning at work, I learned that the client had suddenly and unexpectedly delayed our presentation, giving us plenty of time to work on it.

The next Tuesday, satan raised the stakes. Once again, a major problem arose that would require us to work late. This was not a minor issue—the problem involved getting money into an account to cover the next day's payroll. I felt God's voice strongly in my spirit urging me to hold ground. So I chose to go to the Evangelism Explosion class. The next morning when I came in, I discovered the issue was still unresolved. My CFO informed me it had gone from bad to worse. I still believed I had heard God accurately and that if I took care of His business the night before, then He would take care of mine. As I began to pray, a thought came to me that my CFO had overlooked. One of our clients owed us a series of property tax reimbursement charges that we had already paid on their behalf but not yet billed. We were entitled to a reimbursement, so we could collect it from the trust account that day. The amount was enough to cover payroll.

The lesson I learned was that when you're in God's will, He will take care of the situation. Don't let satan throw you off track. Peter writes:

✠ *Be self-controlled and alert. Your enemy the devil prowls around like a roaring lion looking for someone to devour. **Resist** him, standing firm in the faith...* (1 Peter 5:8-9).

This theme of *resisting* the devil is important in our efforts to obtain victory in the battles for territory in our Promised Land. The concept may *not* be easy to do, but it is simple to understand. If we are doing God's will, then light eliminates the darkness, and the devil can't get a foothold—he *must* flee.

✠ *Submit yourselves, then, to God. Resist the devil, and he will flee from you* (James 4:7).

✠ *Do not give the devil a foothold* (Ephesians 4:27).

✠ *Flee the evil desires of youth, and pursue righteousness, faith, love and peace, along with those who call on the Lord out of a pure heart* (2 Timothy 2:22).

When you are tempted, call on Jesus to help you.

✠ *Because* [Jesus] *Himself suffered when He was tempted, He is able to help those who are being tempted* (Hebrews 2:18).

✠ *No temptation has seized you except what is common to man. And God is faithful; He will not let you be tempted beyond what you can bear. But when you are tempted, He will also provide a way out so that you can stand up under it (1 Corinthians 10:13).*

## ACTION & VISUALIZATION

*When you are being tempted or have a recurring temptation, seek God's wisdom and power for the way out of the temptation.*

## PREPARE FOR TEMPTATION

When satan approached Jesus at the start of His ministry, satan's first target was Jesus' flesh. He used Jesus' physical hunger from a forty-day fast to tempt Him to step out of His Father's will to do evil:

✠ *The devil said to Him, "If you are the Son of God, tell this stone to become bread."*

*Jesus answered, "It is written: 'Man does not live on bread alone'"* (Luke 4:3-4).

Jesus resisted satan, and, in fact, counterattacked by speaking the Word of God. Satan then abandoned that approach and appealed to Jesus' mind, or more specifically, he appealed to His ego. Remember that the Bible says that "praise will test a man's heart." It's okay to strive to be the best in endeavors as long as it is for the right reasons (to live up to your God-given potential, for example) and not because you are seeking praise for your efforts. Satan tempted Jesus with the same thing that made satan himself fall—the desire to be worshiped:

✠ *The devil led [Jesus] up to a high place and showed Him in an instant all the kingdoms of the world. And he said to Him, "I will give You all their authority and splendor, for it has been given to me [by man], and I can give it to anyone I want to. So if You worship me, it will all be Yours."*

*Jesus answered, "It is written: 'Worship the Lord your God and serve Him only'"* (Luke 4:5-8).

Once again, Jesus resisted satan and offered a biblical counterattack. Finally, satan tempted Jesus to test God as His Provider and Protector—he tempted His very trust in God. And, yet again, Jesus resisted and spoke the Word of God as a counterattack. Then Luke tells us:

✠ *The devil led [Jesus] to Jerusalem and had Him stand on the highest point of the temple. "If you are the Son of God," he said, "throw Yourself down from here. For it is written: 'He will command His angels concerning You to guard You carefully; they will lift You up in their hands, so that You will not strike Your foot against a stone.'"*

*Jesus answered, "It says: 'Do not put the Lord your God to the test.'"*

*When the devil had finished all this tempting, he left Him until an* **opportune time** (Luke 4:9-13).

Don't miss this last sentence. Satan is an opportunist, and he will look for the most opportune time and place to tempt you. He will strike at your weakest point and at your weakest time; he will strike when you're seeking and striving to gain new territory.

## THE ULTIMATE TEMPTATION

Satan came to Jesus again in the last hours of His life on earth. God's own creation, humans, had rejected Him and would now become not only the cause but even the instrument of Jesus' death. But read this prayer Jesus prayed in the garden of Gethsemane in which He questions the Father about the necessity to do what God had laid out for Him:

✛ *Going a little farther, He fell with His face to the ground and prayed, "My Father, if it is possible, may this cup be taken from Me. Yet not as I will, but as You will"* (Matthew 26:39).

Soon after this, Jesus was betrayed with a kiss by one of God's own creations—by one of His disciples:

✛ *Now the betrayer [Judas] had arranged a signal with them: "The One I kiss is the Man; arrest Him." Going at once to Jesus, Judas said, "Greetings, Rabbi!" and kissed Him* (Matthew 26:48-49).

The high priest tried Jesus and the crowd declared Him worthy of death.

✛ *Then they spit in His face and struck Him with their fists [while He was blindfolded]. Others slapped Him and said, "Prophesy to us, Christ. Who hit You?"* (Matthew 26:67-68).

From there Jesus was taken to the Roman governor Pilate, where a choice was given to release the very Son of God—the author of love—back into the world, or to release Barabbas, the very image of satan, a lawless thief and murderer. The people *rejected* Jesus. And so Jesus was *flogged* thirty-nine times with a cat-o-nine-tails (a leather strap with pieces of metal that slash the flesh to the bone). Matthew tells us:

✛ *Then the governor's soldiers took Jesus into the Praetorium and gathered the whole company of soldiers around Him. They **stripped** Him and put a scarlet robe on Him, and then twisted together a crown* of thorns and set it on His head. They put a staff in His right hand and knelt in front of Him and **mocked** Him. "Hail, king of the Jews!" they said. They **spit** on Him, took the staff and **struck** Him on the head **again** and **again** (Matthew 27:27-30).

Jesus' hands and feet were *nailed* to the cross, and then the cross was hoisted vertically, so Jesus would hang, *tortured unto death*:

✠ *In the same way the chief priests, the teachers of the law and the elders mocked Him. "He saved others," they said, "but He can't save Himself! He's the king of Israel! Let Him come down now from the cross, and we will believe in Him. He trusts in God. Let God rescue Him now if He wants Him, for He said, 'I am the Son of God'"* (Matthew 27:41-43).

Even with Jesus' own mother looking on, the soldiers *divided* up His clothes and cast lots for His tunic.

After humans did all this evil to Jesus, would He pay humankind back with what they *deserved,* or would He respond with the ultimate act of *love* and give up His own life for people—for you and me? Satan and all of Heaven waited to see how Jesus would respond to this *relentlessly* evil attack on His body, His reputation, His ministry, and His message. In this vulnerable and opportune moment, satan tempted Jesus again and again to *not* follow through with doing His Father's will. One temptation came from the crowd. They shouted:

✠ *Come down from the cross, if You are the Son of God* (Matthew 27:40).

Another temptation came from the soldiers who said:

✠ *If You are the King of the Jews, save Yourself* (Luke 23:37).

And yet another temptation came from one of the thieves on a cross next to Jesus when he said:

✟ *Aren't You the Christ? Save Yourself and us!* (Luke 23:39).

Did Jesus leap off the cross, as He could have done and given human-kind what it deserved for this evil done to Him? No, He gave up His life unto physical death for those who rejected Him, forsook Him, beat Him, spit on Him, ridiculed Him, mocked Him, and then crucified Him, along with all of *us* who also sinned against Him. Peter tells us:

✟ *When they hurled their insults at* [Jesus], *He did not retaliate; when He suffered, He made no threats. Instead, He entrusted Himself to Him* [the Father] *who judges justly. He Himself bore our sins in His body on the tree, so that we might die to sins and live for righteousness; by His wounds you have been healed* (1 Peter 2:23-24).

Satan whipped up a powerful opportunity for Jesus to say to His Father: "They don't deserve it. They don't love You!" Satan was trying to give Jesus a reason to *not* follow through with His Father's will for His life, to not fulfill His destiny. Satan was making every attempt possible to get Jesus to act out of the will of His Father. Jesus could have chosen to do evil, which would have given satan the ultimate victory. It's important to listen carefully to how Jesus responded to the people perpetrating these relentlessly evil attacks on His body, His reputation, His ministry, and His message. Jesus said:

✟ *Father, forgive them, for they do **not** know what they are doing* (Luke 23:34).

You will encounter people who are doing what they *think* is best for themselves but who are instead listening to their flesh or a demonic force and not following the Spirit. They are driven by the *same* motivation as the people who tempted Jesus. Jesus knew these people were spiritually blind, acting without insight, and therefore He asked for forgiveness on their behalf—on our behalf too.

✠ *We know that we are of God, and the **whole** world lies under the **sway** of the wicked one* (1 John 5:19 NKJV).

✠ *But the way of the wicked is like deep darkness; they do not know what makes them stumble* (Proverbs 4:19).

Remember that after the fall of humankind, we lost our direct connection to God and therefore can be led astray from God's plan by both satan and the seduction of the world in which we live. So it is important for us, much like Jesus, to forgive people who harm us, because they too do not know what they do. Also be aware of and alert to people who come into your life and think this way, and to people who are driven by their flesh and/or demonic forces. These people are essentially doing satan's work when they tempt you to go against the will of God.

Even other believers can unwittingly lead you astray from God's will at times. Remember Peter who, right after correctly identifying Jesus as the Messiah, then suggested He *not* go to Jerusalem where He was to be crucified for the sins of humanity. Jesus identified the source of Peter's plea:

✠ *But when Jesus turned and looked at His disciples, He rebuked Peter. "Get behind Me, satan!" He said, "You do not have in mind the things of God, but the things of men"* (Mark 8:33).

I don't mean here that these people's intentions are evil, but if their actions tempt or bait you into behavior that leads you astray—out of the will of God—then steer clear! Also, *forgive* them. Remember, just like Peter, they could turn right around to do great things for God despite their being a stumbling block for you.

The most important fact to remember is that you have a significant advantage over people who do not know God—you have been given spiritual insight and discernment. Satan hoped he could trick, intimidate, or tempt Jesus into responding with His mind or flesh. Satan wanted to get Jesus onto a battlefield where He had no advantage. Jesus was obedient, led by the Spirit, and used His spiritual insight. Don't let satan trick you onto a battlefield where you have no advantage, a battlefield that leaves God behind.

Jesus resisted and followed through with God's will. He forgave the people and gave up His life:

☩ *Jesus called out with a loud voice, "Father, into Your hands I commit My spirit." When He had said this, He breathed His last* (Luke 23:46).

You too will need to do God's will and *forgive* the people who come into your life and hurt, defame, or even mock you.

## Satan's Relentless Pursuit

Just as he did with Jesus, satan will take his best shots at you at your most vulnerable moments. When another driver cuts in front of you on the highway, how do you respond? In love? In God's will? Of course, this seems trivial when compared to the trials Jesus faced, but it is still a test of your mind and body at an opportune time. This is a small place to start, but a good place to start. Victory in the small trials grows us spiritually so we can handle bigger trials, battles, and temptations. And they will come in many ways.

Perhaps you can imagine scenarios involving your boss, a business partner, a customer, a waiter, an auto service mechanic, a customer service attendant, a neighbor, your in-laws, parents, spouse, children—the list goes on and on. We *all* have a long way to go, many battles to fight, and many strongholds to pull down before we fully inhabit our Promised Land—the image and likeness of God.

## DON'T START DOWN THAT ROAD

Don't start down the road of giving over territory to satan, making compromises, and choosing white lies over the truth, because little by little you are losing ground. Eventually, these small, seemingly harmless sins lead you to death. Even our imagination can lead us into sin. We need to be careful in the little things that can trip us up and hurt our spiritual growth.

✠ *Catch for us the foxes, the **little** foxes that ruin the vineyards, our vineyards that are in bloom* (Song of Solomon 2:15).

Satan will coax and finesse you into sin, so be alert. Stay on guard and watch out for those little things for which you know that you have weaknesses. Your weakness is your flesh, mind, and sinful heart; therefore, stay away from areas where you may be tempted, because your flesh is weak and your mind can be tricked. Solomon in his wisdom wrote this warning about temptation:

✠ [The adulteress said], *"I have fellowship offerings at home; today I fulfilled my vows* [beginning her seduction by expressing her godliness]. *So I came out to meet you; I looked for you and have found you! I have covered my bed with colored linens from Egypt. I have perfumed my bed with myrrh, aloes and cinnamon. Come, let's drink deep of love till morning; let's enjoy ourselves with love!"* (Proverbs 7:14-18).

Sounds enticing? Let me be clear: satan is *not* going to appear before you as a red man with a pointed tail holding a pitchfork trying to talk you into sinning. You will be lured into sin in a slow and seductive way. That temptation may even come with an active leader in your church. Remember, satan was the most attractive and beautiful-sounding angel who led worship over God's throne. He knows good and evil, as well as how to manipulate your perception of them—making the truth to appear gray and hazy. By mixing them up with physical beauty, alluring thoughts, sensual emotions, and self-exhilarating images, his temptation is subtle.

As an example, if you are married, you should *not* be confiding in a co-worker or fellow churchgoer of the opposite sex with personal things that are meant for your spouse. Satan knows it is easier to create an inappropriate sexual relationship by beginning with an emotional or romantic (by worldly standards) one that will ultimately lead you down the path toward sin. If you are in business, a little white lie to close a deal will only start you down the wrong path too.

Solomon went on to say, in his warning about the adulterous woman, that falling for her temptation begins with walking down the path that goes *by* her house. It's harder to resist going into her house when you're on the path in front of it than if you are on the other side of town where you're supposed to be. Here is Solomon's warning for you and me: the path to her house leads to sin, which results in spiritual *death*. It's common knowledge that you can't cook a frog by putting it in boiling water; it will jump right out. However, when the frog is placed in room-temperature water and the water is heated slowly, the frog won't realize the fatal change until it's too late. This is satan's approach.

Satan will even take what God meant for good and trick us into taking it in excess beyond the boundaries God intended. Some examples are:

- Communication to gossip

- Self-care to selfishness

- Carefulness to fear

- Physical rest to laziness
- Same-sex friendship to homosexuality
- Loving-kindness to over-protection
- Generosity to wastefulness
- Sexual freedom to immorality
- Cautiousness to unbelief
- Self-preservation to dishonesty
- Discernment to judgment
- Appetite for food to gluttony
- Physical pleasure to sin

We need to be discerning and wise in finding the limits and boundaries within our lives—*even in the good things.*

## ACTION & VISUALIZATION

*Find God's limits in all areas of your life.*
*Don't go down any paths that lead you by temptations.*

## SATAN IS ACTIVE IN THE WORLD

Satan is a master deceiver. He is credited for blinding the minds of unbelievers to the truth of God. Paul wrote about this in 2 Corinthians:

✠ *The god of this age has blinded the minds of unbelievers, so that they cannot see the light of the gospel of the glory of Christ, who is the image of God* (2 Corinthians 4:4).

Here's what that means, in practical terms: When you're sharing your faith with someone who "just doesn't understand," turn your attention to prayer, asking God to pull down the stronghold that is blinding that person to the truth. The lying spirit of satan can come at us from any direction. We need discernment to know whether a spirit is from God, from people, or whether it comes from satan. Jesus said this of the *religious* leaders of His time:

✝ *You belong to your father, the devil, and you want to carry out your father's desire. He was a murderer from the beginning, not holding to the truth, for there is no truth in him. When he lies, he speaks his native language, for he is a liar and the father of lies* (John 8:44).

Peter was recorded as the first one to see Jesus as the Son of God. Jesus said that He would build His church "on this rock" (referring to Peter and the Holy Spirit, who revealed this to Peter). Remember, this same Peter tried to talk Jesus out of going to the cross and was rebuked by Jesus when He said, "Get behind me, satan!"

It's important to have discernment always, because satan mimics God and His followers. Even Christians who have a full revelation of Christ can be deceived and used by satan—that is, if they are *not* discerning.

✝ *For such men are false apostles, deceitful workmen, masquerading as apostles of Christ. And no wonder, for satan himself masquerades as an angel of light. It is not surprising, then, if his servants masquerade as servants of righteousness...* (2 Corinthians 11:13-15).

Satan's prime objective is to distract or sidetrack people from coming to know Jesus Christ as their Savior. He is violently opposed to us reflecting God's image and likeness into the world. Because satan knows that humanity is wandering around unfulfilled with a hole in their hearts where

Jesus belongs, satan has created false "churches" for humanity to join that promise fulfillment, hoping to distract from ones where people will come to know Jesus as their Lord and Savior.

Satan also knows that when people hear any part of God's truths, there is often a powerful witness to that word in a person's spirit. Therefore, when satan creates these churches, while they mimic many of the principles of God, they leave out key truths—primarily that Jesus is the *only* way to life, and that we need to be reconnecting ourselves to the light source. Therefore, not having reconciliation with God and not having the Holy Spirit within them, they have no real power source to spread the light. As God's church, as God's people, we are called to reveal the deception of these so-called churches. Use loving words, loving deeds, and *prayer* instead of arguments and accusations, which will lead you to the *wrong* battlefield.

## ACTION & VISUALIZATION
*Pray regularly for insight and discernment.*

## A UNIFIED BODY OF CHRIST

Does satan have a strategy against God's church? Yes. Satan's four-fold strategy against God's church is to water down the church, divide the body of Christ into fragments, isolate believers from other Christians, and keep believers from receiving, unwrapping, and using the gifts of freedom.

Satan's highest priority is to attack an effective church. He will prey on and exploit the pastor's and leadership's weaknesses. We have blind spots. Much like we do on the highway between the moment when we can see a car in the rearview mirror and the moment when it is suddenly beside us, so we have spiritual blind spots as well. God has *not* given His full knowledge to any *one* person; each of us has blind spots and weaknesses. Because of this, satan can sometimes bring down an effective leader by attacking his or her most vulnerable place. Surely, you've read stories about pastors who have fallen because of some secret weakness that is suddenly revealed.

Similarly, no one church or denomination has been given the *full* revelation of God's knowledge. I travel all the time, which has given me the benefit of attending many different churches around the world. Some are particularly strong in evangelism, teaching, worship, giving, community service, miracles, love, or faith, and yet all are imperfect and vulnerable to satan's attacks. The preventative answer God intended is that we are all one church body, and the greater church body is to spiritually and physically shore up each other's weaker aspects. If you had only been given one eye, your area of vision would be much smaller; however, God designed us to have two eyes so they could work in tandem to cover each other. Indeed, each different functioning part of the body was intended to operate in its strength for the benefit of the *whole*.

One of the most powerful ways satan attacks individual churches or denominations is by sneaking "pride" into them. The belief that "our church is right in certain aspects and yours isn't" divides and fragments the body of Christ into a jealous competition at times, so we don't have the benefits of what the other parts have to offer. Our charge is to follow Jesus, *not* a doctrine. We can turn differences in certain doctrines into insurmountable conflicts. This, of course, is not something Jesus desires. To have a fragmented body with the arms and legs disconnected and the eyes and ears doing their own thing isn't God's plan for a powerful church. Doesn't this make for a dysfunctional body?

Read what Jesus said to His disciples about *not* criticizing or judging others who proclaim His name:

✟ *"Teacher," said John, "we saw a man driving out demons in Your name and we told him to stop, because he was not one of us."*

*"**Do not stop him**," Jesus said. "No one who does a miracle in My name can in the next moment say anything bad about Me, for whoever is not against us is for us. I tell you the truth, anyone who*

*gives you a cup of water in My name because you belong to Christ will certainly not lose his reward"* (Mark 9:38-41).

And the book of James gives this instruction to believers:

✟ *Brothers, do not slander one another. Anyone who speaks against his brother or judges him speaks against the law and judges it. When you judge the law, you are not keeping it, but sitting in judgment on it. There is only one Lawgiver and Judge, the One who is able to save and destroy. But you—who are you to judge your neighbor?* (James 4:11-12).

If a part of the church body believes there is an important reason to attack another part, then it should attack the other's weaknesses in the spiritual realm, *not the physical.* Through prayer and seeking God's will, we can bring down a stronghold, false teaching, and pride. Paul wrote that he prayed for the believers' understanding:

✟ *I keep asking that the God of our Lord Jesus Christ, the glorious Father, may give you the Spirit of **wisdom** and **revelation**, so that you may know Him better. I pray also that the eyes of your heart may be **enlightened** in order that you may **know** the hope to which **He has called you**, the riches of His glorious inheritance in the saints* (Ephesians 1:17-18).

If we are serious about bringing down false teachings and doctrine in the church, then our charge is to pray this prayer for others' wisdom, revelation, and knowledge. That is not to say that false doctrine should not be challenged, but the best way to expose false doctrine is to preach God's Word (sound doctrine) in God's love. I have witnessed churches that have preached unsound doctrine; however, they have many people coming to know Christ through them, and therefore, the entire ministry can't be judged as bad. Salvation is clearly a miracle manifested by God and done in the name of Jesus; therefore, Jesus' instructions are, "Do not stop him."

The body of Christ should join where they have common ground. Our common belief in Jesus as Savior should be enough common ground. Remember what God said in Genesis of humanity's power on earth when we act in unity:

✝ *The Lord said, "If **as one** people speaking the same language they have begun to do this, then **nothing** they plan to do will be impossible for them"* (Genesis 11:6).

God has given His body seemingly impossible tasks to accomplish here in this fallen world, but He has also clearly offered us the gift of human relationship to receive, unwrap, and use. When we do this as believers, then "nothing will be impossible for us."

✝ *So in Christ we who are many form **one** body, and each member belongs to all the others* (Romans 12:5).

✝ *Because there is one loaf, we, who are many, are **one** body, for we all partake of the **one** loaf* (1 Corinthians 10:17).

✝ *There is neither Jew nor Greek, slave nor free, male nor female, for you are all **one** in Christ Jesus* (Galatians 3:28).

✝ *[Gifts of the Spirit were given to us to use] until we all reach **unity** in the faith and in the knowledge of the Son of God and **become*** *mature*, attaining to the whole measure of the fullness of Christ (Ephesians 4:13).

☩ *Make every effort to keep the **unity** of the Spirit through the bond of **peace**. There is **one** body and **one** Spirit—just as you were called to **one** hope when you were called—**one** Lord, **one** faith, **one** baptism; **one** God and Father of all, who is over all and through all and in all* (Ephesians 4:3-6).

Indeed, Paul on many occasions exhorted the church to be unified despite her differences:

☩ *I appeal to you, brothers, in the name of our Lord Jesus Christ, that **all** of you **agree** with one another so that there may be **no** divisions among you and that you may be **perfectly united** in mind and thought* (1 Corinthians 1:10).

☩ *Bear with each other and forgive whatever grievances you may have against one another. Forgive as the Lord forgave you. And over all these virtues put on **love**, which binds them all together in **perfect unity**. Let the **peace** of Christ rule in your hearts, since as members of **one** body you were called to **peace**. And be thankful* (Colossians 3:13-15).

And Peter echoes similar sentiments:

☩ *Finally, all of you, live in **harmony** with one another; be sympathetic, love as brothers, be compassionate and humble* (1 Peter 3:8).

Jesus also prays for our unity as one body in Him:

☦ *That all of them may be **one**, Father, just as You are in Me and I am in You. May they also be in Us so that the world may believe that You have sent Me* (John 17:21).

Just like the early church, we too can become unified. When this happens, the Holy Spirit will pour out signs, wonders, and, most importantly, powerful, authentic *love* in our midst.

## Action & Visualization

*Take advantage of any opportunities you have to bring the whole body of Jesus back together in unity. Spiritually protect and defend the other parts too!*

## You Are Not Alone

Satan doesn't just attack church leaders in his efforts to destroy the church; rather, he attacks all of us, doing his best to distract us from spiritual matters and isolate us from relationships with other believers. But we are not alone as we fight satan's attacks. If you seek God and surrender to Him and follow the leading of the Holy Spirit, then God's power can help you be victorious in the battles for your Promised Land. He also gives you relationships with others to help you stay strong.

☦ *If one falls down, his friend can help him up...* (Ecclesiastes 4:10).

Regularly fellowship with other believers to keep your faith vibrant. Seek people who will pray for you and lovingly hold you accountable in your walk with God.

You also want to rely on your most important relationship by receiving, unwrapping, and using all the gifts God offers you to assist in reaching your Promised Land. Will you gain back all the territory in this life? No, but if you follow the leading of the Spirit and trust God's ability to defeat your foes, then you will gain more and more territory as you spiritually grow in Him.

✠ *The angel of the Lord encamps around those who fear Him, and He delivers them* (Psalm 34:7).

✠ *For the eyes of the Lord range throughout the earth to strengthen those whose hearts are fully committed to Him* (2 Chronicles 16:9).

✠ *He will cover you with His feathers, and under His wings you will find refuge; His faithfulness will be your shield and rampart* (Psalm 91:4).

## ACTION & VISUALIZATION

*Whenever you are having trouble with temptation,
seek God and then submit to His divine knowledge and power.*

## FIND GOD IN THE PRESENT

Finding God in the present will allow you to filter the good out of the past and the future without opening the door to all the negatives, which happens when dwelling in certain ways on the past and future. There are certain watchwords we need to get deep into our spirits and active in our lives when dealing with the past, present, and future: *forgiveness* for the past, *obedience* for the present, and *faith* for the future.

573

It is important for us to know where we find God. While He can experience the past, present, or future at any moment, we, on the other hand, are designed to live only in the present. The present is where we find God and therefore the joy He offers us.

✠ *This is the day the Lord has made; let us rejoice and be glad in it* [not yesterday and not tomorrow] (Psalm 118:24).

God gave us a memory to allow us to review the past so we could gain experience from it, thus enabling us to make positive adjustments in the present. Our memory also allows us to build up our faith by remembering what He has done in our lives. However, God did not intend for us to dwell in the past or to let it paralyze us with guilt over the failures we have had. We will not find God there. He offers us unconditional forgiveness to free us from letting our past paralyze us.

✠ *On the other hand, if we admit our sins—make a clean breast of them—He won't let us down; He'll be true to Himself. He'll forgive our sins and purge us of all wrongdoing* (1 John 1:9 MSG).

✠ *As far as the east is from the west, so far has He removed our transgressions from us* (Psalm 103:12).

Accepting the forgiveness God offers us each day is how we get freedom from our past failures. He desires us to live in that freedom—in the present.

The future is the key feature on which we hinge our faith. We can change our lives by imagining our future differently, then putting our words of faith and efforts into what we imagined. When our faith is lined up with God's promises, then we will obviously see the best results. God also gives us glimpses of the future to help us build our faith. However, without faith in God's goodness and good intentions, our dwelling on the future can paralyze us with fear. We are not to let our faithless fear paralyze us and consume our present with fear of what could happen in the future. Jesus said:

✚ *But seek first His Kingdom and His righteousness, and all these things will be given to you as well. Therefore do not worry about* **tomorrow**, *for tomorrow will worry about itself* [live in the day and have faith in God for tomorrow]. *Each day has enough trouble of its own* (Matthew 6:33-34).

Using the faith God offers us is how He gives us freedom from our fear of the future. He desires for us to live in that freedom—in the present. But how do we live in the present? First, we remember God is *always* with us and there to *help* us:

✚ *For I am the Lord, your God, who takes hold of your right hand and says to you, Do not fear; I will help you* (Isaiah 41:13).

We forget our past mistakes, and each day we start *anew* to pursue God's plan. In so doing, we show confidence in Him and His plan for our lives by obeying in the present. This will allow us to obtain our best life. Jesus said:

✚ *If you* **obey** *My commands, you will remain in My love, just as I have obeyed My Father's commands and remain in His love. I have told you this so that* **My joy be in you and that your joy may be complete** (John 15:10-11).

Living in your present is where you will find God, and where you find God is where you will find His *peace* and *joy*. You should approach every day as a *new* day without any guilt from the past. You can start over by acting in faith and obedience, no matter how you have failed or how many times you have failed.

In summary, stay focused on God in the present, knowing your past failures are forgotten. Only use your past to draw from in constructing a faith-based plan that you can act on today in obedience, using your faith.

## Action & Visualization

*Live with God in the present each day, obeying Him and only using the past and future thoughts in the way He desired so they help you.*

## Our Weapons

It is important to remember that your weapons and armor are *not* the same as the world's. David tried on King Saul's armor and sword to fight Goliath, but they were not right. So he took five smooth stones and his slingshot instead. This is not something you'd think would bring down a nine-foot warrior wearing 125 pounds of armor and carrying a fifteen-pound spear. But those were God's chosen weapons, and therefore, they were *perfect* for the job. Had David trusted in King Saul's armor and sword, he would have *failed*. You will fail too if you use the world's weapons in your spiritual battles—if you trusted the world's temporal systems (physical force, money, power, intelligence, and so on).

God gives us many weapons to fight our spiritual battles. It is up to us to *seek* them out and understand their use under His direction. Paul describes this "battle gear" in Ephesians:

✠ *Finally, be strong in the Lord and in His mighty power. Put on the full armor of God so that you can take your stand against the devil's schemes. For **our struggle is not against flesh and blood**, but against the rulers, against the authorities, against the powers of this dark* *world and against the spiritual forces of evil in the heavenly realms. Therefore put on the full armor of God, so that when the day of evil comes, you may be able to stand your ground, and after you have done everything, to stand. Stand firm then, with the **belt of truth** buckled around your waist, with the **breastplate of righteousness** in place, and with your **feet fitted** with the readiness that comes from the **gospel of peace**. In addition to all this, take up the **shield of faith**, with which you can extinguish all the flaming arrows of the evil one. Take the **helmet of salvation** and the **sword of the Spirit**, which is the Word of God.*

*And pray in the Spirit on **all occasions** with all kinds of prayers and requests…* (Ephesians 6:10-18).

Paul clarifies that it is *not* other humans (flesh and blood) who are your enemies. If you attack them, you are only attacking a *decoy* and doing the will of satan. To achieve victory in the physical realm, you must battle in the spiritual realm and gain your victory there.

Paul then tells us how to outfit ourselves for this spiritual battle so that we can achieve that victory. The "full armor of God" allows us to stand strong in the face of an attack and defeat our real enemies, which are spiritual forces, thoughts, imaginations, and strongholds that are *not* in line with God's will.

When I first read this verse as a new Christian, I immediately prayed for God to put the armor of God on me. I was clearly under attack. I thought that by a simple prayer, God would supernaturally outfit me into this armor. However, God didn't do this. Instead, I eventually embraced a profound revelation later. What I realized was that this verse instructs *us* to put on the armor of God. God wasn't going to outfit me in the full armor of God without my involvement. It was *my choices* and *actions* every day that would *manifest* the full armor of God in my life.

God asks us to be intentional about preparing for spiritual battles. Our *speaking* and *acting* in truth, righteousness, peace, faith, His knowledge, and the Word is what *creates* the armor of God upon us while we are acting in those modes.

## Belt of Truth

Let's look closer at each piece of the armor Paul describes. The "belt of truth" represents God's truth, buckled securely around your waist. This belt holds all your other armor together. Without God's truth at the center of our lives, our remaining weapons are useless. His truth does not supernaturally come upon us. We must speak it and live it out for it to manifest as part of the armor of God around us. Once manifested, God's truth gives us the power and freedom needed to enter battles and win.

✝ *Jesus said, "If you hold to My teaching, you are really My disciples. Then you will know the truth, and the truth will set you free" (John 8:31-32).*

If you are wrapped by any thoughts other than God's truth, then you will not spiritually have the freedom to fully move as required in a battle.

## Breastplate of Righteousness

Paul says that you need to be wearing the "breastplate of righteousness" before you go into battle; however, your righteousness was given to you as a gift from God when you were born again. Paul writes elsewhere:

✝ *But now apart from the law the righteousness of God has been made known, to which the Law and the Prophets testify. This righteousness is given through faith in Jesus Christ to all who believe. There is no difference between Jew and Gentile, for all have sinned and fall short of the glory of God, and all are justified freely by his grace through the redemption that came by Christ Jesus. God presented Christ as a sacrifice of atonement, through the shedding of his blood—to be received by faith. He did this to demonstrate his righteousness, because in his forbearance he had left the sins committed beforehand unpunished* (Romans 3:21-25).

✚ *I have been crucified with Christ and I no longer live, but Christ lives in me. The life I live in the body, I live by faith in the Son of God, who loved me and gave Himself for me. I do not set aside the grace of God, for if righteousness could be gained through the law, Christ died for nothing!* (Galatians 2:20-21).

We are in a battle against strongholds that are too powerful for us to deal with alone. The righteousness that is produced by our own works is flawed and therefore defenseless when under attack. But the righteousness of God—the perfect righteousness we received on the day of our eternal salvation—is a powerful deflector of satan's attacks. I can share from personal experience that when I have suited up in my own righteousness, I've been summarily defeated.

✚ *What does the Scripture say? "Abraham believed God, and it was created to him as righteousness"* (Romans 4:3).

Believe God, even at the height of battle—and *especially* at the height of battle.

## GOSPEL OF PEACE

Next, we are to put on our feet the readiness to spread the gospel of peace. *Gospel* means "good news," and indeed, it is good news to know freedom from bondage to sin. And, as we've already learned, the good news is universally needed, as the world and everything in it has been infected by sin.

✠ *Now the earth was corrupt in God's sight... (Genesis 6:11).*

The Message Translation puts the same scripture a little more bluntly:

✠ *As far as God was concerned, the Earth had become a sewer; there was violence everywhere. God took one look and saw how bad it was, everyone corrupt and corrupting—life itself corrupt to the core (Genesis 6:11-12 MSG).*

✠ *The earth is defiled by its people; they have disobeyed the laws...* (Isaiah 24:5).

Healing should always follow where our feet take us as we spread the gospel everywhere we go. When we sow the seeds of blessing back into the world through spreading the gospel, we in turn will be blessed. This is why Paul declared:

✠ *As it is written, "How beautiful are the feet of those who bring good news!"* (Romans 10:15).

Be ready in word and deed to give the message of "good news" when opportunities present themselves. It may be spontaneous or planned, or it may even be during battle. *So be ready.*

## THE SHIELD OF FAITH

Are there times when it looks like your life is going horribly wrong and it will never right itself? Well, if you feel this way, then be warned. This is a fear-based attack to launch you out of God's will. The best defense to this tactic is to stand in faith despite what you *see, hear,* or *feel.* Faith is your shield. Take hold of it and stand firm. Yes, satan has power, even power to land a blow that can knock us around:

✟ [We are] *struck down, but **not** destroyed* (2 Corinthians 4:9).

✟ *Therefore we do not lose heart. Though outwardly we are wasting away, yet inwardly we are being renewed day by day. For our light and momentary troubles are achieving for us an eternal glory that far outweighs them all. So we fix our eyes not on what is seen, but on what is unseen. For what is seen is temporary, but what is unseen is eternal* (2 Corinthians 4:16-18).

✟ *Take up the shield of faith, with which you can extinguish all the flaming arrows of the evil one* (Ephesians 6:16).

It is faith that absorbs the flaming attacks and allows us to get off the ground and keep moving toward victory. Victory may not seem possible over some strongholds, but this is why we must hang on tightly to the shield of faith. What may seem impossible is in time made possible by *faith*, which is the substance of things not seen.

When I was young and working construction, I saw an electrician working on a high-voltage transformer. He was clearly in a hurry. He didn't shut off the power and put on only one protective glove to work on a 2,800-volt electrical transformer. While he was working, a wire slipped out of the socket and started falling. With an unthinking reflex, he reached out his ungloved hand to grab the falling wire. He died instantly. Had he been properly shielded, he would have lived.

The shield of faith keeps us from being stopped or defeated by what satan and the physical world brings against us. Our faith will keep us focused on our spiritual weapons and spiritual armor rather than natural methods. Some battles may take a long time to win. Some won't be won in our lifetimes. But that is why faith is so important—it allows us to hang on until victory in the battles we are destined to win without being discouraged by those battles that go on a long time, as well as those we may never see an end to in our earthly lifetimes.

Our victories won't come by our strength or timing, but by His. This keeps us dependent on God. By relying solely on God rather than our power or intelligence, we stay close in our relationship with God. The psalmist said:

☩ *Though the Lord is on high, He looks upon the lowly, but the proud He knows from afar* (Psalm 138:6).

The apostle Paul made this observation about dependency on God:

☩ *To keep me from becoming conceited because of these surpassingly great revelations, there was given me a thorn in my flesh, a messenger of satan, to torment me. Three times I pleaded with the Lord to take it away from me. But He said to me, "My grace is sufficient for you, for My power is made **perfect** in **weakness**." Therefore I will boast all the more gladly about my weaknesses, so that Christ's power may rest on me. That is why, for Christ's sake, I delight in **weaknesses**, in insults, in hardships, in persecutions, in difficulties. For when I am **weak**, then I am **strong*** (2 Corinthians 12:7-10).

✠ *God chose the foolish things of the world to shame the wise; God chose the weak things of the world to shame the strong* (1 Corinthians 1:27).

If the world considers you weak, simple, poor, or down and out, then you should consider yourself lucky, because you are in a perfect position for God to work in and through you. So keep up your shield of faith!

## THE HELMET OF SALVATION

The helmet of salvation protects your mind in Christ Jesus. When you were saved, your mind was reconnected to God by the Holy Spirit. It is both the knowledge of your salvation and this Holy Spirit connection that allows you to keep your mind and priorities straight in the heat of the battle. When you are in sync with God, your enemies don't have a chance.

✠ *...be transformed by the renewing of your mind. Then you will be able to test and approve what God's will is—His good, pleasing and perfect will* (Romans 12:2).

## THE SWORD OF THE WORD

Remember that each time satan tried to tempt Jesus, He spoke the Word of God to satan and defeated his temptation. God's Word, which Paul calls "the sword of the Word," is spiritually alive. When used in battle, it can be more effective than a nuclear weapon. The writer of Hebrews says:

✠ *For the word of God is living and active. Sharper than any double-edged sword, it penetrates even to dividing soul and spirit, joints and marrow; it judges the thoughts and attitudes of the heart* (Hebrews 4:12).

And Isaiah declared:

✝ *So is My word that goes out from My mouth: It will not return to Me empty, but will accomplish what I desire and achieve the purpose for which I sent it (Isaiah 55:11).*

This is why studying the Bible is so important. If you know your Bible, when you're in a spiritual battle the Spirit of God can help you recall verses to strengthen your faith and mount a counterattack.

Perhaps the most important thing to remember about the armor of God is that, like all the gifts God offers, they have no value until we in faith receive them, unwrap them, and use them. It is important to note that your armor is designed to assist you when you are moving forward in an attack mode or standing strong in defense. Your armor will give you *no* protection from the backside if you run away in retreat; you will be vulnerable and exposed. Our charge from God is to occupy our territories aggressively. That means we are to maintain what we already have and continually seek to gain that which we do not yet have.

✝ *And from the days of John the Baptist until now the Kingdom of Heaven suffers violence, and the violent take it* [their place in the Kingdom within them] *by force (Matthew 11:12 NKJV).*

## ACTION & VISUALIZATION

*Put on the full armor of God each piece at a time, and then attack to take back your Promised Land.*

## Keep in Communication

How are we to live, and what is our plan once we are fully suited in God's armor? Paul gives us the answer in his closing verse:

✤ *...praying **always** with all prayer and supplication in the Spirit...* (Ephesians 6:18 NKJV).

Prayer invites God to directly join with us in spiritual battle, giving us access to His divine knowledge and power.

✤ *The weapons we fight with are not the weapons of the world. On the contrary, they have divine power to demolish strongholds* (2 Corinthians 10:4).

✤ *If God is for us, who can be against us?* (Romans 8:31).

We are *citizens* of Heaven who are occupying this world as foreigners until Jesus returns. We are Jesus' taskforce, and we are therefore to keep our alliance to the country of our citizenry we will someday fully occupy:

✤ *Dear friends, I urge you, as **aliens** and **strangers** in the world, to abstain from sinful desires, which war against your soul* (1 Peter 2:11).

✤ *Do not love the world or **anything** in the world. If anyone loves the world, the love of the Father is not in him* (1 John 2:15).

✠ *But our **citizenship** is in **Heaven**. And we eagerly await a Savior from there, the Lord Jesus Christ, who, by the power that enables Him to bring everything under His control, will transform our lowly bodies so that they will be like His glorious body* (Philippians 3:20-21).

As citizens of Heaven, we should also be speaking our natural language when communicating with Him whenever possible. While in the battle, it is important that the communications are clear between you and God. Your spirit needs to know His will and know the battle plan. There is no clearer communication than spirit to Spirit—speaking in your heavenly language. Otherwise, your mind will tend to wander or consider its own will. Pray in the Spirit whenever led before and during your spiritual battles, and allow God to communicate what is required and how you need to respond.

## Action & Visualization

*Pray in the Spirit before, during, and after the battle.*

## You're Designed to Be Resilient

Sometimes when you are attacked, you will be wounded. Thankfully, God has made His people generally resilient, but even more so when acting in the will of God. He made us amazingly resilient in the physical realm. Just look at how we heal from injury and sickness. This also applies to our emotional, mental, and spiritual resilience as well. If we aren't careful and allow the infections of sin, envy, pity, unforgiveness, or sorrow into our pain, then we can negatively impact the spiritual healing progress. The reverse is true as well. When we let God's image and likeness flow through us, then He can choose to speed our physical, emotional, mental, and spiritual healing.

✛ *A heart at peace gives life to the body, but envy rots the bones* (Proverbs 14:30).

✛ *A merry heart makes a cheerful countenance, but by sorrow of the heart the spirit is broken* (Proverbs 15:13 NKJV).

✛ *Be kind and compassionate to one another, forgiving each other, just as in Christ God forgave you* (Ephesians 4:32).

✛ *Do not be wise in your own eyes; fear the Lord and shun evil. This will bring health to your body and nourishment to your bones* (Proverbs 3:7-8).

✛ *[God's words of wisdom] are life to those who find them and health to a man's whole body* (Proverbs 4:22).

✛ *Reckless words pierce like a sword, but the tongue of the wise brings healing* (Proverbs 12:18).

✛ *The fear of the Lord adds length to life...* (Proverbs 10:27).

## ACTION & VISUALIZATION

*When hurt in battle, stand on God's Word, stay in God's will, and trust His healing touch.*

## OVERCOME THE WORLD

The way to overcome in this world is to follow in the footsteps of the One who overcame this world—Jesus. Because He overcame, Jesus will make us one with Him, and sharing His victory, we too will overcome. While here on earth, we will have to fight the spiritual battles to overcome each obstacle.

✝ [Jesus said], *"I have told you these things, so that in Me you may have peace. In this world you will have trouble. But take heart!* **I have overcome the world**" (John 16:33).

It is important to note that when Jesus said this, He had not yet gone to the cross and fully manifested His victory over death and sin. Yet Jesus had an insight and a mind-set that gave Him the confidence to make this declaration. You will want to grab hold of this same confidence and mind-set so you can be an overcomer in *this* world by having this same type of confidence. Your victory will manifest. He has made it possible, and He looks forward to it.

✝ *He who overcomes will, like them, be dressed in white. I will never blot out his name from the book of life, but will acknowledge his name before My Father and His angels* (Revelation 3:5).

✝ *Him who overcomes I will make a pillar in the temple of My God. Never again will he leave it. I will write on him the name of My God and the name of the city of My God, the new Jerusalem, which is coming down out of Heaven from My God; and I will also write on him My new name* (Revelation 3:12).

*To him who overcomes, I will give the right to eat from the Tree of Life, which is in the Paradise of God* [the tree taken out of the garden when Adam and Eve sinned so that humanity could not live eternally] (Revelation 2:7).

*But every spirit that does not acknowledge Jesus is not from God. This is the spirit of the antichrist, which you have heard is coming and even now is already in the world. You, dear children, are from God and have overcome them, because the One who is in you is **greater** than the one who is in the world* (1 John 4:3-4).

*...for everyone born of God overcomes the world. This is the victory that has overcome the world, even our faith* (1 John 5:4).

We see from this last verse that all who are "born again" will eventually overcome; however, believing and knowing that can change our lives for the better.

Do you remember where we started? The gift of myrrh? To win our battles, we must die to ourselves. We must learn to follow God's will, taking advantage of the whole armor of God when we face inevitable battles. The gift of myrrh is the gift of dying to self. Our willingness to die is our source for life, which can spring forth from the fruit of the Spirit. Jesus said:

*I tell you the truth, unless a kernel of wheat falls to the ground and dies, it remains only a single seed. But if it dies, it produces many seeds. The man who loves his life will lose it, while the man who hates his life in this world will keep it for eternal life* (John 12:24-25).

# MEDITATION POINT

When you let your flesh and selfishness die, then you will gain your eternal victories.

Go to Chapter 7 Study Guide section on page 643.

Study Guide

# INTRODUCTION

P lease don't think of this study guide as a homework assignment. It *isn't* about giving the "right answer"—it's about giving an honest answer. It *isn't* about "getting it done"—it's about letting the questions stir your heart. It *isn't* about "filling in the blanks," but instead letting the Holy Spirit speak to your soul. Think of this as a spiritual experience or potential encounter between you and God rather than an exercise to check off your to-do list.

We are conditioned to believe that our answers to questions in a textbook will be graded; however, that mind-set stifles the purpose of this study guide. This is an opportunity to write honestly about your faith, to grow and go deeper in God's Word, to pray earnestly about His will for your life, and most of all to cultivate an intimate relationship between you and your Creator.

If possible, devote time for quiet reflection as you read the material, think about your life, and write accordingly. Answer the questions as you truly feel, even if it seems wrong or troubling. Remember that "the truth will set you free" and that growth can only happen when the soil is soft. You get what you give. You could burn through this entire study guide in half an hour if you'd like, but it would offer little to no lasting benefit.

I pray that you will put in the time and effort to maximize this material and actualize the full impact of His Gifts of Freedom into your life. Use the study guide to find the spiritual growth and maturity God desires you to have in your life.

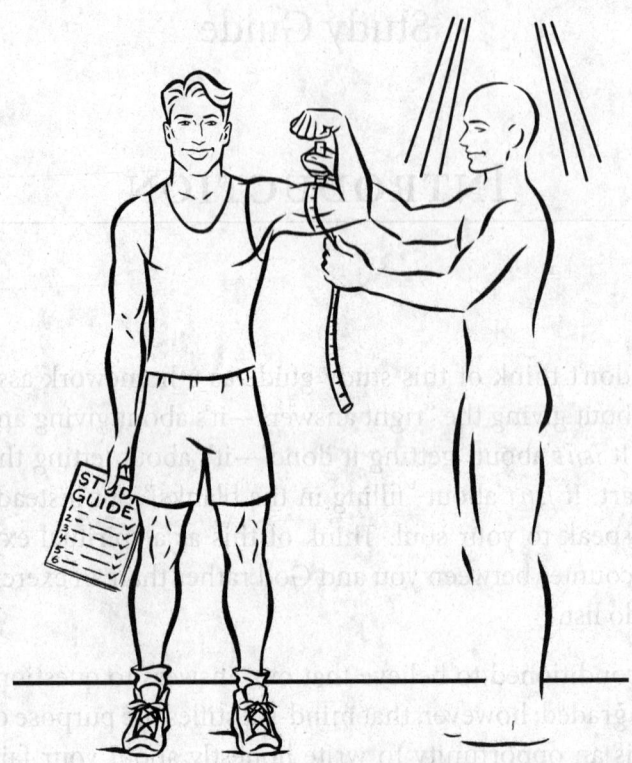

# The Gifts of Freedom Study Guide

# BOOK 2

## GIFTS OF PROVISION, COMMUNICATION, AND DEATH

### HOW TO USE THIS STUDY GUIDE

You can use this study guide in a variety of ways, including individually, as part of a small group Bible study, or in a Sunday school setting. If you are working through this book on your own, then use this study guide to record your personal growth journey. Take the time after each chapter to answer the questions. Some are designed to help you remember the main concepts in the chapter, while others are designed to help you personalize the content and apply it to your own life. At the end, seriously pray in closing that God will fill you with His gifts, and that you will recognize and accept them. You can also visit our website at www.giftsoffreedom.com and see how others have applied this information to their lives.

If you're reading this book in a small group, then use the study questions to prompt lively discussion. Discuss the action steps with at least one other group member to build accountability in your plans for action, then close your time together with prayer. For more information on how to lead a group or Sunday school class and get additional resources, visit our website at www.giftsoffreedom.com.

If you are not currently in a group study of the book, you might want to consider starting one after you finish, so you can spread to others the new freedoms you have discovered. As you help others, you will deepen your understanding and relationship with God, gaining even more freedoms.

Go to www.giftsoffreedom.com for additional resource materials and instructions.

# Chapter 1

# GIFT #5—GOLD (PART 1)

## HOW DOES YOUR RELATIONSHIP WITH GOD RELATE TO GETTING YOUR NEEDS MET?

### STUDY QUESTIONS

1. Do you believe God has gifts specifically designed for you? Why does it take faith to receive these gifts?

_____

_____

_____

_____

_____

_____

_____

_____

_____

Provision is what you really need, not money or gold.

2. Do you see how we can overemphasize and confuse money, bank accounts, and jobs over "God's provision"? Have you done so, and if so, in what ways?

_____

_____

Faith in God as your Provider gives you the power to resist temptation and stay on His path.

3. In what areas do you try to fulfill your own needs instead of trusting that "God will fulfill your needs"? Does this ever lead you to cut corners when you lack full confidence in Him as your Provider? If so, what are some of these ways? If your trust and confidence level were solely rooted in God as your faithful Provider, it would be easier to resist these temptations, wouldn't it?

_____

_____

4. Peace is often intimately linked with trust in the Bible: "May the God of hope fill you with all joy and peace as you trust in Him…" Why do you think this is? How have you witnessed this in your own life with work, friendships, or family?

_____

_____

_____

_____

_____

Trust that God is actively moving you through every experience and new place to fulfill His purposes for your life.

5. "When you face circumstances that overwhelm you, you're only seeing half the picture." What half of the picture do we often see? What do we miss? Where does faith come in? What are some past circumstances you now see have added to your character, knowledge, experience, or opportunity? What are some currently overwhelming situations where you may be only seeing half the picture?

_____

_____

_____

_____

_____

When you are following His leading, you can trust your heavenly Father.

6. How do we live out a "childlike faith"? What are some of the qualities children have that make them a model for our relationship with God?

_____

_____

_____

_____

_____

Trust in the One who never changes for eternal peace and joy.

7. How can God use circumstances (either good or bad) to help us reprogram our thinking? What is one situation you can see His hand in today?

_____

_____

_____

_____

8. Why do we tend to trust our ways and resources instead of God's? What are the dangers of trusting our ways? How does it feel to know you can trust that God *never* changes and that He *always* has good intentions for you? How can this fact change your outlook on life?

_____

_____

_____

God offers you a unique destiny, and with faith and a thankful spirit you can fulfill your purpose and therefore live a joy-filled life.

9. Were we all created to be the same? Were we created as robots or clones to receive and experience the same in life? What might your purpose be and how might that differ from others' purpose?

_____

_____

_____

_____

Cultivate an intimate relationship by sharing your personal experiences with God.

10. Why is it important to have a thankful attitude that God is in control? What does your attitude say about your relationship with God? What is the opposite of "an attitude of gratitude"? If it appears you have nothing to be grateful for, how could you possibly have gratitude?

_____

_____

_____

_____

_____

_____

_____

_____

_____

_____

_____

_____

Go out on a limb to seek a rich relationship with Him, which will illuminate and multiply His gifts.

11. How do you go about seeking God diligently? Why is seeking such an important part of your relationship with God? Why isn't God easy for us to find sometimes?

_____

_____

_____

_____

_____

_____

12. What does it mean to "seek first [God's] Kingdom"? What are the "things" that will be "given to you" when you do this?

_____

_____

_____

## ACTION STEPS

Summarize the content of the first chapter. Based on what you've learned, are there any steps you need to take to seek God first? To learn to trust His ways? List those thoughts here, and plan to work on them in the coming days.

_____

_____

_____

_____

## CLOSING PRAYER

(Pray this prayer, or come up with your own to close this study time.)

Lord, thank You for the gift of gold. Help me to trust You more and find Your peace as I seek first Your Kingdom.

# Chapter 2

# GIFT #5—GOLD (PART 2)

## HOW DOES FAITH IN GOD'S GIFT OF PROVISION BRING THIS GIFT INTO FULL BLOOM?

### STUDY QUESTIONS

If you take His prescription, you can be healthier and live longer.

1. In Matthew 6:25-34, is Jesus calling us to a "revolutionary" life or the American way? Do we worry about our lives because deep down we don't believe God is really in control or doesn't always have our best interests at heart? In what ways will wholehearted trust in God revolutionize your life?

_____

_____

_____

_____

2. Can you describe how the gift of gold becomes two gifts if we use faith? In addition to God giving us provision, how does having faith in this gift change our lives?

_____

_____

_____

_____

_____

_____

3. How does discomfort in our lives cultivate an intimate relationship with God? Does God care more about our physical comfort or our relationship with Him? Why?

_____

_____

_____

_____

_____

_____

_____

God intended a parent's love to mirror His love for us, giving provision when we can't provide for ourselves.

4. What are some examples of God's provision in your life? In the lives of friends and family? What are three of your greatest obstacles in trusting God for His provision?

_____

_____

_____

_____

_____

_____

5. When you share God's message to the world (witnessing), why is it made more meaningful when "personalized with your experiences"? What difficult or miraculous experience could you share?

_____

_____

_____

_____

_____

Life is an open-book test, so pay attention in class and use the Book—it will help you pass to the next level of spiritual growth.

6. What is the best resource you can lean on in life's "open-book test"? How well do you lean on it now? What are some things you can do to improve your "test scores"?

_____

_____

_____

_____

_____

_____

7. What is the state of "quiet expectation"? Can you describe a specific season, person, or area in your life where you have entered this state, waiting on God to do His part?

_____

_____

_____

_____

_____

_____

_____

Put God's priorities first and He will handle what you need to fulfill your purpose.

8. If you don't currently seek God first, what *do* you seek first? (Sometimes it's revealing to look at your check stubs to find out where your priorities are.) What does this say about the importance of God in your life? Is it easy to trust God to take care of you? How is this trust an example of a mature faith?

_____

_____

_____

Things in this temporal world may come and go, but your attitude, love, and joy should remain.

9. Do you at times place more importance on what's provided rather than the Provider? How? Can we effectively love both the Provider and the provided?

_____

_____

_____

You will have to "let go" of some things to get to your Promised Land.

10. What are some of the items you have to "let go" of in order to reach your Promised Land? How will you do this? What is the reward of letting go?

_____

_____

_____

_____

Going upstairs is harder than down, so trust that you will find your reward at the top.

11. Is the trip en route to a destination always easy? Do you make your journeys in life for the trip or the destination? What are some difficult journeys in your life that have ended or could end in a good way?

_____

_____

_____

_____

12. What are some ways God might be working "behind the scenes" in your story? What comfort do you get from knowing God is working out His plan for you?

_____

_____

_____

_____

## ACTION STEPS

Make a list of some ways God has provided for you. Then make another list of things you tend to do for yourself without trusting God. What are some steps you can take to move items from the second list over to the first?

_____

_____

_____

_____

_____

_____

_____

_____

# CLOSING PRAYER

(Pray this prayer, or come up with your own to close this study time.)

Lord, thank You for Your provision. Help me to trust You in all aspects of my life so that I might build a more intimate relationship with You.

# Chapter 3

# GIFT #6—FRANKINCENSE (PART 1)

## HOW CAN PRAISE AND WORSHIP CHANGE YOUR LIFE?

### STUDY QUESTIONS

1. What are some of your strongest positive "scent memories"? How do these affect your mind or heart? Can you see how your faith-filled praise and worship can create memories for God—Kodak moments, as it were?

_____

_____

_____

_____

_____

_____

_____

Jesus again made a way for praise and worship to come from our inside and radiate out, instead of having to go to a temple to worship.

2. What does it mean to worship God in spirit and in truth? How can you do this now?

_____

_____

_____

Let your actions reflect your Maker's image within you and be grateful for His hands on your life. He has a great plan for you!

3. Reflect on this: "He is the Creator, and we are the creation." How does this lead us to a "dramatic perspective shift"? What perspective are we shifting away from? Meditate on this as it relates to the decisions you make in your day-to-day life. In what way could this have an impact on some of your big decisions?

_____

_____

_____

4. What are the two repeated themes that should be in our praise and worship? Outline how praise and worship would incorporate these two themes into your life. Can you see how this builds your confidence in God?

_____

_____

_____

_____

_____

Praise and worship opens your heart to God so He can work His power within you.

5. Do you ever find yourself "going through the motions" with praise and worship? Why isn't that true worship? What are the attributes of true worship? What does true worship and praise do for you?

_____

_____

_____

_____

_____

6. How is "praise" defined in Scripture? Are you misdirecting your praise at times to yourself or to others? How?

_____

_____

_____

7. Do you tend to only offer praise to God when your circumstances are praiseworthy? How can you offer praise to God when you are not in the mood, when you have nothing to give, when you don't feel like singing, or when circumstances don't warrant it? List some ways.

_____

_____

_____

_____

God dwells in a different dimension that allows Him to experience your future now, and He can share it with you through worship.

8. How does our limited perspective impact the way we might choose to praise and worship? How can God's ability to see your past, present, and future enter your worship time?

_____

_____

_____

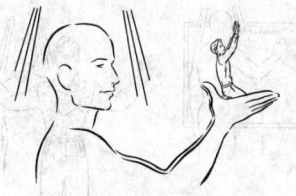

When you lift up God, He will lift you up.

9. Do you expect God to move supernaturally in your times of praise and worship? What is one instance where something amazing happened?

_____

_____

_____

_____

10. What are some circumstances that are holding you back? How could praise and worship affect that situation? Do you believe your praise and worship has the power to help break you free? Where is this power found?

_____

_____

_____

_____

_____

_____

_____

Your provision, healing, understanding, and comfort are all found in your praise and worship.

11. When you're lacking, hurting, confused, or feeling alone, what can you do? Is it easy to praise God in these circumstances? If not, how can you do it?

_____

_____

_____

Sacrifices in your life are a worship offering to God, and obedience is the sacrificial offering of your life itself.

12. Explain in what ways this statement could apply in your life: "God treasures your obedience over your sacrifice." How does that apply in praise and worship?

_____

_____

_____

## ACTION STEPS

What does your praise and worship look like today? Do you experience it only at church? On your own? Plan this week to take time (including some time when you have not done so before) specifically to enter praise and worship. If your church offers a special worship service, be sure to attend and allow God to speak to you through your worship time.

_____

_____

_____

_____

_____

_____

## CLOSING PRAYER

(Pray this prayer, or come up with your own to close this study time.)

Lord, thank You for the fragrant gift of frankincense and the ability to praise and worship You. Help me to meet You, focus on You, and know You in worship times with an open heart and a welcoming spirit.

## Chapter 4

# GIFT #6—FRANKINCENSE (PART 2)

## WHAT ARE THE KEY ELEMENTS OF INTIMATE COMMUNICATIONS WITH GOD?

STUDY QUESTIONS

1. Do you have a relationship with someone that is completely open and honest—one where you know each other well and share a mutual trust? What brought that relationship to that place?

_____

_____

_____

_____

_____

_____

_____

2. Describe what communication was like in the garden between God and humans. How did that change after the fall? What kind of communication is available to us today?

_____

_____

_____

_____

_____

Prayer, no matter the method, time, or place, is simply communicating with God.

3. Simply put, what is prayer? Does it have to be formal? Outside of church activities, can you think of some ways, times, and places you could converse with God?

_____

_____

_____

_____

_____

_____

When you are truly at peace with others, when you are righteous, when you are seeking God, and when you are praying wholeheartedly for His will in faith, then you have good reason to have high expectations.

4. Why does God want us to pray, even though He already knows everything? What are some key elements of successful prayer?

_____

_____

_____

Use the Jesus model for prayer as you pursue communication with God.

5. Describe the example Jesus gave of a prayer structure in Matthew 6:9-13. How can you construct a personalized prayer using this template? In what spirit should all your prayers be offered?

_____

_____

_____

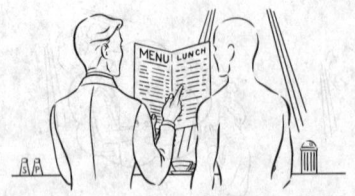

Bring God into the little decisions of your life.

6. What should we pray about? What are some things you could include God in that you haven't been including Him in?

_____

_____

_____

_____

_____

Jesus is our model for prayer. He prayed for direction, for the recharging of His spirit, for others, and for God's will to be done. He prayed before, during, and after His personal battles.

7. What can you do in your life to improve your "odds" of getting the answers you want to your prayers? Or is that even possible? Explain your answer.

_____

_____

_____

_____

8. When should we pray? What does it look like to pray continually?

_____

_____

_____

_____

_____

9. What are the answers you hope to receive from your prayers today? How can communication with God through prayer help you find hope for these circumstances? When prayers don't seem to be answered, what's our checklist for some of the possible reasons? Once we review the checklist and make any necessary adjustments, what did Jesus teach us we should do?

_____

_____

_____

_____

_____

_____

_____

_____

There is synergistic power in the spirit realm when you pray in unity with others. This can cause evil to scatter and strongholds to come down.

10. Matthew 18:20 says that whenever two or three come together in God's name, God is there in the midst of them. How do you go about praying "in one accord"? Do you access the power of prayer with others in your life? Name some ways you could do it more.

_____

_____

_____

_____

_____

11. Describe intercessory prayer. How did Jesus intercede for us? How are we to intercede for others?

_____

_____

_____

_____

_____

Intercessory prayer is powerful and life-changing; it is also beneficial.

12. What is the "sowing and reaping" effect that comes with intercessory prayer? (See Solomon's story in 1 Kings 3:5-14.) How can you utilize this in your own prayer life?

_____

_____

_____

_____

## ACTION STEPS

Review the list of items to pray for at the end of the chapter. Add other items for which you're led to pray. Take time to pray each of these prayers right now. Then make a commitment to pray for each of these things every day.

_____

_____

_____

_____

## Closing Prayer

(Pray this prayer, or come up with your own to close this study time.)

Lord, thank You for the gift of frankincense and the ability to communicate with You through prayer. Teach me how to pray, and help me to rely on prayer every day as I seek to grow closer to You.

# Chapter 5

# Gift #7—Myrrh (Part 1)

## Why Is Dying the First Step to Living in Freedom?

### Study Questions

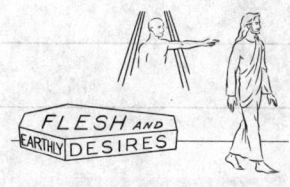

> You must die to the flesh, earthly desires, and selfish ambition to have the freedom and clarity to follow the leading of His Spirit.

1. Have you ever had a relationship or job that looked like "the end" but turned out to be the beginning of something new or better? In what two ways did Jesus die, and how did those ways become the ultimate beginning for Him? What will each of our deaths begin for us?

_____

_____

_____

_____

627

You must first establish a spiritual "bench head" before you can conquer your physical "mountains."

2. Imagine you were among the Israelites prior to Jesus' birth. What sort of Messiah would you hope for? How might you have reacted to the claim that the Messiah was born in a lowly manger, not in the palace of a king? That He would suffer a seemingly physical loss to gain spiritual victory? What does this say about the way God works? What does it say about your current physical needs?

_____

_____

_____

_____

Jesus was establishing an eternal Kingdom, not a temporal one.

3. In what ways did Jesus fulfill the requirement for righteousness? (See Philippians 3:8-9.)

_____

_____

_____

4. After reflecting on Jesus' humble arrival, how does this King's arrival on the scene differ from earthly kings, royalty, dignitaries, and celebrities? What was His purpose in this first arrival that required such an appearance, and how will it differ from His next arrival? Why did they miss God?

_____

_____

_____

_____

_____

_____

_____

5. Why doesn't the world recognize Jesus now? How did you recognize Him? What does this say about God's desire to know you?

_____

_____

_____

_____

_____

_____

_____

_____

_____

The Kingdom of God is just another dimension around us which we too can access from within by doing His will.

6. "The Kingdom of God is found through the Holy Spirit within us and not by physical observation." How do we get there? Is this something this world opposes? In what ways? What does our physical life look like when we enter the Kingdom of God?

_____

_____

_____

God's Spirit went through His Word, which is Jesus, and then into us who receive the Word—and we bring Him into the world.

7. What are the two different kinds of testimonies? How does God build your testimony? What is your responsibility regarding your testimony? When was the last time you shared your testimony with someone else? How does sharing your testimony act as salt and light in the world?

_____

_____

_____

_____

We, like Jesus, need to humble ourselves and serve others if we want to be lifted up by God.

8. How do you humble yourself to serve others? What does a true servant's heart look like?

_____

_____

_____

Carrying someone else's load speaks volumes to them.

9. Describe the concept of "dying to self." How does this allow you to find God's will? To become a servant? To create a testimony?

_____

_____

_____

631

10. Our flesh and the influences of the world are at war with God. "Dying to self" is opposed by both powerful forces; it's unnatural. Ultimately, what does your flesh desire if it always gets its way? What are some practical steps you need to take to "die to self"? Does it take self-discipline? Why?

_____

_____

_____

_____

11. What is your response to the idea that we're to be "ready to die" as Christ-followers? Does this cause you anxiety? What is the opposing message? In what area and how are you going to start implementing this concept into your life so that it is not merely a "nice church saying"?

_____

_____

_____

_____

12. How do you find the "true fulfillment" God intended for you? Does finding "true fulfillment" involve discomfort as we seek God's will? What is the prominent message we hear in the media about "true fulfillment"? Why is it impossible to love or follow both the things of the world and the things of God at the same time?

_____

_____

_____

_____

## ACTION STEPS

A servant's heart comes from the realization that it's "not all about you." This is in line with the idea that we need to die to self to truly pursue God's will. Take a moment to evaluate the ways you serve today. What are some of the things you are doing for others? Are there other ways you can die to self? What are some other ways you can serve with your servant's heart? Make a list of some of these and then commit to working on your service to others in the coming weeks.

_____

_____

_____

_____

_____

_____

## CLOSING PRAYER

(Pray this prayer, or come up with your own to close this study time.)

Father, thank You for coming to die for my sins and for leading the way so I might discover what it means to die to self. Help me to develop a servant's heart and act on that heart as I seek greater intimacy with You. Amen.

# Chapter 6

## GIFT #7—MYRRH (PART 2)

### WHAT ARE GOOD STRATEGIES
### FOR SUCCESSFUL LIVING?

#### STUDY QUESTIONS

1. What are some of the strategies you have in life? Why is it important to have strategies? Does making a battle plan involve the way you live and think?

   My new found strategy and battle plan is to meet every situation in life with Gods word against which nothing can stand.

2. Who is your enemy? What are his strengths and weaknesses? What are your strengths and weaknesses? What is the battlefield on which you fight?

   The enemy is my flesh which I have to war against because of satan. His strengths are only which we allow if we arent filled with the Word, Gods promises.

3. How does our definition of "good" and "evil" differ from God's definition?

*Gods defintion is based on righteousness and is perfect and ours is based on our flesh and is corrupted*

The world may offer many ways to live; however, there is only one way that offers an abundant life, one way that can accomplish His purposes. Look for the signs He gives you and follow His way.

4. What is the path to a victorious life? Where do we find the strategies to get there?

*The path is based on our complete surrender to God and standing on His word as the final authority for our lives*

It is important to discern where the attacks against you are coming from so you can extinguish the source of your problem, not the symptoms.

5. What are some of the specific battles you're facing right now? Are you in sync with God as you fight this battle? If not, what do you need to do to align your will with God's? How will that impact your battle strategy? How about your success on the battlefield?

*One of my biggest failings has always been my faith and doubt. Also my pride after the storm is over but since my complete surrender to Christ I have no doubt. I cast my cares and stand on His word.*

Fasting improves your spiritual insight so you can more clearly see God's will.

6. How is fasting a part of our spiritual growth? How can this act enhance our relationship with God? Is a fast only not eating food, or can you fast from other things as well? Is God leading you to fast from something?

*The seed to learn more about fasting has been planted and I think its my next step to growing with God!*

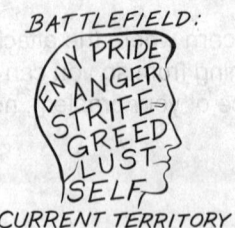

BATTLEFIELD:

ENVY PRIDE
ANGER
STRIFE
GREED
LUST
SELF

CURRENT TERRITORY

BATTLEFIELD:

LOVE PEACE
KINDNESS
CARING GIVING
HELPFULNESS
HOSPITALITY
SELFLESS-
NESS
MEEKNESS

PROMISED LAND

The battlefield is in the mind, and we need to hold every thought captive to the obedience of Christ in order to possess our Promised Land.

7. What does it mean to "bring every thought captive"? Are they just random thoughts, or does your mind have a direct relationship with your heart and/or actions? What are the recurring thoughts you could take captive today to find victory over your strongholds?

It means that we shouldnt be led by our minds to rationalize our lives. We should let our hart thats filled with Gods word be our filter EVERY thought because then we will be leaning on HIS understanding. Our minds cannot be our leader because we rationalize with the Flesh and God with perfect right-eousness.

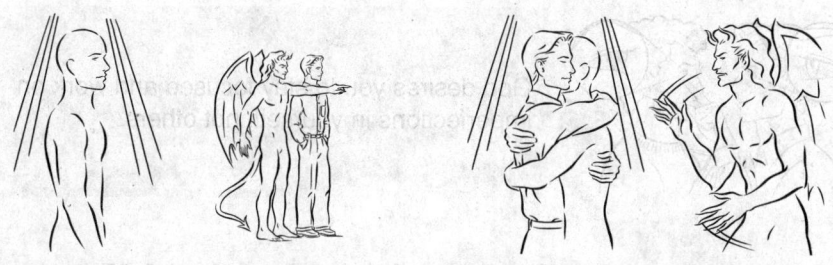

A closer relationship with God makes it easier to overcome temptations.

8. Respond to this quote: "Sin begins in the mind and is powered by desires." What does this suggest about the choices you make? How about the things you fill your mind with? What changes do you need to make in your lifestyle to avoid filling your mind with wrong thoughts? How does having a closer relationship with God help get more of your thoughts under control?

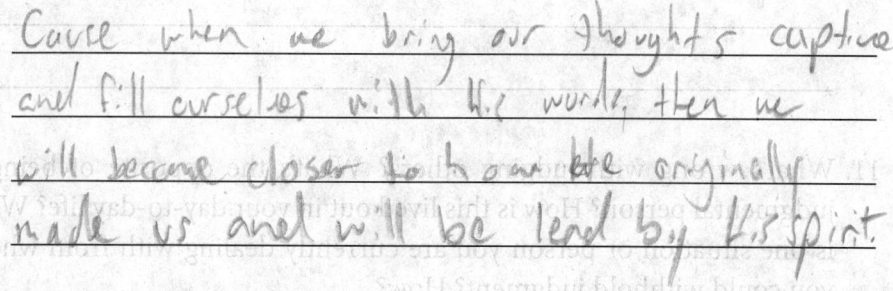

*Cause when we bring our thoughts captive and fill ourselves with the words, then we will become closer to how he originally made us and will be lead by his spirit.*

9. If we are naturally compelled to return "evil for evil," what kind of strategic plan could you make to counteract that impulse? Who or what are your weak points when it comes to seeking revenge?

_____

_____

_____

_____

God desires you to stay focused and work on imperfections in yourself, not others.

10. What causes you to focus on others' imperfections? How can you reverse this habit, looking instead at your own areas for growth and improvement?

_____

_____

_____

_____

_____

_____

11. What's wrong with judging others? What's the opposite of being a judgmental person? How is this lived out in your day-to-day life? What is one situation or person you are currently dealing with from whom you could withhold judgment? How?

_____

_____

_____

_____

_____

_____

Sometimes being still allows God to speak through you to light the way for others.

12. Read Matthew 27:12-14. What kind of message do we send to God when we let Him work on our behalf? Why do we want to step in and take control? Are we trying to be God? When do you find yourself "allowing God to be God," and what environment, thoughts, or actions trigger this kind of heartfelt response?

_____

_____

## ACTION STEPS

What are some of the strategies you're currently using to pursue God's will and live a life of faith? List these. Then consider the areas of your life where you face the greatest battles with satan's desire to turn you from God's will as well as your own thoughts and habits that would cause you to do the same. What are some specific strategies you can implement to better fight those battles? List those here as well and commit to utilizing them.

_____

_____

_____

## CLOSING PRAYER

(Pray this prayer, or come up with your own to close this study time.)

Lord, thank You for the gift of myrrh and for all the truth You have given in that gift. Give me clear insight in my life, and help me to develop a confident battle plan as I continue to pursue an intimate relationship with You.

# Chapter 7

# Gift #7—Myrrh (Part 3)

## Who Is Your Enemy, and How and Where Will He Attack?

### Study Questions

1. Do you understand how our struggle to "fly" is part of God's growth plan? What are some struggles or situations in your life that God could use (irrespective of how they come about) for your growth? Do you see spiritual maturity as a process, or does it happen overnight?

_____

_____

_____

_____

_____

_____

643

Your protection and purpose is on God's path, so don't let satan trick you into wandering off it.

2. Describe the nature of your enemy and some of his schemes. How do you prepare yourself to be ready for him?

_____

_____

_____

_____

Satan is an opportunist and will wait for your weakest moment to tempt you.

3. What are the two most "opportune times" satan might use to tempt you? What are some weak areas of your life for which you need a better plan of defense? What are some new areas you are attacking to gain ground? How will resisting the devil play a part in these?

_____

_____

_____

_____

How will you respond to an attack by satan in the physical realm—physically or spiritually—with a verbal attack, or in love and with prayer?

4. How does satan use other people to get you to fall? Are we to hold them responsible or forgive and pray for them? List some people and events in your life that satan has used to attempt to throw you off God's track. How can you improve your response in these moments of temptation, as satan seeks to throw you off?

_____

_____

_____

Don't be tricked into waters that your flesh will be too weak to get out of when satan turns up the heat.

5. Review the list of things God meant for good that satan often tricks people into taking in excess. What are the items that are tempting for you to take across the line to an excess? What are some practical actions you can do to avoid falling for these temptations?

_____

_____

_____

_____

Satan makes every effort to trick us from turning on or up our light.

6. What are some examples of satan's involvement in today's world? What is his prime objective? How do you see this in action in your own life? How can you be more discerning?

_____

_____

_____

_____

7. What is satan's four-fold strategy against the church?

_____

_____

_____

8. Why is unity of the body so important to God's church? What are the greatest obstacles to such unity? What can you do individually to work toward unity of the body?

_____

_____

_____

You are never alone in your battles—look for God and count on Him always.

9. In what ways are you not alone in your battles? How does this help you as you face challenging circumstances? What does this suggest about your role in helping others who are in the midst of difficult battles?

_____

_____

_____

Don't be misled by the world's battle equipment and strategies. They will lead you into traps and headaches.

10. How important is it to find the right weapons and right battlefield in our fight against our enemy? List some of the weapons you have to fight your spiritual battles. How do you put them on? Which of these do you already use? Which should you learn more about so you can better prepare to fight the inevitable battles?

_____

_____

_____

11. Why is our continued communication so important to fighting our battles? How do you keep in communication with God?

_____

_____

12. What are some ways God makes us resilient? How do we assist or hinder our spiritual and physical healing? How do we overcome?

_____

_____

## ACTION STEPS

List all the weapons you have at your disposal for fighting spiritual battles. Then evaluate how well you're using each weapon. What can you learn from this book and from Scripture to better prepare to fight your battles? Which of the weapons do you need to train with the most? Come up with a plan to work on strengthening your abilities with these weapons, and then implement that plan.

_____

_____

## CLOSING PRAYER

(Pray this prayer, or come up with your own to close this study time.)

Lord, thank You for all the weapons You have given me to help fight spiritual battles. Give me wisdom in using these weapons and strength to wield them so that I can defeat satan and grow in Your image and likeness. Amen.

# Unwrapping Increase, Destiny, Relationships, God, and the Gifts of the Spirit

## Book 3

# PREFACE

Ｗhat does God want you to do with your life? The answers we may get from Christians may vary. One may say, "Good church attendance," another may say, "Giving the church your financial support," or maybe you've heard someone say, "Being active in church programs!" But none of these alone will truly satisfy our hearts.

You were created for relationships, which is what the five gifts in this book are all about. First is your relationship with God. In fact, the church is described as the bride of Christ being prepared for a wedding. After that comes the Bible's definition of how your relationships with other people should look like. Using the gifts God offers will allow your relationships to truly satisfy your heart and give purpose to your life.

This book will answer the question, What does God desire for your life? It is not just being active in His church, but truly becoming His living church.

*As you come to Him, the living Stone—rejected by men but chosen by God and precious to Him—you also, like living stones, are being built into a spiritual house to be a holy priesthood, offering spiritual sacrifices acceptable to God through Jesus Christ (1 Peter 2:4-5).*

# INTRODUCTION

## BOOK 1: IN THE BEGINNING

In Book 1, we looked at how we were created by God to be in relationship with Him—a relationship of mutual love. Originally, this was easy because Adam and Eve were created in His image and likeness, and they enjoyed a spirit-to-Spirit connection with Him, which allowed them to keep His essence of love alive within them. They radiated with God's love, in a pure and intimate relationship with their Creator. God gave them freedom of choice, a free will that allowed them to love and choose perfect love or to reject His will for their lives and thus sin. They rebelled and chose to reject God (see Genesis 3).

Today many people still reject Him, much like Adam and Eve did, because they believe they are wiser, they can work life out on their own, and they have a better plan for their lives than their Creator. However, God's desire is for His creation to *thrive* by walking with His Spirit's guidance and according to instruction from His Word.

When Adam and Eve disobeyed God, they brought sin into the world—that is, things outside of God's perfect plan. They opened Pandora's Box. With sin came death and humanity's bondage in and to this world. Then humanity had to toil, work, and sweat in order to survive, having lost a functioning spirit-to-Spirit connection with God. As humanity, we brought this curse upon ourselves, and our daily experience of it brings us back to the truth that we need God.

The trouble is that we can't find God on our own! Our only hope of getting back on course is in salvation through Jesus Christ. His death on the cross through the gift of grace gives us the opportunity for new life and complete forgiveness of our sins, if we choose to accept it.

When we receive this first gift of life through the gift of grace, we accept the second with it—the gift of the Holy Spirit. Indeed, this spirit-to-Spirit reconnection is the vehicle for achieving real intimacy with Him. His image and likeness can once again exude from our lives with a real-time connection. It is through the Holy Spirit that we receive the other gifts too, except for the gift of faith.

The gift of faith was already given to us at birth, but it must be received, unwrapped, and used in our relationship with God for it to bring forth life. Faith is a verb, an action; that's the only way to use it! An action of faith pleases God; it's the key to His heart (see Hebrews 11:6). This means we live out and act upon His promises as if our lives depended on it. Our actions please God because the gift of faith is the foundation on which we live, allowing us to unwrap and unleash all the other gifts available to us while we're here on earth.

The first gift we can unwrap with our faith is the gift of adversity. In all adversity, no matter what the cause, God has imbedded some form of potential redemption that we can unwrap with our faith.

## BOOK 2: BUILDING YOUR SPIRITUAL HOME

The gift of new life in Jesus is just that, a new and unfamiliar way of living—Jesus called it being "born again" (see John 3:3). If you are truly, spiritually born again, just like a newborn, you need to learn how to crawl, walk, and eat. How do children learn these essential components of life? They learn them only by being willing to accept guidance, teaching, and help until they are mature and can stand and eat on their own.

If Book 1 is about building a spiritual foundation, then Book 2 involves assessing and using those materials to build a solid spiritual home using three additional gifts that God offers each of us. At Jesus' birth, the wise men brought Him gifts of gold, frankincense, and myrrh. These gifts were symbolic, but they also served a practical function for Jesus and His family—they were vital gifts. Today, they are still just as essential to His family, which is you and me!

The gift of gold represents God's promise of provision in our lives. When the gift is fully unwrapped with our faith, then we also find the peace of God that passes our understanding permeating our hearts. Receiving this peace allows us to better resist temptations in the world, and to follow the path that God has laid out for us.

The gift of frankincense represents praise, worship, and prayer, through which we develop our intimacy with God. Praise and worship are designed to clarify and confirm the relationship between God and us. Prayer is a vital communication link that establishes expectation, for in it we hold a two-way dialog with the Creator of Heaven and earth.

The gift of myrrh represents death. Like Jesus, our first death should be a death to ourselves or our decision to give up our will and allow God's will to replace it. This is the primary way to clear the path for God's will and destiny to flow into our lives. This is our first death. Jesus' first death was also successfully used to establish His spiritual Kingdom on earth. But Jesus' second death on the cross, His physical death, was the vehicle used to bring us back into relationship with God and to give us eternal life.

## BOOK 3: BRINGING LIFE TO YOUR SPIRITUAL HOME

Now that you've established your spiritual home, you may be asking, "How do I turn this house into a home? How do I make it vibrant? How do I live an abundant life with everything that God has to offer me?"

The answer to these questions are found in the last five gifts we will discuss in this book, which are all about relationship. The gifts covered in this book are the gift of increase, the gifts of the Spirit, the gift of relationship, the gift of destiny, and the gift of God Himself, who is the head of the Trinity. They each address how we relate to God, living an abundant life and exuding His image and likeness. And they address how we relate to others. The gifts of destiny and of God Himself speak primarily to our ideal relationship with God, while the gifts of the Spirit and of relationship revolve around our connection with others—the quality of which affects our relationship with God. And within the gift of increase, both our earthly and heavenly relationships are intertwined.

A big difference exists between knowing information and becoming a teacher, between reading a baby book and becoming a mom or dad. The difference involves establishing relationships in order to bring knowledge alive. This book is about bringing your house alive.

*The Gifts of Freedom* series was written to turn a spiritual infant into a warrior for God—for this is your true calling. Remember, you do not need to speed through this book. Take the time you need and allow God to interact with you as you consider the biblical truths He presents to you. Also consider how each of the Action & Visualization instructions I offer throughout each chapter can bring long-term change in your life. These spots are meant to be a time to pause and apply what you have read. Perhaps they may provide a good time to lay the book down and to live out what you just read.

Let's unwrap the next five gifts.

# Chapter 1

# Gift #8—Increase (Part 1)

## Where, How, and Why Is There Increase?

Before you begin to read, pray that the Holy Spirit will give you
and all readers of this book understanding and application.

✠ *I planted, Apollos watered, but God **gave** the **increase**. So then neither
he who plants is anything, nor he who waters, but God who **gives** the
**increase*** (1 Corinthians 3:6-7 NKJV).

Who doesn't want to put their time and energy into something
that is going to be successful, something that will show an increase? Financially, we all want to see our investments double
or multiply over time. Whether we have a home, a business venture, an
IRA, or a stock portfolio, we are in many ways gambling when we invest.
We *hope* for an increase, but in most cases, we have no certainty of one.
The investments we make in the physical world are always risky because
the markets are unstable, fluctuate, and sometimes even crash. Open the
business section of any newspaper on any day of the week and you'll nearly
always read something about economic instability.

An investment in God's market, however, is an investment in a Kingdom
where the principles never change and where we are assured of eternal
truths and rewards. With that in mind, consider why we put our trust and

hope in the business market for financial gain. Do we do it for happiness or for security? Isn't God the giver of every good and perfect gift; isn't He the true source and giver of increase? James writes:

✠ *Every good and perfect gift is from above, coming down from the Father of heavenly lights, who does not change like shifting shadows* (James 1:17).

Yes, God is the giver of all increase, advancement, and victory, whether in the spiritual, physical, or financial realms. The gift of increase has the power to free you in many ways. It has a ripple effect, much like a rock landing in the middle of a pond.

In this chapter, we'll explore how increase is rooted in the investment of our time, attention, heart, and yes, even our money, in the Kingdom of God, which is the *only* truly sound investment. You'll discover that, while you do have a role to play in the process (the opening verse of the chapter indicates both planting and watering), the actual increase comes alone by God's hand. It is His sovereign, reserved right to determine when and how it happens and to release the increase. However, it's important to remember your part requires an action of faith, which is what pleases God and is the key to His heart (see Hebrews 11:6). Yes, increase can come to you by the process of enhancing your relationship with God.

## INCREASE FROM THE BEGINNING

God's plan is to give increase and multiplication. From nature, we see that all life has a growth pattern and that it multiplies itself. This is evident from the very beginning of creation:

✠ *God blessed them and said to them, "Be fruitful and increase in number; fill the earth and subdue it..."* (Genesis 1:28).

God gave Noah a similar command regarding the animals:

✝ *Bring out every kind of living creature that is with you—the birds, the animals, and all the creatures that move along the ground—so they can multiply on the earth and be fruitful and increase in number upon it* (Genesis 8:17).

And an angel told Abraham's wife, Sarah, that God would bless them with the gift of increase as well:

✝ *The angel added, "I will so increase your descendants that they will be too numerous to count"* (Genesis 16:10).

## INCREASE IN GENERATIONS

Abram, whose faith God counted as righteousness, was also blessed by God with wealth. Genesis tells us:

✝ *Abram had become very wealthy in livestock and in silver and gold* (Genesis 13:2).

And his son, Isaac, was also blessed with wealth:

✝ *The man became rich, and his wealth continued to grow until he became very wealthy* (Genesis 26:13).

And so too his grandson Jacob was blessed with wealth:

✠ *In this way the man grew exceedingly prosperous and came to own large flocks, and maidservants and menservants, and camels and donkeys* (Genesis 30:43).

In fact, in the Old Testament, increase is often portrayed as a blessing that is carried down from generation to generation. Consider the following verses:

✠ *May the Lord, the God of your fathers, increase you a thousand times and bless you as He has promised* (Deuteronomy 1:11).

✠ *May the Lord make you increase, both you and your children* (Psalm 115:14).

## INCREASE AS BLESSING

When you start receiving God's gift of increase (including wealth) as a *blessing* that comes from Him, then you will discover that it is a trouble-free gift to those who have faith and know it is from God. Proverbs reminds us:

✠ *The blessing of the Lord brings wealth, and He adds no trouble to it* (Proverbs 10:22).

Of course, wealth is not always good unless it is a blessing from God:

✠ *...the abundance of a man permits him no sleep* (Ecclesiastes 5:12).

Increase, both good and bad, comes to both the righteous and wicked *alike*. However, it is our faith in God that makes whatever the gift a true blessing in which we can joyously *rest*. Increase of bad things when we have faith will allow us to see and unwrap the good gift contained inside. Increase of good without *faith* will only cause constant anxiety—the struggle to maintain and protect the gift. Without faith, the rich man will worry about how to keep his wealth. But the righteous know that prosperity is one of many gifts from God; they understand that God has good intentions to freely give us His good gifts.

✝ [God] *who did not spare His own Son, but delivered Him up for us all, how shall He not with Him also freely give us all things?* (Romans 8:32 NKJV).

✝ *We have not received the spirit of the world but the Spirit who is from God, that we may understand what God has freely given us* (1 Corinthians 2:12).

The Bible even gives insight into our ability to enjoy what we receive, whether *little* or *great*. Even our enjoyment is a gift from God.

✝ *Moreover, when God gives any man wealth and possessions, and enables him to enjoy them, to accept his lot and be happy in his work—this is a gift of God* (Ecclesiastes 5:19).

## GOD RELEASES INCREASE

Symbolically speaking, you will have winter and summer seasons throughout your life. However, as you grow closer to God and gain wisdom, you will come to understand that He has a special gift of riches and honor designed just for you, and the gift is within your reach.

✠ *With [God] are riches and honor, enduring wealth and prosperity* (Proverbs 8:18).

✠ *But remember the Lord your God, for it is He who gives you the ability to produce wealth, and so confirms His covenant, which He swore to your forefathers, as it is today* (Deuteronomy 8:18).

Remember, it is by *faith* that we unwrap the gifts of God. In this case, we must have faith that God's gifts are perfect, though they are not always apparent, and they are going to be beneficial and complete.

We need faith to accept that God's provision is sufficient to cover all our needs. Only then will we possess all the benefits of the gift and *all* that God offers. For example, the Israelites were offered access to their Promised Land, but since they did not spiritually receive and unwrap this gift from God, they could not enjoy and maintain possession of the gift and all that God had promised them.

✠ *So we see that they were not able to enter, because of their unbelief* (Hebrews 3:19).

Though many times we can maintain a gift physically, if we do not receive it with faith then we do not get *full* possession of all its benefits (rest, joy, and fulfillment). It's only through an intimate relationship with God that we can understand and, therefore, obtain all the benefits from the gifts that He offers us while on earth. This is one reason we should not be envious when we see the unrighteous gain great wealth, fame, and power—it will not be joyful and fulfilling to them; indeed, it is more often a *curse*. However, those who have exercised their faith through intimacy with God will find rest, joy, and fulfillment in the spoils that come from God (even when the spoils don't seem like much).

✠ *Now we who have **believed** enter that rest...* (Hebrews 4:3).

## ACTION & VISUALIZATION

*Regardless of the gifts you receive, use your faith and relationship with God to get the fullest benefit from them.*

## FAITH HELPS BRING INCREASE

God also works with His followers, combining their faith with His power to bring about multiplication. We see this in the story of Elisha and the widow:

✠ *The wife of a man from the company of the prophets cried out to Elisha, "Your servant my husband is dead, and you know that he revered the Lord. But now his creditor is coming to take my two boys as his slaves."*

*Elisha replied to her, "How can I help you? Tell me, what do you have in your house?"*

*"Your servant has nothing there at all," she said, "except a little oil."*

*Elisha said, "Go around and ask all your neighbors for empty jars. **Don't ask for just a few.** Then go inside and shut the door behind you and your sons. Pour oil into all the jars, and as each is filled, put it to one side."*

*She left him and afterward shut the door behind her and her sons. They brought the jars to her and she kept pouring. When all the jars were full, she said to her son, "Bring me another one."*

*But he replied, **"There is not a jar left." Then the oil stopped flowing.***

*She went and told the man of God, and he said, "Go, sell the oil and pay your debts. You and your sons can live on what is left"* (2 Kings 4:1-7).

The widow said she had nothing left, but only a small amount of oil. We too often start with a small amount of resources—money, energy, talents, education (our seeds may be many or few)—but God wants us to step out and plant those seeds, having faith in His power to give the increase.

In this story, Elisha asked the widow to collect as many jars as she could, as many as her faith would allow. The number of jars she collected, one could say, represented her level of faith. The oil was multiplied by God, filling all the jars, according to the measure of her faith. Indeed, in this case, when her faith ended, *the oil stopped flowing.* Likewise, when we act in faith, God can multiply our resources, sometimes beyond our understanding, allowing us to accomplish His will.

In the gospel of John, we find a similar story. A boy gives Jesus five loaves of bread and two small fish, which Jesus multiplies to feed five thousand people (see John 6:1-13). Not only did Jesus provide increase to feed the crowd, but there were twelve baskets of leftovers. That's far more than the boy brought to Jesus in the first place.

We will note in reading the story that Jesus did not create a big pile of food from the five loaves of bread and two fish. It was only when He and each person thereafter broke the bread and the fish, and then *passed* on the rest, that the act of passing the food created the additional food for the next person to be filled. This is a wonderful analogy of God's intended economy for the world. Our giving creates increase for ourselves and others. When we give, we are expressing an *essence of God's love.*

In fact, the word *give* is spelled with the letter *hey* (grace) and *alef* (God), representing the manifestation of God's grace. Giving also triggers another essence of God, which is *multiplication.* When you are in a similar position, remember that the boy's generosity and willingness to surrender his meal to Jesus in faith allowed him to combine what he had with Jesus' power for God's will to be accomplished. For the part he played, the boy received a return or increase. This is a vivid picture of how God can turn what seems like a little into a lot—it is supernatural multiplication. God can do the same for you when you act in faith by trusting Him with what little you have. *Whatever you give God in faith, He will return it to you in abundance.*

Jesus' disciples acted in faith when they went out with no money and only the clothes they were wearing—and God worked with them and through them.

✠ *Then the disciples went out and preached everywhere, and the Lord worked with them and confirmed His word by the signs that accompanied it* (Mark 16:20).

You can rely on God and His power when you are acting in His will.

✠ *Not that we are competent in ourselves to claim anything for ourselves, but our competence comes from God* (2 Corinthians 3:5).

## ACTION & VISUALIZATION

*Give God what you have so that He can return to you an increase.*

## ONLY GOD GIVES THE INCREASE

God is the only source of increase in wealth, in honor, and in strength:

✠ *Wealth and honor come from You; You are the ruler of all things. In Your hands are strength and power to exalt and give strength to all* (1 Chronicles 29:12).

✠ *To this John replied, "A man can receive only what is given him from heaven"* (John 3:27).

Another type of increase comes in the form of personal victories over the difficulties in our lives. Just as with material increase, we must also trust God for increase in victory.

✠ *With God we will gain the victory...* (Psalm 60:12).

✠ *[God] holds victory in store for the upright...* (Proverbs 2:7).

Not only does God give the increase, growth, and victory, but He also sustains them. All growth (or increase) in our lives must be built up and maintained by God; otherwise, it is meaningless. This is why the psalmist could say:

✠ *Unless the Lord builds the house, its builders labor in vain. Unless the Lord watches over the city, the watchmen stand guard in vain. In vain you rise early and stay up late, toiling for food to eat—for He grants sleep to those He loves* (Psalm 127:1-2).

This passage shows that confidence in God (who is our Provider) will allow us to rest and be comfortable with our gifts when they are delivered. When we see ourselves as our ultimate provider, then we're acting out our disbelief in the Provider. In so doing, we miss the path He intends for us. But when we place our faith in God and obtain His power of increase, growth, and victory, then we effectively allow Him to show Himself in our lives.

✠ *But we have this treasure in jars of clay to show that this all-surpassing power is from God and not from us* (2 Corinthians 4:7).

## WHY ONLY GOD?

Why has God reserved the right to determine increase, growth, and victory? Why is He the sole author? Why can't we just go out and get it ourselves?

To answer these questions, we need to remember that God gave us freedom of choice—*independence*—so that we would have the ability to have a loving relationship with Him. God cannot force or demand love from us. If He did, then it wouldn't be love. We can only exhibit love through our freedom of choice and independence. Without independence, love cannot exist; however, with this independence we have chosen to bring evil into the world. How can God counteract this evil while at the same time allowing our independence? If we have complete independence, how can God have complete control as well?

First, this divine right enables God to remain in ultimate control of the world while at the same time offering us freedom of choice. If He controls the increase, then ultimately, despite our bad choices, He controls the result. Of course, God allows consequences to happen according to our choices, but by controlling the increase, God can imbed an opportunity for redemption, an opportunity for us to get back on track, even when we make the wrong choices. It also gives God room to work in our lives, to be a rewarder, to exercise His grace, to show His love, and to accomplish His will. By controlling the increase, God determines where the power, the money, and the blessings go; thus, He can accomplish His will for us in the end. Consider this example of God using His power of increase as a means to accomplishing His will:

> *I will increase the fruit of the trees and the crops of the field, so that you will no longer suffer disgrace among the nations because of famine* (Ezekiel 36:30).

Second, it pulls us closer to Him. If increase were solely up to our own efforts, would we perceive our need for God? Would as many of us really seek Him, or seek Him as earnestly? However, because we trust God for increase, for our physical sustenance, we are led to realize our dependence upon Him. Since we are also spiritually needy, our realization of our physical dependence leads us to a realization of our spiritual dependence on God and His grace. This dependence compels us to seek a closer and more intimate relationship with Him, and therefore we find fulfillment.

Third, dependence on God keeps us from becoming prideful. Keep in mind that pride was the cause of satan's fall from Heaven:

*You said in your heart, "I will ascend to heaven; I will raise my throne above the stars of God." ...But you are brought down to the grave, to the depths of the pit (Isaiah 14:13,15).*

Ezekiel goes on to describe satan's pride in this way:

*...You [satan] were the model of perfection, full of wisdom and perfect in beauty. You were in Eden, the garden of God; every precious stone adorned you: ruby, topaz and emerald, chrysolite, onyx and jasper, sapphire, turquoise, and beryl. Your settings and mountings were made of gold; on the day you were created they were prepared. You were anointed as a guardian cherub, for so I ordained you. You were on the holy mount of God; you walked among the fiery stones. You were blameless in your ways from the day you were created till wickedness was found in you. ...Your heart became **proud** on account of your beauty, and you corrupted your wisdom because of your splendor. So I threw you to the earth; I made a spectacle of you before kings (Ezekiel 28:12-15,17).*

The lesson here is clear: pride comes before a fall (see Proverbs 16:18). Remember the invisible law of gravity? Well, this is the invisible *law of pride.* Just as slipping off a high ledge will cause your body to fall in the natural, so in the spiritual realm, pride will cause your demise as well. The writer of Proverbs reminds us:

✠ *First pride, then the crash—the bigger the ego, the harder the fall* (Proverbs 16:18 MSG).

✠ *When pride comes, then comes disgrace, but with humility comes wisdom* (Proverbs 11:2).

✠ *Pride lands you flat on your face; humility prepares you for honors* (Proverbs 29:23 MSG).

Pride is not the will of God, but it came as a result of living in a fallen world and being swept up in it. John tells us of this:

✠ *For everything in the world—the cravings of sinful man, the lust of his eyes and the boasting of what he has and does—comes **not** from the Father but from the world* (1 John 2:16).

When we understand that we don't control our increase, then pride takes a back seat and humility kicks in. Only when we are in this state of humility can we see and accept God's plan and purpose for our lives. This applies to all kinds of increase, including our salvation (which is the greatest increase we receive since it grants us the promise of Heaven and an eternity with God):

✠ *For it is by grace you have been saved, through faith—and this not from yourselves, it is the gift of God—**not** by works, so that no one can boast* (Ephesians 2:8-9).

God knows that if we could earn our salvation through works, we would be boastful and proud. Our eyes would be set on ourselves and not on Him. This is one reason our salvation is a *gift*—to help us keep our eyes on Him and on His plan for our lives. It is for this same reason that *all* increase (physical, financial, and spiritual) is a gift that comes from Him (see James 1:17).

The danger of pride is also part of the reason God requires faith to receive His gifts. Just as we had to humble ourselves and have faith in God in order to receive the gift of life, so too our actions of faith can unwrap the gift of increase. Furthermore, we can't fully use the gift until we unwrap all of it. In other words, our levels of action in faith simply represent our levels of intimacy with God. Each step that we walk in faith brings us *closer* to Him. It's what pleases Him, and it is the key to His heart. The writer of Hebrews says:

✝ *And without faith it is impossible to please God...* (Hebrews 11:6).

God arranged it this way because He knew humanity had a prideful spirit. He seeks ways to protect us from ourselves, from our actions against ourselves and His creation. Look at what happened when people thought they could build a tower to get to Heaven without God:

✝ *Then they said, "Come, let us build ourselves a city, with a tower that reaches to the heavens, so that we may make a name for ourselves and not be scattered over the face of the whole earth"* (Genesis 11:4).

They wanted to touch Heaven in a physical, external way without God. But God wants us to reach for Heaven through our relationship with Him, through our internal spirit-to-Spirit connection. Because the people at the Tower of Babel sought to reach Him through the wrong means, God scattered them so that they would have to seek Him in the right way.

✠ *So the Lord scattered them from there over all the earth, and they stopped building the city* (Genesis 11:8).

The Babylonians, approximately seven hundred years later, provide another example. Look at what happened to them when they allowed their pride to take over:

✠ *You have trusted in your wickedness* [operating outside of God's will] *and have said, "No one sees me." Your wisdom and knowledge mislead you when you say to yourself, "I am, and there is none* [no god] *besides me." Disaster will come upon you, and you will not know how to conjure it away. A calamity will fall upon you that you cannot ward off with a ransom; a catastrophe you cannot foresee will suddenly come upon you* (Isaiah 47:10-11).

Simply put, pride in your efforts is not a vehicle toward intimacy with God and will lead to disasters, calamities, and catastrophes. On the other hand, God has designed in the gift of increase a way for us to gain greater intimacy with Himself, if we so choose.

## IMPORTANCE OF CREDITING GOD

Why do these bad things happen when we develop pride? Sadly, it's because we start seeing ourselves as masters of our own universe; essentially, we are trying to dethrone God in certain areas of our lives. In those areas, we put ourselves in His position. When we develop pride, we are saying, at best, "He doesn't matter," or at worst, "He doesn't exist." How can we ever fulfill our purpose of developing a loving relationship with God and exuding His image and likeness into the creation if we think in this way?

Consider God for a moment. How would you feel if you prepared and cooked all day for a dinner party and your spouse took credit for all your hard work? Relationship means acknowledging and giving credit where credit is due. The same is true in our relationship with God. We must not try to take credit for God's work.

✝ *Like clouds and wind without rain is a man who boasts of gifts he does not give* (Proverbs 25:14).

When good things happen to you, it is always important to remember God and to give Him the glory:

✝ *Let them give glory to the Lord…* (Isaiah 42:12).

✝ *Fear God and give Him glory…* (Revelation 14:7).

God does not just demand credit for His gifts for credit's sake alone. He knows this is the first step for us to understand how to find true fulfillment. And by giving Him the credit, it will become a witness to others so they will come to Him. He rewards those who give Him the credit He rightfully deserves:

✝ *Humility and the fear of the Lord bring wealth and honor and life* (Proverbs 22:4).

Conversely, we have read that a boastful and thankless attitude takes the credit away from God and will not be rewarded. Moreover, our boasting about what we have today is in vain because we never know what tomorrow will bring.

✝ *Don't brashly announce what you're going to do tomorrow; you don't know the first thing about tomorrow* (Proverbs 27:1 MSG).

A story in the gospel of Luke illustrates the need for a humble and thankful attitude for you to find and receive the ultimate desire that God has for your life. On the road, Jesus met ten lepers and gave them instructions on how to be healed:

✠ *When [Jesus] saw them, He said, "Go show yourselves to the priests." And as they went, they were cleansed* (Luke 17:14).

They all followed His instructions and were cleansed. This is an example of the first step: acting on faith is the road to your miracle. But read what happens next:

✠ *One of them, when he saw he was healed, came back, **praising** God in a loud voice. He threw himself at Jesus' feet and thanked Him—and he was a Samaritan.*

*Jesus asked, "Were not all ten cleansed? Where are the other nine? Was no one found to return and give **praise** to God except this foreigner?" Then He said to him, "Rise and go; your faith has made you **well**"* (Luke 17:15-19).

Not only was this Samaritan leper cleansed, but he was also *made well* as a result of giving God the glory. Jesus healed the ten lepers' physical diseases, which was a result or physical manifestation of their spiritual sicknesses. One leper came back to praise God for the physical healing and therefore received spiritual healing as well. By so doing, he got to the root of what was creating problems in his life. When you are praising God and giving Him credit for all the things He gives to you, you are developing greater intimacy with God through which His mere presence will free you.

Our best life revolves around an interconnected relationship with God. This creates intimacy and aligns us with our Creator. The better we understand our responsibility and God's nature, the better we are able to align ourselves with God. God does not want to get the credit just to get the credit. He knows that giving Him the credit is good for us because it forces us to align ourselves with Him and the purpose for which He created each one of us. When we are aligning ourselves with God and His plan, we are creating intimacy with which comes His manifestations.

Aligning ourselves with God, of course, also puts us in a better position to receive, unwrap, and use all the increase that He offers. We begin to realize that it is *not* our company, our boss, or our clients who are the providers; it is God *alone*. Therefore, He should be our *only* God and our *main* focus.

## ACTION & VISUALIZATION

*Be humble in all things, always giving God credit,*
*so that your vision will be clear enough to see His will in your life.*

## SOWING AND REAPING

One of the key aspects to finding increase is the principle of *sowing and reaping*. This principle applies spiritually, intellectually, physically, and financially. We have two parts to play in this process: we sow in *faith* and we reap in *thanks*. God has two parts to play as well: He supplies the seed, and once we sow, God then gives the increase.

For us, faith is an essential component to this process—that's why the two chapters on faith in Book 1 are important to understand before you can fully understand and appreciate the principle of sowing and reaping. Like the preceding gifts, faith is the *catalyst* for this gift too.

How do you put faith into this principle of sowing and reaping? Your level of faith will likely determine *what* and *how much* of your resources you're willing to plant. Obviously, if you have no faith in the principle of growth, you will plant nothing that has any value to you. And conversely, the higher the level of faith you have, the more willing you'll be to plant the things of greater value in your life.

I have discovered nine spiritual truths that relate to this principle of sowing and reaping. These nine truths will affect every day of your life, whether you are intentionally acting according to them or not. Therefore, it is important to fully understand their powerful effects and consequences in the same way that you have learned to adjust your life to gravity, allowing it to help you and not harm you.

## TRUTH #1: YOU REAP WHAT YOU SOW

How do we understand the spiritual truths of sowing and reaping? One way that spiritual truths are revealed is through nature. Paul tells us:

*For since the creation of the world His invisible attributes are clearly seen, being understood by the things that are made, even His eternal power and Godhead, so that they are without excuse... (Romans 1:20 NKJV).*

We see the principle of sowing and reaping played out in nature. This first truth on sowing and reaping, along with the second and third, are found in Galatians 6, where Paul writes:

*Do not be deceived, God is not mocked; for whatever a man sows, **that he will also reap** (Galatians 6:7 NKJV).*

Simply put, in nature, when you plant an apple seed, you get an apple tree, and when you plant an orange seed, you get an orange tree. When you sow something, you reap more of the same.

## Sowing Not Just Seeds

This concept applies to all areas of life. You can sow and reap the harvest of many things, even *time*. Yes, time. I learned this after I'd begun planting my time—a tithe, so to speak—by doing work for the church. Sowing our time can allow us to reap what Christian author Mario Murillo calls "God speed."[1] This kind of harvest was demonstrated to me the day I read the chapter on "God speed" in his book *I Am the Christian the Devil Warned You About.*

That day, when I left the thirty-eight-story building in which I lived, I was pressed for time en route to church to help my pastor. Getting an elevator in my building usually took a long time; however, that day as I came down the nineteenth-floor hallway, before I could even press the button, the elevator door opened. I went straight in and it went down. Then when I got to the street, there was only one cab in sight—but it had a customer in it. That cab pulled right up, the passenger jumped out, I got in, and the cab sped off.

As I got in, the cab driver radioed the dispatcher that he was not going to the Ala Moana Mall *anymore*. The previous customer he had—*without explanation*—aborted the trip midway through. He was now headed to the Word of Life Christian Center. It was as if God had ripped that other customer right out of the cab so that I could get to church quickly. When I got back to my building that afternoon, the elevators continued to open on my floor as I approached them, allowing me to do more in less time. I found out later that the building managers had reprogrammed the elevators to go to the nineteenth floor (midpoint of the building) and wait there when not in use.

The elevator's timing was not a miracle intervention by God like the parting of the Red Sea, but it made an impression on me. Every day since then, I have been vividly reminded of the chapter that I had read about God speed. I think the reprogramming was a God-inspired occurrence that helped make the elevators more efficient, illustrating to me that even *time* can be increased when we learn to trust God with it.

Several times it is recorded in the New Testament that Jesus and His disciples experienced supernatural transportation, freak weather occurrences, or other supernatural interventions by God to get from one place to another.

✠ *And [the eunuch] gave orders to stop the chariot. Then both Philip and the eunuch went down to the water and Philip baptized him. When they came up out of the water, **the Spirit of the Lord suddenly took Philip away**, and the eunuch did not see him again, but went on his way rejoicing. Philip, however, appeared at Azotus and traveled about, preaching the gospel in all the towns until he reached Caesarea (Acts 8:38-40).*

✠ *After Paul had seen the vision, we got ready at once to leave for Macedonia, concluding that God had called us to preach the gospel to them. From Troas we put out to sea and sailed straight for Samothrace and the **next** day on to Neopolis (Acts 16:10-12).*

(This 125-mile trip, under natural circumstances, would take two days; however, with freak winds known to the region, God allowed them to make it in one day.)

✠ *All the people in the synagogue were furious when they heard this [what Jesus said]. They got up, drove Him out of the town, and took Him to the brow of the hill on which the town was built, in order to throw Him down the cliff. But He walked right through the crowd and went on His way [to Capernaum to give His time to teaching] (Luke 4:28-30).*

As we continue, I will reveal other areas you can sow that will reap a harvest, and, if you are in God's will, a harvest of life-long blessings.

## How Much Increase?

You probably are wondering if there's a relationship between the amount of sowing and the increase a person experiences. According to the Bible, the answer to this is yes. Read what the apostle Paul writes to the Corinthian Christians:

✝ *...He who sows sparingly will also reap sparingly, and he who sows bountifully will also reap bountifully* (2 Corinthians 9:6 NKJV).

And, of course, what can ultimately happen if we don't sow at all? Proverbs tells us the answer:

✝ *A sluggard does not plow in season; so at harvest time he looks but finds nothing* (Proverbs 20:4).

Does this mean that if you sow a seed you will be guaranteed a harvest? If we look deeper at the analogy in nature, we find that the answer is no. Crops sometimes fail! But, lest we're mistaken, crop failure can be good when we have planted the wrong seed. I have prayed for crop failure at times, for divine mercy. This is why we always need to keep in mind *who* is in charge of the harvest:

✝ *I planted, Apollos watered, but God **gave** the **increase*** (1 Corinthians 3:6 NKJV).

Though Apollos and Paul had a role to play in the sowing, God was still in charge of the results. How hard we work doesn't immediately translate proportionately into the harvest. But that shouldn't dissuade us from planting and doing so bountifully; for when God chooses to provide increase (as you see from the previous verse), He will do so according to our sowing.

## TRUTH #2: SOW SPIRITUALLY TO REAP AN ETERNAL HARVEST

The next verse in Galatians clarifies this second truth, which is that sowing and reaping do not just apply to the physical realm, but also to the spiritual realm:

✦ *For he who sows to his flesh will of the flesh reap corruption* [all flesh is corrupted so that which grows from it is also corrupt], *but he who sows to the Spirit will of the Spirit reap everlasting life* (Galatians 6:8 NKJV).

If you only sow to the flesh—earthly desires, for example—then you will only reap of the flesh, things that are not godly. However, if you follow the leading of the Spirit with your sowing, then you will reap a harvest of everlasting value.

When we take Galatians 6:7-8 together, we see it is possible to sow a single seed that has potential to yield two harvests. For instance, we can sow financially into a ministry and receive both a financial harvest in the physical realm and a spiritual harvest. The spiritual harvest is greater intimacy with God. Flowing out of this harvest is insight, understanding, and knowledge, as well as other blessings for us, our family, and those for whom we pray. When you consider what seed to plant and what seed to consume, it is important to remember that seeds planted can yield two harvests: one harvest will be enjoyed in this life, while the other will last for all eternity!

## Truth #3: Seed + Time = Harvest

In the next verse in the Galatians passage, God highlights the third truth:

✝ *And let us not grow weary while doing good, for in due season we shall reap if we do not lose heart* (Galatians 6:9 NKJV).

When the apostle Paul writes "doing good," he's talking about the sowing process—the planting of *spiritual* seed. "In due season" refers to God's timing, not ours. "We shall reap" refers to the harvest or increase that will come as a result. This is not just a material harvest; it also includes a harvest of spiritual fruit, like love, joy, and peace (see Galatians 5:22-23); spiritual gifts, like prophecy and healing; and gifts of salvation for the people you know.

Yes, God can also return your physical sowing with a spiritual harvest:

✝ *Now He who supplies seed to the sower and bread for food will also supply and increase your store of seed and will enlarge the harvest of your righteousness* [right standing or relationship with God] (2 Corinthians 9:10).

✝ *Do not store up for yourselves treasures on earth, where moth and rust destroy, and where thieves break in and steal. But store up for yourselves treasures in heaven, where moth and rust do not destroy, and where thieves do not break in and steal. For where your treasure is, there your heart will be also* (Matthew 6:19-21).

Galatians 6:9 concludes with the phrase, *"if we do not lose heart,"* which leads us to a critical part of the third truth that we must understand about the principle of sowing and reaping to be successful at living life in God. It's important to not miss the implications of the phrases *"in due season"* and *"if we do not lose heart."* They are God's way of reminding us to hang in there, to use our faith. God makes it clear that our role is keeping our faith steadfast, trusting in what we hope for (His promises), not necessarily in what we see. This is God's way of doing things—*if we don't lose heart.*

Let's consider some of the ramifications of the truth of Seed + Time = Harvest. When you plant an apple seed, you are *not* going to grow an orange tree. Nor will you have apples to eat the next day, because it *takes time* for the tree to bear fruit. Time allows God to work in and through us, growing our faith. This is why James reminds us:

✛ *Meanwhile, friends, wait patiently for the Master's Arrival. You see farmers do this all the time, waiting for their valuable crops to mature, patiently letting the rain do its slow but sure work. Be patient like that. Stay steady and strong. The Master could arrive at any time* (James 5:7-8 MSG).

When the Lord comes, He will bring an increase because His essence is increase. God is the God of increase and multiplication. He has set this spiritual truth of Seed + Time = Harvest to work in everything. For example, if you plant seeds of kindness, then in time you will receive a harvest in kindness. If you plant smiles, then you'll receive more smiles. The truth also applies to bad seeds:

✛ *As I have observed, those who plow evil and those who sow trouble reap it* (Job 4:8).

In the case of the bad seeds we plant, the delayed time gives us the opportunity for redemption and hopefully mercy—a crop failure.

## It Requires Work

When these first three truths were initially revealed to me after I was saved, I felt like I was hearing *bad news*. Honestly, most of the seeds I had sown weren't good. On the other hand, learning these truths gave me a blueprint for how to turn things around. They helped me see what I had to do to work my way out of the hole I had dug for myself. Don't be afraid of the word *work*, for it is with toil that we will reap our harvest. Because of the fall, much effort and toil are required in sowing and reaping (even in the spiritual realm). This is why God told the man after the fall:

☥ *Cursed is the ground because of you; through painful toil you will eat of it all the days of your life. It will produce thorns and thistles for you. ...By the sweat of our brow you will eat your food... (Genesis 3:17-19).*

You will learn through your trials that even the act of sowing and reaping is a simple and powerful way to please God. It will draw you toward intimate relationship with Him because it requires you to use your faith; plus, the great effort that it requires will lead you to seek His rest.

Work is truly important to our faith. While the gift of salvation is free—we can't earn it—God does ask us to work on our spiritual lives. The apostle Paul said that we must each *work* out our own salvation (see Philippians 2:12). As you can see, a key focus for our walk of faith is the principle of sowing and reaping.

## TRUTH #4: GOD DETERMINES THE INCREASE

God has reserved the right to determine the increase that we receive so that He can dispense it for our good. He will not release it at a time that would be bad for us, causing us to stumble. Only He knows the *best* time for release.

Despite the way that I've written out Truth #3, Seed + Time = Harvest, it is not a mathematical formula. It does not say that if we plant $x$ dollars then we will reap $y$ dollars in return. We only need to look at nature to see evidence of this. We can't know all the reasons for the size or the timing of a harvest. But remember, God is working in all things to accomplish His goals, which are often beyond our understanding. What God wants us to remember is this:

✠ *And we know that all things work together for good to those who love God, to those who are the called according to His purpose* (Romans 8:28 NKJV).

What does all this mean? It means we are to have faith! We are to have faith that God is working all things together for our good. How do we have this faith? Remember that faith is an action. Our first action is to plant the seed. Sometimes we live our faith out through being joyful in difficult circumstances (like when a crop fails or when the wait for a promised harvest seems interminably long). And then we plant again. And again. Most of all, faith in action does not lose heart; it always remains steadfast and brave.

Look at the farmer. He has complete trust and confidence in Seed + Time = Harvest. When he experiences a crop failure, he doesn't stop planting. He starts all over again. He trusts that eventually a harvest will come, and he refuses to give up. While he may have to endure tough times, it is his ability to "not lose heart" that keeps the hope of a harvest alive. It's that steadfast hope and faith in the harvest that allows him to toil in the face of seeming setbacks. Remember, faith means *persistence*. And let's not forget that the bigger the setback or the longer the wait, the more we must exercise our faith—and this is a God-honoring position, one that will not go unnoticed by the giver of all increase.

### ACTION & VISUALIZATION

*Plant seeds that you believe God wants you to sow,
and don't lose heart if the harvest doesn't come according
to your expectations. Keep on planting.*

## TRUTH #5: THE SEED IS WITHIN

God puts the seed required for multiplication in each of His creations. This truth is found in this verse:

*Then God said, "Let the earth bring forth grass, the herb that yields seed, and the fruit tree that yields fruit according to its kind, **whose seed is in itself**..." (Genesis 1:11 NKJV).*

*"Whose seed is in itself."* What does that mean? God is saying that fruit has within itself the ability to multiply. Study an apple or an orange and you will see this truth in vivid display. Here's what it means to us spiritually: When God gives the gift of increase, He is simultaneously giving the gift of seed. Our increase is always for the purpose of more sowing according to His plan. This concept applies to many things, including all things that grow (including you and me)— money, actions, and much more. Just like a farmer, we must maintain a *cycle* of sowing and reaping as God gives us increase.

## TRUTH #6: BOTH SUSTENANCE AND SEED

As I wrote earlier, God gives the seeds, and when we plant them, He is the one who is responsible for the *increase*. We are only responsible for the *sowing*. But let's take it a step further. Look at this verse in Isaiah:

✿ *For as the rain comes down...and make*[s] *it* [the seed] *bring forth and bud, that it may give seed to the **sower** and **bread to the eater**...* (Isaiah 55:10 NKJV).

As I understand it, this verse means that God gives us the seeds, and we divvy them up. Which seeds should be planted? Which of those seeds should be used for sustenance? The decision is ours and it's a critical one for our future.

Look at an ear of corn. It is both food and seed. Farmers know that if they consume all their crops and leave nothing for planting, then they will not have any income the following year. Money can also be both food and seed. You can consume it or you can plant it. It is up to you to determine what portion will be *seed* and what will be your *food*. Sometimes we withhold "planting seed" out of fear that our God-given resources will dry up, meaning we store it up or horde it out of fear that God will not continue to give future increase. But planting wisely now is important to both our immediate and our distant future.

## ACTION & VISUALIZATION

*Wisely consider the dispensing of your harvest.*
*What will you use for seed, and what will you use for food?*

## TRUTH #7: LIVE BY FAITH

As discussed at the beginning of this chapter, growth, increase, and multiplication are all part of God's nature, and we position ourselves to receive them when we live by faith. But how do we do this practically?

Since God gives the seed, we do not determine how much we start with. Some begin with abundance while others begin with much less. The woman described in Luke 21:2 had only two small coins to give in an offering, but when she gave those coins Jesus praised her over all the others who gave much more. Jesus said that by giving the two coins, which was all that she had, this woman did more than all the rest.

The message of this is clear: It wasn't the dollar amount of her gift, but what it represented at the heart and faith level. It was all she had! This was a powerful action of faith, and it pleased God so much that He recognized her for all of eternity in Scripture. Remember, God looks at the heart, not at the outward appearance, as the world does.

> But the Lord said to Samuel, "Do not consider his appearance or his height, for I have rejected him. The Lord does not look at the things man looks at. Man looks at the outward appearance, but the Lord looks at the heart" (1 Samuel 16:7).

Likewise, it isn't the appearance or size of the gift you give that impresses Him; it's the intentions (motives) of the giver's heart that finds favor with Him. Neither is it about the amount of money that you have; instead, it's about what you do with the money that He gives you.

This is also illustrated in Matthew 25 through the parable of the talents. In this story, three men are given varying amounts of money (*talents* in the Bible passage). One is given five talents, one is given two, and the third is given one. What was most important in this story was not the number of talents each man was given, but how he invested what was given to him (see Matthew 25:14-30). We all have something to give, something with which to improve the body of Christ, whether it is our money, time, or talents. This is one of our callings as Christians, and God desires that we use these gifts (money, time, resources, abilities, information, emotions, etc.) in ways that build up the body of Christ and, in that process, ourselves. This is done in faith by planting or using what we have been given.

## Faith vs. Flesh

Unfortunately, living by faith is not all that easy. When we seek to embrace God's spiritual realm, we must fight against our flesh and our temporal desires. Our fleshly desires—our sinful nature—usually point us toward comfort and pleasing ourselves. This is in sharp contrast to what God desires: He wants us to follow Him and please Him with all our actions. Our flesh and spirit are at war with each other, which is why Paul wrote:

*For the flesh lusts against the Spirit, and the Spirit against the flesh; and these are contrary to one another, so that you do not do the things that you wish* (Galatians 5:17 NKJV).

We need to be aware of this so that we can make every effort to win the battle over the flesh because:

*...flesh and blood cannot inherit the kingdom of God* [in our daily lives]... (1 Corinthians 15:50 NKJV).

It is not only our fleshly desires that challenge our faith, but also our fleshly minds. The Bible says a mind without the Spirit of God cannot understand spiritual things:

*But the natural man does not receive the things of the Spirit of God, for they are foolishness to him; nor can he know them, because they are spiritually discerned* (1 Corinthians 2:14 NKJV).

Thus, in order to live a life of faith, we must overcome our desires that are not in line with God's. The famous philosopher Aristotle said, "I count him braver who overcomes his desires than him who overcomes his enemies;"[2] for the hardest victory is over self. Only when we allow ourselves to be led by the Spirit are we able to act in faith and please God, thus placing ourselves in a better position to receive whatever increase He has planned for us. For example, take note of this:

✝ *...for God loves a cheerful giver* (2 Corinthians 9:7).

It is not only important to be an obedient planter and giver, but it is also important to be a *willing* and cheerful one. And the ability to be a *cheerful* giver comes only through subduing the flesh and living in faith.

Note also in the verse that follows that God has two requirements of us to allow us to eat the best of the land:

✝ **If** you are **willing** and **obedient**, you will eat the best from the land (Isaiah 1:19).

It's not just your obedience that God desires, but also your willingness. This again is an act of faith, a decision to go one step beyond obedience (which you could perform grudgingly) to willingness (which is a position of trusting in God's goodness). You will then have all that God purposed for you, which is an abundant life.

## TRUTH #8: YOU MUST DIE TO SELF

Proper planting requires that you let go of what you plant in order to let God use both you and your seed for His purposes. This truth was most clearly revealed to me in this verse:

✝ *Foolish one, what you sow is **not** made alive unless it **dies*** (1 Corinthians 15:36 NKJV).

The apple seed must cease to exist as a seed before it can become an apple tree. In other words, you must die to yourself if you are to bear fruit. God's will must come before your own—leaving fleshly desires behind. Think about this in relation to other areas of your life. Perhaps your hold on your money or finances needs to die before you can receive the increase that God desires for you. When you give, are you giving so that you can have some additional control over a person or entity? When you give, is it to be known and to receive praises? Or are you giving simply and quietly, without fanfare, solely to follow God's will in your life and to exude His love?

## ACTION & VISUALIZATION

*Give for God's purposes, not your own.*

## TRUTH #9: THE TIMELINE IS SHORTENING

The spiritual growth timeline, from seedtime to harvest, is becoming shorter and shorter as we approach the return of Jesus. This truth should inspire us to sow generously and often. The Bible says that in the last days, cycles will grow shorter and shorter. For example, Amos prophesied:

✠ *"Behold, the days are coming," says the Lord, "When the plowman shall overtake the reaper, and the treader of grapes him who sows seed..."* (Amos 9:13 NKJV).

We see another vivid example of this in the rate at which human knowledge has increased over time. According to a study by French economist George Anderlo, if all scientific knowledge accumulated prior to AD 1 equaled one unit of information, then it took 1,500 years to double the first time to two units of information. The next doubling of information, from two to four units, took only 250 years or up until 1750. By 1900, only 150 years later, it had doubled yet again up to eight units. The speed of doubling continues to get faster and faster. Sixteen units of information was reached in 1950 with the passage of only fifty years, and this doubled again in just ten years to a total of thirty-two units. Another seven years to sixty-four units, and then in just six years to 128 units of information. This was in 1973, the year of Anderlo's study. The doubling speed of information has continued to accelerate and is now estimated to occur about every eighteen months. With the coming of the Internet, information in certain specialized areas may double every year.[3] Think about it: between the first day of college classes and graduation day, the knowledge in our world will have doubled *four* times. Indeed, since I wrote the first edition of this book, humankind's collective knowledge is now doubling in less than every twelve months. According to IBM, the buildout of the "internet of things" will lead to the doubling of knowledge every twelve hours.[4]

Ninety percent of all scientists who have ever lived are alive today and, as you read this, they are busily involved in the search for facts.[5] Science is a body of knowledge that has been estimated to be the equivalent of some ten million books on science and applications. More important, this body of knowledge is increasing at a rate estimated to be about one million book equivalents a year, or on the order of a hundred books an hour.[6]

This ever-increasing explosion of knowledge is part of the end-time plan for people to be exposed to a greater intellectual understanding to better see God's role in creation. Moreover, science without God in the equation will start coming to an end as scientists realize that the answers to the biggest scientific questions ultimately point to God. This is, of course, already the case on many points. Many of the assumptions that godless science has used to explain the creation without God's involvement defy simple logic and ignore scientific evidence. What I'm suggesting is that it will become harder and harder to maintain this model as knowledge increases because more and more anti-God assumptions will be proven unquestionably wrong.

When prophesying of the time near Jesus' return, Daniel said:

✠ *...Many shall run to and fro, and knowledge shall increase* (Daniel 12:4 NKJV).

The fact that the harvest cycles are getting shorter and shorter, as we grow closer to the end times, also has a planned purpose. Through it, God will provide the required physical resources and the acceleration of spiritual manifestations necessary for the church to be able to reap a great end-time harvest. This truth should spur us on to act boldly on our faith. The good news is that our planted seeds will show a quicker return as we approach Christ's return.

In a spiritual and physical sense, this makes Robert Louis Stevenson's quote more meaningful to me: "Don't judge each day by the harvest you reap, but by the seeds you plant."[7]

## God's Imperishable Seed in You

When you were born again, God planted in you a seed that could not perish. Peter writes:

✠ *For you have been born again, not of perishable seed, but of imperishable...* (1 Peter 1:23).

Even when it feels like you have been buried alive by satan, you should continue to believe that the very same dirt covering you has nutrients in it for you to grow, prosper, and bloom into your destiny.

## In Conclusion

Finally, consider this: the principle of seed, time, and harvest is not something that God prepared just for you and for me. Jesus said this about His death:

✠ *I tell you the truth, unless a kernel of wheat falls to the ground and dies, it remains only a single seed. But if it dies, it produces many seeds* (John 12:24).

God sowed *His* most precious possession, His only begotten Son, so that He could reap a harvest of sons and daughters. That's you and me. And that is something in which we can rejoice.

## MEDITATION POINT

The light of God exudes with power, giving us the means for growth and multiplication. We are to be conduits of His light, providing growth and multiplication to others just as the rest of the world does for us.

Go to Chapter 1 in the Study Guide section on page 931.

## ENDNOTES

1.  Mario Murillo, *I Am the Christian the Devil Warned You About* (Danville, CA: Fresh Fire Communications, 1996), 81–93.

2.  Aristotle, Quotation #29862 from Classic Quotes (www .quotationspage.com).

3.  Daniel H. Johnston, *Lessons for Living: Simple Solutions for Life's Problems* (Macon, GA: Dagali Press, 2001), 72.

4.  D. David Russell Schelling, "Knowledge Doubling Every 12 Months, Soon to be Every 12 Hours," Industry Tap into News, April 19, 2013, http://www.industrytap.com/knowledge-doubling-every-12-months -soon-to-be-every-12-hours/3950, accessed September 5, 2017.

5.  *Christian Science Monitor*, January 23, 1971.

6.  *Science News*, October 18, 1969.

7.  Robert Louis Stevenson, www.quotesandpoem.com/quotes/ slowquotes/author/Robert-louis-stevensen/25967.

# Chapter 2

# GIFT #8—INCREASE (PART 2)

## HOW DO YOU GET THE GOOD KIND?

Before you begin to read, pray that the Holy Spirit will give you
and all readers of this book understanding and application.

*Do not be deceived, God is not mocked; for whatever a man sows,
that he will also reap. For he who sows to his flesh will of the flesh
reap corruption, but he who sows to the Spirit will of the Spirit reap
everlasting life. And let us not grow weary while doing good, for in due
season we shall reap if we do not lose heart* (Galatians 6:7-9 NKJV).

I once heard a story of a young Christian man who was about to graduate
from college. For months, he had admired a beautiful sports car in a
dealer's showroom. Knowing that his father could afford it, he told him
that the car was all he wanted for a graduation gift. As the day approached,
the young man awaited signs that his father had purchased the car. Finally,
on the morning of his graduation, his father called him into his private
study. His father told him how proud he was to have such a fine son, and he
told him how much he loved him. He handed his son a beautifully wrapped
gift box. Curious, but somewhat disappointed, the young man opened the
box and found a lovely leather-wrapped Bible. Angrily, he raised his voice

at his father and said, "With all your money you gave me a Bible?" and stormed out of the house, leaving the "instruction book" behind.

Many years passed, and his life went as many "Christian" lives go—up and down, good and bad, like the ocean tides. He got married, had two kids, and started a business. The business had its ups and downs and never gave him the freedom he sought in life. The effort he put into the business detracted from his family relationships, and, as a result, he got a divorce (like 35 percent of professing Christians). His son wound up in jail because of a drug habit, and his daughter never really forgave him for the divorce because, in her mind, he'd abandoned the family.

Sitting alone at home one day, he got a phone call letting him know that his father had passed away and that he would need to come home to settle his father's estate. When he arrived, sadness and regret filled his heart. He began to search through his father's important papers and saw the still-new Bible, just as he had left it twenty-five years earlier. With tears, he opened the Bible and began to turn the pages. As he read, a car key dropped from an envelope taped behind the Bible. It had a tag with a dealer's name, the same dealer who had the sports car he'd desired. On the tag was the date of his college graduation and the words, "Paid in full."

Are you expecting God to bring increase, blessings, and gifts the way *you* desire? How often do we presume to know the way almighty God, the God who made the heavens and the earth, should work? Honestly, as Christians, most of us know that Jesus is the way, the truth, and the life (see John 14:6), but when it comes to the way we live our lives, we still live by "my way or the highway." What if our increase is embedded in a person, a mission, a teaching, or an encounter that we have yet to experience, that God has yet to give us, or that *we have yet to embrace*?

I found my increase amid God profoundly exercising my faith. Working *through* this process brought it about in a dramatic way. Remember that, just like the man in this story, your increase can only be *found* when, with faith in Him, you receive, unwrap, and then use this life-changing gift offered to you.

## RECEIVING THE GIFT

Early in my Christian walk, I learned the significance of the opening verse of this chapter (Galatians 6:7-9); however, at the time I didn't realize that it would become the cornerstone of my testimony and would profoundly affect my faith. God punctuated this verse in my life in a special way, since only He could know that I would eventually write this book.

In the summer of 1988, I was living well financially, and I was just beginning to develop my personal relationship with Jesus Christ. However, I started getting into financial trouble. I lost my company, my money, my house, and my car—it was a horribly painful series of events that seemed to snowball, leaving little behind. *Where was the God to whom I had just given my life? What was He doing with my life?* I couldn't help but wonder at times, *God, I've given You my life, now why are You trying to take it away—to destroy it?* Every time I thought it couldn't get any worse, it did.

At the time, I felt like my life was a bad Christian witness. I dreaded people asking me to give my testimony. My story seemed so depressing, one people would want to avoid, so I wondered who could possibly be inspired or want to come to know Jesus after hearing it. On the other hand, despite my difficult financial experiences, my life, my relationships, and my outlook had changed for the better, and for the first time in my life everything made sense in light of God's Word.

Yet, despite this profound clarity, I had lost nearly every one of my possessions. At one point, I thought it might be a virtue to be poor. This was taught in the church I attended as a young child; however, I couldn't find any support for it in the Bible. What was happening in my life? Why did it seem like everything was falling apart?

From the time I received Jesus, my wife and I had started praying diligently for faith. As we did, things seemed to get worse. How was that possible? As you recall, faith comes by trusting God, by acting despite what you see (see Hebrews 11:1). The key here is the word *acting*. This is how we exercise our faith and how we grow, by *acting* on our hope *despite* what we *see* or *experience*. So how does this work? Well, for my wife and me to have the opportunity to grow our faith, we had to initially see that for which we had *not* hoped, like losing all our possessions. In our case, this exercise program wasn't a light jog—it was more of a boot camp.

We were supposed to *praise* God because He *had* answered our prayers! God had instituted a faith-building exercise program using our finances, which was probably the easiest way for God to get and keep our attention. I was certainly interested in that area of my life. Like most people, I was *too* interested. My flesh was not too thrilled about this faith exercise program, though God wanted me to be joyous about it.

This was the period of life when I discovered the principle of seed, time, and harvest that you just read about in the previous chapter. Initially, this principle seemed like bad news because, as a new Christian, so many of the seeds I had sown were going to bear fruit that I didn't want. However, this principle and its supporting truths ultimately gave me a blueprint. It gave me hope and encouraged me to *work* my way out of the predicament that *I* had gotten *myself* into.

## Unwrapping the Gift

The *first* step we took to begin living out this principle was to start *tithing*. *Tithe* means one-tenth. The first recorded tither was none other than the father of our faith, Abraham, who gave his king and priest the first *tenth* of everything that he received.

[Melchizedek said], *"And blessed be God Most High, who delivered your enemies into your hand." Then Abram **gave him a tenth of everything*** (Genesis 14:20).

Tithing later became part of the Mosaic Law for the Israelites, who were commanded to give the first tenth of their increase to God's priests, the Levites.

> *A tithe of everything from the land, whether grain from the soil or fruit from the trees, belongs to the Lord; it is holy to the Lord* (Leviticus 27:30).

This verse indicates that this tenth *belongs* to the Lord and is holy. This would suggest that under the Mosaic Law, if they didn't pay their tithe, then they would essentially be stealing from God. The only place in the Bible where God challenges us to test Him is in relation to tithing. He issues this challenge through the prophet Malachi:

> *"Bring all the tithes into the storehouse, that there may be food in My house, and **try Me now in this**,"* says the Lord of hosts, *"**If** I will not open for you the windows of heaven and pour out for you such blessing that there will not be room enough to receive it"* (Malachi 3:10 NKJV).

Some Christians try to justify *not* tithing, saying, "These verses came from the Old Testament, which was a different spiritual season governed by the law. And since we're now in a season of grace, tithing no longer applies." We have been *freed* from the law; however, I knew that it was still important to tithe, even in this season of grace. It was an offering of my obedience, faith, and surrender to God's work—to God's Kingdom and not humanity's—even during financial struggle (*especially* in the midst of financial struggle). Consider this important verse in Galatians that introduces the principle of seed, time, and harvest itself:

> *Anyone who receives instruction in the word **must** share all good things with his instructor. Do not be deceived: God cannot be mocked. A man reaps what he sows* (Galatians 6:6-7).

It was in the context of a discussion in the New Testament on giving (which is the main way that we support those who teach, our church pastors and staff) that God showed me the principle of seed, time, and harvest. In this passage, God's use of the word *must* makes it crystal clear that we should support pastors, teachers, and those who preach God's Word, *even in this season of grace*. Indeed, sometimes this will involve *more* than one-tenth of your income. Paul says that, in return, we will receive a reward for giving to God's work.

> ✠ *I planted, Apollos watered, but God gave the increase. So then neither he who plants is anything, nor he who waters, but God who gives the increase. Now he who plants and he who waters are one, and each will receive his own **reward according to his own labor*** (1 Corinthians 3:6-8 NKJV).

Watering a plant is what brings life to it. We see in the same way giving to God is how you bring the fullness of life to yourself that God desires for you. The same concept is presented in Proverbs:

> ✠ *Honor the Lord with your wealth, with the first fruits of **all** your crops; then your barns will be filled to overflowing, and your vats will brim over with new wine* (Proverbs 3:9-10).

We are not really *giving* to God, but we are *returning* to God what is already His. When my kids were young and bought me birthday and Christmas presents, I knew I paid for them, but it was the love and excitement they exhibited in giving them that made me happy. And it is the same with God.

Interestingly, the first word in the Bible in the Hebrew language is *breeshiyt*, or *beginning* (as "in the beginning"). The first letter of that word is *beth*, which means "house." If you remove that letter from the first word, then you have the word *raishiyt*, which means first fruits. Likewise, the Hebrew word for *tithe* is *maaser*. The first letter of that word is also *mem*, which is a sign for the Holy Spirit. If you remove the first letter of *maaser,* then you have the word *aser,* which means wealth. All of this reinforces the fact that our starting point is to bring our first fruits to the storehouse as our tithe, which will in turn bring us wealth.

As you might guess, the biggest problem with tithing is in following through with it. Your faith *will* be tested on this point because of the time it takes for crops to grow and because of occasional crop failure. Mine was tested in a severe way many times. Of course, these tests will exercise your faith and build it up, which is ultimately a good thing.

## ACTION & VISUALIZATION

*Though it may be a challenge for you, start tithing regularly.*

## USING THE GIFT BY TITHING

When I accepted Christ, I was in the process of moving from a salaried position into commercial brokerage, where deal closings became my paydays. In commercial brokerage, you have the opportunity for big paydays, but these can be irregular and are often spread far apart. Initially, my paydays weren't substantial, and they were spread very, very, *very* far apart. On top of that, I had built up a significant overhead from "better living days" that wasn't easy to get rid of. When I did get paid, it always seemed to be less than what I needed to make it to the next closing. Looking at the numbers, I could see that if I didn't give God His tithe, I *might* just make it if I got "lucky."

Due to the length of time it takes for a deal to close, I would typically know my dire financial picture months in advance. Yet, despite what I saw and the fear I felt, I chose to walk by faith and tithe anyway. Remember that faith is an action that pleases God. As a result, God would at times show me His hand operating in some unusual ways. I admit that it was often a hair-raising period of life, as I was barely making enough to stay afloat. But in God's wisdom, He knew that this would cause me to tightly hang on to Him for my financial survival.

I lost all my nonessential possessions in one physically and mentally painful event after another, while I sank deeper and deeper into debt. I was eventually reduced to riding the bus and living in a *two-room* apartment. Not a two-bedroom apartment, but a *two-room* apartment. One room was our living room, the kids' bedroom, kitchen, and dining room, while the other was a bedroom for my wife and me, as well as my office. Because I was in Hawaii, I had to get up at 3:00 AM to make calls to the East Coast.

I would sit on the corner of my bed all day with files spread across it, occasionally staring out the small window in the cinder block walls, thinking, *How will I get out of this hole?* As is the case with many Christians, my freedom to go places and do things was severely restricted because of my lack of financial increase. My life was clearly in a winter season.

Though I was unable to save, in debt, and barely providing for my family, I knew that God was calling me to tithe. Do you think that was challenging to my faith? Yes, *unbelievably* so. Yet we did not lose heart and we continued to tithe and give anyway, believing for a change of season. We were planting good seed; however, what we were experiencing was the truth that "due season" is something God determines, not us. I was still reaping the not-so-good fruit from the seeds I had planted before; the *good* seeds I'd planted were not yet bearing fruit. God uses time to let us put our faith into *action*. My wife and I had to keep heart and *continue* planting seed in faith for the future despite the drought.

Of course, every time things got worse, we prayed for *more* faith. (We didn't initially realize the intense exercise program we were putting into motion.) The apostles did something similar when they asked Jesus for more faith.

✝ *The apostles said to the Lord, "Increase our faith" (Luke 17:5).*

Only a short time later, their friend, teacher, and leader, Jesus, was *crucified*. Suddenly, everything they had dedicated their lives to was *gone*. Their world was *completely* and *forever* changed. Their faith was *severely* tested. Three days later, Jesus delivered on His promise by defeating death and rising from the dead. And, in *time*, He will fulfill His promises to you and me too.

For my family, at our lowest point, we were living in Waikiki in our two-room apartment with no car. Our refrigerator was one of those tiny mini-bar refrigerators with no freezer, so my wife had to endure the adventure of riding the bus to purchase food and ice, and then lug them home, *daily*.

Sometimes we would get a little extra money. My instinct was to buy a used car. However, my wife had a vision of a new green Nissan van. One day when she was walking in Waikiki, she saw one come around the corner, and it seemed to be moving in slow motion, glistening in the sun. She was convinced that it was God speaking to her in that circumstance. We began trusting God for that Nissan van and nothing but the Nissan van. We were so sure of God's direction that we took any extra money—at first $1,000, then $5,000—and gave it to God beyond our tithes. This was "seed money" for the Nissan van. One July, it looked like I was going to close the biggest deal of my career, beyond my wildest expectations: *$800,000* in commissions.

However, it became clear that my co-broker, despite an agreement to the contrary, was going to double-cross me and keep the entire $1.6 million commission for himself. My client was sympathetic and agreed to pay me $100,000 directly. However, the $1.6 million went to the other broker. I was crushed, yet here again, it was another opportunity to *exercise* my heart and my faith.

I owed money to the IRS and other creditors, so after I paid the back taxes and old bills, there wasn't enough to get the Nissan van. In hopes of getting the van, I told the co-broker that instead of taking him to court on the $800,000 he rightfully owed me, I would settle for just $25,000. He refused. You can imagine, given our situation, how *hard* this was to accept.

I was heartbroken—all my hard work seemed wasted. As I struggled for understanding and direction about what to do next, I wanted to kill the co-broker in some slow and torturous way.

It was a difficult decision, one I had to *work* at, but I wound up *not* suing him. I knew the long and costly process of litigation would keep anger burning in my heart. I don't know about you, but I am simply not spiritual enough to avoid letting anger get the best of me. My anger, justified or not, would *not* have been beneficial. Knowing that *my* heart was weak, I needed to protect it.

☦ *Keep your heart with all diligence, for out of it spring the issues of life* (Proverbs 4:23 NKJV).

Furthermore, Jesus had this advice for me:

☦ *And from him who takes away your goods do not ask them back* (Luke 6:30 NKJV).

As much as I didn't want to admit it, I had not spiritually earned the money yet as all things are created in the spirit realm first.

☦ *To this John replied, "A man can receive only what is given him from heaven"* (John 3:27).

I can guarantee you that *nobody*, and I repeat, *nobody*, can take away what God intends for you. And no lawsuit was going to get for me what God hadn't yet intended for me. Only a *generous, forgiving* heart would help me receive what God was preparing.

☦ *Good will come to him who is generous...* (Psalm 112:5).

✠ *Give, and it will be given unto you. A good measure, pressed down, shaken together and running over, will be poured into your lap. For with the measure you use, it will be measured to you* (Luke 6:38).

God is not going to turn around surprised one day and say, "Oops, how did you get that $800,000 in your account?" Nor is He going to say, "Oops, what happened to that $800,000 I meant for you? Did someone cheat you out of it?" It was clear that I needed to wait on Him.

## USING THE GIFT BY GIVING

About a month after the deal closed, my wife, still without a car, was taking her Bible out of the nightstand to pray when a letter fell onto the floor. She had placed the envelope there a few days earlier without looking at it. Though it was clearly junk mail, God impressed on her that it was important that she open it. Inside was an offer to get a car financed with bad credit, which was a new concept at the time. I was leaving for Mexico the next morning, but because she felt so strongly about it, I made the call.

I quickly confirmed an arrangement to buy a new Dodge minivan—bad credit and all. Then it struck me—my wife's vision was for a green Nissan van, *not* a Dodge. I called the Nissan dealership and asked if they had a similar bad credit loan program, and sure enough, they did. I went in and met with the representative from the lending company, who *happened* to be there that day. After everything was arranged, a man explained to me the surprising nature of this car deal: "This is our first day of the bad credit loan program, and you're our first customer." Had I called even one day earlier when we received the letter from Dodge, the Nissan dealer would have said no because this lending program didn't exist! *And* because the lender was there setting up the program that first day, I got an even *better deal.* I happily drove the glistening green Nissan van home that day, knowing that God was fulfilling His promise:

✠ *To guide our feet into the way of peace* [contentment] (Luke 1:79 NKJV).

About six months after I bought the car, I received the largest commission I had ever received—$200,000. I had $100,000 left after paying current taxes, back taxes, and old debts. We had been praying for and trusting God for a home so that we could get out of the two-room apartment, but the remaining $100,000 was not enough for a house in Hawaii, especially given my credit problems. Additionally, we weren't hoping for just any house, we had high expectations!

✠ *He who sows sparingly will also reap sparingly, and he who sows bountifully will also reap bountifully* (2 Corinthians 9:6 NKJV).

✠ *Now may He who supplies seed to the sower...**multiply** the seed you have **sown**...* (2 Corinthians 9:10 NKJV).

We knew that if we wanted to get the kind of home we dreamed of, then finding a way to *multiply* our money was the key. I could only get a 10 to 20 percent return from traditional investments. And even with $100,000, at those return rates, it would take a long time to earn enough money for the home we wanted. But I knew that because God was the God of *multiplication*, He could choose to give us a much greater return (increase) if I invested the money with Him.

Did my flesh think this was a good idea? No! It *hated* the idea. I am sure a professional advisor would have also found fault with this investment concept as well. My natural mind thought it would be foolish to give away the most money that I'd ever had in our bank account. However, despite my natural mind's fears, I decided to walk in the Spirit and in faith.

Out of that original $200,000 commission, this is what I did: I gave $20,000 tithe; I paid off my debts and taxes with $100,000; I gave $50,000 as a gift to my church for their building program; I gave a gift of $25,000 to my former pastor so that he could put a down payment on a house in Denver; and I gave $5,000 to another church. I sowed everything I could, leaving nearly nothing in the bank account. With a warrior's spirit, I followed the lead of the widow with the two coins and gave *all that I had* to God. My spirit soared with expectations.

My flesh and mind didn't stop working. In fact, pride began to seep in when I calculated that the contribution I had made to my church made up a noticeable amount of the entire building fund. Well, you guessed it: I still had more spiritual shaping-up to do in the gym. A year went by and nothing happened—there was *still no harvest*.

## God Surprises Us

Though discouraged at times, I remained confident in the seeds I had planted. A little more than a year later, while I was seeking a retail location for a ministry, I ran into an out-of-town commercial broker I knew. I'd met him previously while trying to sell a beautiful townhouse complex to a developer. At the time, I had hoped that I might be able to get one of the units in the complex if I sold the complex to a developer. Now two years later, the broker told me that the townhouses had all sold, except for one—a particularly nice unit—which was still personally owned by the developer. He thought the developer might be interested in selling it.

Out of courtesy and curiosity, I made an appointment to look at it with the broker. Though it was *perfect* and even more wonderful than we expected, I didn't have enough for a down payment, nor could I qualify for a standard loan. I did *not* call him back again after the showing.

The next Sunday at church, I noticed the same broker sitting in the row in front of me. Interesting *coincidence*, don't you think? He turned out to be a fellow Christian who, when in Honolulu, would visit our church. After church, he asked me if I liked the townhouse. I said yes and then explained my problem. He said he thought he could do something to help. Ultimately, he got the owner to hold a large second mortgage, which made getting a low-leverage first mortgage easy, even with my credit problem.

We purchased the townhouse with almost no money down. One month later, the value went up by more than $50,000. God did what I thought was impossible. In that same week, I found out that my former pastor had sold his house (the one he'd purchased a year earlier with my $25,000 gift) for a $70,000 profit. He then bought a bigger house that had room for his entire extended family. That *very same month*, he took advantage of a lower interest rate to pull $30,000 of equity out of his current house (without raising his payments) so that he could divide it between his three children so that they could each get a condo. Amazingly, that *same month* I was also placed in a position to help my current pastor acquire his dream house, giving me the same favor that I had given up a year earlier when I decided to follow God's leading to help my former pastor instead.

## The Surprising Increases

Wait! God wasn't finished yet. About a month later, I sold a $115 million portfolio of hotels, for which I received a $1.6 million commission (enough to pay off my new high-leverage mortgage). This showed me God's sense of humor. He was driving His point home in a dramatic way: He could do the *impossible* with credit *or* cash. Remember the broker who double-crossed me for $800,000? This commission was double that amount!

✠ *If a man delivers to his neighbor money or articles to keep, and it is stolen out of the man's house, if the thief is found, he shall pay* **double** (Exodus 22:7 NKJV).

This verse can apply to anything that the devil steals from you, which is illustrated in the book of Job. After the season of trouble created by satan, God blessed Job by doubling the possessions that satan had taken and destroyed. Yes, you *really can* count it all joy when satan steals your possessions, because God can double what was stolen.

My harvest had begun, and it was beyond what I would have projected because it was clearly God's power at work. After a rapid series of other amazing examples of God's increase, I sold a $233 million resort hotel portfolio in Mexico. A month after that, I closed a $65 million joint venture hotel deal in Denver with the biggest hotel-buying company in the world. The seeds that I had been planting over the years were now bearing fruit in rapid succession.

✝ *He who goes out weeping, carrying seed to sow, will return with songs of joy, carrying sheaves with him* (Psalm 126:6).

Then the biggest hotel-buying company asked if I could scout out European hotel chains that they could buy. What an incredible opportunity. Any intelligent businessperson would make time for a meeting with the world's largest hotel-buying company. All I needed was a hotel owners' directory. I called and asked the presidents of the European hotel companies if they were interested in going to lunch with the director of real estate for the largest hotel-buying company in the world. It was a no-brainer; who wouldn't say yes? God was orchestrating my increase, and it was clear to everyone around me that this was supernatural. God likes to show off in your life when you truly make room for Him to show up.

This fruit-bearing journey was not the result of hard work (though I always worked hard) or education (anyone could read a phone number, and I knew very little about hotels at the time). Instead, God was allowing me to operate well beyond my means, well beyond my high school education, and well beyond my intellect and abilities.

Some of you might be thinking, *I could never have that kind of faith*, or, *I could never give up everything like you did.* Both of those thoughts are wrong. First, I was no spiritual superman. I made many errors—I still committed sins against God after I was saved. For those sins, I also reaped an unfruitful harvest in my life. Second, it may be that God gifted me initially with a large measure of faith, but *anyone* can build his or her faith with exercise. However, as I was soon to discover, keeping that faith strong takes continued exercise and commitment. Don't get lazy and avoid the gym.

## TRUSTING GOD'S PATH

After my first wave of faith, I blinked. Yes, I *blinked*. God had rewarded me financially with substantial increase. I had more money than I needed or could even spend. My flesh—my mind and my body—*liked* having money in the bank. It felt good. It felt safe. But is it God's ultimate goal to make us feel good and safe? Yes, but only if He is our source and sustainer. God wanted me to feel good and safe *in Him*, even when money was going in and out of my bank account like the ocean's tide, because instability is part of a fallen world. He wanted me to trust in *Him*, not in my bank account.

✝ *Command those who are rich in this present world not to be arrogant, nor to put their hope in wealth, which is so uncertain, but to put their hope in God...* (1 Timothy 6:17).

✝ *The wealth of the rich is their fortified city; they **imagine** it an unscalable wall* (Proverbs 18:11).

I knew deep down that I was in for more spiritual training, but my mind made a convincing argument. With so much money in the bank, I could rely on traditional investments with lower returns. Maybe I didn't need to continue my aggressive faith-based investments into spiritual things, into His Kingdom's work. Making this mistaken rationalization, I changed strategies and stopped walking in aggressive faith. This new reliance on what I could see was, of course, not pleasing to God. I shrank back, and my flesh took over.

Admittedly, I had also become somewhat proud. I felt like, at my level of faith, I had "arrived"—I had reached faith's peak. Yet faith never reaches an end and becomes idle—there is no such thing as "coasting" with God. Instead, we should simply reach for new plateaus from which to launch into new and unknown territory. Unfortunately, my financial comfort led to less and less communication with God. I began to put my faith in bank statements rather than in His voice and His Word. It didn't take long for my new investment strategy to have the potential to wipe out much of God's increase in my life. Things went so bad in one investment that I wound up having to take out a $4-million business loan with my investing partners to cover the cash shortfall. The business was going so badly it looked like I would soon be heading back to a two-room apartment. My, how chatty I can get with God during these kinds of circumstances. But I sure became a better listener too. I don't know about you, but hanging over a boiling pit of grease by a thin thread causes me to be more communicative with God.

After I began listening to God, He led me back to my original investment strategy. Sure enough, things started to turn around again in amazing and miraculous ways. I learned that when I was obedient and following the leading of the Spirit, following the path God set before me, amazing God-driven things would come my way:

✠ *In the way of righteousness is life, and in its pathway there is no death* (Proverbs 12:28 NKJV).

✠ [God's] *paths drip with abundance* (Psalm 65:11 NKJV).

This abundance does not necessarily mean material wealth (although it can); rather, it means experiencing all that God has offered you according to your unique destiny, which, of course, makes life full of what is the most fulfilling. I also learned that, for our own good, God does not want us to place our love, trust, or hearts in the gifts that He gives us; instead, He wants us to place our love, trust, and hearts in Him. When we do this, Jesus gives this corrective command:

*Sell your possessions and give to the poor. Provide purses for yourselves that will not wear out, a treasure in heaven that will not be exhausted, where no thief comes near and no moth destroys. For where your treasure is, there your heart will be also* (Luke 12:33-34).

## God's Path Drips with Abundance

In 1998, God took someone off a flight from Honolulu to Chicago the day before my own flight to Chicago. The next day we were on the same red-eye flight, seated next to each other. Because of a casual conversation, I sold him what many consider to be the best city hotel in the world for *$275 million*. He didn't own a hotel at the time, nor was he seeking to buy one. But God's path drips with abundance. And I ran into that *same* man in another "fluke" encounter at a mall in Oakbrook, Illinois. This encounter grew into a business relationship that has resulted in over *$1 billion* in hotel sales, as well as in an asset management assignment, which has provided me regular income for some time.

About four years before meeting this man on the plane, I had met an investment banker on a red-eye flight to Mexico City. In 2005, I decided to introduce my two plane-encounter friends to each other, and this resulted in a mutually beneficial transaction for both of them, as well as the largest loan placement I have ever done to that date: *$425 million*.

Due to another "chance" encounter at the Tokyo Airport, and another set of unusual circumstances, I entered a distribution business in Japan for the man I originally met on the flight to Chicago. While in Japan, this allowed me to assist in lining up a Japanese satellite for the first twenty-four-hour Christian broadcasting network in Asia. I knew I was on destiny's path when I learned that the name of the satellite was JC3. This satellite now beams twenty-four-hour Christian programming into over 7.5 million households in Asia. The network is responsible for many people receiving the gospel and coming to know Jesus Christ. I consider this to be one of the most important things that God has allowed me to do in my life to date.

God's path *drips with abundance* and leads to *destiny*. But it all starts with an *action* of faith. Are you willing to act by faith?

✠ *A gift opens the way for the giver...* (Proverbs 18:16).

Your gifts will open ways and paths designated by God for you too. It's become clear to me in my own life experiences and through God's Word that He is *actively* involved in all aspects and details of my life's journey. The Bible says:

✠ *You enlarged my path under me; so my feet did not slip* (2 Samuel 22:37 NKJV).

✠ *Your word is a lamp to my feet and a light to my path* (Psalm 119:105 NKJV).

By walking in faith, through the actions of our hearts, we are creating the circumstances that we will run into in our future. This is because we are constantly manufacturing things in the spirit realm that will *in due time* manifest in the realm of the physical.

I ran into the broker who cheated me out of an $800,000 commission again several years later. He had become the exclusive listing agent for a chain of hotels. Had I sued him, he would not have spoken to me. Instead, when I brought my client to look at his listings, he was helpful and gave me an edge over other bidders to push things in my favor. As a result, I closed the deal, selling *more* hotels than ever before in one transaction. This is a great reminder for us to guard our hearts, because our actions are setting into play our future circumstances.

✛ *Keep your heart with **all** diligence, for out of it spring the issues of life* (Proverbs 4:23 NKJV).

My wife and I have chosen the path of relentless sowing. We've learned to continue down this path regardless of what we are seeing with our natural eyes. This is the path with the greatest kind of rewards—eternal rewards.

## Action & Visualization

*Walk in faith, and be consistent with the actions of your heart.*

## Seek First God's Kingdom

The Bible says in Matthew 6:33 that if you seek first the Kingdom of God, then all things will be added unto you. Jesus paints this picture of the Kingdom of God:

✛ *He said, "To what shall we liken the kingdom of God? Or with what parable shall we picture it? It is like a mustard seed which, when it is sown on the ground, is smaller than all the seeds on earth; but **when*** *it is sown*, *it grows up and becomes greater than all herbs, and shoots out large branches, so that the birds of the air may nest under its shade*" (Mark 4:30-32 NKJV).

Now that my prior giving is returning a harvest, I can plant new seeds into people and ministries, going well beyond what would be possible from my own efforts. It is a blessing as a Christian to be able to make a positive impact on the world and to give to the body of Christ.

For the past sixteen years, I have been able to provide funds for several ministries in ever-increasing amounts. I can only do this because I planted seeds that God grew into a towering oak tree, which now provides rest and shade for others. I could *not* have created these with my own efforts. There is indeed a *power beyond our own efforts* that can make a difference for the Kingdom—this is the power of faith, which is evidenced in the principle of seed, time, and harvest.

✠ *Wealth and honor come from You; You are the ruler of all things. In Your hands are strength and power to exalt and give strength to all* (1 Chronicles 29:12).

✠ *Therefore do not cast away your confidence, which has great reward* (Hebrews 10:35 NKJV).

## ACTION & VISUALIZATION

*Seek God first by confidently sowing into His Kingdom. Then you will be rewarded with the fullness of His power, releasing freedom in your life.*

## The Importance of Generosity

God wants His body on the earth to be a blessing to the world and to other Christians who are in need. God needs Christians who will be *open conduits* through whom He can pour out His provisions and gifts. We are blessed when increase and gifts come to us, but we create further blessings when we allow them to flow to others *through* us. God blesses those who trust Him to use them for His purposes. It is good and right to become a blessing to others in this way. The Scriptures are full of verses about the importance of generosity:

✠ *Freely you have received, freely give* (Matthew 10:8).

✠ *I want each of you to take plenty of time to think it over, and make up your own mind what you will give. That will protect you against sob stories and arm-twisting. God loves it when the giver delights in the giving* (2 Corinthians 9:7 MSG).

✠ *...remembering the words the Lord Jesus Himself said: "It is more blessed to give than to receive"* (Acts 20:35).

✠ *Mercy to the needy is a loan to God, and God pays back those loans in full* (Proverbs 19:17 MSG).

✠ *One person gives freely, yet gains even more; another withholds unduly, but comes to poverty* (Proverbs 11:24).

✠ *A generous man will prosper; he who refreshes others will himself be refreshed* (Proverbs 11:25).

✠ *A generous man will himself be blessed, for he shares his food with the poor* (Proverbs 22:9).

For me, the harvest keeps coming, and I am able to re-sow the seeds in order to give more back to God. Indeed, some seeds even multiplied themselves. Remember the pastor to whom I gave $25,000 that returned to him $70,000, and then later $30,000 more? The last time I spoke to him, he said that he was able to refinance his house yet *again*. With that money, he built a Bible college in Burma and a home for the director of an orphanage—all for $25,000! Shortly after that, his uncle gave him his house that was worth over $400,000.

Why was all this happening to him? He told me that, when he moved to take the pastoral job where I met him, he had sowed the equity from his house—valued at approximately $25,000. The day that I originally called him to tell him that I was going to give him $25,000 for a house, he and his wife had spent the afternoon looking at houses they couldn't afford. His wife had asked him, "Do you think we will ever be able to afford a house again?" Before he could answer, he received my call and the $25,000 gift. *The seed you sow* can reap a harvest beyond your imagination, and it can continue multiplying itself like a ripple in a pond. It all *begins* when you toss your pebble of faith into the water.

God wants us to focus on giving because it's a fundamental principle in how the Kingdom of God works. Jesus tells a parable in Luke about a successful man who was rich:

✠ *The ground of a certain rich man produced a good crop. He thought to himself, "What shall I do? I have no place to store my crops."*

*Then he said, "This is what I'll do. I will tear down my barns and build bigger ones, and there I will store all my grain and my goods. And I'll say to myself, 'You have plenty of good things laid up for many years. Take life easy; eat, drink and be merry.'"*

> *But God said to him, "You fool! This very night your life will be demanded from you. Then who will get what you have prepared for yourself?"*
>
> *This is how it will be with anyone who stores up things for himself but is not rich toward God* (Luke 12:16-21).

Despite the rich man's apparent worldly success, Jesus called him a fool because he was *not* generous toward God. Being rich, even famously so, is not synonymous with being wise. I am sure you can think of some examples who are in the media today. It's interesting that the rich man's wealth came from crops, a profession in which the increase clearly comes from God. Did you notice that the rich man's favorite word in the parable is *my*? Our money, talents, intellect, abilities, power, and authority all come from God, and we should generously give of them to help His other children. And we should also be giving back to God for the blessings and gifts that He has given to us:

✝ *Each of you **must** bring a gift in proportion to the way the Lord your God has blessed you* (Deuteronomy 16:17).

The apostle Paul wrote this encouragement to the Corinthians who had been supporting God's work through giving to his ministry:

✝ *Now...[God] will also supply and increase your store of seed and will enlarge the harvest of your righteousness. You will be made rich in every way **so that you can be generous** on every occasion...* (2 Corinthians 9:10-11).

## Action & Visualization

*Be a generous giver.*

## YOUR GIFT IS YOUR SWORD

In the Old Testament, there is a story of God calling Gideon to save Israel from the Midianites who were preparing to attack Israel. Gideon, not feeling he was physically qualified for this calling, answered God this way:

✠ *"But Lord," Gideon asked, "How can I save Israel? My clan is the weakest in Manasseh, and I am the least in my family"* (Judges 6:15).

In preparation for this great battle, Gideon prepares an offering of meat and *bread* to give to God (see Judges 6:16-21). God could clearly show that the battle would be won in His power alone, not by the strength of Gideon's army (from the weakest clan). God moved Gideon through several events, paring his army down from thirty thousand to three hundred men (see Judges 7:1-8). Then Gideon, with just his three hundred men, was on the hill above the camp of the Midianites and Amalekites. Once there, God instructed Gideon to go down and ambush the enemy's encampment. Just prior to their attack, God instructed Gideon and his servant to sneak into the enemy's camp so they could listen to what the enemy was saying about him.

✠ *The Midianites, the Amalekites and all the other eastern peoples had settled in the valley, thick as locusts. Their camels could no more be counted than the sand on the seashore.*

*Gideon arrived just as a man was telling a friend his dream. "I had a dream," he was saying. "A round loaf of barley **bread** came tumbling into the Midianite camp. It struck the tent with such force that the tent overturned and collapsed.*

*His friend responded, "This can be nothing other than the **sword** of Gideon son of Joash, the Israelite. God has given the Midianites and the whole camp into his hands"* (Judges 7:12-14).

Gideon's offering of *bread* had become his *sword*, which was powerful enough to defeat this seemingly undefeatable enemy. In 1 Kings 18:16-46, there is a similar story of where the prophet Elijah singularly took on 450 prophets of Baal. Elijah first made a sacrifice to God, and then God delivered Elijah from his enemy in a truly miraculous way. You, too, by wielding the weapon of your offerings and sacrifices, can find victory even when the odds are against you.

## Action & Visualization

*Remember that when your enemy is encamped around you,*
*your offering to God can be your sword. Make sure it is a powerful*
*one that can take down any enemy that may come your way.*

## Not Just Money

I want to point out here that, while I have primarily focused on the ways in which God provided increase to my finances, this is certainly not the only way in which God applies the principle of seed, time, and harvest. I highlight the financial aspect only to show how God used this area to teach me (He knew it would most effectively catch my attention). What is God using to catch your attention? Where do you need to plant seeds? In what area or areas are you seeking increase?

The gift of giving is also my calling and the area where He knew I could serve Him best. But as I expressed in the previous chapter, when we sow good seeds of *any* kind, God will use them and provide a *rich* harvest.

Indeed, sowing grace and mercy has had the most tangible and impactful harvest in my life. Since I am imperfect, the one thing I need the most in my relationships with others is grace. When I judge people for their actions, I am sowing judgment, and I will reap judgment in my own earthly relationships. However, if I sow grace, I will reap that much-needed grace from others. Just like sowing financially, you may have to sow repeatedly in faith, but eventually you will receive a crop of grace and mercy in your life.

✠ *Blessed are the merciful, for they will be shown mercy* (Matthew 5:7).

Another great example of sowing is in missionary work. When Mother Teresa began sowing kindness and care to the unwanted in Calcutta, she was one of only twelve who were called to serve that community. Today, the order she founded has more than four thousand members, each dedicated to giving sacrificially to help those in need. Her seed of faith multiplied into other workers while bringing countless others to faith in Christ.

You will always have seeds of some kind to sow into another's life. When you step out and sow with your faith into others' lives, then you will bring a harvest of faith into your own. You have read my testimony. You now know what I know. You have read God's words. If you act on what you have read and if you sow, this gift of increase will set you free from the restrictions of this world. There is one thing you can count on:

✠ *As long as the earth endures, seedtime and harvest, cold and heat, summer and winter, day and night will never cease* (Genesis 8:22).

# MEDITATION POINT

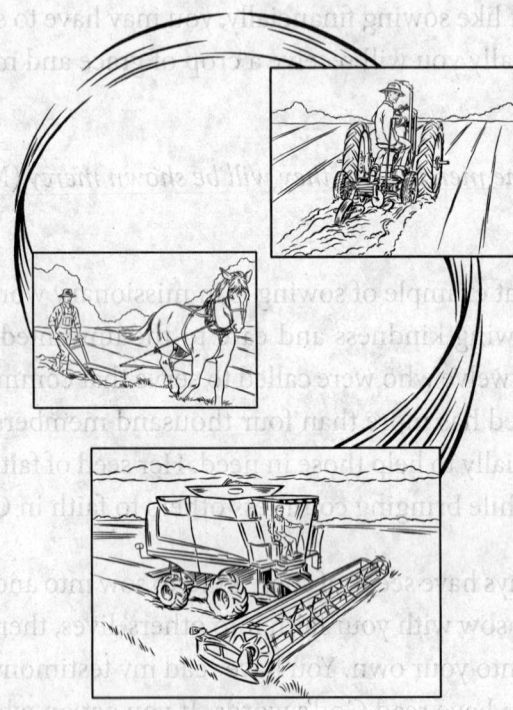

Seed, time, and harvest will never cease.

Go to Chapter 2 in the Study Guide section on page 943.

# Chapter 3

# GIFT #9—GIFTS OF THE SPIRIT (PART 1)

## HOW DO YOUR GIFTS BRING LIFE TO YOUR LIFE?

Before you begin to read, pray that the Holy Spirit will give you and all readers of this book understanding and application.

[God's] *intent was that now, through the church* [you and me], *the manifold wisdom of God should be made known to the rulers and authorities in the heavenly realms* (Ephesians 3:10).

Holding your own newborn child is an amazing experience. Your heart is flooded with love and affection for this precious life. As a new dad or mom, you realize that life is beyond you and that it is bigger than just your own personal needs. You now have another life that is dependent on you, and your attention and focus change dramatically. At first, parenthood is awkward; your sleep, meals, and lifestyle are turned upside down. You begin to see life through new eyes—the eyes of a mother or father—and your vision is permanently altered.

But what about our new life in Christ? What new responsibilities do we have that will shift our vision, desires, goals, and lifestyle? How do we adjust and walk into those changes, into that new life? God has given us the Holy Spirit, who offers each of us certain gifts, for this very reason. This chapter is devoted to explaining the new adventures of a life in Christ and the ways that these gifts of the Spirit will assist in this new life so that you, as well as all those with whom you live out life, experience the abundance God intended.

Look again at the verse at the beginning of this chapter. What an awesome responsibility. We live in this world, and the spirit (heavenly) realm exists all around us. Activities in one realm affect the other, and vice versa. This passage says that God will make known His manifold wisdom *through us* to both realms. In the book of Hebrews, when speaking of the prior patriarchs of the Bible who showed great faith, it says that their acts still live as a witness in the atmosphere (see Hebrews 11:4). Your acts of faith will live on beyond you. The writer of Hebrews goes on to remind us:

*Therefore, since we are **surrounded by such a great cloud of witnesses** [actions of faith by Old Testament patriarchs], let us throw off everything that hinders and the sin that so easily entangles, and let us run with perseverance the race marked out for us (Hebrews 12:1).*

When I first read these verses, I marveled at their implications. You may be asking, "How do I do this? How do I make God known to the spirit realm? How do I create an eternal witness? I have enough trouble just looking after the daily challenges of the earthly realm." And yet, these passages say that life is more than feeding ourselves, caring for our families, or pursuing our careers. We will not all be full-time apostles, pastors, and evangelists, yet even through our earthly jobs we are working for Him, fulfilling His greater plan.

*Whatever you do, work at it with all your heart, as working for the Lord, not for men, since you know that you will receive an inheritance from the Lord as a reward. It is the Lord Christ you are serving (Colossians 3:23-24).*

No matter what we do for a living, we all have simultaneous goals to attain as they relate to the *spiritual realm*. Let's examine how we can partner with the Holy Spirit to accomplish these and our other responsibilities as Christians.

## GOD REVEALS HIMSELF

Before beginning our discussion of the gifts of the Spirit, I want to emphasize one of their key purposes. Through the gifts God gives, God reveals Himself in you to the world in which you live. And this is one of our key responsibilities as Christians. As we read about the many ways that God reveals Himself, we need to remember that He has chosen us to be a part of His revelation. This is why Paul writes:

✝ *We are therefore Christ's ambassadors, as though God were making His appeal through us* (2 Corinthians 5:20).

As you manifest the gifts of the Spirit through your life, you reveal His power and presence on earth. You will find in the church that Christians and pastors can sometimes overly rely on words to try and persuade people of God's existence and love for them. The apostle Paul said this about his preaching to others:

✝ *My message and my preaching were **not** with wise and persuasive **words**, but with a demonstration of the **Spirit's power**, so that your faith might not rest on men's wisdom, but on God's power* (1 Corinthians 2:4-5).

Having a close, intimate relationship with God like the apostle Paul had will strengthen God's Spirit within you—His Spirit working through you in *power* and *love* is far more persuasive and powerful than any human words or sermons you can minister to others. Since the beginning of the world, God has revealed His divine truth to His creation in many ways. He reveals His truth through nature:

✠ *The heavens declare the glory of God; the skies proclaim the work of His hands* (Psalm 19:1).

✠ *For since the creation of the world God's invisible qualities—His eternal power and divine nature—have been clearly seen, being understood from what has been made, so that men are without excuse* (Romans 1:20).

God also reveals His truth through the conscience of each person:

✠ *They show that the requirements of the law are written on their hearts, their consciences also bearing witness, and their thoughts now accusing, now even defending them* (Romans 2:15).

He wrote the truth on stone tablets:

✠ *The Lord said to Moses, "Come up to Me on the mountain and stay here, and I will give you tablets of stone, with the law and commands I have written for their instruction"* (Exodus 24:12).

God spoke the truth through Jesus Christ, who is the living Word:

✠ *The Word became flesh and made His dwelling among us. We have seen His glory, the glory of the one and only, who came from the Father, full of grace and truth* (John 1:14).

He revealed the truth in all of Scripture. Paul wrote:

✠ *For everything that was written in the past was written to teach us, so that through endurance and the encouragement of the Scriptures we might have hope* (Romans 15:4).

God writes His truth on people's new hearts through the Holy Spirit:

✠ *This is the covenant I will make with the house of Israel after that time, declares the Lord. I will put my laws in their minds and write them on their hearts...* (Hebrews 8:10).

✠ *I will give you a new heart and put a new spirit in you; I will remove from you your heart of stone and give you a heart of flesh. And I will put my Spirit in you and move you to follow my decrees and be careful to keep my laws* (Ezekiel 36:26-27).

And finally, God writes His truth through your very life and testimony:

✠ *You yourselves are our letter, written on our hearts, known and read by everybody. You show that you are a letter from Christ, the result of our ministry, written not with ink but with the Spirit of the living God, not on tablets of stone but on tablets of the human hearts* (2 Corinthians 3:2-3).

✠ *[God's] intent was that now, through the church [you and me], the manifold wisdom of God should be made known to the rulers and authorities in the heavenly realms* (Ephesians 3:10).

What a privilege this is! God wants to reveal Himself through you! Are you wondering how you can express God's wisdom and truth in your life, how you can show His power, or how you can create your personal testimony? God offers us the many gifts of the Spirit to assist us.

## The Gifts Have a Purpose

God has woven the church together by His Spirit into one body. As parts of that body, we are the only physical representation of God on the earth. Each member of the body is designed to serve a unique function that will ultimately benefit the whole. To achieve His plan, God offers different gifts in varying amounts to each member of the church body—to you and to me.

Each of us is given specific gifts, some in greater measure, some that grow over time, and one that may be primary and dominant. In the course of your life, you will have opportunities to use your gifts for the glory of God and the good of others. In fact, this is critical. If you don't use and exercise your gifts, then the entire body can't function properly, and you won't fulfill your purpose. As with the other gifts, we must receive, unwrap, and use them if we want them to benefit us and others.

## Proper Gift-Wrapping

In this chapter, I want to remind you of the proper context (wrapping) for the gifts of the Spirit. The gifts of the Spirit ignite when they are wrapped in the fruit of the Spirit. This is crucial if we want them to be properly received and opened by others. If they are *not* wrapped in the fruit of the Spirit, then the gifts are *not* likely to be received well. The gifts must be exercised with character and maturity, which is what the fruit of the Spirit is all about: love, joy, peace, patience, kindness, goodness, faithfulness, gentleness, and self-control (see Galatians 5:22-23). Are you exhibiting these traits as you manifest the gifts of the Spirit given to you?

Think of yourself as a tree for a moment. Each limb is a gift of the Spirit. As you read the following verses, you will understand that those limbs are only useful when they bear fruit—in our case, the fruit of the Spirit.

## THE GIFTS

Let's examine the biblical passages that reveal the twenty-one primary gifts of the Spirit. In the next chapter, we will look at each gift in-depth to help you locate your specific gifting, which will be given to you in larger measure by the Holy Spirit. Before doing that, however, we will examine the proper way to operate in the gifts. Though the following passages are long, I choose to quote them in their entirety because they demonstrate the right context (healthy body life) in which the gifts belong. Using them in the right context is what makes them powerful and effective for the fulfillment of God's purpose.

Paul, in his letter to the Ephesian church, identifies five positions (the five-fold ministry) needed by a church to begin and maintain both its spiritual and physical growth:

*As a prisoner for the Lord, then, I urge you to live a life worthy of the calling you have received. Be completely humble and gentle; be patient, bearing with one another in love. Make every effort to keep the unity of the Spirit through the bond of peace. There is one body and one Spirit—just as you were called to one hope when you were called—one Lord, one faith, one baptism; one God and Father of all, who is over all and through all and in all.*

*But to each one of us grace has been given as Christ apportioned it [in various degrees].*

*…It was He who gave some to be **apostles**, some to be **prophets**, some to be **evangelists**, and some to be **pastors** and **teachers**, to prepare God's people for works of service, so that the body of Christ*

*may be built up until **we all reach unity in the faith and in the knowledge of the Son of God** and become mature, **attaining to the whole measure of the fullness of Christ.***

*Then we will no longer be [spiritual] infants, tossed back and forth by the waves, and blown here and there by every wind of teaching and by the cunning and craftiness of men in their deceitful scheming. Instead, speaking the truth in love, we will in all things [spiritually] grow up into Him who is the Head, that is, Christ. From Him the whole body, joined and held together by every supporting ligament, grows and builds itself up in love, as each part [you and I] does its work.*

*So I tell you this, and insist on it in the Lord, that you must no longer live as the Gentiles do, in the futility of their thinking. They are darkened in their understanding and separated from the life of God because of the ignorance that is in them due to the hardening of their hearts. Having lost all sensitivity, they have given themselves over to sensuality so as to indulge in every kind of impurity, with a continual lust for more [walking in the flesh and not in the Spirit].*

*You, however, did not come to know Christ that way. Surely you heard of Him and were taught in Him in accordance with the truth that is in Jesus. You were taught, with regard to your former way of life, to put off your old self, which is being corrupted by its deceitful desires; to be made new in the attitude of your minds; and to put on the new self, created to be like God in true righteousness and holiness.*

*Therefore each of you must put off falsehood and speak truthfully to his neighbor* [in your words and deeds, despite possible resulting persecution], *for we* [believers] *are all members of one body. "In your anger do not sin": Do not let the sun go down while you are still angry, and do not give the devil a foothold. He who has been stealing must steal no longer, but must work, doing something useful with his own hands, that he may have something to share with those in need.*

*Do not let any unwholesome talk come out of your mouths, but only what is helpful for building others up according to their needs, that it may benefit those who listen. And do not grieve the Holy Spirit of God, with whom you were sealed for the day of redemption. Get* rid of all bitterness, rage and anger, brawling and slander, along with every form of malice. Be kind and compassionate to one another, forgiving each other, just as in Christ God forgave you (Ephesians 4:1-7,11-32).

In Romans 12, Paul speaks about the qualities and characteristics of a faithful follower of Christ, attributes that are required for the church body to properly function. These are a second wave of gifts, which, when used, will show God to the world through you!

✞ *Therefore, I urge you, brothers, in view of God's mercy, to offer your bodies as living sacrifices, holy and pleasing to God—this is your spiritual act of worship. Do not conform any longer to the pattern of this world, but be transformed by the renewing of your mind. Then you will be able to test and approve what God's will is—His good, pleasing and perfect will.*

*For by the grace given me I say to every one of you: Do not think of yourself more highly than you ought, but rather think of yourself with sober judgment, in accordance with the measure of faith God has given you. Just as each of us has one body with many members, and these members do not all have the same function, so in Christ we who are many form one body, and each member belongs to all the others. We have different gifts, according to the grace given us. If a man's gift is **prophesying**, let him use it in proportion to his faith. If it is **serving**, let him serve; if it is **teaching**, let him teach; if it is **encouraging**, let him encourage; if it is contributing to the needs of others, let him **give** generously; if it is **leadership**, let him govern diligently; if it is showing **mercy**, let him do it cheerfully.*

*Love must be sincere. Hate what is evil; cling to what is good. Be devoted to one another in brotherly love. Honor one another above yourselves. Never be lacking in zeal, but keep your spiritual fervor, serving the Lord. Be joyful in hope, patient in affliction, and faithful in prayer. Share with God's people who are in need. Practice **hospitality**.*

*Bless those who persecute you; bless and do not curse. Rejoice with those who rejoice; mourn with those who mourn. Live in harmony with one another. Do not be proud, but be willing to associate with people of low position. Do not be conceited.*

*Do not repay anyone evil for evil. Be careful to do what is right in the eyes of everybody. If it is possible, as far as it depends on you, live at peace with everyone. Do not take revenge, my friends, but leave room for God's wrath, for it is written: "It is mine to avenge; I will repay," says the Lord. On the contrary: "If your enemy is hungry, feed him; if he is thirsty, give him something to drink. In doing this, you will heap burning coals on his head." Do not be overcome by evil, but overcome evil with* [a response of] *good* (Romans 12:1-21).

Finally, Paul lists additional gifts that the overall church body needs to exhibit to become life-giving and effective in our witness of God.

*Now about spiritual gifts, brothers, I do not want you to be ignorant. You know that when you were pagans, somehow or other you were influenced and led astray to mute idols. Therefore I tell you that no one who is speaking by the Spirit of God says, "Jesus be cursed," and no one can say, "Jesus is Lord," except by the Holy Spirit. There are different kinds of gifts, but the same Spirit.*

*There are different kinds of service, but the same Lord. There are different kinds of working, but the same God works all of them in all men.*

*Now to each one the manifestation of the Spirit is given for the common good. To one there is given through the Spirit the message of* **wisdom,** *to another the message of* **knowledge** *by means of the same Spirit, to another* **faith** *by the same Spirit, to another gifts of* **healing** *by that one Spirit, to another* **miraculous** *powers, to another* **prophecy,** *to another distinguishing* [**discernment**] *between spirits, to another speaking in different kinds of* **tongues,** *and to still another the* **interpretation** *of tongues. All these are the work of one and* *the same Spirit, and He gives them to each one* [of us], *just as He determines.*

*The body is a unit, though it is made up of many parts; and though all its parts are many, they form one body. So it is with Christ. For we were all baptized by one Spirit into one body—whether Jews or Greeks, slave or free—and we were all given the one Spirit to drink. Now the body is not made up of one part but of many.*

*If the foot should say, "Because I am not a hand, I do not belong to the body," it would not for that reason cease to be part of the body. And if the ear should say, "Because I am not an eye, I do not belong to the body," it would not for that reason cease to be part of the body. If the whole body were an eye, where would the sense of hearing be? If the whole body were an ear, where would the sense of smell be? But in fact God has arranged the parts in the body, every one of them, just as He wanted them to be. If they were all one part, where would the body be? As it is, there are many parts* [each of us uniquely different for the function we are made to perform], *but* [working together as] *one body.*

*The eye cannot say to the hand, "I don't need you!" And the head cannot say to the feet, "I don't need you!" On the contrary, those parts of the body that seem to be weaker are indispensable, and the parts that we think are less honorable we treat with special honor. And the parts that are unpresentable are treated with special modesty, while our presentable parts need no special treatment. But God has combined the members of the body and has given greater honor to the parts that lacked it, so that there should be no division in the body, but that its parts should have equal concern for each other. If one part suffers, every part suffers with it; if one part is honored, every part rejoices with it.*

*Now you are the body of Christ, and each one of you is a part of it. And in the church God has appointed first of all apostles, second prophets, third teachers, then workers of miracles, also those having gifts of healing, those able to help others, those with gifts of administration, and those speaking in different kinds of tongues* (1 Corinthians 12:1-28).

We see in these passages that the gifts of the Spirit, within the context of mature and healthy relationships, enable us to display the manifold wisdom of God in our lives. And even beyond His wisdom, these passages offer us the supernatural power of God's Spirit. So how do we locate and utilize the gifts of the Spirit meant for us? Those specific gifts meant for us would, of course, be the greater gifts for us. Paul, in 1 Corinthians 12, goes on to instruct us on how to start finding and utilizing them:

✠ But **eagerly desire** the greater gifts. And now I will show you the most excellent way (1 Corinthians 12:31).

Finding and utilizing your specific gift will *begin* with your *heart*. The strength and intensity of your desire to manifest them will translate into the outpouring and display of the Spirit's gifts in your life.

## THE CHURCH BODY

These three passages, which provide Scripture's main discussion of the gifts of the Spirit, discuss in detail the importance of body life. As a Christian, you are part of a larger body, and you are expected to coordinate with the other members to enact God's overall plan in the earth. This is a *major* purpose in each of our lives. This concept is simple to understand. All who have accepted Jesus into their hearts and have received the Holy Spirit have become part of a greater body of believers. The Holy Spirit could be compared to the body's central nervous system. Jesus Christ is the Head and we are the body—together we work to accomplish God's will.

✠ For the husband is the head of the wife as Christ is the head of the church, His body, of which He is the Savior. Now as the church submits to Christ, so also wives should submit to their husbands in everything (Ephesians 5:23-24).

✚ *And God placed all things under His feet and appointed [Jesus] to be head over everything for the church (Ephesians 1:22).*

✚ *Consequently, you are no longer foreigners and aliens, but fellow citizens with God's people and members of God's household, built on the foundation of the apostles and prophets, with Christ Jesus Himself as the chief cornerstone. In Him the whole building is joined together and rises to become a holy temple in the Lord. And in Him you too are being built together to become a dwelling in which God lives by His Spirit (Ephesians 2:19-22).*

✚ *As you come to [Jesus], the living Stone—rejected by men but chosen by God and precious to Him—you also, like living stones, are being built into a spiritual house to be a holy priesthood, offering spiritual sacrifices acceptable to God through Jesus Christ (1 Peter 2:4-5).*

Moreover, Paul says that the gifts play a major role in bringing maturity and wholeness to the larger body of Christ. In fact, that is one of their key purposes:

✚ *...to prepare God's people for works of service, so that the body of Christ may be built up until **we all reach unity** in the faith and in the knowledge of the Son of God and become mature, **attaining to the whole measure of the fullness of Christ** (Ephesians 4:12-13).*

✚ *Now I rejoice in what was suffered for you, and I fill up in my flesh what is still lacking in regard to Christ's afflictions, for the sake of His body, which is the church. I have become its servant by the commission God gave me to present to you the word of God in its fullness. ...We* proclaim Him, admonishing and teaching everyone with all wisdom, so that we may present everyone perfect in Christ. To this end I labor, struggling with all His energy, which so powerfully works in me [to show Himself through me] (Colossians 1:24-25,28-29).

Finally, the apostle Paul makes two important points about the body of Christ. First, he says that God alone chooses who receives what gift and how we all fit together as a whole:

God has arranged the parts in the body, every one of them, just as He wanted them to be (1 Corinthians 12:18).

All these [gifts] are the work of one and the same Spirit, and He gives them to each one, just as He determines (1 Corinthians 12:11).

Second, he says that we must suffer and rejoice together. We must stand with each other, even when we have different gifts and callings, because that is what a body does—it works together for its overall greater good:

If one part suffers, every part suffers with it; if one part is honored, every part rejoices with it (1 Corinthians 12:26).

Yes, we have the lead role in our own lives—and are fully responsible for it—but we also have a role to play in the larger body. We are accountable to both believers and nonbelievers alike, and this is a great responsibility.

[God said], "And for your lifeblood I will surely demand an accounting. I will demand an accounting from every animal. And from each man, too, I will demand an accounting for the life of his **fellow man**" (Genesis 9:5).

✠ *The entire law is summed up in a single command: "Love your neighbor as yourself"* (Galatians 5:14).

It's no wonder that we are told to love our neighbors as ourselves—we were intended to be part of the same body. Jesus Himself gives this important command:

✠ *Love one another. As I have loved you, so you must love one another. By this all men will know that you are My disciples, if you love one another* (John 13:34-35).

Remember that the kind of love Jesus had for His disciples led Him to the cross. That's a tall order that we cannot attain on our own. It is only through the power of the Holy Spirit flowing in us that we can live that kind of love.

Our purpose is to create a Heaven-like experience for everybody on earth (for Christians and non-Christians alike). If we want them to receive this heavenly experience, then we need to exude God's love (His will and essence) to everybody with whom we come into contact. This means that we, through the Holy Spirit, work in concert with all the other parts of the body, thus *eliminating* collision and friction between the parts.

The brain and central nervous system keep all your body parts working in unison without bumping into each other. This is what Christ (the Head of the church) and the Holy Spirit (the Central Nervous System) do for the church. The Trinity models this for us through their perfect coordination and submission to one another's will. Only through submission to God will the parts of the church body coordinate and operate in unison. This is why we all need to accept Christ as our Head and follow the leading of the Spirit daily. Indeed, without reliance on the power of the Holy Spirit within us, we falter in producing God's kind of love, especially in the face of trying circumstances and people.

In this life, we will fail at times; this is why we all need to be purified and perfected before we begin our actual Heaven experience. God's plan is that Heaven will be a perfect, trouble-free experience, which of course *cannot* happen if we are *not* all operating in God's love and will. Indeed, this is what creates the prerequisite of voluntarily being born again to get to Heaven and knowingly allowing God to conform us to His image and likeness. Otherwise, Heaven, as described in the Bible, couldn't exist.

## ACTION & VISUALIZATION

*Submit yourself to Christ's headship and the leading of the
Holy Spirit so that you can be a functioning member of His body.*

## BEARING FRUIT

A major part of participating with the body in unity is bearing fruit. Without fruit, we will experience only friction and division. But if we are operating in the leading and fullness of the Holy Spirit, we will bear much fruit. Wherever the Holy Spirit is, there fruit grows. However, when we attempt to exercise our gifts through pride, the logic of our own minds, out of duty, or out of mindless repetition, then the fruit of the Spirit will be absent. When we exhibit our gifts in this way, our gifts cannot bear fruit and they will receive a poor reception from others because their purpose is only to build up the church body in both size and spiritual strength:

✝ *...since you are zealous for spiritual gifts, let it be for the edification of the church that you seek to excel* (1 Corinthians 14:12).

God did *not* give you specific gifts of the Spirit for bragging rights or because you earned them. Rather, He gave you these gifts when He originally designed you because He knew they would enable you to complete *your* purpose in His plan. Be transparent with people that you have weaknesses, and that it is only through the Holy Spirit and the gifts of the Spirit that you can successfully live out your purpose. As parts of the body of Christ, we have an *individual* purpose, and when we are *united together,* we are also working toward a *corporate goal.*

Our individual purpose can be completed with the specific gifts that we have been offered. But from a corporate standpoint, we must work interdependently with other Christians and their gifts to accomplish God's overall purpose. This interdependence helps us keep our pride in check. Avoid the temptation of pride in your gifts at all costs, for it is satan's ultimate snare for believers. Gifts are given to enable you to lift people up, not put them down for not having your gift.

When we use our gifts with humility, the distribution of different gifts to specific members orchestrates a beautiful and complete body—a body that is working together, *using* the gifts of the Spirit. Each part may be individually weak and incomplete, but when we work together in unity, the result is a masterpiece of God's design.

## THREE THINGS TO GIVE

Your ability to complete your individual and corporate purpose boils down to having a close relationship with God. We see in Peter's relationship with Jesus that he had to take three major steps before he could fulfill his purpose. Likewise, you too will have to take these steps before you can fulfill yours.

Initially, Peter had a mental recognition or revelation of who Jesus is:

*Simon Peter answered, "You are the Christ; the Son of the living God."*
   *Jesus replied, "Blessed are you, Simon son of Jonah, for this was not revealed to you by man, but by My Father in heaven"* (Matthew 16:16-17).

The Holy Spirit gave you a revelation of who Jesus is when you were first saved. Let your revelation of Him be complete as you fully embrace His nature and intentions for you so that you can also fully embrace His purpose. In other words, you must give your *mind* to Him. This is why Paul writes:

*Do not conform any longer to the pattern of this world, but be transformed by the renewing of your mind. Then you will be able to test and approve what God's will is—His good, pleasing and perfect will* (Romans 12:2).

Later, Peter had to give Jesus his *heart*:

*When they had finished eating, Jesus said to Simon Peter, "Simon son of John, do you truly love Me more than these?"*

*"Yes, Lord," he said, "you know I love You."*

*Jesus said, "Feed My lambs."*

*Again Jesus said, "Simon son of John, do you truly love Me?"*

*He answered, "Yes, Lord, You know I love You."*

*Jesus said, "Take care of My sheep."*

*The third time He said to him, "Simon son of John, do you love Me?"*

*Peter was hurt because He asked him the third time, "Do you love Me?" He said, "Lord, You know all things; You know that I love You."*

*Jesus said, **"Feed My sheep"** (John 21:15-17).*

The way Jesus asks for Peter's love shows Peter and us that He desires a kind of love that is more than spoken love. Jesus desires us to have a living love that manifests itself through our demonstration of God's love to His children. Whatever God calls us to do for the body should not be only a job. We should strive to model our attitude for ministry after Jesus, to take ownership, to be passionate, and to pursue a full heartfelt commitment.

✟ *I am the Good Shepherd. The Good Shepherd lays down His life for the sheep. The hired hand is not the shepherd who owns the sheep. So when he sees the wolf coming, he abandons the sheep and runs away. Then the wolf attacks the flock and scatters it* (John 10:11-12).

Jesus knows that we will be attacked by our enemy when we try to care for people. If our hearts aren't committed, then we will flee when the inevitable trouble comes.

At this point, Peter has now given Jesus his head and his heart; however, there is still one more requirement to bring that relationship to full life. He must give Jesus his *hands.* Do you remember the story in Book 1 about John and Peter running into the lame beggar as they passed through the gate called Beautiful?

✟ *Then Peter said, "Silver or gold I do not have, but what I have I give you. In the name of Jesus Christ of Nazareth, walk." Taking him by the **hand**, he helped him up and instantly the man's feet and ankles became strong* (Acts 3:6-7).

To bring Jesus' living love alive in the world, we must give our minds and hearts to Him, and we must be His hands on earth as well. By so doing, we are enlivening our relationship with God at the same time—because everything in the creation is interconnected through Him.

## ACTION & VISUALIZATION

*Follow the three steps Peter took in his relationship with Jesus.
Give Him your head, heart, and hands.*

## Be Fruitful with Love

As we said earlier, the effective Christian life requires the fruit of the Spirit. So how do love and the other fruit of the Spirit mix? How do they truly become real, effective, and alive? This is how Paul continued his discussion of the gifts of the Spirit in 1 Corinthians:

✠ *And now I will show you the most excellent way.*

*If I speak in the tongues of men and of angels, but have not love, I am only a resounding gong or a clanging symbol. If I have the gift of prophecy and can fathom all the mysteries and all knowledge, and if I have a faith that can move mountains, but have **not love, I gain nothing**.*

*…Love is patient, love is kind. It does not envy, it does not boast, it is not proud. It is not rude, it is not self-seeking, it is not easily angered, it keeps no record of wrongs. Love does not delight in evil but rejoices with the truth. It always protects, always trusts, always hopes, always perseveres. **Love never fails**…* (1 Corinthians 12:31–13:1-2,4-7).

Jesus was the act of love. In fact, I would encourage you to reread the definition of love and insert His name each time it says or refers to *love*. A good exercise is to now replace *your* name where it says love, and then imagine how you would reproduce each of these attributes in your own life. God's definition of love should be committed to memory (create a reminder card with your name in each place the verse says love and post it around your house if necessary) so you can prophecy it to yourself regularly. Each day consider how you are dealing with people and apply it to all aspects of your life. If you do, then your life will be different in ways that you can't even imagine. Love is the binding, vital force to all our virtue.

✠ *Therefore, as God's chosen people, holy and dearly loved, clothe yourselves with compassion, kindness, humility, gentleness and patience. Bear with each other and forgive whatever grievances you may have against one another. Forgive as the Lord forgave you, and over all these virtues put love, which binds them all together in perfect unity* (Colossians 3:12-14).

Love is the primary fruit out of which all other gifts grow. Pride about how well our gifts work is dangerous, particularly if we begin to think our gifts are somehow more important or have a greater impact. Another danger is using our gifts for personal gain—for applause, money, love, favor, or other self-interests. We are then seeking glory for ourselves, not the giver of the gifts—our gifts will become powerless in our lives and ineffective in the body. His gifts are designed to be delivered in love, not out of pride or greed.

✠ *God is love. Whoever lives in love lives in God, and God in him. In this way, love is made complete among us so that we will have confidence on the day of judgment, because in this world we are **like Him*** (1 John 4:16-17).

And again, if we are to be *like Him* in this world, then what is He?

✠ *...God is love* (1 John 4:8).

We live in a created world that is full of objects, so our tendency is to think of God as an object; however, this verse is describing God as an *action*—the action of *love*. His *physical* presence is the *living action of love*, which is patient, kind, humble, sensitive, gentle, compassionate, forgiving, truthful, and yet merciful. Ponder this for a minute. Is this you? If we are going to be *like Him*, then our actions are what's important, not how we look.

Indeed, it is our actions that are supposed to give life to the creation itself, to bring it alive in splendor and beauty. Remember the three-step process Peter went through that will help us in achieving His likeness here on earth. We should use all aspects of our personal physical creation in concert with God's Spirit within us to manifest real love to the world—true love, *God Himself.*

## ACTION & VISUALIZATION

*Memorize each attribute of God's love. Rely on the Holy Spirit to assist you in manifesting each attribute in all aspects of your daily life.*

## DECIDE TO LOVE

It is easy to show love in return when someone is showing love to us. But how about when someone is unkind, rude, mean, or even harmful to us? As Christians, we know we are *not* to return evil with evil, but to show love to our enemies (see Matthew 5:44; Luke 6:27; Romans 12:17). How do we adjust our habit of reacting in anger or retaliation? The only way is to look at other people through God's view, not through our own view. We are to fix our eyes on Jesus, who is our example, our coach, our strength, and our source of love, for His sacrifice has set our course here on earth and beyond until we all join Him in heaven.

✠ *Therefore, since we are surrounded by such a great cloud of witnesses, let us throw off everything that hinders and the sin that so easily entangles. And let us run with perseverance the race marked out for us, fixing our eyes on Jesus, the pioneer and perfecter of faith. For the joy set before him he endured the cross, scorning its shame, and sat down at the right hand of the throne of God (Hebrews 12:1-2).*

✠ *Since, then, you have been raised with Christ, set your hearts on things above, where Christ is, seated at the right hand of God. Set your minds on things above, not on earthly things. For you died, and your life is now hidden with Christ in God* (Colossians 3:1-3).

Even when people are doing wrong to us, we need to see them the way Jesus sees them. We only need to remember the way God looked at us when we were going against His will and desires:

✠ *All of us also lived among them at one time, gratifying the cravings of our flesh and following its desires and thoughts. Like the rest, we were by nature deserving of wrath. But because of his great love for us, God, who is rich in mercy, made us alive with Christ even when we were dead in transgressions—it is by grace you have been saved. And God raised us up with Christ and seated us with him in the heavenly realms in Christ Jesus, in order that in the coming ages he might show the incomparable riches of his grace, expressed in his kindness to us in Christ Jesus* (Ephesians 2:3-7).

God showed us *grace* because of His love for us, despite the fact that we did not love Him. This is what we need to do when people don't act the way we feel they should toward us. They will have to suffer the consequences of their actions and be responsible for what they have done; however, we can still decide to show the love of God to them as God did to us. This was such great love that He gave the life of His only Son to bring us to Heaven though His grace. We did not have to act differently to receive His love, so we should not require people to act differently to us to receive our love. Paul reminds us:

✠ *For it is by grace you have been saved, through faith—and this is not from yourselves, it is the gift of God—not by works, so that no one can boast* (Ephesians 2:8-9).

I know you are asking, how could I possibly show this level of grace to those who harm me? Well, the only way is for you to stay alive in your faith, and this is best done by repeating these verses of God's grace over and over in your mind as you go through your Christian walk. These verses not only should motivate you to show grace to others, but they also tell you how you should see other people. In Psalms, it says we are wonderfully made:

✠ *For you created my inmost being; you knit me together in my mother's womb. I praise you because I am fearfully and wonderfully made; your works are wonderful, I know that full well* (Psalm 139:13-14).

Yes, God made you for wonderful works, but he also made others as well. We must decide to love them even before they are good toward us. This is hard, but it should be your goal and one you should set your mind on doing each day. Think of when you knew you were having a baby— you decided to love your baby. When he or she came, he or she cried all night and demanded things of you all the time, yet you continued to love that baby because you already decided to love him or her no matter what. All the unconditional love you showed, he or she eventually returned as that baby grew up. Likewise, you need to reset your mind and see that people were made to be wonderful so you see them as God sees them. When we show them unconditional love, we are doing God's will, bringing God's love into their world, which can bring them to change. God wants us to change the world, but sometimes we need to change our minds before we can change other people's minds.

Racism is defined as having a forgone negative conclusion of what you will think about someone of a particular race before you get to know him or her. As Christians, we are to have the reverse of that. We are to have a forgone conclusion that people are God's handiwork and are wonderfully made to eventually do God's work, no matter what they do now. Therefore, I like the saying that we are to practice grace*ism* to all people we encounter. We need to be known as grace*ists* if we are going to capture the attention of all people. If our love is not louder than our opinion and preaching, then people will not hear our opinion or our preaching. This all seems hard to do, but we were created in Jesus Christ, so if we set our minds to stay focused on Him and in Him, then we will be surprised as to what we can do with His power working through us in the manifestation of the gift of the Spirit.

✙ *For we are God's handiwork, created in Christ Jesus to do good works, which God prepared in advance for us to do* (Ephesians 2:10).

## ACTION & VISUALIZATION

*Decide each morning to show love and kindness to all those you encounter today.*

## LOVE FULFILLS THE LAW

When you act in love, you become like the source of love, you grow closer to Him, and your confidence in salvation grows too (see 1 John 4:17). Indeed, when you exude love, you are fulfilling the law by fulfilling a higher law, which is the law of love. Paul writes:

✙ *Let no debt remain outstanding, except the continuing debt to love one another, for he who loves his fellowman has* **fulfilled** *the law* (Romans 13:8).

✙ *The entire law is summed up in a single command: "Love your neighbor as yourself"* (Galatians 5:14).

You are fulfilling the law because, at that moment, you are becoming the image and likeness of God. This is why John could write:

✠ *No one has ever seen God; but if we love one another, God lives in us and His love is made complete in us* (1 John 4:12).

When Adam was created, he had the Spirit of God (the source of love) in him, but he did not have the knowledge of good and evil. He was created to do everything through God—through love—so that God could manifest Himself in His creation through man. However, when Adam ate from the Tree of the Knowledge of Good and Evil, he lost his eternal guidance system. With this knowledge of good and evil he then had the illusion that he could guide himself, but he was no longer in sync with God's will, and God's love no longer freely flowed in and through him. Because humans lost their eternal guidance-by-love system, they projected their broken selves into the creation to bring all kinds of evil into the world through their misguided actions. So God had to institute the law.

The law is an imperfect definition of love. Real love is a complex and living thing and cannot fully be defined by words. For example, real love is kind and knows how to find the proper balance between mercy and truth. Finding this balance in love is what allows truth's full benefits to be recognized. Because the law is only an attempt to define love, love itself fulfills the law.

Jesus' eternal purpose was to fulfill the law through simply loving, in addition to providing our salvation. By following His Father's leading, who is love, Jesus automatically fulfilled the law; indeed, Jesus went beyond the law because God's essence is perfect love, which is *higher* than the law. We also should follow Jesus' example and be guided by the Father's love, through the Holy Spirit:

✠ *If you are led by the Spirit, you are not under the law* (Galatians 5:18).

✠ *...he who loves his fellowman has fulfilled the law* (Romans 13:8).

✠ *The fruit of the Spirit is love, joy, peace, patience, kindness, goodness, faithfulness, gentleness and self-control. Against such things there is no law* (Galatians 5:22-23).

Therefore, *any* action that is done in God's love fulfills the law, even if it seems to contradict the letter of the law. What determines the difference between *real* love and those actions that masquerade as love? God's love comes through His Spirit and is manifested from your heart, and only God knows what is in a person's heart.

✠ *All a man's ways seem innocent to him, but motives are weighed by the Lord* (Proverbs 16:2).

You must be careful not to stretch this truth, that love fulfills the law. Some have used this as a justification to kill abortion doctors who are killing unborn babies. What these people miss is that the *whole truth* of the Word that embodies God's wisdom is love. You can't merely take a piece of God's truth to justify your actions. True love gives us a different plan of attack for stopping the senseless killing of babies. Consider these passages:

✠ *Submit yourselves for the Lord's sake to every authority instituted among men: whether to the king, as the supreme authority, or to governors, who are sent by Him to punish those who do wrong and to commend those who do right* (1 Peter 2:13-14).

✠ *For our struggle is not against flesh and blood, but against the rulers, against the authorities, against the powers of this dark world and against the spiritual forces of evil in the heavenly realms. ...And pray in the Spirit on all occasions with all kinds of prayers and requests...* (Ephesians 6:12,18).

✛ *A wise man attacks the city of the mighty and pulls down the stronghold in which they trust* (Proverbs 21:22).

Perhaps the wisest, most loving, and most effective way to stop this slaughter is for God's people to pray and thereby change the heart of the nation. This is why God declares:

✛ *If **My** people, who are called by **My** name, will humble themselves and pray and seek My face and turn from their wicked ways, then I will hear from heaven and will forgive their sin and will **heal** their land* (2 Chronicles 7:14).

God does not hold the nonbelievers responsible to change what is happening in our country. He holds *believers*—those who should be operating by the Spirit (in love)—responsible for making spiritual changes that can then manifest as changes in the physical realm. Hear this warning to us from the Lord:

✛ *Son of man, I have made you a watchman for the house of Israel; so hear the word I speak and give them warning from Me. When I say to a wicked man, "You will surely die" and you do not warn him or speak out to dissuade him from his evil ways in order to save his life, that wicked man will die for his sin, and I will hold **you** accountable for his blood. But if you do warn the wicked man and he does not turn from his wickedness or from his evil ways, he will die for his sin; but you will have **saved yourself*** (Ezekiel 3:17-19).

There are two principles I want to call to your attention. First, we must warn those who live in sin, using *love*, of course. Second, once we have done this, we are *not* required by God to *physically* stop them. Remember, God gave us *all* freedom and independence to choose for ourselves. Taking things into our own hands preempts God and doesn't allow the offender time to repent. It also *distracts* us from using our spiritual weapons, the weapons that have *real* power to make changes in both the spiritual and natural worlds. By aligning our will with His will, we allow Him to work through us.

Instead of using our individual physical efforts, together we can work in one accord with God, evoking His power to pull down the spiritual strongholds of evil. As we covered in the previous books, strongholds are thoughts, mind-sets, actions, habits, and forces (individual or corporate) that are not in the will of God. These strongholds should be the point of our attack, and we should be unified in fighting against *them*, not against each other.

Many strongholds are too powerful for you alone to bring down, particularly ones established by a collective action, thinking, or belief. That's why God intends us to all join as one body to work with Him in pulling them down. No stronghold is more powerful than a unified body of Christ on earth.

✠ *And the Lord said, "Indeed the people* **are one**...*now nothing that they propose to do will be withheld from them"* (Genesis 11:6 NKJV).

Remember from Book 1 that God originally gave Adam and Eve authority over earth (see Genesis 1:28) and that would now be collectively the case for humankind—we are gifted with the authority of God.

## POWER IN UNITY

Clearly, because of this power in collective authority, the church should be unified against all strongholds and operate in *one accord*. We should unite ourselves under the banner of love, which is the very nature and purpose of God. Jesus Himself prayed for our unity:

✟ [I pray] *that all of them* [believers] *may be* **one***, Father, just as You are in Me and I am in You…* (John 17:21).

In speaking to the body of believers, Paul said:

✟ *I appeal to you, brothers, in the name of our Lord Jesus Christ, that all of you agree with one another so that there may be no divisions among you and that you may be perfectly united in mind and thought* (1 Corinthians 1:10).

Remember from Book 2 that the early church had a supernatural power of God manifesting through their unity.

✟ *All the believers were one in heart and mind…* (Acts 4:32).

✟ *The apostles performed many miraculous signs and wonders among the people…* (Acts 5:12).

This same power is available to us today if we follow their example.

✟ *So continuing daily with* **one accord** *in the temple, and breaking bread from house to house they ate their food with gladness and* **simplicity of heart** (Acts 2:46 NKJV).

Notice that the early church was not caught up with arguments over doctrine. Rather, they built unity around the simplicity of His message—*love from the heart*. If we want Him with us in our efforts, then, as the apostle Paul says:

✠ *Accept him whose faith is weak* [or you may perceive as weak], *without passing judgment on disputable matters* (Romans 14:1).

✠ *...avoid foolish controversies and genealogies and arguments and quarrels about the law, because these are unprofitable and useless* (Titus 3:9).

✠ *Aim for perfection, listen to my appeal, be of **one mind** and live in **peace**. And the God of love and peace will be with you* (2 Corinthians 13:11).

In unity of spirit, God's Spirit will empower our collective agreement. With His Spirit, we as a united body have added power to do miraculous wonders and pull down the strongest of strongholds, allowing us to give people a most convincing case for God's presence and love for them. One of the ways we are called to demonstrate unity is through our response to our earthly authorities. Paul reminds us:

✠ *Everyone must submit himself to the governing authorities, for there is no authority except that which God has established. The authorities that exist have been established by God* (Romans 13:1).

While submitting in obedience to authorities, we can pull down strongholds and (through that act of submission) release punishment for acts of disobedience to Christ. For example, in our response to abortion, we should be praying against the deceiving spirit that makes people believe that abortion is not murder. We should be praying against the spirit of lust that leads to unintended pregnancies. And we should be praying that our leaders and politicians would see the wisdom of God.

Rather than acting in illegal ways (like attacking abortion doctors or burning down clinics), we must submit ourselves to the laws of our government, and with God bring change through appropriate means, like prayer and fasting (as well as other forms of petition and communication allowed by our government). If we want to change the direction of our nation, it is important to also change the hearts of the people (and not just the laws), because people will break the laws. Indeed, all people break even God's laws—including Christians.

When you use the gifts of the Spirit as a member of the unified body who operates in love (and the rest of the fruit of the Spirit), then you will show God's wisdom to the world and the spiritual principalities in heavenly realms. Attacking evil powers in the spirit realm while loving their victims in the physical realm will give you great success. If *all* followers of Christ join in this effort, then God's plan will surely be carried out.

## Action & Visualization

*Unite with other believers, even across denominational lines,*
*so that you can bring down the strongest of strongholds.*

## Why the Law?

God gave us the law because we lost relationship with Him; yet, we have already learned that we cannot get back into relationship with God through the law because:

✝ *All have sinned and fall short of the glory of God* (Romans 3:23).

So why did God give us the law in the first place? These verses provide some insight:

✠ *Therefore no one will be declared righteous in His sight by observing the law; rather, through the law we become conscious of sin (Romans 3:20).*

✠ *What shall we say, then? Is the law sin? Certainly not! Indeed I would not have known what sin was except through the law. For I would not have known what coveting really was if the law had not said, "Do not covet" (Romans 7:7).*

The law brought us face to face with our sin; it showed us how we fell short of His image and likeness, how we fell short of our intended purpose. The law made us conscious of the fact that we had rejected God's will and that we needed a Redeemer. Because our flesh was too weak—to live in love and to fulfill the law—we needed a Redeemer.

✠ *God went for the jugular when He sent His own Son. He didn't deal with the problem as something remote and unimportant. In His Son, Jesus, He personally took on the human condition, entered the disordered mess of struggling humanity in order to set it right once and for all. The law code, weakened as it always was by fractured human nature, could never have done that (Romans 8:3-4 MSG).*

✠ *The former regulation [the law] is set aside because it was weak and useless (for the law made nothing perfect), and a better hope [Jesus] is introduced, by which we draw near to God (Hebrews 7:18-19).*

✠ *What, then, was the purpose of the law? It was added because of transgressions until the Seed [Jesus] to whom the promise referred had come... (Galatians 3:19).*

✚ *So the law was put in charge to lead us to Christ that we might be justified by faith. Now that faith has come, we are no longer under the supervision of the law* (Galatians 3:24).

We were originally created to be in an eternal intimate relationship with God. The law could only lead us to this relationship but not replace the relationship. It is our faith in Jesus that replaces the law and reestablishes our relationship with God. Jesus describes the eternal life we've been given in this way:

✚ *Now this is eternal life: that they may know You* [know as in have an intimate relationship with], *the only true God, and Jesus Christ, whom You have sent* (John 17:3).

If you look at the law (the Ten Commandments, in Exodus 20:1-17, are God's most important laws), you will see that they define right and wrong in a way that attempts to express this loving relationship we are to have first with God (the first five) and then also with His other children on earth (in the next five). The problem is that relationships and love are dynamic; they cannot be expressed adequately on paper or stone tablets. Additionally, no one using human effort alone can keep every law perfectly. Can you also see how a constant attempt to keep every letter of the law would keep you a slave in your efforts to perform it?

Instead, God needed to change our imperfect stone hearts into living hearts so that we could understand and live out the same living love that God offered us when He sent His Son to die on the cross for our sins. God said through Ezekiel:

✚ *I will give them one heart, and I will put a new spirit within them, and take the stony heart out of their flesh, and give them a heart of flesh* (Ezekiel 11:19 NKJV).

Now it is simply a matter of using our new spirit and heart. God desires that we operate in love so that we can be free from adherence to the law. This freedom comes to us through *faith* in our Redeemer, whose perfect adherence to the law freed us from slavery to it. This *faith* in our Redeemer then frees us from the bondage of the law by allowing God's Spirit to reside in us again.

> ✠ *Before this faith came we were held prisoners by the law, locked up until faith should be revealed* (Galatians 3:23).

Once led back to God, we in *faith* are given His Spirit. It is the Holy Spirit who gives us freedom to conform to His likeness, which in turn enhances our relationship with Him. In love, He became sin for us to remove the curse from us and on to Himself.

> ✠ *Now the Lord is Spirit, and where the Spirit of the Lord is, there is* **freedom**. *And we, who with unveiled faces all reflect the Lord's glory, are being transformed into His likeness with ever-increasing glory, which comes* **from** *the Lord, who is the Spirit* (2 Corinthians 3:17-18).

## JESUS FULFILLS THE LAW

As you have seen, it is through Jesus that we are again allowed to have an eternal relationship with God. How did Jesus do it? How did He overcome the law of sin and death? He, in love, became sin for us to remove the curse from us and unto Himself. Paul tells us in Galatians:

> ✠ *Christ redeemed us from the curse of the law by becoming a curse for us, for it is written, "Cursed is everyone who is hung on a tree"* (Galatians 3:13).

Does this mean that Jesus' actions got rid of the law? Not at all. Rather, Jesus' action of love *fulfilled* the law. As He said:

✝ *Do not think that I have come to abolish the Law or the Prophets; I have not come to abolish them but to fulfill them* (Matthew 5:17).

By becoming both fully man and fully God, Jesus lived a perfect life, fulfilling the law so that, when He went to the cross, He could pay for our sins. Only someone who had not sinned could fulfill the law.

✝ *Through Christ Jesus the law of the Spirit of life set me free from the law of sin and death. For what the law was powerless to do in that it was weakened by the sinful nature, God did by sending His own Son in the likeness of sinful man to be a sin offering. And so He condemned sin in sinful man, in order that the righteous requirements of the law might be fully met in us, who do not live according to the sinful nature but **according to the Spirit*** (Romans 8:2-4).

While Jesus came to earth as a man, Paul notes that He still had the fullness of God within Him:

✝ *For God was pleased to have His **fullness** dwell in Him* [Jesus] *and through Him to **reconcile** to Himself **all things**, whether things **on earth** or things **in heaven**, by making peace through His blood, shed on the cross* (Colossians 1:19-20).

Because Jesus was fully man and fully God, He could fuse humanity and the Spirit back together through His life and His death:

✝ *For* [Jesus] *Himself is our peace, who has made the **two one** and has destroyed the barrier, the dividing wall of hostility, by abolishing* *in His flesh the law with its commandments and regulations. His purpose was to create in Himself one new man out of the two, thus making peace, and in this one body to reconcile both of them to God through the cross, by which He put to death their hostility* (Ephesians 2:14-16).

Through this fusion process, Jesus fulfilled the law for us so that it could not condemn us or enslave us in the future.

✠ [Jesus], *having canceled the written code, with its regulations, that was against us and that stood opposed to us; He took it away, nailing it to the cross. And having disarmed the powers and authorities, He made a public spectacle of them, triumphing over them by the cross* (Colossians 2:14-15).

We too should *not* walk according to our flesh, but according to the Spirit of God within us.

✠ *It is for freedom that Christ has set us free. Stand firm, then, and do not let yourselves be burdened again by a yoke of slavery* (Galatians 5:1).

The yoke of slavery is the law; as a child of God, don't ever let yourself become a slave to it. You will see in your walk of faith that both Christians and Christian leaders, much of the time, lose sight of this *important* point. We were not created to adhere to a law that would enslave us. We were created to be in relationship, to freely react to life's situations in God's love, according to our own unique personalities. If we only had a standardized legal requirement to perform in every situation, then why would we need a living relationship with God?

Your own religious precepts or even religious leaders will, at times, lead you back into the slavery of the law even though Jesus has set us free from the law. Religiosity can keep you busy with a bunch of dos and don'ts, but relationship is all about finding *intimacy* and *oneness*. Driving for that oneness is our only true goal. However, this does not mean that we should use our new freedom for selfish reasons.

✝ *You, my brothers, were called to be free. But do not use your freedom to indulge the sinful nature; rather, serve one another in love* (Galatians 5:13).

We should utilize the gifts of the Spirit that He offers to bring down strongholds in the spiritual realm and to make public spectacles of them in both the physical realm and the heavenly places. The strong presence of the Holy Spirit working through you can help keep you free as well as assist in setting others free, because wherever the Spirit of the Lord is, there is real freedom (see 1 Corinthians 3:17).

## Action & Visualization

*Develop a most intimate relationship with God in you so that*
*He can better make spiritual statements through you.*

## Fruit-Bearing Condition

When preparing to use the gifts of the Spirit, it's important to be in good fruit-bearing condition. To do this, we must walk in the Spirit.

✝ *But now, by dying to what once bound us, we have been released from the law so that we serve in the new way of the Spirit, and not in the old way of the written code* (Romans 7:6).

To sum it up, the best way to operate in this world is by walking by the Spirit, by being in fruit-bearing condition. This truly contradicts the ways of the world; however, through God's power, will, and nature, you will be able to convincingly show the world the way they should walk. Walking in contradiction to the world when you're not in fruit-bearing condition will only be a bruising experience for you and for others.

We previously explored what it means to be fruit-bearing. Here I want to summarize the four-step process for fruit bearing.

The first step is to maintain a receptive spirit and heart always. Jesus reminds us:

☩ *But the one who received the seed that fell on **good soil** is the man who hears the word and understands it. He produces a crop, yielding a hundred, sixty or thirty times what was sown* (Matthew 13:23).

The second step is to die to your old life, which allows God's life in you to flourish. Again, Jesus said:

☩ *I tell you the truth, unless a kernel of wheat falls to the ground and dies, it remains only a single seed. But if it dies, it produces many seeds* (John 12:24).

The third step is to remain open to the inevitable and valuable cutting or pruning process.

☩ *[God] **cuts off** every branch in Me that bears no fruit, while every branch that does bear fruit He **prunes** so that it will be even more fruitful* (John 15:2).

Finally, the fourth step is to abide in Christ always. Jesus said:

✠ *I am the vine; you are the branches. If a man remains **in Me** and I in him, he will bear much fruit; apart from Me you can do nothing* (John 15:5).

Clearly, the gifts of the Spirit will be in the best fruit-bearing condition when you are operating in the fruits of the Spirit.

## ACTION & VISUALIZATION

*Work the four-step fruit-bearing process into your everyday life.*

## CULTIVATE YOUR GIFTS

God has endowed you with the right measure of gifts to accomplish what He wants you to do while in your physical body upon this earth (see Ephesians 2:10). The truth is that God gave you specific gifts according to your function in life. But your performance is not automatic. Just as preparation for a race requires exercising muscles, so too your God-given gifts need to be exercised if you want to perform your calling well. Jesus illustrated this in a parable:

✠ *Again, it will be like a man going on a journey, who called his servants and entrusted his property to them. To one he gave five talents of money, to another two talents, and to another one talent, each according to his ability. Then he went on his journey. The man who had received the five talents went at once and put his money to work and gained five more. So also, the one with the two talents gained two more. But the man who had received the one talent went off, dug a hole in the ground and hid his master's money.*

*After a long time the master of those servants returned and settled accounts with them. The man who had received the five talents* brought the other five. "Master," he said, "you entrusted me with five talents. See, I have gained five more."

His master replied, "Well done good and faithful servant! You have been faithful with a few things; I will put you in charge of **many things**. Come and share your master's happiness" (Matthew 25:14-21).

Likewise, we share in our Master's happiness by receiving, unwrapping, and using the gifts He gives to each one of us. By doing this, we are giving God a gift in return that He will surely receive, unwrap, and use, perhaps to craft the gift of increase for you.

If we are going to live out the full potential that God offers, then we must recognize and utilize His gifts. If we do not use them, then we may find ourselves getting the same sort of treatment given to the man who, in Jesus' parable, did *not* invest what God had given to him.

✠ [His master replied], *"Take the talent from him and give it to the one who has the ten talents. For everyone who has will be given more, and he will have abundance. Whoever does not have, even what he has will be taken from him. And throw that worthless servant outside, into the darkness, where there will be weeping and gnashing of teeth"* (Matthew 25:28-30).

When we use our gifts in the way God intends, they will increase; however, when we don't use them, then we will lose them. Paul exhorted Timothy in this way:

✠ **Do not neglect your gift,** which was given you through a prophetic message when the body of elders laid their hands on you (1 Timothy 4:14).

763

The Bible suggests that the laying on of hands can be a possible catalyst to manifest your gifts:

✛ *For this reason I remind you to fan into flame the gift of God, which is in you through the laying on my hands* (2 Timothy 1:6).

✛ *When Paul placed his hands on them, the Holy Spirit came on them, and they spoke in tongues and prophesied* (Acts 19:6).

Remember that you were baptized in the Holy Spirit, perhaps even by the laying on of hands by an elder. From that point on, it's important for you to seek revelation about your gifts that the Spirit gives to you. You may not discover them right away, but if you are seeking from the heart, then knowledge will come. You may receive a prophetic word from a prophet or from God directly. Perhaps you or others will simply notice your exceptional abilities. It is important as you read about each of these gifts to pray for discernment.

A website that contains a lot of good information on the gifts of the Spirit (including spiritual gift tests to assist you in determining which gifts God may have given you) can be found at www.buildingchurch.net. When you know what gifts God has offered to you, it is up to you to start using them. Paul told Timothy (when talking about using his gifts) to be bold and to step out in faith:

✛ *For God did not give us a spirit of timidity, but a spirit of power, of love and of self-discipline* (2 Timothy 1:7).

We need to be diligent in self-discipline and focused on building our gifts in order to succeed in the race we are running. We are in this for the long haul. Therefore, it is important to review your gifts and start fanning the flame that God has deposited within you. No matter your age, look for new gifts. I did not know that I had the gift of teaching until I wrote this book series in my fifties, almost twenty years after I was saved. Always be open to new things, because some gifts develop as you grow and, therefore, they may not be noticeable when you first begin looking. Of course, they all become stronger as you use them. The gift of teaching within me grew substantially in the years of completing these books.

## Lessons from Elisha

To further cultivate your gifts, you will need to stay close to your teacher and mentor: the Holy Spirit. The Old Testament includes the story of Elisha, to whom God gave the gift of prophecy. Elisha sought a double portion of the gift of prophecy that his teacher and mentor, the great prophet Elijah, had. Just prior to the time when Elijah was taken to Heaven, he told Elisha that he was going to *Bethel* and asked Elisha to not come with him (he was testing him).

What's important to note here is that *Bethel* means "house of God." Approximately seven hundred years earlier, the city received its name from Jacob, who had a vision from God in which angels were ascending and descending in that location (see Genesis 28:10-22). But Elisha responded to Elijah, "I will not leave you" (see 2 Kings 2:2). Likewise, your gifts will be cultivated in the house of God.

Once Elijah and Elisha reached Bethel, Elijah again asked Elisha to stay behind while he went to Jericho. Jericho, of course, as you may remember from Book 1, represents the strongholds in our lives that need to come down for us to fully inhabit our Promised Land. Again, Elisha responded, "I will not leave you" (see 2 Kings 2:4). Likewise, you need to bring down the strongholds in your life in order to increase your gifts.

Finally, Elijah said that he was going to the Jordan River, and he asked Elisha to not come along with him. Of course, as we learned in Book 1, the crossing of the Jordan River represents the baptism of the Holy Spirit. And once again, Elisha responded, "I will not leave you" (see 2 Kings 2:6). Likewise, you need to follow the leading of the Spirit to manifest and increase your gifts. The gifts are always there.

We too have a choice every day: will we follow, or will we be led astray from our teacher and mentor, the Holy Spirit? Following Him into the house of worship, into battle against our strongholds, and into our Promised Land will cultivate our gifts and enable them to grow in exponential ways.

The Bible describes the handing over of Elijah's mantel to Elisha in this way:

*Fifty men of the company of the prophets went and stood at a distance, facing the place where Elijah and Elisha had stopped at the Jordan. Elijah took his cloak, rolled it up and struck the water with it. The water divided to the right and to the left, and the two of them crossed over on dry ground.* [The Israelites had originally gone across the same river to enter the Promised Land.]

*When they had crossed, Elijah said to Elisha, "Tell me, what can I do for you before I am taken from you?"*

*"Let me inherit a double portion of your spirit," Elisha replied.*

*"You have asked a difficult thing," Elijah said, "yet **if you see me when I am taken from you, it will be yours**—otherwise not."*

*As they were walking along and talking together, suddenly a chariot of fire and horses of fire appeared and separated the two of them, and Elijah went up to heaven in a whirlwind. Elisha saw this and cried out, "My father! My father! The chariots and horsemen of Israel!" And Elisha saw him no more. Then he took hold of his own clothes and tore them apart.*

*He picked up the cloak that had fallen from Elijah and went back and stood on the bank of the Jordan. Then he took the cloak that had fallen from him and struck the water with it. "Where now is the Lord, the God of Elijah?" he asked. When he struck the water, it divided to the right and to the left, and he crossed over (2 Kings 2:7-14).*

Simply put, Elisha *saw* God working in his circumstances—he had *insight* about what was happening in the spiritual realm while living in the physical world. Because of this *insight*, he was granted (or you might say, *he automatically had access to*) a double portion of his gift. When you keep an eye on the spirit realm and how it interplays with your daily life, then your gifts will automatically have more impact in the physical realm.

It is interesting to note that Elijah and Elisha were almost like twins. They lived similar lives, and the miracles they performed were also similar. But they had differences too. Elijah was more of a loner, one who was in an unavailing struggle against the evils of the time. He suffered serious bouts of depression. On the other hand, Elisha's double portion of the prophetic gift allowed him to live a more triumphant life. He was more involved with the people of his time. There is no record of him ever fleeing from his enemies, complaining, or losing courage as Elijah did from time to time. You too can have this same increased manifestation of the gifts in your own life if you will learn to see what is happening in the spiritual realm when you look at your physical circumstances.

The first miracle that Elisha performed after receiving the double portion of his gift has an important message in it, if we choose to unwrap it:

⊕ *The men of the city said to Elisha, "Look, our lord, this town is well situated, as you can see, but the water is bad and the land is unproductive."*

*"Bring me a new bowl," he said, "and put salt in it." So they brought it to him.*

*Then he went out to the spring and threw the salt into it, saying, "This is what the Lord says: 'I have healed this water. Never again will it cause death or make the land unproductive.'" And the water has remained wholesome to this day, according to the word Elisha had spoken* (2 Kings 2:19-22).

The message is clear—we must have salt in our lives (water represents life) if we want to be productive, if we want to become salt in the world, bringing healing to it and stopping death's increase. Our lives are salted when our gifts are manifested in *love*.

Now that I have shared with you this additional perspective (God's perspective) on exercising your gifts in love, I would like to return to the original passages that you read from Romans. This time, I would ask you to pause and meditate on each point that emphasizes the application of love as it applies to the different aspects of your life. Take your time and talk with God about it.

✝ *Love must be sincere. Hate what is evil; cling to what is good. Be devoted to one another in brotherly love. Honor one another above yourselves. Never be lacking in zeal, but keep your spiritual fervor, serving the Lord. Be joyful in hope, patient in affliction, faithful in prayer. Share with God's people who are in need. Practice hospitality.*

*Bless those who persecute you; bless and do not curse. Rejoice with those who rejoice; mourn with those who mourn. Live in harmony with one another. Do not be proud, but be willing to associate with people of low position. Do not be conceited.*

*Do not repay **anyone** evil for evil. Be careful to do what is right in the eyes of everybody. If it is possible, as far as it depends on you, live at peace with everyone. Do not take revenge, my friends, but leave room for God's wrath, for it is written: "It is mine to avenge; I will repay," says the Lord. On the contrary: "If your enemy is hungry, feed him; if he is thirsty, give him something to drink. In doing this, you will heap burning coals on his head." Do not be overcome by evil, but overcome evil with good* (Romans 12:9-21).

Yes, transforming your attitude will not be easy because you will be giving up your human attitude for God's attitude—indeed, His very essence, which is love. Of course, we can only grow in love by getting closer to its true source, who is God. And really, that is our primary goal in all of life. It is only by God's love that we are saved, and through that expression of love, we become His intimate sons and daughters.

## ACTION & VISUALIZATION

*Operating in your gifts, start exuding love whenever and wherever you can.*

## MEDITATION POINT

The rulers and authorities of the heavenly realms look to see the wisdom of God manifested through you.

Go to Chapter 3 in the Study Guide section on page 953.

# Chapter 4

# GIFT #9—GIFTS OF THE SPIRIT (PART 2)

## HOW DO YOU FIND YOUR GIFTS?

Before you begin to read, pray that the Holy Spirit will give you and all readers of this book understanding and application.

✝ *His intent was that now, through the church, the manifold wisdom of God should be made known to the rulers and authorities in the heavenly realms...* (Ephesians 3:10).

If you've ever been to the symphony, then you're familiar with the warm-up that happens before the conductor comes out. Each member tunes up his or her instrument—the violins play in different keys, the drums bang, and the horns blast out random notes. It doesn't sound so enjoyable, and, in fact, it might sound like fingernails across a chalkboard to some. However, when the conductor comes out and raises his arms, the individual instruments are hushed and then *perfect harmony* occurs. They are unified in rhythm, pitch, and volume, sounding beautiful together, creating a *moving* experience for the listener. Each individual part plays and complements all the others.

You have read about the twenty-one gifts of the Spirit that Paul lays out for us as disciples of Christ. Because you are God's follower, God has fashioned you with gifts to ring out in *harmony* within the body of Christ. You are instrumental in God's orchestra, His church, whose mandate is to create a moving experience for the world to hear. This chapter is dedicated to finding and tuning the gifts He has given you—gifts that, when used to their fullest potential in concert with others, will complement the whole and bring joy and fulfillment to your life and to others.

What part does God want you to play in His body? What gifts did He specifically give to you in good measure? You may not know for sure until you try some out, experiencing each gift through trial and error. Perhaps, when you were a child, your parents exposed you to different sports, music, and arts in order to discover areas in which you were gifted. In that case, it was up to your parents to expose you, but it was up to you to sharpen your gifts once they were found. In this case, I'm going to lay out all of God's gifts for you to choose which ones you will pursue and sharpen. If you try teaching and notice everybody sleeping, then move on to the next, and so on; however, if you get some positive response on one gift, then stay with it awhile. Remember, gifts gain strength with exercise.

As you read these verses, remember that we're all members of one body (Jesus' body on earth), and that each member is called to do his or her part for the greater good of the whole. If all parts perform well, then the whole—the global church—can have a powerful impact on the world. But if the parts don't perform well, then the whole body suffers, and so does the rest of world.

As I said in the last chapter, it's important that we are led by the Spirit and are flowing in love when exercising these gifts. This is what helps hold the body of Christ together. Actions performed in love can have a greater impact than the most persuasive words of wisdom delivered without it. Also, if our motivation becomes pride or self-interest, the gift backfires, falling flat because it is void of God's power. Paul writes:

✠ *If I speak in the tongues of men and of angels, but have not love, I am only a resounding gong or a clanging symbol. If I have the gift of prophecy and can fathom all mysteries and all knowledge, and if I have a faith that can move mountains, but have not love, I am nothing. If I give all I possess to the poor and surrender my body to the flames, but have not love, I gain nothing.*

*Love is patient, love is kind. It does not envy, it does not boast, it is not proud. It is not rude, it is not self-seeking, it is not easily angered, it keeps no record of wrongs. Love does not delight in evil but rejoices with the truth. It always protects, always trusts, always hopes, always perseveres.*

*Love never fails… (1 Corinthians 13:1-8).*

## ADMINISTRATION

The gift of *administration*, when used in love, gives you the skills to identify goals and to organize people to accomplish those goals.

✠ *And in the church God has appointed…those with gifts of **administration**… (1 Corinthians 12:28).*

✠ *Suppose one of you wants to build a tower. Will he not first sit down and estimate the cost to see if he has enough money to complete it? For if he lays the foundation and is not able to finish it, everyone who sees it will ridicule him, saying, "This fellow began to build and was not able to finish" (Luke 14:28-30).*

✠ *The reason I left you in Crete was that you might straighten out what was left unfinished and appoint elders in every town, as I directed you (Titus 1:5).*

# Apostolic Ministry

The gift of *apostolic ministry*, when used in love, gives one the ability to exercise skillful leadership over several churches.

✝ *And in the church God has appointed first of all* **apostles**... (1 Corinthians 12:28).

✝ *It was He who gave some to be* **apostles**... (Ephesians 4:11).

✝ *Truly the signs of an apostle were accomplished among you with all perseverance, in signs and wonders and mighty deeds* (2 Corinthians 12:12 NKJV).

✝ *Consequently, you are no longer foreigners and aliens, but fellow citizens with God's people and members of God's household, built on the foundation of the* **apostles** *and prophets, with Christ Jesus Himself as the chief cornerstone* (Ephesians 2:19-20).

# Discernment

The gift of *discernment*, when used in love, gives you the ability to identify the root cause of someone's actions—whether their actions are divinely, humanly, or satanically inspired. This is an important gift because determining the source of someone's actions allows you to react correctly in your efforts to help them and the overall church body.

✠ *...to another* [there is given] **distinguishing between spirits**... (1 Corinthians 12:10).

✟ *From that time on Jesus began to explain to His disciples that He must go to Jerusalem and suffer many things at the hands of the elders, chief priests and teachers of the law, and that He must be killed and on the third day be raised to life.*

*Peter took Him aside and began to rebuke Him. "Never, Lord!" he said. "This shall never happen to you!"*

*Jesus turned and said to Peter, "Get behind me, satan! You are a stumbling block to Me; you do not have in mind the things of God, but the things of men"* (Matthew 16:21-23).

✟ *"But what about you?"* [Jesus] *asked. "Who do you say I am?"*

*Simon Peter answered, "You are the Christ, the Son of the living God."*

*Jesus replied, "Blessed are you, Simon son of Jonah, for this was not revealed to you by man, but by My Father in heaven"* (Matthew 16:15-17).

✟ *"Sir,"* the [Samaritan] *woman said, "I can see that You* [Jesus] *are a prophet"* (John 4:19).

✟ *My dear friends, don't believe everything you hear. Carefully weigh and examine what people tell you. Not everyone who talks about God comes from God. There are a lot of lying preachers loose in the world. Here's how you test for the genuine Spirit of God. Everyone who confesses openly his faith in Jesus Christ—the Son of God, who came as an actual flesh-and-blood person—comes from God and belongs to God. And everyone who refuses to confess faith in Jesus has nothing in common with God. This is the spirit of antichrist that you heard was coming. Well, here it is, sooner than we thought!*

*My dear children, you come from God and belong to God. You have already won a big victory over those false teachers, for the Spirit in you is far stronger than anything in the world. These people belong to the Christ-denying world. They talk the world's language and the world eats it up. But we come from God and belong to God. Anyone who knows God understands us and listens. The person who has nothing to do with God will, of course, not listen to us. This is another test for telling the Spirit of Truth from the spirit of deception* (1 John 4:1-6 MSG).

✝ *The man without the Spirit does not accept the things that come from the Spirit of God, for they are foolishness to him, and he cannot understand them, because they are spiritually discerned* (1 Corinthians 2:14).

✝ *But solid food is for the mature, who by constant use have trained themselves to distinguish good from evil* (Hebrews 5:14).

## EVANGELISM

The gift of *evangelism*, when used in love, gives you the special ability to present the gospel to unbelievers in ways that have a great effect.

✝ *It was He who gave...some to be **evangelists**...* (Ephesians 4:11).

✠ *Leaving the next day, we reached Caesarea and stayed at the house of Philip the **evangelist**...* (Acts 21:8).

✠ *Philip went down to a city in Samaria and proclaimed the Christ there. When the crowds heard Philip and saw the miraculous signs he did, they all paid close attention to what he said* (Acts 8:5-6).

✠ *They preached the good news in that city and won a large number of disciples. Then they returned to Lystra, Iconium and Antioch...* (Acts 14:21).

✠ *But you, keep your head in all situations, endure hardship, do the work of an **evangelist**, discharge all the duties of your ministry* (2 Timothy 4:5).

## EXHORTATION

The gift of *exhortation*, when used in love, is the God-given ability to administer words of meaningful, life-changing encouragement, growth, or warning to another.

✠ *...if [a man's gift] is **encouraging**, let him encourage...* (Romans 12:8).

✠ *Each of us should please his neighbor for his good, to build him up* (Romans 15:2).

✠ *Let us not give up meeting together, as some are in the habit of doing, but let us **encourage** one another—and all the more as you see the Day approaching* (Hebrews 10:25).

✠ *[They returned], strengthening the disciples and **encouraging** them to remain true to the faith. "We must go through many hardships to enter the kingdom of God," they said* (Acts 14:22).

✠ *He must hold firmly to the trustworthy message as it has been taught, so that he can **encourage** others by sound doctrine and refute those who oppose it* (Titus 1:9).

✠ *And we urge you, brothers, warn those who are idle, **encourage** the timid, help the weak, be patient with everyone. Make sure that nobody pays back wrong for wrong, but always try to be kind to each other and to everyone else* (1 Thessalonians 5:14-15).

✠ *I long to see you so that I may impart to you some spiritual gift to make you strong—that is, that you and I may be mutually **encouraged** by each other's faith* (Romans 1:11-12).

## FAITH

The gift of *faith*, when used in love, is an extraordinary confidence that moves you to act on what you believe but can't yet see.

✠ Now **faith** *is being sure of what we hope for and certain of what we do not see. This is what the ancients were commended for.*

*By faith we understand that the universe was formed at God's command, so that what is seen was not made out of what was visible.*

*By faith Abel offered God a better sacrifice* [a sacrifice of shed blood, which represented a sacrifice of one's own life] *than Cain did. By faith he was commended as a righteous man, when God spoke well of his offerings. And by faith he still speaks, even though he is dead.*

*By faith Enoch was taken from this life, so that he did not experience death; he could not be found, because God had taken him away. For before he was taken, he was commended as one who pleased God. And without faith it is impossible to please God, because anyone who comes to Him must believe that He exists and that He rewards those who earnestly seek Him.*

*By faith Noah, when warned about things not yet seen, in holy fear built an ark to save his family. By his faith he condemned the world and became heir of the righteousness that comes by faith.*

*By faith Abraham, when called to go to a place he would later receive as his inheritance, obeyed and went, even though he did not know where he was going. By faith he made his home in the promised land like a stranger in a foreign country; he lived in tents, as did Isaac and Jacob, who were heirs with him of the same promise.* **For he was looking forward** *to the city with foundations, whose architect and builder is God. By faith Abraham, even though he was past age—and Sarah herself was barren—was enabled to become a father because he considered Him faithful who had made the promise. And so from this one man, and he as good as dead, came descendants as numerous as the stars in the sky and as countless as the sand on the seashore.*

*All these people were still living by faith when they died. They did not receive the things promised; they only saw them and welcomed them from a distance. And they admitted that they were aliens and strangers on earth. People who say such things show that they are looking for a country of their own. If they had been thinking of the country they had left, they would have had opportunity to return.*

Instead, they were **longing for a better country**—a heavenly one. Therefore God is not ashamed to be called their God, for He has prepared a city for them.

By faith Abraham, when God tested him, offered Isaac as a sacrifice. He who had received the promises was about to sacrifice his one and only son, even though God had said to him, "It is through Isaac that your offspring will be reckoned." Abraham reasoned that God could raise the dead, and figuratively speaking, he did receive Isaac back from death.

...By faith Moses' parents hid him for three months after he was born, because they saw he was no ordinary child, and they were not afraid of the king's edict.

By faith Moses, when he had grown up, refused to be known as the son of Pharaoh's daughter. He chose to be mistreated along with the people of God rather than to enjoy the pleasures of sin for a short time. He regarded disgrace for the sake of Christ as of greater value than the treasures of Egypt, because **he was looking ahead** to his reward. By faith he left Egypt, not fearing the king's anger; he persevered because he saw Him who is invisible. By faith he kept the Passover and the sprinkling of blood, so that the destroyer of the firstborn would not touch the firstborn of Israel.

By faith the people passed through the Red Sea as on dry land; but when the Egyptians tried to do so, they were drowned.

By faith the walls of Jericho fell, after the people had marched around them for seven days.

...And what more shall I say? I do not have time to tell about Gideon, Barak, Samson, Jephthah, David, Samuel and the prophets, who through faith conquered kingdoms, administered justice, and gained what was promised; who shut the mouths of lions, quenched the fury of the flames, and escaped the edge of the sword; whose weakness was turned to strength; and who became powerful in battle and routed foreign armies. Women received back their dead, raised to life again. Others were tortured and refused to be released, so that they might gain a better resurrection. Some faced jeers and flogging, *while still others were chained and put in prison. They were stoned; they were sawed in two; they were put to death by the sword. They went about in sheepskins and goatskins, destitute, persecuted and mistreated—the world was not worthy of them. They wandered in deserts and mountains, and in caves and holes in the ground.*

*These were all commended for their faith, yet none of them received what had been promised. God had planned something better for us so that only together with us would they be made perfect* (Hebrews 11:1-18,23-30,32-40).

✢ *Against all hope, Abraham in hope believed and so became the father of many nations, just as it had been said to him, "So shall your offspring be." Without weakening in his **faith**, he faced the fact that his body was as good as dead—since he was about a hundred years old—and that Sarah's womb was also dead. Yet he did not waver through unbelief regarding the promise of God, but was strengthened in his faith and gave glory to God, being fully persuaded that God had power to do what He had promised* (Romans 4:18-21).

✢ *In the same way, **faith** by itself, if it is **not** accompanied by **action**, is **dead*** (James 2:17).

## GIVING

The gift of *giving*, when used in love, is the ability to give generously and to receive satisfaction in doing so.

✢ *...if [a man's gift] is contributing to the needs of others, let him **give** generously...* (Romans 12:9).

✠ *Jesus sat down opposite the place where the offerings were put and watched the crowd putting their money into the temple treasury. Many rich people threw in large amounts. But a poor widow came and put in two very small copper coins, worth only a fraction of a penny.*

*Calling His disciples to Him, Jesus said, "I tell you the truth, this poor widow has put more into the treasury than all the others. They all gave out of their wealth; but she, out of her poverty, put in everything—all she had to live on"* (Mark 12:41-44).

✠ *The disciples, each according to his ability, decided to provide help for the brothers living in Judea* (Acts 11:29).

✠ *And now, brothers, we want you to know about the grace that God has given the Macedonian churches. Out of the most severe trial, their overflowing joy and their extreme poverty welled up in rich generosity. For I testify that they **gave** as much as they were able, and even beyond their ability. Entirely on their own, they urgently pleaded with us for the privilege of sharing in this service to the saints. And they did not do as we expected, but they gave themselves first to the Lord and then to us in keeping with God's will. So we urged Titus, since he had earlier made a beginning, to bring also to completion this act of grace on your part. But just as you excel in everything—in faith, in speech, in knowledge, in complete earnestness and in your love for us—see that you also excel in this **grace of giving*** (2 Corinthians 8:1-7).

## HEALING

The gift of *healing*, when used in love, gives one the ability to share God's healing power with others and to cure them of various infirmities—whether those infirmities are physical, emotional, or spiritual.

✠ *And in the church God has appointed...also those having **gifts of healing**...* (1 Corinthians 12:28).

✠ *[Jesus] called His twelve disciples to Him and gave them authority to drive out evil spirits and to **heal** every disease and sickness* (Matthew 10:1).

✠ *[In Jesus' name], they [believers] will pick up snakes with their hands, and when they drink deadly poison, it will not hurt them at all; they will place their hands on sick people, and they will get well* (Mark 16:18).

✠ *The apostles performed many miraculous signs and wonders among the people. And all the believers used to meet together in Solomon's Colonnade. No one else dared join them, even though they were highly regarded by the people. Nevertheless, more and more men and women believed in the Lord and were added to their number. As a result, people brought the sick into the streets and laid them on beds and mats so that at least Peter's shadow might fall on some of them as he passed by. Crowds gathered also from the towns around Jerusalem, bringing their sick and those tormented by evil spirits, and all of them were **healed*** (Acts 5:12-16).

## HELPS

The gift of *helps*, when used in love, gives you the ability to help others in a variety of practical ways.

✠ *And in the church God has appointed…those able to* **help** *others…* (1 Corinthians 12:28).

✠ *Some women were watching from a distance. Among them were Mary Magdalene, Mary the mother of James the younger and of Joses, and Salome. In Galilee these women had followed Him and cared for His needs. Many other women who had come up with Him to Jerusalem were also there* (Mark 15:40-41).

✠ *Jesus answered by telling a story. "There was once a man traveling from Jerusalem to Jericho. On the way he was attacked by robbers. They took his clothes, beat him up, and went off leaving him half-dead. Luckily, a priest was on his way down the same road, but when he saw him he angled across to the other side. Then a Levite religious man showed up; he also avoided the injured man. A Samaritan traveling the road came on him. When he saw the man's condition, his heart went out to him. He gave him first aid, disinfecting and bandaging his wounds. Then he lifted him onto his donkey, led him to an inn, and made him comfortable. In the morning he took out two silver coins and gave them to the innkeeper, saying, 'Take good care of him. If it costs any more, put it on my bill—I'll pay you on my way back.'*

*"What do you think? Which of the three became a neighbor to the man attacked by robbers?"*

*"The one who treated him kindly," the religion scholar responded.*

*Jesus said, "Go and do the same"* (Luke 10:30-37 MSG).

## HOSPITALITY

The gift of *hospitality*, when used in love, is the ability God gives you to be unusually welcoming to those in need of food or lodging.

⊕ *Love must be sincere. Hate what is evil; cling to what is good. Be devoted to one another in brotherly love. Honor one another above yourselves. Never be lacking in zeal, but keep your spiritual fervor, serving the Lord. Be joyful in hope, patient in affliction, faithful in prayer. Share with God's people who are in need. Practice **hospitality*** (Romans 12:9-13).

⊕ *One of those listening was a woman named Lydia, a dealer in purple cloth from the city of Thyatira, who was a worshiper of God. The Lord opened her heart to respond to Paul's message. When she and the members of her household were baptized, she invited us to her home. "If you consider me a believer in the Lord," she said, "come and stay at my house." And she persuaded us* (Acts 16:14-15).

⊕ *Keep on loving each other as brothers. Do not forget to **entertain** strangers, for by so doing some people have entertained angels without knowing it* (Hebrews 13:1-2).

⊕ *Offer **hospitality** to one another without grumbling* (1 Peter 4:9).

## INTERCESSION

The gift of *intercession*, when used in love, is the ability to pray on behalf of others with unusual intensity as the Holy Spirit leads.

⊕ *In the same way, the Spirit helps us in our weakness. We do not know what we ought to pray for, but the Spirit Himself intercedes for us with groans that words cannot express* (Romans 8:26).

✠ *Therefore [Jesus] is able to save completely those who come to God through Him, because He always lives to **intercede** for them* (Hebrews 7:25).

✠ When [Peter realized he had been rescued], *he went to the house of Mary the mother of John, also called Mark, where many people had gathered and were praying* (Acts 12:12).

✠ *Are you sick? Call the church leaders together to pray and anoint you with oil in the name of the Master. Believing-prayer will heal you, and Jesus will put you on your feet. And if you've sinned, you'll be forgiven—healed inside and out. Make this your common practice: Confess your sins to each other and pray for each other so that you can live together whole and healed. The prayer of a person living right with God is something powerful to be reckoned with* (James 5:14-16 MSG).

✠ *The first thing I want you to do is pray. Pray every way you know how, for everyone you know. Pray especially for rulers and their governments to rule well so we can be quietly about our business of living simply, in humble contemplation. This is the way our Savior God wants us to live* (1 Timothy 2:1-3 MSG).

## KNOWLEDGE

The gift of *knowledge*, when used in love, is the ability God gives you to know things that you would have no other way of knowing except through the Spirit.

✛ *...to another [there is given]* **the message of knowledge** *by means of the same Spirit...* (1 Corinthians 12:8).

✛ *The Lord told [Ananias], "Go to the house of Judas on Straight Street and ask for a man from Tarsas named Saul, for he is praying. In a vision he has seen a man named Ananias come and place his hands on him to restore his sight"* (Acts 9:11-12).

✛ *While Peter was still thinking about the vision, the Spirit said to him, "Simon, three men are looking for you. So get up and go downstairs. Do not hesitate to go with them, for I have sent them"* (Acts 10:19-20).

✛ *He told [the Samaritan woman], "Go call your husband and come back."*

*"I have no husband," she replied.*

*Jesus said to her, "You are right when you say you have no husband. The fact is, you have had five husbands, and the man you now have is not your husband. What you have just said is quite true"* (John 4:16-18).

✛ *My purpose is that they may be encouraged in heart and united in love, so that they may have the full riches of complete understanding, in order that they may know the mystery of God, namely, Christ, in whom are hidden all the treasures of wisdom and* **knowledge** (Colossians 2:2-3).

## LEADERSHIP

The gift of *leadership*, when used in love, is the ability God gives you to lead others in accomplishing God's will.

☩ *...if* [a man's gift] *is **leadership**, let him govern diligently...* (Romans 12:8).

☩ *Then I heard the voice of the Lord saying, "Whom shall I send? And who will go for Us?" And I said, "Here am I. Send me"* (Isaiah 6:8).

☩ [God] *rescued him from all his troubles. He gave Joseph wisdom and enabled him to gain the goodwill of Pharaoh king of Egypt; so he made him ruler over Egypt and all his palace* (Acts 7:10).

☩ *As they traveled from town to town, they delivered the decisions reached by the apostles and elders in Jerusalem for the people to obey. So the churches were strengthened in the faith and grew daily in numbers* (Acts 16:4-5).

☩ *The elders who direct the affairs of the church well are worthy of double honor, especially those whose work is preaching and teaching* (1 Timothy 5:17).

☩ *Whoever wants to be first must be your slave—just as the Son of Man* [Jesus, our best example of leadership] *did not come to be served, but to serve...* (Matthew 20:27-28).

## MERCY

The gift of *mercy*, when used in love, enables you to have an unusual compassion for those who are hurting.

✦ *...if [a man's gift] is showing **mercy**, let him do it cheerfully...* (Romans 12:8).

✦ *Blessed are the **merciful**, for they will be shown mercy* (Matthew 5:7).

✦ *At that hour of the night the jailer took them and washed their wounds; then immediately he and all his family were baptized. The jailer brought them into his house and set a meal before them; he was filled with joy because he had come to believe in God—he and his whole family* (Acts 16:33-34).

✦ *Then Peter came to Jesus and asked, "Lord, how many times shall I forgive my brother when he sins against me? Up to seven times?"*

*Jesus answered, "I tell you, not seven times, but seventy-seven times.*

*"Therefore, the kingdom of heaven is like a king who wanted to settle accounts with his servants. As he began the settlement, a man who owed him ten thousand talents was brought to him. Since he was not able to pay, the master ordered that he and his wife and his children and all that he had be sold to repay the debt.*

*"The servant fell on his knees before him. 'Be patient with me,' he begged, 'and I will pay back everything.' The servant's master took pity on him, canceled the debt and let him go.*

"But when that servant went out, he found one of his fellow servants who owed him a hundred denarii. He grabbed him and began to choke him. 'Pay back what you owe me!' he demanded.

"His fellow servant fell to his knees and begged him, 'Be patient with me and I will pay you back.'

"But he refused. Instead, he went off and had the man thrown into prison until he could pay the debt. When the other servants saw what had happened, they were greatly distressed and went and told their master everything that had happened.

"Then the master called the servant in. 'You wicked servant,' he said, 'I canceled all that debt of yours because you begged me to. Shouldn't you have had **mercy** on your fellow servant just as I had on you?' In anger his master turned him over to the jailers to be tortured, until he should pay back all he owed.

"This is how My heavenly Father will treat each of you unless you forgive your brother from your heart" (Matthew 18:21-35).

✠ ...And what does the Lord require of you? To act justly and to love **mercy** and to walk humbly with your God (Micah 6:8).

✠ Be **merciful**, just as your Father is merciful (Luke 6:36).

## MIRACLES

The gift of *miracles*, when used in love, gives you God's power to change circumstances in supernatural ways.

✠ ...to another [is given] **miraculous powers**... (1 Corinthians 12:10).

✠ ...*This salvation, which was first announced by the Lord, was confirmed to us by those who heard Him. God also testified to it by signs, wonders, and various **miracles**, and gifts of the Holy Spirit distributed according to His will* (Hebrews 2:3-4).

✠ *Everyone was filled with awe, and many wonders and **miraculous signs** were done by the apostles* (Acts 2:43).

✠ *Now Stephen, a man full of God's grace and power, did great wonders and **miraculous signs** among the people* (Acts 6:8).

✠ *I [Paul] will not venture to speak of anything except what Christ has accomplished through me in leading the Gentiles to obey God by what I have said and done—by the power of signs and **miracles**, through the power of the Spirit...* (Romans 15:18-19).

✠ *The things that mark an apostle—signs, wonders and **miracles**—were done among you with great perseverance* (2 Corinthians 12:12).

## PASTORAL MINISTRY

The gift of *pastoring* or *shepherding*, when used in love, is the ability and willingness to assume the personal responsibility for a group of Christians' spiritual development and welfare.

✠ *It was He who gave...some to be **pastors**...* (Ephesians 4:11).

✠ *Then I will give you **shepherds** after My own heart who will lead you with knowledge and understanding* (Jeremiah 3:15).

✠ *To the elders among you, I appeal as a fellow elder, a witness of Christ's sufferings and one who also will share in the glory to be revealed: Be **shepherds** of God's flock that is under your care, serving as overseers— not because you must, but because you are willing, as God wants you to be; not greedy for money, but eager to serve; not lording it over those entrusted to you, but being examples to the flock* (1 Peter 5:1-3).

✠ *Here is a trustworthy saying: If anyone sets his heart on being an overseer [**pastor**], he desires a noble task. Now the overseer must be above reproach, the husband of but one wife, temperate, self-controlled, respectable, hospitable, able to teach, not given to drunkenness, not violent but gentle, not quarrelsome, not a lover of money. He must manage his own family well and see that his children obey him with proper respect. (If anyone does not know how to manage his own family, how can he take care of God's church?) He must not be a recent convert, or he may become conceited and fall under the same judgment as the devil. He must also have a good reputation with outsiders, so that he will not fall into disgrace and into the devil's trap* (1 Timothy 3:1-7).

## PROPHECY

The gift of *prophecy*, when used in love, is the ability to receive and communicate God's message to others.

✠ *...to another [there is given] **prophecy**...* (1 Corinthians 12:10).

✝ *…If a man's gift is **prophesying**, let him use it in proportion to his faith* (Romans 12:6).

✝ *It was He who gave some…to be **prophets**…* (Ephesians 4:11).

✝ *Judas and Silas, who themselves were **prophets**, said much to encourage and strengthen the brothers* (Acts 15:32).

✝ *He [Philip] had four unmarried daughters who **prophesied**. After we had been there a number of days, a **prophet** named Agabus came down from Judea. Coming over to us, he took Paul's belt, tied his own hands and feet with it and said, "The Holy Spirit says, 'In this way the Jews of Jerusalem will bind the owner of this belt and will hand him over to the Gentiles'"* (Act 21:9-11).

✝ *I will pour out My Spirit on all people. Your sons and daughters will **prophesy**, your old men will dream dreams, your young men will see visions* (Joel 2:28).

✝ *In the past God spoke to our forefathers through the **prophets** at many times and in various ways, but in these days He has spoken to us by His Son, whom He appointed heir of all things, and through whom He made the universe* (Hebrews 1:1-2).

## Service

The gift of *service*, when used in love, is the God-given heart to help meet people's needs by serving them sacrificially.

✠ *If* [a man's gift] *is **serving**, let him serve...* (Romans 12:7).

✠ *In those days when the number of disciples was increasing, the Grecian Jews among them complained against the Hebraic Jews because their widows were being overlooked in the daily distribution of food. So the Twelve gathered all the disciples together and said, "It would not be right for us to neglect the ministry of the word of God in order to wait on tables. Brothers, choose seven men from among you who are known to be full of the Spirit and wisdom. We will turn this responsibility over to them and will give our attention to prayer and the ministry of the word."*

*This proposal pleased the whole group. They chose Stephen, a man full of faith and of the Holy Spirit; also Philip, Procorus, Nicanor, Timon, Parmenas, and Nicolas from Antioch, a convert to Judaism. They presented these men to the apostles, who prayed and laid their hands on them.*

*So the word of God spread. The number of disciples in Jerusalem increased rapidly, and a large number of priests became obedient to the faith* (Acts 6:1-7).

✠ *May the Lord show mercy to the household of Onesiphorus, because he often refreshed me and was not ashamed of my chains. On the contrary, when he was in Rome, he searched hard for me until he found me. May the Lord grant that he will find mercy from the Lord on that day! You know very well in how many ways he helped me in Ephesus* (2 Timothy 1:16-18).

✠ *Carry each other's burdens, and in this way you will fulfill the law of Christ* (Galatians 6:2).

✠ *Therefore, as we have opportunity, let us do good to all people, especially to those who belong to the family of believers* (Galatians 6:10).

## TEACHING

The gift of *teaching*, when used in love, is the ability God gives you to effectively communicate truth in such a way that brings others closer to God.

✠ *And in the church God has appointed...third **teachers**...* (1 Corinthians 12:28).

✠ *It was He who gave...some to be pastors and **teachers**...* (Ephesians 4:11).

✠ *...if* [a man's gift] *is **teaching**, let him teach* (Romans 12:7).

✠ *Meanwhile a Jew named Apollos, a native of Alexandria, came to Ephesus. He was a learned man, with a thorough knowledge of the Scriptures. He had been instructed in the way of the Lord, and he spoke with great fervor and **taught** about Jesus accurately, though he knew only the baptism of John. He began to speak boldly in the synagogue. When Priscilla and Aquila heard him, they invited him to their home and explained to him the way of God more adequately.*

*When Apollos wanted to go to Achaia, the brothers encouraged him and wrote to the disciples there to welcome him. On arriving, he was a great help to those who by grace had believed. For he vigorously refuted the Jews in public debate, proving from the Scriptures that Jesus was the Christ* (Acts 18:24-28).

✠ *You know that I have not hesitated to preach anything that would be helpful to you but have* **taught** *you publicly and from house to house. I have declared to both Jews and Greeks that they must turn to God in repentance and have faith in our Lord Jesus* (Acts 20:20-21).

✠ *Therefore go and make disciples of all nations, baptizing them in the name of the Father and of the Son and of the Holy Spirit, and* **teaching** *them to obey everything I have commanded you...* (Matthew 28:19-20).

✠ *Not many of you should presume to be* **teachers**, *my brothers, because you know that we who teach will be judged more strictly* (James 3:1).

## TONGUES

The gift of *tongues*, when used in love, is the ability God gives you to speak in a heavenly language to help your spirit discern and accomplish God's will.

✠ *...to another* [there is given] *speaking in* **different kinds of tongues**... (1 Corinthians 12:10).

✠ *When the day of Pentecost came, they were all together in one place. Suddenly a sound like the blowing of a violent wind came from heaven and filled the whole house where they were sitting. They saw what seemed to be tongues of fire that separated and came to rest on each of them. All of them were filled with the Holy Spirit and began to speak in **other tongues** as the Spirit enabled them.*

*Now there were staying in Jerusalem God-fearing Jews from every nation under heaven. When they heard this sound, a crowd came together in bewilderment, because each one heard them speaking in his own language. Utterly amazed, they asked: "Are not all these men who are speaking Galileans? Then how is it that each of us hears them in his own native language? Parthians, Medes and Elamites; residents of Mesopotamia, Judea and Cappadocia, Pontus and Asia, Phyrgia and Pamphylia, Egypt and the parts of Libya near Cyrene; visitors from Rome (both Jews and converts to Judaism); Cretans and Arabs—we hear them declaring the wonders of God in our own tongues!" Amazed and perplexed, they asked one another, "What does this mean?"*

*Some, however, made fun of them and said, "They have had too much wine"* (Acts 2:1-13).

✠ *While Peter was still speaking these words, the Holy Spirit came on all who heard the message. The circumcised believers who had come with Peter were astonished that the gift of the Holy Spirit had been poured out even on the Gentiles. For they heard them **speaking in tongues** and praising God* (Acts 10:44-46).

✠ *For then I will restore to the peoples a pure language, that they may all call on the name of the Lord, to serve Him with one accord* (Zephaniah 3:9 NKJV).

✟ *For anyone who **speaks in a tongue** does not speak to men but to God. Indeed, no one understands him; he utters mysteries with his spirit* (1 Corinthians 14:2).

## Interpretation of Tongues

The gift of the *interpretation of tongues*, when used in love, is given to be able to hear tongues in a corporate or group setting, and to interpret them for the benefit and nourishment of others.

✟ *...to still another* [there is given] *the **interpretation of tongues*** (1 Corinthians 12:10).

✟ *What then shall we say, brothers? When you come together, everyone has a hymn, or a word of instruction, a revelation, a tongue or an **interpretation**. All of these must be done for the strengthening of the church. If anyone speaks in a tongue, two—or at the most three— should speak, one at a time, and someone must **interpret**. If there is no interpreter, the speaker should keep quiet in the church and speak to himself and God* (1 Corinthians 14:26-28).

## Wisdom

The gift of *wisdom*, when used in love, is the ability to receive insight and spiritually meaningful knowledge from God that allows you to become supernaturally solid in your walk of faith, thus creating a powerful testimony for others.

☩ *To one there is given through the Spirit the message of* **wisdom**... (1 Corinthians 12:8).

☩ *And He said to man, "The fear of the Lord—that is* **wisdom**, *and to shun evil is understanding"* (Job 28:28).

☩ *Therefore everyone who hears these words of Mine and puts them into practice is like a* **wise** *man who built his house on the rock* (Matthew 7:24).

☩ *Bear in mind that our Lord's patience means salvation, just as our dear brother Paul also wrote you with the* **wisdom** *that God gave him. He writes the same way in all his letters, speaking in them of these matters. His letters contain some things that are hard to understand, which ignorant and unstable people distort, as they do the other Scriptures, to their own destruction* (2 Peter 3:15-16).

☩ *If any of you lacks* **wisdom**, *he should ask God, who gives generously to all without finding fault, and it will be given to him. But when he asks, he must believe and not doubt, because he who doubts is like a wave of the sea, blown and tossed by the wind* (James 1:5-6).

Truly, the gifts of the Spirit are the tools that God gives us in order that we might show Him and His intentions to the world—we are His body on earth. We are called by God not only to identify our gifts, but also to use them in their fullness, and to exercise them correctly. Indeed, to the extent that we are able, we are to use our gifts in love wherever opportunities arise. Paul eloquently describes the *attitude* we should have as we use these gifts, as members within the body of believers, the church:

✠ *My purpose is that they may be encouraged in heart and united in love, so that they may have the full riches of complete understanding, in order that they may know the mystery of God, namely, Christ, in whom are hidden all the treasures of wisdom and knowledge* (Colossians 2:2-3).

## ACTION & VISUALIZATION

*Locate and use the gifts of the Spirit that God has given to you, in love, wherever opportunities arise.*

## FINDING ALL THE GIFTS

Since the gifts are all used to build up the body of Christ, and since you are part of the body, once you have determined what gifts you have been given in good measure, then you need to locate and expose yourself to people gifted in the *other* areas. It is important to have exposure to *all* the gifts of the Spirit (especially the gifts of prophet, pastor, and teacher), whether through yourself, a friend, or a church leader. We need each other's gifts to reach perfect maturity:

✠ *It was He who gave some to be apostles, some to be prophets, some to be evangelists, some to be pastors and teachers, to prepare God's people for works of service, so that the body of Christ [including you] may be built up until we all reach unity in the faith and in the knowledge of the Son of God and become mature, attaining to the whole measure of the fullness of Christ* (Ephesians 4:11-13).

✠ *He who walks with the wise grows wise...* (Proverbs 13:20).

## ACTION & VISUALIZATION

*Expose yourself to all the gifts of the Spirit, so that you can become mature and perfected into the image of Christ.*

## MEDITATION POINT

Alone you may not make moving music, but in concert with others it will have a beautiful, powerful impact.

Go to Chapter 4 in the Study Guide section on page 961.

# Chapter 5

# GIFT #10—RELATIONSHIP

## HOW DO RELATIONSHIPS COMPLETE YOU AND YOUR DESTINY?

Before you begin to read, pray that the Holy Spirit will give you and all readers of this book understanding and application.

✢ *Two are better than one, because they have a good return for their work: If one falls down, his friend can help him up. But pity the man who falls and has no one to help him up! Also, if two lie down together, they will keep warm. But how can one keep warm alone? Though one may be overpowered, two can defend themselves. A cord of three strands is not quickly broken* (Ecclesiastes 4:9-12).

The government recently calculated the cost of raising one child from birth to age eighteen, and they came up with the figure of $249,180![1] Imagine what kind of exotic vacation, sports car, or boat you could buy with that kind of money. Looking at it strictly from an economic position, one might wonder if the best financial advice would be to avoid having children altogether. If you're a parent, though, I suspect you can attest to the truth that the money you've invested in your children has given you a truly rich return. At all stages—from the loss of their first tooth to their high school graduation, from their first step to their first day driving a car—children are priceless.

Yet parents, friends, husbands, and wives are prone to ignore the kinds of returns that we can receive when we relentlessly invest in relationship. How often do we think about what we can take from our marriage or our friendships? Do we sometimes just think about what we will lose or gain? With Christ as our example, true relationship—the richest relationship—seeks to pour our lives into others. For our Savior, this sort of relationship took Him to the cross so that He could offer us an eternal relationship with Him. How do we live this out as parents, friends, husbands, wives, sons, and daughters?

If we break it down, we see that God offers us two kinds of relationships: a relationship with Himself and relationships with others here on earth, which is the subject of this chapter. We will discuss our relationship with God in Chapter 7, although you will see that our relationship with other people is a part of our relationship with God and a vehicle to help us achieve a deeper relationship with God. He is in them as He is in you.

God offers us earthly relationships for many reasons. Companionship, of course, is one of the most important. Imagine what life would be like if you had nobody to talk to or share things with. Relationships also help us complete our destinies, giving us the critical support we need to help us execute our callings and, thereby, impact the world. Imagine our world without the relationships of parents, teachers, pastors, mentors, spouse, children, or friends. What would fill us with information, instruction, life's joyful moments, and, most importantly, love? We would be empty without relationships.

Just as we needed parents to raise and provide for us when we were young, so too as adults we need relationships to strengthen, support, and encourage us throughout life. Not only do we find personal support through relationships, but we also give support; our earthly relationships enable us to help one another in times of trouble. This is another way we find purpose in life.

God has created us for synergy with others. We can see this even at the most basic levels. Have you ever scooted close to someone just to stay warm? Shared body heat is a wonderful, physical example of a spiritual truth. In challenging times, two or more people have a better chance than one of persevering through the trial. Together we create something each one of us individually doesn't have alone.

Spiritually speaking, we find incredible power in a prayer of agreement with others, in joining our faith together as one. We are each uniquely gifted, as we've already explored in previous chapters, so another benefit of human relationships is that we can team up with those who are strong where we are weak. This happens in business partnerships all the time, and it can be a wonderful truth in married life as well. This is why God said:

✠ *"It is not good for the man to be alone. I will make a helper suitable for him"* (Genesis 2:18).

Perhaps this seems obvious, but the very truth that the continuation of civilization requires the union of man and woman (through the living out of a God-ordained human relationship in marriage) is evidence of the value and necessity of relationship.

There is another wonderful phenomenon that comes about as a result of relationships too. Each of us is created uniquely different and we each have different positions and areas of interests (parent, teacher, pastor, mentor, spouse, child, sibling, friend, servant, boss, entertainer, etc.). As two people interact to create a relationship, they draw out of each other and react to each other in their own unique ways, thereby making every relationship unique! What an interesting life God offers us, an opportunity where no two relationships are the same. Parents can even tell you that the relationships with each of their children have a different give-and-take component, thereby manifesting a unique relationship with each.

In Book 1, I make the analogy that we are each like crystals that create a unique pattern of colors when God's light shines through us. Likewise, when we line up in relationship and God's light shines through us, there is yet another pattern of colors created by our relationship—one that matches no other.

Now let me pause for a moment and remind you that much of what has already been explored in this series of books is all about relationships. Jesus' ministry, the work of the Spirit, and the heart of God is focused around relationships with you and me—in turn, we affect the world because of our relationship with Him. The other Gifts of Freedom are aimed to impact the way you relate to friends, family, coworkers, and even strangers. You have already learned how God uses your relationship with other believers (the body of Christ) to accomplish His greater purpose. Now, let's take it a step deeper. I'd like to highlight a few of the reasons why all kinds of relationships are vital to our spiritual growth. Applying these truths will enhance and enrich our earthly relationships as well as our relationship with God.

## For Self-Improvement

Relationships can help us improve ourselves in ways that make success in all areas much easier and likelier:

✝ *As iron sharpens iron, so one man sharpens another* (Proverbs 27:17).

✝ *If the ax is dull and its edges unsharpened, more strength is needed...* (Ecclesiastes 10:10).

I also like how the *Message Translation* puts this verse:

✝ *Remember: The duller the ax the harder the work; use your head: The more brains, the less muscle* (Ecclesiastes 10:10 MSG).

✝ *Where there is no counsel, the people fall; but in a multitude of counselors there is safety* (Proverbs 11:14 NJKV).

✝ *Plans fail for lack of counsel, but with many advisors they succeed* (Proverbs 15:22).

It's important to have someone in your life who will hold you accountable for your Christian walk and the goals that you set for yourself. This person (or people) should be someone who knows you and someone you are free to be honest with—to discuss your trials, your victories, and your defeats. We have spiritual blind spots, so accountability partners give us perspective, which can help reveal these if we are open to it.

We will all face times when we need the help of others. We may need physical help or prayer or encouragement or a rediscovery of the right perspective when the schemes of satan get us turned around. The presence of others can create both a physical and a spiritual synergy to help keep us "warm." We learned in the last two chapters that all believers possess different gifts that are meant to build up the whole body and bring us to a greater revelation of Christ. Let us not forget that there is a special kind of power in praying in agreement with others—combining our faith with theirs. This is just a few of many reasons why it's good to be part of a Christian fellowship where we can regularly *give* and *receive* support.

## OUTWARD FOCUS

Paul exhorts us to have the same attitude Jesus had when it comes to making friends. When you focus on the needs of others, you forget what you are lacking. And when you forget about what you're lacking, you give God room to deal with it. But, as Paul addresses in this passage, it's not always easy to be a good friend. Listen to his definition:

✠ *Then make my joy complete by being like-minded, having the same love, being one in spirit and purpose. Do nothing out of selfish ambition or vain conceit, but in humility consider others better than yourselves. Each of you should look not only to your own interests, but also to the interest of others.*

*Your attitude should be the same as that of Christ Jesus: who, being in very nature God, did not consider equality with God something to be grasped, but made Himself nothing, taking on the very nature of a servant, being made in human likeness. And being found in appearance as a man, He humbled Himself and became obedient to death* [of His self-interest]—*even death on a cross!* **Therefore** *God exalted Him to the highest place and gave Him the name that is above every name* (Philippians 2:2-9).

You will be tempted to set yourself above others in situations because of power, authority, money, or even a gift that you have received, which would seem to make you "better" than someone else. In these situations, Jesus is our example. He certainly could have set Himself above mere humans. Instead, however, Jesus elected to be equal and to be a servant to His brothers and sisters, even though by human standards He would have been considered better. We too are called not to set ourselves above other people, but to serve them:

✠ *Whoever wants to be first must be your slave—just as the Son of Man* [Jesus] *did not come to be served, but to serve...* (Matthew 20:27-28).

✠ [Jesus said], *"For who is greater, the one who is at the table or the one who serves? Is it* **not** *the one who is at the table? But I am among you as one who serves"* (Luke 22:27).

## SERVANTHOOD

Jesus showed us how to be a servant by washing the feet of the disciples. He also said:

✠ *Whoever wants to become great among you must be your servant, and whoever wants to be first must be slave of all* (Mark 10:43-44).

When you are serving, you will be given stronger friends, and strong friends help you become the person God intends you to be. The Bible includes many stories about strong friendships. One of the most familiar is the friendship between David and Jonathan. First Samuel tells us:

✠ *After David had finished talking with Saul, Jonathan became one in spirit with David, and he loved him as himself. From that day Saul kept David with him and did not let him return to his father's house. And Jonathan made a covenant with David because he loved him as himself. Jonathan took off the robe he was wearing and gave it to David, along with his tunic, and even his sword, his bow and his belt* (1 Samuel 18:1-4).

In the end, Jonathan laid down his own *right* to the throne and instead helped David become the king God wanted him to be. The way you become a strong and serving friend is by putting the interests and needs of others before your own. Jesus teaches that this loving service is second in importance only to our relationship with God (the first commandment):

✠ [Jesus said], *"The second is this: 'Love your neighbor as yourself.' There is no commandment greater than these"* (Mark 12:31).

In a conversation with an expert in the law, Jesus described what the act of loving your neighbor as yourself looks like:

✠ *In reply Jesus said, "A man was going down from Jerusalem to Jericho, when he fell into the hands of robbers. They stripped him of his clothes, beat him and went away leaving him half dead. A priest happened to be going down the same road, and when he saw the man, he passed by on the other side. So too, a Levite, when he came to the place and saw him, passed by to the other side. But a Samaritan, as he traveled, came where the man was; and when he saw him, he took pity on him. He went to him and bandaged his wounds, pouring on oil and wine. Then he put the man on his own donkey, took him to an inn and took care of him. The next day he took out two silver coins and gave them to the innkeeper. 'Look after him,' he said. 'And when I return, I will reimburse you for any extra expense you may have.'*

*"Which of these three do you think was a neighbor to the man who fell into the hands of robbers?"*

*The expert in the law replied, "The one who had mercy on him."*

*Jesus told him, "Go and do likewise"* (Luke 10:30-37).

Jesus offers clear instructions about how to respond when we meet people with *physical* needs, even when those people are not *desirable*, and *even* when those people dislike us. During this time, the Jewish people looked down on the Samaritans. In fact, the Jews considered them less than human. But this Samaritan went out of his way to help the Jewish man who hated him.

Like much of the Bible, these stories have meaning on several levels. In Chapter 7, I will show you how this story pertains to your relationship with Jesus. However, as it pertains to being a friend in your earthly relationships, all of us are to consider all people friends—yes, even our enemies. Jesus is *also* giving us clear instructions about how to care for each other's *spiritual* needs. We are not to leave others by the side of the road to spiritually die.

Reread this passage, but look at it from a spiritual perspective. Assume that the robbers are satan or satanic forces. The priest and Levite are religious leaders who portray themselves as caring for the spiritually sick, but they're wrapped up in their own interests of the day (the playground where satan likes to keep our attention), and who also look down at people of other colors or other beliefs. Who is the Samaritan? He is an example of who we are called to be. With oil (the Holy Spirit) and wine (the blood of Jesus), we can minister to a spiritually sick person. It's important to remember that it is up to us to work out our own salvation. This is why we are to put him back on his own donkey so he can go forward spiritually on his own. We are only asked to pour on the oil and wine, which, of course, begins with addressing any required physical needs.

Now look at the innkeeper. In our spiritual rethinking of the story, the innkeeper represents the pastor of a local church who spiritually cares for the injured man. We aren't finished when we drop the man off at the church. Jesus asks us to financially support those churches that are spiritually caring for hurting people. We are also to return and make sure that they become healthy. When we do this, what do you think we are showing people, especially those who don't like us?

With that in mind, imagine yourself *going and doing likewise*, just as Jesus instructed. This sounds impossible—to go and be such a friend to those who hate you or in some way have abused you, right? Being this kind of friend to an enemy is only something Jesus can do, right? So why does Jesus tell us to go out and do the same?

The next story that Luke tells is Jesus visiting the house of two sisters, Mary and Martha (see Luke 10:38-42). Martha was so overwhelmed preparing the house and meal for Jesus' visit, while Mary was singularly focused on Jesus, listening to His word while sitting at His feet. Jesus told Martha that Mary was doing the right thing in focusing on Him. When the required task either overwhelms you or seems too difficult to accomplish, Jesus is telling you to stop what you are doing and place your focus on Him. That is the one source for power, love, and a sound mind. It is only through His power that the hardest tasks in being a friend will be accomplished.

## Fulfilling the Law

Paul said that the act of friendship fulfills the Old Testament law and Christ's command:

✠ *Let no debt remain outstanding, except the continuing debt to love one another, for he who **loves** his fellowman has **fulfilled** the law* (Romans 13:8).

✠ *Carry each other's burdens, and in this way you will **fulfill** the law of Christ* (Galatians 6:2).

Friendship fulfills the law because becoming a true friend is an act of loving, and loving is serving (just as Jesus served). Cultivating good friendships through serving can create stronger relationships, even beyond those within our own families. The book of Proverbs tells us:

✠ *Do not forsake your friend and the friend of your father, and do not go to your brother's house when disaster strikes you—**better a neighbor nearby than a brother far away*** (Proverbs 27:10).

✠ *A man of many companions may come to ruin, but **there is a friend who sticks closer than a brother*** (Proverbs 18:24).

✠ *A friend loves at all times, and a brother is born for adversity* (Proverbs 17:17).

✦ *A wise servant will rule over a disgraceful son, and will share the inheritance as one of the brothers* (Proverbs 17:2).

## How to Win Friends

How do we find meaningful friendships and people on whom we can rely? Well, as you probably already know, they don't just appear. The answer to this question is a familiar one: *we reap what we sow.* If we want friends, then we need to offer friendship to others. If we want a strong friendship, then we must be a strong friend to others. The degree in which we unselfishly sow and plant within relationships will be revealed in the harvest of strong friendships. Jesus, of course, is the ideal model for this too. He said:

✦ *Greater love has no one than this, that he lay down his life for his friends* (John 15:13).

In regular everyday "day in and day out" context, this simply means putting your friend's interest above your own interests and goals. This even means putting the interests of people who do not yet think of us as a friend above our own. Before we were saved, we were not Jesus' friends and likely we did not deserve His friendship, but He invested Himself in becoming our friend. This is Paul's point when he writes:

✦ *You see, at just the right time, when we were still powerless, Christ died for the ungodly. Very rarely will anyone die for a righteous man, though for a good man someone might possibly dare to die. But God demonstrates His own love for us in this: While we were **still** sinners [not yet friends], Christ died for us* (Romans 5:6-8).

In Hebrew, the word for *love* is *a'hab*, which is made of the letters *aleph* or God, *hey* or grace, and *bet* or son. The letters can read "God's grace through the sacrifice of His Son is love." The numerical number for *aleph* is one and *bet* is two. *Hay* also means "giving" and "becoming." We could say that love is built on one giving for the benefit of the two, and the two becomes one. Paul instructed us to imitate Christ's love in this way:

✠ *I try to please everybody in every way. For I am not seeking my own good but the good of many, so that they may be saved* (1 Corinthians 10:33).

✠ *Do nothing out of selfish ambition or vain conceit, but in humility consider others better than yourselves. Each of you should look not only to your own interests, but also to the interests of others* (Philippians 2:3-4).

This means that you may have to show friendship to people who are not being friendly to you. That is why Paul says the following:

✠ *Do not repay anyone evil for evil. Be careful to do what is right in the eyes of everybody* (Romans 12:17).

We should also actively seek to do good, both for those who deserve it and for those who are not able to help themselves.

✠ *Never walk away from someone who deserves help; your hand is God's hand for that person. Don't tell your neighbor "Maybe some other time" or "Try me tomorrow" when the money's right there in your pocket* (Proverbs 3:27-28 MSG).

✠ *Blessed is he who has regard for the weak; the Lord delivers him in times of trouble. The Lord will protect him and preserve his life; He will bless him in the land and not surrender him to the desire of his foes* (Psalm 41:1-2).

Essentially, as you, like Christ, reach out in love to others, many faithful and strong friends will be attracted to you. And as you become closer to the image and likeness of God, then you will attract friends who will reflect that *light* back to you, making them the best kind of friend to have.

## ACTION & VISUALIZATION

*Be a friend to others in faith and in love.*

## MARRIAGE: THE ULTIMATE EARTHLY RELATIONSHIP

The strongest earthly relationship that God offers to us is that between a *man* and a *woman* in the covenant of marriage. Through this relationship, that of a parent and child can also grow. I could fill a few books on the topic of what makes a great marriage. Thankfully, however, there are plenty of great books that teach what a biblically-based marriage ought to look like. But because this is such an important aspect of the gift of relationship, I wanted to be sure to introduce some of the *key* biblical concepts that make a marriage flourish.

Marriage is the ultimate expression of companionship, as two are spiritually tied together in such a way that they practically become *one person*. This combining of two is also a simple model of the ultimate spiritual relationship that God desires to have with us—a combining into one—Him in us and us in Him. Let's start at the beginning so we can understand the marriage relationship.

✜  *...But for Adam no suitable helper was found* [among the creation]. *So the Lord God caused the man to fall into a deep sleep; and while he was sleeping, He took one of the man's ribs and closed up the place with flesh. Then the Lord God made a woman from the rib He had taken out of the man, and He brought her to the man. The man said, "This is now bone of my bones and flesh of my flesh; she shall be called 'woman,' for she was taken out of the man." For this reason a man will leave his father and mother and be united to his wife, and they will become* **one flesh** (Genesis 2:20-24).

The Hebrew word for *man* is spelled with the letters *aleph, yod,* and *shin,* while woman is spelled with *aleph, shin,* and *hey.* Each has a letter the other doesn't contain, and those two letters together spell God's name. This gives us a good picture of the purpose of marriage, which is to show God to the world. The man has the letter *yod,* which represents hand and thought; this is a picture of the man working. The woman has the letter *hey,* which is a sign for grace or giving, which is so vital for children and a family to flourish. When you take out the extra letter of each of these, it spells the word *fire.* When you put the two fires together, then you have an explosion. Or better said, a marriage without God's love being exhibited will result in an explosion.

## Two Unique Roles

God created man and woman to have interlocking abilities and weaknesses, which, when combined in marriage, could help them accomplish their combined God-given purpose. Likewise, spiritually speaking, they also interlock to become one. Let's look first at God's intent for each in creation.

✜  [Man] *is the image and glory of* **God**; *but the woman is the glory of* **man** (1 Corinthians 11:7).

This does not imply in any way that men are more important than women. Rather, it merely tells us that each has a distinctly different purpose and role. It's like asking what's better, the light bulb or the socket it fits in? Neither. To light an area, both the socket and the bulb require the electricity and require each other to function as one. If any one of the three are missing—socket, bulb, or electricity—there will be no light.

Marriage is much the same. The two in the marriage require each other, as well as God's power, to give the marriage life and proper function. Spiritually, men and women are equal in God's eyes; He doesn't play favorites. His love reaches out to both genders, encouraging us to seek His purpose for our lives. This is why Paul writes:

✠ *There is neither...male nor female, for you are one in Christ Jesus* (Galatians 3:28).

Indeed, *both* are *equally* needed to accomplish God's purpose; in the case of married couples, the Bible tells us they become "one flesh" in God's eyes anyway (see Genesis 2:24). It is helpful to look at the differences between men and women so that we can better understand God's individual plan for each as He intended them to complement the other.

## Role of Men

Men were designed primarily for function, which God talks about immediately after the fall:

✠ *To Adam [God] said, "Because you listened to your wife and ate from the tree about which I commanded you, 'You must not eat of it,' cursed is the ground because of you; through painful toil you will eat of it all the days of your life. It will produce thorns and thistles for you, and you will eat the plants of the field. By the sweat of your brow you will eat your food until you return to the ground, since from it you were taken; for dust you are and to dust you will return"* (Genesis 3:17-19).

This description of a man's role is not unlike that of a workhorse. Think of a heavy-duty truck used for hauling, the kind you see at construction sites. For *thousands* of years, history has demonstrated that we naturally grade a man on his ability to *perform*, because that is what we intuitively *know* he was designed to do. Paul reminds us:

✟ *If anyone does not provide for **his** relatives, and especially for **his** immediate family, **he** has denied the faith and is worse than an unbeliever* (1 Timothy 5:8).

Regardless of the increased number of women in the workplace, men are still primarily responsible to be the providers for their families. Another verse, which is directed at women, further describes the man's role in spiritual matters too:

✟ *Your desire will be for your husband, and he will rule over you* (Genesis 3:16).

For the man, this might at first seem like the "best" position to hold, the position with all the "glory" and power, so to speak. But *think about it*: in business, who is responsible when something goes wrong? It is the person who is in charge. God gives men authority, but He also gives them the responsibility that goes with it. If things go wrong, God holds the man *responsible* for his actions and the leadership direction to those under his authority.

Some men may be thinking that, because God put them in charge, they must have all the answers. Men, for you to have the right perspective, it's worth reviewing the sobering words that God used when He looked at the man He made:

✟ *And the Lord God said, "It is not good that man should be alone. I will make him a **helper** comparable to him"* (Genesis 2:18 NKJV).

Yes, God knew in His infinite wisdom that men could not make it alone. All men, like Adam, are lacking and need help.

## Role of Women

It was to cover the lack of men that God gave a very different role to women. One of the key differences, as we all know, is that she is the sole child-bearer and primary child-care provider.

✟ *To the woman* [God] *said, "I will greatly increase your pains in child-bearing; with pain you will give birth to children..."* (Genesis 3:16).

But the Bible also says that women are the glory of men. Instead of that heavy-duty truck, think of a beautiful, unique sports car—the sort of car that you take great pride in, that you take great care of, and that you like to take out for Sunday drives. As the glory of man, her sheer beauty shines from the *inside out*, much like that sports car, glistening in the light from the sun.

The truck has a rather straightforward method to perform its function. You just turn on the ignition switch and then drive. But the sports car requires more attention, more finesse. All those switches, gauges, dials, and buttons have to be just right for it to perform at its optimum level.

Even our symbols for marriage—the rings—reflect these distinct differences between the man and the woman. The simpler design of the husband's ring conveys, in a straightforward, no fanfare way, the fact that he is married, while the wife's more intricate wedding ring reflects the beauty that the husband feels for and through her.

## Celebrate Your Differences

The differences in the way that God made men and women help each to fulfill their roles within their relationship. Man alone was incomplete—lacking—so women were made with *differences* that, when combined with men, completed them. *Together* they can achieve God's perfect plan.

Consider this: If we were designed exactly alike, how could one possibly help the other's weakness? How would it make sense that we could combine and become one? It can be tempting to blur those differences and attempt to conform one to the other. However, instead we should celebrate those *differences*. Indeed, isn't it those very *differences* that make the marriage relationship interesting?

Let's look at some of the less obvious differences. According to one understanding of the science behind gender differences, during the eight weeks in development within the womb, a man receives more of a testosterone wash in his brain that causes the brain to suffer a kind of damage. (Of course, my wife tells me that she knew that all along.) Simply put, this results in men having fewer nerve cells that connect the brain than women. The basic effect of this is that women are much more physically connected to the world and to their bodies. Information from the senses (sight, sound, touch, and taste) are being processed in the brain in greater quantity all the time. Moreover, the area of the brain that handles language in a woman is better connected to the right hemisphere, allowing it to pitch in on language.[2]

Because of this, women generally have the ability to simultaneously notice and process more of what's happening around them and to them. They have an acute sense of their surroundings—their radar is fine-tuned far beyond a man's. Men were to receive real-time information about the world through their wives, which is why women are also wired for communication. This natural gift of communication is fed by a *desire* to communicate the information they are receiving; indeed, women are fulfilling a God-given purpose when they pursue this desire. This is why their need to know that their communication is being received is so *vital* and *fulfilling*.

My wife is enviably more communicative than I am. Substantially so! I have read books and articles that compare the number of words a woman speaks in an average day to that of a man. While the findings differ from one study to the next, all seem to agree that women speak more words than men—twice as many, or even more. When I told my wife this, she said, "Of course! We have to repeat everything twice for you men to hear!" While this may not always be true, it is interesting and significant that many women believe it to be true. Regardless of the actual difference in the number of words spoken, the average man clearly comes up short in communication skills—according to many women, most men either don't listen or don't *properly* acknowledge that they were listening.

Men, on the other hand, having less exterior information to process, tend to be more cerebral than women in their approach to the world—much more detached. This is a result of having more white matter in the brain, allowing men to be superior at spatial reasoning.[3] They process information in a different manner, conceptualizing and strategizing life into linear goals. In conversation, they are more likely to leap right to "the point" and skip over an explanation of the bigger and more-detailed picture, which usually requires fewer words. This habit of leaping right to the point without first properly acknowledging a woman's input can leave her feeling that her input wasn't heard at all, thereby making her feel *incomplete* and *unfulfilled*.

Let's look at an example of how these different views play out in everyday life. When my wife and I are heading to the mall so that she can buy a new pair of shoes, I am thinking about the layout of the mall and the best place to park. I'm doing this so that I might get home in time for the next game on TV. She, on the other hand, is enjoying the ride and the nice day out as she seeks to engage me in conversation about some relational issue with our kids. After she has finished a vivid blow-by-blow of the issue, she waits for my comments, and, of course, I respond with a quick, to-the-point (and thereby probably unsatisfying) yes as I'm trying to figure out, based on traffic at the mall that day, whether it is worth driving closer or not in hopes of getting a better parking spot.

When we get into the mall, my attention is still on the practical: the hunt for shoes. My goal is to find them, grab them, bag them, and go. She, on the other hand, is fully engaged in the experience: enjoying the walk through the mall, the window-shopping, the people watching, the smells, the sounds, the sights. Indeed, she stops in front of a display window looking at a pretty dress that caught her attention.

"I thought we came for shoes," I say in protest of this distraction from our *original objective*. In the end, she doesn't find any shoes she likes, so we head for home. For her, the whole shopping experience was stimulating and enjoyable and, therefore, *complete*. I, on the other hand, experience a sense of incompleteness. Something is missing: where are the shoes we came to buy?

Understanding these basic differences can help us as we attempt to relate to one another. Instead of seeing our differences as a point of conflict, we can learn from each other. For example, the man can learn more about the world around him through her senses, and the woman can learn interesting ways to navigate through that world from a man's perspective. When we respect and honor these differences, we allow the other to complete us, equipping us to complete God's plan.

The *key* to enjoying these differences is *allowing* each partner to be who he or she is. Compromise is important, but acknowledging that we're not going to change the other person from what God intended him or her to be is also vital to a healthy relationship. We must work in tandem, balancing one another, viewing our individual differences as a means to growth, not as a point of conflict.

## COMBINATION MAKES WHOLE

The abilities and characteristics that God gave men and women allow them to combine into one flesh, fulfilling a family's needs. Man is designed to provide for the family and will generally feel some level of incompleteness when he is not successful at doing this. The man is also designed to be the head of the family:

*Now I want you to realize that the head of every man is Christ, and the head of the woman is man, and the head of Christ is God* (1 Corinthians 11:3).

From a purely biological sense, this seems logical. A mind primarily focused on strategy and survival would be critical to the success of a family. But the role of the woman is no less important in the process. The body gives the mind *critical* feedback that it *needs* to properly perform its function. A woman's feedback and insight can give critically needed information and light to the man's strategic and linear thinking. Simply put, when God said, "It's not good for man to be alone," He knew what He was talking about.

This brings up a point I need to emphasize to the men reading this book. Please listen to your wife and acknowledge that you're listening. Remember that a woman's sense of completeness is based on being heard, as well as being taken seriously for the thoughts that she offers. If you surveyed married couples at any point in history, you'd find that the most common problem is a "communication problem." Usually, this means that either the man isn't listening, or he isn't doing a very good job of acknowledging that he's listening, or both. When this happens, there will be a lack of completeness in the marriage, leading to relational problems.

And don't miss this: what she offers is of *great* value. Women's "radars" tend to detect nonverbal information better than men's. This is particularly the case when it comes to feelings. God created women to be sensitive and nurturing, knowing, for example, what a baby needs simply by the sound of his or her cry. Because of this, she is usually best at seeing and responding to family fractures. Indeed, many women weave themselves into the entire experience of the family relationship, and that broader experience of "family" becomes a significant part of their identity. This is why she may feel that you're personally criticizing or attacking her when you identify things that you may feel are shortcomings with the house or family. Remember the heightened, fine-tuned radar allows her to incorporate the greater experience of house and family into herself in such a way that the line between where one ends and the other begins is less defined. Choose your words carefully and seek to be an encourager to your wife. When you do so, she will respond positively, like a plant being watered.

I want to reiterate that God doesn't see either role as more important than the other—*just different*. Both the man and woman need each other in marriage to be *complete*. When you think about it, you realize that God has made marriage a beautiful circle. Woman originally came from man, but man comes from woman; and it takes the union of them both, as one flesh, to plant the seed to create a new life. God designed that very union of planting the seed to be the most satisfying and unifying experience that a husband and wife can share.

## Action & Visualization

*Acknowledge and enjoy your differences in the gift of marriage that God offers you.*

## A Word to Husbands

Husbands, your role as the head of the family should never be exercised by physical force, mental leveraging, or even by the exertion of God-given spiritual leadership. Your role is to *inspire* your wife to *follow* your lead as you travel down the path of life together. If you are behind her, pushing her down the path, then you are not inspiring her (or perhaps you are not listening enough). To instill this trust, you need to have an open dialogue. You will successfully inspire her if you have the same attitude as Christ:

✠ *Husbands, love your wives, just as Christ loved the church and* **gave Himself up for her***…* (Ephesians 5:25).

✠ *In this same way, husbands ought to love their wives as their own bodies. He who loves his wife loves himself. After all, no one ever hated his own body, but he feeds and cares for it, just as Christ does the church…* (Ephesians 5:28-30).

✠ *Husbands, in the same way be considerate as you live with your wives, and treat them with respect as the weaker partners and as heirs with you of the gracious gift of life, so that nothing will hinder your prayers* (1 Peter 3:7).

Your role as leader in the marriage relationship is that of a servant-leader. Let's go a little deeper with this. First, consider this Scripture:

✠ *Wives, submit to your husbands as to the Lord. For the husband is the head of the wife as Christ is the head of the church, His body, of which He is the Savior. Now as the church submits to Christ, so also wives should submit to their husbands in everything.*

*Husbands, love your wives,* **just as Christ loved the church and gave Himself up for her to make her holy,** *cleansing her by the washing with water through the word, and to present her to Himself as a radiant church, without stain or wrinkle or any other blemish, but holy and blameless. In this same way, husbands ought to love their wives as their own bodies.* **He who loves his wife loves himself.** *After all, no one ever hated his own body, but he feeds and cares for it, just as Christ does the church—for we are members of His body. "For this reason a man will leave his father and mother and be united to his wife, and the two will become one flesh." This is a profound mystery—*

*but I am talking about Christ and the church. However, each one of you also must love his wife as he loves himself, and the wife must respect her husband* (Ephesians 5:22-33).

The first thing to note here is that God created a structure where everyone is submitted to someone else: wife to husband, husband to Christ, and Christ to God. Your success as a husband will be directly proportional to your submission to Christ and your willingness to follow His example. Indeed, if you are not already married, keep in mind that one of the most attractive qualities to Christian women is a humble and contrite spirit, which is demonstrated through your obedience to God.

The second point to note in the above passage is that the better we treat our wives, the better our wives will be. If you treat your wife meanly, then you will probably have an unhappy and spiteful wife. What you put *in* her is you will get *out* of her; so be *wise* and *invest wisely*.

## · Action & Visualization

*Men, respect your God-given role in your marriage.*

## A Word to Wives

God created the world to have order and structure. Unfortunately, humankind has brought chaos to that order. If you are married, you decided to join with a man to drive down the highway of life. There's only one steering wheel in the car. You can strive for relational equality, but in the *end*, when a turn needs to be made to avoid disaster, only *one* person can drive. God has clearly designed and designated this position for man. Considering the differences between men and women, this makes sense, doesn't it?

Women, because of your design, being so strongly connected to your senses, it is important that you do not let them sway you from spiritual realities, as happened with Eve.

✝ *Then the Lord God said to the woman, "What is this you have done?"*
*The woman said, "The serpent **deceived** me, and I ate"* (Genesis 3:13).

And Paul later wrote to the Corinthians:

✝ *But I am afraid that just as Eve was **deceived** by the serpent's cunning, your minds may somehow be led astray from your sincere and pure devotion to Christ* (2 Corinthians 11:3).

In some ways, because of your design, you have the tougher road in holding your spiritual ground. Knowing this, God holds men more responsible for their actions than He does women. Even though the Bible says that the woman sinned *first*, God held the man *responsible* for *headship*—it was actually *not* her sin but *his* sin that brought sin into the world. The woman was *deceived*, but the man *disobeyed* God. Paul spells this out for us in Romans 5:

✝ *Sin entered the world through one **man**, and death through sin, and in this way death came to all men, because all sinned* (Romans 5:12).

It is, therefore, important that you do not allow yourself to be deceived about what your real priorities are in life and marriage. Outer beauty and worldly pursuits should not be your primary goal; your spiritual development and obedience to God should be your focus. Peter writes:

✠ *Your beauty should not come from **outward** adornment, such as braided hair and the wearing of gold jewelry and fine clothes. Instead, it should be that of your **inner** self, the unfading beauty of a gentle and quiet spirit, which is of great worth in God's sight. For this is the way the holy women of the past who put their hope in God used to make themselves **beautiful**. They were submissive to their own husbands, like Sarah, who obeyed Abraham and called him her master. You are daughters if you do what is right and do not give way to fear* (1 Peter 3:3-6).

If you are an unmarried woman, remember that your most attractive quality to Christian men will be your inner beauty that shines God's love out of you. It is also important that a wife speaks God's life and word to her husband. The writer of Proverbs says:

✠ *She speaks with wisdom, and faithful instruction is on her tongue* (Proverbs 31:26).

## ACTION & VISUALIZATION

*Women, respect your God-given role in marriage.*

## MARRY A BELIEVER

If you are not currently married, then it is critical for you to only consider marrying another Christian. The Bible is clear on this point:

✠ *Do **not** be yoked together with unbelievers. For what do righteousness and wickedness have in common? Or what fellowship can light have with darkness? What harmony is there between Christ and Belial?*

*What does a believer have in common with an unbeliever? What agreement is there between the temple of God and idols? For we are the temple of the living God...* (2 Corinthians 6:14-16).

It is particularly important for a woman to have a believing husband because of his spiritual leadership in their marriage (as noted in the previous section). His submission to Christ should be your main concern if you want to enjoy a prosperous marriage. Indeed, it is through your husband that you and your family will obtain your spiritual covering in the battles that you are sure to face in this fallen world. Men, you need to marry a strong Christian girl who shows God's image and likeness from the inside out so that she will be your glory.

☦ *A wife of noble character is her husband's crown...* (Proverbs 12:4).

However, for wives who already are married to an unbelieving husband, the Bible offers the following course of action:

☦ *Wives, in the same way be submissive to your husbands so that, if any of them do not believe the word, they may be won over without words by the behavior of their wives, when they see the purity and reverence of your lives* (1 Peter 3:1-2).

## Staying the Course

Paul, who was not married, expressed his belief that those who did not get married could fully dedicate themselves to the Lord and His work. There is certainly great value in this truth. However, he also cautioned that, because of the weakness of the flesh to sexual sin, it is better in most cases to get married if you don't possess the God-given gift of celibacy. Due to our shared sexual weaknesses, Paul exhorts us to give our bodies exclusively to each other in marriage to eliminate the temptation for sexual or emotional satisfaction outside of this sacred union.

✞ *Now for the matters you wrote about: It is good for a man not to marry. But since there is so much immorality, each man should have his own wife, and each woman her own husband. The husband should fulfill his marital duty to his wife, and likewise the wife to her husband. The wife's body does not belong to her alone but **also to her husband**. In the same way, the husband's body* [including his ears and mouth] *does not belong to him alone but **also to his wife**. Do not deprive each other except by mutual consent and for a time, so that you may devote yourselves to prayer. Then come together again so that satan will not tempt you* [with inappropriate emotional or sexual relations] *because of your lack of self-control. I say this as a concession, not as a command. I wish that all men were as I am. But each man has his own gift from God; one has this gift, another has that* (1 Corinthians 7:1-7).

Today, primarily because of so many women entering the workplace, there is an epic shift in the way sexual infidelity is mutating before our eyes. Traditionally, for men, love is one thing and sex is…well, sex. Now, men as well as women are forming deep emotional attachments before they even slip into an extramarital bed together. It often happens as they work long hours together in the office. This kind of an affair, where emotional attachments are involved, is more likely to end in divorce, as it can bind two people together way beyond a sexual encounter.[4]

You need to be alert and careful in setting boundaries where you have extensive interaction with the opposite sex, whether it's at work, at church, or in any other setting. Be wise about the sharing of intimacy meant strictly for your spouse. Most affairs begin as seemingly honest, innocent conversations between two people that grow into inappropriate emotional attachments.

Paul in his discourse on marriage goes on to give other relevant advice on the subject:

✠ *Now to the unmarried and the widows I say: It is good for them to stay unmarried, as I am. But if they cannot control themselves, they should marry, for it is better to marry than to burn with passion.*

*To the married I give this command (not I, but the Lord): A wife must not separate from her husband. But if she does, she must remain unmarried or else be reconciled to her husband. And a husband must not divorce his wife.*

*To the rest I say this (I, not the Lord): If any brother has a wife who is not a believer and she is willing to live with him, he must not divorce her. And if a woman has a husband who is not a believer and he is willing to live with her, she must not divorce him. For the unbelieving husband has been sanctified through his wife, and the unbelieving wife has been sanctified through her believing husband. Otherwise your children would be unclean, but as it is, they are holy.*

*But if the unbeliever leaves, let him do so. A believing man or woman is not bound in such circumstances; God has called us to live in peace. How do you know, wife, whether you will save your husband? Or, how do you know, husband, whether you will save your wife?*

*Nevertheless, each one should retain the place in life that the Lord assigned to him and to which God has called him. This is the rule I lay down in all the churches* (1 Corinthians 7:8-17).

## MARRIAGE'S ULTIMATE PURPOSE

Marriage can benefit and bless us in many ways. But is marriage just about our comfort and happiness in this world, or is it about something greater? Does it have an eternal purpose?

Adam and Eve related to God in tandem, and in His image and likeness they exuded God's love into the world. Then came the fall. Man and woman became full of sin, and their perspectives were distorted by sin. Their focus became more on self—not on God and not on others. Marriage, from that point forward, would become difficult (at times). However, God embedded an opportunity in those difficulties.

Remember that within every wrong path that we choose to walk, God has embedded signs that point us back to Him. Marriage, though we have distorted it with sin, has the call of God embedded within its very nature. It reflects our intended relationship with Him—one of ultimate love, trust, and sacrifice, a holy union of two into one.

Because you are a fallen person who is married to a fallen spouse, marriage will at some point challenge your character in a profound way. My wife and I can certainly attest to this. Becoming successful at marriage requires you to become Christlike—to become forgiving, selfless, and serving (as she has learned and I am learning to be). You will face moments of "sink or swim" as you develop and strengthen your character through the exercise of marriage. It is a *molding* and *shaping* experience *if* you seek to do it as God instructs. The intensity of a close relationship 24-7 will exercise your *faith* and *heart*, because *selflessness* is a requirement for a healthy marriage relationship.

Our problem is that we have a selfish approach to marriage. That is to say that we want to know what we can get out of it. God meant marriage to be a place where we practice our relationship with Him. We need not worry about our needs getting met, but must focus instead on satisfying our spouse's needs (sowing seeds). Then and only then will we reap satisfaction in some surprising ways. Marriage gives us a real opportunity to practice subjecting our will to another's.

Throughout Scripture, our relationship with Christ is compared to a marriage, and earthly marriage is one main way that we make ourselves ready for our ultimate marriage with Him.

☩ ...*For the wedding of the Lamb has come, and His bride* [you and me] *has made herself ready* (Revelation 19:7).

A healthy earthly marriage will help prepare us for an eternal wedding, an everlasting union.

Most believers miss the eternal and spiritual benefits of marriage—the enhancing of their relationship with God while they are molded into a better person. Instead, most are merely seeking happiness or romance. We already know from Book 1 that happiness can't be maintained in this world because it is temporal. Likewise, our spouses will eventually make us unhappy. This puts too much weight on something temporal and will leave us susceptible to wanting a new spouse when the happiness in the current relationship can't be maintained any longer. If we are basing our marriage solely on happiness, then our marriage is doomed to fail.

And how about romance? How many times have we heard "there's no romance left in our marriage"? What are they saying? What exactly is romance anyway?

The tricky thing about romance is that it's subjective; it means different things to different people. Our definitions of romance also tend to *change* as we grow and mature. You will have problems in your marriage if it's based on movie-theater romance. Don't blame your lack of romance on your marriage partner (which is what the world does). Instead, if you want more romance in your marriage, plant seeds of romance. *Sow it!* The beautiful part of this concept is that you can sow the exact type of romance you desire. Just like sowing anything else, it may take some time for those seeds to grow, and you may suffer crop failure at times, but if you don't lose heart and if you keep on sowing, you will eventually reap a harvest. If you want romance in your marriage, it is *your* responsibility to create it.

Another problem with basing a marriage on romance is that, like happiness, it is only temporal. Some people attach that fluttering feeling of infatuation to romance. I have heard people suggest that this is the feeling of love that God gives us. In my case, I felt that toward more than one woman before I was married. Does that mean God wanted me to have more than one wife? Of course not. Indeed, I think we all have experienced, at some time, even after we were married, that same feeling toward someone else.

Does that mean that God wanted us to get a divorce and marry another person? Of course not. He says:

✠ *"I hate divorce," says the Lord God of Israel...* (Malachi 2:16).

What is that feeling that we get sometimes? In my case, this has happened less and less my marriage has matured and as I've grown closer to God. Perhaps it is simply a warning system, much like when you start moving your hand close to a fire and it begins to get warm, signaling you to be cautious about your approach. I am not suggesting that this feeling is always a warning away from someone at the first signs of attraction. What I am saying is that, because there is a natural attraction to a particular person, which could lead to desire, God has provided a warning system for us.

If you are single, approach carefully and be alert; don't let yourself fall into temptation. If you are married, stop and reverse course. If you live as if this concept is true, then you will be better off. It is certainly true that such romantic feelings will not sustain a marriage. Just like fear, which can momentarily be an exciting feeling for those who like roller coasters or scary movies, trying to sustain these romantic feelings will be unsatisfying and ultimately impossible to sustain—a long-term healthy marriage requires *choosing to love the other even through difficult circumstances.*

The marriage relationship is built on love, not love that is a feeling, but love that is a decision to serve the other, a decision to sow ourselves into the relationship with steadfast *perseverance* as we deal with the inevitable ups and downs of a shared life between two imperfect people.

✠ *Therefore encourage one another and build each other up...* (1 Thessalonians 5:11).

✠ *May the Lord direct your hearts into God's love and Christ's perseverance* (2 Thessalonians 3:5).

To err is human, but to forgive is the nature of God; a happy marriage is the union of two good forgivers operating in the Spirit of God. That Spirit also leads us into servanthood and putting the other first:

*Don't push your way to the front; don't sweet-talk your way to the top. Put yourself aside, and help others get ahead. Don't be obsessed with getting your own advantage. Forget yourselves long enough to lend a helping hand. Think of yourselves the way Christ Jesus thought of himself* (Philippians 2:3-5 MSG).

What was the nature of Jesus? He had a servant's attitude, washing the feet of His disciples, including the one who would betray Him. Jesus died for us while we were still sinners so that He could have an eternal relationship with us. Your spouse is also a sinner, and you will have to die to yourself at times so that you can bring life to the relationship.

This death to ourselves allows us to enter and take possession of our Promised Land. Christians must be obedient and commit to their marriage vows, which are made before God, by acting selflessly in love. Indeed, Jesus says that we are to love our enemies, so we are certainly to love our spouses too (see Matthew 5:44). No matter how wonderful your spouse is, he or she is still infected with sin, which will lead to selfish actions at times. This will stretch your ability to love—and that is a good thing.

## ACTION & VISUALIZATION

*Take every opportunity to approach your spouse in a selfless, serving way.*

## UNTIL DEATH DO YOU PART

God holds the marriage union between two believers as sacred. In times of trouble, remember that God does not want you to divorce and change to another spouse. Most likely, He wants you to *change yourself and trust in Him*; this puts your faith into action, and it will eventually change the spouse you already have. It is through marriage that you, your spouse, and your children will find life and freedom to the fullest.

Satan brings chaos into our world, and he will try everything he can to tear you away from your marriage union through fleshly and emotional temptations, as well as through pride. You must remain focused on wholeheartedly giving yourself to your marriage. Don't let the enemy distract or discourage you. For good reason, God sets a high goal for you to stand by:

✠ *Some Pharisees came and tested [Jesus] by asking, "Is it lawful for a man to divorce his wife?"*

*"What did Moses command you?" He replied.*

*They said, "Moses permitted a man to write a certificate of divorce and send her away."*

*"It was because your hearts were hard that Moses wrote you this law," Jesus replied. "But at the beginning of creation God 'made them male and female.' 'For this reason a man will leave his father and mother and be united to his wife, and the two will become one flesh.' So they are no longer two, but one. Therefore what God has joined together, let man **not** separate."*

*When they were in the house again, the disciples asked Jesus about this. He answered, "Anyone who divorces his wife and marries another woman commits adultery against her. And if she divorces her husband and marries another man, she commits adultery"* (Mark 10:2-12).

The sanctity of marriage is important to God. But what if you fail? This does not mean that you lose your eternal salvation. However, it does mean that you will not have the most abundant life possible while on earth. Holding on to your relationship may involve fighting in spiritual warfare and pulling down strongholds. It might mean swallowing your pride or seeing your faith tested beyond what you ever expected. If you are with an abusive spouse, healing and your safety may require time apart. A successful marriage will involve much prayer and trust in God. It will often involve offering forgiveness. And it will always require actions of faith to last until "death do you part."

If you are divorced, you shouldn't lose heart. God may hate divorce, but He loves those who have been through divorce. He offers you forgiveness and hope.

## ACTION & VISUALIZATION

*Respect and honor your marriage. Base it on obedience*
*to God so that it will stand the unavoidable storms.*

## MARRIAGE BENEFITS YOUR CHILDREN

God created the relationship of marriage not only for your benefit but also for the benefit of your children. God's plan was that children would have both a father and a mother through whom they would experience the attributes of God. Divorce, therefore, distorts children's perception of God. God holds both parents responsible for providing for, nurturing, training, and sculpting their children, because it takes both parents to fully complete the job in the way that God intends. Statistics show us that a break-up in a marriage causes a breakdown in the fulfillment of these God-given responsibilities. The results show that their children will not be as likely to fulfill their purpose. In fact, a study shows that 75 percent of youth suicides are from homes where a parent has been absent.[5]

One study shows that children of divorce are *twice* as likely to drop out of school, *three* times as likely to have babies out of wedlock, *five* times more likely to be in poverty, and *twelve* times more apt to become incarcerated.[6]

## Teach Your Children

Of course, there's more to good parenting than simply avoiding divorce. Listen to what the Word of God has to say about our responsibility as parents. The Bible says that training your children will produce a good result, even though it may not seem so at the time:

✠ *Train a child in the way he should go, and when he is old he will not turn from it* (Proverbs 22:6).

A parent is responsible to know, believe, and implement God's Word. And parents must also teach God's Word to their children:

✠ *Fix these words of Mine in your hearts and minds; tie them as symbols on your hands and bind them on your foreheads.* **Teach them to your children***, talking about them when you sit at home and when you walk along the road, when you lie down and when you get up. Write them on the doorframes of your houses and on your gates, so that your days and the days of your children may be many in the land that the Lord swore to give your forefathers, as many as the days that the heavens are above the earth* (Deuteronomy 11:18-21).

God promises that, if you know and live according to God's Word, then your children will be blessed:

✠ *The righteous man leads a blameless life; blessed are his children after him* (Proverbs 20:7).

We are also told to teach our children about the blessings and miracles that God has done in our lives and in the lives of those who went before us:

✠ *Only be careful, and watch yourselves closely so that you do not forget the things your eyes have seen or let them slip from your heart as long as you live. **Teach them to your children and to their children after them*** (Deuteronomy 4:9).

✠ *In days to come, when your son asks you, "What does this mean?" say to him, "With a mighty hand the Lord brought us out of Egypt, out of the land of slavery. When Pharaoh stubbornly refused to let us go, the Lord killed every firstborn in Egypt, both man and animal. This is why I sacrifice to the Lord the first male offspring of every womb and redeem each of my firstborn sons." And it will be like a sign on your hand and a symbol on your forehead that the Lord brought us out of Egypt with His mighty hand* (Exodus 13:14-16).

## Action & Visualization
*Teach and train your children in the ways of God.*

## Discipline Your Children

We are also encouraged to discipline our children so that they will learn God's ways and choose to follow Him.

✠ *Do not withhold discipline from a child; if you punish him with the rod, he will not die. Punish him with the rod and save his soul from death* (Proverbs 23:13-14).

✠ *Discipline your children while you still have the chance; indulging them destroys them* (Proverbs 19:18 MSG).

✠ *Folly is bound up in the heart of a child, but the rod of discipline will drive it far from him* (Proverbs 22:15).

✠ *A refusal to correct is a refusal to love; love your children by disciplining them* (Proverbs 13:24 MSG).

✠ *Discipline your son, and he will give you peace; he will bring delight to your soul* (Proverbs 29:17).

To be effective, discipline *must* be applied in *love* with peace, patience, kindness, goodness, faithfulness, gentleness, and self-control. Discipline applied in any other way can be damaging to both your relationship with your child as well as your child's relationship with God and others.

## ACTION & VISUALIZATION

*Only discipline your children in love.*

## HONOR YOUR PARENTS

Finally, God wants us to respect our parents (even as adults):

✠ *Listen, my son, to your father's instruction and do not forsake your mother's teaching. They will be a garland to grace your head and a chain to adorn your neck* (Proverbs 1:8-9).

✠ *A wise son brings joy to his father, but a foolish man despises his mother* (Proverbs 15:20).

Even if your parents were not good parents because of the sin and self-focus of their own lives, you still can (and should) honor them and show them God's love. The fifth commandment promises long life and blessings for those who honor their father and mother:

✜ *Honor your father and your mother, as the Lord your God has commanded you, so that you may live long and that it may go well with you in the land the Lord your God is giving you* (Deuteronomy 5:16).

To those without parents or who were forsaken by them, God offers this comforting promise to you:

✜ *Though my father and mother forsake me, the Lord will receive me* (Psalm 27:10).

✜ *...You [God] are the helper of the fatherless* (Psalm 10:14).

## RELATIONSHIPS ARE A PRIORITY

Establishing good relationships in life is your highest priority—your relationship with God being your highest. It's a given that each relationship will take time and effort to properly develop and maintain. This leads us to ask *how* we do this and everything else when twenty-four hours doesn't seem to be enough time in a day.

Consider this story: A teacher stood before his class one day with some items in a box on his desk. He began by picking out of the box a large glass mayonnaise jar, and he proceeded to fill it with golf balls. He then asked the students if the jar was full. They agreed that it was full. The teacher then picked out of the box a container of pebbles and poured them into the jar. He lightly shook the jar. The pebbles rolled into the open areas between the golf balls. He then asked the students again if the jar was full. They agreed it was full.

The teacher next picked out of the box a bag of sand and poured it into the jar. Of course, the sand filled up everything else. He asked the students once more if the jar was full. At this point, perplexed, the students agreed. The teacher reached one more time into the box and pulled out a bottle of wine and proceeded to empty it into the jar, effectively filling the empty spaces between the grains of sand. The students were amazed.

"Now," the teacher said, "the jar represents your life and the golf balls all your important relationships—with God, your spouse, your children, your family, your friends, and yourself (your physical, mental, and spiritual health). So if everything else in life was lost and these things remained, your life would still be full. The pebbles are the other things important to you, like your ministry, your job, and your favorite passions. The sand represents everything else in life—your possessions and everything else you do.

"If you put the sand or pebbles in the jar first, then there is no room for the golf balls. The same is true in life. If you spend all your time and energy on your ministry, your job, your pastimes, etc., then you will never have time for the developing of the things most important to you—your *relationships*. You need to set your priorities in life from the beginning, filling your life with good relationships by paying attention to and dealing with the small things required to maintain and develop each one of those relationships."

A student then asked, "What does the wine represent?"

The teacher responded, "The wine represents having Christ in everything so that you can have joy in everything you do because you are doing it in the freedom of His blood."

I terribly wish I had understood this analogy early in my life. For once you fill up your jar with the wrong things, you will find life very unsatisfying, because nothing else fits. You will also find it more difficult to change the contents of your life once it is already full. Of course, the part of your life that has gone by and the opportunities it represents can never be brought back, so start now to set your priorities straight.

God offers us freedom and blessings in earthly relationships if we receive, unwrap, and use them the way God intended. The gift of relationship is worth the time, effort, and energy that relationships take to nurture and grow. Unwrap this special gift and invest your life in those whom God has placed into your story.

## ACTION & VISUALIZATION

*Take full advantage of the relational gifts that God offers you.*

✦ *It was just before the Passover Feast. Jesus knew the time had come for Him to leave this world and go to the Father. Having loved His own who were in the world, He now showed them the **full extent** of His love* (John 13:1).

Go out and show the full extent of your love to the people God gives you, just as Jesus did.

## Meditation Point

God offers and encourages us to lean on healthy relationships amid struggles.

If you are married or planning on getting married, I recommend further reading on this subject. Here are a few books to consider: *Sacred Marriage* by Gary Thomas; *Making Love Last Forever* by Gary Smalley; *The Five Love Languages: How to Express Heartfelt Commitment to Your Mate* by Gary Chapman; *Every Man's Marriage: An Every Man's Guide to Winning the Heart of a Woman* by Stephen Arterburn, Mike Yorkey, and Fred Stoeker; and *The Act of Marriage* by Tim and Beverly LaHaye.

Go to Chapter 5 in the Study Guide section on page 967.

# ENDNOTES

1.  *Consumer Expenditure Survey* (US Department of Labor conducted 1990–92 updated to 2001 dollars using the Consumer Price Index), www.moneycentral.msn.com/articles/family/kids/tlkidscost.asp.

2.  Hara Estroff Marano, "The New Sex Score Card," *Psychology Today* (July/August 2003).

3.  Ibid.

4.  Ibid.

5.  Jean Beth Eshtain, "Family Matters: The Plight of America's Children," *The Christian Century* (July 1993), 14–21.

6.  Judith Wallerstein, Julia Lewis, Sandra Blakesley, *The Unexpected Legacy of Divorce: A 25 Year Landmark Study* (New York, NY: Hyperion, 2000).

# Chapter 6

# GIFT #11—YOUR DESTINY

## HOW DO YOU FIND YOUR DESTINY?

Before you begin to read, pray that the Holy Spirit will give you
and all readers of this book understanding and application.

✝ *My frame was not hidden from You [God] when I was made in the
secret place. When I was woven together in the depths of the earth,
Your eyes saw my unformed body. All the days ordained for me were
written in Your book before one of them came to be (Psalm 139:15-16).*

✝ *So will it be with the resurrection of the dead. The body that is sown
is perishable [our current bodies], it is raised imperishable [our new
heavenly bodies]; it is sown in dishonor, it is raised in glory; it is sown
in weakness, it is raised in power; it is sown a natural body, it is raised
a spiritual body...* (1 Corinthians 15:42-44).

If you've ever traveled around Christmas season, you know how challenging a trip to the airport can be. There's the drive to the terminal, the
hunt for a parking spot, long lines at check-in, luggage to cart around,
airport security, crying babies, disgruntled passengers, and lots and lots of
waiting. Of course, that's if everything goes smoothly. So why do we put

ourselves through such torture year after year? We endure this hardship because there's something on the other side of the chaos, the discomfort, the challenges, and the long lines. We've planned and prepared to reach a goal, a destiny—typically, it's a Christmas reunion with family and loved ones.

Our pursuit of our earthly destiny as followers of Christ is similar. However, many believers are content to sit at home for the holidays—they're content to make a phone call or send an e-mail. But if they don't make that flight, they'll miss the wonder and fulfillment of face-to-face communication! They'll miss the joy that is on the other side of this important journey. This chapter is for those who truly want to take flight.

*Webster's New World Dictionary* defines *destiny* as "the seemingly inevitable succession of events or [one's] fate." The question many of us wonder about is, Who decides our destiny: God, us, or chance? This is the profound question we will explore in this chapter. This is a question the greatest minds have sought to answer. When considering this question, it is interesting to note that in Hebrew there is no word for coincidence.

## Two Destinies

God offers us two destinies that we can receive, unwrap, and use. The first verse of this chapter speaks to our *earthly* destiny, and the second to our *eternal* destiny. Our eternal destiny is received and unwrapped when we accept the gift of eternal life. However, the full experience of our eternal destiny will not be realized until Jesus' return. We will explore in this chapter the other destiny that God offers is the one we have in this world of chances, where "in the beginning" man's decision to put his will above God's opened Pandora's Box. Once opened, this box released sin, which goes against the will of God, resulting in an infected world:

✝ *The creation waits in eager expectation for the sons of God* [born-again believers] *to be revealed. For the creation was subjected to frustration, not by its own choice, but by the will of the one who subjected it, in hope that the creation itself will be liberated from its bondage to decay and brought into the glorious freedom of the children of God.*

*We know that the whole creation has been **groaning** as in the pains of childbirth right up to the present time. Not only so, but we ourselves, who have the firstfruits of the Spirit, groan inwardly as we wait eagerly for the adoption as sons, the redemption of our bodies* (Romans 8:19-23).

While we await the full manifestation of this eternal destiny, God offers each of us a unique and specific destiny. Jesus had a destiny that He could embrace or reject when He came to earth; likewise, we each have a unique destiny for which God made us—we too can embrace or reject it.

✦ *Listen to Me* [Jesus said prophetically through Isaiah], *you islands; hear this, you distant nations: Before I was born the Lord called Me; from My birth He has made mention of My name. He made My mouth like a sharpened sword, in the shadow of His hand He hid Me; He made Me into a polished arrow and concealed Me in His quiver* (Isaiah 49:1-2).

Jesus knew His destiny and offered His followers a life with purpose too. Have you ever considered God's destiny for your life? What plans has He laid out for you individually? You were designed to be a sharp arrow in God's quiver, crafted by Him for a specific purpose; however, because God gave you the freedom of choice, you can choose to be used by Him or not. The truth is that God has embedded within you what you will need to complete that destiny *with* Him. You can't achieve your destiny alone. From this day forward, you will be faced with a choice: will you choose to live out your destiny or deny it?

## Your Destiny on Earth

Receiving, unwrapping, and using the gift of your earthly destiny is a lifelong process. And it is this gift that all the other gifts work toward. They all work in conjunction with each other to enable you to fulfill your God-given destiny. Without receiving, unwrapping, and using the other gifts, you cannot fully unwrap and use your gift of destiny.

You can choose to follow God's will, as Jesus did, or you can be distracted by the desires of your flesh. If you choose the latter, you will be on your own in a world of chance. You will be left to your own devices, and you will miss out on God's *perfect plan* for your life. If you only opened the gift of life (salvation) and not the gift of destiny, God will still be in you, but you won't know the fullness or abundance of the earthly life that He offers those who die to self and follow His will. It is in this abundant life (the manifestation of your earthly destiny) that you will find *true fulfillment*, regardless of the circumstances you encounter.

The apostle Paul and others in the Bible spoke about this sort of life. When you give yourself over to God's plan, your life becomes inevitable. Hear what the Bible says toward this end:

✠ *For we are God's workmanship, created in Christ Jesus to good works, which God prepared in advance for us to do* (Ephesians 2:10).

✠ *He who began a good work in you will carry it on to completion until the day of Christ Jesus* (Philippians 1:6).

✠ *Many are the plans in a man's heart, but it is the Lord's purpose that prevails* (Proverbs 19:21).

✦ *The Lord will fulfill His purpose for me; Your love, O Lord, endures forever—do not abandon the works of Your hands* (Psalm 138:8).

✦ *This is what the Lord says—He who made you, who formed you in the womb, and who will help you: Do not be afraid, O Jacob, my servant, Jeshurun, whom I have chosen* (Isaiah 44:2).

✦ *I know that You* [God] *can do all things; no plan of Yours can be thwarted* (Job 42:2).

✦ [God] *will not let your foot slip—He who watches over you will not slumber* (Psalm 121:3).

✦ *I cry out to God Most High, to God, who fulfills His purpose for me. He sends from heaven and saves me, rebuking those who hotly pursue me; God sends His love and His faithfulness* (Psalm 57:2-3).

✦ *In his heart a man plans his course, but the Lord determines his steps* (Proverbs 16:9).

✦ *A man's steps are directed by the Lord. How then can anyone understand his own way* (Proverbs 20:24).

For those who decide to answer God's call, Paul raises an important question to which we need to know the correct answer and have full confidence in the answer as we grab hold of God plan for our lives:

☩ *And those [God] predestined, He also called; those He called, He also justified; those He justified, He also glorified. What, then, shall we say in response to this? If God is for us, who can be against us? (Romans 8:30-31).*

Fully believing this will allow you to be bold and travel down the path of your destiny.

## ACTION & VISUALIZATION

*Have faith that God can deliver to you the destiny He offers you.*

## GO WITH THE FLOW

Your earthly life is like a river, and your destiny in life should be to go within the flow of that river to its intended end. At the center of the river, the water flows at a faster pace; at its sides, the water flows slower and slower as you get closer to the edge. You can try to fight the currents and swim upstream, but this will only tire you out, and you will have little fulfillment to show for much effort. Or you can choose to swim through your life downstream, either in the middle where the current is strong, or by the bank where it's weaker.

If you choose the sides of the river, you may have some semblance of control in your progress and direction, but if you choose to find the center of God's will—your destiny—then He will take you for an unbelievable ride in His power. The ride in the strongest currents won't be easy, and it will be scary at times, especially when you face challenges that bounce you around on the rapids; however, it will be the most exhilarating and fulfilling life possible. God desires for us to choose the strongest current and then, letting go, to give our direction over to Him so that we can experience the excitement of the life He desires for us.

When you do this, you will know deep inside the progress that you are making toward your destiny, even in adversity and trials. Living out your destiny is God's will for your life—at the center of the river of life.

As you find the strong current, you will know more and more that God is working in and through you in a progressive way. Our lives can be powered in supernatural ways by the strongest current, which is destiny. You must be a consummate seeker, always searching for the center, because it is so easy to slip into idle habits or to succumb to fears, fleshly desires, and the demands of life that take you back to the sides of the river. You must consciously reprogram your thinking and actions. Once your earthly destiny is offered to you, it will take your persistent faith to fully manifest it. So if you always seek God's will for your life and continue to receive, unwrap, and use all of the Gifts of Freedom, then you will find your way to the center of the river.

## TRUE FULFILLMENT

Once you set out on God's journey, He will be there to encourage you when you run into troubles. As you know, the apostle Paul had a challenging destiny to fulfill, but he came to understand his purpose and kept the end in sight:

⸙ *You've all been to the stadium and seen the athletes race. Everyone runs; one wins. Run to win. All good athletes train hard. They do it for a gold medal that tarnishes and fades. You're after one that's gold eternally. I don't know about you, but I'm running hard for the finish line. I'm giving it everything I've got. No sloppy living for me! I'm staying alert and in top condition. I'm not going to get caught napping, telling everyone else all about it and then missing out myself* (1 Corinthians 9:24-27 MSG).

⸙ *Therefore, since we are surrounded by such a great cloud of witnesses* [on earth and in the spiritual realm], *let us throw off everything that hinders and the sin that so easily entangles, and let us run with*

*perseverance the race **marked out for us** [the destiny God offers us].
Let us fix our eyes on Jesus, the author and perfecter of our faith, who
for the joy set before Him endured the cross, scorning its shame, and
sat down at the right hand of the throne of God. Consider Him who
endured such opposition from sinful man, so that you will not grow
weary and lose heart.*

*In your struggle against sin, you have not yet resisted to the point
of shedding your blood* (Hebrews 12:1-4).

The writer of Hebrews goes on to say that we should see the hardships
we encounter in life as a necessary part of moving us from where we are
into our destiny. He then directs us to find God's path to avoid danger and
to receive healing instead:

✠ *Therefore, strengthen your feeble arms and weak knees. "Make level
paths for your feet," so that the lame may not be disabled, but rather
healed* (Hebrews 12:12-13).

Look at how he concludes, exhorting us to have confidence in our final,
eternal destination:

✠ *You have come to Mount Zion, to the heavenly Jerusalem, the city of
the living God. You have come to thousands upon thousands of angels
in joyful assembly, to the church of the firstborn [Jesus], whose names
are written in heaven. You have come to God, the judge of all men,
to the spirits of righteous men made perfect, to Jesus the mediator
[between us and God] of a new covenant, and to the sprinkled blood
[of Jesus] that speaks a better word than the blood of Abel.*

*...If they did not escape when they refused Him who warned
them on earth, how much less will we, if we turn away from Him who
warns us from heaven? At that time His voice shook the earth [in the*

day of Moses], *but now He has promised, "Once more I will shake not only the earth but also the heavens." The words "once more" indicate the removing of what can be shaken—that is, created things—so that what cannot be shaken may remain* [our eventual home will only consist of that which is eternal].

*Therefore, since we are receiving a kingdom that cannot be shaken* [even while on earth, by obeying the Word, we build our house on the unshakable solid rock], *let us be thankful, and so worship God acceptably with reverence and awe, for our "**God is a consuming fire**"* (Hebrews 12:22-29).

Paul had an intimate relationship with God, so when he encountered situations that appeared to be setbacks, his intimate relationship with God was vital and encouraging.

✝ *Last night an angel of the God whose I am and whom I serve stood beside me and said, "Do not be afraid, Paul. You must stand trial before Caesar; and God has graciously given you the lives of all who sail with you"* (Acts 27:23-24).

As I've already mentioned, Paul had many ups and downs in life; he had bouts with satan and his flesh that he didn't always seem to win. But in his second letter to Timothy, Paul wrote about the satisfaction and fulfillment that he had in living out his story as God had written it:

✝ *For I am already being poured out like a drink offering, and the time has come for my departure* [physical death]. *I have fought the good fight, I have finished the race, I have kept the faith. Now there is in store for me the crown of righteousness, which the Lord, the righteous Judge, will award to me on that day—and not only to me, but also to all who have longed for His appearing* (2 Timothy 4:6-8).

Paul was an ordinary human with all the frailties that you and I experience. Yet he still encourages us through the trials of life to keep our eyes fixed on Jesus, who is the author and finisher of our faith, *not* on our present circumstances. Clearly, we should not count on our own strength or brilliance to win this race:

✠ *The race is not to the swift or the battle to the strong, nor does food come to the wise or wealth to the brilliant or favor to the learned; but time and chance happen to them all* (Ecclesiastes 9:11).

## Action & Visualization

*Despite trying circumstances, let God be in control of fulfilling your destiny.*

## Keep the End in Sight

Our success at living out God's will is dependent on our faith, and, specifically, on our ability to exercise it to the maximum while keeping our earthly and eternal destinies in sight. If you wore a blindfold and were told to walk in a long, straight line to a location that was far away, you'd probably end up walking in circles because you are imperfect. One of your legs is stronger than the other, and that would cause you, over time, to stray from walking the straight line. To get to our destination, we need to keep our destinies locked in sight, always pressing on toward our goal and adjusting when our weaknesses try to pull us off course.

What happens if we lose our focus? The problems and pleasures of our earthly life will turn us every which way until we are completely lost. Pride will also turn us away from God's destiny:

✠ *We all, like sheep, have gone astray, each of us has turned to his own way...* (Isaiah 53:6).

✠ *The seed cast in the weeds is the person who hears the kingdom news, but weeds of worry and illusions about getting more and wanting everything under the sun strangle what was heard, and nothing comes of it* (Matthew 13:22 MSG).

✠ *For everything in the world—the cravings of sinful man, the lust of his eyes and the boasting of what he has and does—comes not from the Father but from the world* (1 John 2:16).

✠ *Pride goes before destruction* [of your life and destiny]... (Proverbs 16:18).

When you are experiencing the same thing over and over in your life, it's time to consider whether you're moving in circles rather than truly moving toward your destiny. Taking our eyes off God leads us to a self-focused life that lacks purpose and direction. We should not confuse what we believe our destiny should be with what God says it is to be. Of course, knowing the difference isn't always easy. How do we know with certainty that we're hearing Him correctly? How do we find the powerful current that He created at the center of the river, at the center of His will?

## ACTION & VISUALIZATION
*Keep your destiny in sight so that you don't drift off course or make unnecessary circles.*

## Finding the Path

God wants us to live our lives through Him. God Himself unfolds His will for us, but it is our job to continually seek that developing path.

✟ *This is what the Lord says: "Stand at the crossroads and* **look; ask** *for the ancient paths,* **ask where the good way is,** *and walk in it..."* (Jeremiah 6:16).

Like the psalmist, you must ask for and seek out God's assistance to keep your focus. The psalmist prayed:

✟ *Turn my eyes away from worthless things; preserve my life according to Your word* (Psalm 119:37).

Your growing relationship with God is the context in which He begins to unfold your destiny.

✟ *Whether you turn to the right or to the left, your ears will hear a voice behind you saying, "This is the way; walk in it"* (Isaiah 30:21).

✟ *But eagerly desire the* **greater gifts**. *And now I will show you the most excellent way* (1 Corinthians 12:31).

It's all about God in you and you in Him, as well as receiving, unwrapping, and using all the Gifts of Freedom to find growth in your relationship and communication with Him. This allows you to receive and manifest your God-given destiny directly from Him:

✠ *You [God] have made known to me the path of life…* (Psalm 16:11).

✠ *As for God, His way is perfect…* (2 Samuel 22:31).

For many years, I was stuck on the bank of the river. I was not only spiritually dead, but I was recklessly headed for physical death. I had an addiction to alcohol, to many different drugs, to the earthly pleasures of life, and to extreme living. Even in high school, my friends had a running bet that I wouldn't live to see my twenty-first birthday. So when I turned twenty-one, it only encouraged me to test fate with even harder living—it seemed that I could go beyond the edge.

However, God clearly had other plans for my life. He held my destiny out for me when I was ready to receive, unwrap, and use it. As we have read, God has long-suffering patience, and this was certainly true in how He related to me. He waited for me to get into the river. I did not live for God for the first thirty-six years of my life. Indeed, I was involved in a wide range of sin, including the murder of my unborn child. Yes, God was patient with me as He watched me choose to waste away day after day. Even as a father and a husband, I did not deserve or qualify to enter the river in any way. (None of us qualify, by the way. This is what God's grace is all about.)

How then did I get into the river? One day I simply decided to seek God. I said yes to a relationship with Him. That day in church, God became real to me. I did not know how or why God did it that morning—I can only describe my experience as supernatural. My life had radically changed. I was now in the river.

✠ [Jesus said], ***"On that day you will realize*** *that I am in My Father, and you are in Me, and I am in you"* (John 14:20).

Even though I was in the river and my heart had changed, I still had *my mind* dwelling on the places *I* wanted to go. I still had *my* pride and *my* old selfish habits. I thought, "Surely now that I'm a Christian, Jesus will help me accomplish *my* goals and dreams in life." I didn't understand that God does not fill us with His power to help us accomplish *our* goals, but to fulfill *His* goals for our lives. And, in so doing, we assist others whom God puts in our path in living out the life God desires for them as well.

For years after I was saved, I tried swimming upstream! As you can imagine, I eventually grew tired. However, as I tired, I eventually started receiving, unwrapping, and using the additional Gifts of Freedom. These gifts brought me into a closer relationship with God. This close relationship enabled intimacy with God—communication with Him in my daily life that led to a better understanding of His power, His will, and what it looked like to live out my God-given destiny.

I eventually stopped swimming upstream and started letting His current carry me. Initially, I stayed close to the riverbank so that I could keep some control. (It's hard to let go of control when you're used to being "in control.") Little by little, I learned how to swim out into the current for a while. I continued growing closer to God. I started trusting and surrendering my work, my family, my finances, my relationships, and my future to God. Consequently, I moved closer to the center of the river where the rapids were faster and much more powerful.

Now it's important to note that as I was getting closer to the center of the river, it became harder for me to accomplish *my* goals because the current often took me in another direction. At the same time, however, God was putting new desires in my heart. I realized that I needed to let go of *my goals* and find His will; I needed to relax and start *going with the flow—His flow.*

When I did this, life started falling into place. In some ways, it became easier, but *not* any less scary. In fact, the ride started getting more thrilling and exciting because I had to navigate by faith and *not* by sight. New and unfamiliar obstacles and challenges were coming at me faster all the time. The stakes became higher and higher, so now, clearly, I had a lot to talk to

God about in the midst of all the excitement and obstacles that came my way. *I grew in intimacy with God.*

I learned that, as I got closer to the center of God's will, I could only navigate by letting go. Also, the farther from the center I was, the harder it was to see my destiny. However, as I found the center of the river, it was generally easier to see farther down the river to my earthly goals. I became better at navigating down the center of the river. It was all about surrendering control of my life through receiving, unwrapping, and using the Gifts of Freedom. As I became more successful at this, I began moving at full force—centered within God's will.

## ACTION & VISUALIZATION

*Receive, unwrap, and use the Gifts of Freedom while seeking your earthly destiny. Think about how you will use each gift to find your earthly destiny.*

## EXPECT THE UNEXPECTED

Then, out of nowhere, came this book series. The idea of writing a book never even crossed my mind. I wasn't a qualified writer. If you talked to people who know me, they'd tell you that I'm not a writer. Could I write an entire series of books? "Highly unlikely," or "Impossible," they might say. It is not something I dreamed of doing or something I had the knowledge or ability to do. I am actually a very poor writer. In fact, in my business, I prefer to communicate by e-mail whenever I can (and when I do write letters, I have my assistant or administrator draft or at least edit them).

When I began writing, however, I didn't have the spiritual insight or knowledge to write. And yet, as I began writing the chapters, I was amazed at what my hand was putting on the page. The more I wrote, the more the books took shape, the more inevitable they became, and the closer I came to God. I was *receiving* His gift of destiny in the very work of writing this book.

I became a consistent seeker of God and a constant finder of Him as I walked and worked out my own story. When I first began writing, I was far from perfect, but I was a seeker—I had a heart for God. I thought that's why God had given them to me. When I arrived at this chapter, it became clear that my consummate seeking had helped me *find* my destiny—the center of the river.

However, it was also clear that the privilege of writing these books was *not* something that I earned or deserved as a result of my seeking; it was simply my destiny—God's choice, and only He knows the reason. *A gift!* Indeed, a *surprise* gift that I found in the center of my river. There will certainly be a *surprise* for you too when you find the center of your river. In fact, God's gift of your destiny will have *many* surprises in it.

The greatest joy that God offers us through His gifts is that they keep on giving. For example, these books hold a battle plan that I can continue to strive toward and conform my life to. Let me be clear: I may have written this book, but I am *not* fully living it in all areas of my life. I can tell you that successfully living out what I have written is a far greater task than writing it. Though, when I let go and relax in quiet and stillness before God, He helps me conform. God will help you conform too. Remember that life is a journey; you don't automatically get to your destination just because you decide to go somewhere. It takes a persistent pursuit in faith to be successful at conforming yourself in such a way as to be able to find God's will for your life. The apostle Paul said it this way:

✠ *I plead with you to give your bodies to God because of all He has done for you. Let them be a living and holy sacrifice—the kind He will find acceptable. This is truly the way to worship Him. Don't copy the behavior and customs of this world, but let God transform you into a new person by changing the way you think.* **Then you will learn to know God's will for you**, *which is good and pleasing and perfect* (Romans 12:1-2 NLT).

## GETTING ON AND LETTING GO

Getting on the road toward your destiny is not easy because it takes faith. It is by the Spirit that we receive the gifts, and it is by faith that we unwrap and use all of them. The same is true with our gift of earthly destiny too—we receive God's will by the Spirit of God and unwrap it by faith. In order to go on a trip to the Grand Canyon, you would need to use your faith to plan, pack, and check the car. Once you are on the road, you will run into challenges that your faith can help you overcome. In the pursuit of your earthly destiny, you'll find that the devil may even challenge you. Only your *intimate relationship* with God will allow you to resist the enemy's attempt to pull you off the path to your destiny:

✝ *With flattery he* [the enemy] *will corrupt those who have violated the covenant, but the people who* **know** *their God will firmly* **resist** *him* (Daniel 11:32).

✝ *I* **know** *whom I have believed and* [therefore] *am persuaded that He is able to keep what I have committed to Him until that day* (2 Timothy 1:12 NKJV).

The world will also try to lead you off your road. Again, your *intimate relationship* with God and your ability to allow the Holy Spirit to lead you down the right path are the keys to finding your destiny:

✝ *Enter through the narrow gate* [you start by doing something that may be difficult in the physical realm—walking in the Spirit]. *For wide is the gate and broad is the road that leads to destruction* [living life in the flesh and mind], *and many enter through it. But small is the gate and narrow the road that leads to life, and only a few find it* (Matthew 7:13-14).

On the right road to your destiny is also where you will find your abundant life:

✠ [God's] *paths drip with abundance* (Psalm 65:11 NKJV).

When you're living an abundant life, you will walk out the destiny God offers you, one in which you will seek His will above all else. Your will must die to make room for His will in your life:

✠ *Foolish one, what you sow is not made alive unless it dies* (1 Corinthians 15:36 NKJV).

## Jesus' Example

Just as we all have a specific, God-offered destiny, so Jesus had one as well. His destiny was to come to earth as a man and die for our sins:

✠ *All that the Father gives Me will come to Me, and whoever comes to Me I will never drive away. For I have come down from heaven not to do My will but to do the will of Him who sent Me. And this is the will of Him who sent Me, that I shall lose none of all that He has given Me, but raise them up at the last day. For My Father's will is that everyone who looks to the Son and believes in Him shall have eternal life, and I will raise him up at the last day* (John 6:37-40).

Receiving your destiny requires a great action of faith. In Jesus' case, this act of faith was unto death. Walking out this brutal death was not easy for Jesus. He asked His Father three times if He could follow a different path to fulfill His destiny:

✠ [Jesus] *went away a second time and prayed, "My Father, if it is not possible for this cup to be taken away unless I drink it, may Your will be done."*

*When He came back, He again found them sleeping, because their eyes were heavy. So He left them and went away once more and prayed the* **third** *time, saying the same thing* (Matthew 26:42-44).

There will be times when you need to pray for strength to help you move forward to fulfill your destiny, and there will be times when you will ask Him if there is another way, another path to take. God will encourage and strengthen you, just as He did His Son:

✠ *An angel from heaven appeared to* [Jesus] *and strengthened Him. And being in anguish, He prayed more earnestly, and His sweat was like drops of blood falling to the ground* (Luke 22:43-44).

Clearly, Jesus was wrestling to let go of His will and to do the Father's will so that He could fulfill His destiny. At times, you will have to overcome the difficult task of letting go of your will. This may involve you also letting go of multiple issues that are keeping you from freedom to fulfill your destiny.

Let me illustrate this with a story from nature. A certain type of monkey is so enamored with bananas that it will make a decision that puts its life at risk—refusing to let go. This allows its predators to *catch* and *kill* it in a most unique way.

In Africa, poachers will place a cage filled with bananas in the jungle, a cage with bars just wide enough for a monkey to slip its open hand in, but not wide enough for it to pull the banana out with a closed fist. The poachers know the monkey will forfeit its freedom just to clutch the precious bananas. With its fist wrapped around the fruit, the monkey cannot escape, and it becomes easy prey. The acrobatic monkey becomes stationary, a slave to its own desires, and it needlessly gives itself over to be captured or killed.

Sounds foolish, doesn't it? Why give up your freedom needlessly? Yet how often do we get ourselves into this same predicament? Can you see how this applies to our own lives? When we hang on to things so tightly that they hold us in bondage, we're easy prey for our predator— satan. I've already mentioned some of these areas—drugs, smoking, an expensive lifestyle, overworking, pride, stress, overeating, toxic friends or relationships, sexual habits, a stingy attitude—the list goes on and on. If we don't learn to let go of these, we will be hindered from fulfilling our full destiny. Remember what Paul wrote:

✙ *"Everything is permissible for me"—but not everything is beneficial. "Everything is permissible for me"—but I will not be mastered by anything* (1 Corinthians 6:12).

This can be confusing at times. Just like bananas are good for monkeys, so too what we are holding on to seems like a good thing. However, we need to be sensitive to the possibility that what we are holding on to, no matter how good it seems, could be creating another problem in our lives or keeping us from achieving a most intimate relationship with God and thereby keeping us from reaching our destiny.

Refusing to let go of hindrances can cause us to fall short of our earthly destinies. But don't be misled: once we have the incorruptible seed of Jesus in us, our *eternal* destiny is assured.

## ACTION & VISUALIZATION

*Let go of what is hindering you.*

## Against the Flow

You may find that your destiny leads you against the customs of your time (which is another example of a contradiction), but you still must say yes to destiny as Mary, the mother of Jesus, did when visited by an angel:

✠ *The angel went to her and said, "Greetings, you who are highly favored! The Lord is with you."*

*Mary was greatly **troubled** at his words and wondered what kind of greeting this might be (Luke 1:28-29).*

Yes, it is possible that, when you receive God's call, you will initially be troubled by what you hear, but keep on listening. Do not shut off God's messenger, whether it be the Holy Spirit within you, your circumstances, a prophet, an angel, or any other method that God uses. Luke goes on to tell us:

✠ *But the angel said to her, "Do not be afraid, Mary, you have found favor with God. You will be with child and give birth to a son, and you are to give Him the name Jesus. He will be great and will be called the Son of the Most High. The Lord God will give Him the throne of His father David, and He will reign over the house of Jacob forever; His kingdom will never end."*

*"How will this be," Mary asked the angel, "since I am a virgin?"*

*The angel answered, "The Holy Spirit will come upon you, and the power of the Most High will overshadow you. So the Holy One to be born will be called the Son of God. Even Elizabeth your relative is going to have a child in her old age, and she who was said to be barren is in her sixth month. For nothing is impossible with God" (Luke 1:30-37).*

What an incredible destiny God offered to Mary. She does not respond by asking, "Why me?" or by questioning her worthiness. Rather she says:

✠ *"I am the Lord's servant," Mary answered. "May it be to me as you have said." Then the angel left her* (Luke 1:38).

The destiny that God offered Mary defied *physical logic*, and yours may as well. It presented Mary with a real dilemma. It was customary in her time for an unmarried, pregnant woman to be *stoned to death*. And yet, in the face of this grave possibility, Mary's answer to God was, "I am the Lord's *servant*. May it be to me as you have said." For Mary, unwrapping the gift of destiny meant being a servant to God. Her destiny was to serve Him as the mother of His Son.

This seems to have been Mary's destiny from the beginning. As I previously mention in the Hebrew alphabet, each letter has a numerical meaning. The study of the letters' numerical number values taken together in a word is called *gematria*. If we take the letters of the name of God in Hebrew, which are *yud, hey, vav,* and *hey,* then add them together, we get twenty-six. If we then take the numerical value of Mary's name in Hebrew (*Mariam*) and add them together, we get 290. Adding God's plus Mary's number values together, we get 316, which is the numerical value of Jesus' Hebrew name. It is also an interesting reference to a key Bible verse referencing Jesus:

✠ *For God so loved the world that he gave his one and only Son, that whoever believes in him shall not perish but have eternal life* (John 3:16).

Your prescribed destiny has also been known to God, and it is *no less* important to Him. Your role in His redemptive plan is equally essential. I urge you to get this truth into your spirit and to live in confidence of your calling, because that confidence will produce great joy and peace.

## Take the Ball and Run with It

Look at the next line after Mary's response to God's messenger: "Then the angel *left* her." At some point, God will tell or show you a piece of your destiny, and then it is up to you to *take* the ball and *run* with it. The message has been given; now the messenger is *gone*; that is all that you may get for a while. By *faith* and through your connection with God, you are expected to take the next steps.

Remember the verse that tells us not to worry about what to say or how to say it? Jesus tells us that, at the necessary time, we will know what to say, for it will not be us speaking, but the Spirit of our Father speaking through us (see Luke 12:11). Likewise, when you are in the center of the river—His will—then you will not have to speak in your own words or act in your own power. God will provide the words and the power with which you are to speak and act. This *reliance* on God will further enhance your relationship with Him, and you will begin to really live your life through Him.

## A Little at a Time

Think for a minute about how little God initially told Mary about the destiny that He was offering to her. He didn't tell her where to have the baby, how to deal with the impending persecution, how to raise the baby, what to teach the baby, where she would raise the baby, what her relationship would be with the baby, what the baby would do, and, most importantly, what the future would bring for her and the baby. Sometimes God may give you as little as *one word* and expect you to *run* with it. Remember the verse:

*Your word is a lamp to my feet and a light for my path* (Psalm 119:105).

God is only lighting the immediate path set before you, perhaps only the spot where your foot is to land next. It does not say that He uses a beacon or floodlight to light your whole journey at one time. This little-by-little method serves God's purpose because the unwrapping process, which is continually unfolding in your life, keeps your faith vibrant. This creates a foundation for growing your relationship with Him, which is His reason for creating you.

Listening to the angel's simple message, Mary had no way of knowing how the circumstances would work out. And certainly, she could not tell what it would mean to give birth to the Messiah. Her natural mind could not conceive of this. Yet when she received this word from God, she did not look at her circumstances, but kept her focus on God's *words*. Mary had faith that *nothing* was impossible with God, and she stayed focused on His promises.

Your destiny will start to unfold at some point and time. It may take time, or it may come quickly once you are saved. Every person is different and is on a *unique path*; avoid comparing yourself to other Christians and how their destinies unfold. Do not be jealous. Celebrate with others what they receive from God and where He sends them. Resenting or envying another's path and relationship with God will only lead you out of His will, as Jesus illustrated in this parable:

✟ *For the kingdom of heaven is like a landowner [God] who went out early in the morning to hire men to work in his vineyard.*

*He agreed to pay them a denarius for the day and sent them into his vineyard. About the third hour he went out and saw others standing in the marketplace doing nothing. He told them, "You also go and work in my vineyard, and I will pay you whatever is right." So they went.*

*He went out again about the sixth hour and the ninth hour and did the same thing. About the eleventh hour he went out and found still others standing around. He asked them, "Why have you been standing here all day long doing nothing?"*

*"Because no one has hired us," they answered.*

*He said to them, "You also go and work in my vineyard."*

*When evening came the owner of the vineyard said to his foreman, "Call the workers and pay them their wages beginning with the last ones hired, and going on to the first."*

*The workers who were hired about the eleventh hour came and each received a denarius. So when those came who were hired first, they expected to receive more. But each one of them also received a denarius. When they received it, they began to grumble against the landowner. "These men who were hired last worked only one hour," they said, "and you have made them equal to us who have borne the burden of the work and the heat of the day."*

*But he answered one of them, "Friend, I am not being unfair to you. Didn't you agree to work for a denarius? Take your pay and go. I want to give the man who was hired last the same as you. Don't I have the right to do what I want with my own money? Or are you envious because I am generous?"* (Matthew 20:1-15).

## ACTION & VISUALIZATION

*Take your instructions from God and start the process, by faith, of unwrapping and living out your destiny.*

## UNUSUAL WAYS

Our destinies aren't all revealed in the same way. Take the apostle Paul's destiny, for example. It started unfolding quickly, wrapped up with his salvation, and arrived in a very dramatic fashion. In fact, there is a term, "Damascus road experience," that refers to the beginning of Paul's conversion and his introduction to God's destiny for his life. At the time Paul was called Saul, and he was a vigilant, well-known persecutor of Christians. Here is the beginning of His spiritual journey, as recorded by Luke in Acts:

☥ *Meanwhile, Saul (would later change his name to Paul) was still breathing out murderous threats against the Lord's disciples. He went to the high priest and asked him for letters to the synagogues in Damascus, so that if he found any there who belonged to the Way [the church], whether men or women, he might take them as prisoners to Jerusalem. As he neared Damascus on his journey, suddenly a light from heaven flashed around him. He fell to the ground and heard a voice say to him, "Saul, Saul, why do you persecute Me?" [Jesus said this about His body, the church.]*

*"Who are You, Lord?" Saul asked.*

*"I am Jesus, whom you are persecuting," He replied. "Now get up and go into the city, and you will be told what you must do."*

*The men traveling with Saul stood there speechless; they heard the sound but did not see anyone. Saul got up from the ground, but when he opened his eyes he could see nothing. So they led him by the hand into Damascus. For three days he was blind, and did not eat or drink anything (Acts 9:1-9).*

There are three things I would like to call to your attention in this passage. First, God did not initially give Saul a vision of his entire destiny. Second, after Saul's initial contact with God, his sight was removed from him. It is not unusual for God to remove some physical aspect of our lives to enable us to see more clearly spiritually, thus making way for His gift of destiny. Third, the men traveling with Saul could not see what he saw. It was something personal between Saul and God. Saul was having an individual experience. You too are a unique individual before God, and He will give you experiences specific to who you are. Again, do not focus on how God speaks to others, rather keep your focus on God.

Let us continue with the account:

☥ *In Damascus there was a disciple named Ananias. The Lord called to him in a vision, "Ananias,"*

*"Yes, Lord," he answered.*

*The Lord told him, "Go to the house of Judas on Straight Street and ask for a man from Tarsus named Saul, for he is praying. In a vision he has seen a man named Ananias come and place his hands on him to restore his sight."*

*"Lord," Ananias answered, "I have heard many reports about this man and all the harm he has done to Your saints in Jerusalem. And he has come here with authority from the chief priest to arrest all who call on Your name"* (Acts 9:10-14).

Ananias and Saul each had a destiny that crossed paths with the other. In fact, the verse indicates that Saul at this point already had a vision where he saw Ananias would restore his sight. Ananias was scared to follow through with his assigned destiny, and rightfully so. Remember, Saul had a reputation as a violent, hostile man—especially toward Christians.

✠ *But the Lord said to Ananias, "Go! This man is My **chosen instrument** to carry My name before the Gentiles and their kings and before the people of Israel. I will show him how much **he must suffer for My name**"* (Acts 9:15-16).

Before Saul was saved, God told Ananias that He had a specific destiny in mind for Saul—one we know (through the biblical accounts) that he lived out as Paul. Even though at that exact moment, Saul was an enemy of the church, God still said he was *destined* to become a messenger to facilitate growth in the church.

Perhaps you may have been an enemy of the church, but that does not preclude or hinder you from receiving your destiny from God and doing great things for His Kingdom. Also note that God described for Ananias the unusual sufferings that Saul would experience. Likewise, God had spoken to Saul about Ananias' prayer to restore his sight even before He spoke to Ananias. As the story continues, we see how Ananias is responsible for catching up with his future—that which Saul had already seen in a vision. Here's how the story continues:

✠ *Then Ananias went to the house and entered it. Placing his hands on Saul, he said, "Brother Saul, the Lord—Jesus, who appeared to you on the road as you were coming here—has sent me so that you might see again and be filled with the Holy Spirit." Immediately, something like scales fell from Saul's eyes, and he could see again. He got up and was baptized, and after taking some food, he regained his strength* (Acts 9:17-19).

You too will have to catch up to your future if God's will is going to be manifested in and through your life.

## Knowing through Relationship

God did not give Saul a detailed account of his destiny or specific instructions for how to unfold his destiny. God simply installed in Saul His guidance system, the Holy Spirit. Through that relationship, Saul's destiny began to unfold:

✠ *Saul spent several days with the disciples in Damascus. At once he began to preach in the synagogues that Jesus is the Son of God. All those who heard him were astonished and asked, "Isn't he the man who raised havoc in Jerusalem among those who call on this name? And hasn't he come here to take them as prisoners to the chief priests?" Yet Saul grew more and more powerful and baffled the Jews living in Damascus by proving that Jesus is the Christ* (Acts 9:19-22).

God started growing Saul into his destiny right away, even though for several years Saul had to be discipled by others. God converted him from being an enemy of the church to being one of the leading apostles of the church—writing approximately *one-third* of the New Testament. Saul, who would soon change his name to Paul, received pieces of his destiny as he went through his life's journey. He learned where he would go, what he was supposed to do, and what would happen to him in different ways as he unwrapped and used his destiny.

These Scriptures all highlight times when Paul received further understanding of his destiny through his *relationship* with God:

✠ *While* [the disciples] *were worshiping the Lord and fasting, the Holy Spirit said, "Set apart for me Barnabas and Saul for the work to which I have called them." So after they had fasted and prayed, they placed their hands on them, and sent them off. The two of them,* **sent on their way by the Holy Spirit,** *went...* (Acts 13:2-4).

✠ *Paul and his companions traveled throughout the region of Phrygia and Galatia, having been kept by the Holy Spirit from preaching the word in the province of Asia. When they came to the border of Mysia, they tried to enter Bithynia, but* **the Spirit of Jesus would not allow them to** (Acts 16:6-7).

✠ *After Paul had seen the vision, we got ready at once to leave for Macedonia,* **concluding that God had called us to preach the gospel to them** (Acts 16:10).

✠ *About midnight Paul and Silas were praying and singing hymns to God* [witnessing to the other prisoners, despite their troubles]*, and the other prisoners were listening to them. Suddenly there was such a violent earthquake that the foundations of the prison were shaken. At* *once all the prison doors flew open, and everybody's chains came loose* (Acts 16:25-26).

While Paul was in Corinth, after a bad experience with an abusive crowd:

✞ *One night the Lord spoke to Paul in a vision:* "*Do not be afraid; keep on speaking, do not be silent. For I am with you, and no one is going to attack and harm you, because I have many people in this city.*" *So Paul stayed for a year and a half, teaching them the word of God* (Acts 18:9-11).

✞ *And now,* **compelled by the Spirit**, *I am going to Jerusalem, not knowing what will happen to me there. I only know that in every city the Holy Spirit warns me that prison and hardships are facing me. However, I consider my life worth nothing to me, if only I may finish the race and complete the* **destiny** *the Lord has given me—the task of testifying to the gospel of God's grace* (Acts 20:22-24).

It is clear in Scripture that Paul received, unwrapped, and used the Gifts of Freedom. Paul ran his race and learned to be satisfied with receiving his instructions one step at a time from the Holy Spirit. May you also take hold of that kind of faith and listen to that *one word* God may share with you.

## ACTION & VISUALIZATION

*Live out your destiny, step by step,*
*when God presents it to you that way.*

## OWNING YOUR DESTINY

In 1 Samuel is the story of Samuel the prophet anointing David to be the next king of Israel. God instructed Samuel to go to the house of Jesse of Bethlehem where Samuel would anoint with oil one of Jesse's sons to be the next king. As each of Jesse's sons passed by Samuel, God would not allow the anointing oil to be placed on them, no matter how logical of a choice for king they seemed to be. In the same way, your anointing oil is meant for you, and God will not let it be poured out on someone else. If you receive this gift of anointing, then the anointing God has given you will enable you to complete your destiny.

The gift of destiny is the most fulfilling gift that you can receive here on earth, a unique gift that God has specially designed just for you. But it is meaningless unless you receive, unwrap, and use it. Remember that when you receive, unwrap, and use a gift from God, you are in turn giving God a gift as well. The gift of destiny is also the most fulfilling gift that you can give to God while you are still on earth because it fulfills His purpose for you as well as for others. Even with God, your life will never reach perfection here on earth, but you can fulfill your destiny.

No matter who you are or how much faith you have, you will have times when you question your destiny. That is natural because you are merely human. John the Baptist illustrates this for us. Jesus said of him:

✠ *I tell you the truth: Among those born of women there has not risen anyone greater than John the Baptist...* (Matthew 11:11).

John the Baptist's destiny was to be the voice announcing to the world the coming Messiah:

✠ *This is the one about whom it is written: "I [God] will send My messenger [John the Baptist] ahead of You [Jesus], who will prepare Your way before You"* (Matthew 11:10).

877

This was John the Baptist's destiny from the beginning, and, indeed, even from before his birth. Look at what happened when Mary, who was pregnant with Jesus at the time, visited John's mother, Elizabeth, while she was pregnant with John:

✠ *When Elizabeth heard Mary's greeting, the baby leaped in her womb, and Elizabeth was filled with the Holy Spirit. In a loud voice she exclaimed: "Blessed are you among women, and blessed is the child you will bear! But why am I so favored, that the mother of my Lord should come to me? As soon as the sound of your greeting reached my ears, the baby in my womb* [John] *leaped for joy"* (Luke 1:41-44).

John the Baptist should never have had a question about whether he was fulfilling his destiny, right? Well, keep in mind he was human, just like you and me, so when he found himself in a *prison*, he questioned whether he was fulfilling his destiny. Indeed, he sent a messenger to Jesus, questioning Him:

✠ *When John heard in prison what Christ was doing, he sent his disciples to ask Him, "Are you the one who was to come, or should we expect someone else?"* (Matthew 11:2-3).

You may have times when it seems as if you've hit a lowly place and begin to question your destiny; nonetheless, you should never give up or lose faith. Remain persistent in your pursuit. When you are confused, seek Jesus and rest in Him so Jesus can carry you to your destiny in His river. Remember Joseph? God gave Joseph his destiny through a dream, telling him that his brothers would someday bow down to him. But first he was left in a pit, sold as a slave, wrongfully accused, and sent to jail. Through it all, however, Joseph never gave up; indeed, all those unlikely, tragic, and painful events were required to put Joseph into a position to *receive* his destiny. They were all an integral part of his destiny.

Your circumstances may cause you to question your destiny, but regardless of what you encounter along the way, if you follow God's will, He will illuminate His specific, unique path for you to follow. Your destiny awaits....

## MEDITATION POINT

Opening all the other gifts will allow you to piece together the destiny your Creator intended for you.

Go to Chapter 6 in the Study Guide section on page 975.

# Chapter 7

# THE GIFT—GOD OF THE TRINITY

## WHAT WILL YOUR RELATIONSHIP ULTIMATELY BE WITH HIM?

Before you begin to read, pray that the Holy Spirit will give you
and all readers of this book understanding and application.

✠ *The Lord had said to Abram, "Leave your country, your people and
your father's household and go to the land I will show you. I will make
you into a great nation and I will bless you; I will make your name
great, and you will be a blessing. I will bless those who bless you, and
whoever curses you I will curse; and all peoples on earth will be blessed
through you" (Genesis 12:1-3).*

✠ *Now we who have believed enter that rest...* (Hebrews 4:3).

L et me tell you a classic story about a poor married couple, whose
names are Jim and Della. As Christmas approached, they began to
think of gifts for each other—wonderful gifts that would accurately
represent the depth of their love for one another. But they could barely afford rent and food, let alone expensive gifts! Jim wasn't content to show up
giftless on Christmas morning, so he sold his most prized possession—a

gold watch. Sadly, he had never worn the watch because the band was broken and it was too costly to repair. After selling the watch, however, he bought Della a most wonderful gift.

Unbeknownst to Jim, Della was also selling her most prized possession—her beautiful hair—in order to buy him a gift. They were both eager to give each other their gifts. On Christmas Eve, Della threw the door open, holding up her gift for Jim: a gold watch band. Jim stood there, stunned, motionless. Without a word, he slid a wooden box across the table to Della so that she could open his gift to her: a most elegant ivory hair comb. They had sold their most prized possessions to give each other seemingly unusable gifts.

Were Jim and Della fools? Some might say so. And some might also call us fools for giving up our lives—our most prized possessions—to follow Jesus Christ into His world. However, what we get in return for our sacrifice is of infinite value—real love.

Remember that God is the action of love. When we surrender our lives, which is our most valuable possession, to God, He gives it back, but He gives us back much better. We find a renewed life that has real *intimacy* with Him, real love, and real freedom—the kind of *life* that is only found when we are willing to truly return His love by giving up everything in this world or "land" and move into God's world whose underpinning revolves around the action of love. It is our unwrapping of all the gifts of freedom that leads us to this deeper intimacy with God and the people around us that He has made, many of whom God is or will be inhabiting.

## THE ULTIMATE RELATIONSHIP WITH GOD HIMSELF

Who is this God for whom we're to give up our lives? You have read about the three persons or personalities of God—the Father, the Son, and the Holy Spirit. We often think of them as three separate persons, yet the Bible repeatedly tells us there is clearly only *one* God.

✠ *So then, about eating food sacrificed to idols: We know that an idol is nothing at all in the world and that there is no God but **one**. For even if there are so-called gods, whether in heaven or on earth (as indeed there are many "gods" and many "lords"), yet for us there is but **one** God, the Father, from whom all things came and for whom we live; and there is but one Lord, Jesus Christ, through whom all things came and through whom we live* (1 Corinthians 8:4-6).

✠ *Make every effort to keep unity of the Spirit through the bond of peace. There is one body and one Spirit—just as you were called to one hope when you were called—one Lord, one faith, one baptism; one God and Father of all, who is over all and through all and in all* (Ephesians 4:3-6).

✠ *Hear, O Israel: The Lord our God, **the Lord is one**. Love the Lord your God with all your heart and with all your soul and with all your strength* (Deuteronomy 6:4-5).

Since we relate to the rest of the world through our bodies, which seem to separate us from all else in this physical world, it is difficult for us to fully understand the concept of the Trinity. We learn about the members of the Trinity as separate individuals, but they are all part of our *one* God. The last verse may give us some clues on how we can understand God as three in one, specifically when it describes how we're to love Him: with all our heart and with all our soul and with all our strength.

Couldn't Jesus be the heart of God, couldn't the Father be the soul or mind of God, and the Holy Spirit the strength (or accomplishing mechanism) of God all working in concert with one another and all yielding in perfect harmony to one another? We also have a hard time understanding how God can reside in us and how we are to yield to each other so we work in perfect sync with those with whom we are in relationship. We also have similar divisions of heart, soul, and strength within ourselves. We are called to love with our heart, mind, and strength, though in our life we have a general tendency to rely on our physical strength rather than spiritual strength that only the Holy Spirit can provide for us if we let Him. It is hard for us to understand this concept of three in one, but even the Hebrew alphabet tells us this. *Aleph* is the letter in Hebrew that signifies God is made up of three parts, but is one letter. Likewise, all the letter values on God's name spelled out total 111.

Do you remember what three gifts Peter had to offer Jesus to develop his relationship with God—mind, heart, and hands? Clearly, our understanding of the Trinity and their interworking relationship is very limited, as well as our understanding of how the Trinity relates to us; however, this process of discovery will make exploring the whole universe of knowledge and eternity exciting. Imagine the limitless exploration we will have available to us once we get to Heaven.

✠ *One God and Father of all, who is over all and through all and **in** all* (Ephesians 4:6).

The fact that God is everywhere and in all things says that we will be able to experience everything through Him, that is through our intimate relationship with Him. And how do we achieve an intimate relationship with God? For most of us, intimacy with God is a journey. It is a process, a Spirit-to-spirit connection that happens between us and our Creator, which opens a new world for us. However, to fully experience it we must leave the old one behind.

For example, Abram, whom God would later change his name to Abraham, modeled this for us nearly six thousand years ago. The name Abram, in Hebrew, has four letters. The first and second letters spell *abba* or *father,* while the second and third letters spell *son,* and the fourth letter is the sign of the Holy Spirit. Abram's name is identified with the triune nature of God, as well as our triune nature. Abram began with these elements; however, when God called Abram to become the father of many nations, He spoke this into being by calling him Abraham.

In Hebrew, this change of name is simply done by adding one letter (*hey*, which means grace) after the second and third letters, meaning son, who indeed brought grace to humanity. He also brought us the Holy Spirit, which was signified by the last letter of Abraham's new name. Most importantly, it is God's grace that allows intimacy with God, and that knowledge of His grace allows our faith in God. For God to find faith in us, we must know and believe in His grace.

Abraham's journey with God was much like yours and mine. He had doubts, insecurities, and areas of disbelief, but when God spoke, he obeyed. In fact, God called Abraham to leave his country, family, friends, and job, and move to a foreign country—a Promised Land. What was the purpose of this move? Why would God call him to leave behind what *he loved*? Well, Abraham didn't know, but he obeyed because of a promise God made to him: "Pursue the Promised Land and you will be greatly blessed." Sound familiar?

Isn't our Promised Land to dwell in an intimate relationship with God and see His image and likeness develop in us as we live out our destinies? Isn't this the source of life's *greatest blessing*? However, just like Abraham, we will face resistance both from our own hang-ups as well as the world in which we live. Like Abraham, it will cause us to leave the comfort and familiarity of our homeland, which in our case is the habits, thoughts, and surroundings familiar to us, to relocate somewhere different and unfamiliar. It will be a place where we step out and take chances, relying on the nature of God's grace to follow through. This is the journey of walking by faith toward intimacy with God.

The Gifts of Freedom are all about helping you reach your Promised Land. Of course, you won't enter the fullness of the Promised Land until you receive a renewed body and you are welcomed into the physical presence of God Himself in the Kingdom of Heaven. It is impossible at this point to fully imagine and comprehend eternity with Him, especially in our current state. In Heaven, God's image and likeness reign supreme—pure love! If we consider how far we are from perfect love, we will realize just how far we are from the closeness and intimacy that God desires.

In Heaven, we will have complete intimacy with our Creator. An *infinite* God can meet and exceed every one of our individual expectations, not just daily or hourly but minute by minute. I truly believe it will blow our minds and surpass even our wildest dreams—no words or feelings we have on earth come close to describing it. In that place, His fullness will be on us and we will enjoy a face-to-face relationship with God, the fullness of the Trinity. John writes:

*And I heard a loud voice from the throne saying, "Now the dwelling of God is with men and He will **live with them**. They will be His people, and **God Himself** will be with them and be their God"* (Revelation 21:3).

At that time, He will complete our transformation into His image and likeness, as well as bring us into His perfect rest. But those two wonderful aspects are *not* just for Heaven. God Himself invites us to begin this incredible journey toward intimacy with *Him* now.

*God, who got you started in this spiritual adventure, shares with us the life of His Son and our Master Jesus. He will never give up on you. Never forget that* (1 Corinthians 1:9).

Where are you headed? Where is your journey taking you today? As a believer, you are asked to set out for His Kingdom, beginning the journey of moving closer and closer to His image and likeness, toward intimacy with Him. As we *grow* in our spiritual relationship with God, we can start possessing our Promised Land *now* in His presence—this is the Kingdom of God inside of us. But like Abraham, to answer this call, we too *may* have to leave our countries, families, or jobs. In other words, are you willing to face discomfort to find your Promised Land?

Listen to what Jesus said about sacrifice in the Kingdom:

✠ *I have come to bring fire on the earth, and how I wish it were already kindled! But I have a baptism to undergo, and how distressed I am until it is completed! Do you think I came to bring peace on earth? No, I tell you, but division. From now on there will be five in one family divided against each other, three against two and two against three. They will be divided, father against son and son against father, mother against daughter and daughter against mother, mother-in-law against daughter-in-law and daughter-in-law against mother-in-law* (Luke 12:49-53).

✠ *"I tell you the truth," Jesus replied, "no one who has left home or brothers or sisters or mother or father or children or fields for Me and the gospel will fail to receive a hundred times as much in this present age...and in the age to come..."* (Mark 10:29-30).

How do we get to our Promised Land? We follow what is sometimes a slow, winding, and difficult journey. Like Abraham, to receive this gift, we must start out on the journey with an action of faith, and then continue to walk in faith despite the adversity that will come upon entering our Promised Land.

✠ *By faith Abraham, when called to go to a place he would **later** receive as his inheritance, obeyed and went, even though he did not know where he was going* (Hebrews 11:8).

✝ *Though you have not seen Him, you love Him; and even though you do not see Him now, you believe in Him and are filled with an inexpressible and glorious joy* (1 Peter 1:8).

To receive this joy, you need to know God in an intimate way so that you will automatically have the kind of faith that trusts God to take you to your Promised Land:

✝ *I am with you and will watch over you wherever you go, and I will bring you back to this land. I will not leave you until I have done what I have promised you* (Genesis 28:15).

This applies as well to our transformation into His image and likeness when, as believers, we partner with Him:

✝ *Because of your **partnership** in the gospel from the first day until now, being confident of this, that He who began a good work in you will carry it on to completion until the day of Jesus Christ* (Philippians 1:5-6).

## Action & Visualization

*On this long journey of faith, which may take you through unfamiliar and difficult territory, get to know God better so you can have confidence that He is with you and that He will complete your journey to your Promise Land.*

## God's Presence Now

In Jesus' first recorded sermon (commonly referred to as the Sermon on the Mount), He presented clear instructions on how to start this journey toward receiving, unwrapping, and using the gift of God:

✠ *Blessed are the poor in spirit,*
  *for theirs is the kingdom of heaven.*
*Blessed are those who mourn,*
  *for they will be comforted.*
*Blessed are the meek,*
  *for they will inherit the earth.*
*Blessed are those who hunger and thirst for righteousness,*
  *for they will be filled.*
*Blessed are the merciful,*
  *for they will be shown mercy.*
*Blessed are the pure in heart,*
  *for they will see God.*
*Blessed are the peacemakers,*
  *for they will be called sons of God.*
*Blessed are those who are persecuted because of righteousness,*
  *for theirs is the kingdom of heaven* (Matthew 5:3-10).

In construction, if you compromise the foundation or the superstructure, you create an unstable building. The same thing is true of your relationship with God. Each step that Jesus outlines in His sermon needs to be properly completed in order to create a stable relationship. God took the first step in building this relationship by offering the greatest gift one could give—the gift of eternal life given in an ultimate act of unselfish love before we deserved it.

✠ *For God so loved the world that He gave His one and only Son, that whoever believes in Him shall not perish but have eternal life* (John 3:16).

In this eternal life, which is a gift God offers everyone, we have a promise to receive, an invitation to a relationship with God Himself forever, which is the *ultimate* gift. If we choose to unwrap this gift, it will assure us of an eternal relationship with God into our next life and forever. However, there is more to the gift than an eternal life in the hereafter—we can enjoy and benefit from this "eternal" life in the here and now, if we choose to unwrap it.

## NEED GOD CONSTANTLY

Let's look at the first step of this journey that Jesus establishes for receiving this aspect of the gift of life, the gift of God. (I've included three translations of this verse to help illuminate its meaning.)

✟ *Blessed are the poor in spirit, for theirs is the kingdom of heaven* (Matthew 5:3).

✟ *You're blessed when you're at the end of your rope. With less of you there is more of God and His rule* (Matthew 5:3 MSG).

✟ *Blessed (happy, to be envied, and spiritually prosperous—with life-joy and satisfaction in God's favor and salvation, regardless of their outward conditions) are the poor in spirit (the humble who rate themselves insignificant) for theirs is the kingdom of heaven* (Matthew 5:3 AMP).

If you want to go from point A to point B, you first need to determine where you are: the location of point A. Remember what God asked Adam: "Where are you?" (see Genesis 3:9). Well, this is a question to which He asks you *every* single day of your life on earth. It is not a question He doesn't know the answer; rather, it is a question He is asking for your benefit. He knows where you are. However, you need to know the answer to that question to properly navigate from where you are toward Him. If you don't know where you are at (point A), how could you possibly know how to get to Him (point B)? Would you even know you need to move to get there? Look at this parable:

> To some who were confident of their own righteousness and looked down on everybody else, Jesus told this parable: "Two men went up to the temple to pray, one a Pharisee and the other a tax collector. The Pharisee stood up and prayed about himself: 'God, I thank You that I am not like other men—robbers, evildoers, adulterers—or even like this tax collector. I fast twice a week and give a tenth of all I get.'
>
> "But the tax collector stood at a distance. He would not even look up to heaven, but beat his breast and said, 'God, have mercy on me, a sinner.'
>
> "I tell you that this man, rather than the other, went home **justified before** God..." (Luke 18:9-14).

The second man, who was humble and contrite, correctly knew where he was at in relation to God, and in so doing allowed himself to be justified before God. He did not rely on his actions, but instead relied 100 percent on God's grace. Likewise, you need to begin your journey with God by *conceding* that you are poor in spirit, that you need something more that only He can give you. That more you need is God, and, therefore, you reached out to Him for your salvation.

Here is the important part: You need to have this realization *every* morning when you wake up, even *after* you have received the gift of salvation. You need to realize that, while you have gained something wonderful, you are *still* spiritually *lacking*. You are incapable of real success without Him, minute to minute, hour to hour, and day to day. If you know you need Him every day, every hour, and every minute, then you will *seek* Him in everything all the time. This is the catalyst for the growth process that leads to an *intimate relationship* with God and allows you to spend more time to resting in Him in true peace.

## Mourn the Loss of His Presence

Jesus then instructs us in the next verse to appreciate and appropriately respond to where we are versus where we *should be*. Doing this produces a *mournful* spirit:

✞ *Blessed are those who mourn, for they will be comforted* (Matthew 5:4).

✞ *You're blessed when you feel you've lost what is most dear to you [God's fullest presence in you]. Only then can you be embraced by the one most dear to you* (Matthew 5:4 MSG).

If we did something that seriously offended our spouse, we would experience some grief as a result of our actions. Likewise, when we are not walking and operating in the Spirit, we lose the most precious thing—*intimacy* in our relationship with God. If we recognize and wrestle with this, we will experience a spirit of sorrow about missing God and His mark for us, prompting us to change our behavior. Paul said it this way:

✞ **Godly sorrow** *brings repentance that leads to salvation and leaves no regret...* (2 Corinthians 7:10).

When Jesus used the word *mourn*, it was the strongest possible word that He could have used to describe inner pain expressed in an outward way. However, mourning under the conviction of the Holy Spirit over that which we long for will *not* end in discouragement. James reminds us:

✞ *Grieve, mourn and wail. Change your laughter to mourning and your joy to gloom. Humble yourselves before the Lord, and He will **lift you up*** (James 4:9-10).

We are *not* to dwell on our sins and failures, for God knows that we are weak and will fall. Indeed, we are simply to acknowledge that weakness and to respond by bringing Him into the picture to help us change. *Godly* sorrow produces a *change* in behavior that will *lift us up*; it will *not* bring crippling regret.

The word used in the Bible when John the Baptist told the people they should repent was *metanoeo* (met-an-ah-eh-oh) (see Matthew 3:1-2). This meant that the people should change their minds and actions, or reverse their course. The word *repent* comes from two words: *meta* ("after") and *noeo* ("to think"). Repentance is a decision that results in a change of mind, which in turn leads to a change in our purpose, our actions, and our course.[1]

It's interesting that today the word *repent* breaks down into *pent*, meaning "top" (as in penthouse or top house), and *re*, meaning "get back." The word *repent* means "*to get back to the top*." And that's where God wants our focus when we fail—on getting back to the top. Of course, getting there sometimes means letting go of things that weigh us down so that we can more easily move in the right direction, which is *up*.

When we see what holds us down, we should have the sorrow that's produced by the conviction of the Holy Spirit. Then we let go so that God can lift us up, *back to the top*. You will find that, when you are successful at doing this, your top will ascend higher and higher each time.

You may wonder, "How long must I mourn?" I would suggest you should mourn as long as it takes to make a change. Mourning must come from the *heart* in order to bring change—a change of heart. And with a change of heart, there is a change of direction. There is a strong connection between our heart and mind in our decision-making process. When our heart changes, our minds are guided by its direction.

Your heart is not just a pump; it also acts like a mini brain. Science demonstrates that our hearts have their own independent nervous system, a complex system with at least forty thousand neurons, as many as are found in various subcortical centers of the brain. In effect, our "heart's brain" acts like a checking station or conscience for all the emotions generated by the flow of chemicals from our thoughts.

Science is discovering that our "heart's brain" is a real "intelligent force" behind the intuitive thoughts and feelings we experience. It produces an important biochemical substance called ANF, or arterial peptide, the balance hormone that regulates many of our brain's functions and motivates behavior.

Your heart is in constant communication with your brain and the rest of your body in three scientifically documented ways: neurologically (through transmissions of nerve impulses), biochemically (through hormones and neurotransmitters), and biophysically (through pressure waves). A growing body of scientific evidence also suggests that your heart communicates with the brain and body in a fourth way: energetically through electromagnetic field interaction.

Through all these biological communication systems, the heart has a significant influence on the function of your brain and all your other body systems. The signals the heart sends to your brain influence not just perception and emotional processing, but higher, cognitive functioning as well. New scientific evidence on the heart's neurological sensitivity points to feedback loops between the brain and the heart that checks the accuracy and integrity of our thought life.[2] We find confirmation for this in the Bible:

✠ *...the Lord searches every **heart** and understands every motive behind the **thoughts**...* (1 Chronicles 28:9).

✠ *Jesus knew what they were thinking and asked, "Why are you **thinking** these things in your **heart**?"* (Luke 5:22).

Your brain alone can have endless thoughts and therefore needs an anchoring mechanism that comes from your innermost soul. The direction of your mind and actions are set by your heart:

✠ *For as he thinks in his heart, so is he...* (Proverbs 23:7 NKJV).

✠ *Keep your heart with all diligence, for out of it spring the issues of life* (Proverbs 4:23 NKJV).

✠ *...doing the will of God from your heart...* (Ephesians 6:6).

✠ *...for out of the overflow of his heart his mouth speaks* (Luke 6:45).

Indeed, our very salvation comes from the faith and belief that resides in our hearts:

✠ *That if you confess with your mouth "Jesus is Lord" and believe in your **heart** that God raised Him from the dead you will be saved. **For it is with your heart that you believe** and are justified...* (Romans 10:9-10).

Since love comes from the heart, God intended our heart to be our true guide for our actions with Him and other people. When we only use our heads, it can be calculating and self-serving. When we ponder our actions with our hearts, however, we tend to think of other people's feelings and how our actions affect them. And when we have done something wrong, it is our hearts that should lead us in mourning or pondering our actions so we can find peace in a resolution.

I want to be clear on something: Mourning is different from regret, which denotes something of the mind. God does not want us to cripple ourselves in regret, but we do need to remember that it was you and me who nailed Jesus' hands and feet to that cross. It was *our* sin for which He paid the price and suffered. Remembering this should produce a meaningful attitude of mourning that will change the direction of our hearts. Indeed, it will lead to life, freedom, and greater intimacy with our Creator. This change will get us to where we want to go—back to the *top*.

## Take Your Proper Place

Jesus' next instruction is for us to accept our proper place in this new relationship. It is from this place, and only this place, that we can have access to all the things in the world that God created for us to enjoy in this life on earth. So what is our place? What should our attitude be in the relationship? Jesus tells us:

✛ *Blessed are the meek, for they will inherit the earth* (Matthew 5:5).

Some translations of the Bible use different words for *meek*, such as *gentle* (NASB), *content* (MSG), and *lowly in spirit* (NLT). All these words are meant to convey the idea that we're to be sensitive to the Spirit of God's teaching and leading in our lives. When we do this, a greater world opens to us, a world where we can obtain our full inheritance from God. This includes a greater awareness of God's presence and a greater intimacy with Him.

It is important to note that the word *meek* does *not* mean weak. Think of *meek* as being bridled like a horse. A Belgian mare is not weak, but when you put a bridle in its mouth, the horse can be guided to places it would not go otherwise. Similarly, when we allow ourselves to be bridled by the Holy Spirit, we are able to go to places where we can receive more of God in our lives. For it is then that we will inherit the earth, and the whole world will open to us. The contradiction is that we are not fully free in this life until we allow ourselves to be fully bridled, until we surrender our lives to God. Choose to find that vital place in relationship with God, the place of humility and contentment.

✠ *"...God opposes the proud but gives grace to the humble." Submit yourselves, then, to God. ...Come near to God and He will come near to you. ...Humble yourselves before the Lord, and He will lift you up* (James 4:6-8,10).

✠ *You're blessed when you're content with just who you are—no more, no less. That's the moment you find yourselves proud owners of everything that can't be bought* (Matthew 5:5 MSG).

## Hunger and Thirst for Him

The next thing that Jesus teaches us about fulfilling our relationship with God is that we must be hungry and thirsty for righteousness, or right standing with Him.

✠ *Blessed are those who hunger and thirst for righteousness, for they will be filled* [satisfied] (Matthew 5:6).

As we covered in Book 1, God loves those who *seek* Him, and those who do so will find Him, and, therein, they will also find true satisfaction. If we don't seek Him, then He will not become intimately real in our lives; however, if we do seek Him, He will draw closer to us. This is why James tells us:

✠ *Come near to God and He will come near to you...* (James 4:8).

Take note: God does not say that we can achieve our *own* righteousness. God is *not* seeking perfect people. You will fail at that and put yourself back into bondage trying to follow the law. Rather, He is seeking people who are *hungry* and *thirsty* for Him. This attitude is embodied by the writers of these psalms:

✟ *As the deer **pants** for streams of water, so my soul pants for You, O God. My soul **thirsts** for God, for the living God. When can I go and meet with God? (Psalm 42:1-2).*

✟ *My soul **yearns**, even faints, for the courts of the Lord; my heart and flesh **cry out** for the living God (Psalm 84:2).*

It's *not* your current location as it relates to Him that's important to God; rather, it's your desire to move closer that moves Him. It's your desire to continue the journey into Him that God desires. He encourages us to *seek* righteousness (relationship/likeness) now and to not just wait for Him to shower it on us as He will do in the next life. We should not passively wait for Him to perfect us. Hosea reminds us:

✟ *Sow for yourselves righteousness, reap the fruit of unfailing love and break up your unplowed ground; for **it is time to seek** the Lord, until He comes and showers righteousness on you (Hosea 10:12).*

Remember that the key to achieving righteousness is not by simply seeking it (i.e., avoiding sinful actions), but it is achieved by seeking *Him* and making His heart your heart. It is achieved by showing a constant hunger and thirst for *Him*.

One of the keys to maintaining that hunger and thirst is making sure that you don't fill yourself up with the *wrong* foods. Remember the Samaritan lady Jesus spoke to at the well? She was trying to fill the hunger in her life with men. But Jesus offered her *living water*, real sustenance, instead (see

John 4:1-26). Jesus also said that we *cannot* live by bread alone (by the things of the world that satisfy our flesh and ego). Instead, Jesus said that He is the Bread of Life (see John 6:35-38), and that real sustenance is found only in the Word of God (see Matthew 4:4). Also remember that Jesus is identified as the Word in John 1:1 and 1:12. He is telling us not to fill ourselves up with worldly pursuits, but to remain hungry for His spiritual nourishment.

We must be careful in our pursuits because much of what we pursue in this world can fill up our time, attention, mind, and heart. But a continued hunger and thirst for right standing with God Himself above all else will allow us to be truly fulfilled.

✚ *Come, all you who are thirsty, come to the waters; and you who have no money, come, buy and eat! Come, buy wine and milk without money and without cost. Why spend money on what is not bread, and your labor on what does not satisfy? Listen, listen to Me, and eat what is good, and your soul will delight in the richest of fare* (Isaiah 55:1-2).

We will be happiest when we accept the free things in this life which God offers us.

## OFFER MERCY

The next instruction Jesus gives us, in building our relationship with God, is to be merciful:

✚ *Blessed are the merciful, for they will be shown mercy* (Matthew 5:7).

To understand the meaning of *mercy*, we can consult the meaning of the Latin root word from which it is derived, *misericordia*. It is composed of two words: *miserans*, meaning pitying, and *cor*, which means the heart; or *miseria cordis*, pain of heart.

Mercy supposes two things: 1) a distressed object; and 2) a disposition of another's heart, through which it is affected at the sight of such object.[3] In other words, mercy is an aspect of love involving an emotion that one feels when he or she sees the trial or distress of another. It is shown when we enter the miseries of our neighbor, feel for and mourn with them. It is as if you get into someone else's skin and are feeling what they feel. Have you ever wished you could take away the pain of a loved one by actually taking on the pain yourself?

Mercy and *hesed* (God's covenant love) are closely related. In the Bible, *hesed* is viewed in terms of mercy. In this relationship, mercy then comes to be seen as the quality in God that directs Him to forge a relationship with people who absolutely do not deserve to be in relationship with Him.[4] Offering mercy means "refraining from giving people what they deserve."

Truly, seeking to understand where someone is coming from or having a similar experience makes it easier for us humans to have mercy on that individual. Jesus Himself embodied this. He came and got into our skin, living as we live. He dealt with all the same temptations that we deal with (see Hebrews 2:17-18). Jesus extended mercy to us; therefore, we should do the same to others, especially since they answer to God and *not to us*:

> ☩ *Who are you to judge someone **else's** servant? To his own master he stands or falls...* (Romans 14:4).

We are no one's master. However, God is everyone's Master, and He has elected to judge no one until after they die and the final chapter of their lives has been written:

> ☩ *Just as a man is destined to die once, and **after that** to face judgment...* (Hebrews 9:27).

God Himself has given everyone an inalienable right to *not* be judged until their final chapter is closed, a right of redemption. How then can *you* judge someone, and even before that person's time has come? It is because of sin—because we ate from the Tree of the Knowledge of Good and Evil— that we are so quick to judge others. That very act of judging has caused us to *lose* our innocence. This is because when we judge others, we're also judged by the *same* measure. What you plant or sow you will also reap:

⨯ *Don't pick on people, jump on their failures, criticize their faults— unless, of course, you want the same treatment. That critical spirit has a way of boomeranging* (Matthew 7:1-2 MSG).

⨯ *You, therefore, have no excuse, you who pass judgment on someone else, for at whatever point you judge the other, you are condemning yourself, because you who pass judgment do the same things* (Romans 2:1).

⨯ *Why do you judge your brother? Or why do you look down on your brother? For we will all stand before God's judgment seat* (Romans 14:10).

On the other hand, showing mercy will likewise bring you mercy. It will bring God lovingly into your circumstances, sharing your pain. Your own expression of mercy allows you to avoid judgment. Our own lack of mercy validates our disobedient acts as sins that require punishment. Without our mercy interceding for us, we rely solely on His mercy, which can only be obtained through our acknowledgement of our need for it. This is confirmed in an exchange that Jesus had with a Pharisee:

⨯ *Jesus said, "For judgment I have come into this world, so that the blind* [who cannot judge good and evil] *will see* [life] *and those who see* [and judge things as good and evil] *will become blind* [to life]."

*Some Pharisees who were with Him heard Him say this and asked, "What? Are we blind too?"*

*Jesus said, "If you were blind, you would **not** be guilty of sin; but now that you claim you can see, your guilt remains"* (John 9:39-41).

This is why innocent children who die before receiving Christ will be able to enter the Kingdom of God. It is their very innocence (or lack of judging) that keeps them blind from judgment, and, therefore, judgment will be blind to their sins.

In our dealings with other people, we must remember that God has personal relationships with many of them and that He seeks oneness with others. God wants the best for them, just as He wanted the best for us even before we knew Him and were cleansed by Him.

Perhaps when you see someone acting outside of God's will, you will be tempted to judge them. Well, guess what? You're not qualified for that job. First, you are not sinless. Remember, Jesus said, "Let the one without sin throw the first stone" (see John 8:7). Second, you can't see the future like God can. Only He knows where that person is heading. Third, you don't know how much God loves that individual. This is why He does *not* want you to see yourself as his or her judge, but rather as his or her *friend*. This is also why the second greatest commandment (after loving God) is about loving others:

✝ *The second is this: "Love your neighbor as yourself." There is no commandment greater than these* (Mark 12:31).

Simply put, we enhance our relationship with God by enhancing our relationship with others. Jesus Himself offers this account of the final judgment to show us how our relationship with God is intricately tied to our relationships with others:

✠ *Then the King will say to those on His right, "Come, you who are blessed by My Father; take your inheritance, the kingdom prepared for you since the creation of the world. For I was hungry and you gave Me something to eat. I was thirsty and you gave Me something to drink, I was a stranger and you invited Me in, I needed clothes and you clothed Me, I was sick and you looked after Me, I was in prison and you came to visit Me."*

*Then the righteous will answer Him, "Lord, when did we see You hungry and feed You, or thirsty and give You a drink? When did we see You sick or in prison and go to visit You?"*

*The King will reply, "I tell you the truth, whatever you did for one of the least of these brothers of Mine, you did for **Me**."*

*Then He will say to those on His left, "Depart from Me, you who are cursed, into the eternal fire prepared for the devil and his angels. For I was hungry and you gave Me nothing to eat, I was thirsty and you gave Me nothing to drink, I was a stranger and you did not invite Me in, I needed clothes and you did not clothe Me, I was sick and in prison and you did not look after Me!"*

*They also will answer, "Lord, when did we see You hungry or thirsty or a stranger or needing clothes or sick or in prison, and did not help You?"*

*He will reply, "I tell you the truth, whatever you did not do for one of the least of these, you did not do for Me."*

*Then they will go away to eternal punishment, but the righteous to eternal life* (Matthew 25:34-46).

Show mercy to others where you are able, and you will receive mercy where needed.

## SEE BETTER WITH PURITY

The next thing that Jesus says we need to do to fully receive God is to put our hearts and minds in the right place. Without righteous hearts and minds, our spiritual vision will be too distorted to see God.

✟ *Blessed are the pure in heart, for they will see God* (Matthew 5:8).

If our temple is not clean, then we won't see God in the way that we should. An impure heart distorts our insight, blocking clear vision of God:

✟ *God hasn't invited us into a disorderly, unkempt life but into something holy and beautiful—as beautiful on the inside as the outside* (1 Thessalonians 4:7 MSG).

✟ *For it is written, "Be holy, because I am holy"* (1 Peter 1:16).

✟ *Make every effort to live in peace with all men and to be holy; without holiness **no one will see the Lord*** (Hebrews 12:14).

✟ *You're blessed when you get your inside world—your mind and heart—put right. Then you can see God in the outside world* (Matthew 5:8 MSG).

Unfortunately, what we don't see is what we don't know is missing or distorted. This is why we are exhorted to keep a pure heart. It has a fundamental effect on our relationship with God, which affects every other aspect of our lives.

You see, our hearts represent the innermost part of ourselves, which gives direction to the mind and body. A good book to read on this subject is *Who Switched Off My Brain? Controlling Toxic Thoughts and Emotions* by Dr. Caroline Leaf. Dr. Leaf goes through the scientific data that shows the need for us to have "positive faith-based emotions" (love, joy, peace, happiness, kindness, gentleness, self-control, forgiveness, and patience) versus "negative fear-based emotions" (hate, worry, anxiety, anger, hostility, rage, ill-will, resentment, frustration, impatience, and irritation). These "negative fear-based emotions" produce toxic attitudes, which produce toxic chemical responses in the body, causing sickness and disease. Through the book, Dr. Leaf shows us how to use "positive faith-based emotions" to detox our minds and hearts, which allows us to detox our bodies and be healed.[5]

When our hearts are pure and in *tune* with God (which is the key), our whole life benefits, both physically and spiritually, allowing us to see and experience the life God desires for us. This is why the Bible reminds us:

✠ *A cheerful heart is good medicine...* (Proverbs 17:22).

✠ *Above all else, guard your heart, for it is the wellspring of life* (Proverbs 4:23).

✠ *Dear friends, if our hearts do not condemn us, we have confidence before God and receive from Him anything we ask, because we obey His commands and do what pleases Him* (1 John 3:21-22).

God looks at your heart and He *knows* your heart. He wants to uphold the innermost part of your being, which makes guarding the purity of your heart vital. We can't do this by our efforts alone—we need Jesus' help. Peter reminds us:

✠ *His divine power has given us everything we need for life and **godliness through our knowledge of Him** who called us by His own glory and goodness. Through these He has given us His very great and precious promises, so that through them you may participate in the divine nature and escape the corruption in the world caused by evil desires* (2 Peter 1:3-4).

We see, in this passage, that to escape the corruption of the world, we must embrace His divine nature and purity that is within us. Our purity will only come through our knowledge of Him or intimacy with Him. We cannot achieve purity alone. It only comes through our willingness to better understand who He is and then surrender ourselves to Him so He can work in and through us.

Also, being holy is *not* simply a matter of doing good. For example, you can give someone money to leverage them or for selfish recognition. Purity is all about the motives of your heart, as you can do seemingly "good things," even "Christian things," with worldly intentions.

☩ *All a man's ways seem innocent to him, but motives are weighed by the Lord* (Proverbs 16:2).

☩ *...[God] will expose the motives of men's hearts* (1 Corinthians 4:5).

When our heart is holy, sin does not distort our vision, and when our vision is clear we can see God in our world and everyday circumstances. This allows us to do His will and to fulfill our purpose in sometimes-confusing situations. He will lead and guide you into righteousness if you allow Him.

☩ *He [God] guides me in the paths of righteousness for His name's sake* (Psalm 23:3).

## Practice Peace

The next step that Jesus gives us, toward our efforts to unwrap our relationship with God, is to be at peace with God and those around us.

✠ *Blessed are the peacemakers, for they will be called sons of God* (Matthew 5:9).

We are called to foster peace, first with our Father God and then with those whom He created:

✠ *Peacemakers who sow in peace raise a harvest of righteousness* (James 3:18).

You will not have peace with God until you have peace with other people. This is because you cannot separate your relationship with people from your relationship with God—they are intertwined. God is inseparably in other people, just as they are in Him. Jesus prayed:

✠ *Father, just as You are in Me and I am in You, may* **they** *also be in* **Us**... (John 17:21).

When you were a child, I'm sure your earthly parents were upset when you and your siblings would fight. If a fracture happens in a family, that fracture interrupts the will of God for that family. Lack of unity denies relationships their full potential. Remember, Heaven on earth can't exist unless *all* relationships reach their full potential.

*Love* and *humility* are a critical part of becoming a true peacemaker. A peacemaker doesn't just avoid arguing with others, but he or she also refrains from speaking negatively about those same people behind their backs. *All* your actions should seek unity among your brothers and sisters in Christ:

✠ *You're blessed when you can show people how to cooperate instead of compete or fight. That's when you discover who you really are, and your place in God's family* (Matthew 5:9 MSG).

## Endure Persecution

The last thing that Jesus teaches in this portion of His sermon is that we will face persecution in this world because of the relationship we have with God. Not only that, but that we're to hang in there and endure it. Let's look at two translations of this verse:

*Blessed are those who are persecuted because of righteousness, for theirs is the kingdom of heaven* (Matthew 5:10).

*You're blessed when your commitment to God provokes persecution. The persecution drives you even deeper into God's kingdom* (Matthew 5:10 MSG).

Let me be clear that, if you are on track with the other seven ingredients for a deeper and more intimate relationship with God, then you *will* encounter persecution. This is because you'll be living in contradiction to the way that the world is living. Indeed, if you are *not* encountering persecution, then you may want to review whether you're pursuing the other seven ingredients as readily as you ought. As I have said before, if you and satan are going in the same direction, you won't encounter any problems with him. However, if you're going in the opposite direction, then he will attempt to oppose you. Listen to what Jesus said about persecution:

*Remember the words I spoke to you: "No servant is greater than his master." If they persecuted Me, then they will persecute you **also**...* [assuming you have made Him the Master of your life] (John 15:20).

Therefore, Jesus goes on to encourage us in His Sermon on the Mount to rejoice in persecution:

✛ *Blessed are you when people insult you, persecute you and falsely say all kinds of evil against you because of Me. Rejoice and be glad, because great is your reward in heaven, for in the same way they persecuted the prophets who were before you* (Matthew 5:11-12).

The apostle Peter said it this way:

✛ *Dear friends, do not be surprised at the painful trial you are suffering, as though something strange were happening to you. But rejoice that you* **participate** *in the sufferings of Christ, so that you may be overjoyed when His glory is revealed. If you are insulted because of the name of Christ, you are blessed, for the Spirit of glory and of God rests on you. If you suffer, it should not be as a murderer or thief or any other kind of criminal, or even as a meddler. However, if you suffer as a Christian, do not be ashamed, but praise God that you bear that name. For it is time for judgment to begin with the family of God; and if it begins with us, what will the outcome be for those who do not obey the gospel of God* (1 Peter 4:12-17).

## ACTION & VISUALIZATION

*Build your relationship with God carefully, using all the steps
that Jesus teaches in His Sermon on the Mount.*

## SERVICE AND OBEDIENCE = LOVING GOD

Accepting the gift of an intimate relationship with God should be our primary focus and concern in life:

*One of the teachers of the law came and heard them debating. Noticing that Jesus had given them a good answer, he asked Him, "Of all the commandments, which is the most important?"*

*"The most important one," answered Jesus, "is this: 'Hear, O Israel, the Lord our God, the Lord is one. Love the Lord your God with all your heart and with all your soul and with all your mind and with all your strength'"* (Mark 12:28-30).

So how do we express loving God with all our heart, soul, mind, and strength? In its simplest definition, the expression of our love for God can be summed up in two words: *serve* and *obey*. Before the Israelites were about to enter the Promised Land, Moses recalled all that God had commanded them throughout the wilderness:

*And now, O Israel, what does the Lord your God ask of you but to fear the Lord your God, to walk in all His ways, to love Him, to **serve** the Lord your God with all your heart and with all your soul, and to **observe** the Lord's commands and decrees that I am giving you today **for your own good**?* (Deuteronomy 10:12-13).

Remember that the greater degree in which you serve and obey, the greater God's presence will be in your life. Of course, the reference here to obeying does not mean ritualistically enslaving ourselves to the law for obedience's sake alone, but it means we are to obey in love. True obedience comes from the heart; it is led by the Spirit and thirsts for that which leads to a deeper commitment to God.

When we reach Heaven, God will completely purify our temples, at which time we will walk perfectly with Him; however, until then we obey Him to please Him and complete our purpose here on earth:

*What agreement is there between the temple of God and idols? For we are the temple of the living God. As God has said: "I will live with them and walk among them, and I will be their God, and they will be My people"* (2 Corinthians 6:16).

Until then, we look to Jesus as our example for how to relate to God:

✟ [Jesus] *replied, "Blessed rather are those who hear the word of God and **obey** it"* (Luke 11:28).

✟ *As the Father has loved Me, so have I loved you. Now remain in My love. If you **obey** My commands, you will remain in My love, just as I have **obeyed** My Father's commands and remain in His love. I have told you this so that My joy may be in you and that your **joy may be complete*** (John 15:9-11).

Note that *when* you obey to please God and enter a deeper relationship with Him, not only will you be expressing your love to God, but you also will experience joy, as you will be living out that for which you were created. God ties things together in amazing ways, all of which are for our benefit.

## ACTION & VISUALIZATION
*Look for ways you can serve and obey God.*

## DEPENDENCE BRINGS YOU CLOSE

When we serve and obey God's will (even when we don't fully understand God's plan at the time), we are acknowledging our dependence on God. Dependency is a virtue that enhances our relationship with God because it allows more of Him in us. Paul offered these conclusions:

✠ *But He said to me, "My grace is sufficient for you, for My power is made perfect in weakness." Therefore I will boast all the more gladly about my weaknesses, so that Christ's power may rest on me. That is why, for Christ's sake, I delight in weaknesses, in insults, in hardships, in persecutions, in difficulties.* **For when I am weak, then I am strong** (2 Corinthians 12:9-10).

Paul knew that his weaknesses caused him to be dependent on God in those areas, which then became his strengths. It was the same for all the Bible heroes who knew they were not the star of their story, but that God was the star. The writer of Hebrews tells us of:

✠ *Gideon, Barak, Samson, Jephthah, David, Samuel and the prophets, who through faith conquered kingdoms, administered justice, and gained what was promised; who shut the mouths of lions, quenched the fury of the flames, and escaped the edge of the sword; whose* **weakness** *was* **turned to strength***; and who became powerful in battle and routed foreign armies* (Hebrews 11:32-34).

Paul also wrote that Jesus is our model for how we become weak in order to gain God's strength:

✠ *For to be sure, [Jesus] was crucified in* **weakness***, yet He lives by God's power. Likewise, we are* **weak** *in Him, yet by God's power we will live with Him to serve you* (2 Corinthians 13:4).

God finds His place in your weaknesses to form a partnership with you. This happens when you realize that you cannot find victory on your own. God wants this type of relationship with you, a oneness where you depend on Him as He invests His power in you. The more room you give God to inhabit your efforts, the more of God (and the less of you) will dwell in them.

As you have learned, an important part of growing with God is preparation. I am referring to the inner you; the part of you that God is most concerned with is not your strength or exterior beauty. Rather, He is concerned with your heart:

✠ *But the Lord said to Samuel, "Do not consider his appearance or his height, for I have rejected him. The Lord does not look at the things man looks at. Man looks at the outward appearance, but the Lord looks at the heart"* (1 Samuel 16:7).

✠ *The lamp of the Lord searches the spirit of a man; it searches out his innermost being* (Proverbs 20:27).

✠ *Woe to you, teachers of the law and Pharisees, you hypocrites! You are like whitewashed tombs, which look beautiful on the outside but on the inside are full of dead men's bones and everything unclean* (Matthew 23:27).

✠ *Stop judging by mere appearances, and make a right judgment* (John 7:24).

God is most concerned about what's on the inside of you because He expects His children to live from the inside out, thus outwardly reflecting what is inside of them (Him) for the world to see. Remember that even Jesus' appearance was described as ordinary (see Isaiah 53:2). Sometimes we get so caught up in preparing our outward appearances that we place little focus on preparing our hearts. The outward appearance is only temporal. Confidence in exterior things will *eventually* disappoint, for in time our outward self grows old and wears out. Instead, we need to be focused on improving our inner selves because, in contrast, our inner selves can become better and better, brighter and brighter, every year that we live.

Your effort will not go unnoticed by others. As you operate, fully connected to your primary purpose, projecting His image and likeness, others will notice. On the other hand, Paul said that such people who seem outwardly powerful are of no account to God or His message to the world:

✝ *As for those who seemed to be important—whatever they were makes* **no** *difference to me; God does not judge by external appearance—those men added nothing to my message* (Galatians 2:6).

What *is coming out* of us is *more* important than the *outside* of us. Remember the light bulb analogy from Book 1? What is inside of us determines what comes out. God is the spirit in actions and not an inanimate object, so it is only by our actions we can be like Him, and not by our physical presence. Therefore, we need to keep God at the center of our lives, being fully dependent on Him who is in us so that He can perform His great works *through* us.

✝ *I can do everything through Him who gives me strength* (Philippians 4:13).

✝ *Do not grieve, for the joy of the Lord is your strength* (Nehemiah 8:10).

✝ *Be strong in the Lord and in His mighty power* (Ephesians 6:10).

✝ *In all these things we are more than conquerors through Him who loved us* (Romans 8:37).

Obeying God and preparing yourself for Him will not only make your relationship with God stronger, but it will also give you much more *freedom* in your life.

✚ *To the Jews who had believed Him, Jesus said, "If you hold to My teaching, you are really My disciples. Then you will know the truth, and the truth will set you free"* (John 8:31-32).

---

## ACTION & VISUALIZATION

*Work at obediently preparing yourself so that you can project the right image and likeness.*

## INTIMATE UNION

Our relationship with God begins as a spiritual one that will eventually manifest itself as a holy union. The Bible likens this union to that of a husband and wife; Jesus, the husband, marries His bride, the collective church (see Ephesians 5:23). This infers that we will become one with God, just as God says that husbands and wives are one. Indeed, just like a husband and wife prepare for their marriage union, so we are betrothed to Christ and are commanded to prepare for and respect our union with Him:

✚ *Let us rejoice and be glad and give Him glory! For the wedding of the Lamb has come, and His bride has made herself ready* (Revelation 19:7).

✚ *At that* [end] *time the kingdom of heaven will be like ten virgins* [the church] *who took their lamps and went out to meet the bridegroom* [Jesus] (Matthew 25:1).

✝ *At midnight* [the end times] *the cry rang out: "Here's the bridegroom* [Jesus]*! Come out to meet Him"* (Matthew 25:6).

This is why the Bible exhorts us to keep ourselves clean and pure:

✝ *"Food for the stomach and the stomach for food"—but God will destroy them both* [when we get our heavenly bodies]. *The body is not meant for sexual immorality, but for the Lord, and the Lord for the body. By His power God raised the Lord from the dead, and He will raise us also. Do you not know that your bodies are members of Christ Himself? Shall I then take the members of Christ and unite them with a prostitute? Never! Do you not know that he who unites himself with a prostitute is one with her in body? For it is said, "The two will become one flesh." But he who unites himself with the Lord is one with Him in spirit* (1 Corinthians 6:13-17).

✝ *I saw the Holy City, the new Jerusalem, coming down out of heaven from God, prepared as a bride beautifully dressed for her husband* (Revelation 21:2).

✝ *I am jealous for you with a godly jealousy. I promised you to one husband, to Christ, so that I might present you as a pure virgin to Him* (2 Corinthians 11:2).

Relationship with Jesus is an invitation to the water of life. This living water, which Jesus spoke of with the Samaritan woman, is actually Jesus Himself.

✠ *The Spirit and the bride say, "Come!" And let him who hears say, "Come!" Whoever is thirsty, let him come; and whoever wishes, let him take the **free gift** of the water of life (Revelation 22:17).*

## ACTION & VISUALIZATION

*Begin preparing yourself now for your holy union with Jesus.*

## YOUR ETERNAL DESTINY

There remains one unanswered question. Was our salvation predetermined from the beginning? Consider these verses:

✠ *Therefore He has mercy on whom He wills, and whom He wills He hardens.*

*You will say to me then, "Why does He still find fault? For who has resisted His will?" But indeed, O man, who are you to reply against God? Will the thing formed say to him who formed it, "Why have you made me like this?" Does not the potter have power over the clay, from the same lump to make one vessel for honor and another for dishonor?*

***What** if God, wanting to show His wrath and to make His power known, endured with much longsuffering the vessels of wrath prepared for destruction, and that He might make known the riches of His glory on the vessels of mercy, which He had prepared beforehand for glory...* (Romans 9:18-23 NKJV).

✠ *For [God] chose us in Him before the creation of the world to be holy and blameless in His sight. In love He predestined us to be adopted as His sons through Jesus Christ, in accordance with His pleasure and*

917

*will—to the praise of His glorious grace, which He has freely given us in the one He loves* (Ephesians 1:4-6).

Was the current so strong, the way so clear for those of us who have received Jesus? Was saying yes to God inevitable for you and me? Whatever the case, those who received the gift of salvation have an eternal destiny, an eternal future with God. John writes:

✠ *They will make war against the lamb, but the lamb will overcome them because He is Lord of lords, and King of kings—and **with** Him will be His called, chosen and faithful followers* (Revelation 17:14).

At that time, we will receive the fullness of our Promised Land (transformation into the image and likeness of God) and live eternally in His very presence. All that has been infected by sin on the earth will be destroyed, burnt up, and God will replace it with a new Heaven and a new earth; however, all of His promises to us will remain:

✠ *Heaven and earth will pass away, but My words will never pass away* (Matthew 24:35).

✠ *Behold, I will create new heavens and a new earth. The former things will not be remembered, nor will they come to mind* (Isaiah 65:17).

✠ *By calling this covenant "new," He has made the first one obsolete; and what is obsolete and aging will soon disappear* (Hebrews 8:13).

✦ *All the stars of the heavens will be dissolved and the sky rolled up like a scroll; all the starry host will fall like withered leaves from the vine, like shriveled figs from the fig tree* (Isaiah 34:4).

✦ *Lift up your eyes to the heavens, look at the earth beneath; the heavens will vanish like smoke, the earth will wear out like a garment and its inhabitants die like flies. But My salvation will last forever, My righteousness will never fail* (Isaiah 51:6).

✦ *"As the new heaven and the new earth that I will make endure before Me," declares the Lord, "so will your name and descendants endure"* (Isaiah 66:22).

✦ *I tell you the truth, until heaven and earth disappear, not the smallest letter, not the least stroke of a pen, will by any means disappear from the law until everything is accomplished* (Matthew 5:18).

✦ *But the day of the Lord will come like a thief. The heavens will disappear with a roar; the elements will be destroyed by fire, and the earth and everything in it will be laid bare.*

*Since everything will be destroyed in this way, what kind of people ought you to be? You ought to live holy and godly lives as you look forward to the day of God and speed its coming. That day will bring about the destruction of the heavens by fire, and the elements will melt in the heat. But in keeping with His promise we are looking forward to a new heaven and a new earth, the home of righteousness* (2 Peter 3:10-13).

All evil will be consumed from earth, which leaves only His unshakable promises standing. Only His Kingdom will remain, where we can be the people He wants us to be, fully consumed in our relationship with Him.

✠ *Therefore, since we are receiving a kingdom that cannot be shaken, let us be thankful, and so worship God acceptably with reverence and awe, for our "God is a consuming fire" (Hebrews 12:28-29).*

## IMAGE AND LIKENESS

Not only will the current world we live in be purified, but also our very own bodies will be purified as well. Consider these verses about our eternal bodies:

✠ *But our citizenship is in heaven. And we eagerly await a Savior from there, the Lord Jesus Christ, who, by the power that enables Him to bring everything under His control, will transform our lowly bodies so that they will be like His glorious body (Philippians 3:20-21).*

✠ *And after my skin has been destroyed, yet in my [new] flesh I will see God (Job 19:26).*

✠ *According to the Lord's own word, we tell you that we who are still alive, who are left till the coming of the Lord, will certainly not precede those who have fallen asleep [died]. For the Lord Himself will come down from heaven, with a loud command, with the voice of the archangel and with the trumpet call of God, and **the dead in Christ*** *will rise first. After that, we who are still alive and are left will be caught up together with them in the clouds to meet the Lord in the air. And so we will be with the Lord forever* (1 Thessalonians 4:15-17).

✠ *Now we know that if the earthly tent we live in* [our body] *is destroyed, we have a building from God, an eternal house* [body for our mind and spirit] *in heaven, not built by human hands. Meanwhile we groan, longing to be clothed with our heavenly dwelling* [God's glory shining from the inside out], *because when we are clothed, we will not be found naked. For while we are in this tent, we groan and are burdened, because we do not wish to be unclothed but to be clothed with our heavenly dwelling* [God's glory], *so that what is mortal may be swallowed up by life. Now it is God who has made us for this very purpose and has given us the Spirit* [which we received when we were saved] *as a deposit, guaranteeing what is to come* [complete fulfillment of our intimate relationship and transformation into His image and likeness] (2 Corinthians 5:1-5).

✠ *I consider that our present sufferings are not worth comparing with the glory that will be revealed in us. The creation waits in eager expectation for the sons* [and daughters] *of God to be revealed. For the creation was subjected to frustration, not by its own choice, but by the will of the one who subjected it, in hope that the creation itself will be liberated from its bondage to decay and brought into the glorious freedom of the children of God.*

*We know that the whole creation has been groaning as in the pains of childbirth right up to this present time. Not only so, but we ourselves, who have the firstfruits of the Spirit, groan inwardly as we wait eagerly for our adoption as sons* [and daughters], *the redemption of our bodies* (Romans 8:18-23).

✛ But someone may ask, "How are the dead raised? With what kind of body will they come?" How foolish! What you sow does not come to life unless it dies. When you sow, you do not plant the body that will be, but just a seed, perhaps of wheat or of something else. But God gives it a body as He has determined, and to each kind of seed He gives its own body. All flesh is not the same: Men have one kind of flesh, animals have another, birds another and fish another. There are also heavenly bodies and there are earthly bodies; but the splendor of the heavenly bodies is one kind, and the splendor of the earthly bodies is another. The sun has one kind of splendor, the moon another and the stars another; and star differs from star in splendor.

So will it be with the resurrection of the dead. The body that is sown is perishable, **it is raised imperishable**; it is sown in dishonor, **it is raised in glory**; it is sown in weakness, **it is raised in power**; it is sown a natural body, **it is raised a spiritual body**.

If there is a natural body, there is also a spiritual body. So it is written: "The first man Adam became a living being"; the last Adam [Jesus], a life-giving spirit. The spiritual did not come **first**, but **the natural**, and **after that the spiritual**. The first man was of the dust of the earth, the second man [Jesus] from heaven. As was the earthly man, so are those who are of the earth; and as the man from heaven [Jesus], so also are those who are of heaven. And just as we have borne the likeness of the earthly man, **so shall we bear the likeness of the man from heaven** [Jesus].

I declare to you, brothers, that flesh and blood cannot inherit the kingdom of God, nor does the perishable inherit the imperishable. Listen, I tell you a mystery: We will not all sleep [remain dead], but **we will all be changed in a flash, in the twinkling of an eye, at the last trumpet**. For the trumpet will sound, the dead will be raised imperishable, and we will be changed. For the perishable must clothe itself with the imperishable, and the mortal with immortality. When the perishable has been clothed with the imperishable, and the mortal with immortality, then the saying that is written will come true: "Death has been swallowed up in victory."

> *"Where, O death, is your victory?*
> *Where, O death, is your sting?"*
> The sting of death is sin, and the power of sin is the law. But thanks be to God! He gives us the victory through our Lord Jesus Christ (1 Corinthians 15:35-57).

✝ *Dear friends, now we are children of God, and what we will be has not yet been made known. But we know that when He appears, we shall be like Him, for **we shall see Him** as He is. Everyone who has this hope in Him purifies himself, just as He is pure (1 John 3:2-3).*

## YOUR FUTURE

What will this new Heaven be like? Well, the Bible gives us some exciting clues; however, when reading these descriptions, remember that the authors could only use words and concepts that they and we could relate to and understand. The reality is that Heaven will be so different from anything we have ever experienced that the words we now know cannot fully or properly describe it in an accurate way. Here is what the Bible says about Heaven:

✝ *Then I saw a new heaven and a new earth, for the first heaven and the first earth had passed away, and there was no longer any sea. I saw the Holy City, the new Jerusalem, coming down out of heaven from God, prepared as a bride beautifully dressed for her husband. And I heard a loud voice from the throne saying, "Now the dwelling of God is with men, and **He will live with them**. They will be His people, and **God Himself** will be with them and be their God. He will wipe every tear from their eyes. There will be no more death or mourning or crying or pain, for the old order of things has passed away."*

*He who was seated on the throne said, "I am making everything new..."* (Revelation 21:1-5).

✠ *The ransomed of the Lord [Christians] will return. They will enter Zion [God's presence] with singing; everlasting joy will crown their heads. Gladness and joy will overtake them, and sorrow and sighing will flee away* (Isaiah 51:11).

✠ *Never again will they hunger; never again will they thirst. The sun will not beat upon them, nor any scorching heat* (Revelation 7:16).

✠ *The Lord their God will save them on that day as the flock of His people. They will sparkle in His land like jewels in a crown. How attractive and beautiful they will be! Grain will make the young men thrive, and new wine the young women* (Zechariah 9:16-17).

✠ *Then the angel showed me the river of the water of life, as clear as crystal, flowing from the throne of God and of the Lamb [Jesus] down the middle of the great street of the city. On each side of the river stood the Tree of Life, bearing twelve crops of fruit, yielding its fruit every month. And the leaves of the tree are for the healing of the nations. No longer will there be any curse [brought on by man]. The throne of God and of the Lamb will be in the city, and His servants will serve Him. They will **see His face**, and His name will be on their foreheads. There will be no more night. They will not need the light of a lamp or the light of the sun, for the Lord God will give them light. And they will reign for ever and ever* (Revelation 22:1-5).

✟ *I did not see a temple* [place of worship to meet God] *in the city, because the Lord God Almighty and the Lamb are its temple. The city does not need the sun or the moon to shine on it, for the **glory of God gives it light**, and the Lamb is its lamp* (Revelation 21:22-23).

The Bible is clearly telling us here that our final destination will be in direct relationship with *God Himself* and that we will see *God's face*. Remember God told Moses that Moses could not see His face, for no one could see it and live (see Exodus 33:20). How can we truly comprehend that, given our current limitations and understanding of time and space? Remember, God does not have a physical presence. He is, for lack of a better term, an action—love, life, goodness, mercy, etc.

What does the face of God look like? For us, of course, it would be the experience of pure love, as well as the full knowledge of His thoughts and knowledge. Think of the infinite mind of God that imagined and then created every physical *detail* you see in nature, right down to the smallest molecule and the furthest galaxy. This is something we really can't fathom. Consider the unique design of every butterfly, snowflake, or even feelings. Because of His infinite capacity, God is always with each of us now; however, in our heavenly experience, we will have a face-to-face intimate relationship that allows us to personally explore the depths of His love, knowledge, and power. Put the book down for a few minutes to let your imagination flow, and dwell on what it means to see the face of God.

The verse also says He will be our temple, or, we could say, the place in which we experience Him (see Revelation 21:22). The verse continues with:

✟ *The nations will walk by its light, and the kings of the earth will bring their splendor into it. On no day will its gates ever be shut, for there will be no night there. The glory and honor of the nations will be brought into it. **Nothing impure** will ever enter it, nor will anyone who does what is shameful or deceitful, but only those whose names are written in the Lamb's book of life* (Revelation 21:24-27).

How is this heavenly experience, where everything goes well and no one feels disappointment, possible? What does a "perfect world" look like? Well, perfection can only happen when everything and *everyone* are acting in complete obedience to the will of God, when all people are only experiencing love from God and giving God's love to *one another*. We all will help create the heavenly experience, as revealed in the Bible, for each other, because God will conform us back into His image and likeness. We will be heavenly beings.

We enter Heaven when we accept the gift of salvation, when we accept Jesus as our Savior and have our names written in the Lamb's book of life. This starts the process of our transformation that is required to get to Heaven. We volunteer, allowing Him to conform us into His image and likeness, into heavenly beings. We become heirs of our Father's Kingdom. And when we reach this Promised Land, after we are transformed into His image and likeness, we will no longer know evil. We will all be in *perfect harmony* with God and with each other.

## Improve Your Eternity

While salvation gets us into Heaven, we do *not* all have the same experience in Heaven. The gift of God Himself can begin to be unwrapped on earth, enabling us to walk in greater obedience, submission, and love. Remember that when we receive, unwrap, and use a gift God offers, we are in turn giving Him a gift. Gift-giving is the manifestation of intimacy, as in a marriage, which is the *most* intimate earthly relationship. God's goal is to have an ultimate intimacy with you for all of eternity. The Bible suggests that, while on earth, we can influence our future relationship with God by how well we unwrap our relationship with Him now:

✠ *Behold, I am coming soon! My reward is with Me, and I will give to everyone according to what he has done* (Revelation 22:12).

✠ *But store up for yourselves treasures in **heaven** [by planting good seeds on earth], where moth and rust do not destroy, and where thieves do not break in and steal* (Matthew 6:20).

✠ *Then I heard a voice from heaven say, "Write: Blessed are the dead who die in the Lord from now on."*

*"Yes," says the Spirit, "they will rest from their labor, **for their deeds will follow them**"* (Revelation 14:13).

✠ *Blessed are you when people insult you, persecute you and falsely say all kinds of evil against you because of Me. Rejoice and be glad, because great is your reward **in heaven**, for in the same way they persecuted the prophets who were before you* (Matthew 5:11-12).

✠ *The Lord has made proclamation to the ends of the earth: "Say to the Daughters of Zion, 'See, your Savior comes! See, His reward is with Him and His recompense accompanies Him'"* (Isaiah 62:11).

✠ *Do not work for food that spoils, but for food that endures to **eternal life**, which the Son of Man will give you...* (John 6:27).

✠ *Sell your possessions and give to the poor. Provide purses for yourselves that will not wear out, a treasure in heaven that will not be exhausted, where no thief comes near and no moth destroys* (Luke 12:33).

✠ *"I tell you the truth," Jesus replied, "no one who has left home or brothers or sisters or mothers or fathers or children or friends for Me and the gospel will fail to receive a hundred times as much in this present age... **and the age to come**..."* (Mark 10:29-30).

✠ *For the Son of Man is going to come in His Father's glory with His angels* [at His second coming], *and then He will reward each person **according to what he has done*** (Matthew 16:27).

Another theme that runs through the Bible is that our actions of faith earn us *crowns* that we will wear in Heaven. Some we gain simply by placing our faith in Jesus as our Savior, and some come by other *actions* of faith.

✠ *Everyone who competes in the games goes into strict training. They do it to get a **crown** that will not last; but we do it to get a **crown that will last forever*** (1 Corinthians 9:25).

✠ *Now there is in store for me the **crown** of righteousness, which the Lord, the righteous Judge, will award to me on that day—and not only to me, but also to all who have longed for His appearing* (2 Timothy 4:8).

✠ *Blessed is the man who perseveres under trial, because when he has stood the test, he will receive the **crown** of life that God has promised to those who love Him* (James 1:12).

✝ *And when the Chief Shepherd appears, you will receive the **crown** of glory that will never fade away* (1 Peter 5:4).

✝ *I am coming soon. Hold on to what you have, so that no one will take your **crown*** (Revelation 3:11).

An interesting passage in the book of Revelation says that the twenty-four elders lay down their crowns before Jesus' throne as an act of submission and worship:

✝ *The twenty-four elders fall down before Him who sits on the throne, and worship Him who lives for ever and ever. They lay their **crowns** before the throne...* (Revelation 4:10).

The question I would ask you now is, How many *crowns* would you like to lay at the feet of Jesus on that day?

God is going to complete His promise to you.

✝ *Being confident of this, that He who began a good work in you will carry it on to completion until the day of Christ Jesus* (Philippians 1:6).

What will you do for Him? Now is the time to consider what *gifts* you can receive to lay at His feet.

# Meditation Point

In Heaven, your relationship with God will become one in presence and spirit.

Go to Chapter 7 in the Study Guide section on page 981.

## Endnotes

1.  Jack Hayford, ed., *Spirit-Filled Life Bible for Students* (Nashville, TN: Thomas Nelson Publishers, 1995), 1188.

2.  Dr. Caroline Leaf, *Who Switched Off My Brain? Controlling Toxic Thoughts and Emotions* (Dallas, TX: Switch on Your Brain USA Inc., 2008), 123–124.

3.  Adam Clarke, "Commentary on Matthew 5," *The Adam Clarke Commentary*, http://www.studylight.org/com/acc/view.cgi?book=mt& chapter=005. 1832.

4.  Ibid.

5.  Dr. Caroline Leaf, *Who Switched Off My Brain*, 119–120.

# Study Guide

## INTRODUCTION

Please don't think of this study guide as a homework assignment. It *isn't* about giving the "right answer"—it's about giving an honest answer. It *isn't* about "getting it done"—it's about letting the questions stir your heart. It *isn't* about "filling in the blanks," but instead letting the Holy Spirit speak to your soul. Think of this as a spiritual experience or potential encounter between you and God rather than an exercise to check off your to-do list.

We are conditioned to believe that our answers to questions in a textbook will be graded; however, that mind-set stifles the purpose of this study guide. This is an opportunity to write honestly about your faith, to grow and go deeper in God's Word, to pray earnestly about His will for your life, and most of all to cultivate an intimate relationship between you and your Creator.

If possible, devote time for quiet reflection as you read the material, think about your life, and write accordingly. Answer the questions as you truly feel, even if it seems wrong or troubling. Remember that "the truth will set you free" and that growth can only happen when the soil is soft. You get what you give. You could burn through this entire study guide in half an hour if you'd like, but it would offer little to no lasting benefit.

I pray that you will put in the time and effort to maximize this material and actualize the full impact of His Gifts of Freedom into your life. Use the study guide to find the spiritual growth and maturity God desires you to have in your life.

# The Gifts of Freedom Study Guide

# BOOK 3

## INCREASE, GIFTS OF THE SPIRIT, RELATIONSHIPS, DESTINY, AND GOD HIMSELF

### HOW TO USE THE STUDY GUIDE

You can use this study guide in a variety of ways, including individually, as part of a small group Bible study, or in a Sunday school setting. If you are working through this book on your own, then use this study guide to record your personal growth journey. Take the time after each chapter to answer the questions. Some are designed to help you remember the main concepts in the chapter, while others are designed to help you personalize the content and apply it to your own life. At the end, seriously pray in closing that God will fill you with His gifts, and that you will recognize and accept them. You can also visit our website at www.giftsoffreedom.com and see how others have applied this information to their lives.

If you're reading this book in a small group, then use the study questions to prompt lively discussion. Discuss the action steps with at least one other group member to build accountability in your plans for action, then close your time together with prayer. For more information on how to lead a group or Sunday school class and get additional resources, visit our website at www.giftsoffreedom.com.

If you are not currently in a group study of the book, you might want to consider starting one after you finish, so you can spread to others the new freedoms you have discovered. As you help others, you will deepen your understanding and relationship with God, gaining even more freedoms.

Go to www.giftsoffreedom.com for additional resource materials and instructions.

# Chapter 1

# Gift #8—Increase (Part 1)

## Where, How, and Why Is There Increase?

### Study Questions

1. What is the primary purpose of an investment? How do earthly investments differ from investments in God's Kingdom? What does this suggest about a successful investment strategy?

_____

_____

_____

_____

2. Does an investment in knowing God cause increase in other areas of our lives? Are we prone to ignore this? Why?

_____

_____

_____

_____

The measure of your faith is found through the actions of your faith.

3. What does your measure of faith look like today?

_____

_____

_____

_____

_____

Knowing and believing that God gives you all your increase will enhance your relationship with Him each day.

4. How does pride get in the way of increase? What changes when you trust God to be the sole provider of increase?

_____

_____

_____

_____

_____

Regardless of what the world and your ambition may tell you, it is God whom you need to trust and see as your Provider.

5. Who is your ultimate provider? Why is understanding this important? How is it vital to what you will receive?

_____

_____

_____

_____

_____

6. If you reap what you sow, what are some seeds that you would like to uproot? What are some seeds you would like to see growing in your life that you need to begin planting? (Also consider nonphysical things, such as love, mercy, and truth.)

_____

_____

_____

_____

_____

_____

_____

Allow time to be the opportunity to grow your faith as you wait for your seeds to bear fruit.

7. Reflect on this verse: *"And let us not grow weary while doing good, for in due season we shall reap if we do not lose heart"* (Galatians 6:9 NKJV). Why did Paul write, *"if we do not lose heart"*? What is he talking about? What are some seeds you have planted in faith you may have to not lose heart over before you see growth? Following the analogy, what are some ways that you can water, nourish, and facilitate growth?

_____

_____

_____

_____

_____

_____

_____

_____

_____

_____

> What we sow and what we consume as bread is up to us; one will give us an additional return. Choose wisely what you will consume and what you will replant for long-term reward.

8. What is the best way to determine which portion of our increase we should consume and which portion we should use for seed?

_____

_____

_____

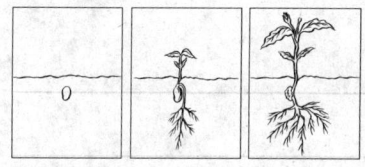

> Just like the seed must die to be made alive as a plant, so you as well must die to yourself so you can have spiritual growth that brings life.

9. What does it mean to "die to yourself"? Why is this important for bearing fruit? Conversely, how does living for self stifle growth?

_____

_____

_____

10. Why is the spiritual growth timeline from seed to harvest becoming shorter and shorter? What does this mean for you, practically speaking?

_____

_____

_____

_____

_____

God sowed His Son into physical death so that He could receive a spiritual harvest of eternal sons and daughters.

11. Why was it important for God to sow His most precious possession? What can we learn about sowing and reaping from this most precious gift?

_____

_____

_____

_____

_____

_____

12. Most of us believe that God is the source of increase, but our lives often suggest that we are the ultimate source of increase, not Him. What areas can you change to reflect this new, abundant way of thinking and living?

_____

_____

_____

_____

_____

## ACTION STEPS

Summarize the nine spiritual truths of sowing and reaping contained in this chapter. What have you learned about sowing and reaping that can help you in your day-to-day walk of faith? How will these truths help you grow closer to God? Consider practical ways that you can put this new knowledge into practice every day.

_____

_____

_____

_____

_____

_____

## CLOSING PRAYER

(Pray this prayer or come up with your own to close this study time.)

Lord, thank You for the gift of increase. Teach me how to use these steps in my own life and to wait patiently on Your increase.

# Chapter 2

# GIFT #8—INCREASE (PART 2)

## HOW DO YOU GET THE GOOD KIND?

### STUDY QUESTIONS

1. After reading the story that opens this chapter, what do you think the sports car could represent in your life? What do you think caused the son to miss his father's gift? Is your ultimate desire for the "bigger gift" first and foremost, blinding you to the gift that God is offering you?

_____

_____

_____

_____

_____

_____

_____

_____

_____

After the fall, increase was found in hard work; yet our true increase is found when we accept, unwrap, and use God's help.

2. How do you go about exercising faith? What are some principles with physical exercise that relate to your spiritual growth? Can you see some possible areas in your life where this may apply?

_____

_____

The only challenge God makes to you in the Bible is to bring your tithe into His house. He promises that He will open the windows of Heaven and pour out such a blessing that there will not be enough room to receive it.

3. Why do you think God challenges us to "test" Him when it comes to tithing? How do you do this? What kind of blessings could come from God's response to your obedience?

_____

_____

_____

A dire financial situation may not really be a need for money, as much as a need for more of God's presence in your life.

4. What are some examples of *dire situations* you've experienced that have compelled you toward God? Do difficult times always send people toward God? Why or why not?

_____

_____

_____

A generous heart will help build up your eternal account and impede the devourer.

5. What does a *generous heart* look like in your story? How have others been generous toward you? How are you generous toward others? What are the spiritual benefits of generosity?

_____

_____

_____

When the enemy is stealing your possessions, you can count it joy because your retribution can be double.

6. Think of times when you've been troubled by satan. What would a doubled repayment look like in these times? How has God blessed you or others after times of trial and testing? Why do God's blessings typically follow a winter season, a period of trial and testing?

_____

_____

_____

_____

_____

_____

_____

_____

_____

_____

_____

_____

946

Listen to God and His advice during the good times so you won't have to experience things He didn't intend for you.

7. "If God wants to say something to me, I'm right here." Is this attitude different from actively seeking and listening to God? How do you go about listening to Him? Are there other ways you could seek His input? Why is this important in relation to increase?

_____

_____

_____

A gift opens the way for the giver to generously receive.

8. What are the gifts that you can give to God? What spiritual doors are *opened* by giving gifts to God?

_____

_____

_____

947

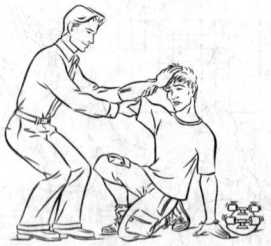 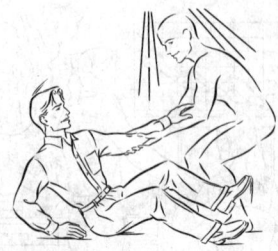

The actions of our hearts put spiritual principles in motion that create the situations in life that we later run into.

9. What are some ways that you need to guard your heart in current relationships? How might this play into future circumstances?

_____

_____

_____

_____

_____

_____

_____

_____

_____

_____

God can use your planted seed to give you and others rest and shade in ever-increasing amounts.

10. What are some Kingdom-building seeds you have planted? Imagine how and in what way these could grow.

_____

_____

_____

_____

_____

_____

_____

_____

11. Jesus said that we should seek first God's Kingdom (see Matthew 6:33), yet most of us, in all honesty, seek God's Kingdom only when there's time or when it's not too stressful. What if a farmer had this attitude with his or her crops? How could this apply to you?

_____

_____

_____

_____

_____

_____

12. In the author's story, God used money to bring increase after intense and repeated testing. What is God using in your life? What good seeds are you planting right now in faith that will bring increase?

_____

_____

_____

_____

_____

_____

## ACTION STEPS

Look at the way you currently give to God. Are you tithing? Are you generous with your increase (look at your check stubs for the answer)? Even if you don't have much money, you can give to God from what you do have. Consider adjusting your giving habits if you need to. Then trust God to deliver on His promises to bless you. Consider all the other areas in which you can give too.

_____

_____

_____

_____

_____

_____

## CLOSING PRAYER

(Pray this prayer or come up with your own to close this study time.)

Lord, thank You for Your blessings. Help me to become a generous giver and to trust Your hand as I learn to obey and anticipate Your increase in my life.

# Chapter 3

# GIFT #9—GIFTS OF THE SPIRIT (PART 1)

## HOW DO YOUR GIFTS BRING LIFE TO YOUR LIFE?

### STUDY QUESTIONS

1. What are some ways in which becoming a parent alters your perspective on life and, therefore, the way you live it? What similar changes take place when you become a follower of Christ? Can you do it on your own? Who can help?

_____

_____

_____

_____

_____

_____

_____

Let the world see God through your actions and reactions.

2. What does it look like to let the world see God through your actions and reactions? In tense or stressful situations, what do your actions and reactions say about your faith? Give an example of this from your own life.

_____

_____

_____

_____

_____

3. True or False: God gives Christians gifts when they deserve them and can properly use them. Why or why not? What happens if you don't exercise your gifts?

_____

_____

_____

_____

_____

Jesus, as the Head of the church body, orchestrates it through the Holy Spirit to fulfill God's plan for the world. You are God's hands to reach a dying world.

4.  How do the different gifts work together to make something beautiful? How does unity in the body of Christ impact the reach of God's hands into our world? How well have you done at submitting your head, heart, and hands to God as Peter did? What could you do to improve?

_____

_____

_____

_____

_____

_____

_____

_____

_____

_____

_____

Our words and gifts will be received based on how well they are wrapped with God's Spirit.

5. Of what value are the gifts when love is not a part of the process? Why? How do you infuse love with the gifts?

_____

_____

_____

_____

_____

6. How does love fulfill the law? Are we called to love or to live by the law? How does love develop our relationship with God?

_____

_____

_____

_____

_____

_____

We are to pray in unity to bring down the spiritual strongholds that operate and have control over our land.

7. How do we pray to bring down spiritual strongholds? What is a Christian's role in changing the world? What specific sicknesses or sins do you feel led to pull down? List some ways of praying for those strongholds.

_____

_____

_____

Jesus lived a perfect life so He could fulfill the law and die to pay for our sin, allowing oneness again between humans and the Spirit of God.

8. How did God completely fulfill the law? How did that change our relationship with God? Why?

_____

_____

_____

When you can see, in your everyday life, what is happening in the spirit realm, using your gifts will become much easier.

9. What does it mean to contradict the world? When we do this and want people to follow us, what condition should we live in? Plan for when, where, and how you are going to be in fruit-bearing condition.

_____

_____

_____

_____

_____

Wrapping your gifts in God's love will allow them to be accepted and therefore used.

10. Think of some of God's gifts and how you would wrap them in pure love. What's likely to happen when you do? What's likely to happen when you don't?

_____

_____

_____

_____

11. List ways that you could be tempted to use your gifts for applause, personal gain, power, or other self-focused means. How do you guard yourself against these temptations?

_____

_____

_____

_____

_____

12. Love is God's essence, and our charge is [to make known] *"the manifold wisdom of God to the rulers and authorities in the heavenly realms, according to His eternal purpose which He accomplished in Christ Jesus our Lord"* (Ephesians 3:10-11). If Jesus returned today and asked how you're fulfilling this mandate, what would you say? Where are you lacking, and how could you become more active?

_____

_____

_____

_____

_____

_____

## Action Steps

Think about how well you're using your gifts in love. Are there some attitudes or actions you need to change to better live them out with God's love? Make those needed changes and watch to see how God will use you in surprising and powerful new ways.

_____

_____

_____

_____

_____

## Closing Prayer

(Pray this prayer or come up with your own to close this study time.)

Lord, You have given me unique and important gifts from Your Spirit. Help me to exercise them only in love so that they will impact the world in powerful ways.

# Chapter 4

# Gift #9—Gifts of the Spirit (Part 2)

## How Do You Find Your Gifts?

### Study Questions

1. Have you ever been to the symphony? What are some areas in which you may be unpracticed, out of sync, or out of tune with the Conductor?

_____

_____

_____

_____

_____

_____

_____

Gifts offered in anything other than God's love will be rejected or even backfire.

2. What are some examples of what happens to our gifts when our motivation becomes pride or self-interest? How does this damage our relationship with God? With others?

_____

_____

_____

3. What if you have a gift, such as teaching, but never use it? If you have a gift, does that automatically make you a good teacher, prophet, leader, etc., from the start? Or does it take time to fully develop your gifts? How do we sharpen and refine our gifting?

_____

_____

_____

4. As you read about the different gifts, which one(s) did you identify with most clearly? How can you experiment with all the different gifts to see which ones you may possess?

_____

_____

_____

Use discernment to identify the root cause of someone's heart and actions.

5. Do you have or know someone who has the gift of discernment? How can this gift help your own life story?

_____

_____

_____

_____

The gift of knowledge can allow you to know the core issues in a person's life.

6. If you had the gift of knowledge, how would you use it to glorify God? What is the value of seeking this gift out?

_____

_____

_____

_____

7. How do you see the gift of leadership exercised by the leaders in your church? God's idea of a leader can be much different from the way that many corporate leaders lead. How so? How did Jesus show leadership?

_____

_____

_____

Acts of mercy will be noticed by others who will question their source.

8. Mercy is something that we're all supposed to have in some measure. What can someone who has this gift offer that the rest of us can't?

_____

_____

Prophecy will encourage others and build their faith in the face of struggle and pain.

9. Do you have or know of someone who has the gift of prophecy? How can finding those who have this gift help you?

_____

_____

Using wisdom will allow your decisions to be on a rock-solid foundation.

10. What are some areas in your life where you could benefit from the gift of wisdom? Why is this particular gift important to you? Why is it important to the body of Christ?

_____

_____

_____

_____

11. The saying "receive, unwrap, and use the gifts" is written throughout this book. How does this apply to spiritual gifts? What steps are you taking toward finding, trying out, and developing your specific gifting?

_____

_____

_____

12. Have you exposed yourself to those who possess these powerful gifts so that you can mature and become perfected in Christ? List the people who have blessed you with their use of specific gifts. Which ones are missing? How will you expose yourself to these missing yet vital gifts?

_____

_____

_____

## Action Steps

Do you know what your gift(s) are? Take time to review the descriptions in this chapter and at www.buildingchurch.net. They have a questionnaire that can help you determine which gifts you possess in greater quantities. You may have gifts that you didn't know you had, or they may be right in line with what you expected. Learn all you can about your gifts and how they may benefit the body of Christ. Talk with church leaders about how you can make better use of your gifts.

_____

_____

_____

_____

_____

## Closing Prayer

(Pray this prayer or come up with your own to close this study time.)

Father, thank You for the gifts that You've given me. Help me to identify them and use them fully, according to Your purpose.

# Chapter 5

# GIFT #10—RELATIONSHIP

## HOW DO RELATIONSHIPS COMPLETE
## YOU AND YOUR DESTINY?

### STUDY QUESTIONS

1. Why do we talk about *investing* in relationships? How does that investment look in your life with those closest to you? What do you potentially gain and lose? Are you too busy to make the investment, or do you just think it is too much work? If so, how could you change?

_____

_____

_____

_____

_____

_____

_____

2. How do the gifts that you've already learned about impact the way you relate to friends, family, coworkers, and strangers? How do you make friends and improve the friendships that you already have?

_____

_____

_____

_____

Relationships can remove limits and thereby give us more freedom, both physically and spiritually.

3. How do relationships help improve us? What are some of the ways relationships can give us more freedom?

_____

_____

_____

_____

_____

_____

Focusing on others' needs and lack rather than your own will make the journey more enjoyable. It will ultimately open a gift of freedom for you to walk to further places in life.

4. What are some practical ways you can focus on others' needs? How does this impact your relationship with them? How does this impact your relationship with God?

_____

_____

_____

_____

5. What does it look like to love your neighbor as yourself? Is this always easy? Why or why not? Looking at the parable of the Good Samaritan, how can you "go and do likewise," as Jesus said (see Luke 10:25-37)?

_____

_____

_____

_____

_____

Only relationships can birth real life here on earth.

6. How can God's love, exuding through you, bring life to others?

_____

_____

_____

_____

_____

7. God spiritually binds a man and a wife together as one; however, physically speaking, each of them must take actions that keep the bond together. List some ways you can see this happening in a marriage.

_____

_____

_____

_____

_____

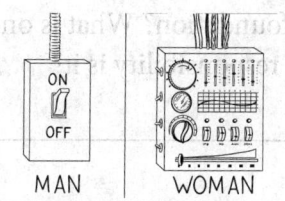

MAN | WOMAN

Man's design and function is more straight-forward and to the point, while the woman's function is more complex and robust.

8. Think of some examples that support the truth about the specific differences between the way men and women are wired. How does knowing this help you in your relationships? In what ways do you think you can benefit and enjoy these differences?

_____

_____

_____

The fall distorted our view of the world and made it difficult to see beyond ourselves. However, in marriage, seeing beyond ourselves is essential.

9. Describe some of the ways that a marriage on earth is like our relationship with God. What are some of the truths about our relationship with God that we can discover through marriage? How can marriage help build your character? If you are married, what are some things that you can change to build a better marriage?

_____

_____

_____

10. Why is basing a marriage on romance a poor foundation? What is one way to add romance to your marriage? Whose responsibility is it?

_____

_____

_____

When you could not take care of yourself, God gave you the wonderful gift of relationship—respect and treasure this God-given gift.

11. How can you respect your parents even when you disagree with them or when you've been hurt by them?

_____

_____

_____

_____

12. What are some of the blessings and freedoms that you can gain when you receive, unwrap, and use the gift of relationship?

_____

_____

_____

## Action Steps

Take a close look at the relationships that you are involved in today. If you're married or dating, consider how well you're living out the sort of relationship that God would desire for you as a couple. What are some ways you can work on improving all your earthly relationships? What steps do you need to take to avoid unnecessary conflict? To grow a deeper friendship? Make plans to enact these steps in the days to come.

_____

_____

_____

_____

_____

_____

## Closing Prayer

(Pray this prayer or come up with your own to close this study time.)

Lord, thank You for the gift of relationship. Give me wisdom in relating to family, friends, coworkers, and strangers. And show me Yourself through these relationships so that I might learn more about You and grow closer to You.

# Chapter 6

## GIFT #11—YOUR DESTINY

### HOW DO YOU FIND YOUR DESTINY?

**STUDY QUESTIONS**

1. What are some ways that you've sought your own earthly destiny? Are you seeking to live out the destiny God offers you or are you trying to create your own? What happens when you reject the one God offers? What do you have to do to find the one God offers?

_____

_____

_____

_____

2. What are some of the desires of the flesh that can distract you from discovering or fulfilling your destiny?

_____

_____

_____

Keep your end in sight so you can keep on your course.

3. How can you keep your eyes on your destination? What weaknesses (in faith, trust, prayer, worship, dying to self, etc.) do you think might have you going in circles, repeating the same mistakes over and over, causing you to cover the same ground repeatedly?

_____

_____

_____

Attaining goals outside of God's will is a struggle without fulfillment. Instead, find your destiny in the river of life, for it will be far more exhilarating and fulfilling.

4. What are some of the ways that you've tried to swim upstream? What was the result for your efforts? What was the motivation for your direction during these times? What are some things that you might need to do to move into the current where God wants you?

_____

_____

The closer to the center of the river you are, the easier it will be to see your destiny.

5. Why is it more difficult to see your destiny when you are farther from the center of God's will? What are some things you need to do in order to see better?

_____

_____

_____

_____

You will find surprise gifts en route to your destiny.

6. What are some different ways God surprises us as we seek our destiny? How have you been surprised so far? How can you live your life so that you're prepared for and welcoming of God's surprises along the way? Why is it hard for our flesh to recognize His surprises?

_____

_____

_____

_____

7. What was Jesus' destiny on earth? What can we learn from how He lived out His destiny? How can it help us with our own?

_____

_____

_____

_____

This is not what God wants for you, but rather the result of not "letting go" of what He didn't intend for you.

8. What are some things that you might need to let go of to reach your God-intended destiny?

_____

_____

_____

9. Could your appointed destiny defy physics and logic, contradict customs, lead you into new areas, be unbelievably challenging, and be a tall order all at the same time? How would God ask you to respond to these potentially uncomfortable circumstances? Do you see parts of your destiny starting to unfold yet? What challenges might come with it?

_____

_____

_____

_____

10. Respond to this quote regarding your destiny: "Do not worry about what to say or how to say it. At that time, you will be given what to say, for it will not be you speaking..." (see Matthew 10:19-20). How does this encourage you as you pursue your destiny? In what ways does it lead you to grow in faith?

_____

_____

11. Review Paul's destiny as described in this chapter. How do you see God working through Paul's life in surprising or creative ways? Are you looking for and expecting God to reveal your path in surprising ways? How are you doing this?

_____

_____

_____

Your gift of destiny, if received and used, is the most fulfilling gift that you can receive from God and is the most fulfilling gift that you can give God in return.

12. In what ways is the gift of destiny the most fulfilling gift that you can receive, open, and use? How can you best deal with those times when you question whether your destiny even exists? What is the Holy Spirit's vital role in this? How about all the other Gifts of Freedom—what part do they play?

_____

_____

## Action Steps

Spend some time thinking about the life you've lived thus far. Then write down ways that you think God might have used your circumstances to bring you to where you are today. What might He be preparing you for? In what areas could you become a witness to others? In what areas could you show compassion? Talk with a friend about what you discover, and then spend time together in prayer, inviting the Holy Spirit to reveal to you what is next in your pursuit of your unique God-given destiny. Keep checking back with God so that you can stay focused on this destiny and so that you can be aware of His hand in your life and the creative, evolving ways that He continues to shape your future.

_____

_____

_____

_____

_____

## Closing Prayer

(Pray this prayer or come up with your own to close this study time.)

Lord, thank You for my unique destiny. Help me to discover Your will for me in everything I do. Give me purpose and clarity as I seek Your will and uncover the plans that You have for my life—my earthly destiny.

# Chapter 7

# THE GIFT—GOD OF THE TRINITY

## WHAT WILL YOUR RELATIONSHIP ULTIMATELY BE WITH HIM?

### STUDY QUESTIONS

1. What is the primary purpose of the Gifts of Freedom?

   _____

   _____

   _____

   _____

2. What are some of the steps you need to follow to create a stable foundation for your relationship with God? How will living this out help you discover the Promised Land that God has in mind for you?

   _____

   _____

   _____

   _____

Before you can figure out how to get to point B, you need to know where you currently are at—point A.

3. What is your current point A in life? Where is that in relation to Him, to your Promised Land? What do you need to do to properly reposition yourself?

_____

_____

Godly sorrow brings you to a change in the way you do things that will lift you up and, unlike regret, that will bring you down.

4. Where have you known or felt godly sorrow in your life? How has that changed you in good ways? If you haven't known godly sorrow yet, how do you think you can find it? How can you use it to bring about spiritual growth and not despair?

_____

_____

_____

5. What does Jesus mean when He says, "Blessed are the meek"? What is the difference between being meek and weak? What will you find when you're meek?

_____

_____

_____

_____

Your heart sets the issues of life in motion, issues you will encounter in the future.

6. How does an "unclean temple" keep us from clearly seeing God? What do you need to do to clean your heart? To cleanse your mind?

_____

_____

_____

_____

_____

_____

When you are ablaze with the light of Jesus, the devil will attempt to dim or snuff you out.

7. What are some ways that satan tries to persecute or distract those who are seeking an intimate relationship with God? How are we to respond to these attacks? How does God help us respond to them?

_____

_____

_____

_____

_____

_____

8. How do we express our love to God? How are you serving Him? If you are not, what is stopping you? How are you obeying Him? What are the signs of someone who is obedient to God?

_____

_____

_____

_____

_____

_____

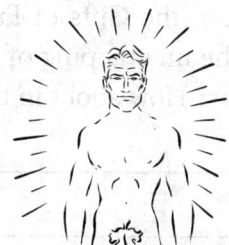

At the resurrection, God will restore you with a new body that is free from sin and shame.

9. What are you most looking forward to when you receive new life after the resurrection? How can this future Promised Land help encourage you toward obedience, love, and holiness?

_____

_____

_____

_____

_____

10. What does the Bible tell us about what this new Heaven will be like? (List your favorite verses describing this.) What are some reasons you could think of that would make Heaven indescribable?

_____

_____

_____

_____

_____

11. How can the Gifts of Freedom affect your Heaven experience? How does the unwrapping of your relationship with Him now impact your life now? How about in the future?

_____

_____

_____

_____

_____

_____

How many gifts will you have to give when you get to Heaven?

12. How many crowns would you like to lay at the feet of Jesus? Are you living to praise Jesus in the end? What can you do to gain more crowns for Him?

_____

_____

_____

_____

_____

## ACTION STEPS

Review the Gifts of Freedom in this and the other two books. Then plan to read these books again in several months to review what you've learned and to remind yourself of your goals as you seek to discover God's plan for your life. How well are you doing so far in all that you've committed to? What are some things that you can work on in your pursuit of God? Plan to keep working on these in the coming months and years. It will be a process that never ends in this life, as long as you remain a seeker.

_____

_____

_____

_____

_____

_____

_____

## CLOSING PRAYER

(Pray this prayer or come up with your own to close this study time.)

Lord, thank You so much for the gift of You and all the Gifts of Freedom. Give me both the desire and the wisdom necessary to receive, unwrap, and use these gifts so that I can enter my Promised Land and live out the unique destiny that You have planned for me.

# ABOUT THE AUTHOR

Greg Rice began his real estate business in 1971; however, God has taken him on a most unusual journey since that time. In 1988, he gave his heart to Jesus Christ—the gift of salvation began to grow, heal, and restore his life. Greg's continual seeking to know God and develop a most intimate relationship with Him has led to many discoveries.

As God was healing him, Greg began to share his new life and successes with others through several ministries. He has now focused much of his ministry efforts through Solid Rock Media (see www.solidrockmedia. com), and its vision is to illuminate the life and light of Jesus to a dying world through various media outlets. The Gifts of Freedom book series grew out of this pursuit. In November 2005, the Holy Spirit began to give the words. God's message was clear: "Offer Christians a clear path toward living in wholehearted freedom."

God has an answer for those who find themselves bound in life by what is not of God. God's desire is for everyone bound and held captive to be set free so they can achieve their purpose and fulfill their destiny. The Gifts of Freedom was written to illuminate the gifts God offers so we can achieve our God-given purpose and calling in this life. Yes, the heart of the book is to shine this light of freedom into churches, marriages, and families. And, indeed, this light can even penetrate the steel and cement of prison walls and jail bars.

Men and women held in prison also have a God-given purpose and destiny. With this in mind, Greg's mission is to distribute the Gifts of Freedom free of charge to prisons and jails around the world to facilitate salvation, discipleship, healing, and growth. To this end, Greg has already donated 120,000 copies to prisons across the United States.

It is Greg's prayer that the Spirit of God would bring change within, working from the inside out, as only He can bring true rehabilitation and freedom. Partner with Greg by giving a donation to distribute additional copies of the books, bringing spiritual nourishment to spiritually hungry men and women in prisons worldwide. In the US alone, there are over seven thousand incarceration facilities now holding almost 2.5 million prisoners. If this were a city, it would be the fourth largest city in the United States after Chicago and before Houston. Certainly, these men and women have the time to consider this life-changing message. What better way is there to positively influence the crime statistics as well as the negative human results of those crimes?

Write a check to "Gifts of Freedom" and mail it to:

Gifts of Freedom
P.O. Box 62459
Colorado Springs, CO 80962
Visit our website at www.giftsoffreedom.org

✝ *I, the Lord, have called you in righteousness; I will take hold of your hand. I will keep you and will make you to be a covenant for the people and a light for the Gentiles, to open eyes that are blind, to free captives from prison and to release from the dungeon those who sit in darkness* (Isaiah 42:6-8).